Great Times
Good Times

JAMES KOTSILIBAS-DAVIS

GREAT TIMES
GOOD TIMES

The Odyssey of
MAURICE BARRYMORE

1977
DOUBLEDAY & CO., INC.
GARDEN CITY, NEW YORK

Grateful acknowledgment is made for permission to use excerpts from the following copyright material:

Confessions of an Actor by John Barrymore. Copyright 1926 by John Barrymore. Reprinted by permission of the Bobbs-Merrill Co., Inc.

Memories: An Autobiography by Ethel Barrymore. Copyright © 1955 by Ethel Barrymore. By permission of Harper & Row, Publishers, Inc.

We Barrymores by Lionel Barrymore, as told to Cameron Shipp. Copyright 1951 by Lionel Barrymore and Cameron Shipp. Reprinted by permission of Hawthorn Books and the William Morris Agency, Inc.

"The First of the Barrymores—A Trouper's Reminiscence" by Virginia Tracy: Reprinted by permission; © 1938, 1958 The New Yorker Magazine, Inc.

We Three by John Barrymore. New York: Saalfield Publishing Co., 1935 (Big-Little Book).

Library of Congress Cataloging in Publication Data

Kotsilibas-Davis, James.
    Great times, good times.

    Bibliography: p. 504
    Includes index.
    1. Barrymore, Maurice, 1849–1905. 2. Actors—
United States—Biography. I. Title.
PN2287.B35K6   792'.028'024 [B]
ISBN 0-385-04953-6
Library of Congress Catalog Card Number 72–76182

This book is dedicated
to the memory
of my father,
HARRY KOTSILIBAS DAVIS,
who sustained it five years
but missed the finish.

Foreword

There is a new generation now which would ask not merely *who was Maurice Barrymore?* but *who were the Barrymores?* The concept of a Royal Family of a kingdom called Broadway, or indeed the existence of such a kingdom, is alien to them, even ridiculous. Some of them, possibly, have read that John was a great *Hamlet*. Others, thanks to old movies on television, may recall Lionel as a benevolent curmudgeon, Ethel as an imperious old lady with startling blue eyes. But Hollywood was the end, perhaps the only feasible end, of an incredible odyssey begun by strolling players in Shakespeare's time: three hundred years to develop three siblings who achieved glory in their lifetimes. How is such achievement possible?

This is the story of the man who fathered them.

Contents

Illustrations will be found following pages 82, 202,
  322 and 442. (Unless otherwise credited, illustrations are from the collection of the author.)

There was a shout from adoring Lambs whenever Maurice Barrymore entered. This founder of the house of Barrymore was English-born, Herbert Blyth—preëminently a man's man, and beyond question a woman's man, of wit so telling and yet so good-hearted that even the objects of his keen satire, joined in laughter at their own expense. On the stage he was always a picture—in private, an Apollo in a slop suit. Amateur champion middleweight boxer, narrator of a thousand stories, quick in resentment of an insult, generous to a foe, burner of candles at both ends, Bedouin of Broadway, this was the Barrymore that I knew.

Otis Skinner

Great Times
Good Times

Prologue

A Brief Chronicle of the Blyths

There was the matter of my fate in me when I was fashioned first, and given such life as goes with a sad end.

ALGERNON CHARLES SWINBURNE*

---

*First of three quotations chosen by Maurice Barrymore to introduce his play *Nadjezda*.

SNEATING HALL COMMANDED the highest hill in the Tendring Hundred. On downcast mornings its flintstone towers became one with gray heaven, and if mist cleared, you could follow the land of Squire William Edward Blyth, sprawling out from his great house, almost as far as the eye could see. Sheep grazed his hills like broken clouds. His fields lay green and advantageous. The Squire desired no farther view.

As second son to the Blyths of Beaumont Hall, he had been born to the privilege and power of the Essex landed gentry; but when his elder brother inherited the family estate, William was obliged to seek independence. There was no need to venture far. He had secured the lease of Sneating Hall, the neighboring estate, by the clever manipulation of wit and family name, and of his wife's dowry. It became William Edward Blyth's greatest point of pride that Beaumont Hall rested in the valley far below his towering acquisition.

Between 1783 and 1800 the baptism records of St. Michael's Church in Kirby-le-Soken burst with the thirteen children of William and Mary Carrington Blyth. As his fortune increased, he was determined that each of them would be worthy to share in it. He acquired, for a substantial fee, the exclusive services of St. Michael's parson. The scholarly cleric had come down from Christ Church, Oxford, which enhanced his position so far as William Blyth was concerned. The Squire could afford the luxury of having one or two sons pursue the academic life, and the parson could arrange that for him at Christ Church.

It was obvious from the beginning that his second son, John, born in 1785, was the potential scholar. He was quick and perceptive in the predominantly classical studies offered by the parson. He was also willful and easily bored; but a handsome face and a winning obstinacy easily mistaken for strength of character endeared him to father and tutor alike.

3

Let the eldest son, Will, and the third son, Daniel, work the land, John would be a learned man. His studies were intensified and plans laid to send him to Christ Church. There, the Squire decided, his son would qualify as a prince of the church.

John was of a different mind. Propped up against the stone weary wall of the back kitchen, safe from the parson's fussy solicitations, he could sight the distant port of Harwich. His restless eyes, Northern gray, his father called them, strained to follow sailing ships that left the busy port.

It was behind the kitchen, also, where the future prince of the church, in his sixteenth year, seduced the daughter of a Sneating Hall cottager. She proved as fond of the diversion as was her transgressor, and the boy took his pleasure regularly until the eve of planned departure for Oxford. On that autumnal afternoon, as they lay together for the last time, John felt a decided bulge in the belly of his confederate. His initial shock was replaced by pride in the achievement. Acting in a manner unusual and indeed unsuitable for a gentleman's son, he proposed to wed the girl.

William Blyth was staggered, but his violent opposition merely turned John's lighthearted decision to resolve. The father, however, would not see plans for his son dashed by the trivial matter of a cottager's whelp with child. That evening, the Squire rode out over his darkening fields to the girl's father. He gave his cottager a horse and cart and ten gold sovereigns, a fortune to one who paid yearly rent in shillings and capons, and bid the frightened fellow be gone with his family before daybreak.

Early the next morning, John saddled Hotspur, his father's prize chestnut colt, and rode not in pursuit of the girl who carried his child, but with the rising sun to London.

He had visited the city with his father, but now its immensity struck him for the first time. It was a crowded place of nearly a million inhabitants, not beautiful, but wonderful for its bigness. Immaculate crescents and whitewash squares were immediately backed by crumpled "Gin Lanes." Primped and powdered gentlemen, complacent in sedan chairs, passed unheeding the gaunt beggars and bewildered children who littered the streets like so much rubbish. Tradesmen spilled out of the spindly clutter of terraced shops. Everywhere, even in the sacred confines of St. Paul's, they bartered, hawking wares from morning till far into the noisy night. By comparison, Essex was a well-tended garden, but to a young man in his eighteenth year, London was intoxicating.

That night he stopped at the Swan with Two Necks in Lad Lane, giving his last few shillings for a room and a supper of sack, pigeons, Westphalia ham and cabbage. Afterward, in the "darke parlour" of the inn, he sat contentedly sipping porter amid the heavy smoke and tavern talk of his fellow travelers. One among them, who was taking the morning coach to Staffordshire, mentioned that he had that day vacated a room in the house of a tailor's widow, an accommodating woman, on Ludgate Hill.

In the morning, John sold his father's colt to an ironmonger for a goodly sum and headed for Ludgate Hill. The widow Mrs. Collie was accommodating indeed. She not only proffered his bed and board, but the pleasures of her bed, as well, a convenience bound to please any lad newly arrived in the big city. The good widow admitted to five and thirty, but she was well past forty. Her hair was too black, her cheeks too red, and her bosoms too limp for the exposure to which she subjected them. But she was well provided for by her deceased husband and did not press the issue of rent.

Once settled with Mrs. Collie, John ventured down to the docks, but his longing had succumbed to the intoxication of London. A tangle of netting and masts and bloated cargo seemed to choke the river breathless, muting for a time the call of the sea. Instead, he established himself on Ludgate Hill as tutor to the scions of neighboring commercial families, tradesmen and shopkeepers, mainly, who were discovering education as a means to profit and polite society. Latin and Greek successfully occupied his mornings and afternoons, but at night, when he could disarm his glowering mistress, John headed for the night cellars and brothels around Covent Garden. Fitted into the late Mr. Collie's wardrobe, he became a prominent fixture in this underground world of fruity port and roistering rakes. He frequented the cavernous spaces under Leicester Square devoted to late-night orgies of men of fashion, and riverside taverns near the level of the Thames bed.

While not averse to keeping her amorous boarder, Mrs. Collie resented his nocturnal ramblings. The arrangement endured nearly three years, however, until the misguided widow began to talk of marriage. It was not long before John Blyth's thoughts returned once more to the sea.

The mysteries of the East, elaborated at the taverns which he frequented, intrigued the young man from Essex. Since the Honourable East India Company held a monopoly on these mysteries, it was to their docks opposite Deptford that he ventured. When he signed on the *Tigris* bound for Calcutta, the twenty-one-year-old, obviously of gentle birth, received the prestigious post of assistant to Purser Archibald MacDowell.

On the first leg of their journey, as they rode the southerly wind full press for Madeira, John Blyth satisfied his childhood longing for the sea. He was not reprimanded when he lingered in the bows. His job was not taxing, and MacDowell had taken a fancy to him.

Beyond Madeira, in the latitude of the Canary Islands, they picked up the northeast trade wind and steered a course westward of the Cape Verde Islands. When they lost the northeast trade the ship was in the region of the variables. They met unsteady breezes, long calms and heavy rain.

Long before they rounded the Cape of Good Hope the wind had turned bitter, and the stifling tedium of a long sea voyage had set in. Scurvy had killed eleven Lascar crewmen before the cape was sighted. Beyond were twelve thousand treacherous islands between Madagascar and the Indian mainland. The French had outposts among them, and guarded their charts from the English under penalty of death. English charts, based on hearsay and legend, were hopelessly unreliable.

During this ponderous leg of the journey, traveling in fear of attack or scurvy or boredom, John befriended some cadets shipping to Calcutta for the company's army. Most of them were of his age, and of more or less gentle extraction. He was impressed by their sense of imminent adventure, moved by their words of untempered enthusiasm for the life awaiting them.

When the *Tigris* reached Calcutta, John Blyth went ashore for what appeared to be an ordinary evening's leave. Archibald MacDowell did not notice that his assistant had donned three layers of Mr. Collie's finest costumes.

Calcutta struck John as a hand-colored caricature of London. Once he left the clutter of the docks it took on Western symmetry. The wide main thoroughfare was fringed by the neat façades of the Old Court House and the Writers Building. St. John's steepled Church of England reached beyond the shining temples of the East. Nor did the European inhabitants concede to their environment. They seemed to prefer an imitation of London fashion to comfort. One gentleman, brocaded and bewigged, reclined in a sedan chair borne by four native servants wearing loincloths, while another servant ran alongside with a parasol to shade his master. He must have been fleet, for the sun could never have crossed the lily white face of the passenger. Two ladies in muslin and ostrich plumes paused their liveried barouches side by side to barter fresh gossip. A scantily clad native traversed the late-morning throng with his master's six white whippets on gilded leashes.

It was English stamina that supported such frivolity in a land where oppressive climate and rampant disease killed eighty per cent of the European inhabitants. But overtaxation of that stamina was responsible for another prime mortality factor: dissipation, not exposure to sun and plague but to Hodgson's pale ale, claret, and native women. When the *Tigris* sailed, John ventured out of hiding to partake liberally of all three. With the aid of his cadet friends, he gained entry to Calcutta's fashionable salons, where good looks and lively tales of London night life won him the favor of the bored elite.

In the less rarefied company of dedicated civil servants, surveyors, and active military, he saw beyond the transplanted refinement of the city. While Calcutta frolicked, the Bengal Artillery secured the interior, and adventurers charted land and settled it for Company and Country. He soon lost patience with imitation society.

On July 21, 1808, the gentleman from Essex appeared for the first time on the *List of the Non-Commissioned Officers and Privates composing the Hon'able Company's European Army on the Bengal Establishment.* He was no longer John Blyth, but "John Blake" to avoid being traced as a deserter. His assignment as Writer in the Arsenal at Fort William allowed him three comfortable years. But during that time his longing for adventure grew stronger. He pressed for active duty; but educated men were rare in the service. He was promoted corporal and appointed to fill a staff shortage at the Lower Orphan School. This might have proved tedious had it not been for a willowy, black-haired young lady with a mind of her own.

Mary Butterworth had been born in Calcutta twenty-three years before, the daughter of a Bengal Army major. She had shown unusual willfullness for a well-born young lady by refusing to be shipped to England for schooling and a proper marriage. Continuing to rebel, she refused offers of marriage from eligible members of the Calcutta Establishment, preferring the useful occupation of teaching at the Lower Orphan School. She had been there nearly a year when the handsome twenty-six-year-old Englishman arrived to assist in Greek and Latin.

They were married at the Fort William Garrison chapel on the second of July, 1812. Without any particular effort, the Blakes became acknowledged members of the British community. Society was still based on the values of the homeland, and John was of the landed gentry, Mary a major's daughter. Their first child lived only long enough to be baptized Mary Anne. On the ninth of November, 1815, Mary Butterworth Blake died bearing a second daughter, who did not survive infancy.

For solace, John sought the nocturnal world which he had known; but the mood of Calcutta had changed. When Crown replaced Honourable Company as the ruling force in India, the gay society of rakes and second sons paradoxically gave way to a tight professional bourgeoisie. John Blake could no longer be assured standing because he spoke the King's English and walked with a memory of land.

The following summer, at the home of Chaplain Thomas Robertson, he married Sophia Tubbs, a sixteen-year-old ward of the Lower Orphan School. She was dark and shy, with wide, soft features that belied her ready strength and gentle assurance. She was in awe of the gentleman that had wed her, but as the rogue abated, Sophia became the quiet power of their household. The first of their eight children was born a year later. Sickly and weak, named for his father, he managed to survive infancy. But when a second son was born in 1818, a robust, animated child, he assumed in John Blake's eyes the position of first-born. John named him William Edward, for the father that he had left at Sneating Hall fifteen years before.

There was concurrent talk in the city about Sophia Tubbs Blake. It was rumored that her birth had resulted from the dalliance of one Lieutenant Tubbs, Bengal Infantry, with an unidentified native girl, a mixture considered untenable by the British community. No proof could be found to substantiate such claims, but in 1823, John Blake gratefully accepted the post of Conductor of Ordinance in the fort at Allahabad. The city was administrative headquarters for a rambling district of a thousand villages heavy with black soil and dhāk jungles. It stood desolate at the junction of the Ganges and the Jumna rivers. But the malicious tongues of Calcutta were 512 miles away. The ordinary shade temperature between April and November reached 117 degrees. But the rank of conductor in the artillery carried with it most of the privilege, much of the respect of an officer, and here, at least, his rapidly increasing progeny were assured education with the children of officers.

Their education became the Conductor's obsession. He supplemented it at home, impelling them to repeat Latin declensions until the weakest among them wept. His second son did not weep. He thrived. Studious and alert, William Edward was always ahead of his brothers, sisters, and the rest of the class. The Conductor concentrated particularly on their English. If a grammatical error or a vulgar pronunciation crossed their lips, they would be scrupulously corrected and punished. The prodigal was determined to bequeath to his children the refinements of ladies and gentlemen. Concerned with their right to a proper heritage, he resumed the name of Blyth in 1828.

Early in the summer of 1833, he was felled by typhoid fever. He was strong, only forty-eight, but the attack was severe, and lucid moments few. William Edward was summoned to the bedside. The Conductor struggled to tell his second son tales of misspent youth, and of a mansion high on a hill in the Tendring Hundred. Barely audible between empty breaths, he urged the boy to contact the family which he had abandoned thirty years before.

Toward the end of July, John Blyth of Sneating Hall was buried within the high sandstone walls of Allahabad Fort, five hundred miles from the Eastern Sea.

To Captn. James Bedford
Deputy Surveyor General
Western Provinces, Allahabad
10 August, 1833

Sir,

We have a case of real distress at present in The Fort by the death of one of my conductors, who, has left a widow and seven or eight children in utter penury. The oldest [sic] is a boy of fifteen, well behaved and intelligent. Enclosed is a specimen of his handwriting.

Were it not for the distress of the family I would not have taken upon myself thus to trouble you, but it would really be a charity could you by and by in the event of a Survey being got up here, gave him some trifling employment. His name is Blyth.

[*A True Extract*]
[*Signed*]   *L. Burroughs*
Commissary of Ordinance
Allahabad

There were no surveys being fitted at the time, but Captain Bedford took the boy into his own drawing office. William Edward Blyth proved to be intelligent indeed, with more of his mother's quiet perseverance than his father's restless spirit. He resembled Sophia in feature as well. He was a good-looking boy, with none of his father's striking attributes, but with a wide, dependable face that hid the machinations of a precise mind and inspired trust in his associates. He learned quickly the intricacies of revenue surveying and the benefits of an ingratiating nature. He employed both to insure himself and his family against the kind of shattering uncertainty that had followed John Blyth's death.

The Conductor's dependents survived on William's small monthly salary of thirty rupees, the equivalent of three English pounds, about fifteen dollars. They were allowed to remain in army quarters, and, somehow, Sophia Blyth managed to dress and feed her eight children, and to educate them.

When an employee was pensioned off, leaving a possible opening for William in the field, Captain Bedford wrote immediately to the Sudder Board of Revenue: "The boy has been attending my office for some time past, gained good general knowledge of what he will have to do, and appears both docile and intelligent," the captain assured his superiors. "I propose therefore that he be brought on the strength of the Department in lieu of Mr. Jenkins and for the present receive 50 Rupees (from the balance which remains after payment of the pension) to be increased hereafter, if he prove deserving, to 100, when an opening admit of it, without augmenting the general expense."

The Board of Revenue readily accepted Captain Bedford's proposal, and William was dispatched to the Furruckabad Survey under Lieutenant Henry Lawrence. Lawrence, a prodigious worker, took time to train the eager recruit. Revenue surveying was a painstaking process of evaluating the vast land of India to set its boundaries and taxes, requiring distant journeys into uncharted areas, culminating often in months of arduous jungle living. The compensation hardly equaled the task. It was difficult, indeed, for a man to keep himself, even under camp conditions, starting with Rs. 50 a month, and maybe reaching Rs. 250, about $120, at the end of his career. Not that most of them ever achieved that. Promotion did not always keep pace with merit, for the Establishment charges of each survey party had to be kept strictly within a definite allotment.

In his twentieth year, William was assigned to a survey outside Ghazipur, a city of roses, where the chief industry was scent-distilling. Blossoms spread for miles around like red plush carpeting to be plucked and drained for rose water and otto of roses. The local Apothecary for the Bengal Establishment, Henry Chamberlayne, a talkative Irishman, was greatly impressed by the businesslike young revenue surveyor. (Chamberlayne had no sons. His wife had died the previous year, leaving two daughters. The eldest was of marrying age, beautiful, but home-bound, content since her mother's death to tend father, sister, and garden.)

When William Edward Blyth was introduced to Charlotte Matilda de Tankerville Chamberlayne, she was sixteen. He later contended that he had loved her from that moment. It was probably so. Wherever she went, Matilda left a memory of beauty. Indians marveled, English eyes followed as she walked to church each week, fine-boned Parian with emerald eyes, soft-spoken and slim. The worst said of her, usually by disappointed mothers of less gifted girls, was that instead of wearing a proper bonnet she twined white roses in her pitch-black hair.

The Blyth-Chamberlayne wedding, in August of 1839, was considered a social event by the Ghazipur gentry. The Deputy Surveyor General sent a fine bronze coronation bust of Victoria, the new Queen. Henry Chamberlayne, smiling uncontrollably, presented his new son-in-law with a massive Regency secretary of high-polished oak.

The Blyths moved from one remote town to another during their first years of marriage. Usually a surveyor's wife would remain in one place while he moved with his assignments. Matilda Blyth preferred to be with her husband. In each new place she would set up housekeeping with their few wedding gifts or whatever bits she could afford to purchase. Somehow she would make it, with flowers, with her own warmth, a haven for her husband.

Their first child was born at Gyah. Her grave lies shaded in the churchyard there, marked by a small stone.

Sacred
to the Memory of
ALICE
Beloved Child of
William & Matilda Blyth
who departed this life
on the 8th of June, 1843.
aged 1 year, 1 month and 9 days.

Three months later, William Henry was born in Dinapore; Evelin Agnes was born there the following year.

It was no mean accomplishment that in his twenty-fifth year William Edward Blyth had reached the honorable position of Assistant Revenue Surveyor in the Uncovenanted Service at Rs. 250 a month, and had managed to bring three of his brothers into the department with him. He arranged a suitable job for his older brother, John, who had been weakened in mind and body by childhood fevers. John became a dispatcher at the Courts of Sudder, where he remained until his early death. His younger brothers, Daniel and George, robust, intelligent boys, joined William in the surveys when they came of age.

In 1846, William was sent on a new survey of the Trans Sutlej Territory. It was to be a long stay, so he moved his family into a big white house in Amritsar, where the children would have room to grow, and for the first time since their marriage, Matilda could have a proper garden. William's pay was raised to Rs. 500, he was made nominal head of the survey, and rose to the appointment with precise reports to the Surveyor General bearing the seal of authority. ("The progress of this survey depends upon the employment of elephants," he wrote; "have engaged nine and request permission to entertain a further number that may be essential . . . Also require sanction to employ Coolies for jungle clearing, and masons for erecting masonry pillars as boundary marks." The account for the following month showed that his request had been granted: "500 rupees—expenses incurred for clearing jungle and feed of elephants.")

He arranged to have his brother, George, transferred to the same survey, and, consequently, in February of '49, there was another Blyth-Chamberlayne merger. George married Matilda's younger sister, Amelia. It was a marriage made in heaven, although William and Matilda had helped it along. George was a steady, uninspired young man, overshadowed by his elder brother. Amelia was a plain girl, relentlessly mild, who worshiped her sister. During the wedding breakfast, William announced proudly that his wife was again with child.

It was a difficult pregnancy for Matilda, and toward the middle of July she began having frequent fainting spells. The doctor ordered her to bed; Amelia moved in to care for her. Convinced that the child would be a boy, Matilda sat for hours during the long summer rains mulling over names for him, taking no notice whatsoever of her sister's suggestions for girls' names. By end of summer, the confident twenty-six-year-old had decided: Herbert, because she fancied it; Arthur, after the legendary King of Camelot, whom she had loved in storybooks; Chamberlayne, to honor her father, who had died the year before. She also decided that Major James Hunter and his wife, Sarah, old family friends from Agra, should be his godparents. William saw no reason for her to plan so far ahead, but she was unusually persistent in getting his approval.

The rains subsided considerably in September, winds were light, days grew fair and luminous. Matilda longed to be in the garden again, working, while Eva and Will played nearby. It was time to sow larkspur and mignonette, to put down cuttings of roses and violets and heart's-ease. Returning from town on September 20, Amelia found her sister fallen in the garden. With the help of servants, she carried her into the house, sending for the doctor and for William.

A boy was born in the early hours of morning. Barely conscious, Matilda called out for her new child. She was allowed to hold him for a moment before he was taken away. Then, an hour before dawn, she died.

For three years, Amelia admonished her brother-in-law to consider baptizing the child, but he would not be bothered. Finally, in 1852, she took it upon herself to contact the Hunters, whom Matilda had designated godparents. The event was set for the thirteenth of June at St. Paul's, the Hunters' church in Agra. With a minimum of ceremony, the three-year-old was baptized Herbert Arthur Chamberlayne Hunter Blyth. When the presiding chaplain requested date of birth for his register, the child's father could not recall it. For Revenue Surveyor Blyth, the twenty-first of September, 1849, would remain irrevocably the day he lost Matilda Chamberlayne.

ACT
FIRST

Life has been compared to a race; but the allusion still improves, by observing, that the most swift are ever the most apt to stray from the course.

OLIVER GOLDSMITH*

*Part of a quotation to have been translated in H. A. Blyth's Fifth Form French examination.

I

A MONTH AFTER his wife's death, William Edward Blyth became Extra Assistant Commissioner on Settlement Duties. It did not satisfy him. He was concerned now by the second-class connotation of the Uncovenanted Service. The distinction between local recruits and London-appointed servants of Her Majesty was disappearing, but William felt it nonetheless. It strengthened his determination to see his sons educated and properly covenanted, his daughter well married.

Considering also the social standing of his siblings, he arranged advantageous marriages for his three sisters. When the last of them was married in 1850, he sent his mother to live with his brother, Daniel, who had been assigned to the distant outpost of Jhansi. There had been a recurrence of talk in Amritsar about Sophia Blyth's parentage, and her son thought it best to send her away. The Extra Assistant had his career to consider.

Emboldened by his increased station, he wrote, as his father had willed, to the Blyths of Sneating Hall. His aunt, Charlotte Blyth, the youngest child of Squire William, answered. Her father had died in 1812, she related, unaware that his second son had settled in India. Sneating Hall, the lofty estate which the Squire had leased, was no longer in the family, since his descendants had finally acquired Beaumont Hall, their ancestral home. Charlotte assured her long-lost nephew that his children would be welcome there if they were sent to the homeland for schooling. It pleased William Blyth inordinately that his three children would be accepted at the ancestral home of his forebears. Before Herbert was five, his brother, Will, had already sailed for England to begin his education at Blackheath Proprietary School.

The children had all been devotedly raised by their late mother's sister, Amelia Chamberlayne Blyth. But Herbert, the youngest, hers since the hour Matilda died, was the favorite. He was a Chamberlayne, the boy, she had decided at first glance, the image of his mother. But the fine-boned features were startled by Northern gray eyes. Spirit, too, recalled his grandfather, John Blyth.

The child was quick to sense his aunt's favor, and adjusted accordingly. Initial willfulness developed into temper, usually vented upon his doting aunt. She fretted no end about it, but afterward, he would always win her back with easy charm, as frequent and natural as his tantrums. Then they would celebrate with tea in Aunt Amelia's "English" kitchen. She had never been to England, but she had contrived, with flowered chintz, braided mats and a collection of English cookery books to re-create the homeland which she imagined. It was Herbert's favorite room, and he spent many hours there poring over the engraved delicacies in Aunt Amelia's kitchen library. This privilege was suspended, however, when his father was about. The Extra Assistant did not approve his children's loitering in the realm of servants.

Paradoxically, Herbert was docile and mannerly toward his father. William Blyth had little time for the boy. He neither showed affection nor malice. If he disapproved his son's behavior, his native playmates or numerous stray animals, Amelia was dispatched to attend the situation. She became her brother-in-law's agent in all matters concerning his second son.

Aunt Amelia managed to obtain clemency for one of Herbert's strays. Even William Blyth was taken by the parti-colored mongrel that his son had named Rahj. There had undoubtedly been an English sheep dog in his line somewhere, but it had been hopelessly mixed in the alleys of the East. He was small and wiry, with enormous ears that flopped over large, expressive eyes, making visibility unlikely. Herbert was usually there, however, to lead the way.

Amritsar offered them a fair field for adventure. It lay flat and comparatively temperate on the Grand Trunk Road near Lahore. Gilt minars and domes of the Sikhs' Golden Temple dominated the skyline, and forty acres of public gardens filled the center of the city with scent and color. Persian lilac, banyan, mulberry and horseradish trees had been imported to line the streets. Limes and oranges, mangoes, China peaches, and an inferior sort of pomegranate were commonly cultivated. In the fields, muskmelon and tarbúz abounded, while English gardeners prided themselves on grapes and strawberries.

The district was well stocked with antelope and ravine deer, and wild pigs occasionally appeared in the jhand forests. Wolves were the only beast of prey. Eight of them were brought in for bounty in Herbert's sixth year. Black partridges, sand grouse and peafowl were plentiful. Twice yearly, at harvest times, quail visited the fields. Uncle George often allowed Herbert to accompany him on a morning shoot. When the crops were being cut at the beginning of May, if they placed call-birds in a field overnight, the hunters often returned before breakfast with twenty or thirty brace.

Herbert more frequently managed unsupervised excursions with Rahj, usually leading to the bazaar in the center of the city. Rahj resented its familiar odors, afraid of being left again where he had once roamed hungry. Herbert understood the whimpering and carried his pet through the jumble of counters and carpets heaped high with fresh tobacco, oil seeds, raw silk. The young Sahib was known by the wily beggars and obsequious merchants, who vied for coins, and the barefooted boys his own age, who strained to work gigantic looms. Molders in the open air cast ornaments: rude zinc for the natives; refined brass for the raj. Circles of bent old women, eyes slit from ragged pouches, embroidered timelessly in gold thread and silk. Morning sun caught silver threads and spangles, jewels of colored glass, and the son of the Extra Assistant Commissioner crawling carelessly with native children through the dust and din. Stall keepers understood that returning the wayward boy to his home meant baksheesh. Allowance was made for it in Amelia Blyth's housekeeping expenses.

One afternoon, Deputy Commissioner F. H. Cooper, William Blyth's direct superior, discovered the boy cavorting in the bazaar. When his father was informed, contrary to his usual policy, he lectured the vagabond himself. Herbert was severely reprimanded, not so much for wandering, but for where his wandering led. He was told that it did not become the son of an Extra Assistant to fraternize with natives. After all, there were children of respectable civil servants and officers with whom to associate. To avoid further contamination, William Blyth decided not to send his son to the district school, but to have him tutored at home by Church of England missionaries.

Herbert proved to be an exceptional student with little effort. Rev. Strawbridge was impressed, and visions of academic glory appeased the Extra Assistant Commissioner for a time. Herbert was even allowed to accompany him to Agra for the funeral of his godfather, James Hunter.

Seeing opportunity for advancement and prestige, William Blyth resigned to the Judicial Department as an Assistant Commissioner early in 1857. His salary was raised to Rs. 800, but he had already become a rich man from the extras of revenue surveying: land speculation and polite bribery from landowners. He further secured his position, when some of the Sepoy regiments in British pay mutinied at Meerut to protest the severity of incompetent officers, the use of cartridges greased with the fat of the cow which they worshiped and the pig which they despised. Reverberations were swift. Before the end of May, the renegades had taken the strategic cities of Delhi, where there was no British regiment, Cawnpore and Lucknow.

In the Punjab, good government had won the confidence of the native Sikhs. The Amritsar area was considered a potential place of arms for the British, a bastion for the reconquest of the warring Sepoys. Diplomatic handling was required, and William Blyth was called upon to contribute. Amritsar was commanded by the lofty fortress of Govindgarh, occupied by a detachment of the 59th Native Infantry, with only seventy additional European artillery men. This became a source of great uneasiness. Deputy Commissioner Cooper called a meeting of the top Indian and European officials to discuss tactics of disarming the Native 59th without offending them. It was decided that a body of European foot must be got into the fort.

On May 13, Cooper, Captain of Police Lawrence, and William Blyth rode to Lahore for a conference with Brigadier Corbett. He complied with half a company of the 81st Foot. They were run across late the same night in *ekkas*, native one-horse gigs, and arrived in Amritsar before dawn on the fifteenth. Herbert had awakened his aunt to watch the discreet entry from the cover of garden shrubs. When the company had passed, Aunt Amelia noticed that Herbert had slipped off with Rahj in the morning mist. A dispatched servant caught up with them just as the boy and his dog were about to enter Fort Govindgarh, marching smartly in the dust of the 81st.

The Native 59th remained in the fort, and as they seemed loyal, no attempt was made to disarm them. Then, at the end of June, William and George Blyth were notified that their mother, Sophia, and their brother, Daniel, his wife and four children had been slaughtered with sixty other Europeans in the massacre of Jhansi. Distraught, and afraid that such a tragedy might occur in Amritsar, they urged that the 59th be disarmed. The continuing bloodshed and butchery in the South helped the cause of the brothers. On the ninth of July, Brigadier Nicholson peacefully disarmed the Natives.

Assistant Commissioners Blyth and Mac Naghton took to the Grand Trunk Road to raise the country against passing deserters. William Blyth, perhaps recalling that he had sent his mother to Jhansi to avert gossip, was particularly passionate in his denunciation of the wanton marauders, offering rewards for the capture of any Sepoy who had deserted. Every village became a nest of hornets for a deserter; escape was hopeless. The loyalty of the people made the Amritsar district famous in the annals of 1857.

With the Mutiny under control by the end of autumn, William Blyth, much honored for his participation, returned to the business of the Judicial Department. He and Sarah O'Conner Hunter, Herbert's widowed godmother, began keeping company. Friendship never quite ripened into love, she was a severe, unyielding woman, but he grew dependent and devoted. Colonial life was baseless and lonely for a man without a wife.

On the twenty-eighth of November, they were married at St. Paul's Church in Amritsar. Amelia Blyth, Deputy Commissioner Cooper, and Victoria Strawbridge, the chaplain's wife, were the only witnesses. After the wedding, Aunt Amelia continued to supervise the upbringing of her sister's children. Sarah Hunter Blyth, childless herself, did not particularly care for the children of others.

Herbert continued to excel in his studies, displaying particular acumen in the classics. There was every indication, according to Rev. Strawbridge, that the boy would be a scholar. Transcending his original plan for Civil Service glories, William Blyth contacted a friend in the Judicial Department at Lahore, an old Harrovian. Months of correspondence ensued across the oceans, and after the boy had written an excellent entrance examination under supervision at Lahore, he was accepted at Harrow for autumn term of 1860. When passage was booked on the sailing ship *Nile*, his father announced that Rahj would have to stay behind: It was impractical to bring a dog across the ocean; he would not be allowed at school. Aunt Amelia promised to care for the dog, but the boy was inconsolable. On the morning of departure, his eyes were riveted to some intangible target. He did not look at his father during their farewell.

His aunt and uncle accompanied Herbert to Calcutta, Amelia fussing all the way about the boy being sent across the water by himself. He would nevertheless have supervision. He was joining the sons of eight prominent Anglo-Indian families who were being sent to the homeland for proper schooling in the care of Mr. Payne, a tutor hired at combined expense. Aunt Amelia was not satisfied. She presented the boy with one of his father's leather-bound account ledgers, admonishing him to jot down every detail of the voyage and send it to her when he arrived in England. Before visitors were called ashore, she collared the cabin steward, an old man named Potter, handed him five rupees, and implored him to watch over her nephew.

When the *Nile* cast off, Amelia Blyth waved frantic arms from the receding quay. "Herbert did not notice," she complained to his father in a letter to Amritsar. "He had turned his eyes toward the open sea."

II

THE BOY ASKED to be awakened when the coast was made. He had slept in his clothes, and reached the bows a few minutes after Potter had called him. Leaning against the forward bulwarks, he scrutinized the white mist. Swaddled somewhere in the distance, the coast of England lay.

Potter brought tea, which Herbert sipped absently while jotting notes in his ledger book. As the mist cleared, he was astonished by the traffic around them: lines of ocean ships, holiday boats brimming toward Margate, coasting vessels, war monsters, little open boats fishing for Billingsgate Market. When they entered the Thames, there were guard ships making a glittering bracelet around Sheerness. They passed one port after another along the river until Greenwich, where tugs hitched on to guide them through the crowded Pool of London.

There was no one to bring definition to his first sight of London; no one to point out this or dismiss that. Other passengers had gathered on the quarter deck for the approach, but Herbert remained aloof. He had endured quite enough of Mr. Payne's patronizing guidance during the six-week crossing. As his notes for Aunt Amelia indicated, the boy was prodigiously capable of his own perceptions. "I was taken first by the unbroken line of masts stretching as far as one could see," he wrote, "like the Native 59th presenting arms." He described a shapeless black landing stage lying motionless beside some twisting waterman's stairs. Beyond he glimpsed a dark lane lined with massive warehouses and broken tenements. From deep within came the halfhearted cry of a child, reminding him of "hungry cries one hears in Amritsar." That concerned the boy, until he was startled by the impudent dome of St. Paul's.

The school at Harrow held its hilltop with monastic calm. The similarity did not end there. It was a closed world of fierce superiority protected by thick walls of stone and tradition. It could be dreadfully lonely for any ten-year-old new boy, but somehow more so for an assistant commissioner's son from the Punjab. His school clothes, ordered by mail, were awaiting him at the Knoll, the boardinghouse to which he had been assigned. His Eton jacket was too large, his Harrow straw hat, with dark blue ribbon, too small; his regulation black tie hung precariously around his neck, since he had never learned to manipulate such an object. He became fair game for the fifty other boys who boarded at the Knoll.

"Nabooby" was the name they coined for him, and at the sound of it Herbert Blyth leaped into action. He had not yet the wit for combat, but he had the fists. He struck out at his tormentors with a pale-eyed ferocity which might have frightened them had not their number made it unnecessary. His persistence merely encouraged repetition, until the authorities began to notice. They were soon concerned also with the boy's scholastic standing. Although he was clever, there seemed a reluctance to learn. They considered, of course, that the child was young and undisciplined and far from home. Herbert was warned.

Second term he was moved to the Foss, a "small" house "for boys for whom more individual attention is desired." The Amritsar adventurer did not seem to benefit from the change. He distributed enough black eyes and bloody noses to be reckoned a challenge by tormentors and faculty alike. As his reputation grew, his confidence grew with it. Defensive fisticuffs were replaced by belligerent assaults on his original attackers when he found one or two of them alone. His scholarship continued to diminish while faculty concern increased. The housemaster was advised to give him extra moral instruction before bedtime. In the dim gaslight of his cubicle, he would hear each parable told and retold until he fell mercifully asleep. Notwithstanding the Bible, the boy would not be broken. It was decided that he was a bad influence on those around him.

A letter was dispatched to his father pointedly suggesting that the boy should not be returned after midsummer holidays. William Blyth rose to the occasion:

> . . . I lament the waste of the opportunities set before you. I have sent
> you to Harrow, a school for the sons of gentlemen, so you will be able
> to meet them on equal ground in the Great World, but instead you
> brawl like a guttersnipe and ignore your studies . . .
>   I close now unable to dwell longer on this most painful topic, having
> to labour to make other accommodations for the education of a
> thankless son.
>
> > Your Father,
> >
> > Wm. Ed. Blyth

Herbert and his elder brother were strangers when they met at Beaumont Hall that summer of 1861. They got on well enough, but Will was nearly sixteen, purposeful and reserved, with the look and manner of his father. They were spending the holidays with their great-aunt, Charlotte Blyth Denys, the last living child of Squire William Edward Blyth. She was tall and very thin, as old as the century. In feature, she resembled the brother who had escaped Sneating Hall when she was not yet five. There was a mystery about her, a suggestion that she had lived far beyond the faded chintz of her drawing room. She had married late in life, but that was not it. Colonel Denys had been a widower when they married, a boon companion rather than a *grande passion*.

She and her grand-nephew were immediately drawn to one another. It was not only their similar looks, but kindred spirits which brought them close together. Every day of Herbert's visit, they would venture out for long walks in the countryside. When she brought him to Sneating Hall, his grandfather's birthplace, the great house was in the throes of a massive Victorian renovation. She led him behind the house to an old stone kitchen. When Great-aunt Charlotte made a sweeping gesture toward the distance, the boy sighted Harwich and the silver thread of sea which had won his grandfather seventy years before.

Blackheath Proprietary School held two precise advantages for the refugee that autumn: an older brother already established there; a congenial atmosphere in which to apply the severe lessons of Harrow. For a lower school boy, Herbert walked with great assurance.

Blackheath's neo-Gothic school building stood on a rise above, but not beyond, the prosperous village which had given the school its name. It had been capitalized in 1830 by a hundred public-spirited Englishmen with shares of twenty pounds each. The intent of those proprietors was "to provide a Course of Education for Youth, comprising Classics, Mathematics, and such Modern Languages, and other Branches of Science and General Literature, as may from time to time be introduced; combined with Religious and Moral Instruction in conformity with the principles of the Church of England." After Victoria's accession, the school had gained favor with the growing upper middle class as slightly more practical and accessible than more venerable institutions. Herbert's fellow pupils tended to be wellborn but not overbred.

Blackheath had the further advantage, so far as the twelve-year-old was concerned, of not being a proper boarding school. Life there did not require the monastic privation of Harrow. Herbert joined his brother in the home of Mrs. Valentine, a widow whose late husband had been a school proprietor. She boarded five boys in her square white Regency mansion with wrought-iron window guards and a park planted with roses, holly trees, and lilac. Her spacious house dominated the Glebe, a small circle of large dwellings, a mile from the school. Mrs. Valentine, who employed a tutor to take charge of the boys in the evening, charged eighty pounds per annum. William Blyth also paid for each of his sons an entrance fee of ten pounds, and twenty pounds "in full for Tuition, Stationary, and other matters connected with the course of Education, with the exception of printed School Books, which shall be supplied to the Pupils at the net cost price, and charged accordingly."

Herbert took immediate advantage of his new freedom. On school days, he stayed in bed until the last possible minute, jumped into his clothes, dipped his nose in the basin, fell on his knees and said, "The same as yesterday." When the worthy widow asked the usual questions about his toilet and his prayers, he most politely answered "yes" to everything.

William Blyth, to avoid the stigma of the Uncovenanted Service, had enrolled his eldest son in a Special Department devoted to the instruction of candidates for direct appointments to Her Majesty's or the East India Company's service. It was in this Special Department also that Herbert was entered. His father's hopes for loftier pursuits had been set aside after the failure at Harrow.

Upon the completion of Herbert's first term, the Headmaster, Reverend Doctor E. J. Selwyn, sent off an enthusiastic report to William Blyth: ". . . Therefore," he concluded, "I make so bold to suggest that the boy be removed from the Special Department to a course which would promote his aptitude for Classical Studies, and prepare him for one of the Universities." Flushed with his recent promotion to Deputy Commissioner at Jhang, William Blyth dispatched immediate approval. The Commissioner's hope for glory from his youngest child was rekindled.

In 1862, Herbert entered the First Form. His scholarship was generally excellent, although he was noticeably weak in mathematics. Mathematics, however, was considered merely an expedient. Certainly it was not placed on a level with classical studies. When he finished the year as Prize Boy in classics and history, and won a special French Award, the usually reticent Rev. Dr. Selwyn made note of it in his annual report. "In the First," he observed simply, "Blyth has done well."

For the six-week midsummer holiday, Herbert returned to Beaumont Hall, where his father and stepmother, on leave from Jhang, were also in residence. Father and son had not met for three years, but time had not mellowed William Blyth. He expressed little pride in the boy's performance at Blackheath, dwelling, instead, on the humiliation at Harrow, and the shame that it had brought.

When Herbert returned for autumn term, he displayed an erratic side which alarmed his masters. He seemed generally depressed, belligerent, and particularly bored with his studies. His standing fell disastrously in the class of twenty-five. He had finished the previous school year first in classics, French and history, third in divinity, fifth in marks, and eighteenth in mathematics. Now he stood thirteenth in classics, tenth in history and French, seventeenth in divinity, fourteenth in marks, and last in mathematics. When one of the masters caught him brawling with some townies in the main street of Blackheath, he was sent to the Headmaster. No punishment resulted. It transpired that Herbert had interfered to protect a smaller schoolfellow from being bullied. He was allowed to accompany Will to Beaumont Hall for Christmas holidays; but at the request of the Headmaster, Herbert returned to school a week before the other boys.

The Rev. Dr. E. J. Selwyn was a spare, bespectacled scholar whose shoulders stooped decidedly earthward, while his face rose conspicuously toward heaven. These characteristics mirrored a spirit which struggled to be true to both man and God without offending either. He had reached a state of spiritual truce when Herbert arrived. The Reverend Doctor said nothing of the boy's academic decline, nor did he probe for deep-seated reasons. He set out to build the boy's confidence to insure his performance, welcoming Herbert into his home for the last week of Christmas holiday, a restful week with a pupil for whom he held great expectations.

The benign strategy of the Headmaster had the desired effect. Herbert reached the top of the Second Form during spring term. At home, however, the fluctuations of the student were eclipsed by other matters. A letter from Aunt Amelia excitedly announced his sister Evelin's marriage to Edward George Wace. "He comes of a fine Oxfordshire family," she related, "and your father is extremely proud. Edward is a Lieutenant of Her Majesty's 33rd Regiment of Native Bengal Infantry, assigned as an Assistant Commissioner to your father at Jhang. Eva was the picture of your lamented mother in the same pretty bridal dress she wore on her wedding day at Ghazeepore."

Herbert returned for his Third Form year an undisputed favorite with the faculty, Mrs. Valentine, and his fellows. He was no longer considered Will Blyth's younger brother. Herbert had already eclipsed him when Will went up to London that autumn to coach for the Civil Service examination. At fifteen, Herbert was strikingly handsome, a trifle husky, perhaps, but cricket and rugby were already streamlining bulk into muscle. He was also something of a clown, and his schoolroom humor brought forth some enduring sobriquets. For the French master, M. Sueur, he devised from *S'il vous plaît* the nickname "Soup-plates" Sueur. For the English and writing master, Mr. Earland, who was hard of hearing, he coined the more obvious "Misty Earlobe." As for the proprietors who decided against central heating in the schoolroom. ("However well adapted the system of dry heating by hot water may be for Hot and

Green Houses," they proclaimed, "it is certainly unfit for human habitations.") They became "The Hot Air Gang."

Cricket also absorbed the young humorist, and his performance further endeared him to the academic community. Dick Irwin, a famous "pro," coached the Blackheath team. He was a colorful character who came to the field clad in enormous boots, and breeches so incredibly tight that Herbert wrote a jingle about them:

> *We grant those boots are practical*
> *With room for plenty more*
> *Feet and socks and cricket bats*
> *And any other store.*
> *But let us take those breeches, now,*
> *They make a handsome sight,*
> *But (excuse the trifling skit, Dick)*
> *Can you get them off at night?*

Despite his attire, Irwin was a painstaking coach, who appreciated Herbert's ability. He often spent an hour after regular practice bowling a steady, medium-paced ball to his young protégé, training him for forward play. It was not suprising that Herbert became the youngest boy ever to make the first XI.

He also proved adaptable off the playing field. Mrs. Valentine would sometimes have young ladies in to tea when her boys had half-days. She felt, with the blessing of the Headmaster, that her young gentlemen would benefit from well-chaperoned meetings with young ladies of good family. Emily Shortrede was of good family indeed; her uncle was a major general and a school proprietor, as well. More to the point, Herbert remembered that Will had said, rather scornfully, that she was a "kisser." She was seventeen, nearly two years older than he, but he stared mercilessly at her throughout teatime.

Being the youngest in the house, Herbert was usually charged with passing the tray. When he stopped before Emily Shortrede, she hesitated perceptibly reaching a biscuit. They smiled. By the time he had returned to his place on the sofa beside Mrs. Valentine, Emily had brought the conversation around to gardening. She was well aware that the widow took extraordinary pride in her gardens, and asked if she might take some rose cuttings for her uncle. The flattered lady dispatched Herbert for the garden shears.

There was a locked garden house behind a row of holly trees. Budding vines covered a row of trellises along the wall facing away from the main house. Herbert dropped the shears as Emily pushed him up against the roses. ("When I plucked my first sweet rose of love," Maurice Barrymore recalled years later, "thorns were appropriately pricking my buttocks.")

Herbert's academic enthusiasm was clearly flagging at the end of his Fourth Form year. When he and a schoolfellow were discovered off limits, cheering an illegal prize fight on Blackheath Common, he was again sent up before the Headmaster. Anticipating that Herbert's boredom with secondary school success might again affect him scholastically, Selwyn told the boy that a superior Fifth Form year could mean going up early to Lincoln College, Oxford. The Headmaster felt that university curricula would be more profitable for the precocious sixteen-year-old than another year at school polishing up classical composition. After five years at Blackheath, the routine of school, even the warm supervision of Mrs. Valentine, had indeed become suffocating. Even his furtive meetings with Emily Shortrede ended that spring when she married a solicitor from Tunbridge Wells. The possibility of eliminating Sixth Form year and the promising freedom of university life spurred him on.

When he entered the Fifth Form in 1867, he was elected Captain of the first XI. In Christmas examinations, he made Honour List in classics, history, and divinity. During Prize Day ceremonies that spring, he was named Prize Boy in all three, with an honorable mention for writing, and a special award for fluency in French presented by "Soup-plates" Sueur.

The Moral Conduct Prize was the last to be presented on Prize Day. Since the recipient was known only to the Headmaster, an aura of anticipation pervaded as he read the familiar preface. "The Moral Conduct Prize," he flatly recited, "arises from the investment of fifty guineas in the Funds by the late Rev. Doctor Spence. The Prize is awarded to the boy who, in the opinion of the whole School and of the Masters, most commends himself, by his high moral and religious character, influence, and example."

When Herbert rose to accept the award, there came a spontaneous cheer from his fellows. The Rev. Dr. Selwyn was visibly moved when he presented the parchment scroll and the five-pound check. As for the Prize Boy, he discerned a fair amount of irony in the situation.

III

Herbert A. Blyth found the manicured core of Lincoln College protected behind old high walls. His two-tailed commoner's suit was rumpled from the train ride, but he was formidable among the thirty-odd freshmen. The Dean asked him to muster the others, and led them all off single file in their requisite outfits to Pembroke College. They scurried like choir boys after the old man, as he billowed down the High Street in his scholar's robe, until they reached the sudden gateway of Pembroke. When they entered the Great Hall, the sound of new leather heels on worn stone echoed through the vast chamber. The Vice-Chancellor, sitting in state at a high table, proffered an austere greeting in Latin. Presenting each boy with a bound copy of the University Statutes, he bid them write their names and their fathers' professions in Latin in the Great Matriculation Book.

Old boys were not due for another day, so freshmen dined alone that evening in the hall at Lincoln College. Emptiness emphasized its ugly lath-and-plaster wagon roof, added by some misguided rector to hide the original chestnut timbers. Herbert sat securely with a few fellow Black-heathans, while others found the comfort of their own school groups or sat awkwardly alone. After dinner he went to his rooms, stared for a while from his window at the main quandrangle below, thumbed absently through the Jacobean Latin of the Statutes. A passage stopped him. Something to the effect that freshmen must at all cost avoid the society of *histriones et funambuli*. He laughed out loud. It had not even occurred to him to associate with actors and rope dancers.

When the other students had returned to the cloisters of Lincoln, bitter memories of Harrow returned with them. Here were those same superior Harrovians, older but hardly changed. They were not only from Harrow, of course, but they all preserved the smug superiority and closed circles of their first-rated public schools. Herbert was no longer a victim. He was impressive now, well schooled and self-assured, much sought after by the worst of them, but he made little effort to secure their friendships. He resented them, and, more acutely than he cared to admit to himself, he felt the fall from upper school hero to ordinary freshman. He easily fixed a reputation for repartee, but most of his time was spent boxing or rowing in the Torpids. Rare were nights of undergraduate camaraderie, vintage wine and mellow voices raised in song along the dark High Street.

Studies proved to be a greater disappointment to the young man. He was supposed to prepare for Moderations under the surveillance of two classical tutors. One he hardly saw. The other merely drew perfunctory red lines under parts of his weekly translations. One old resident tutor, however, was more agreeable. Herbert turned up in hall one day at lunchtime obviously having "looked upon the wine when it was red." Some of his fellows wondered how he had managed to reach that happy state so early in the day.

"In quest of knowledge, I assure you," Herbert explained. "I have been reading through the second extant decade of Livy with Senior Tutor, and during the session he placed a bottle of port and two glasses on a table before us. As you know, Livy frequently mentions Hannibal. Whenever we came to the name of that venerable Carthaginian, Senior Tutor replenished our glasses, crying, 'Here's that old fellow again; we must drink his health,' never failing to suit the action to the word." His gathered colleagues chortled. "This is no complaint, mind you," Herbert was quick to add, "I heartily approve his method of tuition."

As Christmas holidays approached, Herbert was convinced that all his energy for scholastic achievement had been spent at Blackheath. He accepted an invitation to spend Christmas in London with his sister Evelin's brother-in-law, Henry Wace, whom he had met at Beaumont Hall. Herbert had been impressed by "Harry," who was not only curate of St. James's Church, Piccadilly, but was on the regular staff of leader writers at the London *Times*. Three nights in the week he labored from 10 P.M. to 3 A.M. at the *Times* office, while he continued his busy parish work during the day. He had also rowed three in the Torpids and bow in the Eights at Oxford. Herbert headed for the Wace house in Portland Place confident that he would find a sympathetic listener.

The intensity with which the young man broached his subject seemed to Wace excessive for the grievances expressed. Herbert worked himself into a rage denouncing the snobbery of public schools and the limitation of their product. The good reverend, disturbed by the performance, attributed it to the fervor of youth. When rage ran out, Wace empathized with his guest. He had been through the same crisis in his first term at

Oxford, he explained. It was best to return for another term, and if there was no improvement something could then be done about it.

Harry's wife Elizabeth made an effort during the holiday to introduce Herbert to some young ladies and gentlemen of quality. He was a success at their gatherings, rather enjoyed them, but they left him unsatisfied. At the end of the holiday, he spent a pleasant week with Great-aunt Charlotte at Beaumont Hall. Coercion was not necessary, but the Commissioner had reminded him that it was an obligation. "You must be respectful," he had written, "to those who have patronised you."

Spring term was not an improvement. Studies seemed merely a continuation of those at Blackheath, now diluted by repetition and the lack of congenial supervision. The interlude was spiced, however, by a chambermaid at an inn around the corner from Lincoln in the High Street. She was a generous, overspilling girl, who inconveniently lived with her grandmother. They were obliged, therefore, to meet mornings at the inn while the girl was doing her daily rounds. It was an Elizabethan building of half-levels and abortive corridors, which Herbert could enter without witness to search for his waiting accomplice. Standing prim in starched white cap and apron, with bed sheets bundled in her arms, she would beckon him into an empty room.

Done with pleasure, he would depart as stealthily as he had arrived. The girl would adjust her cap, change the linen, and go on about her chores. When they were discovered by the housekeeper one spring morning, Herbert was not particularly concerned. He had already decided to leave Oxford at the end of that term.

Herbert posted a diplomatic explanation to Jhang, suggesting the inevitable alternative—the Indian Civil Service. His father replied in hearty agreement, establishing a year's ample income while he prepared for the examination. Herbert was surprised and strangely disappointed at the unusual lack of opposition. A letter from Aunt Amelia indicated the reason for William Blyth's magnanimity. (The Commissioner and his eldest son had recently returned from a walking tour of New Zealand, where a girl had turned Will's head at a reception given for his father by the Deputy Commissioner of Mongonin. The young lady was of exceedingly good family. So much so that William Blyth looked to his own position, and decided to purchase an impressive estate for his son in Auckland. There was not the slightest objection when marriage was discussed. Flattered by his own acceptance in local society, the Commissioner purchased a second estate for himself before sailing for India.) Herbert assumed that his father had not been ungrateful to eliminate the expense of a lingering classical education.

Walter Wren's coaching school in London was where one crammed for the Indian Civil Service examination. Will had studied with Wren when the gentleman was a dedicated tutor without a school of his own. Now, Wren was concerned with obtaining quick results rather than imparting substantial knowledge. To the amusement of his schoolfellows, Herbert characterized the rather stout educator. "Wren's mind," he observed, "is like the trunk of a bull elephant, which will pick-up pins and peanuts."

The reluctant student bought a plucky fox terrier, christened him Rahj II, and took lodgings, three rooms of an early Georgian house just off Russell Square in Bloomsbury. He shared the rooms with Paul Potter, an oldish young man of seventeen, who seemed an unlikely companion for Herbert Blyth. "Why study life," Paul questioned, "when it is all so thoroughly written and pigeonholed and catalogued by men so superior to any of us?" Herbert was of a different mind, but Paul's penchant for brilliant debate, his quick wit, and colorful knowledge of London made him stimulating company. Together, they meandered through Bloomsbury, down Lamb's Conduit Street and Museum Street, browsing in curio shops and "twopenny" bookstalls, filling their rooms with Hindoo idols, yellow dragons and rare volumes. Paul's literary tastes ran to the Expurgatorius and Diderot, Herbert's to Dickens, Thackeray, and Fielding.

Paul's parents had urged him to Wren's, but his overriding ambition was to write plays. He naturally gravitated toward the theatrical aspects of the city. Herbert was a willing companion. In the West End, they were taken by the smooth comedies of T. W. Robertson, particularly when acted by Squire Bancroft and his wife at the Prince of Wales's Theatre. Herbert and Paul saw *School* three times to indulge the popular pastime of cheering H. J. Montague when he proclaimed: "Some women would kill gallantry and chivalry by something called equality with men. What is equality with men? Having their clothes made by a he-tailor instead of a she-milliner. How pleasant for a man and wife to be measured together; or, at an election, for him to walk arm-in-arm to the meetings with a wretched, half-mad, who-mannish creature who votes for the candidate you wish to exclude."

They were drawn also to seedier theatricals at the Garrick Theatre in Leman Street, where one could procure a box for threepence. Herbert, Paul, and whichever friends would condescend to join them straddled chipped gilt side chairs, attending with equal interest the pit or the stage. During *Starving Poor of Whitechapel,* when stage policemen were getting the worst of a free-for-all, Herbert joined some wildly transported patrons who climbed onstage to validate the battle.

He particularly relished the infamous "penny gaff" where poverty and crime met, usually to the advantage of both. Paul and Herbert, with Rahj glowering from under his arm, elbowed their way down foul, narrow passages past hawk-eyed pickpockets. From filthy seats in the littered hall, they watched a tattered trio sing in true street style with mimes and gestures and hinted indecencies. Crowding around the platform, endangering its makeshift proscenium, Whitechapel loafers and ladies of the evening lent rough, raucous punctuation. In a music-hall and refreshment-bar era, only the "gaff" recaptured the grandeur of London's underworld. The caves and night cellars once frequented by John Blyth had vanished thirty years before.

Patronized by the Waces, the Denyses, and the families of school friends, H. A. Blyth, Esq., found himself on many of the London *Lists*. He received invitations to what was left of dancing evenings, although the ballroom was on the decline in fashionable society. It had been observed by Blanchard Jerrold that "only very young men could be got to stand up at a ball, therefore 'devotion for life, dearest' was becoming bad form during dance music." Herbert was invited to the *déjeuner*, garden parties and croquet parties which were replacing the dance as popular matrimonial market places. "What peculiarity of temperament," Herbert wondered in a letter to Aunt Amelia, "decrees a hand on the mallet a more potent stimulant than an arm round the waist?"

He was a novelty at these functions, his intense good looks enhanced by an increasing disregard for style of dress. Fluttering young ladies were attracted to him; but resentful young men wrote him off as a Bohemian. Herbert offended their refined sensibilities by expressing the republican sentiments of Sir Charles Dilke, who was aiming to abolish the monarchy, or by dramatizing the lot of the poor. "The St. Pancras workhouse authorities have entered upon a crusade for the extinction of pauperism," he confided to an unsuspecting group around a punch bowl. "Their method is founded on a perfectly intelligible principle: make them worse off in the workhouse, than they would be outside and pauperism will soon disappear. One old woman there was good enough to illustrate the theory the other day by dying of starvation."

He was amused for a while by the world of polite society and its obsequious young ladies who gave blushing consent to trysts behind clipped boxwood hedges. But the role of resident Bohemian soon wearied him and, although he did not admit it to himself, offended him, as well.

In the more rarefied malt- and tobacco-scented atmosphere of the Mitre in St. Martin's Lane, he found his *métier*. Lionel Brough, scion of a noted theatrical family, who became assistant publisher of the *Daily Telegraph*, innovated the selling of papers by newsboys in the streets, and resumed the family trade; C. P. Flockton, a Bohemian zither-playing actor-manager; sportsman Micky Slater, of the West London Rowing Club; politicians, athletes, writers mingled there for warm beer and talk usually more heated. Good talk was the particular fare of the Mitre, and Charles Vandenhoff was by far its leading exponent. Having returned recently from five years of acting in America, he regaled Wren's student with tales of his tour and glorified theatrical shop talk. Though a year younger than Herbert, he had seen far more of the world. While young Blyth romped on the playing fields of Blackheath, Charley had claimed his heritage as a boy actor at the Drury Lane. Son of George Vandenhoff, nephew of Henry Vandenhoff, noted Shakespearean actors of the day, Charley was a good all-around performer, a little undersized, and just a trifle stagy, but thoroughly experienced and sound. As a loyal friend and teller of tales, he was without peer.

One evening at the Mitre, Herbert held forth halfheartedly to his uninterested companions on the merits of Dilke's crusade against the Throne. He was spurred on by voices from a shadowed corner table. Attention inspired him to rhetoric, rhetoric fired him to participation. When he joined his public, they were outlining a plan to smash a Conservative meeting at Knightsbridge Riding School the following evening.

The conservative portion of Dilke's constituency in Chelsea had been trying to repudiate the sentiments of their quixotic M.P., but the radicals continually thwarted them. Although special tickets had been issued to prevent them from gaining entry to the riding school, Herbert and his boisterous companions forced their way into the meeting. They quickly gained the upper hand in a brief period of turbulent contention. Then, bored with debate, they carried the platform by violent assault. Herbert joined in the amiable distribution of black eyes and bloody noses, driving the conservatives from the building. Dilkites had been reduced to mauling one another when, *The Sportsman* reported, "the police concluded the proceedings by the extinction of gas."

Herbert escaped to the Mitre, where he recounted the exploit with the flushed excitement of a triumphant cricketer. During the monologue, one of his cohorts returned. When the fellow pointed furtively to the door, Herbert followed him to the street. "That little exercise tonight was only a start," the fellow began in an overconfidential whisper. Between excited breaths he outlined a fantastic plot to assassinate Queen Victoria. Herbert's eyes paled. With his right fist, he knocked the startled conspirator up against the front wall of the pub. Unconscious of his own strength, Herbert kept up a barrage of left jabs. There was blood. Shouting. Micky Slater and Charley Vandenhoff rushed to the street. They restrained their raging friend with great effort, while the would-be assassin stumbled down St. Martin's Lane.

"At Wren's," observed Paul Potter, "Blyth became a sort of fleeting shadow with the reputation of being a brilliant scholar, of knowing how to manage his 'dukes,' and of never attending any class save when Professor Thorold Rogers was talking scandal against Queen Elizabeth."

Walter Wren remembered Will Blyth with the special affection that an uninspired but dutiful teacher has for an uninspired but dogged pupil. Will had brought honor to his tutor by placing high in the Indian Civil

Service examination for his year. The professor was frustrated by the younger brother, just turned twenty, who seemed to possess more native ability but far less interest. He admonished the prodigal for failure to memorize his lessons: "Remember, Blyth, that only that knowledge can be properly called so which can be produced ready for use instantly. Whether you are in the examination room or the House of Commons, you must be able to do without books." Herbert reminded the professor that he had no intention of spending his time in either place. He need not have troubled. The scarlet fever felled him that spring, and he never went up for the examination.

While Herbert convalesced at Beaumont Hall, his father made another attempt at respectability for him. When Harry Wace was appointed Chaplain of Lincoln's Inn, a college for the study of law, the Commissioner had written asking if he could use his influence to place the wayward boy in chambers with a barrister. Wace arranged for a clerk's position, to train the boy, in the offices of Messrs. Grover and Humphreys, solicitors to the Blyths and the Waces. The position satisfied William Blyth. He established another year's income for his son, to be administered by Harry Wace.

Herbert approached warily the tired terrace that held 4 Kings Bench Walk within the courts and closes of Inner Temple. But after a few weeks, he developed a theatrical sense of his new profession, swaggering each morning in his cutaway and topper from Russell Square to the City, through the ancient stone archway to his offices. He made an effort to concentrate. Messrs. Grover and Humphreys were impressed by the attractive young man so quick to grasp the intricacies of their calling. But after a few months, the repetition began to bore Herbert. The small neat office with its narrow leaded window suffocated him.

It was not long before the clerk strayed far from the sanctity of Inner Temple.

IV

THERE WAS IN London a convivial circle of amateur sportsmen, boxers and swimmers, rowers and runners and footballers. They ran with the Thames Hare and Hounds or rowed with the Leander Club or dozens of other organizations dedicated to amateur athletics. They trained assiduously for the Amateur Boxing Championships or the Metropolitan Regatta and Diamond Sculls, competing for Grand Challenge Cups or Silver Goblets and Medals, mainly for the sport of it. Their names are not immortal, but in the sixties and seventies the best of them inspired the envy of challengers and the devotion of schoolboys: "Bat" Murphy; young "Dutch Sam" Abison of Bowlea, who held the mile record for many years; Teddy Mills, a beautiful distance runner, of Bethnal Green; Hayward, the Billingsgate fish porter and long-distance walker; Miles of Brighton, the "walking coachman"; Jack White of Gateshead, the best man from four to ten miles who ever put on a shoe.

The ruling spirit of this devoted lot was Micky Slater, president of the West London Rowing Club and patron of the Mitre, whose father, a Yorkshire sporting squire, had run through a fortune at all sorts of sport, but raised his son to be a rare hard one. Impressed with Herbert Blyth's potential for sport and struggle, Micky got him into the W.L.R.C. and urged him to join a four that he was making up for the Wyford Challenge Cup at Henley. The others of the foursome were salesmen in the "rag trade" in the big drapery warehouses around St. Paul's Churchyard. They usually worked late, so training had to be done early in the morning.

Herbert would rise at five o'clock to dress in the sunless chill of his Russell Square rooms. By half-past the hour, with Rahj shivering under his arm, he would be heading in a cab toward Cheney Walk. There, he rallied with his fellows to jog three miles to the Feathers, an ancient waterman's pub and training place at the mouth of the Wandle. Silence prevailed on the dark journey, broken only by the idle yapping of their mascot or the bell of an occasional Thames barge.

It was usually light enough when they arrived to get into their boat. With little time to spare, they rowed hard at a slow stroke up to Putney Bridge. Slater thought it unprofessional, but Rahj was allowed to accompany them. Herbert trained him to sit upright in the bow. He stayed still as a figurehead, surveying the oncoming river, barking only if another boat veered close to them. At Putney, they turned around and pegged away down to West London Railway Bridge, a little over one and three-quarters miles, as hard as they could lick. They returned to the Feathers at a hard slow stroke.

There were no showers at the ancient pub, so they used either to have a dive in "the Cut," the barge entrance of the Wandle, or in the clear cold Thames itself at low water, or have buckets of water thrown over them. They would rub down, dress quickly, and snatch a hasty breakfast of cold meat, stale bread, watercress, if available, and two cups of tea, before hustling back to their workaday worlds of warehouses and offices.

Herbert would return to the Feathers on boxing night to participate in amateur matches. He became infatuated with the sport which had been merely a flirtation at Oxford, and began taking lessons at Angelo's Fencing Academy to perfect his style.

"In order to gain further experience," he remarked, "I would go to various public houses kept by retired pugilists, and by paying a sovereign would get them to box with me and give me points." Dressing himself in rough clothes, he spent some hard nights at the Blue Anchor in Shoreditch, where publican Bill Richardson offered instructive pommeling. For several months, once or twice a week, Herbert left these encounters in thoroughly battered condition. But he stuck gamely to his task until he had pretty much mastered the tricks of hard fighting. With technique came confidence, and he started taking on all challengers from the rough trade of the pub. Agile and hard from mornings on the river and afternoons at Angelo's, he bested the toughest opponents.

Three nights running during Herbert's performance, a stranger watched intently from a ringside table. Although he could not have been much older than Herbert, and was quite a bit shorter, there was a worldly way about him. His round Irish face supported a large mustache and a silk top hat, both at rakish angles. He wore a massive black frock coat trimmed generously with Persian lamb. His gloves were still fragrant, and he carried a monstrous silver-headed cane. When Ned Donnelly stood up full height to challenge the Blue Anchor exhibitionist, the hem of his frock coat touched the floor.

Donnelly muttered instructions as they sparred: "Now yer left 'and . . . over with yer right . . step back and come again . . ."

Herbert announced, rather grandly considering his short breaths, that he knew quite well what to do.

"'old yer 'ands a little 'igher, can't yer?" Donnelly continued.

Herbert stepped back to rattle his presumptuous opponent with some long-arm hitting, dropping his guard as he maneuvered for a hit. Donnelly stepped in about twelve inches, countered with a left uppercut. The public house hero fell flat on his back in the center of the makeshift ring.

Ned Donnelly, still in his thirties, was considered London's Royal Professor of the Art of Self-Defence. He could neither read nor write, but was steeped in the lore of the prize ring when it had approached horse racing in the estimate of the sporting public. He remembered his own boxing days, when gentlemen would gather on Sunday mornings within a stone's throw of Covent Garden to cheer hot and strong knuckle fights. Donnelly would have been a champion—if the prize ring had not been outlawed. In twenty-two-year-old Herbert Blyth, he envisioned not only a talented boxer, but a gentleman who might elevate the image of his beloved sport.

That night at the Blue Anchor, they sipped ruby port, Ned's particular drink, long after closing time, outlining an elaborate plan for Herbert's boxing career. The first step would be the Marquis of Queensberry's Amateur Championships, only a few months away. It was almost daylight when they finally reached the pavement. A dray stacked high with barrels had pulled up, its two stately horses snorting daggers into the cold, while leathered draymen carried another week's beer to Bill Richardson. The Royal Professor and the Prize Boy sowed visions of glory along the dawning streets to Bloomsbury.

Herbert did not officially break his ties with Messrs. Grover and Humphreys, but he became merely a visitor in their offices, making what amounted to courtesy calls to satisfy Harry Wace, the administrator of his income. With some regret, he also dropped out of Micky Slater's Wyford four. Boxing obsessed him. His days and nights were given to intensive training at Mr. Waite's School of Arms in Golden Square, where the Professor gave lessons. Donnelly was somewhat concerned by the ferocious intensity of his protégé, but the results justified the method.

He was duly entered for the boxing championships of 1872 to be held on Thursday, the 21st of March. Weighing 150 pounds, he qualified as a gentleman amateur in the middleweight division between ten stone and eleven stone, four pounds. The committee, headed by the Marquis of Queensberry, reserved the right of requiring a reference, or of refusing an entry, but Herbert's credentials conformed to their definition of a gentleman amateur: "Any gentleman who has never competed in any open competition, or for public money, or with professionals for a prize; and who has never taught, pursued or assisted in the pursuit of athletic exercises as a means of livelihood, nor is a mechanic, artisan, or labourer."

Mr. Waite kept a cottage on a farm in Surrey, where hopefuls from his School of Arms could train. Six weeks before the scheduled match, the Professor traveled the Surrey Road with his star pupil and a dog. When they arrived at the secluded cottage, Donnelly went briskly about his business. He fastened a well-blown-out bullock's bladder by a string to a high beam, carefully adjusting it to the height of an opponent's head. "Practice wif a swinging bladder," he announced, "makes yer quicker than if yer practice wif a stuffed sack."

He ceremoniously poured pints of whiskey and vinegar into a pot, added horseradish, rock salt, juice of five lemons, and brought it to a boil. When it had cooled, he poured the remarkable brew into a large bottle, with the satisfaction of a French chef over perfect hollandaise, advising his pupil to rub himself with it, arms, hands, face, chest, three times a day. After final instructions, the Professor left Herbert to voluntary confinement. Apart from the occasional visits of Donnelly, his only companions for six weeks, besides Rahj, would be a deaf daily woman to cook and clean for him, and a chestnut gelding, Moonlight, hired from the owner of the farm.

The Queensberry hopeful began his mornings at six with a cold bath—without soap, since the Professor deemed it harmful. He threw out a pair of two-pound dumbbells in the position of infighting until he was tired, then broke his fast with a single gingerbread nut steeped in Hollands. He took a brisk morning walk with Rahj, not more than a mile, through the surrounding woods, returning slowly to avoid heating his body.

His morning refreshment—rennet-whey and hard white biscuits without seeds—came at nine, after which he rubbed himself with the Professor's precious mixture, and rode or ran out for his sweat. On wet days, when it was impossible to go out, he put on a couple of flannel suits, a flannel mask, a warm cap, woolen scarf, thick gloves, and skipped rope for an hour or more, at intervals, before a large fire. At eleven, he had a glass of jelly, a rusk and wine.

He amused himself walking moderately and sparring before dinner at one, which was alternately stewed veal and well-fed fowls. (Red wine mixed with water was allowed at dinner, and a glass of hock afterward, but porter, ale, any sort of beer or spirituous liquors, as well as salts, red meats and acids, were not. Nor was tea to be taken in the afternoon; but a rusk and hot chocolate were allowed early in the evening as compensation.) He would sleep for an hour, then work with the dumbbells or pommel the bullock's bladder. He rubbed down again, bundled up to

37

avoid a chill, and walked out over the fields, or rode Moonlight through the darkening woods.

At seven, he would sup on rennet milk pottage, some bread, a chicken, or some food that was nourishing but not gross. Another bath and a claret posset mulled were taken before retiring. By nine o'clock he was usually deep in his feather bed with the works of Dickens, Thackeray, and Fielding. *Oliver Twist* made him weep. *The Newcomes* brought him "the fair Miss Ethel," his first literary infatuation. And he found his favorite of fiction in *Tom Jones*—of character and temperament not unlike his own.

"It was rather like quarantine," Maurice Barrymore recalled years later, "but I never again had such peace, or such good companions."

The day before the scheduled championships, the Professor rode out to collect his hardened contender, bringing along some mail from Russell Square. Donnelly navigated his gig precariously over the rutted road to London as Herbert, Rahj cowering in his lap, read a letter from his father.

"Will it never end, this constant degrading of yourself and your family? Boxing is for street-corner ruffians, not for a young man of education and background . . ." The gig jerked to the right, as Donnelly, crouched like a jockey, maneuvered his brown mare around a lackadaisical farm wagon. "You must terminate this foolishness, and sever ties with bad companions who lead you into such pastimes. I would prefer a son of mine to be an honourable clerk, than a champion of the boxing ring . . ."

That night he slept fitfully in Donnelly's rooms above the School of Arms, awakening long before dawn. The Professor rubbed him down, gave him breakfast of unbuttered toast and half a pint of mulled red wine. It was still dark when they walked up Piccadilly through light snow. At Hyde Park Corner, they hailed a cab. When they arrived at Lillie-Bridge, Donnelly complained to the driver that a shilling and sixpence to West Brompton was highway robbery.

The snow had stopped in the first hour of daylight. Three workmen pitched the ring, driving stakes to mark a twenty-four-foot square, running two rows of heavy rope through them. A shivering woman was setting up her refreshment booth. A youth lined up coconut and doll targets for a makeshift Three-Throws-A-Penny. Some gypsies in gaudy finery were already prowling, while tricksters and mountebanks polished up their acts. Competitors were arriving, and spectators, when a messenger appeared from the Secretary of the Amateur Athletic Club. The meeting was postponed because of inclement weather. Donnelly noticed that Herbert's eyes paled as his voice rose to denounce the A.A.C. He tried to quiet his protégé, but spectators and boxers alike joined in rattled agreement. Three days later, a letter from H. A. Blyth was published in *The Sportsman:*

Sir, In the name of many—I may, I believe, say most—of the competitors and of all the intending spectators who were present on the ground on Thursday, I beg leave to protest against the deferment of the Boxing Championship Meeting.

One of the fundamental principles of all such meetings prescribes that the day originally fixed should be adhered to. This abandonment of the rule has in many notable instances caused the greatest dissatisfaction and excited the loudest protests. It has been the ruin we know of regattas and prize meetings of various sorts, and if it is not checked at once will be the ruin of the A.A.C. Competitors will never take pains to prepare themselves to set apart a day for the race or competition if it is in the power of a secretary to adjourn the whole affair arbitrarily, without even a day's notice. Extraordinary circumstances may excuse such an irregularity but such cases occur very rarely.

Now on Thursday there was no such case. At the time when the meeting would naturally have begun the weather was perfectly fine overhead . . . The best proof that the meeting could have been held with perfect ease is that every professional man on the ground strongly urged that the competition should take place, and that the competitors themselves supported the same view . . .

I now come to what was the evident motive for this proceeding. It was feared that the weather would prevent, or, had prevented spectators from coming. It was apparent that the gate money would not amount to a very magnificent sum, and for the paltry, petty-fogging economy—the miserable desire to get a few more shillings—the convenience of all the persons most genuinely interested, who, of course, were present, was disregarded. The competitors were seriously inconvenienced, and some of them deprived of their chance (as they were unable to stay longer in London); and, what is worse, the character of the club for holding to its engagements lost. Such poor and miserable policy cannot but ruin the club if persevered in. This time, it is true, a sovereign or two may be gained by the device, but in the long run members will be shy of joining, and spectators of attending, the meetings of a club on whose engagements so little reliance is to be placed.—I am, sir, & c,

                                                                One of the Competitors

The meeting, rescheduled for the following Tuesday, promised "to afford more than usually good sport," predicted *The Sportsman.* "Mr. E. B. Mitchell appears again for the middle weights, which he won in '70, and we hear he has learnt better style." Style was imperative, and Mitchell was favorite. Queensberry Rules specified that the decision of the judges depended on the best style and the most points achieved by a competitor. ("The points shall be for 'Attack,' direct clean hits with the knuckles of either hand on any part of the front or sides of the head, or body above the belt; 'Defence,' guarding, slipping, ducking, counter-hitting, or getting away. Where points are otherwise equal, consideration to be given to the man who does most of the leading off.") There were three rounds in all open competitions, with an interval of one minute between them. The first two rounds were of three minutes each, the final round of four minutes.

Doors opened at 1:30. By 2:00, there were no more than five hundred spectators, a somewhat select attendance. Herbert considered the fruits of "petty-fogging economy" while Donnelly and Micky Slater helped him to dress. Slater was acting as second, since the Queensberry Rules forbade trainers to do so. The Professor pushed "Registered Champion" gloves over Herbert's knuckles, bemoaning the demise of knuckle fighting.

There were spontaneous cheers when H. A. Blyth entered the ring for the first heat. They did not know him, but he seemed one to be reckoned with, twenty-two years old, six feet tall, lean and hard in white knee breeches belted with the yellow-and-blue-striped sash of the West London Rowing Club. They noted the natural swagger, the head held high.

He felt goose flesh. He was unsure if the cheers or the afternoon chill had brought it. When he performed the formal handshake with E. B. Mitchell, Herbert was irritated by the fellow's complacent gaze. They assumed smartly the starting position. The timekeeper gave the signal. Before the crowd realized it, there came a right-hand body blow. Then a left-hand uppercut.

"H. A. Blyth," reported *The Sportsman*, "opened a spacious firmament to the bewildered eyes of the favourite."

Herbert was overconfident when he entered his second heat, but F. M. Chappell, the Oxford champion, soon had him working very hard. Although he went down twice in the last round, partly from blows, but chiefly because he slipped, the judges decided in his favor. "Blyth displayed the best points unmistakably, and hit his man oftener than he received," explained *The Sportsman*. "Chappell seemed to have got slower since last year. He waited and waited, but had few chances of countering, as Blyth stopped him well . . ."

To give breathing time until the finals commenced, there was a Two Miles Race between the professional bicycle champion and a pony, Black Bess. During the break, Donnelly was informed that W. J. West, Herbert's opponent in the finals, was an instructor of boxing in Northampton. He was considered a semiprofessional, technically ineligible to compete. The Professor felt that his pupil was tired, could lose the championship now. He urged him to enter a protest against West. Herbert refused.

West was a hard man to put down. Being a little too "tricky" with his hands, he caused Herbert to spar a trifle nervously at first. "Blyth, however, soon warmed to his work," *The Sportsman* added reassuringly, "and there was some good countering and stopping, Blyth being very straight in deliveries. The neatest points of the day, including the light and heavy weight competitions, were displayed during this bout, and the Londoner won easily at the finish, notwithstanding his opponent's 'dancing.' "

When Herbert entered the winner's circle, he observed that Black Bess, the victorious pony, had preceded him there, leaving a pungent token. The studied dignity of the Marquis of Queensberry was somewhat undermined as he presented the honored cup. The exultant Professor could not understand the amusement of his champion, nor his lack of excitement when offered a staff position at Mr. Waite's school. The champion was grateful to his mentor, but the School of Arms was a far cry from Donnelly's vision of a Prize Ring renaissance. "My craving for athletic glory is satisfied now," Herbert told him; "I'll pay more attention in future to my law books."

That night, publican Nat Langham gave a tumultuous victory celebration at the Mitre. The small pub was stacked with jovial bodies unable to move but able to shout. At three in the morning, Nat was still trying to move the last hangers-on out of his private upstairs room. C. P. Flockton put a hand on the shoulder of the champion. Their bleary eyes met.

"First season Windsor Easter Monday, Herby," offered the actor-manager in alcoholic cablese. "Ought to come down try your hand. Good utility part. Must be there tomorrow. Guinea for the week." Herbert considered. He knew that leaving Messrs. Grover and Humphreys would mean final estrangement from his father. He had a stifling memory of leaded windows.

Late the next morning, the Middle Weight Champion of England and his small dog boarded the South-Western Railway for Windsor.

THEATRE ROYAL, WINDSOR
SOLE LESSEE & RESPONSIBLE MANAGER . . . MR. FLOCKTON
Notice!—The above named theatre having been taken for a term by
Mr. Flockton, he begs to inform the public that the Spring Dramatic
Season will commence on Easter Monday, April 1st, 1872 with an
Efficient Company selected from the London and principal
Provincial Theatres.

Windsor's Theatre Royal, one of the most elegant and complete establishments in the provinces, had been built to house a local stock company. But that common practice was becoming unprofitable, since the rapid advance of railways made it possible to transport complete London productions throughout the country, exposing audiences to the high standards of the metropolis. Notwithstanding loyalties to familiar favorites, and the local color generated by a regular company, it became impossible for them to compete, even with a nightly change of bill.

The owners of the Theatre Royal were attempting a compromise in the face of the current trend: a season produced by a London actor-manager with a selection of well-known metropolitan players. In the *Windsor and Eton Press*, Flockton promised "a succession of the best London novelties, supported by talented artistes and embellished by handsome scenery and dresses, to tender the establishment in every way worthy of the town." At the end of his generous prospectus he did not neglect to mention "H. A. Blyth, the Middle Weight Boxing Champion, in his first dramatic role."

Flockton was commencing his season with a revival of Dion Boucicault's *London Assurance*, first produced in 1841, a witty exposition of city versus country life in Regency England. Herbert was cast as *Cool*, valet to *Sir Harcourt Courtly*. It was not a large part, but he appeared regularly to spice Boucicault's contention that the servant was often master of the man.

He approached rehearsals lightheartedly, as a wonderful adult game played on the exotic field of a bare stage. He learned his few lines quickly, and had little trouble delivering them. Flockton was pleased with his voice and movement, but Herbert noticed a change in his convivial comrade of the Mitre. He was stern and rather aloof during rehearsals, considerations of friendship laid aside. Rahj was not allowed inside the theater, nor could he enter the boardinghouse where the company stayed. To the misery of pet and master, he was tied in a shed at the bottom of the garden.

Others in the company, who had proved congenial away from the theater, were also quiet and businesslike within its darkened precincts. It had not occurred to the Commissioner's son that actors had these moments, like solicitors or civil servants. With rehearsal done, they adjourned to the Bells of Ousely by the river, becoming once more the colorful storytellers and conjurers he had known. It was the challenge of their wit and the warmth of their company which held the newcomer.

On Easter Monday, the day of their opening, Herbert joined the many holiday visitors to Windsor who took boats out on the Thames. He had hired a pair-oared skiff to take the leading lady, Miss Gainsborough, for an afternoon row. She had seemed at rehearsals to take more than professional interest in him. He intended to try her that afternoon. She reclined on the cushioned seat facing him; between her strait-laced shoes and her long green skirt, an inch of silk stocking tantalized him. He maneuvered away from the other boats to a bank of willows.

As he started to put up the oars, she placed both hands firmly on his, urging him to start back. It was barely four o'clock, but he realized that the lady was not being coy. She made it plain that she was not averse to an amorous afternoon on the river, but concerned about the eight-o'clock curtain. Her nearly desperate insistence made him relent. Herbert rowed back to shore against a trying northeast wind, puzzling over his partner's anxiety. The opening of the Theatre Royal that evening had been far from his thoughts.

As the opening coincided with the arrival at Windsor of Queen Victoria, Flockton was anticipating Royal patronage. None was forthcoming. As usual since the death of the Prince Consort ten years before, Her Majesty left Windsor Castle only to walk or drive in the gardens with Princess Beatrice, Lady Churchill, or inevitable German cousins.

Despite the lack of Royal patronage, the opening was well attended, critical response favorable. "*London Assurance* and the burlesque of *Aladdin* were performed by one of the most talented companies that have performed in Windsor for some years . . ." noted the *Express*, adding, however, that "The young man who impersonated the valet was far too handsome." This inconclusive observation was H. A. Blyth's only notice as *Cool*, but he could not resist turning it into a good line, even at his own expense. Back at the Mitre, Charley Vandenhoff asked if his performance had been reviewed.

"Yes," replied the debutant, "one of the critics consigned me to a place where I would never be *Cool* again."

Harry Wace did not find the line amusing when it was repeated before dinner at Portland Place. He warned the young man that a life upon the stage would not be condoned by his father. It would probably necessitate a complete break from the Blyths, and in all decency, if he persisted in this folly, a change of name as well. He insinuated that it was not only the Blyths but the Waces, also, who would be disgraced. His father's reaction could be predicted, of course, but Herbert had expected more of Harry Wace. He did not stay for dinner. After hasty apologies to Elizabeth, he returned to the warmth of the Mitre.

Charley Vandenhoff understood. (Recently, when he had started to become well-known as a leading man in comedy and melodrama, his father had written a public letter denouncing him: "Only two men have any right to use the historical theatrical name of Vandenhoff," the Shakespearean actor had concluded, "myself and my illustrious brother Henry." Charley had written a dignified and intensely human reply, signed "the natural son of a most unnatural father." The letter was ignored. In a way, it seemed to embitter Charley's whole life.) About to depart for a summer as leading man to a stock company in Scarborough, Charley asked his distressed friend to come along. He was sure that they could get him the job of utility man, the small parts actor, at a guinea a week with room and board. Herbert liked the idea of a summer by the seashore with his gregarious friend. The income would also be welcome.

The last of the money allotted by his father had been received that month, and little of it remained. Money, for young Blyth, was merely something to be spent.

Concurrently, Herbert had an offer from a dramatic agent to go on as one of the clubmen in a revival of Bulwer-Lytton's *Money*. Squire Bancroft's production of that comedy standard at the Prince of Wales's might well have made a name of H. A. Blyth in the West End.

"I declined the honour," he said, "to go with my friend to Scarborough."

V

O N   T H E   T W E N T Y - F I R S T of June, 1872, the Great Eastern Railway deposited the two young actors at Scarborough, "Queen of English Watering-places." Rahj had been left at Russell Square with Paul Potter. Charley had convinced the reluctant master to do so. "An actor's life," he warned, "is no life for a dog." The leading man was to stay in style at the new Grand Hotel on the bay. The utility man retired to Mrs. Hogg's boardinghouse, 12 Aberdeen Walk, with his immediate superiors, J. H. "Handsome Jack" Barnes, first walking man, and Dalton Stone, second walking man.

Mrs. Hogg reminded them that she was a respectable widow, who would not have taken actors were she not acquainted with the owner of the Londesborough Theatre. It was true that she did not usually accommodate theater people, but her house resembled the establishments that did. In her determination to prove that she was not obliged to take boarders, small refinements had given way to studied shows of affluence, creating the impression of a middle-class home gone commercial.

Mrs. Hogg completed their indoctrination, turned toward the kitchen, and called, "Elsie, bring the Register." A nervous chambermaid entered with a morocco-bound, gold-embossed book nearly too large for her to carry. She offered it in turn to each of the actors. Herbert hesitated. Then he leaned over, quickly scrawling "G. H. Blythe." That, he assumed, should satisfy the Blyths and the Waces.

He dined and strolled with his colleagues along the Yorkshire coast that evening. The tide was out, leaving a wide gray beach nearly deserted. Some truant local children still played in the smooth sand, but small visitors had been swept off hours ago by their nannies to supper and safety in the Grand Hotel. There was a suggestion of light and music

45

from the Spa Promenade above them. The actors resisted the temptation. There was a meeting with their new employer in the morning.

The Londesborough Theatre was W. A. Waddington's gift to the Muses. After making his fortune at the manufacture of pianofortes in York, he had cultivated a relentless kinship with the worlds of music and drama. He was fortunately a man of taste. That, combined with ready money, had made his new theater the admiration of visitors and the pride of Scarborough. Waddington had gathered around him a group of sound professionals. Assured of their capabilities, he did not interfere with them. His house manager, E. J. George, was courteous and obliging, his stage manager, C. A. Cowdery, painstaking and accomplished. Messrs. Gordon and Jones, of the Queen's Theatre, London, designed all of his scenery, and most of his company were seasoned players with vast repertoires of popular plays committed to memory.

When rehearsals commenced ten days before opening, it was necessary for Herbert to work harder than any one of his colleagues. He found the challenge invigorating, sharing, from the outset, a sense of quality in the proceedings and a commitment to them. "We can testify to the praiseworthy energy and unremitting labour which has been displayed on the part of each individual member of the company," wrote the *Express* critic. "They have been incessantly at work for at least the week previous, and although they were at rehearsal till midnight on Saturday, they were at it again early on Monday morning, the day of the opening." Unbeknownst to the *Express*, or to the city fathers, who prohibited it, the company rehearsed long after midnight, well into the Sabbath. They were overwrought and ready for opening night.

LONDESBOROUGH THEATRE

SOLE PROPRIETOR & LESSEE . . . . MR. W. WADDINGTON

MANAGER . . . . MR. EDWARD J. GEORGE

THIS NEW AND ELEGANT THEATRE WILL OPEN FOR THE SEASON
ON MONDAY NEXT, JULY 8TH, 1872
UNDER THE IMMEDIATE PATRONAGE OF THE WORSHIPFUL
THE MAYOR, (W. F. ROOKE, ESQ., M.D.,)
AND THE MAYORESS

The Performances will commence at Eight precisely
with a New Comedy Drama, in Three Acts, by H. T. Craven, Esq.,
entitled COALS OF FIRE. To conclude with the successful Burlesque
by R. Reece, Esq., entitled LITTLE ROBIN HOOD;
or QUITE A NEW BEAU.

Orchestra Stall, 4s.; Pit Stalls, 2s.6d.; Reserved Seats, 2s.;
Balcony, 1s. Doors open at Half-past seven.
CARRIAGES MAY BE ORDERED AT 10.45

Mr. Waddington himself could not have written a more affectionate review than did the *Express* critic. "To say that an unqualified success has attended the opening of this elegant place of entertainment," he began, "is to convey but a very imperfect idea of the enthusiastic reception which greeted the initiatory performances on Monday evening. The whole scene was brilliant, and the large and fashionable audience assembled never wearied in evincing its unbounded delight in the magnificent fittings and decorations of the spacious hall, the superb scenery, and above all, the really high class and accomplished company of artistes who occupied the boards . . ."

The Scarborough *Gazette*, in its equally glowing notice, mentioned that "Mr. Blythe in the small part of the detective also came in for his meed of praise."

After the opening, the work load increased, the challenge with it. The Londesborough bill was changed two and three times every week, playing usually a farce, a comedy, and a burlesque every night, with a drama on Saturday. It was light entertainment for the holiday crowd, but no less strenuous for the actors. The quality was kept at a high level, and popularity seemed assured. Charley Vandenhoff gained great favor as the leading man, displaying great versatility at comedy or drama. In *Woodcock's Little Game* his *Mr. Woodcock* was deemed "a piece of comic acting which needs to be seen to be appreciated." His *Bob Brierly* in Tom Taylor's popular drama *The Ticket-of-Leave-Man* was pronounced "a matchless performance."

"G. H. Blythe" was also attracting favorable attention in smaller parts. On July 22, he was advanced to juvenile leads at three guineas, over fifteen dollars, per week. His first chance at a character part, in *The Corsican Brothers*, brought with it his first taste of disaster.

Mr. George had telegraphed to London for trick swords, which did not arrive in time. He promised the actors that if they would file their own swords to break at the right moment, he would reimburse them. They did so. Herbert, heavily made up, played *Chateau-Renaud*; Charley was *Fabian di Franchi*; "Handsome Jack" Barnes was *Montgiron*. The high point of the piece, the duel scene, approached:

Montgiron: The fight cannot proceed; Monsieur de Chateau-Renaud's sword is broken; the weapons are not equal.

Fabian: You are mistaken, sir. I shall make them equal. (*He puts his sword beneath his heel to break it.*)

Montgiron: Implacable!

Fabian: As destiny!

The sword would not break under Charley's foot. He placed it over his knee with a heroic flourish, and tried again. It bent double. "As destiny!" he repeated a little less loudly, trying to break it the other way. It seemed as if the weapon could be tied in a knot without yielding. He sat frustrated, a misshapen, unusable dueling piece in his lap.

"Ah, monsieur," Herbert ad-libbed, proffering half of his own broken sword, "it appears that destiny is never implacable."

Wielding the butt end of the wrong sword, Charley proceeded to duel with his friend amid derisive and amused shouts from the house.

It was generally regarded as the proper thing during the season to be seen upon the Spa Promenade at least once a day, either between eleven and one o'clock, or in the evening between seven and nine, when a German band conducted by Herr Wm. Meyer Lutz played in the Music-Saloon. Sir Joseph Paxton, creator of the Crystal Palace, had designed this graceful, colonnaded rotunda, which seemed to revolve with the music of Offenbach, his last and lightest, and lilting snatches of Rossini and Mozart. At the height of the season, at the right times of day, three or four thousand promenaders passed and repassed between Paxton's colonnade and the thick sea wall of Whitby stone. When the tempo of the music quickened, the pace of the promenaders, the stir and hum and merriment, seemed to quicken with it.

Between eleven and one, Herbert and Charley were fashionable regulars at the Spa, sporting the short, broad-buttoned, bobtailed coats and skin-tight trousers so popular with young men in London. The leading man carried an ebony walking stick, wore a proper top hat. The juvenile lead had neither, but he usually wore a brightly colored cravat, tied spontaneously in the irreverant manner of the French artists, giving him a romantic Bohemian air. They made a striking pair, searching the length of the Promenade for unchaperoned ladies in light summer frocks.

While Herbert was sitting for Oliver Sarony, a celebrated local photographer, one particularly fair morning, Charley awaited him at the Spa with Tilly Wright and Lottie Moreton, the musical ingénues of the Londesborough. They had proved during the season to be loyal and generous companions. The threesome turned many heads as they strolled along the Promenade. The young ladies both stood nearly a head taller than their escort, the difference exaggerated by picture hats and parasols. Charley was undaunted. He walked head relatively high, a lady on each arm.

The proper entrance to the Promenade was over the Cliff Bridge, where an admission of sixpence each insured the exclusion of undesirables. Any enterprising fellow, however, could gain entry by climbing down the side of the cliff. Three ruffians, having done so, were leaning against the base of an ornate gas lamp, when the colorful threesome passed.

"Yer think yer can 'andle 'em bof, shorty?" one of them called.

Charley hurried his charges along; the bullies followed, insulting as they went. Charley was scared. He had never been a fighting man, but the honor of the ladies was being questioned, and his as a result. He was spared the necessity of action. His friend arrived.

Herbert sauntered up to the bullies, advised them to move on. They moved closer together, plunged thumbs under their belts, and informed the dandy that they liked it where they were. One of them made another allusion to the ladies. Herbert lunged at him. Charley moved the ladies away. Promenaders scattered, as ladies and gentlemen do, quickly, but not too far. They watched excitedly as the Middle Weight Champion made a quick job of the three toughs.

After some light refreshment, the Promenade hero escorted the grateful Miss Moreton back to his room. Elsie, the maid, was late getting to Mr. Blythe's room that day, but she knew that he was never in at that hour. When she unlocked the door, the startled twosome scrambled for the bedclothes. Elsie's scream filled the house as she stumbled down the stairs, leaving a trail of clean sheets and pillow cases behind her.

Mrs. Hogg understood perfectly, but she certainly could not speak to her impudent boarder directly. Besides, she knew Mr. Waddington socially, and since he had become a widower, she had wanted to know him better. It had been suggested to her by mutual acquaintances that they would be a good match. She plunged a hatpin into her most somber creation, green felt with a few discreet pheasant feathers, and forged down Aberdeen Walk.

The good widow was put out to find E. J. George sitting in for Mr. Waddington at the Londesborough. The manager did his courteous best to soothe her, but the indignant lady insisted upon seeing the proprietor. She reminded him that her late husband had been a close friend of Mayor Rooke, insinuating that it might be necessary to consult him. Mr. George offered to telegraph his employer at York.

Mr. Waddington arrived on the afternoon train, and called immediately at Mrs. Hogg's. Her indignation had developed some refinements. Presenting a perfect counterfeit of the shocked gentlewoman, she was careful not to offend him personally, but denounced Herbert, actors in general, the entire acting profession. She wondered how a proper gentleman like Mr. Waddington could have entered into such a world. She mentioned the Mayor often, finally requesting, in the name of propriety, that Herbert be discharged. Mr. Waddington had no choice. He said that he would do so, but could not replace him for that evening's performance. The widow agreed that tomorrow would be soon enough, but insisted, eyes demurely cast down, that the young bounder leave her house immediately.

Having got Lottie away without anyone discovering her identity, the culprit was packing when his employer knocked on the door. He apologized to Waddington, expressing hope that the theater would not be hurt by his indiscretion, acknowledging that Mr. Waddington was taking the only possible course by firing him. He finished packing, and walked to the theater, where he sat alone in the men's dressing room. It seemed forlorn and cold, suddenly unfamiliar; without players and the excitement of preparation, it held no charm of its own. Paint and powder rested neatly in their containers where the dresser had placed them. In big wicker hampers along cream walls, costumes lay folded, not to be given life until eight precisely. When Charley arrived, Herbert told him what had happened. Charley advised the outcast to take his things to the Grand Hotel after the performance, and not to worry. That evening, during *Little Robin Hood*, Lottie Moreton offered her featured song, "I'm So Awfully Clever," with less than her usual conviction.

After the final curtain, the leading man and two walking men of the Londesborough Theatre went to see the proprietor. They told him that if Blythe went, they went with him. Mr. Waddington implored them to understand his position. They assured him that they did, but remained adamant. Their harassed employer said that he would try to arrange something.

Early the next morning, the Waddington Melody Master, his latest and most expensive pianoforte, was delivered to 12 Aberdeen Walk. There was a good deal of commotion in the street when the polished fruitwood instrument with real ivory keys was carried into the parlor. Mrs. Hogg assured her curious neighbors that Mr. Waddington was a close personal friend. She decided that it would be silly to bother the Mayor with the trivial matter of a promiscuous boarder.

The receipts of the Londesborough Theatre were not keeping pace with its quality. "The attraction of this fashionable place of entertainment has been amply sustained during the present week," affirmed the *Express* critic on July 20, "although the attendance of the public has scarcely been commensurate with the talents of the admirable company brought together by Mr. Waddington. We are scarcely prepared to account for this seeming apathy on the part of the public for the entertainment is certainly one which for excellence is seldom to be met with in the provinces . . ." Nor was Mr. Waddington prepared to account for it. He considered the competition, abundant resort fare for privileged Britons and visitors from the Continent.

The Theatre Royal was giving much the same kind of entertainment. Although its quality was inferior to the Londesborough, the older house enjoyed a loyal following from years past. The Spa Saloon occasionally imported touring companies, bringing the latest London plays to seaside audiences. There was also a weekly *Grand Gala* at the Cliff Bridge Grounds, which included the "Great Feast of Lanterns," Professor Brown's "Ride Out to Sea On His Brilliantly Illuminated Water Bicycle," and a "Grand Pyrotechnic Display"—all for one shilling.

Poole & Young's Great Panorama at the Hunter's Row Assembly Rooms displayed "Paris,—In Grandeur, On Fire, And In Ruins!" accompanied by the English Opera Company. At Mechanics' Hall, *Turner's Diorama* presented scenes of the Holy Land enhanced by the vocal and instrumental Turner Family. Even the local Floral and Horticultural Exhibition advertised three hundred pounds in prizes, music by the band of the 5th Dragoon Guards and three other bands, and spectacular fireworks.

Mr. Waddington announced a surprise for the competion on August 6: But he quickly found a remedy and announced it on August 6:

SPECIAL NOTICE

The Eminent Comedian, Mr. J. Clarke, of the Olympic, Strand and Princess's Theatres, London; and the Charming Actress Miss Furtado, of the Adelphi Theatre, London, will appear in the late T. W. Robertson's Military Comedy *Ours* on Monday Night, August 12th, For Six Nights Only.

Charley Vandenhoff took it badly. He would now be reduced to second leads in plays chosen by Clarke to accent himself and Miss Furtado, his bride of a week. Mr. Waddington assured him that the arrangement would last only a week, just long enough to help establish his new theater with the public, but Charley brooded and, just in case, sent off a cable to his London dramatic agent asking him to find another engagement.

During rehearsals with Clarke, Charley grew petulant, grumbling and finding fault with the comedian, usually behind his back. "Is there no scene in *Ours*," he asked his colleagues, "that does not require that ungodly cur to be in the middle of it?"

"Come now, Charley," replied Jack Barnes, "Clarke happens to be a very pious fellow."

"I repeat 'ungodly cur,'" Charley countered. "You care to contradict it?"

"All right, gentlemen," interrupted Herbert, averting disaster, "Clarke is an actor who believes in God and the centre of the stage."

There was a furor at the Londesborough on the week of August 12. On opening night, the large building was sold out, and many potential patrons had to be turned away. In one scene, when Crimea-bound troops filed past a window in Hyde Park to the March of the British Grenadiers, the audience was roused to such a pitch of excitement that a thundering recall resulted. Mr. Waddington was a richer and happier man by the end of the week.

When the regular company regained the stage, business returned to normal. On Friday, Waddington announced that Clarke and Miss Furtado would return for six nights only the following Monday. Charley Vandenhoff gave a week's notice.

On Saturday, Herbert received a reply from Aunt Amelia to a letter that he had written about his new career:

Dear Herbert,

Your letter left me deeply aggrieved . . . I have not spoken to your Father of it, for he is travelling to England next Spring, and is in hopes of meeting with you to plan a respectable future for you in some honourable profession. He must never know that his youngest child by my lamented sister has ventured upon the stage, for it would be the end of that good man, and the end of many things, I fear. How in good faith could I be aunt to an actor upon the stage?

Aunt Amelia did not mention that the Commissioner, seriously ill, was coming to England for treatment.

Herbert awakened after noon on Sunday. Finding Charley still asleep, he dressed, had some tea in the lounge, and walked out alone. He covered the length of the harbor, climbed high to the ancient ruins of Scarborough Castle. He looked out over the city and the sea from a broken set of stone steps that ended in midair. He ran as fast as he could down the winding path to the beach, continuing at the same pace back to the Grand Hotel. He climbed the long stone stairway past the hotel to the top of the South Cliff, and sat there at the exact center of the huge curve formed by the bay. His eyes followed the twisting paths and rocky steps lined with ornamental shrubbery and rustic seats sacred to novel reading. Low down the face of the steep declivity were the Spa buildings.

Great waves dashed themselves to spray against the battlemented walls, while visitors heedlessly strolled the Promenade. They walked a bit, sat or stood or lounged, talking, flirting, and laying plans for the not too distant future. There would be a quick flurry of skirts if an impetuous wave threw a shrill shower over the wall, but the sea usually kept its place. "One stone's breadth between the restless sea and the restless pursuit of pleasure," Herbert observed, "one step from the sublime to the amiable and the petty."

He would have expected such a letter from his father, but Aunt Amelia had always been Herbert's ally. Something of what he had felt for his aunt disappeared with that letter; something for his new profession went with it. A heavy gray mist had fallen, seeming to bring night as a result

52

of its weight. At the end of the crescent, Scarborough Castle turned into its rock cliff, as he walked back slowly to the Grand Hotel.

Charley Vandenhoff had been offered a season as leading man at Leicester. A juvenile lead was also needed, Charley told him; they could wire the agent in the morning. Herbert was quick to accept the proposal. He had no alternative.

VI

The Commissioner's son was reluctant to consider the stage his calling, but the company of actors and the immediate rewards for a part well played held him. His natural gifts were augmented by techniques of performance, easily mastered during two seasons at Leicester. Most of the popular roles for second leads were added to his repertoire, and although the management offered the usual provincial fare—T. W. Robertson, Dion Boucicault, H. J. Byron, Tom Taylor; comedies, melodramas, burlesques—he was given his first chance at Shakespeare. As *Bassanio* in *The Merchant of Venice*, observed a local critic, "His recitation of 'So may the outward shows be least themselves/The world is still deceived with ornament . . .' brought forth spontaneous applause from the audience, so forthright was it, and pure of speech."

When Charley urged the management to produce *Hamlet*, Herbert proved a worthy *Laertes*. One critic even suggested that the roles might have been reversed to advantage: "Mr. Blythe might have lent the heroic bearing so lacking in the Dane of Mr. Vandenhoff." Herbert cringed at this observation, and attempted to hide it from his friend. When Charley finally came across it, he smiled inscrutably without comment.

In June of 1873, the two actors were at liberty for a month before starting a summer season at Bradford. They headed to London for the first time in a year. Paul Potter, still in the Russell Square rooms, gave warm welcome to his friends. Rahj, however, was cool toward his old master, obviously more attached to Paul. Herbert, upset by the indifference of his pet, conceded that it would be best for the dog to stay with Potter.

The prodigal called hesitantly at the Waces' during his visit, not admitting it to himself, but in search of family news. Elizabeth divulged that his father and stepmother were in London. They had taken a house in St. Aubyn's Road, Upper Norwood, near the Crystal Palace. She told him also that Colonel Denys had died at Beaumont Hall early in May, that Great-Aunt Charlotte was dying.

There was no carriage waiting when the train left him at Kirby Cross. He was already late for the funeral, but there was a short cut through the fields to St. Michael's Church. Great-aunt Charlotte had shown it to him during his first summer at Beaumont Hall. When he reached the pasture bordering the churchyard, a flock of sheep sat crowded in the shade of a solitary tree. As he passed, one sheep stood, setting off a chain reaction. By the time he reached the end of the pasture, they were all standing in dumb wonderment at what had disturbed them. He jumped over a stream, into the churchyard. There were stray sheep grazing around the gravestones, and a small black clump of mourners. The coffin had already been lowered. Someone, he assumed his father, as new head of the family, was casting earth upon it. As he approached, the flat voice of the vicar finished the service. "The grace of our Lord Jesus Christ, and the love of God, and the fellowship of the Holy Ghost, be with us all evermore. *Amen.*" The Commissioner lifted his head. Their eyes met for the first time in ten years. Instinctively, his father turned away. The others, led by Sarah Blyth, who had followed her stepson's approach with cold eyes, started to move off. Herbert rounded the open grave of Squire William Blyth's last child.

"You should not have come here," said William Blyth without facing his son. "You are not a welcome member of this family." He started to walk away.

"Father," Herbert called. William Blyth hesitated, visibly struggling with himself. Finally, he turned to his son. He walked very close to him. Herbert was astonished by his face. It hung pale and worn, as if, at fifty-five, it had been used too long. It had never occurred to him before that his father could grow old.

"Leave behind this foolishness, Herbert," he pleaded, "and I shall help you. This humiliation—I cannot face it. We are a proud family. To have a son of mine upon the stage. We are connected with other proud families. Better a common labourer, an artisan . . ."

His father had not finished when Herbert turned and walked without stopping back over the fields to Kirby Cross.

Unhappy with the management at Bradford, the two actors readily accepted an engagement for a season at the Theatre Royal, Hull. Their last performance at Bradford was Bulwer-Lytton's *Lady of Lyons* on September 6. As they were leaving for the station the next morning, a wire was delivered. It had reached Herbert eight days late by way of Russell Square.

REGRET TO INFORM OF DEATH OF YOUR FATHER 31ST AUGUST. INTRO THORACIC TUMOUR. BURIAL 2ND SEPTEMBER UPPER NORWOOD.

MESSRS. GROVER & HUMPHREYS

He did not speak until they were seated in the train. Without looking up he asked Charley for theater stories. Charley was not sure that his pre-occupied companion was listening, but after each story there would be an urgent request for another. One tale made a particular impression.

"There occurred a little incident that was called the Grecian fizzle," Charley began, "because it amounted to the failure of a play founded on Bulwer-Lytton's great Greek novel of *The Last Days of Pompeii*. An actor called Barrymore had charge of this piece, and he determined to make a big show piece out of it. So he got a lot of powder and a quick match, and arranged everything for a big eruption of Vesuvius—at the end of the piece. But when the end came—the match wouldn't work; it just fizzled and made a fuss, and darted round a bit, and then all was darkness, a big lot of smoke and no fireworks at all. The audience hissed and cat-called, and Barrymore was wild. Down went the curtain on a bad failure.

"But Barrymore wouldn't let the matter rest. Seizing a lamp, at the imminent risk of setting himself and all the theatre on fire, he blazed away at the fireworks under Vesuvius, and at last got them to blaze away all right. The eruption went off splendidly, and Barrymore looked around in triumph. But horror of horrors, all this time that the fireworks had been doing so splendidly the curtain had been down. Nobody had pulled it up. The audience hadn't seen anything, except perhaps some red light behind a green curtain.

" 'Ring up that curtain! Pull up that curtain, for God's sake!' yelled poor Barrymore, while his fireworks were all flashing away, with nobody to see them. But there was nobody to 'ring up' or 'pull up'. All the stage hands had left. With the assistance of the call boy Barrymore pulled up the curtain himself. But just as it rose the last bit of fireworks in Vesuvius gave out, and all that the tag end of the audience who still remained in the theatre could see was just nothing at all. Down went the curtain on a worse failure than the first. And from that night anybody who wanted to get Barrymore into a fight had only to say something to him about *The Last Days of Pompeii*."

Herbert's eyes were closed. Charley assumed that he was sleeping.

56

"Which Barrymore was it?" He did not open his eyes.

"I reckon it was William," replied the storyteller, "before he went to the 'Old Vic.'"

"Tell it once more, will you, Charley?"

THEATRE ROYAL, HULL
MR. SEFTON PARRY, PROPRIETOR & MANAGER

The manager begs to announce that this elegant theatre
will open for the season on Saturday evening, September
13th when the following ladies and gentlemen will have
the pleasure of appearing:

Mr. W. Blakeley

Mr. Charles Vandenhoff

Mr. William Etton

Mr. Edward J. George

Mr. M. H. Barrymore . . .

Herbert never mentioned why he had changed his name, or where he had got it, but Charley Vandenhoff knew. He did explain that "M." was for Maurice, to be pronounced in the French manner with the accent on the last syllable. He thought that had a romantic ring. English flattened it, however, and, tired of correcting, he left it that way. New acquaintances, avoiding the Maurice altogether, began to call him "Barry."

During his year at Hull, Herbert's reputation as a good fellow was circulated by the players who traveled from one provincial company to another. Acceptance into this intimate society pleased him, and he took special delight in meeting old comrades in new places. He and Charley were particularly pleased when E. J. George, bitten by the acting bug, quit managing the Londesborough to join them at Hull.

On stage, M. H. Barrymore became a favorite in a variety of roles. Local ladies took to sending flowers after matinees; Hull's critics singled him out for praise: "There is no weak point in the cast of Burnand's Classical Extravaganza *Ixion*, but it is only fair to point to the creditable and noble manner in which Mr. Barrymore sustained the part of *Mars*." And in an "adequate presentation of *She Stoops to Conquer*, Mr. Barrymore acted *Hastings* admirably." During Hull Fair Week his performance as a swashbuckling young officer in *Sailor of France: A Story of the Revolution of 1792* was enthusiastically received, as was his clever lawyer in the celebrated political satire *Extremes: Or, Men of the Day*. The *Merchant of Venice* was presented to acclaim; but Charley, recalling his poor reception in the role at Leicester, discouraged plans for a new production of *Hamlet*.

Before the autumn season of 1874 commenced, Charley received an offer to play in America. He accepted immediately, urging his colleague to join him. Herbert, unable to afford the journey without a firm engagement, decided to accompany Charley to London. It was time, he reckoned, to try his luck in the West End.

Herbert stood nervously at the heavy gate of 18 St. Aubyn's Road, wondering if he should enter. Ornate wrought-iron railing, newly pointed brickwork, cream reveals repeated down the terrace until the Church of England abruptly halted them. Only the numbers distinguished each residence, until one got inside. A young housemaid opened the door. She announced the caller.

The parlor was sparsely furnished. The Blyths had not planned a long stay. He noticed the massive oak secretary holding the same coronation bust that it had held in Amritsar, gifts from his parents' wedding that had always traveled with his father. The Commissioner's widow sat with her back to Herbert in a chair which seemed too small for her. She was staring straight ahead through a flimsy curtain toward the repeated brick fronts of St. Aubyn's Road.

"So you have finally come, Herbert." She did not turn. "I suppose it is about the will?" Herbert was startled. Had he even considered a will, he would not have imagined being cited in it. "They all want to know about the will," she continued. Sarah Hunter Blyth was the only child of two only children. She had no living family. Now, she had been widowed for the second time. She had money of her own, but the fear of loneliness made her cling to William Blyth's bequest, alienating his family, and forfeiting the solace which they could have given. As she turned toward a small table beside the chair to grasp a few sheets of official-looking foolscap, he glimpsed the small reaching hand, the side of her dead-white face. She stood suddenly, faced him. He noticed for the first time that his stepmother was draped from her head to the floor in heavy black crepe.

"You are a handsome boy, Herbert," she said, almost accusingly. Then she began to read the will. It seemed more of a recitation. Sarah Blyth knew the document by heart.

This is the last Will and Testament of me William Edward Blyth of Her Majesty's Uncovenanted Civil Service and Deputy Commissioner of Jhelum in the Punjab but now on furlough residing in St. Aubyns Road Norwood in the County of Surrey Esquire I direct all my just debts funeral and testamentary expenses to be fully paid and satisfied And whereas some time ago I purchased an estate called Blythsdale situate in the County of Mongonin in the Province of Auckland New Zealand with the intention of giving one moiety thereof to my son William Henry Blyth and of retaining the other moiety thereof myself Now I give and devise the whole of the said estate and interest therein

unto and to the use of my said son William Henry Blyth . . . And
whereas I have contracted to purchase another estate called Wharn-
cliffe situate in the County of Mongonin aforesaid and have transmitted
the amount of the purchase money thereof and interest to certain
Bankers in New Zealand for the purpose of completing such purchase
at the proper time Now I give and devise the said estate and all my estate and interest whether equitable or legal therein and all my rights
and interest in the contract for the purchase thereof unto and to the use
of my son Herbert Arthur Chamberlayne Hunter Blyth . . .

Astonished, Herbert looked up at his stepmother. She met his eyes with
quiet contempt.

And in the event of the said contract for purchase not being carried
out then I bequeath the said contract unto my said son. . . . And
whereas I purchased some time ago an estate called Kikurangi Hill situate in the County of Mongonin aforesaid with the intention of giving
one moiety thereof to my said son William Henry Blyth and of retaining the other moiety thereof myself Now I give devise and confirm one
equal undivided moiety to that son . . . And I give and devise the other
one equal undivided moiety in the same estate unto and to the use of
my said son Herbert Arthur Chamberlayne Hunter Blyth . . .

Sarah Blyth took an exaggerated breath, and proceeded with emphasis,
never once consulting the paper she held.

And as to all the rest and residue of my real and personal estate . . . I
devise and bequeath the rents and profits interest dividends and annual
income thereof unto my said wife Sarah Blyth for her sole and separate
use for and during the term of her natural life . . .

She faced her godson triumphant, smiling for the first time that afternoon. She continued to the end of the document, but Herbert no longer
listened. He felt a sickening guilt. The unreasonable guilt of a child accused of stealing something he did not steal. Considering their relationship, he wondered if his father had remembered him merely to punish
him firmly and finally. Perhaps he was expected to go off to New
Zealand and become a gentleman farmer as his brother had. His thoughts
were confused when Sarah Blyth finished her recitation.
"Your brother and your sister's husband will be the executors when I
am gone, but until that time *I* control the will. You will be thankful now
for your great-aunt." When Herbert reacted with surprise, she informed
him grudgingly that he was also a beneficiary in Charlotte Blyth Denys's
will. She advised him to consult Messrs. Grover and Humphreys. Herbert
thanked her, walked to the door.

"Your father was a good man, Herbert," she called after him; "he remembered even you."

A few days after his family visit, Herbert called at the offices of Messrs. Grover and Humphreys. There were no warm memories inspired by his return to 4 Kings Bench Walk. The notification of Aunt Charlotte's, 1,500-pound bequest pleased him, because he had admired her, and she had remembered him. When Solicitor Clerk Cortlandt Mahon offered to read the entire will, Herbert declined with thanks. Nor was he particularly interested when Mahon informed him that Her Majesty's Court of Probate had granted "administration of all and singular the personal estate and effects" of his father's will to Sarah Blyth. She would be executrix for life, and had contested certain aspects of the will. Mahon said that Herbert's inheritance was safe, but would probably be some time in coming to him. Replying that he was sure it was all in capable hands, the beneficiary made to go before the inevitable small talk. He was too late. At the door, the solicitor clerk asked what he had been doing since leaving Messrs. Grover and Humphreys. Herbert looked at the floor, muttered something about traveling, and excused himself.

Once outside the Temple walls, the realization struck. He was rich. Fifteen hundred pounds, over seven thousand dollars, was enough to buy first-class passage to America for himself and Charley, and live well for at least a year. He ran all the way to Russell Square.

Charley shared the enthusiasm of his friend. Not only would he have Herbert's companionship, but they could afford now to depart soon enough to participate at a Boston benefit for C. Leslie Allen. Allen had been a good and helpful friend to Charley during his time in America. Appearing at the benefit would be a chance to repay that kindness, and also, Charley presumed, a perfect showcase for Herbert in the new country. The only available booking that would get them there in time, and directly to Boston, was on a freighter leaving Southampton on December 29. There were two double cabins with an adjoining stateroom for passengers. Herbert booked them both. Even on a freighter, they could travel in style.

Herbert bought out the Mitre on the eve of their departure, and all drank the health of the voyagers. His roommate from Wren's, Paul Potter, was among them, actors C. P. Flockton, Lionel Brough, and, differences at Scarborough forgotten, John Clarke. Ned Donnelly made expansive toasts with Nat Langham's best ruby port, growing maudlin as the drinking progressed, tearfully imploring his champion not to desert London and the Prize Ring. Squire Bancroft, stopping for a nightcap after the theater, was moved by the spirit of the occasion to offer Herbert a place in his Prince of Wales's company when he returned to England.

Herbert was flattered, but said that he would probably not return to the stage after his trip. Micky Slater wondered if he would seek employment in America.

"Charley has a good engagement," Herbert told him, "but I am only going over on a pleasure trip. I would never dream of staying there. After all, Micky, England is my home." After he had said it, Herbert Arthur Chamberlayne Hunter Blyth wondered about it.

The S.S. *America* cast off from Southampton early the next morning. A few loyal leftovers from the Mitre made a bleary-eyed huddle on the pier. Charley and Herbert leaned over the railing, waving, as the steamer sailed down Southampton Water, through the West Solent, and on past the chalk Needles to open sea.

ACT
SECOND

Poor handful of bright spring water,
Flung in the whirlpool's shrieking face.

DANTE GABRIEL ROSSETTI*

* Second of three quotations chosen by Maurice Barrymore
to introduce his play *Nadjezda*.

VII

MESSRS. BARRYMORE AND Vandenhoff were the only passengers aboard S.S. *America*, but tedium had been averted by the seasoned humor and expansive stories of the crew. Herbert and Charley traded generously theatrical anecdotes, which seemed meager by comparison, for lore of the sea. Some of the old-timers regaled them with memories of the port of Boston: colored pennants on Telegraph Hill flapping the news when a clipper was sighted; newsmen, agents and owners and crimps running to the wharves; counting-room clerks hanging out of windows to watch the full-plumed entry. Herbert listened especially as they described the gaudy gathering of Ann Street tarts and hussies. The company of sailors had been pleasant, but after fifteen days at sea, the possibility of compliant women was appealing.

Old Boston had passed with the clipper ships. The port was business-like, relatively sedate. Tarts and hussies no longer waited with splendid effrontery along the wharves. Moral zeal had pent them up years before in shuttered houses along dark streets. Instead, the voyagers found Charley's actor friend, Leslie Allen, waiting with his two little daughters.

Allen had arranged for the new arrivals to board with Miss Amelia Fisher at 2 Bulfinch Place. It was indeed an honor to be admitted to these quaint clapboard premises. Miss Fisher entertained but one permanent guest—William Warren, Boston's admired senior citizen and one of America's foremost actors. He had never married. Since the time of his Boston debut in 1846, Warren had lived in the house of his honored friend.

Mr. Warren and Miss Fisher greeted the actors at the front door, and ushered them into the kitchen, where the teakettle was singing and a wary Boston terrier was watching from his corner. Floors were covered with colored braided mats, the flour barrel dressed in flowered chintz, walls hung with shining dish covers. Herbert was reminded of a similar room in Amritsar. He confided his memory to the lady of the house, and took to calling her "Aunt" Amelia, an intimacy which delighted the maiden lady. She and Warren watched with pleasure that afternoon as the young Englishman, crouching on the kitchen floor, won the confidence of their suspicious pet.

William Warren took it upon himself to introduce Herbert, or "Barry," as he called him, to his beloved city. The visitor was struck with the brightness of things—streets, buildings, signs. Cities in England were dark by comparison, dingy and massive. They stopped at the Boston Museum, where Warren had acted for thirty years. "Boston was at a low ebb theatrically when the Museum was opened in 1841," Warren explained, "so Moses Kimball called his establishment the Boston Museum and Gallery of Fine Arts on the assumption that the public could be made to take very kindly to a new theater if the thing were broken to them gradually."

Warren hailed Mr. Murphy's omnibus at the museum. He and Barry scurried aboard as Murphy called, "Visitors, visitors, step lively! This 'bus goes on down through Washington Street, on off up through Roxbury! Fare twelve-and-a-half cents." The two gentlemen were bound for the clapboard village of Roxbury, where the pleasures of tea with Mrs. J. R. Vincent awaited them. The museum's veteran "character lady" was a culinary specialist, delighting her guests with mincemeat, plum pudding, pickles, jellies and jams put up by her own hands. Side by side in the small top seat of the 'bus they made an incongruous pair, the oversized, kind-eyed old actor and the lithe, stirringly handsome young Englishman, as they bounded along toward Roxbury.

Charley chided his friend for this curious choice of companion. Barry paid it no mind. Nights had to be filled as well, and Charley introduced him to Bohemian Boston. There were stimulating sessions of good talk and drink at Cloud's Rest, Erroll Dunbar's studio on Beacon Hill. Talk and drink also abounded at meetings of the Macaroni Club at the Parker House; but exotic cuisine prevailed. Joe Rammetti of the museum orchestra was elected "chef," his particular function being to instruct the members in manipulating the stringy Italian delicacy from plate to mouth. Fred Williams, stage manager at the museum, and his actress wife were noted for their Sunday night entertainments. Their salon comprised the wittiest and most colorful of the city's artistic people. Literary men had once reigned aloof when Boston was the "Athens of America." But few had come to replace the glorious native sons of decades past. Literature had lost its fascination to railroads and oil wells. Writers now banded with actors and musicians and painters to preserve, at least, the society of their lost world. This commingling of arts and temperaments gave substance to the Bohemian life of Boston.

Barry had not considered an acting career, or employment of any sort, since his arrival. Great-aunt Charlotte's money held out, and the new city offered sundry diversions. Not the least of them was a comely young lady in the Boston Theatre Company. Miss Savory, as an offering to propriety, insisted upon address by her last name. Christian names, she felt, were outward shows of intimacy. Privately, however, she had not the slightest aversion to the most intimate displays. Barry gratefully complied. It was noticed at Bulfinch Place that the young gentleman of the house no longer appeared for the customary after-theater suppers. Amelia Fisher did not comment, but since Mr. Warren was the only guest permitted the use of a latchkey, she waited up for her roving boarder. She never scolded. She would brew a fresh pot of tea when Barry returned, and sit up with him in the kitchen, chatting sometimes till dawn.

When Leslie Allen asked the preoccupied newcomer to perform at his benefit, Barry obliged his new friend, playing the hero in *Under the Gaslight*. Augustin Daly's new melodrama had recently caused a sensation in New York with its spectacular presentation, for the first time on stage, of a moving railroad train. Daly himself, noted manager of the Fifth Avenue Theatre, arrived in Boston to superintend the production of his masterpiece. Impressed by the two Englishmen during rehearsals, he approached the possibility of employment at his theater in New York. Charley was interested. Barry was not anxious to leave Boston.

Saturday, January 23rd, 1875

AMUSEMENTS

ENTERTAINMENTS THIS EVENING

BOSTON THEATRE

That ever-excellent actor, Mr. C. Leslie Allen, his host of appreciative friends, will bear in mind, will receive company tonight for his benefit, the entertainment including *Under the Gaslight*, *Mary, Queen of Scots* and *The Middy Ashore*. Messrs. C. H. Vandenhoff, his first appearance after an absence of nearly four years, and M. H. Barrymore, the talented juvenile actor, from the London Theatres, his first appearance in America, and the entire company of the theatre assisting.

In spite of a snowstorm, the attendance was excellent, the response overwhelming. Charley was welcomed back to the city with an ovation unusual in Boston theaters. Barry, the juvenile "from the London Theatres," who had never played a London theater, captured whatever imagination was available from local devotees of drama. Being English helped in Boston, where the West End successes of T. W. Robertson and Tom Taylor were in vogue, but the romantic *Ray Trafford* of M. H. Barrymore was winning on its own.

He was asked to appear in the Boston Theatre's production of *The Shaughraun*, which Dion Boucicault, author and star of the play, was to direct for its first Boston presentation. Charley left for New York to fulfill the commitment at Wallack's Theatre which had brought him from England. Barry accepted the Boston offer. It was a chance to work with the celebrated Boucicault, whose play, *London Assurance*, had introduced the middleweight champion to acting. Besides, Barry did not wish to leave the city and friends who had taken him so quickly to heart.

The Boston Theatre company dreaded the arrival of Dion Boucicault. His value as a stage director was unassailable, but he was a fabled martinet. He had a way of completely changing his ideas at each rehearsal, a practice somewhat perplexing to actors, and delighted in confusing actresses to the point of tears. During the first walk-through of *The Shaughraun* on a bare stage, he shrieked at Mrs. Thomas Barry, "Are you going to walk over that table?" The startled actress, the first lady of the Boston stage, stepped aside quickly. "Here, here," Boucicault jabbed, "don't run about like a chicken with its head cut off!" Imaginary or not, a table was a table to Mr. Boucicault.

He was a curious fellow to look upon, this Boucicault, glittering eyes, scrubby mustache, bald dome fringed with hair dyed very black. Cold and bilious, he could also be a seductive conversationalist. Sharp and sarcastic, he was the most prolific playwright of his time. At the age of fifty-three, he had already authored, translated or adapted one hundred and fifty plays. Theater people tended to overlook Dion Boucicault's social limitations.

It was the author's custom when away from New York and his wife, Agnes Robertson, to avail himself of the favors of any willing actress in his company. During rehearsals at the Boston Theatre, his eye fell upon Miss Savory. There was the complication this time of the Englishman playing *Captain Molyneux*. Mr. Boucicault made Barry his special target for harassment.

"Young man," reprimanded the author, "the business you are performing is worthy of a schoolboy."

"Mr. Boucicault," Barry answered, somewhere between admiration and contempt, "I have written the directions as you gave them to me yesterday, and performed them accordingly."

"Ah!" replied Boucicault in his sweetest Dublin brogue, "yesterday, certainly, my boy, I told you to do it that way, but the world is just twenty-four hours older, and we have advanced that much; so do it this way today."

Before rehearsals had finished, animosity turned to interest, finally to friendship. The author and his romantic lead became boon companions, almost to the exclusion of poor Miss Savory. She had to content herself with sharing her two suitors on rare nights when they were not drinking at Atwood's Chop House or wenching in Ann Street.

The immense chandelier of the Boston Theatre, composed of thousands of cut-glass prisms, resembled a great glowing jewel. Patrons crowded beneath it to their seats on opening night, seeming to overbalance the parquet. The *Evening Transcript* reported their response after the rousing climax of the third act: "*The Shaughraun* had carried the house by storm, and its triumph was signalized by solid and ringing cheering, such as men are only betrayed into by a real triumph."

The newspaper went on to praise the jovial *Conn* (the "Shaughraun" or ne'er-do-well) of Boucicault, and made particular mention of "M. H. Barrymore, who has all the requisites for his part, in his broad shoulders, manly stride, clean-cut features, handsome teeth, gentlemanly bearing, and refined self-possession, lacking only a little in masculinity in his voice. Still there is little doubt that this youthful hero, with his 'sweet' manners and hair parted in the middle, is fated to be as extensively fallen in love with by young ladies . . ." The review infuriated the newcomer. His first reaction was to pommel the critic; his second, which he implemented, was to lower the pitch of his stage voice. Barry aspired to avoid romantic roles in future, but his attributes made the possibility unlikely. The *Courier* critic, at least, did not find him "sweet": "Mr. M. H. Barrymore, as *Captain Molyneux*, a young English officer, is the ideal young lover of the better class, and his interviews with the lady of his heart were given with a delicacy that never degenerated into namby-pambyism."

Because of Boucicault's previous commitments, the run of the play was limited to four weeks. The house was booked to capacity every night, and Wednesday matinees were instituted by popular demand. The final performance, a benefit for the author, was deemed by the *Transcript* a "warm affair." It was a sad one, too, for the actors, closing a play which Boston's Irish population alone would have kept running for months.

Charley quit Wallack's company in April after instigating an unreasonable issue over money. He returned to Boston, expecting to collect his friend and bring him to New York, where profitable bookings were available. But Barry was still not ready to leave. They settled in at Bulfinch Place, devoting themselves to sociable rambles about town until the end of May, when offers from Augustin Daly arrived. Charley was wanted for the six-week autumn season at one hundred dollars a week. Barry was offered seventy-five dollars a week for the same season, and for a summer tour of the West, leaving from New York in July. From the clapboard cottage in Bulfinch Place, M. H. Barrymore and C. H. Vandenhoff wired acceptance to Daly, autocrat of the famous Fifth Avenue Theatre.

VIII

At SUNRISE, FROM the wheelhouse of the Fall River boat, Barry sighted a golden cluster of low buildings in the distance—Manhattan. He approached the island with eyes squinted, attempting to distinguish landmarks in morning mist along the East River. Two lonely, looming structures startled him as the side-wheeler passed Blackwell's Island. The helmsman explained that they were to be "apartment houses," so-called by their builder, who had put them up on Fourth Avenue at Fifty-sixth and Fifty-seventh streets. He was urging authorities to change the name of the avenue to Park, but that would hardly make the location more desirable. New Yorkers were merely amused by the man's folly: Who would ever consent to live across the street from a ramshackle farm where cows and chickens roamed at will, making intolerable country noises?

From the river it all seemed naïve and wonderful to Barry compared with London's ceaseless accordion rows. Here were vitality of growth, excitement of unfinished landscape, isolated architecture on a plain between two rivers. The sensation of space was challenged as the boat neared lower Manhattan. They docked amid a clutter of wharves and warehouses and bustling shops at Pier 28, North River, at the foot of Murray Street.

The "Rapid Transit Galop" became the rage that summer. Elevated railroads had just been completed, steaming from the Battery along Sixth Avenue to Central Park, and along Third and Ninth avenues to the Harlem River. There was no need to go farther; in fact, fashionable citizens wondered who would go that far. *They* seldom ventured north of Murray Hill. For the two weeks before his tour with Daly would begin, Barry established headquarters in Union Square, the theatrical hub of the adolescent city. Around an imposing equestrian bronze of George Washington, theaters and hotels consorted with the better shops, while omnibuses and coaches, four-in-hands, drays, any manner of vehicle horse could pull, circled the heroic general. Barry and Charley took large rooms at the Morton House with windows on the square. From one of these, shaded by a bright yellow awning, the young man from England gazed down with pleasure on the perpetual motion of his new city.

New York looked back. Barry became a familiar figure, promenading lively blocks between Union and Madison squares. "Anyway, along came Barrymore," noted *Vanity Fair*, "the finest looking youngster you could find in a day's ride, and with the highest spirits, the keenest wit, the completest courage that anybody ever saw in a single human envelope. He was highly educated, perfectly bred, a charming companion, and he could put on full dress clothes which had been lying in a heap for twenty-four hours and look like a prince of the purple." Before he even appeared on the New York stage, the newcomer attracted attention from nonprofessionals who flocked the Rialto to see their footlight favorites. Debutantes, well chaperoned in their family four-in-hands, shopgirls, strolling in their Sunday best, became so obvious in their admiration that certain denizens of theatrical New York began to take umbrage. One among them was Barry's future employer.

Augustin Daly was noted and noticed as he strode each day to his theater at Twenty-eighth Street near Broadway. Not only the reputation but the striking appearance of the thirty-five-year-old manager inspired glances from passers-by. His tall, lanky frame and awkward stride were accentuated by a peculiar stiff black hat of conical shape, which he had designed and always wore. His hatter supplied facsimiles at regular intervals, and the old hats would go to Richard, Daly's faithful black servant. They made a picturesque pair walking down Broadway, sporting identical chapeaux. Daly, well aware of his own impact, wished no competition from the young Englishman whom he had recently employed.

Daly's features were indeed compelling—prominent nose, driving blue eyes, unruly chestnut hair—but resolutely impassive, befitting an advocate of strict discipline and cast-iron rule. There was a singular method of accomplishment at the Fifth Avenue Theatre; that, simply and irrevocably, was the method of Augustin Daly. He employed capable lieutenants but proceeded alone, leaving the merest drudgery to them. He was self-centered, crude, usually repellent, and suspicious of the loyalty of those about him, but his capacity for work was limitless, his quest for excellence unswerving. Every detail of his establishment inspired his devoted attention, from ticket office to costume workshop to stage door. The make-believe world outside his theater did not interest him. Once, after a marathon twelve-hour rehearsal, some of the exhausted actors asked to be excused from the theater for a short break. "And where would you be," asked the ubiquitous manager in all innocence, "if you weren't in the theater rehearsing?" His company, with grudging endearment, called him "Governor," but never to his face.

As the Fifth Avenue Company crossed the vast American continent, perceptible animosity grew between the avid manager and the cavalier actor. Barry was not one to exert blind reverence, and blind reverence was exactly what his new employer required. Close quarters intensified their antipathy. Travel by rail from New York to San Francisco took seven days in 1875. Daly was the first manager to attempt the journey with a full company since the recent meeting of the Central Pacific and Union Pacific had made it possible. There were no dining cars, so the monotony of travel was somewhat relieved by meal-station stops. The interim was spent studying and rehearsing, gossiping, bickering and laughing. Fortunately, Barry's fellow actors proved congenial companions, notwithstanding an initial proclivity to "come up to Englishness."

"Americans," he observed, "have a self-effacing tendency to become 'English' when passing so much as a 'how d'j'do' with an Englishman."

The journey was particularly lightened by the troupe's leading character man, James Lewis. A lean, spry little man, religiously superstitious, he was always nursing some real or fancied illness, but "the more he kicked," observed Barry, "the better you liked him." Mrs. Gilbert, Lewis's partner in stage comedy, was only fifty-three, but due to her affectionate nature and artful playing of dear old ladies and eccentric spinsters, she was "Grandma" to the company. Her career had been long and varied; her repertoire of theater stories was inexhaustible. When Barry questioned the lady about John Wilkes Booth's assassination of Abraham Lincoln, she answered with equanimity. Mrs. Gilbert was perhaps the only member of the theatrical profession with the courage to do so.

"He was very handsome, most lovable and lovely," said the Fifth Avenue "Grandma." "He was eccentric in some ways, and he had the family failings, but he also had a simple, direct and charming nature . . .

"I know from my own limited experience how high feeling could run in those days," she recalled. "A man lived so wholly with people who thought as he did that any one on the other side was hateful to him. Whatever drew Wilkes Booth into the plot, it was not quite daredeviltry. And if the lot fell to him to do the thing, I feel sure that he went through with it without a backward thought. He had that kind of loyalty, that kind of courage. Perhaps the devotion of a high-strung Nihilist, who believes in his cause, comes nearest to expressing it."

Barry also took to John Drew, the twenty-two-year-old juvenile of the company, a bright-eyed, self-possessed young man of wit and gentlemanly bearing, from a famous theatrical family. His mother was the renowned actress-manageress of Philadelphia's Arch Street Theatre, where Jack had acted until his successful Fifth Avenue debut the previous season. Barry found his stiff-backed dignity rather touching in one so young. Jack admired, was somewhat in awe of his colleague from England.

Barry found the leading lady, Fanny Davenport, beautiful and preoccupied, dependent on the Governor, who was grooming her for stardom. Another colleague, however, readily responded to him. When Omaha was reached, he was already spending much of his time with Emily Rigl, a young actress from Germany, possessing fine black hair and Teutonic will.

Beyond Omaha, a new world opened before the Englishman. As they crossed the broad prairies of Nebraska, he was stirred and saddened by American Indians. Squatting in the shade of freight sheds, their tepees clustered in the distance, or riding on the steps of the cars, as they were allowed to do, they seemed bewildered and strangely out of place on their own ancestral earth. He was disappointed not to see buffalo—they had practically disappeared—but he spotted several herds of antelope. In the evening, it was not unusual to see wolves and coyotes slinking away in the gloaming.

Prairies gradually became hills, hills mountains, as the train neared the crest of the Rockies. They descended the western slope, through Echo and Ogden canyons to the Great Salt Lake, across the great American Desert to the Sierra Nevadas, headed up again and across those majestic mountains, descending into the flowers and fruit of the Sacramento Valley. Reporters descended at Sacramento to interview overland passengers for the San Francisco papers. Then came the last stage of the journey—a ferry ride from Oakland across the bay of San Francisco, and finally the great Western metropolis, shining like a vision in afternoon sun.

Once settled at the Occidental Hotel, the company set out to explore the city. Emily Rigl consulted her German *Baedeker*, translating its enumeration of San Francisco's delights for her companions. One sentence— "It is not advisable to visit the Chinese quarter unless one is accompanied by a guide."—intrigued Barry. "Another of those highbinder wars is going on," warned Daly's agent-in-advance; "three chinks killed yesterday." The highbinders were the killers of the tongs, he explained, secret organizations controlling the gambling and slave-girl rackets. Barry convinced a wary Jack Drew that the Chinese quarter deserved their immediate attention.

They came abruptly upon Chinatown, an oasis two blocks wide and seven long within a block and a half of the city's business center: a maze of streets and alleys and painted balconies hung with wind bells, swarming with people in native garb. Drew remarked that the quarter was unlike anyplace he had seen before. To Barry it recalled prodigal mornings long ago in the bazaar of Amritsar. On the sidewalks, tailors worked at Melican sewing machines, a rare concession to the West, while cobblers patched high-soled shoes. Gamblers bought in a lottery; opium eaters purchased their thimblefuls of ecstasy. Bright-eyed creatures in gaudy headdress gazed from windows and doorways in the "Street of the Sing-song Girls." Jack waited nervously below while Barry climbed a dark stairway to try their wares.

When rehearsals began, it was evident that the Governor had begun an overt campaign to break the arrogant newcomer from England. In the opening play, *London Assurance*, Barry was handed the small role of *Cool*, the role that he had played at Windsor in his first appearance on the stage. He had come quite a distance since then. Daly had promised leading roles, was paying him the salary of a leading man. Barry refused to play the valet. Assigned an even smaller role in *Weak Women*, he made his entrance on cue at the first rehearsal, walked to the edge of the footlights, faced the Governor in the first row.

"Mr. Daly," he questioned in a perfectly civil tone, "what do you mean by insulting me? What have I done to deserve this? I came at your request to play leading parts in your company, and play them I shall." Actors, stage carpenters, scene shifters froze. Daly was astounded. No one in his employ had ever before dared to address him that way. The company rallied. There was light applause from a courageous few. The rehearsal was adjourned.

Later that afternoon, Augustin Daly knocked at the door of Barry's hotel room. He was admitted graciously. He said that part of the company would be returning to the Fifth Avenue to fill a booking gap between the Volkes family of actors and the Mexican Juvenile Opera Troupe. Barry would have the leading role of *Bob Ruggles* in a revival of *The Big Bonanza*. The newcomer was agreeable; the two men parted with a handshake. No mention was made of their confrontation, but the Governor had not surrendered without good reason. The Fifth Avenue needed a dashing leading man to challenge the popularity of H. J. Montague at Wallack's Theatre. This arrogant Barrymore, Daly considered, had the real stuff in him.

Barry did not gloat over his apparent victory, nor even consider it such. His thoughts fell to quite another matter. He knew that Emily Rigl was also returning to New York. The pretty German, at least, would break the monotony of another cross-country journey.

Rehearsals for *The Big Bonanza*, guided by one of Daly's Fifth Avenue lieutenants, progressed smoothly and untaxingly for Barry. Although his role was essentially a romantic lead, it offered a welcome chance for character comedy, and allowed time to investigate New York under

Charley Vandenhoff's tutelage. Their headquarters became the Hoffman House, north of Fifth Avenue at Madison Square, an imposing marble structure boasting an enormous open mahogany bar, the first in the city, where the elite of theater, sports, and literature, railroad barons, oil kings, horse breeders and horse players, politicians, and the more liberal notables of society congregated with the likes of General Sherman, future Senator George Hearst, "Buffalo Bill" Cody, and Colonel Joe Rickey, a Washington lobbyist, who courted immortality by inventing the gin Rickey at the Hoffman bar.

The conviviality of such places delighted the Englishman, but the American capacity for hard drink disconcerted him. Barry had been content with English ale until his recent trip to San Francisco. "I was arrested there for violation of the liquor law," he told Charley. "I refused to take a drink." In New York, he attempted to keep up with the whiskey drinkers. His condition after one all-night bout prompted a friend to ask if he wanted a doctor. "No," Barry replied, "I want a *snake charmer*."

He entered the Hoffman bar one afternoon with Charley and H. J. Montague. Harry Montague, Barry's would-be competitor for the hearts of matinee ladies, was an old friend of Charley's from London, whom Herbert Blyth had cheered at the Prince of Wales's Theatre. He was a handsome fellow of unusual wit and warmth, a natural comrade for Maurice Barrymore. The three dashing actors stood at the crowded bar, Barry alternately sipping English ale, to which he had exclusively returned, and drawing on a cigarette of fine Virginia tobacco, a fresh box of which was rolled for him daily by the Hoffman House tobacconist. Close by, a hulking Texan was making loud and lewd conversation. He aimed a cruel remark at the chief bartender concerning that employee's "inferior" station in life. Barry turned to the offender, asked him to keep a civil tongue. The bully stood where he was.

"If I had you in Texas," he replied, a little too loudly, "I'd blow your head off."

"Then your courage is a matter of longitude," Barry observed, walking straight up to the fellow. The Texan backed away. Drinkers approached the victor with curiosity and admiration, leaving another Hoffman House regular nonplussed. Herman Oelrichs, of New York and Newport society, champion swimmer and all-around sportsman, was not used to competition on his home ground. Moving away from the bar, he called to the upstart in an exaggerated English drawl:

"I say, Percy, in this country we don't interfere in the disputes of others. I suppose that is the *English* way, wot?"

"Oh no," replied Barry, impatient with bullying, "allow me to show you." He demonstrated with a sharp, jolting right to the chin. "That is the *English* way!"

Barry ordered an ice pack and, kneeling beside his fallen opponent, massaged him. Oelrichs responded to treatment. He lifted himself from the hardwood floor to face his adversary. Simultaneously, they proffered friendly hands to one another. When they parted in the wee hours, friendship was understood between the actor and the sportsman.

Oelrichs introduced Barry to the city's sporting district. Near the tip of Manhattan, within a tangle of cobble streets, drinking houses abounded where patrons put up purses of five dollars, sometimes even a "tenner," as prizes for boxing and wrestling bouts. Owney Geoghegan's Bastile on the Bowery and Allen's Bal Mabille on Bleecker Street were popular, but Barry was drawn to another place, a place recalling the Blue Anchor in Shoreditch where a good evening's pommeling for a young solicitor clerk had been easy to come by.

A sign hung over the door of English Harry Hill's, lighted by a swinging lantern:

PUNCHES AND JULEPS, COBBLERS AND SMASHES
TO MAKE THE TONGUE WAGGLE WITH WIT'S
MERRY FLASHES

The low two-story building stood on Houston Street, corner of Crosby, one block east of Broadway, surrounded by notorious dives and dens. Hill's, the gayest, most prosperous establishment along "Murderer's Row," as Houston Street came to be called during the Civil War, was comparatively respectable. Harry Hill kept it that way. Stocky, muscular, very English, he saw that his patrons behaved themselves. "Smoking is not allowed while dancing," said a sign over the bar, "and any rough stuff is discouraged by the proprietor—with a club if necessary." There was no shortchanging or taking advantage of customers who were in their cups. Their money was placed in the house safe and returned, every cent of it, the next day.

Inevitable moments of violence occurred at Hill's, but an atmosphere of good cheer prevailed. Rather than the usual slicked-down barroom waiters, there were sixteen comely barmaids and waitresses to serve the customers, and satisfy English Harry's keen eye for beauty. The women patrons were what they were, the men generally of a sporting character, but the clientele included men from every walk of life. P. T. Barnum, owner of the property, Oscar Wilde, when touring in America, and most of Tammany Hall frequented the place. Thomas Edison was a regular customer. As a favor to the struggling young inventor, Hill installed electric illumination, the first in a public place, reaping further fame as "Harry Hill's Electric Light Hall."

Barry's first night there, he and Oelrichs were greeted by the proprietor himself. English Harry was cordial to his countryman, and, when Oelrichs mentioned the newcomer's middleweight title, downright obeisant. Some newspaper reporters, G. M. Pullman, originator of the Pullman palace car, and "Paper-Collar Joe," an infamous confidence man, joined them. "We never try to bunco a man with snap in his walk," Joe assured Barry. "We gotta look out for guys like you. But the slumpy, slouchy, foot-draggy, hands-in-their-pockets guys, they interest us—they're our meat."

The entertainment at Hill's was a heady mixture of song and fisticuffs. Barry heard the sweet tenor of little Billy Scanlan, the boisterous innuendo of Maggie Cline, and watched, impressed, as the "Iron-Chested Man" broke stones on his bare chest, unimpressed as pugilists demonstrated their skill. The main attraction was yet to come.

Sporting men with an eye for style frequented Hill's to see that popular young wrestler, William Muldoon, take on all comers. "Handsome Billy" was gentle and well spoken, with unbroken features belying his hulky, muscular superiority. Four years older than Barry, he had joined the Union forces at eighteen to serve with Company I, 6th Regiment, New York, under General Phil Sheridan, distinguishing himself beside George A. Custer in the battle at Toms Brook. Now Harry Hill's wrestler was a policeman as well, "the most popular 'copper' walking a beat."

Barry was first that night to challenge Billy Muldoon, inspiring mutual respect and admiration by some hot-blooded battle: first, the wrestling bout, which Billy took; then, a boxing match, which was Barry's. They parted friends, resolved to coach one another in their respective specialties.

Even in the heat of summer, a Fifth Avenue first night attracted an impressive audience; so, whatever fashionable folk happened to be in the city on August 23, 1875, witnessed Maurice Barrymore's unheralded New York debut. The patrons greeted him enthusiastically, delighting particularly in his comedic playing of the courting scene. As *Bob Ruggles*, an "impecunious scapegrace," he falls in love with the daughter of a rich banker, borrows a friend's clothes to make a good impression, and limps into the presence of his beloved with the aside, "Jack's clothes fit me pretty well, but his shoes—!" A line which elicited prolonged laughter followed by applause. Despite shoe trouble, he proceeded to illuminate the courting scene in the drawing room with *Eugenia*. There seem to be no candles, so they begin burning matches, each lighting one in turn until the girl burns her fingers. Of course, they have to be kissed and made well, and the rest logically follows. With Barrymore playing *Bob*, one never doubted that it would.

"*The Big Bonanza* was reproduced on Monday, with an almost entirely new cast, which included Messrs. Whiting, Fawcett, Morse, Barrymore, and Ringgold," reported the *Spirit of the Times.* "Mr. Barrymore, who made his debut in New York, is quite an accession to the troupe. He is a gentlemanly-looking young man, and acts exceedingly well, being a pleasant and graceful personage, of evidently gentle breeding and culture." This review was indicative of the debutant's critical reception. Nevertheless, Augustin Daly, in Salt Lake City with the touring company, wrote in his notebook: "Barrymore was liked fairly." It appeared that the Governor's surrender was not unconditional.

At the first meeting of the entire Fifth Avenue company after Daly's return, Barry stood among forty of the finest actors in America. Charley Vandenhoff was not one of them. Having disagreed with Daly over the roles assigned to him, he decided, with the manager concurring, to accept a more congenial offer. It remained a glittering aggregation employed by the onerous Governor, rivaled only by Lester Wallack's company at his theater and A. M. Palmer's at the Union Square.

Anticipation ran high at a Fifth Avenue opening. They were like huge family parties, the Governor standing at the ticket taker's wicket like a benevolent patriarch, greeting the more illustrious members of his audience. Once past the formidable manager, they gathered beneath paintings, engravings, and historic playbills hung in the elegant lobby. Warmth and expectation were evident in their chatter, as they scanned programs announcing old favorites in new parts, and the orchestra played a "Medley of American Airs."

"If hearty laughter and enthusiastic applause are criterions of success, then Byron's comedy of *Our Boys*, produced at Daly's Fifth Avenue Theatre last evening, is in for a long run," predicted the *Dramatic News.* "It was well put upon the stage, and in some instances capitally acted, notably so by Mr. Barrymore and Mr. Fisher, Mrs. Gilbert and Miss Jeffreys-Lewis." Some of the other papers took exception to Barry's interpretation, "in a wondrous blonde wig," of the honest, pig-headed, faithful hero. In his zeal to stress the "character" aspect of another essentially romantic lead, he irritated them.

The crucial review for theater people was William Winter's in the *Tribune.* Though not yet forty, Winter was considered the dean of New York critics. He was powerful, pompous, professorial, and as likely to attack the personal life of an actor as his acting. He was often accused of favoritism toward Daly's theater. The accusation was justified, but favoritism did not color Winter's view of Maurice Barrymore. An advocate of the heroic school, the critic quashed any attempt at naturalism. "Mr. Maurice Barrymore has neither the hauteur nor the elegant reticence of manners implied in the circumstances of his identity and position; yet, particularly toward the close," conceded Mr. Winter, "he acted well."

James Lewis, as usual, receiving unreserved admiration from the critics, sought to encourage Barry after his mixed notices had been read. "Don't allow the critical carping to upset you, Barry," consoled Lewis.

"Not a bit of it, Jimmy," replied the newcomer; "they approached me as an actor, at least, not as a walking codpiece."

Edwin Booth was to begin a six-week engagement at the Fifth Avenue on October 3, but an accident prevented it. The great tragedian was thrown from his carriage, breaking an arm and sustaining internal injuries. At first, the gravest results were feared. Fortunately, they were not realized. Daly was informed that the engagement could commence at the end of October. While Booth convalesced in his home at Cos Cob, Connecticut, he bombarded Daly by mail with explicit directions. They were heeded. Edwin Booth was one man that the Governor did not contradict.

The engagement was reduced to four weeks because of Booth's health; but ten plays were to be presented in that time, with the Fifth Avenue company supporting the actor. Daly was lavish in mounting the plays, providing new tableaux, wardrobe, and mechanical devices, finishing any profit which he might have realized from the venture. Booth demanded "six thousand dollars per week (seven performances) or: half the gross receipts up to fifteen hundred dollars and two thirds of all over that." Booth was investing his towering talent in the enterprise. The other contributions were Daly's, and he fretted about the enormous repertoire for such a brief season. "The cry is still for *Hamlet*," lamented the Governor, "yet Booth persists in varying his performances." Although Barry was to appear in all of Booth's plays, two roles particularly interested him. The *Duke of Aumerle* in *Richard II* (being produced in New York for the first time in half a century), and *Laertes* to Booth's *Hamlet*, the opening play of the season.

The company had been rehearsing without Booth during his convalescence. When the actor arrived, he found their playing much more of Daly than Shakespeare. Patiently, his arm still in a sling, obviously in pain, he went over the play with the company schooled in modern comedy and melodrama. Barry responded to this greatest of *Hamlets*, this serious, kind and gentle man, who had borne the insanity of his father, the infamy of his brother, Wilkes. A man whose art had transcended the early death of Mary Devlin, his beloved first wife, and, currently, the insanity of his second wife, Mary McVicker.

On October 25, 1875, the foremost actor of the American stage stood pale and composed, clad in the mourning garb of *Hamlet*, to receive an extraordinary ovation from a crowded house. In his *Tribune* review, William Winter rhapsodized for several paragraphs before concluding that "Mr. Booth seems to live *Hamlet* rather than to act it." The support, according to Winter, had two "excellent features"—the *Polonius* of Fisher, the *First Gravedigger* of Davidge, and three "tolerably commendable features—the *Laertes* of Barrymore, the *Horatio* of Ringgold, the *Osric* of Parkes. The other performances were "indifferent or worse."

Barry took greater satisfaction from this qualified praise than from any he had garnered during his career. For Booth, somehow, he had wanted to succeed.

After Booth's departure, Clara Morris returned to the Fifth Avenue stage, which she had departed in anger two years before. She had made a tremendous hit there with her strong, intuitive playing, but Daly had not rewarded her fairly. The gifted actress had moved to the Union Square Theatre, where she achieved stardom. Her return to the Daly fold for a starring engagement was a victory for the irrepressible Miss Morris.

Barry first met the actress at a reception in her honor in the Fifth Avenue greenroom. The Governor had invited some businessmen to partake of backstage atmosphere in hopes of financial return. Barry and Clara Morris were trapped by one of these visitors, a particularly pompous fellow who had come from the slums, reached out and grabbed enough to make himself rich, and took great delight in recounting the tale. He glorified his own accomplishments, allowing his bored victims no retreat. "I am a self-made man, Mr. Barrymore," he boasted; "yes, sir, a self-made man."

"What interrupted you?" Barry wondered.

Clara asked Barry to accompany her the following afternoon to one of William Winter's semiliterary "at homes." The *Tribune* critic tended toward the prosy and ponderous on these occasions, entertaining himself and boring his guests with all sorts of padded-cell questions on Shakespearean subjects. "What relation was *Ophelia* to the queen mother?" and so on. Clara's attendance was a professional necessity. She hoped that Barry would enliven the proceedings.

The host's drawing room, cluttered with the relics of forty stage-struck years, resembled the property room of a provincial theater. Thus enshrined, Winter introduced an exhausting dissertation on the bearing of the character of *Goneril* upon the moral development of *Cordelia*, climaxing it with hypothetical questions. When an unusually pedantic query had been aimed at him, Barry lifted a weary eyelid toward the critic. "I used to know a blind beggar," he drawled, "great student of the drama. Blind beggar had a brother. Brother died." There was a silent pause broken only by a murmured "God bless us!" from Winter's direction. "Now," concluded Barry, "what relation was the blind beggar to the deceased?"

The guests, enlivened by a new voice, believed that they were brothers. When this was denied, an animated discussion ensued, leaving Winter pouting in his chair beside a bust of Sarah Siddons. After lengthy argu-

ment, Barry reluctantly yielded the answer: "The beggar was the dead man's sister." The reverential gathering broke up in refreshing disorder.

When Clara Morris opened in *The New Leah*, the lack of public interest was a startling surprise in and out of the theater. It proved to be one of the most ghastly failures in the careers of both actress and manager. After a week of diminishing returns, in spite of Daly's offer to revive one of her past successes, Clara Morris retired on a plea of ill health. She humorously described the experience to Barry as "a brilliant failure."

Daly had planned to open an original play of his own after Clara Morris's season, but it was not ready. To keep the theater open, he hurriedly revived *Our Boys*. The original cast was assembled, excepting Fanny Davenport, who was on tour. Miss Davenport's absence, combined with a national financial scare, struck the Fifth Avenue box office. For a fortnight, Mr. Daly did what he recorded as the worst business in his management.

The famine ended on December 4. The Governor presented *Pique*, achieving one of the greatest successes of his career. The "play of today," as Daly called his creation, introduced Fanny Davenport as a full-fledged star and gave Barry his best role at the Fifth Avenue. His pleasure with the part of a charming villain reflected in his performance. "Mr. Barrymore," said the *Times*, "merits great praise for his *Raymond Lessing*, the handsome and treacherous lover, whose villainies are condoned by the ladies and faintly condemned by the gentlemen."

After two months, Wednesday matinees were inaugurated, at one o'clock, for the benefit of suburban ladies. Daly made the week of the hundredth performance a Gala Centennial Celebration. The theater was festively decorated for the occasion, and four special matinees were given. Harvey Dodsworth, the musical director, composed a "Pique Waltz." Souvenir programs, printed on pink satin, were distributed, and the ladies received photographs of Miss Davenport and Mr. Barrymore in a provocative clinch. Since specie payment had been resumed by the Government, Daly announced another proud feature of his celebration: "On and after March 13th, change in silver will be given at the box office, and, on the hundredth night, change in gold!"

On the afternoon of April 16, a special rehearsal of the *Pique* company was called. Jack Drew's sister from Philadelphia was to make her New York debut, replacing Jeffreys-Lewis in the role of *Mary Standish*. When she was presented in the greenroom, Barry noted a tall, supple figure. Upon further inspection, the young lady appeared fair and gay, striking for more than beauty. Enormous blue eyes animated and dominated her features, possessing, it seemed, flashing life of their own. She stood with her brother in the center of the room. Barry approached the friend, anxious to address the sister. He bowed, presenting a most courtly self.

"This is indeed an honor, Miss Drew."

"No, Barry," she cautioned, with beguiling impudence, "my name is Georgie. I will not have you bogging down things with formality."

Her charming nonchalance delighted Barry, but the young lady was in earnest. Jack had spoken of his colleague, and the sight of him confirmed her suppositions. She had decided that M. H. Barrymore, this Barry whom her brother so admired, would be more than a mere acquaintance. Anyone who knew Georgie Drew could have warned Barry that his freedom was precarious.

She was, after all, her mother's daughter.

Above, the strapping eighteen-year-old in the center of the front row is Herbert A. Blyth, captain of Blackheath's Cricket Team in 1867. Below, his sister, Evelin Blyth, embodies the British colonial gentlewoman on the eve of her marriage to Lieutenant Edward G. Wace at Jhang, India.

In 1872, during his first months as an actor, Herbert sat for Oliver Sarony in Scarborough *(above)*. Below, a view of that Victorian watering place, its castle and natural harbor.

Herbert's first London friends were his school-fellow, Paul Potter, seen at left as the successful playwright which, with his friend's help, he later became, and actor Charles H. Vandenhoff *(right)*, whom he accompanied to America.

Actor-manager C. P. Flockton *(left)* introduced Herbert to acting at the Windsor Theatre Royal, after Ned Donnelly *(right)*, the Royal Professor of British Boxing, had groomed him for the Queensberry Cup championships.

With a new mustache and a new name, "M. H. Barrymore," Herbert made his American debut in *Under the Gaslight*, later appearing as the dashing Captain Molyneux *(right)* in Dion Boucicault's *The Shaughraun*.

facing page: Dion Boucicault, the most prolific playwright of his time (above as *Conn* in *The Shaughraun*), and William Warren *(below)*, Boston's beloved comedian, befriended "Barry," as Herbert came to be called, upon his arrival in America.

Wearing a "wondrous blonde wig" in Augustin Daly's production, *Our Boys,* Barry mugged for noted theatrical photographer Napoleon Sarony, who managed to capture the famous Barrymore smile *(bottom, right).*

John Drew.

John Drew *(above, left)*, who be-
came Barry's brother-in-law, and
Ada Rehan *(above, right)* were the
staples of Augustin Daly's Fifth
Avenue Theatre Company. When
Edwin Booth (pictured at left as
Hamlet) played the Fifth Avenue,
Barry supported him in a repertoire
of ten plays.

Barry appeared, respectively, in the companies of New York's foremost nineteenth-century managers: Lester Wallack *(top, left)*, A. M. Palmer *(top, right)*, and Augustin Daly.

Episode

A Brief Chronicle of the Drews

At twelve months old my mother took me on the stage as a crying baby; but cry I would not, but at the sight of the audience and the lights gave free vent to my delight and crowed aloud with joy. From that moment to this, the same sight has filled me with the most acute pleasure, and I expect will do so to the last glimpse I get of them, and when no longer to be seen, "Come, Death, and welcome!"

MRS. JOHN DREW

GEORGIANA EMMA DREW did not enter the Fifth Avenue green-room as an unknown aspirant. She was the daughter of Mrs. John Drew, manageress of Philadelphia's Arch Street Theatre, the most respected woman on the American stage. That heritage alone promised greatness; a promise hard won and worn like laurel on her mother's indomitable brow.

Mrs. Drew had begun life as Louisa Lane far from the respectable brick fronts of Arch Street. "I was born in Lambeth Parish, London, England, on January 10, 1820," she recalled; "my father, Thomas Frederick Lane, was an actor of considerable provincial fame, and my mother, née Eliza Trenter, a very pretty woman and a sweet singer of ballads. That was an eventful year for theatrical people. The old King, George the Third, died, and all the theatres were closed for one month; and there was considerable suffering among our kind, as I have been told since."

Thomas Frederick Lane died before his daughter turned five. He bequeathed an acting heritage which reached back to strolling players in Shakespeare's time, and little else. The destitute young widow and her child headed for the provinces, enduring hardships and privations as they sought work in provincial stock companies. Poor theaters, shabby accommodations, the loneliness of restless travel did not deter them. They performed together sometimes, or alone when mutual engagements could not be found; but no matter what the arrangements on stage might be, during the long mornings in rickety coaches, or dark nights in unfamiliar boardinghouses, Mrs. Lane never left her child. ("Nothing can compensate a well brought up girl for loss of home and all that word means," said Mrs. Drew in later years. "To a child actress, who grows up in the

85

profession and absolutely knows nothing else, it is good, but not to the young girl educated in a refined home.")

At Cooke's amphitheatre, Liverpool, horses were the main actors. As *Prince Agib* in *Timour, the Tartar,* the six-year-old had to perform a daring rescue on horseback. On opening night, her mount stumbled down four stage levels, nearly killing the child. "There was a universal wish on the part of the audience to know if 'the dear little girl was much hurt,'" Louisa remembered of herself, "but she was insensible to the kind wishes of her audience, I believe I may truly say for the first and only time in her life."

Undaunted, she soon earned loyal following in towns beyond memory, playing popular children's parts; but Eliza Trenter Lane wanted more for herself and her child. She shared the goal that most English provincial actors cherished in those days: "America," as she put it, "that El Dorado to an imaginative class, which assuredly theatrical people are." When an agent from New York engaged mother and child as part of an entire company, they set sail for the New World on the packetship *Britannia.*

After an exceptionally fine passage of four weeks, they landed in New York on June 7, 1827. Mrs. Lane made her American debut at Philadelphia's Walnut Street Theatre. "The symphony of her entrance song is a long one," wrote Louisa, "and the orchestra had to play it twice, her reception was so hearty and her nervousness so great." The fair young widow captured more than local audiences. Soon after her debut, she married John Kinloch, stage manager and actor.

Louisa's first assignments in the new land were in support of two of its foremost actors. On September 26, she appeared at the Walnut Street as the little *Duke of York* to Junius Brutus Booth's *Richard III.* She was only seven, but Booth's performance made a powerful impression. "His dramatic force and magnetism were like a giant whirlwind," she recalled, "sweeping all before it." The whirlwind also swept the audience with the power of his playing, imbuing them with the belief that he was *Richard* himself. On occasion, the eccentric Booth shared that belief, particularly during the fight with *Richmond,* when he chased his stage adversary over the footlights through the audience, taking broadsword whacks at his brainpan.

Later, with her mother and new stepfather, Louisa was sent to Joe Cowell's Theatre in Baltimore to play *Albert* opposite Edwin Forrest's *William Tell.* Still in his early twenties, Forrest was already considered one of America's great actors—with towering temperament to match his talent. He was nonetheless beguiled by the little professional from England. At the end of their mutual engagement, she received a fine silver medal "Presented by E. Forrest to Miss L. Lane as a testimonial of his admiration for her talents."

86

Louisa was beginning to make a name, when the successes of Little Clara Fisher started a great vogue for child performers. The Kinlochs at once arranged a starring tour for their own talented child. Just after her eighth birthday, she made her debut as a star at the Bowery Theatre in New York: "Shall I ever forget my stage-fright whilst waiting to hear my cue as *Little Pickle* in *The Spoiled Child?* But when the time of entrance came every feeling but exhilaration vanished—only the certainty of success remained." Louisa toured as a star with varying degrees of financial success, winning unqualified praise in such roles as *Dr. Pangloss* in *The Heir at Law.* When she stood by the orchestra and, looking around the pit, inquired if anyone there wanted the instructions of an LL.D. and A.S.S. at three hundred a year, the effect was irresistible, and the house shouted with laughter. The elder Joseph Jefferson was *Zekiel Homespun* in this production. "Think of that great old actor," exclaimed Louisa, "playing with a child of nine years old!"

While playing Washington, Louisa was invited to the President's Levee. Andrew Jackson was extremely kind, and said that Louisa was "a pretty little girl." ("Need I say," Mrs. Drew confirmed sixty years later, "that I was a Jackson Democrat from that hour, and have remained one up to date?")

When the vogue for juveniles waned by 1830, John Kinloch ventured into management, the better to provide for his growing family. Besides his wife and stepdaughter, there were two infant daughters, born during Louisa's starring days. He engaged a first-rate company to tour the West Indies. They set sail for Jamaica in November, and ten days out, on a clear moonlit night, they struck a hidden rock off the coast of San Domingo. The vessel remained standing, allowing everyone to be taken safely ashore, baggage intact. Ascertaining that the nearest settlement was forty miles distant, the captain ordered his crew to use the ship's deck load—shingles and staves—to erect sturdy tents, and started for the city in hopes of finding a brig to get them off. Camped on that desolate beach for six weeks, subsisting on stores from the ship and scant provisions sent overland, Louisa celebrated her eleventh birthday.

Eventually, the company reached the city of San Domingo, traveling from there to Kingston, Jamaica, where they played successfully until yellow fever struck. John Kinloch died there, followed by the youngest daughter, ten months old. Mrs. Kinloch was nearly taken with them. Alone in unfamiliar tropical surroundings, in the midst of epidemic and quarantine and hysteria, Louisa nursed her mother, cared for her frail half sister, Adine. Fortunately, the doctor was solicitous. While treating the fever, he discovered that the widow was with child. He advised them to go north to Falmouth, where the climate would hasten her recovery.

They met with kindness at Falmouth. Louisa performed to acclaim from the British population; but the interlude was brief. When alarming rumors of native insurrection began to circulate, Mrs. Kinloch was advised to leave the city. She fled with her daughters back across the island to Kingston. From there, with the money Louisa had earned in Falmouth, they booked passage to New York.

> *New York, April 26, 1832—To Messrs. Forrest and Duffy—*
>
> *Gentlemen:*
>
> *Myself and daughter arrived on Sunday last from the West Indies, after a voyage of twenty-two days. I presume it is needless to mention Mr. Kinloch's death, as you have doubtless heard of it long before now. Me and Louisa are at liberty to make an engagement with you. Should there be a vacancy I should be most happy to treat with you—that of first singing or singing chamber-maids—indeed, a general round of business. As to Louisa, you are aware what she can do. Your answer by return will oblige your obedient and humble servant,*
>
> *Eliza Kinloch*
>
> *Please to direct to 194 Hudson Street.*

William Forrest, Edwin's brother, answered from Philadelphia that there were no vacancies at his Arch Street Theatre. Eliza Kinloch nevertheless returned with her daughters to that city, the only home she had known in America. The wayfarers settled at a local boardinghouse, where Louisa made her first friend. Pretty Alexina Fisher was of the same age, also an actress. Together, they played the only game that they knew. Climbing stairs to the empty attic of the boardinghouse, they play-acted —stabbing each other with imaginary daggers with great dramatic fury, falling on the floor with groans and grimaces. When the third-story boarders called for quiet, the girls would effect a mock-reconciliation with tears and embraces.

Mrs. Kinloch found it difficult to secure congenial engagements for herself and her daughter. Louisa had reached the awkward age for actresses—no longer a child and certainly not yet a woman, there was little chance of her acting anything of importance. While at liberty, she and Alexina Fisher haunted the theaters of Philadelphia where they were granted "privilege of the stage." Curiosity drew them particularly to Forrest and Duffy's Arch Street, which boasted an entire company of American actors, the first of its kind.

After the birth of another daughter, christened Georgiana, Mrs. Kinloch found work for herself and Louisa. They would be separated for the first time: Mrs. Kinloch with Adine in Baltimore; Louisa in Washington. Reluctantly, the baby was left with a nurse in Philadelphia.

Mother and daughter were soon reunited in Richmond, Virginia, under the management of "Nosey" Phillips. The manager had made a success there by bringing in stars to augment his stock company. The first of these, after Louisa and her mother joined the organization, was Junius Brutus Booth. In the six years since Louisa had last acted with him, Booth's great sad eyes had grown wider and wilder, his melancholy more evident and touching. It was said that the tragedian had a streak of insanity in him. Whether or not it was true, there was no questioning his eccentricity. (While in London in 1820, playing with Edmund Kean at the Drury Lane, he had fallen in love with Mary Ann Holmes, a Bow Street flower seller. Returning with her to America, deserting his legal wife, he had lived with Mary Ann ever since. Their seventh child, Edwin, was born during the Richmond engagement.) Yet his power as an actor was awesome. "I never heard anyone read just like the elder Booth," said Louisa. "It was beautiful; he made the figure stand before you! Some of the passages of *Lear* were touching in the extreme."

"Nosey" Phillips went off to New York one day to secure talent, and never returned to Richmond. The abandoned company continued to act, but the public neglected to attend. When some of the actors booked passage on a schooner, Mrs. Kinloch and her daughters gladly joined them.

Far off course, on a stormy night, they were wrecked on a sand bar in Egg Harbor, West Indies. Danger at sea was not new to Louisa and her mother, but this time disaster was imminent. As the vessel swayed ominously, they awoke and dressed in a few minutes, watching and listening for the planks to give way. "Mama," asked little Adine with unsuspecting calm, "if we all go in the water, will God give us breakfast?" After a perilous rescue, they were packed for the return to New York into a "wood boat," a vessel without bulwarks, loaded with lumber.

They played a short engagement at the Bowery Theatre, collected Georgiana in Philadelphia, went on to the Warren Theatre in Boston. There, as members of the company for two seasons, mother and daughter received a joint salary of sixteen dollars per week. Eliza Kinloch and her three girls spent two happy seasons there, living at "Ma" Lenthe's boardinghouse, a gable end at the corner of Bowdoin Square. "I don't know how we lived; but mother was a splendid manager," Louisa remembered; "we had a large room on the second story, a trundle bed which went under the other for the accommodation of little children, a large closet in which we kept a barrel of ale and all our dresses." Summers were spent playing in Portland, Maine, and in Halifax, Nova Scotia, with the Garrison amateurs. "We saw a good deal of human nature there," confided the seasoned fourteen-year-old, "all the petty strife of real actors without their ability."

Mrs. Kinloch and her daughters made a gay and easy voyage on the good ship *Star* to New Orleans to open the St. Charles Theatre. On board were Clara Fisher, her husband James Gaspard Maeder, Charlotte Cushman, and others bound for the St. Charles. As they entered the Belize, another ship met them, carrying George Holland, James E. Murdoch, and Henry Blaine Hunt, among others, also bound for the new theater. There was a festive volley of shouted greetings, tossed like garlands between the ships, as they neared the bustling wharves of New Orleans.

Henry Blaine Hunt was captivated by the fifteen-year-old Louisa Lane, who seemed old beyond her years. That was indeed fortunate, considering the age of Mr. Hunt when he began to court the girl. Mrs. Kinloch thought him a good man, and Louisa found him "a very good singer, a nice actor, and a very handsome man of forty." He was certainly a handsome man, and his voice, as befitted a fine Irish tenor, had made him a favorite of operagoing Londoners during the Regency. "He had been a member of the fast set which surrounded George IV before his ascent to the throne," noted the *Dramatic Mirror*, "and was a gentleman of dashing manners and great animal spirits." When he lost favor in England, he had come to the New World, gaining rapid success as the singing hero of popular melodramas and light operas. The Lanes of Lambeth Parish were understandably impressed by the gentleman, even if he was twenty-five years older than the young lady of his choice. Two months after her sixteenth birthday, Louisa Lane became the wife of Henry Blaine Hunt.

Sunday performances were adopted during their second season in New Orleans. Since Mrs. Kinloch and her daughter refused to play on the Sabbath, their engagements were terminated. The enlarged family, Mr. and Mrs. Hunt, Mrs. Kinloch, Adine, Georgiana, took to the road again. In Vicksburg, Mississippi, Louisa was reduced to chambermaid parts. In Natchez, she was elevated to leading lady, achieving a pinnacle of her early career with Edwin Forrest. Ten years before, he had shot an apple from her head in *William Tell*. Now, at eighteen, she was *Lady Macbeth* to his Thane.

She returned to the Walnut Street Theatre, Philadelphia, for a season as leading lady at the highest salary known there—twenty dollars per week. Touring resumed after this season, always with her mother and half sisters, less frequently with her husband. There was, ostensibly, an inability to secure joint engagements; but they had not been making a particular effort to secure them. Louisa divorced Harry Hunt in 1847.

Afterward, she joined the Albany Museum company, in which George Moosop, another Irishman, was a singing comedian. It was difficult to see what Louisa saw in Moosop. He was somewhat younger than Mr. Hunt, light and trim-built, but he drank heavily and acted badly. In fact, if his acting was remarked at all, it was only because offstage he could not speak without stuttering badly, while before the footlights his enunciation became relatively flowing. Mrs. Hunt must have found this anomaly endearing. She married the fellow in 1848. The union proved to be short-lived. In 1849, George Moosop died, some said, of drink.

Louisa at thirty was not beautiful. It did not matter. She made the beholder think that she was. Her blue-black hair, pulled back severely over her ears, accentuated small, sharp features and thrusting blue eyes. And her voice, that was the towering feature. She seemed to exert herself not at all, but her voice was always more distinct than others around her, musical in tone, yet commanding. She was small, under five feet, but none looked down on her. She was erect and formidable; men six feet high stood in her shadow.

There was a young man in the Albany Museum company named John Drew, who was not particularly tall. He was rather short in stature, slender, unpretending in his manners or dress; but he had blazing black eyes, lilting Irish humor. There was a restlessness in his demeanor; but he was easy to approach, having a pleasant word and an agreeable smile for everyone. The young widow took a fancy to him.

Louisa and John were not quite strangers. They had met in New York when she was Mrs. Hunt, playing at the Bowery Theatre, and he was a romping ten-year-old in his father's house. Louisa and her mother had often taken Sunday tea with the Drews and their large family, staying on to join them in evenings of music and recitation. The Drews were also a theatrical family. John's father, in 1837, had sailed with his wife and their six children from Dublin to New York, where he became treasurer of William Niblo's theater at Broadway and Prince Street.

The progeny of Niblo's treasurer were allowed "privilege of the stage" in most New York theaters. By the time John turned thirteen, this world had become commonplace to him. When he informed his parents that he was "bound to be a sailor boy," they did not object. Rather than have their restless thirteen-year-old bolt and meander, Mr. Drew arranged to have him apprenticed to a whaler. The boy sailed in 1841 from New Bedford on a three years' cruise.

John returned home discouraged with a sailor's life but not yet ready to settle down. When work at Niblo's was suggested, he ran away to New Orleans, shipped on a Liverpool packet. Another year at sea satiated John Drew, resolving him to trade "spike and tar bucket for sock and buskin."

Jobs were not forthcoming in the New York theaters which he had known as a boy. His lack of experience closed whatever doors his father's reputation might have opened, until he finally talked himself into the company of the Richmond Hill Theatre on Greenwich Street, where the manager, a stage-struck railroad contractor, was in need of willing actors.

The eighteen-year-old novice played everything and anything, frequently assuming five or six roles in the same piece. The salary was slight and imperfectly paid, the experience invaluable. He stayed on till bankruptcy closed the doors of the Richmond Hill.

Several similar engagements decided John to return to Ireland, where relatives helped him to open a small dry-goods store in Dublin. Business was promising, prospects bright until he was tempted to meddle in local politics, then, as usual in Ireland, running high. "Taking a conspicuous stand on the side of the 'Agitators' on some forgotten issue," he said, "I was at last compelled to become once more an 'Absentee.'"

He sailed again for America, determined this time to make a name upon the stage. After a season at Rochester, he toured extensively in the East, making his first hit as *Dr. O'Toole* in *The Irish Tutor* at the Bowery Theatre. "Mr. Drew owes his success altogether to originality," observed the New York *Clipper;* "he assumes the part and invests it with truth; thus, he displays the very elements of the art . . . his voice, manner, and *abandon* invest such characters with life, real, natural." He continued to tour the country, gaining popularity, being cited by critics as successor to the late Tyrone Power, who had been the finest Irish comedian of his day.

It was early in the spring of 1850 that John Drew had joined the Albany Museum company.

While Louisa nurtured her infatuation for John Drew, he took a fancy to Georgiana Kinloch, Louisa's half sister, who had grown fair and flirtatious. Drew asked Mrs. Kinloch if he might court her youngest daughter. The lady was inclined to consent, recalling with fondness the young man's people. When she consulted Louisa about Drew's proposal, her eldest daughter objected vehemently. She insisted that Georgiana was far too young, Drew far from settled in the profession.

That was in June of 1850. Georgiana was eighteen, her would-be suitor twenty-two. Louisa was thirty.

"Time rolled easily along," observed *The City Item*, "and our hero, having been fortunate in his *Theatrical* engagement, resolved to enter into another, of a different nature . . . This last *engagement* proved the most fortunate and lucky of any he ever effected."

On the twenty-seventh of July, Louisa Lane Hunt Moosop became Mrs. John Drew.

The marriage was not immediately made public. Louisa had several commitments to fulfill before she could join her husband. Once reunited, they played a season together in Chicago, followed by one in Buffalo, where John's father, after thirteen years at Niblo's Garden, was managing a theater. Louisa was welcomed with affection and respect into the numerous household of the theatrical Drews.

92

Louisa's established reputation enhanced John's rising popularity, bringing profitable offers from all quarters. When, in the summer of 1852, they accepted a prestigious engagement at Niblo's Garden, Drew family friends insisted that John and his new wife stay with them in New York. The Judsons owned a vast red-brick house on Gramercy Park, stately and rather forbidding from the outside. Inside, Miss Alice Judson presided over a cheerful ménage of her brothers and sisters, their respective husbands, wives, and various children. Her father had been a great friend of John's father, and Miss Alice, a devotee of all things theatrical, wished to continue the association. She was ten years older than Louisa Drew, tall, erect, fine-boned, her Old World dignity tempered by a satirical appreciation of its obsolescence. Miss Alice did not regret her maidenhood. It was self-imposed. After the passing of her parents, she had chosen to run the house in an attempt to keep the family and its dwindling fortune intact.

The generation of Judsons which was young when John and Louisa Drew first came to stay adored the generous, storytelling husband. "In private life," observed Miss Alice, "he was social, unassuming and open-hearted. No needy actor ever asked his aid in vain, and needy actors in those days, were as plentiful as Falstaff's blackberries. They say that every man has his enemies, but I never knew that John had any—unless it were his own overly-warm heart."

His formidable wife was another matter. Louisa Drew's clear, sharp eyes seemed always to rest upon a missing button, or an inkstain, or something hanging which had no business to hang. That she never mentioned these things, far from reassuring the children, merely confirmed their mistaken idea of her aloofness. They even distrusted her laughter, not sure that it was inspired by amusement. When their antics wrung an unexpected, trenchant "ha!" from Mrs. Drew, they mistook it for disapproval and crept away in panic.

"Our awakening was rapturous," recalled one of Miss Alice's nieces. "We learned that beneath her reserve and surface sternness there was an emotional, tender heart as responsive as a child's to any claim upon its sympathies." Among Mrs. Drew's philanthropies was a young girl who sometimes helped with chores at the Judson house. She was pretty but so poor that it was a struggle to keep herself in neat attire. Adornment of any sort was out of the question. On the girl's birthday, when the children were preparing to deliver a present that they had made for her (a watch case of perforated cardboard with "Love the Giver" on it), Mrs. Drew asked them to take along a little remembrance from her. When the poor maid opened it, she gazed with almost pathetic delight at its contents—a splendid array of neckwear, combinations of real lace, satin ribbons, velvet bows.

That evening at the Judson dinner table, one of the grownups suggested that a more sensible gift might have been given. "Sensible! Bah!" snorted Louisa Drew. "And it *is* sensible! The only sensible thing to give a poor young girl is something pretty."

Autumn season of 1852, the Drews joined Philadelphia's Chestnut Street Theatre company, opening their engagement in Colley Cibber's comedy *She Would and She Would Not*. Louisa, as *Donna Hypolita*, was zealously received in the city of her childhood triumphs. As *Trapante*, John "was so gay, animated and easy," said his wife, "that he made an immediate hit."

Their first child was born in Philadelphia. She was named for her mother, and called "Wisa." Now Louisa Lane Drew wanted to settle. She wanted a place in which her child could grow in familiar surroundings, not on tour never knowing a home; a place where her mother could rest after a lifetime of strain; where her half sister Adine, frail and weak in heart, might recover, and where Georgiana, mourning her loss of John Drew, might find a proper husband. When William Wheatley asked her husband to become co-lessee of the Arch Street Theatre, Louisa urged him to accept.

The Arch, imposing, of classical design, opened under the management of Drew and Wheatley on the twenty-fifth of August, 1853. Their production of Bulwer-Lytton's *Money* met with unqualified success, although it was regretted that Mrs. Drew had not been in the cast. An imminent arrival had prevented her appearance.

A son was born on November 13. He was named for his father, and called "Jack." The Drews and the Kinlochs moved into a house at 269 South Tenth Street, but Louisa was not left to housekeeping. In December, she made her debut under her husband's management, continuing the season in a wide variety of roles, played to great success.

The highlight of the Drew-Wheatley management proved to be their elaborate production of *The Comedy of Errors*. It was something of a family party, what with Drew, his wife, his brother, Frank, his mother-in-law, and his sister-in-law, Georgiana, comprising the cast. The Drew brothers played the *Dromios*, while William Wheatley and L. R. Shewell were the *Antipholuses*. "It is very doubtful if that performance has ever been equalled," Mrs. Drew stated. "The two *Dromios* were so perfect a facsimile of each other, as were also the two *Antipholuses*, that it was impossible even for the actors to distinguish them."

One night, Mrs. Drew called her brother-in-law aside behind the scenes after he had made up and dressed for his part. She talked to him of domestic affairs for ten minutes before realizing that he was not her husband. Sometimes, when the brothers changed their scenes, and *Dromio of Syracuse* would be and act *Dromio of Ephesus*, and vice versa, their own masters didn't know the difference. Backstage, when John went about telling racy stories, his brother would be blamed for them. When Frank was ill for one performance, John played both *Dromios* until the last scene, where the characters meet. Frank recovered sufficiently for the final encounter. The audience never suspected the doubling that John had done.

The *City Item* lauded the Drew-Wheatley management for the "distinguished success which has crowned their exertion,—the debt of gratitude due to them from the profession, and the thankful responses of the public, in thus catering so elegantly for their pleasure and amusement," adding that "Mr. Drew has fully contributed his share in point of attraction, energy and industry, and has an equal hold upon the public and their affectionate regard and praise." But John Drew was growing restless in management. In 1855, when his agent proposed a starring tour of Ireland and England, he withdrew from the Arch. To appease his furious wife, he invited her mother to come along. Mrs. Kinloch was elated. In a flurry of anticipation, she faced the prospect of visiting her homeland after twenty-eight years. Two weeks before their scheduled departure, Louisa discovered that she was again with child. She did not speak of it. Her mother would have canceled the long-awaited journey had she known.

A daughter was born on the twenty-first of May, 1856. She was christened Georgiana, after her aunt, who had stood by Louisa during her months of confinement. When John Drew returned triumphant from the British Isles, the child was already a year old, and "Georgie" to her doting mother. The wandering father presented his three children with a little Irish donkey. To the children's sorrow, the congenial creature was allowed to roam in the back garden for only a few days before it was sold. Mrs. Drew was not fond of animals.

John Drew, urged by his wife, reluctantly returned to the responsibilities of management. He leased the National Theatre on Walnut Street, opening on May 16, 1857, with an unusually strong company, including Joseph Jefferson, whose father Louisa had acted with as a child, and Mary Devlin, who later married Edwin Booth. The venture was unsuccessful. The doors were closed after three months of losing business.

During the 1857–58 season, the Drews joined the company of the Walnut Street Theatre, moving their expanded family into a bigger house on Buttonwood Street. Adine Kinloch was given a bright new room with bay windows on the garden, something she had wished for. After less than a month in it, her weak heart finally gave out. Louisa was grieved by the passing of her little half sister; though timid and retiring, she had given gentle continuity to the sprawling years.

John Drew returned restless from a starring tour of Canada late in 1858, and accepted what looked to be a lucrative tour of California and Australia. He proposed to have Georgiana Kinloch accompany him.

Wary of recurring ardor between her husband and half sister, Louisa sent eight-year-old Wisa along to serve, she hoped, as deterrent. On December 6, after a farewell benefit at the Walnut Street, John Drew, his sister-in-law, and his eldest daughter sailed for San Francisco. He made his first appearance in that city at the American Theatre, continuing to acclaim throughout the state.

They sailed for Melbourne on the twelfth of March, 1859, beginning in that city a tour which was considered one of the most brilliant in Australia's history. He sent a letter to his son from that distant continent, enclosing some pages from a volume of children's verse. "I went the other day to buy a book for your dear little sister Louisa," he wrote, "and among the others I found this. I have cut these leaves out and send them to you because they speak of a little boy named John Drew."

While in Melbourne, Georgiana Kinloch was courted by Robert L. Stephens, a local actor. Although she still preferred her brother-in-law, Georgiana consented to marry the fellow in the spring of 1860. Louisa Drew was particularly pleased when word of the marriage reached Buttonwood Street. Any ardor remaining between her husband and her half sister, she assumed, would now disappear.

During her husband's absence, Louisa Drew had joined the Arch Street Theatre company, still under the management of William Wheatley. She became Philadelphia's favorite that season, culminating a series of comedy portrayals with the tragic *Queen Katherine* to Charlotte Cushman's *Cardinal Wolsey* in *Henry VIII*. "The *Katherine* suffered nothing by comparison with the *Wolsey*," stated the Philadelphia *Public Ledger*. "The exquisitely queenly bearing, commingled with the scarcely concealed mental suffering of the trial scene, reached its climax in the stately exit from the courtroom when the crier whispers, 'Madame, you are called back,' and the Queen's pent-up indignation found vent in an angry smiting of the cushion borne before her, as, with thrilling tones, she replied: 'What need you note it . . . When you are called, return.' "

In June of 1860, John Drew and party sailed from Melbourne, bound to play London's Theatre Royal, Adelphi. Georgiana Kinloch Stephens traveled with her brother-in-law and his daughter, leaving her new husband to a summer engagement in Melbourne with plans for a reunion in London the following autumn. Weather and hazard plagued John Drew's voyage to England. They did not sight Liverpool until September, just in season for John to originate, in London, the role of *Myles-Na-Coppaleen* in Dion Boucicault's new play *The Colleen Bawn*. The success of the London production decided Boucicault to send out a touring company, with his drama, rather than a star, billed as the main attraction. Boucicault's notion proved successful, heralding the beginning of the end of stock companies.

John grew impatient after a month's popular run in London. Without bothering to wait for Georgiana's husband, they departed with Wisa on a tour of Ireland. He opened at the Theatre Royal, Dublin, on October 22, and embarked on a tour of the provinces. Irish audiences were understandably responsive to an "honest child of the Green Isles of Ocean."

While John was conquering the land of his birth, William Wheatley was counting his days as manager of the Arch in Philadelphia. He was leaving to replace William Niblo, who was retiring from the active management of his theater in New York. Under Wheatley's rule, after John Drew's departure, the Arch had depreciated. The theater had been mortgaged for twenty thousand dollars. The Board of Directors were searching scrupulously for a replacement.

Philadelphia's leading citizens looked to their theaters for relief. Otherwise, propriety limited night life to the Philadelphia Club at Thirteenth and Walnut. The stockholders at the various theaters, with boxes set apart for their use, sought relaxation and amusement of an evening by dropping in and out of the different houses, sitting through an entire new play, or a portion of an old one, discussing topics of the day between the acts. When Adam Everly, amateur actor and son of the board's president, suggested Mrs. John Drew, the directors deliberated at length before entrusting their investment and relaxation to a woman. Laura Keene's fortunate management in New York was cited. Young Everly argued that Mrs. Drew's "experience, ability, good taste and judgment would probably make the Arch not only more popular, but Philadelphia's most fashionable theatre."

Louisa Drew was surprised and gratified by the offer. "Little did she think as her mother knocked at the doors of the Arch Street Theatre in the springtime of 1832, and for that time knocked in vain," remembered the Philadelphia *Times*, "that thirty years later she would be the lessee of the house." Before accepting, she wrote to Ireland for her husband's approval. Permission received, contracts signed, she set about engaging a company of seasoned professionals for her theater, astutely augmenting it with amateur actors from various dramatic associations in the city—a policy contrived to delight Philadelphians.

Saturday night, the thirty-first of August, 1861, Mrs. John Drew inaugurated her management of the stately Greek temple on Arch Street. The bill was *Aunt Charlotte's Maid* and *The School for Scandal*. Her *Lady Teazle*, the company she had assembled, the production she had staged inspired unremitting bravos. Louisa Drew worked tirelessly to maintain that standard, introducing numerous novelties and new plays that first season, playing forty-two leading parts herself. "A good deal was done to beautify the theatre," confided the lady. "It was a hard season to meet. I borrowed money every week to meet the salaries." But bravos continued for the redoubtable manageress. Debts were paid. Success was insured by her second season. "When she assumed the reins of supreme control at the Arch Street Theatre," the local *Times* explained, "a new era dawned upon the history of stage management in this city."

Six months later, John Drew and party arrived in New York from Liverpool on the steamship *Kangaroo*. He had been away for three years.

At Buttonwood Street, Wisa ran ahead into the house to embrace her anxious mother and grandmother, brother and sister. John Drew followed slowly with his sister-in-law, Georgiana Stephens. In her arms, she held a newborn infant. He explained, haltingly, that Georgiana had given birth to the baby en route. She had been married in Australia, John reminded his wife, without adding that she had not seen her husband for eighteen months. Louisa Drew surmised as much. With queenly reticence, she took the baby from her irresponsible half sister, named her Adine Stephens, and from that moment raised the girl as her own. She did not need to ask who had fathered the child.

The contrite husband commenced a starring engagement at his wife's theater, filling the house one hundred nights. With the War Between the States raging, the Drews offered numerous benefits for the Union cause. Audiences included the wounded and those about to leave for the front; emotion ran high. During the playing of John's most famous role, *Tim O'Brian* in *The Irish Emigrant*, noted *The City Item*, "Many a wet eye and beating heart waited sympathetically over his scenes, a quiet impressive illustration of sickness, hunger, grief and joy, each in their turn so touchingly given, without one ever over-crowding or choking the other; the little gentle expressions of feeling . . . like rainbow shining joyously upon the cloud of trouble."

At his wife's insistence—he would not have bothered otherwise—John alternated his popular Irish parts with *Meddle* in *London Assurance*, *William* in *Black-Eyed Susan*, *Sir Lucius O'Trigger* in *The Rivals*, *Goldfinch* in *Road to Ruin* (which Louisa had played as a child), and his two favorite Shakespearean parts—*Sir Andrew Ague-Cheek* and *Dromio*. During the engagement, Mrs. Drew received a warm note from President Lincoln, regretting that business in Washington kept him from accepting an invitation to the Arch, but commending her efforts for the Union cause. That note became her most cherished possession.

John's brother, Edward, stopped at Buttonwood Street on his way to the front. A captain in Berdan's Sharpshooters, he wore a uniform with long, blue single-breasted frock coat and brass buttons. The children were fascinated by their uniformed uncle. Georgie insisted upon pulling his long side whiskers, giggling when he called them "Piccadilly weepers." Young Jack was overwhelmed when Uncle Edward showed his father the brand new sighting device which was to be distributed to his men. Now Jack had something to tell his schoolfellows! He had felt somewhat left out at school until his uncle's visit, since class had been much interrupted by the abrupt disappearance of classmates with fathers or brothers or close relatives fighting. It had all seemed exciting, even when those boys returned in a day or two, subdued, with evidence of mourning.

Soon after the heroic visit, Jack came down to breakfast to find his mother and grandmother in tears, reading aloud a letter. Edward Drew had been killed in action. "I hurried to school to declare myself in the 'movement' because I, too, had lost someone," rejoiced the thoughtless eight-year-old. "My uncle had seemed to me very smart with his brass buttons and wonderful whiskers, but the satisfaction of being in the 'game' with my companions out-weighed the loss of an uncle I really did not know. Still, the fact that he was killed in action affected me more than the death of my uncle, George Drew, who had been sent back to Buffalo, where he died of wounds."

John Drew ended his hundred nights at the Arch on Friday evening, the ninth of May. A crowded house called him before the curtain for a speech. He thanked them for the kindness that he had received, and for encouraging his wife in her venture. "I am about to leave you to fulfill engagements in England," he concluded, "but I hope to have the pleasure of appearing before you again, ere long."

He visited New York the following Thursday to see his agent, Mr. Reese, who was sailing for England ahead of him to make arrangements for the impending tour. After seeing Reese off, John frolicked with friends, attended Bryants' Minstrels' Hall on Friday, returned to Buttonwood Street on Saturday.

Tuesday was spent at home with his children, preparing a celebration for Georgie's sixth birthday the next day. While carrying Adine to the nursery, his foot caught under the hall carpet. For fear of injuring the baby, he cradled her firmly in his arms as he fell. His head struck full force against a corner of the carved-oak newel.

Wednesday, May 21, 1862, at four in the afternoon, John Drew died: congestion of the brain, superinduced by the fall.

"Had he lived to be forty-five, he would have been a great actor," acknowledged his widow. "But too early success was his ruin; it left him with nothing to do. Why should he study when he was assured on all sides (except my own) that he was as near perfection as was possible for a man to be? So he finished his brief and brilliant career at thirty-four years of age, about the age when men generally study most steadily and aspire most ambitiously."

Austere widow's weeds lent even more dignity to the Arch Street manageress. Mrs. John Drew was a figure to be reckoned with in Philadelphia, to be respected. She moved her family to a large white-shuttered, white-stepped row house at 119 North Ninth Street, ostensibly to be nearer the theater. There was another reason. That hall in the house on Buttonwood Street returned the horror each time she walked it. Louisa Drew did not display emotion, but she did possess it.

Every Sunday at St. Stephen's Episcopal Church on Tenth Street, Mrs. Drew and Mrs. Kinloch, black bonnets and dolmans, adorned the pew marked "L. Drew." They sat erect, one at each end of the long bench, like sentinels. The children squirmed between them, giggling at their grandmother's loud responses to the service. Georgie, invariably the instigator, was usually dismissed by her mother before the sermon. The Sabbath was not to be taken lightly. Mrs. Kinloch's idea of occupation for the day of rest was reading *The Spirit of Missions* cover to cover. The children's toys and books were put away. Only meditative visitors were encouraged. She was appalled when Georgie boasted that she had seen a woman sewing during a Sunday call.

Jack was eight when his father died. He had met the calamity, attempting to be the man in a house of women. His counterfeit of adult seriousness was broken only by Georgie's chronic pranks and hilarities. For a short time, he was sent to a military boarding school, Valley Green. His mother wrote often to him there, fretting about the fit of his shoes, his dressing in the early morning cold, his homesickness. He was soon transferred to Episcopal Academy, a day school in Philadelphia.

The girls attended its sister school, where Georgie excelled in mischief. She was very blond, in full possession of her mother's omniscient blue eyes and strength of will, and her father's impish spirit. Mrs. Drew would not show it, of course, but her second daughter was her favorite child.

Wisa, hurt in infancy through the carelessness of a nurse, was delicate and suffering, but possessed extraordinary, soulful beauty. Little Adine, always called Tibby, became the image of her namesake as she grew. Her mother, Georgiana, died in 1864, when Tibby was only two. The Drews were her family. Gentle and shy, she adored her older brother and sisters, was content to serve them.

The Drew children rode at Madame Minna's Riding School, danced at the city's best dancing school, and received the other advantages of little ladies and gentlemen to the manor born. Occasionally, on Friday evenings, there was a special treat. Jack, sporting a facsimile of a Union soldier's uniform, Wisa and Georgie in matching dimity pinafores, were allowed to join their black-clad grandmother in the Drew family box at the Arch. If the lobby was crowded, they entered their box from the stage; but this was the only glimpse of the world backstage allowed Louisa Drew's children.

Of the first plays Georgie saw, she was most impressed by *Peter Wilkins*, because her mother played a boy and had a hazardous sword fight with a large, powerful man. "Naturally," remarked Georgie, "she vanquished him." Jack remembered his mother's *Lady Macbeth* opposite a fiery twenty-four-year-old. John Wilkes Booth, said Mrs. Drew at the time, had the greatness and eccentricity of his late father. Jack remembered running home one morning hardly two years later to tell his mother that President Lincoln had been shot, and that young Booth had done it. She stood on the stairs, her face drained white, her body stiffened, as if that murder had taken place there, before her, on the landing.

Not long after her husband's death, Mrs. Drew paid off the mortgage on the Arch with a surplus left for the directors. The stock, which had a par value of $500 a share, reached a value of $780. The theater had grown fashionable and prestigious. The finest actors of the day played with Mrs. John Drew's stock company, considering it top of their profession. "It was, without exception, the best-conducted, cleanest, most orderly and most all-around comfortable theatre that I ever acted in," attested Rose Eytinge. "Of Mrs. Drew herself, eulogy from me is not necessary. She was a woman whom it was an honor for a fellow-woman to call a friend."

Mrs. Drew had an arrangement with Lester Wallack in New York, allowing her first choice, for presentation in Philadelphia, of any British play imported by the manager. She often traveled there to see these plays and judge them worthy or not of the Arch. When Jack, thirteen, and Georgie, three years younger, accompanied their mother on one such excursion, she presented the metropolis at its most glittering. They stopped at the elegant Irving House at Broadway and Twelfth Street, called at the imposing Judson mansion on Gramercy Park, and dined at Delmonico's palm-shaded epicurean shrine. When William Winter, a young drama critic, stopped at their table one evening, their mother's renown was impressed upon the two children for the first time. The critic's nervous, almost obsequious deference assured them that she was known far beyond the brick fronts of Arch Street. After dinner, the family hurried to Wallack's Theatre, where Mrs. Drew's children gazed securely on the proceedings from Lester Wallack's private box.

In Philadelphia, Mrs. Drew brought her family to see Charles Dickens read from *Pickwick Papers* on his second American tour. Mrs. Kinloch, Jack, Georgie, Wisa, and Robert Craig, a young comedian in the Arch Street company, were spellbound, but Mrs. Drew studied the author's performance with an actor's eye. "He characterizes," she astutely observed, "by acting all the voices, thus giving the imagination no opportunity. There is no relief,—no chance for the imagination of the listener to play. The reading becomes monotonous." Nevertheless, she invited the author to visit the Arch. To spare him the bother of curious crowds, she assured him that no advance announcement would be made. Charles Dickens, unmolested, watched *Ours* from the Drew family box, afterward writing a gracious letter of thanks to his hostess.

The night of Dickens' reading, Robert Craig had arrived late from re-hearsal. He still managed to get what he wanted of the author's manner-isms, intonation, and appearance, and the skit which he wrote and per-formed as Dickens became a popular feature at the Arch. It was unusual for Mrs. Drew to fraternize with young members of her company, par-ticularly so to include them in family gatherings, but the handsome young imitator of Dickens was the exception. He spent a great deal of leisure time with his employer. "Robert Craig," she explained, "is one of the most talented young men I have ever met."

During the season of 1867–68, Craig was abruptly asked to leave the Arch Street company. Soon after, Mrs. Drew quit Philadelphia for a long rest in the country. She returned with babe in arms—adopted, she said—and christened him Sidney White. Even when the child grew to be a mir-ror image of his adoptive mother, no one dared to question. Louisa Lane Drew was above reproach.

Rehearsals began promptly at ten at Mrs. Drew's theater. She always arrived five minutes before the hour. Old Mr. Fisher, the doorman, set his watch by her. Sitting on stage at the prompt table, the manageress reigned unquestioned. She was called the Duchess. ("Appropriately enough, I suppose," Georgie said, "but who, then, could possibly be Queen?") She was skilled in every detail of her trade, from the direction of actors to the building of a set. "Why, sir," admitted her principal car-penter to critic Allston Brown, "there ain't a carpenter in the theatre whom she can't sometimes teach how to do a thing."

Mrs. Drew's children, surrounded by such earnest professionalism, were not encouraged to follow theatrical careers. Georgie needed no en-couragement. She had decided to be an actress, and nothing else would do. Even her mother proved helpless against the young lady's will: A debut was announced in Georgie's sixteenth year.

On October 21, 1872, the youngest daughter of Mrs. John Drew made her acting debut as *Leona* in *The Ladies' Battle*. She was the first of the Drew children to do so; another generation of actors in the long line of Lanes and Trenters. The Philadelphia audience greeted her with extreme warmth that night, partly because she was her mother's daughter, but mostly because she was irresistible: fair and animate, with slender grace that took naturally to the stage, and a guileless way of tossing lines like nosegays to the house. Mrs. Drew was proud of her daughter, but flattery was not her way. "Backstage, when I passed my mother after my debut," Georgie said, "she inclined her chin slightly toward her neck, and mur-mured something. It seemed a positive murmur, so I assumed my mother was praising me."

Wisa was not interested in acting. The year of Georgie's debut, her mother hired Charles Mendum, stage-struck scion of a Boston banking family, as business manager of the Arch. The young man's mind wandered from business to a more congenial preoccupation. Mrs. Drew lost a business manager, gained a son-in-law, when Mendum married her eldest daughter and took her to live in Boston.

Jack, as man of the family, was determined to make a place for himself in business. While his younger sister was winning a following at the Arch, he was making a misguided attempt to sell clocks at Wanamaker's department store. It was not a position designed to hold the imagination of a Drew. On March 22, 1873, John Drew's son made his debut at a benefit for Georgie. He took the occasion lightly, remarkable since the nineteen-year-old had never before played in a theater. As the maid, *Wiggins*, Mrs. Drew ushered the debutant on for his first entrance. There was prolonged applause from the house. His first lines as *Plumber* were meant to show the character's self-confidence. Instead, his reading showed only Jack's self-esteem. His mother, exasperated, turned to the audience and shook her head slowly. "What a dreadful young man!" she interpolated. "I wonder what he will be like when he grows up?"

Patrons and critics were more indulgent. Jack was allowed to join the Arch Street company, chastened, and more seriously inclined toward acting. Occasionally, though, he was party to his sister's pranks, usually becoming the scapegoat. One night when they were playing together, Georgie devised a scheme, which she induced her brother to implement. According to her instructions, Jack filled the speaking tube, leading from the prompter's box to the orchestra leader, with face powder. Just as the orchestra was about to play, Georgie lured the prompter from his place. Jack signaled the conductor, blowing through the tube when he answered. Throughout the overture, the baffled, powder-coated conductor endured the derisory laughter of orchestra and audience. "The calling down that I got from an infuriated manager-mother," Jack advised, "had better be left to the imagination."

Ada Rehan, a talented seventeen-year-old in the company, became Georgie's confidante, sharing gossip and intrigues. Mrs. Drew was often forced to reprimand them. "I can distinctly remember the icy politeness of my mother's tone," Georgie said, "as she would turn to me at rehearsal, when I was gossiping away in a corner, instead of attending to my cue, and remark: 'Now, Miss Drew, if you are quite ready, we will resume.'"

Their pranks notwithstanding, Mrs. Drew's children were becoming actors. Georgie was developing a technique of her own; natural and relaxed on stage, she seemed hardly to be acting at all. Jack was growing into all manner of roles. When their mother produced *Women of the Day*, during the fall of 1874, they were shown to advantage in fine light comedy roles. As Augustin Daly's company happened to be playing Philadelphia at the time, the New York manager attended a performance.

Daly was impressed. He wrote to Mrs. Drew, asking if she would allow her son and daughter to join his company. She discussed the matter with them, advising acceptance of the offer.

In January of 1875, John Drew reported to the greenroom of the Fifth Avenue Theatre in New York. His sister decided to remain in Philadelphia. Mrs. Drew was facing a distressing professional crisis. Georgie intended to be with her.

During the last several years, stock companies had given way to touring companies around the country. Sadly, Louisa Drew watched as, one by one, managers capitulated to this new, impersonal system of presentation. She was one of the last holdouts in the provinces; but as business waned, it seemed inevitable that she, too, must submit. Georgie understood how deeply this, the death of theater as she had known it, touched her mother. Even an offer from the renowned Mr. Daly, and her mother's insistence that she accept, could not lure Georgie from the Arch.

The daughter of the Drews learned her trade that season as leading lady to the likes of Edwin Booth, Lawrence Barrett and John McCullough, great stars who played guest engagements with Mrs. Drew's company. The season of 1875 climaxed on April 9 with Georgie's benefit. Philadelphians cheered her *Galatea*, her mother's *Cynica*. But the manageress could hold out no longer.

That season ended the venerable stock system at the Arch Street Theatre. Thereafter, she would run a combination house playing traveling companies. Louisa Lane Drew deplored the change. It made of a theater, she felt, nothing more than a hired hall. "I have seen the stock company system pass through its palmiest days to give place to the present horde of wandering combinations or companies of strolling players," she lamented; "always on the road like Eugene Sue's *Wandering Jew*; condemned to a wearisome round of performances of the same play year in and year out; deprived of a settled home, doomed to play week after week of one night stands; compelled to rise at all hours of the night and morning from uncomfortable beds in queer hotels to take trains on which they must travel all day long and reach a destination barely in time to appear supperless on the stage."

Georgie was called again to the Fifth Avenue the following spring. At her brother's side, she entered a splendid room hung with paintings, engravings, and mezzotints of famous players. Beneath these likenesses of illustrious predecessors, but not outshone by them, sat Fanny Davenport, Mrs. Gilbert, James Lewis, Emily Rigl, and Maurice Barrymore. John Moore, the stage manager, introduced her.

"Ladies and gentlemen," he said simply, "this is Miss Drew of the Arch."

IX

GEORGIE DREW SET two goals for herself at the Fifth Avenue Theatre: recognition in Daly's company, and Maurice Barrymore. The first of these was accomplished by her successful debut in *Pique*, relatively easy for the talented daughter of the Drews. Her second goal required considerably more effort, and straightway took precedence.

Her brother, Jack, had mentioned Barrymore's attraction to Emily Rigl during the Western tour. The affair had continued without any particular intensity in New York, but Georgie soon discovered that the German actress was more intent on career than romance. Early in the quest, Georgie realized that her greatest obstacle was not another woman. It was Barry's devotion to sport and the Bohemian life, to the conviviality of clubrooms and bars that would present her greatest challenge.

The newcomer had joined vigorously into the life of his new city. He had become a regular at English Harry Hill's in "Murderer's Row," where he trained with Billy Muldoon, still a policeman, but increasingly diverted from duty by challenges from professional wrestlers. On Billy's days off from the force, he and Barry ran together and sparred. In milder months, they usually rounded out a day of training by swimming back and forth across the East River from Rhinelust, a resort at the foot of Fifty-fifth Street, to Blackwell's Island. His pursuit of sport was inexhaustible. "Barrymore keeps himself in fine physical trim," reported the *Journal*, "and is always eager for a bout with the gloves. Sometimes the love of a fight leads him to seek a friend who is similarly inclined and they go out in the highways seeking battles with cabmen."

In the company of Charley Vandenhoff, Harry Montague, Billy Floyd, stage manager at Wallack's Theatre, and several other actors and laymen, he also traversed the theatrical heart of New York. The Hoffman House, Maison Dorée, the Union Square Hotel, the Matchbox, at 848 Broadway, opened rosy gaslit spaces to the restless Englishman, returning warm memories of London and the Mitre. These were the night gathering places of Barry and his colleagues. In the afternoon, when he wasn't playing a matinee or training with Billy Muldoon, Union Square was his clubroom, offering benches and sidewalks for shop talk and strolling. If weather turned bad, it was never more than seventeen steps to a bar.

Augustin Daly inadvertently became Georgie's primary ally in the pursuit of Maurice Barrymore. The rigorous schedule at the Fifth Avenue brought them together continually during her first months there. Not only did they appear eight times a week in *Pique* but they were cast in numerous benefits. Benefits involved additional plays during the regular run, requiring the company to be together constantly in the month of May—studying, rehearsing, performing. The month of May was all the time that Georgie Drew needed.

On the sixth, they appeared in *Money* for the benefit of D. H. Harkins. After the first rehearsal, Barry found himself forgoing drinks at the Hoffman House with Charley for tea at Delmonico's with Georgie and her brother. Jack became informal chaperon for his sister, "to protect me from myself," she explained. Barry also suspended an abiding distaste for the functions of the four hundred to escort Georgie to the first public parade of the New York Coaching Club. They made a splendid pair, standing in front of the Brunswick Hotel at Fifth Avenue and Twenty-sixth Street, Barry sporting a bottle-green coat with gilt buttons, yellow-striped waistcoat, silk topper and fresh boutonniere, *de rigueur* for the occasion, Georgie gleaming in a frilled yellow frock with matching hat and parasol. Even Colonel William Jay glanced from the lead coach with haughty admiration for the striking couple.

"Both tall, handsome, and strongly individual, they were observable anywhere," noted Amy Leslie, a genial drama critic from Chicago, "but in their hundred amiable battles of wit they were perhaps as unique and dazzling a couple as ever entertained diverging opinions." Georgie's infatuation deepened by contact into love. Barry responded, but she was never quite sure of his intensity. She felt from the beginning a necessity to compete with him, to match wits, and to banter, never relaxing her defenses for fear of losing his interest. Barry found her challenge invigorating, not a strain, because, as he suddenly realized, he wished to win *her*. "Their courtship was a continual bombardment of wit, clever queries and answers which are classics," added Miss Leslie. "One was quite the match for the other, and the pair incomparable."

On May 13, they were scheduled to participate in *The Serious Family* for the benefit of John Brougham. Barry was *Charles Torrens*, Georgie his devoted wife. The Governor stood before them at rehearsal blocking a light love scene. "Now, Mr. Barrymore," he ordered, "after Miss Drew finishes her line, go to her, place your left arm about her right shoulder, and with your right hand lift her chin, gently, so that your eyes will meet hers. Then, Miss Drew, would you . . ." The Governor broke off. Barry had performed as directed; but when he lifted her chin so tenderly, and she turned those enormous Drew eyes up toward his, Daly acknowledged that even *his* direction had been transcended. A spontaneous hush befell those near enough to see. They all turned away, as if embarrassed to observe such intimacy. Clearing his throat perceptibly, Daly called to Mrs. Gilbert, who stood frozen in the wings. She was to enter briskly, he directed, and address her amusing line to the *Torrenses*.

Pique ended a phenomenal run on July 29 with its two hundred and thirty-eighth performance. The Drews asked Barry to accompany them to Philadelphia during the four-week break between seasons. Georgie and her brother had already signed three-year contracts with Daly. Barry was hesitating to do so. He had initially signed for one season on a trial basis. Now, the Governor wanted him for the usual three-year term. Even with Daly's assurance that he would be leading man, the prospect of a three-year commitment intimidated Barry. He told Daly that he would return with an answer in two weeks.

Barry ceased conversing altogether as the train approached Philadelphia. Georgie and Jack continued chattering, lowering their voices in deference to their preoccupied companion. He had been unusually quiet during the journey; his gaze seemed far from that clattering railroad car. Not often given to introspection, he had lately seemed to be jousting with himself. Georgie Drew had captured his imagination. She had become to him what no other woman had been: necessary. He was content to be with her, even at the expense of his active night life. Somehow, besides the enticing gifts of a woman, she offered the easy delight of a comrade. But the daughter of the Drews would not bestow her favors lightly; he knew that love and marriage were essential. There was also the question of the Fifth Avenue to consider. When it occurred to him that his decision could also affect Georgie, the realization startled him. The possibility of his destiny being bound to another's absorbed him as the train reached the depot at West Philadelphia.

Mrs. Drew's brougham was waiting. The coachman gathered their bags and led them to the shiny black vehicle just in time to stop eight-year-old Sidney from mounting the tired hackney. Georgie and Jack greeted their precocious "adopted" brother, introduced him to their dashing friend. Barry was bombarded with exacting juvenile questions all the way to 119 North Ninth Street.

Mary Aggie, the Irish maid, opened the door of the roomy row house. Adine Stephens, called Tibby, fifteen and frail, darted forth to embrace her returning cousins. (The children were never apprised of the fact that they shared the same father.) In the parlor, Mrs. Kinloch sat uncommonly rigid for her eighty-seven years, making a throne of a high-backed chair. Beside her, compelling and erect, stood Mrs. John Drew. Georgie and Jack, in turn, kissed their grandmother on a cheek, embraced their mother. They presented Maurice Barrymore.

The young man's visit was not unheralded. Georgie had mentioned him in letters, passingly, but Mrs. Drew surmised. Georgie was her favorite, just twenty and willful; she did not intend to hand her daughter over to this "talented amateur," as the veteran actress described him, from England. She was determined to resist, yet the young man was disarming.

The first home Barry had known since holidays at Beaumont Hall embraced him and warmed him more than any clubroom could. He became a stalwart hero to Sidney and Tibby, and Mary Aggie instinctively blushed when she passed him. When Mrs. Garrett, the cook, peeked from behind her swinging door to glimpse Miss Georgie's suitor, he squeezed an apple cheek, sending her scurrying back to the kitchen. Mrs. Kinloch brazenly flirted with the young visitor, contriving to wink outrageously whenever he came within her range. She took to trading her antique memories of English provincial tours with his fresher ones. Even Mrs. Drew, against her considerable will, found herself breaking a stern countenance. Once, to the surprise of those gathered at one of her teas, he inspired a trenchant "ha!" from the reticent lady. On that rare occasion, a visiting Englishman was holding forth belligerently on the superiority of his country to America. There were a number of Philadelphians present, offended, but too polite to contradict the jingo. During a loud declaration of the British Army's prowess, he turned to his countryman.

"Why, the British could sail over here," he predicted, "and lick this country overnight."

"What, again?" Barry countered.

On the eve of Barry's departure for New York, he and Georgie strolled out before dinner to the old Ronaldson Cemetery. This resting place of Revolutionary War heroes had no morbid mark upon it. The stones were blanketed by cool velvet moss, obscured by stray cedar; tufted grass was dotted by enterprising moss pink and myrtle. Georgie said that she had come there to play as a child.

She settled upon thick grass near a cannon rusted dull gold. He sat down close by, leaning his shoulders against the discarded implement of old wars. Stillness under the ash trees was disturbed only by the insistent friction of crickets, challenging the windless August evening. Suddenly, at the same moment, they turned toward one another. He asked her, simply, with the conventional phrase. She accepted with just one word.

After dinner, Barry sought Mrs. Drew's consent. She was not surprised by the inevitable. "And what are your professional plans in future, Mr. Barrymore?" she asked.

"Augustin Daly has offered me a three-year contract, ma'am, he answered, sentencing himself without thinking, "with the promise of leading roles and excellent remuneration."

"Well, Mr. Daly will certainly teach you your trade, young man," and the matter was settled.

The Fifth Avenue contract, with its agreements, rules, regulations, reminded Barry of the Blackheath Annual Report. In small print on the back of the document, were "Rules of the Fifth Avenue Theatre" explicit in eighteen sections and twenty-two articles. They were the Governor's rules of order, meticulously devised and staunchly enforced. Actors were at the mercy of manager from the first section ("No lady or gentleman shall talk loudly in the Green Room . . .") to the last ("Any member of the Company, who, by gossip or remarks about the 'Cast' of a play or the business in any performance, which the Manager sees fit to assign, shall create ill-feeling or pain, or cause any dissatisfaction whatever, will be liable to a fine, light or heavy, according to the mischief caused, or discharge, or both, at the discretion of the Manager.").

With misgivings, Barry signed "for a period of three seasons commencing on or about the first day of September 1876 '77 '78 and terminating on or about the first day of June 1877 '78 '79 . . ." The phrase which followed, "or at any time after two weeks' notice from the party of the first part posted in the Green Room" was stricken from his contract. He had insisted upon its removal, and Daly had grudgingly complied. His salary was to be $80 per week the first season, $100 the second, $125 the third, making him the fifth highest paid of the company's twenty men.

The Governor reaffirmed his intention to make of his new employee a matinee idol. That term rankled Barry, as it did his friend, Harry Montague, for whom it had recently been coined. Hundreds of women gathered at Wallack's stage door after matinees just to watch Montague get into his carriage, while scrubby Bowery boys taunted them with insults and cheeky ditties. When an old lady whacked one of the truants across the ear with a whalebone umbrella, the resulting publicity increased Montague's following and Wallack's receipts. The Governor hoped that *his* Englishman could inspire such passion from Fifth Avenue matinee ladies.

The Drews were not returning to the city for another two weeks, so Barry began again his convivial rounds. Charley Vandenhoff was bewildered by his comrade's decision to marry. When his chiding about it took a sarcastic turn, Barry realized that his old friend felt somewhat abandoned. He assured Charley that their friendship was unshakable, but his continued jibes grew tedious. The old gathering places paled, as well, for Barry's thoughts were elsewhere. Two days after the Fifth Avenue contract had been signed, he returned to Philadelphia.

At the season's first meeting, the Governor delivered a mortal blow to his would-be matinee idol. Charles Coghlan was coming over from England to be leading man for the new season. Barry was livid. For the first time in his theatrical life, he felt the sting of ambition. He had a fiancée to consider, her exacting mother to impress. The coming of Coghlan would mean automatic demotion to glorified "juvenile" of the troupe. As he angrily approached Daly, he experienced another reaction to new responsibilities: caution. If he angered the Governor, lost his place at the Fifth Avenue, Mrs. Drew would certainly withdraw her consent. He felt frustrated and humiliated. Georgie understood, but before she could reach him, he bolted with fellow company member, Louis James, destined obviously for the nearest drinking establishment.

Jack escorted his sister back to Gramercy Park, where they were staying at the home of Alice Judson, the Drews' old friend. She went to her room at once, assuming that Barry would not be keeping their dinner engagement. She changed into night clothes but could not sleep. Sometime after midnight, there was commotion outside. Georgie went to the window. There, in the street below, swayed her fiancé, supported by an equally infirm Louis James, attempting to reach her window with pebbles. She grabbed her robe and rushed downstairs.

"I see you've brought your 'squarer' with you," she accused.

"No, darling," said Barry, putting a hand on James's shoulder; "I have brought my 'rounder' with me." They sat laughing together on the Judsons' front steps, as Louis James went staggering off toward Irving Place.

The Fifth Avenue Theatre opened its season on September 13 with Bulwer-Lytton's *Money*. To accommodate Charles Coghlan, the Governor was attempting old English plays, usually the province of Wallack's Theatre, and, to facilitate his potential patrons, a wire was installed in the box office so that tickets could be secured through any of the offices of the Atlantic and Pacific Telegraph Company. Neither innovation helped. Reviewers commended the first production of Daly's eighth regular season, but Coghlan proved to be no Harry Montague. The critics found him comely and tall, modest of bearing, graceful and expressive, yet lacking, as William Winter put it in the *Tribune*, "the force and glow of exceptional imagination or poetical emotion in either his individuality or his art."

Winter found Barry "very tame" as *Sir Frederick Blount*. Other critics, while offering faint praise, seemed aware that the spark was missing from the promising actor. Disappointment, not indifference, had colored Barry's performance, but his playing perked up somewhat when Georgie replaced Jeffreys-Lewis in the female lead. Her *Clara* was greeted with enthusiasm by the critics who had found her predecessor wanting in the role. While Georgie's presence made the situation more agreeable, Barry was still aggravated by his compromising position at Daly's. He proposed that they marry as soon as a break in the schedule allowed. Then he could proceed without fear of Mrs. Drew's disapproval.

Daly replaced *Money* with *Life*, a new comedy which he had adapted from the French. Barry played *Frank Dodge*, "with a new way to win a widow," and Georgie *Mrs. Gresham*, "type of the Injured." She also understudied Amy Fawcett, the new leading lady, who once had been the "Toast of London," beautiful and seemingly assured, playing *Lady Teazle* for four hundred nights and *Lady Gay Spanker*, in *London Assurance*, for two hundred. When she arrived at Daly's, attempting to recapture old glories in a new land, drink had puffed her beautiful face and distorted her mind; she was morbid and ill, fancying herself the victim of professional conspiracy. Georgie befriended this poor shadow of a woman, coaching her in her parts, covering for her at rehearsal. Because of her formidable reputation in England, Daly overlooked the woman's behavior, assuming that she would revert to her former excellence in performance.

The critics gave Miss Fawcett the same benefit of doubt when reviewing her opening-night performance. "She will probably be seen to better advantage in a part that will give her greater scope," said the *Post*. "Last night she was evidently nervous, and she was unfortunate enough to trip and fall heavily on the stage in her first scene—an accident which evidently caused her some physical pain and no little mental discomposure." Daly, with good reason, was less charitable. He wrote in his account book that she was "an undoubted failure, sloppy in style, waddily [*sic*] and indistinct."

On October 10, Amy Fawcett withdrew from the company, and Georgie replaced her in the lead. Daly advised Amy to return to England, providing passage money, but she lingered on. Sinking lower and lower, she ended up in a cheap Eighth Avenue boardinghouse near Thirty-third Street. Her devoted maid, who had come with her from England, called on Georgie, seeking help for her former mistress.

Georgie ventured alone, without telling Barry, to the fringes of what reformers called "Satan's Circus," where Amy's boardinghouse stood among brothels, dance halls, garish saloons, shabby and forlorn in the revealing light of day. The cabby consented to wait only after a sizable tip was promised. Climbing three flights of filthy stairs to a small room, she found the soiled "Toast of London" on a bare mattress.

Georgie implored the actress to come with her, offering decent lodgings and passage to England. She met with cold and vulgar abuse. Love, it seemed, had come to Amy Fawcett in the person of a fellow boarder. She had no wish to leave. As Georgie was about to go, a smooth, pale man entered the room. His manicured right hand rested on the handle of a pistol placed securely under his belt. Ordering the visitor from the room with threats of violence, he dropped into Amy's waiting arms.

Georgie left her name with the landlady, asking to be notified if she were needed. Before the performance that evening, she consulted the Governor. He had offered aid, he said, but the woman was obviously beyond salvation. Next day, in answer to Georgie's query, the police said that nothing could be done if the woman was there of her own free will. Georgie considered bringing Barry into it. She had heard stories of his courage in the face of adversity, but remembered the evil glint of Amy Fawcett's companion, his ready pistol. The possibility of saving the dissipated actress, she decided, was not worth the risk of her fiancé's life. She skirted the issue when he asked after the actress, feeling guilt without regret.

Daly presented an elegant remounting of *The School for Scandal* on December 4, in which Coghlan repeated his London success as *Charles Surface*. Barry was not in the cast; but Georgie's *Maria* won praise. As the audience left the theater, newsboys were shouting extras: "Brooklyn Theatre Burnt to Ground." Like most theater fires during a performance, the blaze began with the stage gaslights. The lower part of the house had been emptied, but the upper circle was blocked at the first turning of the stairs by crowding and falling bodies. Police saw no one coming down the stairs, assumed that everyone was out, closed and locked the doors without bothering to check. Three hundred people burned alive in the Brooklyn Theatre.

Business was ruined in theaters all across the country that season. Daly's houses fell off more than half, the few patrons who braved the perils, demanding seats not near the stage but near the street. Notwithstanding its brilliant production, *The School for Scandal* played to poor business for only twelve performances.

Daly's next presentation, *The American,* had a capital part for Coghlan, but his failure to capture Fifth Avenue audiences, coupled with the recent fire, inspired no rush on the box office. Playing another virtuous lover, albeit the title role, irritated Barry's frustration at Daly's. His acting showed it. "Mr. Barrymore's *Gerard* was positively bad," stated the *Times.* "It was bad in conception and execution; bad in delivery, attitude and dress. The spectacle of a pink and white youth, with shoulders extended almost from wing to wing by vast lambrequins, accompanying every word with a pose, may be cheerful enough when a fop is to be portrayed, but was scarcely to be looked for in *The American.*"

Georgie toured Brooklyn and the suburbs in *Pique* during the brief run of *The American.* She was playing matinee and evening performances at the Brooklyn Academy of Music on Christmas Day when a note arrived. Amy Fawcett, in critical condition, had been rushed to a hospital. Georgie went to her after the evening performance, and sat with the unconscious actress through the night in the charity ward. The nurse told her what had happened. Her lover, the man Georgie had seen, had gained complete control of her. Keeping her constantly drunk, he had stolen what remained of her money and jewelry. "Two days ago," whispered the nurse, "in a fit of drunken rage, he dashed her headlong over the balustrade and down a long flight of stairs." Georgie remembered climbing those stairs. "Then he carried her back to her room, beat her and left her locked up all night."

She died the day after Christmas. Georgie arranged for a funeral at the Episcopal Church of the Transfiguration, the "Little Church Around the Corner," whose rector, Dr. George Hendric Houghton, was the only New York clergyman who willingly buried actors. Besides Georgie and Barry, only a handful of others attended the service, among them, Harry Montague, who had known Amy Fawcett as the glittering "Toast of London."

During a ten-day break between productions at the Fifth Avenue, Barry and Georgie headed for Philadelphia to convince Mrs. Drew that a small family wedding was in order. The New York *Clipper* reported their success:

> Miss Georgiana Emma Drew, the youngest daughter of the late John Drew, was united in the bonds of holy matrimony on the 31st of Dec., 1876, to Maurice Herbert Blythe (Barrymore) of London, Eng., at the residence of the bride's mother in Philadelphia, the Rev. Dr. Rudder, rector of St. Stephen's Church, in that city, officiating on this happy occasion . . . We wish them all possible prosperity in their new roles in *Married Life*.

They returned to New York that evening. With unusual attention to detail, Barry had reserved the appropriate suite at the Union Square Hotel. When John Drew called on his sister and new brother-in-law three days later, he was informed that the Barrymores did not wish to be disturbed. "They have not left their rooms since the night of arrival," confided the imprudent desk clerk. "Mr. Barrymore communicates with the staff only to order an occasional repast."

A week later, the newlyweds moved from the Union Square to the Judsons' house on Gramercy Park. For twenty-five years, the top floor of the vast red-brick residence had been reserved for the Drews when they played New York. The cheerful domain, still presided over by Miss Alice Judson, had been replenished by a new generation of grandnieces and nephews. The family had fallen over the years into a state of genteel poverty, making difficult the maintenance of their splendid home, without dampening their spirits.

When Georgie had lived there during her first Daly season, she had won the hearts of the children, becoming a zany comrade and staunch ally. Even when her use of slang, so delightful to the children, had shocked the adults, she had continued to spice her conversation with startling expressions from the slums. Since she went off to be married, they had awaited her return anxiously, with a touch of concern, wondering if she might have changed altogether. Would there still be times of late hours and laughter, matinees, carriage drives, unlimited candy?

On the morning of the Barrymores' scheduled arrival, the children stationed themselves behind the drapes of a low front window to watch the cab pull up. Mr. Barrymore, first to step down, seemed taller and more heroic than he had previously to the hidden reception committee. As he helped his bride out of the carriage, they noted that she was even more radiant than they remembered, magnificently tall, costumed like a lady in a fashion book. She was utterly unmoved by the ill temper of the trunk man, who was grumbling about having to take a Saratoga up the narrow stairs. Mr. Barrymore said something to the fellow which sent him at once to the stairs with his burden. Mrs. Barrymore, with a swish of silken drapery, started to follow. "No princess could be grander nor more haughty-looking," observed one of the children, fearing that marriage had indeed changed their audacious friend. Georgie was following the trunk man so closely that the Saratoga slipped precariously near her head. She glanced at it with a queenly Drew quality that was unmistakable. "I hope you are holding tight to that trunk, my good man," she cautioned, "for if you once let go *my* name is mud."

"Georgie!" cried Miss Alice at the door, struggling vainly to make disapproval conquer amusement. It was too late. The children had heard, and came running out to embrace their friend. Of course, she hadn't changed. If she could enter their slang-forbidden house with a new phrase like "my name is mud," nothing had changed.

If any juvenile doubts remained, they were dispelled forever by the appearance of Mr. Barrymore. There could be no question that he was a proper sort of man: One of his coat pockets held very dead meat, the other a very live weasel.

On January 15, Daly opened *Lemons*, which he had adapted from the German. Mrs. Gilbert, the Fifth Avenue "Grandma," made the hit of the season as a lady who believed that half the persons in the world were like lemons—to be squeezed by the other half. Daly's only potential hit that season was cut short by a disastrous *Hamlet* rendered by Charles Coghlan at his own benefit on March 10. The comedian's inadequate playing cast a pall over the Fifth Avenue from which it did not recover that season.

The Barrymores were spared the consequences of Daly's Fifth Avenue failures. Barry's full-fledged dissatisfaction had led to repeated disagreements with the Governor. In order to keep peace in his ranks, and to placate Barry until Coghlan's contract expired, Daly made him leading man of his touring company, with Georgie as leading lady. Together they toured New York City's outlying theaters, Brooklyn, Williamsburg, Greenpoint, Queens County, Staten Island, building a following for themselves and bolstering Daly's reputation. Autonomy brought Barry a satisfaction in performance which had eluded him at the Fifth Avenue.

Gramercy Park remained a welcome base as they toured the boroughs. The privacy of their top-floor apartment was sacred, but the Barrymores were usually downstairs contributing to the buoyant ménage. Barry fell easily into its merry pace, bringing more warmth, more merriment, and other gifts as well. "Like all Bohemians," stated Miss Alice, "we gyrated between extremes of hilarious abundance and just as hilarious a destitution. When the family fortunes were at their lowest and the Barrymores were inmates of the house, we used to make odd finds of greenbacks in a teacup, or bits of silver in pockets that had long been empty—it was very exciting and pleasant."

Barry watched, amused and content, as his wife imperiously ordered the lives of the Judsons into an unending picnic. "Such an audacious, buoyant, care-dispelling creature she is!" effused Miss Alice. "How she kept the house ringing with laughter! Yet her witticisms did not stand repetition. Shorn of the witchery of her voice, lacking the ridiculous insinuations which she gives by mobile eyebrow or curving lip, removed from the immediate exigencies of the occasion that called them forth, they sound most awfully bald and commonplace. Half the time she is intensely serious, and these are the times when she is the funniest to other people." These were the times, also, when she was funniest and most appealing to her husband.

One Sunday, the Barrymores and the entire Judson clan made an excursion to Washington Heights in two open carriages. At the highest point of the rocky precipice, they halted the drivers, stepped down, ventured dangerously near the sheer edge. As they gazed rapturously across the Hudson River to the unbroken sweep of the Palisades, an odd crunching sound distracted them, as if someone were trying to scale the precipice from below. Georgie moved nearer the edge to investigate. She spied a wind-blown woman in sporting tweeds clawing up the wall of rock, "at immense discomfort to herself," reported the lookout, "and doing no earthly good to anybody." As the stranger's complacent visage rose above the sharp rim, Georgie crouched down and looked straight into its eyes. "You ought to get six months for such an act," cried Mrs. Barrymore with angry conviction, stalking off as the climber tottered on the brink. Amid the stifled laughter of the Judsons, Barry lifted the sporting lady onto safe ground before she fell over her own tracks at the shock.

Festivity also prevailed at Mrs. Drew's summer house at Long Branch, New Jersey, which had become something of a theatrical resort after J. W. Wallack, the New York manager, and Mrs. Drew had established residences there in the '60s. A break between seasons left the Barrymores free to participate. Besides Drew kin and retainers, the roomy, gray-shingled dwelling by the sea intermittently harbored Judsons and Bakers. Alexina Fisher, Mrs. Drew's childhood playmate, had married John Lewis Baker, an actor from Philadelphia, the same year that Louisa had married John Drew. She remained Louisa's closest friend over the years. The next generation followed suit. Josephine Baker, their pretty daughter, had been Georgie's best friend since childhood; their son Lewis had been Jack's.

Charley Vandenhoff came out from the city one weekend. He was unusually contentious with Barry, strangely diffident with the others. His attitude toward Georgie, polite but cool, distressed Barry and irritated him. To be upset by the marriage of a boon companion was all very well, but this was excessive. Farewells were amiable enough when Charley left after the weekend, but he was not asked to return.

When Barry returned to the Fifth Avenue, Daly was in urgent need of a hit. He had made an honorable attempt that summer to redeem a year of doubtful prosperity with the much-heralded première of *Ah Sin*, a new play by no less a team than Bret Harte and Mark Twain. "I never saw a play that was so much improved by being cut down," admitted Twain in his first-night curtain speech, "and I believe it would have been one of the very best plays in the world if Augustin Daly's strength had held out so that he could cut out the whole thing." Twain's intimations of mortality were echoed by the press. To a man they found his curtain speech delightful, his play wanting. Patrons agreed. Receipts dwindled week by week for five weeks with considerable loss to Daly.

The Governor was convinced that he had his hit in *The Dark City*, a new compilation of his own on the order of his greatest success, *Under the Gaslight*. Reviews of the September 5 première praised Barry's "excellent" playing of another "virtuous hero," although, ironically, one of them chided him for "a little ineffectual imitation of the mannerisms of Mr. Charles Coghlan." The play was an utter failure.

It had been Daly's last hope; unable to meet the September rent, he was threatened with eviction from the theater which he had nurtured. At once, in moral indignation, he surrendered the place. By giving up the furnishings, which he had provided, he satisfied the claims of the Gilsey estate, owner of the property. "Negotiations concluded," he wrote in his account book, "$45,000 for $8,300, and peace and quiet."

On September 10, 1877, the Governor called his company to the greenroom. He announced that they would withdraw from the theater when the curtain fell on Saturday night. They were free to leave his employ, he stated, whether or not their contracts had lapsed. Any who stayed must do so at a reduction of pay. They must also be prepared to go with him on the road.

Coghlan went to Wallack's. Fanny Davenport departed on a starring tour. James Lewis, after a battle with Daly, sought greener pastures. Even Mrs. Gilbert, with the Governor's approval, accepted a lucrative bid from A. M. Palmer at the Union Square. Barry had been offered an engagement at Wallack's for nearly double his present salary, but the plight of the Governor touched him. Along with his brother-in-law and several others, he decided to stay.

Georgie had not returned to the Fifth Avenue at all that season. Her decision to stay quietly in Philadelphia had little to do with the fortunes of Augustin Daly. Mrs. Barrymore was with child.

X

A LETTER FOLLOWED Barry from theater to theater as he toured with Daly. It reached him in Baltimore: News from his brother in New Zealand via Grover and Humphreys in London.

Kikurangi Hill, the estate in the province of Auckland left jointly to the brothers by their father, had finally become theirs. Their stepmother, Sarah Blyth, had contested the will, but Grover and Humphreys had won this first battle with the vindictive widow. (Other bequests were still in contention. Although they would eventually come to the sons, the Commissioner's widow fought on out of bitterness and fear.) Will Blyth offered to buy his brother's half of Kikurangi Hill for £ 1,500, just over $7,000. Mr. Humphreys added that the price was more than generous. The prospective father was elated by the windfall.

Other news tempered his reaction. Will informed him also that Amelia Blyth had died in Amritsar. The death of the aunt who had raised him left Barry disheartened. Communication between them had ended when her admonitory letter about his acting career reached him in Scarborough five years before. Now, their rift seemed so futile. It was too late. He wrote to his brother accepting the offer, and asking if it would be possible to obtain the old cookery books that Aunt Amelia had kept in her "English" kitchen at Amritsar.

Business was no better on the road for the remnant of Daly's once noble force, "late of the Fifth Avenue, New York," as their billing pointed out. The country was in the throes of financial distress, recovering from a paralyzing railroad strike the previous summer. The Governor decided to return to New York to fulfill an old agreement with Joseph Jefferson. The illustrious actor, who had not played New York for two years, would return in *Rip Van Winkle*, his most popular role. Daly hired Booth's Theatre for the occasion. The arrangement was similar to the previous one with Booth: Jefferson's talent and prestige; Daly's money and company—what was left of them. The critical reception was unanimously favorable. Barry's *Hendrick Hudson* was praised by reviewers, admired by Jefferson himself. But the engagement yielded only fair returns until it ended on December 1.

A week of Shakespeare followed, with Fanny Davenport returning to the Daly fold in *As You Like It* and *Twelfth Night,* and Barry as leading man. He was listed on the bills as Herbert Barrymore for these performances, a tentative nod to his heritage prompted by Will's letter. Miss Davenport's *Rosalind* was not well received by reviewers or patrons on opening night. Barry's *Orlando* was praised, and his playing of the bored *Duke* in *Twelfth Night* inspired kudos as well. When matinee ladies responded with bouquets and other stage-door attentions, the Governor harbored some bitter second thoughts about Mr. Charles Coghlan, his would-be matinee idol.

When his lease at Booth's expired, Daly embarked with his company on a tour of the South—Richmond, Raleigh, Charleston, Savannah, New Orleans, Mobile, Nashville—still emerging from the desolation of war and reconstruction. "My waking sight of ole Virginny from the car window," wrote Daly, "fell upon puddly lands, broken fences, lonely-looking frame houses and sleepy-looking darkies driving depressed-looking teams." Reminders of postwar depression and Old World elegance abounded. Savannah was silent, overspread with web-like moss, evoking a vast, untended cemetery, while the center of Charleston displayed stately terraced mansions surrounded by orange trees, protected by old-fashioned fences with tinseled iron ornaments. Barry was curious about this sad and exotic land of strange dialects, syrup pie, and third tier "Nigger Heavens."

With the close of the Southern tour, Barry and Jack had fulfilled their Fifth Avenue contracts. The Governor, unsure of his theatrical future, was soon to sail for the Continent. The two actors bid him bon voyage and headed for Philadelphia.

The inmates of 119 North Ninth Street were in a state of well-ordered frenzy awaiting the Barrymore heir. Mrs. Drew was in command, arranging her domain for the arrival of her grandchild. Georgie lay calmly in the midst of it all, wishing only to end her long confinement. Barry, from the moment he entered the house, was in a state of perpetual wonder, bordering, toward the end, on panic. Dr. J. Nicholas Mitchell was summoned into the melee on the afternoon of April 12, 1878. He left behind him that evening a grateful and replenished household.

Remembering the name of a London acquaintance which had impressed him, Barry decided to call his son Lionel.

A new sense of parental responsibility, unconsciously coupled with old aspersions cast on an actor's life by the Blyths and the Waces, had Barry flirting with middle-class respectability. Spirit, however, was not corrupted by good intentions. No forays into the worlds of business or law were considered. Playwriting, maybe theatrical management were quite respectable enough.

That spring his imagination wandered far from the clutter of Drews and their retainers. Shut in a small top-floor room at North Ninth Street, Maurice Barrymore began to write a play. His labors produced *A Bitter Expiation*, a turgid melodrama of Russian retribution and lust. Hardly the work of a man bent on middle-class respectability. Barry was convinced that he had found his true calling. His wife and her family hoped it was so. Word of the endeavor circulated, bringing at least one local amateur actor to North Ninth Street, who confided to Georgie the hope of playing in the forthcoming Slav epic. She climbed the stairs to her husband's fourth-floor workroom. "Can you make any use of a young man who has never been on the professional stage?" she asked. "He says he feels the dramatic fire coursing through his veins."

"I'm afraid not," replied Barry; "tell him Russian ceilings are too low for his act."

The fledgling dramatist traveled to New York in June to attend a farewell dinner for Harry Montague. The erstwhile matinee idol was leaving for San Francisco to play *Diplomacy*. He and T. Henry French had purchased touring rights for Victorien Sardou's melodrama, which had made a great success at the Prince of Wales's Theatre in London. The tepid response to Wallack's recent New York production, consequently, had been disappointing. Diplomatic intrigue, in general, the title *Diplomacy*, in particular, conveyed little meaning to Americans in 1878. Nevertheless, Montague and French held high hopes for their tour. Frederick B. Warde, a friend of Barry's from London, was also traveling with the *Diplomacy* company. He and Barry talked at length that evening, expressing admiration and a touch of envy for Harry's new role as actor-manager.

That August, Barry received full payment for Kikurangi Hill from his brother in New Zealand. Not long afterward, a crate arrived from his sister, Evelin Wace, in Lahore, containing the old cookery books which had belonged to Aunt Amelia. Mrs. Garrett, the cook, presumed that the books would be added to those in the Drew kitchen; Barry did not offer them. Instead, he carried the crate to the attic and left it there. One afternoon, Georgie, in search of an old summer frock, came across her husband in the attic absently turning the pages of his dead aunt's cookbooks. "It was only then, for the first time," wrote Georgie, "I realized that those childhood years in India, so remote to me, were much with my husband."

An unexpected offer from T. Henry French reached Barry before summer's end. Tragic news came with it. Harry Montague had died suddenly while playing *Diplomacy* in San Francisco. No one had guessed that the stalwart matinee idol, only thirty-five, had been hopelessly afflicted with consumption. French wanted Barry to play Montague's part in Chicago and on the projected tour. Putting aside his playwriting ambitions for the moment, he agreed to do so in memory of his departed friend.

Most of the original *Diplomacy* company had returned, disheartened, to New York with Harry Montague's body. Frederick Warde took charge in Chicago, filling vacancies with local actors. He and Barry, as *Henry* and *Julian Beauclerc*, carried the production for two successful weeks at McVicker's Theatre; but French decided to abandon the tour. Barry saw his chance to take the step from actor to manager: What better way to employ his recent Blyth money? He and Frederick B. Warde entered into partnership, purchasing touring rights of *Diplomacy* for the United States and Canada.

The Warde & Barrymore Combination, as they called themselves, wasted no time engaging their business staff and company. E. E. Zimmerman, agent-in-advance, Phil Simmonds, business manager, were gentlemen of high repute and competence. Signor and Madame Majeroni, talented Italians who had not been as successful as they deserved in America, signed at once for the key roles of *Count Orloff* and *Countess Zicka*. Plum roles were also assigned to John Drew (*Algie Fairfax*), Alexina Fisher Baker (*Marquise de Rio Zares*), and to the wives of the partners: Annie Edmondson Warde (*Lady Fairfax*), Georgie Drew Barrymore (*Dora*, the heroine), making the tour something of a family party. Barry was buoyant, optimistic that this first venture into management held the promise of his future.

The sterling aggregation opened on September 23, 1878, at Colonel Sinn's Park Theatre, Brooklyn. Critical response was excellent, patrons were enthusiastic. Attendance was only fair. Besides the unfamiliarity of the subject, the fact that neither Barrymore nor Warde was a well-known star affected the box office. They were hopeful that word of mouth would bolster their reception, and business did improve as the Combination toured the theaters outlying New York.

When they headed upstate to Albany at the end of October, the train was drafty and cramped. The change from warm Indian summer had been sudden; a severe autumn frost had fallen when they arrived. "That was an admirable production of *Diplomacy*, by the Warde and Barrymore comb., given during the entire week," wrote a local critic. "The fine play was not seen in its best phases by Albanians, owning to the illness of Maurice Barrymore after Monday evening, its first performance . . . The company was singularly unfortunate, almost every member being strongly under the influence of severe colds, which made their arduous efforts painful to witness."

On Tuesday evening, Warde took Barry's role, Jack Drew took Warde's, an understudy Drew's. "It was quite amusing to note the remarks of the uninitiated at the performance during Barrymore's illness," observed the critic, "respecting the merits of the latter, Warde and Drew in their characters as on the bills." Confusion increased. Georgie lost her voice on Wednesday. Annie Warde replaced her, relinquishing her own part to the ladies' understudy. The Barrymores worsened on Thursday; the Majeronis were felled by the same malady.

As there were no other understudies with the company, Phil Simmonds searched the city for replacements. Finally, he found the willing leading lady and gentleman of a local amateur company. They could not, however, be entrusted with the Majeronis' pivotal roles of *Count Orloff* and *Countess Zicka*. H. Rees Davies (*Baron Stein*) and Mrs. Baker (*Marquise de Rio Zares*) assumed the more difficult roles, the amateurs assumed theirs. Though still feverish, Barry returned on Friday to this chaos. He struggled through the evening performance and the Saturday matinee. Then he collapsed, unable to play on Saturday evening. "The company proved the possession of great versatility," added the Albany critic, "to so capitally guard against contingencies of sickness or any other disorder. The whole comb., for a travelling company, is an unusually good one, and deserving much better patronage than they were the recipients of here, although at the end of the week the attendance was fair in numbers."

Next week: The Arch. The Barrymores recuperated at North Ninth Street, and played without calamities at Mrs. Drew's theater. Phil Simmonds left the Combination at this juncture. Randolph Gardiner, who replaced him as business manager, was conveniently in Philadelphia at the time, having recently taken on Mrs. Drew's business affairs at the Arch. He was a bluff, prosperous-looking fellow whom Barry distrusted, without evidence, from the start.

The potential family party was fast deteriorating. Temperaments smoldered, particularly those of Mr. Barrymore and his *Count Orloff*. Signor Majeroni, tall and sharp-featured, swart and extremely nervous, was a fine, disciplined performer on the stage, prone to excessive melodramatics off. His failure to capture the "New World," as he called it, condescendingly, had embittered him, leaving him suspicious and resentful. The young, seemingly careless actor-manager became a target for the disappointed artist. Taken with his new position, however, Barry strove to keep peace. Their antipathy remained unspoken; the undercurrent was tangible. Signor was trying patience none too firm.

Majeroni and his wife, niece of the great Italian tragedienne, Ristori, had contracted for a combined weekly salary of $200. In Pittsburgh,

Randolph Gardiner informed them that the management had ordered a reduction to $150. The transaction was reported in the New York *Clipper* complete with vaudeville accents.

"I vill consent," said the signor, "to have ze salaree reduce for so long time as you can pay me no more zan-a zat. But when you make-a ze moneys, you pay me, eh?"

"How's that?" asked Gardiner.

"You give-a me ze note for ze balance, and when you can, you pay me ze moneys, eh?" Gardiner informed him that Warde and Barrymore would be consulted. Signor did not wait. Suspecting a plot, he cornered Barry after the performance that evening. Temperament erupted. Majeroni worked himself into an incoherent attack. Barry, unaware of Gardiner's manipulations, assumed that the troublesome signor was demanding a raise.

"What!" exclaimed Barry. "Do you suppose I'm going to engage myself to Mr. Wallack or anybody else, and work all season like a horse, just to pay your salary?"

"But your honaire—your reputation, Mr. Barrymore," pleaded Majeroni.

"I don't care a damn for my reputation," shouted Barry. "All I'm looking out for is the welfare of this company; I'll see to that." Majeroni cooled with Barry's ardor.

"You talk like a boy, Mr. Barrymore," he answered with a satiric smile. "I do not do business wiz ze boys. God-a-night, sir."

"What's that you called me?" yelled Barry, launching into a torrent of abuse. The signor raised his nose in the air and walked away.

Half an hour later, over a game of cards, Barry and Gardiner came to blows. Gardiner had cheated, but Barry was prompted by other motives as well. He suspected the business manager of greater inequities, yet he was frustrated by a lack of evidence. So far as the books showed, accounts were in order. And, Gardiner was Mrs. Drew's business manager, a man of considerable reputation in theatrical circles. Warde begged his partner to desist till that leg of the tour ended. They continued on the road in the condition of quiet discontent.

"Route: Newark, O., Nov. 21st; Wheeling, W. Va., Nov. 22nd; Baltimore, Nov. 25th, One Week." Instead of getting his salary in bulk, Majeroni began to receive installment payments. One day he would get five dollars, another ten, or twenty, and so on. At times, in lieu of cash, he would find his hotel bills paid. Gardiner assured him that the management was to blame.

A simple solution to the misunderstanding was not forthcoming. While he remained in the company, Majeroni would address neither Barrymore nor Warde nor anyone save his signora and Randolph Gardiner. When the party reached Washington, the Majeronis demanded a thousand dollars in back pay from Gardiner. They refused to play opening night unless at least five hundred dollars of it was paid. They still believed that Warde and Barrymore were cheating them.

Gardiner informed the partners that the Majeronis were holding out for increased salaries. He brought in two new actors for their roles, giving orders to turn the Italians into the street if they entered the theater. So far, Gardiner had arranged it cleverly. He stood to make a thousand dollars if the scheme worked. But the wily business manager had overlooked the intensity of Italian temperament. The Majeronis made an unyielding uproar outside the theater that evening, denouncing play and players, reviling the management. When startled patrons began turning away, Gardiner was forced to pay the couple $252.90 out of receipts. It cut his profit, but the inexorable Majeronis went away.

At this juncture, Barrymore and Warde differed as to future policy: Barry wanted to go south and west; Warde north and east. They decided to separate and form two companies. The decision was an amicable one, but the partners were men of obviously different temperaments. Conservative Warde characterized Barry as "a most charming and attractive actor, well bred and well read," with "a keen and ready wit and considerable literary ability," adding, rather wistfully, that "he has the courage of his convictions and the mental and physical ability to maintain them."

While plans for the division were being made, Randolph Gardiner disappeared. His reason became apparent when the New York *Clipper* reached Washington. The editorial was a deadly attack on the infamous business manager, dwelling at length on Mrs. Drew's danger in the hands of the villain. "Mr. Gardiner is Mrs. John Drew's agent, and, so far as we can learn, enjoys the right of entrance to Mrs. Drew's parlor. Mr. Gardiner once had a parlor of his own, in Chicago. He called it 'the deadroom,' and any friend of Mr. Gardiner was always welcome to the use of that parlor for purposes which surpassed in indecency the Capuan orgies of Erberius . . . Won't some true friend of Mrs. John Drew point out to her the dreadful injury she sustains, as a virtuous woman, by being the only woman who receives Mr. Randolph Gardiner on equal terms?"

The editorial went on to describe the indignities suffered by the Majeronis. "It is a significant fact," concluded the piece, "that Mr. Warde and Mr. Barrymore never had a word alleged against their integrity until Mr. Randolph Gardiner became their agent." Compliments of Signor Majeroni, even the sums involved were detailed. Before leaving Washington, Barry sent the mistreated couple $747.10 out of his own pocket.

Since the Western wing of the Combination was not scheduled to begin touring until January, the Barrymores, with Jack Drew and Alexina Baker, returned to Philadelphia. They found Mrs. Drew hard at work, making up losses suffered under Randolph Gardiner. Charles Mendum arrived from Boston to help his mother-in-law unravel the clever tangle. Wisa accompanied her husband to introduce their first-born. She was baptized at St. Stephen's; named for her Aunt Georgie, who also became godmother.

The Ninth Street household revolved around two disparate generations. In the nursery, Lionel of nine months, in chorus with Georgiana of six, held court, watched over by his nurse, Kitty Garrett. Appointed by blatant nepotism—she was the cook's daughter-in-law—Kitty proved equal to the task. Below, Eliza Lane Kinloch, at ninety, commanded from her boudoir with a bell. Those within earshot of the insistent ringing responded day or night to the needs of the old lady.

Amid the ringing and the wailing, Barry made arrangements for his tour, while his mother-in-law made a concession to time. On the eve of her fifty-ninth birthday, Louisa Drew had decided to play her first "old woman's part." The event would take place at a special benefit on February 22, 1879; the role would be *Mrs. Malaprop* in *The Rivals*.

Barry, acting as his own business manager, dispatched a Mr. Redpath to Texas as agent-in-advance. Retaining his original part of *Julian*, the actor-manager promoted Jack Drew to Warde's role of *Henry*, while Alexina Fisher Baker continued as the *Marquise*, H. Rees Davies as the *Baron*. Benjamin C. Porter, whom Barry had known in Boston, was cast in the key role of *Count Orloff*. Ellen Cummins, cast opposite him as *Countess Zicka*, had recently made an impression in New York as *Cordelia* to Edwin Booth's *Lear*.

Prior to departure for Texas, Alexina Baker's daughter was called in to replace Georgie. Mrs. Barrymore was again with child.

XI

The Western wing of the Warde and Barrymore Combination met a rigorous schedule of one-night stands, sometimes spending three days or a week in larger cities. In Houston, a critic deemed Barry "a polished actor, giving a perfect portrayal of a high-minded diplomat." John Drew, as his brother, was "cool, natural, unaffected and thoroughly finished." The same man observed that "attendance was not what the company deserved." Nevertheless, the young actor-manager took satisfaction in the proceedings. Profit was minimal, but operating expenses and salaries were met without delay. The company was congenial. Patrons were responsive, critics warm. And, as they continued through Texas, congeniality, for some of the players, turned to romance.

Jack Drew was first to find the Southwest suitable for courting. The object of his quest had been a friend since childhood. They became more than friends. Warm brown eyes and a tintype profile characterized Josephine Baker. During her twenty-two years, it was probable that no one had passed an unkind word about the girl. That she had never spoken unkindly of another was certain; Josephine Baker had never harbored an unkind thought. The courtship of her daughter and the son of her oldest friend delighted Alexina Fisher Baker. Nearly fifty years had passed since she and Louisa Lane play-acted in the attic of a Philadelphia boardinghouse.

Ben Porter and Ellen Cummins were also brought together—by a coffeepot. Porter had returned from the Civil War with an inseparable companion: a satchel containing an old military patent coffeepot, a spirit lamp, and an oft-replenished supply of concentrated coffee. The spirits of the company were cheered on many a night ride by a cup of Porter's coffee brewed in the cars. Ellen Cummins was admitted into partnership with the owner of the precious equipment, in exchange for supplying fresh coffee and fuel. Night train tête-à-têtes blossomed into love, a development which was certainly a godsend for the thirty-seven-year-old Porter. The son of a Worcester, Massachusetts, livery stable owner, Ben had been left with numerous responsibilities after his father's death. For ten years, he had cared not only for his own estranged wife but for his mother, his widowed sister and her son. The wife, who had wed him while he wore Union blue, found his peacetime profession untenable. The marriage had endured in name only, with Ben perpetually touring. In Galveston, he announced that Ellen Cummins had consented to become his wife as soon as a divorce could be secured.

In March, the Combination crossed into Louisiana to play Shreveport, returning to Marshall, Texas, for a one-night stand. Marshall was the "Gateway into Texas." Fort Worth and Dallas could be reached from there over the Texas & Pacific; the International and Great Northern Railways joined there, at Longview Junction, allowing rail connection with San Antonio, Houston, Galveston, Austin, and Waco. Theatrical troupes touring the Southwest had to pass through Marshall, and all of them played its opera house. Audiences there were reputed to be cultured and appreciative.

MAHONE'S OPERA HOUSE
THE SUCCESS OF THE SEASON
ONE NIGHT ONLY
WEDNESDAY EVE, MARCH 19
THE WARDE & BARRYMORE
COMBINATION
In the Great Wallack's Theatre (N.Y.) Success,
Sardou's play of powerful interest
and novel construction
DIPLOMACY
Produced by a magnificent cast of characters,
received everywhere with most flattering
attention by the public and greeted by the press
with recognized encomiums, which stamp it at
once as
THE GREATEST PLAY OF THE DAY
USUAL PRICES
Box sheet now open at Phillip's drug store

Reaching Marshall after dark, they went directly to Mahone's Opera House. There was no unoccupied seat that evening. The response was unanimous pleasure. It had been the same in the last several cities that they played. Barry was optimistic about the future of his troupe.

After the performance, they removed to the passenger waiting room at the Depot Hotel. There would be nearly a three-hour wait for the two o'clock train northbound to Texarkana. The hotel lunchroom was closed, so Barry and Ellen Cummins asked Ben Porter to brew some coffee. He didn't feel like going to the trouble, and suggested that they get it elsewhere. The desk clerk said that Nat Harvey's Lunch-room was open all night. It was on the station platform about thirty feet away. Their colleagues were dozing. The threesome strolled over to the station by themselves.

They entered Harvey's front door from the station platform. The back of the large room, they noticed, was a saloon, two steps above the dining area, separated from it by a folding screen. Nat Harvey had no other customers when the three actors seated themselves at the eating bar. Ben ordered coffee for himself and Ellen. Barry decided to have light ale. He drank his glassful, returned to the hotel to see about the luggage. Ben and Ellen stayed behind to have some supper. As they were ordering, a man entered the saloon through a side door. They saw him reflected, tall and heavy, black mustache and white sombrero, in the mirror which ran the length of the room. Obviously drunk, he called to Nat Harvey for a drink of ice water. Harvey served it right away.

"I guess I better take a little budge with it," said the big man.

"You better go slow, Jim," replied Harvey; "you look like you had enough."

"No. I must have some," the big man insisted, "it's too good a thing around here."

Harvey knew enough not to refuse Big Jim Currie twice. He was a pretty good fellow when sober, but drinking developed feelings of fierce inferiority. He was over six feet tall, weighed 220 pounds. He always carried a ready pair of Smith and Wesson 38's concealed under his frock coat. It was said that Wild Bill Hickok, the most desperate man in the Black Hills, before he was killed there, admitted that he was afraid of but one man, and that man was Jim Currie. As a scout with Custer, he had earned a reputation as a killer, justified by his position. Recently, he had shot three men—in the line of duty, it was said, since he was now a detective for the Texas & Pacific—but the facts of the killings had been glossed over by the railroad. Also, his protective older brother was Mayor of Shreveport. No, Nat Harvey would not refuse Big Jim Currie twice.

As Currie downed his drink, he saw the two actors reflected in the long mirror. His gaze fell on Ellen Cummins. "There's a high-tossed whore, if I ever saw one," he said to Harvey.

"Come on, Jim," urged Harvey, "you don't know if she's a lady or not; she's behaved herself and I rather you didn't make no such remarks."

"That's all right, partner," he replied as he left the bar. He passed through the dining room, glanced toward the eating bar. Ben, while talking to Ellen, had placed his hands on the back of his neck. It was a frequent mannerism of his. "You threw up your hand like this when I passed you," accused Currie, repeating the gesture. "You can't give me any guff like that."

"My friend," answered Ben, "if you allude to me, I hadn't thought of you; I was talking to this lady here."

"If you say that you're a damned liar," countered Currie.

"I'm in company with a lady and would prefer you wouldn't make remarks of that kind in her presence," Ben requested, "and if you want a difficulty you can see me anywhere you like outside the house."

"Hell of a lady she is!"

"Jim, Jim, stop that," cried Harvey from behind the eating bar.

Just then Barry entered, walked up to Currie, and said softly, "Go away; there's a lady here."

"Maybe you want to take it up, you damned whore-monger," challenged the bully. Barry's eyes widened and paled. He turned quickly to Ben.

"Get Miss Cummins out of here," he implored. Porter took the lady outside.

"So you want to take it up?" sneered Currie.

"Well, I'm not particular," cut Barry, "but I *am* unarmed."

"So am I," said the adversary.

"Haven't you a pistol?"

"No."

"Will you swear that you haven't?"

"Yes."

"Then take off your coat," invited Barry, dropping his own, thrown lightly over his shoulders, to the floor. Currie instantly drew two revolvers from under his long coat, leveled them at his unarmed challenger. Barry supposed that the bully only meant to scare him. He assumed the boxing attitude. Currie fired. At the same instant, Barry turned slightly. The ball struck the muscle of his left arm, above the elbow, passing through the arm to the upper part of his chest. Instinctively, he searched for a weapon, a spittoon, he thought. There wasn't one. Even the stools at the bar were fastened down. He ran into the saloon in search of a loose chair, anything, to hurl at his assassin. Currie fired again, hitting the heel of Barry's boot. Functioning on sheer reflex, Barry ran through the saloon, opened the side door, collapsed beside a water barrel in the yard. Currie fired again through the open door, striking the barrel. Water ran through the hole, making a puddle at the feet of the fallen actor.

Ben Porter ran in through the front door. "For God's sake," he cried, running toward the gunman, "don't murder an unarmed man."

Currie turned and fired, yelling, "God damn you; I can kill the whole lot of you." Ben clutched his stomach, staggered to the front door, fell over the threshold. Ellen Cummins, running along the platform, screamed when she saw her prostrate fiancé. She fell to her knees beside him.

Nat Harvey stayed crouched on the floor behind his eating bar. The actors came running from the Depot Hotel. Jack Drew and Harry Davies arrived first. Davies stopped to help Ben Porter. Jack entered the lunchroom in search of his brother-in-law. The big man stood there, his smoking pistols at full cock in each hand. He gave the newcomer a questioning look. For a moment, Jack Drew did not breathe. Then Currie shoved him out of the way and strode to the front door. He stepped over his fallen victim, pushed aside Davies and Ellen Cummins, and started a trail-blazing jaunt around the station platform. He chased the train dispatcher away and stood, legs wide apart, complacently in control, taking random shots into the darkness.

Some forty people had gathered in the vicinity, but no man made a move to take him, until Arch Adams arrived. Separating a path through the crowd, the deputy sheriff walked to the gaslit platform. Adams was a man of calm, unflinching courage, known and feared by local lawbreakers. He held his shotgun at half-mast, ready to go into action with both barrels. "Jim," he said, matter-of-fact, "I've come to arrest you and take you to jail." As Currie gazed into the determined, steel-blue eyes of the deputy, his drunken bravado disappeared.

"All right, Arch," replied Big Jim softly, "I'll go with you." Adams had faith in the reply. He put his shotgun down against the depot building, disarmed his man, and walked him peaceably to jail.

R. W. Thompson, the Texas & Pacific station agent, took charge of the wounded men. They were carried back to the waiting room in the Depot Hotel, where Dr. Elan Johnson attended them. Forty minutes after he was shot in the stomach, Ben Porter died. As he was being undressed, the ball that killed him fell out of his back.

Dr. Johnson could not stop Barry's bleeding. The ball had broken his shoulder blade and lodged in the muscle of his back, endangering an important artery. The ball had to be removed, but Johnson feared the bleeding. Doctors B. F. Eads and John H. Pope, railroad surgeons, were called in for consultation. The patient was moved to a first-floor room of the hotel. There, the doctors operated, while the bewildered survivors of the Combination sat up anxiously in the lobby.

Dr. Johnson sent Jack Drew to Phillip's drugstore to fill an essential prescription. Tension pervaded Marshall after the shooting. The remaining actors, made rather conspicuous by events, were understandably apprehensive. It was dark when Jack started out. The town itself was over a mile from the Depot Hotel. The train dispatcher called him aside before he left, handed him a pistol. As he passed the only lighted house on the road, a frightened woman called, "Where are you going?"

"To the druggist's," Jack answered, "and then back to the hotel."

"When you go back to the station will you tell my husband, he's the train dispatcher, that there are some tramps hanging around here? They've been in here to demand food."

Jack reached town safely. Mr. Phillip, awake and expecting a call, plied him with endless questions about the shooting as he filled the prescription. On the way back, there wasn't a single light. "The pistol gave me confidence of a sort," he recalled, "but of course I didn't want to use it; I never had used one." He put his hand reassuringly upon the weapon whenever strangers passed him on the dark road.

After delivering the medicine, Jack returned the pistol to the dispatcher, and told him what his wife had said. The dispatcher and his assistant left at once to apprehend the loiterers. They were brought to jail without incident. There was no more killing in Marshall that night.

At daybreak, Dr. Johnson emerged from Barry's room with an announcement for the waiting actors: The ball had been removed, the bleeding checked. When the patient finally awoke that evening, still very weak from the ordeal, Dr. Johnson held up the tiny ball that had nearly killed him.

"I'll give it to my son, Lionel," said Barry, "to cut his teeth on."

First train from Shreveport after the shooting brought Mayor Andy Currie, Big Jim's older brother, accompanied by the Crain brothers, renowned criminal lawyers of Caddo Parish. They at once repaired to the offices of Turner and Liscomb, railroad counsels. Major James H. Turner was considered one of the best criminal lawyers in the West. Later, Colonel Alex Pope, a local attorney, joined them. All of that day was spent in consultation.

Meanwhile, news of the calamity reached the nation. "Currie's pistol shots, fired at Marshall last week, re-echoed throughout the Union," editorialized the Waco *Telephone*. "The smoke that betokened the murder of an unoffending man, had scarcely died away, ere the telegraph wires were bearing the tidings north, east, south, and west." The great metropolitan newspapers, New York, Philadelphia, Chicago, St. Louis, San Francisco, had details of the murder in a few hours after it happened. The New York *Herald*, among others, telegraphed its agent at Dallas to wire every word that could be had of the horror, regardless of expense.

"So brutal was the murder, so notorious had the wires made its details," continued the editorial, "that the Union took a breathing spell and turned for a look at Texas. The response in this State was prompt and proper. From press and people went a shudder of horror at the crime that had stained our soil. Texas disowns Currie, and the friends and companions of the murdered man have been afforded every possible evidence of the detestation entertained for the deed, and the sympathy felt for the dead and those who mourn. And Texans have not suffered their sentiments to rest at mere words."

The *Telephone*'s rational commentary was exceptional. Most of the Texas journals vilified Marshall. The nation vilified Texas. The world vilified the "Sins of America."

The coroner's inquest was held on March 21. "The testimony of but one of witnesses of the terrible scene was given," reported the Marshall *Tri-Weekly Herald*. "Mr. Barrymore was wounded and could not attend the inquest, and Miss Cummins was prostrated from the excitement." Nat Harvey's testimony nevertheless established the event as "an unprovoked and cowardly murder." The state's attorney set his investigation for the following Monday.

Georgie reached Marshall on the day of the inquest, distraught and unsure of her husband's condition. She was greeted at the station by R. W. Thompson, the T & P agent, and five of the city's most prominent ladies. "Many of whom," Thompson observed proudly, "had never been inside a theatre." Nodding curtly to her reception committee, Mrs. Barrymore asked to be taken to her husband.

Barry mustered strength to greet his wife. She was heartened by his condition and by Dr. Johnson's assurance that the worst was certainly over. When Mr. Thompson announced that a room was prepared for her across the hall, she asked, instead, for a cot to be placed beside her husband's bed. Relaxing somewhat, she thanked her vigilant reception committee, which stood at the door in an uneasy counterfeit of upper-class hauteur.

"We understand you were born and reared to a theatrical life," accused one of the ladies, painfully articulate. Georgie could not resist. She affected a staunch British accent.

"Oh yes," she replied, "excepting the time spent at a young ladies' academy in Philadelphia, and of course my years at Vassar." This last lie was too much for Barry. The attempt to suppress his laughter nearly endangered his wound.

On Monday, the twenty-fourth, the state announced itself ready for the investigation. Currie's battery of lawyers asked for time to arrange their defense. The request was denied. They then asked until evening to prepare a written statement. This request was granted. At one o'clock, the defendant appeared and waived examination. Ellen Cummins and H. Rees Davies were introduced as witnesses for the state. Representatives of the nation's newspapers gathered in Marshall. They editorialized against Currie.

Reporters from the St. Louis *Globe-Democrat* and the Marshall *Tri-Weekly Herald* were allowed to visit the jail with a local photographer.

Currie was not the only celebrity behind bars. The neighboring cell held Abe Rothschild, scion of a wealthy Cincinnati family, indicted for the murder of his common-law wife, "Diamond Bessie," at Jefferson, Texas, three years before. A team of handsomely paid lawyers still battled to free Rothschild while he awaited a new trial in Marshall. The two accused murderers posed like proud patriarchs for a portrait, but Big Jim "declined to sit for more than one impression." The man from the *Tri-Weekly Herald* reported that Currie expressed "no regret at what he had done, but alleged that he had been insulted and he only regretted that he had not killed the whole party."

Marshall's band traversed the streets on Tuesday evening, urging citizens to the Mahone Opera House for an Actors' Benefit. Barry, unable to attend, requested that the entire proceeds go to Ben Porter's mother. The city took charge of everything, defraying every expense. The *Herald* staff volunteered printing. Fifteen leading citizens served as ushers. The local string orchestra accompanied the performance. The number of actors ambulatory was not sufficient for *Diplomacy*, so two farces were hastily prepared. *My Uncle's Will* and *Little Treasure* played to a full house, yielding $415.25 for Mrs. Porter. Afterward, Ellen Cummins offered "an exquisite little speech of appreciative thanks."

Residents of Dallas arranged for a benefit the following evening. The troupe arrived on the 4:10, compliments of the railroad, were received at the depot by a delegation, and ceremoniously escorted to a hotel. "Dallas, the reckless, roystering town, opened her big heart," wrote the Waco *Telephone;* "people crowded by the hundreds to the theater, to testify to their sympathy. Everything was free—opera house, hotel, licenses . . ."

When Ellen Cummins made her first entrance that evening, Mayor W. B. Simpson went to the footlights, expressedly "to atone for the words of bitter insult offered toward yourself, lady, without provoke, by a drunken desperado . . . We feel the deepest sympathy and respect," the mayor continued, "and as an evidence of that feeling, I beg to present to you, to be held in remembrance of us these jewels—a gift from the people of Dallas . . ." He presented a Roman gold locket and necklace, amid wild applause and cheering from the gathering. "That we are not all ruffians and desperadoes in Texas, lady, let our conduct here tonight attest. Speaking for this great presence for an outraged people, I implore you not to lay the burden of this great offense upon us all . . . In the name of Texas and Texans, lady; in the name of the people of Dallas who feel the profoundest sympathy, do not remember us altogether with feelings of bitterness and reproach."

Ellen, visibly moved, offered thanks. "When the Dallas invitation arrived," she added, "it was believed that Mr. Barrymore would be able to come, but we were reluctantly obliged to leave him on his sick bed, and we hardly know when he will be able to leave it."

Ben Porter was buried in New York that same day. Compliments of the Texas & Pacific, his remains had been embalmed and inclosed in "an elegant casket," and two passes furnished for Albert Murdoch, an understudy of the Combination, to accompany the body to New York. Murdoch had carried $139 in his pocket, raised by the employees of the railroad to help defray funeral expenses, but that gesture was hardly necessary. "The theatrical fraternity of New York, comprising ladies and gentlemen of culture, intellect, and wealth, took the matter in hand," attested the Waco *Telephone*, "and Wednesday Porter's body will be buried in New York with all the theatrical éclat appropriate to his tragical death."

Hundreds of people gathered at the Little Church Around the Corner in tribute to a thirty-seven-year-old actor that they had only known in death. The Park Theatre Company sent a wreath of camellias, white roses, and calla lilies to cover the casket. His body was buried at Evergreen Cemetery in a lot purchased by the Dramatic Fund Association.

The shooting of Porter and Barrymore, the meetings of actors to raise funds for Porter's family, comments of journalists and professionals had filled the New York papers, reaching a crescendo before the funeral. The *Telegram* hoped that the tragedy would "teach actors to omit Texas in future tours." The *Sun* urged that "Texans ought never to carry pistols after this." The Texans themselves telegraphed that they were afraid the murder would "hurt the State." On the day of the funeral, the *Spirit of the Times* attempted equanimity:

> We have been astonished at the various morals deduced from this sad affair. There has been some loud talk of lynching, broiling over slow fires, and otherwise mutilating the murderer; but the talkers have kindly concluded to permit the law to take its course, and Jim Currie will probably hang without the intervention of his New York denouncers . . .
>
> If the whole party had been in any other State, or even in this blessed city of New York, precisely the same outrage would have occurred. If poor Porter and Barrymore had been tourists, traveling for pleasure, or businessmen returning from an inspection of stock farms, they would have been shot at just the same. There was nothing peculiar to Texas, or to the theatrical profession, in the affair.
>
> We have, unfortunately, plenty of drunken ruffians, armed with pistols, right here in New York. We can count up our Jim Curries by the score. There is scarcely a theatre, hotel, or saloon, from Central Park to the Battery, the floor or the threshold of which is unstained with blood. There is scarcely a theatrical company, or a theatrical audience, assembled in this city, which does not contain at least one person known

to have killed his man, or his wife, or notorious as having been accessory to the killing.

Think over the facts, gentlemen, before casting the next stone at Marshall, Texas.

As soon as Barry could be moved, he was taken to the colonnaded Capital Hotel in the center of Marshall. His stretcher was carried the necessary mile by four of the city's elite, while General W. P. Lane walked alongside, holding an umbrella over the actor to shield him from the setting sun. The Barrymores were given the best rooms in the elegant hotel, opposite the parlor. They received every attention from the contrite townspeople. Dick Thompson, the station agent, and his wife tended Barry with affectionate solicitude. Local ladies sent fresh flowers and homemade delicacies to their rooms each day, along with numerous invitations which Georgie tactfully refused. The patient felt well enough to translate and adapt an old French play, *L'Honneur de la Maison*, which he had found before the start of the tour. Retitling it *The Debt of Honor*, he completed a first draft during his convalescence.

His company, meanwhile, played benefits in Bartle and Longview, Galveston, Shreveport, Jefferson and Texarkana, whose citizens had offered their theaters. Others not so well endowed offered whatever they had. "The people of Texas, to show their detestation of the whole affair and their sympathy with the company," attested John Drew, "offered us the hospitality of a number of towns that no touring company would have thought of visiting. Mesquite was one of these, and Eagle Ford another. This was a sort of 'town hall tonight' tour. When there was no theatre, we played in a hall and once in the dining room of a hotel." But houses were good, response hearty. Although Barry had already lost most of his original investment, he insisted that all proceeds from these productions should go to Ben's mother, absorbing any operating costs himself. They amassed nearly $5,000 for Mrs. Porter.

When the survivors left Marshall, Barry gave them what was left of his inheritance to cover operating expenses, and the railroad furnished free transportation to Memphis. They continued on their own from there, playing wherever "benefits" were offered by generous theater managers. The two wings of the Warde and Barrymore Combination would join again in Louisville late in April.

When Barry was judged fit, Charlie Kretz, who lived next door to the hotel, took him and Georgie out for afternoon drives in his surrey. Spring came early to Marshall. Fresh green contrasted white ante-bellum buildings. East Texas was more of South than West, much more of Louisiana than Texas, green and shaded rather than dry and vast. Outside of town was cypress-shrouded Caddo Lake, the link between South and West before the railroads came. Kretz drove the Barrymores down to the lake one afternoon. It was strange and silent, covered with sleepy jade-green moss. They saw an old paddle wheel river boat pass, one of the last that ran the shaded bayous to Jefferson.

The Barrymores left Marshall on April 15. At the depot, free transportation to St. Louis was presented, with a request for reduced rates from there on the Andalusia and Pennsylvania roads. Most of the townspeople crowded the platform to bid them farewell. Barry, his arm in a sling, was helped aboard by what had become his claque of local notables. From the steps of the car, Georgie tried to express thanks for weeks of kindness. Unexpected sobs interfered.

"I didn't know such good people lived," she called out, as the train pulled away from Marshall, Texas.

They were met by reporters in St. Louis. Rumors were rife that Barry had actually been killed in the shooting. Newspapers were understandably anxious for "in person" interviews. "Texas surgical skill," said the survivor, "and Texas attention and care, brought me through all right." The *Globe-Democrat* offered space for a statement. Barry complied on condition that it would also be sent to the Marshall papers. The reporter took down a "card of thanks" dictated by M. H. Barrymore:

> Mr. Barrymore gladly avails himself of the opportunity good-naturedly offered by the *Globe-Democrat* to express in its columns his warm sense of appreciation of the unremitting solicitude and sympathy extended to him by the residents of Marshall, Texas, though he can not but be conscious that any bare words of his must fail to convey how deep is the gratitude he feels for the numberless kindnesses he has experienced at their hands. He desires, however, at all events to make a grateful acknowledgement to Mr. R. W. Thompson, Jr., representing the Texas and Pacific Railroad, for much generous consideration and assistance at a very trying time, and to his many friends there to believe that nothing can efface the remembrance of his heavy obligations.

The Barrymores continued their ride half-rates to Philadelphia.

XII

Reporters crowded round the black brougham at Broad Street Station. Behind closed windows, Mrs. Drew sat impervious with her son-in-law, Charles Mendum. When the train pulled in, newsmen ran as one to the platform, following, hurling questions, as the arrivals made for the waiting carriage. Maurice Barrymore was a celebrity; not for a performance onstage but for one in Harvey's Lunch-room.

A man from the Philadelphia *Times* interviewed him that afternoon "reclining easily on the sofa" in Mrs. Drew's parlor. "His left arm is still entirely helpless," noted the reporter, "but he is able to sit up a portion of the day." Barry was allowed to convalesce in the parlor by special dispensation from his mother-in-law. The room offered sanctuary behind heavy oak doors: Victorian landscapes lined damask walls, a square piano held pictures of Edwin Forrest and his wife, an ornate music box waited to be wound up by Mrs. Drew so that it might, on important occasions, unwind the "Carnival of Venice." Away from the chatter of women and the wailing of babies, Barry revised *The Debt of Honor*.

The house on North Ninth Street was brimming with another project: a week of Old Comedy revivals at the Arch starring Mrs. Drew. For her return, sadly brief, to old stock days, she assembled a company to perform six plays in six days. Otis Skinner, a young actor engaged as "walking men," and awed by association with Mrs. Drew, worked diligently at his six parts for six nights. The leading man, however, overcome by the prospect, disappeared after the first performance. Mrs. Drew was unperturbed. Her convalescent son-in-law could not yet perform, but her son could. Jack had wired his mother that he would be home early Tuesday morning.

Both wings of the Warde and Barrymore Combination had met and played a successful week at Macauley's Theatre in Louisville. They had gone on to Chicago, played to poor houses there, disbanded. The shooting at Marshall might have been parlayed into success, but Ben Porter's death and Barry's disability had broken the spirit of the company. They were relieved for the time being to let *Diplomacy* rest. Jack, after sitting up two uncomfortable nights in a smoking car, arrived in Philadelphia broke and sleepy at two in the morning. His mother met him at the door —playbook in one hand, candle in the other. She handed him the script. "Don't go to bed, Jack," she admonished. "You play this tonight." Jack did not go to bed.

"That evening," Otis Skinner remarked, "he spoke every line of *Mr. Bronzely* in Mrs. Inchbald's *Wives As They Were and Maids As They Are*, a part longer than the moral law." Georgie, five months pregnant, also pitched in. She played *Maria* to her mother's *Lady Teazle* during the week, but thereafter retired to North Ninth Street to await the birth of her second child.

Cheered by news that the Texas grand jury had brought an indictment against Currie, Barry determined to be in Marshall for the June 17 trial. Meanwhile, he became a conspicuous denizen of Philadelphia during his convalescence, strolling along streets near the Drew house, chatting with curious neighbors and stage doormen, embellishing the tale of Harvey's Lunch-room. "He still carries his left arm in a sling," reported the *Times* on May 1, "and he is unable to make any use of it. His was an almost miraculous recovery, as at one time three doctors had given him up, the wound being so near an important artery that at any moment he was expected to bleed to death. A splendid constitution and abstensious habits saved him." (This last attribution particularly amused his wife.)

Offers began to reach the celebrity at North Ninth Street. The manager of the Novelty Theatre in Williamsburg wondered if *Diplomacy* could fill the week of June 2–7. Aware that his colleagues would be glad of summer employment, the defunct actor-manager set about gathering the disbanded Combination. When a note from William Warren arrived, its letterhead, 2 Bulfinch Place, activated warm memories. Warren, after extending sympathy to his young friend, invited him to appear on May 31 at a Boston benefit for Agnes Booth. Barry had concurrently declined numerous offers to mount benefits for himself, but he admired the wife of the younger Junius Brutus Booth, Edwin's brother. He agreed to play *Armand Duval* to Mrs. Booth's *Marguerite Gautier* in the fourth act of "Camille," his first appearance onstage since the shooting.

Reaching Boston just in time to go on, he removed his sling and entered the scene without make-up, wearing his own evening clothes. The Park Theatre audience greated him with a standing ovation—the hero, not the actor. When the scene, played without rehearsal, ended, there was another ovation, warmer and more prolonged than the first—this time for the actor. "His youth, his handsome stage presence, his vitality, and the general excitement of the whole affair created hearty and genuine enthusiasm," observed the *Transcript*. "More than one person said last evening that Maurice Barrymore has a brilliant future before him."

Refusing more colorful invitations, the hero of the evening visited 2 Bulfinch Place to sup with William Warren and Amelia Fisher. Next morning, he departed for New York.

There was a predictable hero's welcome at the Hoffman House, where Barry's cronies gathered to pay tribute. The shooting at Harvey's was told and retold, elaborated far into the convivial night. The ultimate tribute, however, was in the theater. If anything could conceivably render the *Diplomacy* disaster worthwhile, it was the affectionate greeting offered the reunited Combination at the Novelty. It was the first chance for New York playgoers to show their admiration for the benighted company. Patrons and peers ventured to Williamsburg from Manhattan, while Barry's avid suburban followers flocked to see their martyred leading man. He overacted *Julian Beauclerc* brilliantly, enjoyed himself thoroughly.

The Combination ended its eventful career at the Arch. The crowded houses were responsive to Mrs. Drew's son-in-law, but he toned down his playing for Philadelphia audiences. There was, after all, a tradition to consider.

Ellen Cummins made a decision that last week of *Diplomacy*. Mindful of the needs of Ben Porter's family and the rest of the company, she had gone on after the shooting. But the horror of the incident and the death of her fiancé continued to haunt her. After the last performance at the Arch, she returned to her home in Louisville, seldom to set foot upon the stage again.

Diplomacy ended a potential career for Barry as well. His foray into management had been a series of disheartening obstacles from Randolph Gardiner to Big Jim Currie. Receipts on the whole had been poor, losing all of his investment. He had, in fact, to borrow money from his wife when supposedly generous theater managers, who had offered benefits after the shattered Combination left Texas, demanded payment for the use of their establishments. Not wishing further conflict, Barry paid those whose demands seemed justified, left the others deservedly wanting. Management, he decided, was not his escape from acting. Playwriting remained the alternative for the responsible son of the Blyths.

Maurice Barrymore reached Marshall on the 2:15 train, June 23, 1879. He had wired ahead, but no reception committee was waiting that afternoon. No one was waiting at all. He walked alone to the Capital Hotel, noting unexpected reserve on the part of the townspeople. The *Tri-Weekly Herald* reported Ellen Cummins "very ill and laboring under serious mental and physical prostration." Prohibited by her doctor from traveling, she had given her testimony by deposition. The *Herald* further stated that Nat Harvey had been "shipped to Fort Worth," where a telegram was sent ordering his arrest. Before it was delivered, the witness went to Weatherford, "where there is no telegraphic correspondence." An "unknown party," it was reported, had bought Nat Harvey's Lunchroom for an inordinately large sum of money. Barry's confidence in an easy conviction began to weaken.

On July 3, after a week of delays, District Judge A. J. Booty granted a continuance to Currie on the grounds that the witnesses were absent. Straining to control his temper, Barry approached the bench after the decision. "This reminds me of our performances in England," he said. "We commence with a tragedy and end with a farce." The wily jurist made no reply.

Editor Laughery of the *Tri-Weekly Herald*, long an opponent of the powerful railroads, also attacked the court's action. "Since it is evident that the courts of Marshall have determined to turn Currie loose," the editorial concluded, "the citizens of that town could not make a better investment than to buy a strong rope and organize themselves into a vigilance committee and hang Currie on one end and that cowardly judge on the other." Texas newspapers echoed those sentiments, but the national press gave the first trial of Big Jim Currie little attention. The shooting had been news. The application of justice could hardly be expected to capture equal interest. This was exactly what the counsels for the defense, for the Texas & Pacific, for Mayor Andy Currie had anticipated. And if indifference proved inadequate to their requirements, then fear would be employed. Warned that his life might be endangered by returning to Marshall for the postponed trial, Barry knew that even the omnipotent railroad could not withstand the publicity of another murder. He determined to be there whenever it might be, whatever the expense or risk.

At the depot before Barry's departure, District Attorney W. W. Spivy made a startling revelation. "Just as well for us the trial was continued, Mr. Barrymore," Spivy began. "There are so many of Currie's stamp in the town and vicinity it was not possible to impanel a decent jury." The district attorney lowered his voice. "The first panel contained no fewer than eleven murderers."

A prestigious offer awaited him at North Ninth Street: Leading man at Wallack's Theatre—the position that Harry Montague had held so nobly before his death, that Charles Coghlan had taken for a season after leaving Daly—at one hundred and fifty dollars a week. Barry accepted, sent a copy of his play, *The Debt of Honor*, to the manager, and retired to his fourth-floor workroom to study for the coming season. He required an unusual amount of time to learn his parts. "I suppose it was youth," remarked Jack Drew, "but in those days we all had a capacity for memorizing. That is, all of us except Barrymore. My sister, Georgie, could study a part in no time at all, and she couldn't understand why Barry could not commit things to memory easily. She used to hear him say his parts over and over again. While he had a marvelous memory for things he had read, poetry or prose, or anything he had studied while he was at Oxford, he couldn't commit his parts easily."

All work and study suddenly stopped for two weeks in August. The pace of the Drew ménage quickened, tensed, relaxed again. Georgie gave easy birth to a daughter on the fifteenth. She wanted to name the girl Louisa, after her mother, but Barry remembered his old infatuation in Thackeray's *The Newcomes*. His daughter was named for "the fair Miss Ethel."

Georgie became absorbed by the rituals of motherhood. The husband was bewildered by the spectacle of his once carefree wife dashing and fretting, ordering the household to the specifications of Lionel and Ethel. Lionel of eighteen months was making his first bizarre attempts at articulation. Mrs. Drew became "Mummum," Mrs. Kinloch a variation thereof, and Sidney, inexplicably but not inappropriately, "Uncle Googan." "Aunt Tibby" and "Uncle Jack" escaped rechristening, while Georgie and Barry were predictably "Mamma" and "Papa." The young father was delighted by the energetic companionship of his son, awed by his infant daughter, offended by his wife's diversion. He was not unhappy to depart for Wallack's and the city.

Anticipating the dangers of separation, Mrs. Barrymore contrived to minimize them. Her husband would share a flat with her brother at 324 West Thirty-fourth Street. She assumed that this would limit his activities. Jack, conscientious, determined to succeed at Daly's new theater, would be presumably a good influence on his roistering brother-in-law. The opposite proved true. Jack joined Barry in his renewed patronage of New York's night places. They sought the good fellowship of their peers, however, not the company of the ladies. For Barry, his wife still held all womanly charms. For Jack, there was only Josephine Baker. Their marriage would take place whenever the Drew-Baker clans converged at Philadelphia.

Augustin Daly, opening a new theater that season, had offered Barry and Jack positions at salaries considerably less than they had previously received. Lester Wallack had saved Barry from that fate, but his brother-in-law was at liberty.

My Dear Mr. Daly:
I beg to say that I will accept your offer of $30 or $35 per week for next season. Hoping sincerely that it may be in your power—as I am sure it is your inclination—to make it the latter,
I remain yours very sincerely,
John Drew

Daly's Theatre, on the west side of Broadway, just south of Thirtieth Street, opened early in the new season. "There was great pessimism over the location of the theatre, so far uptown," remarked Jack; yet the building had a long theatrical history, having housed Banvard's Museum, Wood's Museum, the Metropolitan Theatre, and the Broadway. The Governor completely reconstructed the building to his specifications. Although his wealthy father-in-law, John Duffy, financed the operation, costs were kept to a minimum by the usually extravagant manager. Failure at the Fifth Avenue had somewhat chastened him. His weekly expenses during that season were low by any standards:

Weekly Salaries:

Seventeen ladies, fourteen gentlemen, $1,077.
Twenty-three chorus, $248.
Stage hands, $236.
Scenic artists, $60.
Ushers, etc., $88.
Advertising, 16 papers, $300.

Despite his salary, Jack was Daly's leading man. His leading lady was Ada Rehan, Georgie's friend, who had played congenially with him five years before at the Arch. She had matured into a tall, striking young woman, a splendid actress. Augustin Daly was taken by her "intelligence and adaptability, aided by her velvet voice."

"The first night of Daly's Theatre was really not an auspicious occasion," observed the leading man. "Daly had failed so completely with the Fifth Avenue Theatre, and his recent attempt to come back with *L'Assommoir* had been so unfortunate that perhaps at no time in his career of management did his name mean so little to the public as when he opened his own theatre on September 18, 1879." Nor was the opening bill a particular success. As the season progressed, however, critics began to notice John Drew and Ada Rehan. By the end of an otherwise mediocre Daly season, the vivid, humorous, romantic playing of the new team had captivated the public. The Governor would concentrate on Drew and Rehan in future, determined to build a strong and successful company around them. His father-in-law would not underwrite another unprofitable season.

It was quite a different matter at Wallack's Theatre, propitiously located at Thirteenth Street and Broadway. When Barry joined the company, it was the best and most successful in America. Built by J. W. Wallack in 1861, the theater had flourished from the start under the creative guidance of his son, Lester, who maintained a policy of staging mostly English plays, particularly those of Dion Boucicault. One critic called the prolific Mr. Boucicault "almost playwright in ordinary to this theatre."

Lester Wallack was no less a master of his craft than Augustin Daly, but success and sense of humor left him far more congenial. Nor was he less meticulous and generous in mounting his productions, but he was also a generous friend and a happy spendthrift. When Barry joined the company, Wallack was sixty, his still youthful physique crowned by bushy black eyebrows, an extravagant black walrus mustache, and a full head of curly white hair. Barry found his new employer as willing to socialize as to work with the members of his company. The manager was not slumming. He employed aristocrats of the theater—John Gilbert, Harry Edwards, E. M. Holland, Harry Beckett, and, on occasion, even Dion Boucicault—stars in their own right who banded together to vivify Wallack's well-bred old-fashioned rendering of the classics. Maurice Barrymore made his debut among such august company on November 6 in Henry J. Byron's *Our Girls*, playing *Tony Judson*, a young sculptor, "with considerable dash and skill."

During the run, he received belated information from Marshall, Texas. Currie's trial had been called on November 25, and again "continued by the state on the ground that all the witnesses were absent." The *Tri-Weekly Herald*, whose railroad-fighting editor had been surreptitiously replaced, reported that the citizens of Marshall were "indignant at the course of Barrymore, which is regarded as disgraceful." The Marshall *Messenger* complained that Barrymore and Miss Cummins were too concerned with "dollars and cents to come here and see that the murder of poor Ben Porter was avenged." The Marshall press neglected to mention one detail: Barrymore and Miss Cummins had not been informed of the trial. The best legal minds in the state were cleverly manipulating public opinion in favor of Big Jim Currie. The case was continued to June 1880. Frustrated by the course of Texas justice, Barry vowed to be there. He accordingly wired the Marshall papers.

Lester Wallack took the center of his own stage in December as *Charles Marlow* in *She Stoops to Conquer*, but "the important novelty was the *Hastings* of Barrymore," decided critic George C. D. Odell, in his *Annals of the New York Stage*. As the season progressed, Barry was winning Wallack's patrons, while more or less pleasing the critics. Some said that he was no Montague, others that he was not as finished in style as Coghlan, but most agreed with Odell that he was "handsome, popular and in many respects an admirable actor." Barry was not particularly concerned. Wallack had accepted his play, *The Debt of Honor*, for production next season. The author was concentrating on a final revision.

Dion Boucicault returned to Wallack's in February, fresh from his failure to manage Booth's Theatre. He opened in his incomparable role of *The Shaughraun*, with Barry again, as in Boston, *Captain Molyneux*. An unqualified success, it alternated with *The Colleen Bawn*, another of Boucicault's popular Irish plays, until March, when playbills proclaimed the appearance of no less a team than Wallack and Boucicault in the latter's *How She Loves Him*, "being the only occasion these artists have ever acted together in this theatre." The cast was advertised as "unprecedented," not the least of which was Barry's *Dick Hartley*. Boucicault's engagement ended uproariously on St. Patrick's Day with an extra matinee for the Herald Fund to aid the starving poor in Ireland.

After performances, Wallack's more congenial denizens would adjourn to Browne's Greenroom, an "English" chophouse directly behind the theater. In this precinct of sanded floors, old theatrical prints, and Toby jugs, fat, jovial George Browne, formerly an actor in Wallack's company, played no part truer than host. Barry felt a sensation of well-being in such places, enhanced during those winter months by a roaring fire and the fragrance of pulpy, baking apples brimming in steaming copper urns behind the bar. A cold winter's night was warmed by the resulting brew—bits of the hot fruit, boiling water and sugar mixed with spirits distilled from orchards and matured in sherry casks—an apple toddy. Lulled by the mellow brew, Barry was startled by an acquaintance from England noted for his lack of generosity. "Don't you know me?" asked the Englishman.

"I didn't at first," Barry replied, "but when you didn't buy, I knew you right away."

But intruders were few at Browne's. A sense of theater united the group surrounding Lester Wallack and Dion Boucicault, recalling the spirit which had first attracted Herbert Blyth to the profession. During those early London days, it had seemed camaraderie and easy humor. As he rounded and worked with the prolific playwright and the illustrious manager, he saw that it was more. It was joy: vital, irrepressible joy in their calling; storied, humorous, witty, compassionate commitment to a world of foibles and glories. At Browne's and at the theater, Barry, not lacking in wit, not without wisdom, stood beside these men in awe, wistfully aware of their unconstrained dedication—dedication which had so far eluded the prodigal son of the respectable Blyths.

Popularity was nevertheless at hand. In the hearts of matinee ladies and gallery girls, if not in the minds of critics, Barry had replaced Harry Montague. It was a niche which he still did not care to fill, but production of *The Debt of Honor*, he assumed, would soon raise him from the rank of matinee idol. He endured "the last novelty of an exceptional season," chosen especially to suit his dashing image. In *A Child of the State*, supported by Gilbert, Edwards, and Wallack himself, he played the swashbuckling *Count de Lancy* to the fluttering fans and beating hearts of his devotees.

While he swaggered by night as *Count de Lancy*, Barry's days were dedicated to the Lambs'. The actors' club, started informally five years before in Delmonico's Blue Room, and recently incorporated, had purchased a brownstone house at 34 West Twenty-sixth Street as its first official headquarters. This expenditure left the club's entire cash assets at $80.40. Prompted by an alien desire to economize, Barry insisted upon moving the Lambs' possessions from the old rooms at Sixteenth Street to the new house on Twenty-sixth. He performed the duty on foot, carrying what he could, stuffing smaller articles into his pockets, under his belt, or wherever he could possibly accommodate them. The frequent trips and generous loads of this carelessly dressed character aroused the suspicions of a policeman. The dutiful officer halted him and searched under his coat, removing piece by piece the components of the Lambs' billiard table—ivory balls, cues, triangles, even chalk. The suspect proceeded with escort to Twenty-sixth Street, where Lester Wallack, Shepherd of the Flock, applied his considerable powers of persuasion to vindicate the circumstantial burglar.

Wallack's season closed with a benefit for W. R. Floyd, stage manager and actor of the company, who had been away ill for most of the season. It was a glittering and profitable benefit for the man who had befriended Barry during his first season in New York, highlighted by the third and fourth acts of *London Assurance*. Barry played the profligate *Charles Courtly* to the hilt; Billy Floyd re-created his famous *Dolly Spanker*. An auspicious ending to a brilliant season, leaving the martyred Barrymore no less a celebrity but more an actor.

On Thursday morning, June 10, 1880, the case of the State vs. James Currie was called. District Attorney W. W. Spivy and the Stedman brothers, local attorneys, represented the state. Currie's five original lawyers had been augmented by Major Crawford of Dallas, and Judge Scay of Shreveport. After a delay on the part of the defense, the court reconvened at 1:30 P.M. From a special venire of sixty men, only four jurors were selected. When District Attorney Spivy challenged the eligibility of the other candidates, the sheriff was ordered to call sixty additional men.

Barry arrived from New York on Friday and went straight to the Capital Hotel. Saturday, the district attorney withdrew his challenge to the array of jurors. Two more were chosen. On Monday at 1:30 P.M., a third venire was brought in, the six additional jurors were obtained, and the trial opened in earnest.

Nat Harvey, finally tracked down by the prosecution, was returned under arrest to testify. The former lunchroom proprietor gave a diluted account of the night of March 19, 1879. Barry underwent lengthy examination, recalling events as they had happened. "As we listened to the cross-examination by the defense," observed the *Tri-Weekly Herald* ominously, "we realized fully the meaning of the term 'modest assurance.' "

Testimony continued for five days in the hot, overcrowded courthouse. By the third day, the state had introduced but four witnesses: Barrymore, Harvey, Dr. Johnson, who had treated the victims, and Colonel T. E. Whittaker, who had seen Currie rampaging around the platform after the shooting. Ellen Cummins telegraphed from Chicago that she would arrive on the morning of the fourth day. She gave testimony on Thursday which incriminated Currie beyond a reasonable doubt.

The defense introduced *twenty-three* witnesses! "The state has made out a strong case," said the *Herald*. "The defense has endeavored to traverse and attempt to show Barrymore was the aggressor, contending that Currie acted in self-defense." As Major James Turner questioned his client along these preposterous lines, Barry shot up from his chair, eyes lightened with rage. "Lies," he cried, "incredible lies . . ." Judge Booty made a bludgeon of his gavel, pounding to drown out his adversary. Any further outburst, warned the learned judge, and Barrymore would be thrown from court. Spivy returned him to his seat. Big Jim Currie sat smugly in the witness chair, "neatly dressed, and looking well, a fine specimen of physical manhood with a good face, with no appearance of the desperado."

Notwithstanding the killer's neat appearance and twenty-three witnesses, the plea of self-defense could not be substantiated. "The next point by the defense is an attempt to prove that Currie was laboring under *mania potu*. Dr. T. G. Ford, of Shreveport, was last on the stand, his testimony not yet concluded, to prove Currie's insanity. Other medical experts will probably be introduced on both sides."

Testimony closed on Friday, the 18, at one. The argument would commence after lunch. "Ladies will be permitted to attend, and comfortable seats allotted them . . . there will scarcely be standing room in the building. We would suggest a change to the opera hall, which is a larger room, well ventilated, and better supplied with seats." The *Herald*'s suggestion was not taken. Spectators crowded back into the hot, airless courthouse.

The argument for the state was opened by Major William Stedman at 2:20 P.M. He spoke eloquently, with conviction, for two hours. Major James Turner followed for the defense. He also spoke exactly two hours, with equal eloquence if not conviction. Then M. S. Crain, also for the defense, addressed the jury for half an hour. Court was adjourned until morning.

N. A. Stedman opened for the state on Saturday. He was followed by the remaining lawyers for the defense: Judge Scay, Alexander Pope, Colonel Crawford, respectively. The district attorney closed for the state. It was 7 P.M. before Judge A. J. Booty offered his charge to the jury. The learned gentleman took one hour to underscore, none too subtly, several ways to find the defendant *not* guilty of first degree murder.

The twelve jurymen, "all farmers," said the *Herald* generously, left the courtroom. "With what may be characterized as indecent haste," they returned in ten minutes. Foreman T. A. Moore stood, looked toward the judge, Barry said, with "unabashed pride," and announced the verdict:

"We the jury find the defendant *not guilty* on the grounds of insanity."

Spectators received the verdict in stunned silence. Barry, in spite of the obvious direction of proceedings, was incredulous; for once speechless. As the courtroom gradually revived, the district attorney saw Mayor Andy Currie, Big Jim at his side, stroll over to Barrymore. The mayor put out his hand to be shaken; the actor did not respond. The elder Currie spoke. Barrymore replied. Big Jim lurched toward him. Barrymore tensed, but Andy Currie took his younger brother's arm. They exchanged glances; then walked away.

The district attorney hurried over to Barry. "He wanted me to shake hands with his brother," the disgusted actor told him, "and invited me to take supper with both of them. I told him that blood was thicker than water and he was a manly fellow to stand by his brother, but that despite the verdict of those twelve intelligent jurymen, I still considered his brother a cowardly murderer."

"But Big Jim was standing right there," remarked Spivy.

"Certainly, and he didn't open his mouth. He wouldn't have caught me unawares a second time."

Barry collected his things at the hotel, went directly to the depot accompanied by William Stedman and District Attorney Spivy. A group of contrite citizens led by Dick Thompson, the Texas & Pacific station agent, was waiting there. Standing on the platform where Ben Porter's body had fallen a year before, Barry vented his frustration on the sympathetic gathering. "A set of blackguards, the whole lot of 'em," he exclaimed, "from that evil-looking judge downwards! They must have been squared by somebody. I guess there wasn't a man in court who wouldn't sell his soul for a whiskey sour!" He averred that the city marshal, in league with the murderer, had done all in his power to defeat justice. He warned them to beware their officials. He was shouting. Spivy told him that he was indiscreet.

"Look at here, Mr. Barrymore," warned the district attorney. "You'd better get 'way back to New York as soon as you can. They think nothing of killing anyone out here." Night was falling. Gaslights would not be turned on until train time.

"I wouldn't be surprised if another shooting took place before the northbound train gets in," added Stedman.

At that moment, the burly form of the marshal in question was seen approaching the party. As was the custom of lawmen in the Southwest, he wore two revolvers exposed in his belt. He walked slowly past the men on the dark platform, slowly back again. "Is Barrymore here?" asked the marshal.

"No," Thompson lied, "he went to Texarkana to get the train."

"No, sah," corrected a Negro, who was lighting the lamps, "Mas'r Barrymore hain't done gone to Texarkana. He over dar in dat crowd." The marshal addressed the group once more.

"Is Barrymore here?" Having undergone the peculiar transition from caution to indifference, Barry stepped out in front of the marshal.

"Yes, I'm Barrymore. What do you want?" The lawman deliberately dropped his hand to one of his revolvers. Barry lunged forward, knocking the weapon to the platform. His right fist was poised.

"No," cried the marshal, "it ain't loaded." Barry held his fist an inch from the man's face. "Kinder thought you'd like to see the gun Currie used on yer friend." The marshal retrieved the pearl-handled revolver and handed it to the actor. Barry glanced at the lethal instrument, returning it without thanks as the northbound train pulled in.

"One of that distinguished jury which turned the tiger Currie loose had just been released from the penitentiary," said the Sherman *Chronicle*. "Another, who never was known to have a cent, was said to be fairly coated with greenbacks after the verdict." William Stedman, one of the prosecuting attorneys, informed newsmen after the trial that "money was probably used with the jury." He said that a leading merchant was prepared to testify that one of the jurors purchased goods after the trial "literally without as much as asking the price, and on making payment exhibited large rolls of $5 and $10." Major John M. Case reported that another juror took a shave after the trial, paying the barber with a $10 bill from "a roll of greenbacks he took from his side pocket." Mr. Phillip, the druggist, stated that "an hour after Currie's acquittal, one of the jurors exhibited a large roll of bills and offered in payment a $10 greenback," boasting that he had not been on the jury "for nothing."

Big Jim Currie was released to the custody of his brother.

Moral indignation flared, mainly in Western newspapers. Marshall's *Tri-Weekly Herald* led off, regaining some of the objectivity lost after the railroad had replaced its outspoken editor: "The onus of proof of insanity was with the defense, and they utterly and completely failed to establish it . . . Harrison County and the State of Texas will be held responsible for that verdict, and yet it meets with universal condemnation."

The Cincinnati *Star* was sarcastic: "Currie is crazy. If any man cherishes an abiding faith in the intelligence of the jury it is Currie."

The Dallas *Times* was cynical: "The jury of Harrison County, be it remembered, announced to the world that there are moments in intoxication when, the intoxicated man has a right greater than all sober men. The right to shoot down whomever he sees fit."

The Arkansas *Gazette* was contemptuous: "What a wretched farce our criminal prosecutions are getting to . . . It is a good thing for Currie that he didn't steal a 'two-bit Mexican pony.' If he had, the jury would have convicted him."

But the furor soon subsided. After the New York *Dramatic News* advised "all theatrical people to abandon Texas," the initially contrite *Tri-Weekly Herald* quickly recovered its Texas pride. "The theatrical profession may as well understand, first as last, that Texas is not under any obligation to the dramatic profession, and if they choose to stay away, no one will be hurt but themselves," the Marshall paper threatened. "A certain class of them have shown our State no consideration or kindness. Texas has been most roundly abused and slandered by them. The New York *Dramatic News*, their accredited organ has been persistent in its libels upon our state and people. Falsehood has appeared in its columns. If this kind of treatment is to be kept up, retaliation will follow and the 'stocks' and 'stars' that may come here will play to empty houses."

Mayor Andy Currie shipped his brother to New Mexico to run a saloon in partnership with a mining prospector. Some years later, Big Jim shot and killed his partner. Convicted this time, he was sentenced to twenty years in the penitentiary at Santa Fe, beginning his term on September 10, 1888. Two years later, Grover Cleveland appointed a Kansas man named Ross governor of New Mexico. Currie was pardoned March 27, 1891, on condition that he leave that territory forever.

Abandoned even by his brother, the pardoned killer drifted over the border into Mexico, ending up in a lawless mining town. During a barroom brawl one night, a Mexican bandit shot him. It was reported that Big Jim Currie writhed on the hard dirt floor for a few minutes before he died.

XIII

W HEN JOSEPH JEFFERSON booked a nationwide tour of his new version of *The Rivals*, he chose the Arch for the première, its manageress for *Mrs. Malaprop*, and her son-in-law for *Captain Absolute*. Mrs. Drew consented to play away from her own theater for the first time in thirty years. The Arch had not been prospering; although she did not speak of it, Mrs. Drew needed to augment her dwindling income. Barry, delighted by the prospect of playing again with Jefferson, and for the first time with his wife's mother, declined another season at Wallack's to accept the invitation. It was no sacrifice. *The Rivals* tour was the most anticipated theatrical event of the 1880–81 season.

The troupe would play south to New Orleans, west to Kansas City and as far north as Montreal, one-week stands in the larger towns, one-night jumps between. This had been routine since the railroads pushed west to the Missouri River. Many first-rank actors played New York for only a week or two during the season, some not at all. The road was the theater and the theater was the road in 1880. Mrs. Drew, in her sixtieth year, would venture out from the Arch to win a new following, still an advocate of the old stock system, but trusting in Jefferson's sound professionalism.

As a child, Mrs. Drew had played with Joseph Jefferson's grandfather, and, as a young woman, with his father. Now, the third actor of that name, at fifty-one, was considered the theater's grand old man. That premature appellation had been won by his portrayal of *Rip Van Winkle*, which stood as one of the most popular characterizations on the American stage. One role had brought his greatest success, but many had nurtured it. From the time of his debut at the age of four, doing a black-face imitation of "Jim Crow," no theatrical experience had eluded him. His deeply creased face and shaggy gray hair suggested a Yankee preacher, but he was all theater. The third Joseph Jefferson and Louisa Lane Drew stood for the tradition and the grandeur of their calling.

Jefferson saw *Bob Acres* in *The Rivals* as a character suitable to follow his popular "Rip." Reworking the eighteenth-century comedy to this end, he managed to streamline and improve the piece. Purists could cavil, but even its author, Richard Brinsley Sheridan, had disowned his early work, asserting that he "would give anything not to have written it." Mrs. Drew had some revisions of her own for *Mrs. Malaprop*, which Jefferson exclaimed "Sheridan himself would have introduced if the idea had occurred to him." She understood perfectly the methods to best realize the character whose "derangement of epitaphs" had given malapropism to English usage.

Tempered though it was by charm and humor, a grand aura surrounded the two veterans, eliciting from their excellent company deference which bordered on the obsequious. Barry, as well, was striving to be worthy of such august leadership, but his distaste for even a hint of the grandiose caused Mrs. Drew some discomfort when she invited her Board of Directors to one of the last rehearsals. Still unsure of his lines, and bound to undermine his imperturbable mother-in-law, *Captain Absolute*, "the very pineapple of politeness," entered for their first scene together.

It began smoothly enough, but Barry's memory did not hold. Instead of the dialogue, he began to speak whatever came into his head—so eloquently that the invited spectators noticed nothing amiss. On stage, it was quite a different matter. Amy Leslie, covering the historic revival for the Chicago *Daily News*, witnessed the confrontation. "Mrs. Drew was confounded," observed the critic, "and in a blaze of anger she whiffed scorn at him throughout the scene, switched indignation at him from the hem of her petticoats, and landed him glares which would have tamed a zebra. But through it all Barry was cool as a sherbet, bowed graciously to her, showed his milk-white teeth, and never blinked an eyelash to admit he had received her subtly but unmistakably delivered shafts of rage. Only the actors who knew what should be done could detect this side drama of mother-in-law and delinquent son, and Georgie, who was in the wings, laughed herself into a fit at the duo her brilliant husband and equally brilliant mother were doing in a minor key."

Nor did Mr. Jefferson escape Barry's chiding. After the spectacular opening at the Arch, amid the praise came some disapproval at Jefferson's revisions. The public and critics were generally ecstatic, but purists were outraged that an American comedian should take such liberties. Barry, aware of the rattling effect that this had on the fastidious Jefferson, was standing beside him while William Winter offered profuse congratulations. "And what must you think of the new *Rivals*, Mr. Barrymore?" concluded the dean of New York critics.

"Well, sir," replied Barry, "it reminded me of that line in Buchanan Read's Civil War poem, 'And Sheridan twenty miles away.'"

Such irreverence reinforced Winter's dislike of the cavalier Barrymore without diminishing his esteem for Jefferson, Mrs. Drew, and the new *Rivals*. His review in the *Tribune* deemed Mrs. Drew's playing "as fine as anything of the kind can possibly be," adding that "It is worth the journey to this place merely to hear her say, "He has developed the plot to me, and he will give you the perpendiculars.'"

Before *The Rivals* left Philadelphia, John Drew and Josephine Baker were married. Drews and Bakers came together festively for the nuptials blessed on all sides, then dispersed in all directions. The newlyweds returned to New York, where Jack's second season at Daly's held great promise. Barry and Mrs. Drew departed on their tour in Joseph Jefferson's private railroad car. Georgie set off in less splendor but with no less enthusiasm to join the Gosche-Hopper Company at Booth's Theatre in New York.

Mrs. Barrymore had been approached that summer by a stage-struck twenty-year-old from Rhode Island, DeWolf Hopper, who had inherited a large sum of money. In partnership with Jacob Gosche, manager of a New York theater orchestra, the hulking youth had commissioned *One Hundred Wives*, a Mormon thriller, from two Chicago newspapermen. Hopper wanted a "name" to head the cast, and offered Georgie the extremely generous sum of $125 per week to do so. Aware that her husband was not particularly charmed by her devotion to motherhood, and frankly missing the stage herself, she had accepted. Barry, after all, would be touring that season under her mother's restrictive eye.

The Barrymores were not parted immediately. Since their New York engagements coincided, they met, along with Mrs. Drew, at the Judsons'. To have their three favorites all stopping at once was a treat for the Judson children. They had talked endlessly about it to their friends. One rather simpering young lady, anxious to meet the famous Mrs. Drew, was invited to do so. Mrs. Drew had demonstrated to succeeding generations of Judsons that her austerity belied warmth. Assuming that this would also be apparent to their guest, the children were aghast when the young lady emerged from the interview looking rather white and frightened. "What! don't you like her?" they chorused.

"Oh, yes; very much," the visitor answered faintly, "only she *chops one off so!*" Georgie overheard this, and the phrase immediately became the first of many family "wheezes."

While in New York, the Barrymores called on W. R. Floyd, approaching his house at 110 Fourth Avenue with trepidation. Billy Floyd was dying of Bright's disease. He had been a friend from Barry's first season in New York and a fellow member of Wallack's company. His wife Ernestine's sister, Mrs. F. S. Chanfrau, was an old friend and colleague of Mrs. Drew. The families had always summered together at Long Branch, where the Floyds also kept a house. Ernestine greeted the callers, while her three pretty daughters gathered around. The youngest, fifteen-year-old Mamie, took Barry by the hand. Mr. Barrymore had long been her special beau. She did not let go until they parted at her father's bedroom door.

They were allowed only a few minutes with the patient. When Ernestine offered tea, Barry made an excuse and hurried Georgie away. The spectacle of sickness unsettled Maurice Barrymore. Three weeks later, Billy Floyd was dead.

The Park Theatre program for the week of October 30, 1880, during the run of *The Rivals*, included a column headed "Stage Gossip." The lead item noted that "Maurice Barrymore is the author of *The Debt of Honor*, the new play which is to be produced at Wallack's right after the election." Another announcement appeared farther down the column. Soon after *The Rivals*, it stated, the Park Theatre would present a new play called *The Legion of Honor*. Barry noted the coincidence, thought nothing of it.

The *Legion of Honor* opened at the Park while Barry was on the road. The play, it turned out, was another adaptation of *L'Honneur de la Maison*. While not a success, the papers nevertheless made much of the fact that Barrymore had used the same source. Lester Wallack, regretfully, decided not to produce *The Debt of Honor*. A setback for the fledgling playwright, but not one which he dwelt upon. He immediately sent off a copy of the manuscript to John Clayton, an acquaintance from his provincial acting days in England. Clayton, he had heard, was to manage the Royal Court Theatre in London next season.

Christmas Eve found the Gosche-Hopper troupe in a Mississippi town where holiday celebration abounded. "I do not care to say that there was no sober citizen in the town on Saturday," declared Georgie Barrymore, "but I speak advisedly when I say that he was not visible." There was no baggage-wagon driver at the station, but fortunately the company carried its own stage carpenter. With the actors' help, he trucked their trunks and scenery from the station. At the theater, an antiquated opera house, they were greeted by a notice posted near the footlights for the benefit of actors: "Don't spit into the foots." It was their only greeting. The entire stage and house crews were missing. With barely two hours to prepare for the matinee—played, as usual in the South, at noon—the actors rallied, setting up the scenery and lighting the kerosene lamps. They manned the box office, the curtain rope, and were prepared to do the ushering.

At twelve o'clock not a penny had been taken at the box office. Georgie hastily printed a sign on a strip of canvas announcing that the performance was postponed until 1:00 P.M. Hopper found an obliging "darky" still able to walk, gave him a dinner bell, and sent him weaving through the streets carrying the makeshift banner and ringing the bell.

At one o'clock the house was still empty. Not even the complimentaries distributed by the advance man had been offered at the door. The canvas was reversed, and Georgie lent an advance man's touch to a new announcement.

MATINEE

OF THE SENSATIONAL DRAMA

ONE HUNDRED WIVES

FRESH FROM ONE HUNDRED NIGHTS

AT BOOTH'S THEATRE, NEW YORK

POSITIVELY TO BE GIVEN AT TWO O'CLOCK

COME ONE, COME ALL!

The sandwich man weaved forth again with his bell. At 2:00, not a solitary patron had materialized. The matinee was canceled.

Only fifty-three dollars was taken that evening, every cent of it drunk and disorderly. In the outmoded opera house, a flight of broad wooden steps led up from the street to the box office and lobby. During the first act, a tardy patron stumbled up the stairs, slapped a quarter down at the window, demanded the best seat in the house. The stage carpenter was filling in at the window.

"Excuse me, sir," he said politely, "but downstairs seats are seventy-five cents. Our twenty-five cent seats are in the gallery." The potential customer announced belligerently that he did not intend to pay more than two bits, and that he expected the best that money could buy. He loudly heaped vulgar abuse upon the stage carpenter. "You'll go down those stairs for nothing," countered the carpenter, proving as good as his word. The repulsed patron bounced down forty-two steps, picked himself up, and departed.

He returned a few minutes later with an armful of firecrackers, hurling them string by string as he lit them up the steps into the lobby. Inside, the fifty-three-dollar audience took the fusillades to be part of the show. They stamped and hollered and clapped wildly. "It was not a troupe of barnstormers that played to these indignities," asserted Hopper, "but a company that included Mrs. Barrymore and Ada Gilman, two of the first actresses of their time." When the ladies took their curtain call that night, walking man William Harris accompanied them with a dagger in one hand and a revolver in the other. He kissed each weapon to the audience, and barely escaped with the ladies.

The gentlemen of the troupe played poker in the smoking car as the Mobile & Ohio speeded toward Mobile. Georgie was in the sleeper getting Vivia Ogden to bed. Since the tour began, she had watched over the little girl who played the child part. Near the State Line station on the Mississippi-Alabama border, there was a sudden, shattering crash. Georgie, the child in her arms, was thrown the length of the car. The M & O had collided head-on with a freight train in a cut. The freight-engine crew, drunk on Christmas cheer, had run a signal at State Line.

The passengers, most of whom had been asleep, were unharmed except for minor cuts and bruises. But the crews were devastated. The engineer of the passenger train was killed instantly; the fireman, badly burned and mangled, lost a leg. All three men in the freight locomotive were dying. The Negro feeder of the freight, crushed under his engine near the blazing firebox, was singing hymns, delirious with pain. A doctor who happened to be aboard did his utmost. The rest was left to the actors, wide awake after their Mississippi adventure. Georgie begged the doctor to give the feeder something to end his hopeless suffering. He passed over a vial of chloroform. "Don't give him all of it," he warned, "or you will kill him."

Will Harris took the vial from Georgie. "He turned his back and emptied the vial into a glass of whiskey, and I," said Hopper, "holding my hat in front of my face to shield it from the blistering heat, held the glass out for the darky's groping hand. He downed it all, and died an easier death."

The actors carried the body of the freight engineer into the sleeper, laying it in a berth. They presumed him dead. Suddenly he seized De-Wolf Hopper's left wrist. With tormented eyes, the man responsible for the disaster sought the actor's face, reviling himself with his last breath, begging, as he died, to be consigned to the farthest reaches of hell.

They laid the cut and scalded fireman across two seats in the smoker. "I remember Georgie Drew Barrymore laying her new and costly fur-lined circular under the head of the dying fireman of the freight," said Hopper. "She sent that fur piece to the cleaners three times later. It would return apparently spotless, but always a day's dust and sun would bring back telltale stains, until she discarded it."

Sidetracked near Chicago, *The Rivals* company spent a less eventful Christmas Eve. "A merry meeting of the company was arranged in the private car after the play," recalled Joseph Jefferson; "a Christmas tree had been erected, and it was understood that each one should hang a present for the other on it, and that no one should know the donor." Barry was elected to take down the different parcels from the tree and present them. "The choice proved an excellent one," Jefferson noted, "as he bestowed the gifts with wit and humor."

The gifts Barry himself had purchased were the last to be presented. The advance agent was given a paste pot and brush, the company manager an extravagantly wrapped bundle of railway guides; Mrs. Drew was ceremoniously offered a bag of peanuts, which, everyone knew, she violently abhorred; Jefferson received a copy of *The Rivals*—with every part cut out except *Bob Acres*. Jefferson always told of this with gleeful appreciation, referring to Barry as "one of the wittiest of men."

The company toured on to glory. Everywhere full houses and rapturous reviewers greeted them. *Bob Acres, Mrs. Malaprop,* and the spruce *Captain Absolute* were invariably singled out for acclaim. Young ladies, not of the gentry, granted, but devoted nonetheless, took to loitering about the private car to glimpse their Mr. Barrymore. Mrs. Drew, not to one to offer idle praise, nor to taint critical objectivity with family loyalties, nevertheless gave an opinion of her son-in-law's portrayal. "I must confess it, Joseph," she told Jefferson; "Mr. Barrymore is the finest *Captain Absolute* I shall ever hope to see."

The Barrymores' reunion in Philadelphia that spring was heightened by news from England. John Clayton had accepted *The Debt of Honor* for production in September. Contracts waited at North Ninth Street for Barry's signature. Clayton suggested some rewriting, but saw no reason for the author to come across; another writer, he explained, could be called in to make adjustments. Barry was elated, running about the house like a schoolboy, waving the contracts in the air, shuffling the foolscap pages before Georgie and Mrs. Drew. He read over the documents, signed and posted Clayton's copy that same day. His accompanying letter pointedly informed John Clayton that he would arrive in London in August to facilitate any "adjustments" himself.

The Barrymores, with Lionel and Ethel, their nurse, Kitty Garrett, Aunt Tibby and Uncle Googan, set out for Long Branch early in June. Soon after, affairs at the Arch in order, Mrs. Drew appeared with Great-Grandmother Kinloch and Mrs. Garrett, the cook. Later, following another successful season at Daly's, Jack and Josephine Drew arrived. The latter was not allowed her Christian name for long. Compliments of Ethel, of twenty months, heir to her brother in the tongue-twisting department, Josephine became "Aunt Dodo."

The gathered clan, augmented by Bakers and Judsons, shared a joyous season in the roomy house by the sea. Barry and three-year-old Lionel became boon companions, the son worshipfully following wherever the father wandered. Uncle Jack remarked that only Lionel's inescapable devotion had inspired the relationship, but Barry refuted the suggestion. "The little fellow just happens to be damned good company," he declared.

The author worked on his play a bit, shortening the title to *Honor,* or

Honour for the English production, and there was some family friction over a puppy that Barry attempted to introduce to the household. Mrs. Drew prevailed. To the immense displeasure of Lionel and Ethel, the little terrier was presented to Mamie Floyd, who lived with her widowed mother and her sisters not far from the Drew summer house. Otherwise, days were lazy and uneventful.

Georgie was particularly gay and carefree that summer, aware that separation had heightened the pleasures of marriage and fatherhood for her husband. Barry suggested that she travel to England with him, but she was committed to another season of *One Hundred Wives*. Besides, before he sailed, Georgie discovered that she was carrying their third child.

XIV

L ONDON'S ROYAL COURT THEATRE was in the throes of redecoration when M. H. Barrymore called there. John Clayton was not particularly pleased to see him. A noted actor, untried in management, Clayton had been placed in charge of the venerable house in Sloane Square by its new lessee, a London merchant, who demanded a return on his investment. *Honour* would be Clayton's first production. He preferred to mold the play to his own needs without being bothered by the frailties of an actor turned author. Barry understood but held tenaciously to his author's rights.

"My dear Barrymore," jabbed Clayton during their first exchange, "I should awfully like you to play *Rene de Latour*, but you know, my dear fellow, with your American accent it is quite impossible."

"When I am in America," replied Barry, "I am twitted with my English accent. Now I'm in England my American accent is considered an obstacle. Hang it all, Clayton, I can't get my living reciting on transatlantic steamers." But Barry had not intended to perform in *Honour*; he did, however, intend to be its sole author. He absolutely rejected Clayton's suggestion to bring in a "play-doctor." Amid barbs and bickering, he adjusted his work to the manager's specifications, agreeing to the advisability of compressing the action from five to four acts, but questioning another of Clayton's suggestions.

As it stood in Barry's adaptation, Clayton considered the leading motive of the play offensive. Twenty years before the action begins, *Helene*, the innocent heroine, has been seduced, impregnated, and deserted by a young officer. To hide the shame, *Helene*'s mother compels her to marry a young manufacturer who loves her. When a son, *Rene*, is born, the deluded husband accepts him as his own, until he overhears the truth at his mother-in-law's deathbed. For the sake of his daughter, born after

Rene, he conceals knowledge of his wife's past. But he shows no tenderness to the boy and, whenever possible, avoids seeing him. This situation between resentful father and unwanted son is what first attracted Barry to this play, recalling his own relationship with the Commissioner.

At the start of the play, *Rene* returns to Paris from an African campaign with the Cross of the Legion of Honor for his bravery. The gallant young man attends *Countess d'Avranches*'s ball, where he is accosted by *M. Verduret*, an effeminate old scandalmonger. "You see that gentleman passing there," commences *Verduret*, "that is M. de Clamavens—he married his cook—there she is—that fat woman in blue! He tries to pass her off for an English lady to account for the horrible mistakes she makes in grammar. He never lets her take her gloves off in company— but I knew her when she was in service, I did sir, and—a damned bad cook she was." This scene, added by Barry to parody the kind of flighty, superficial society that he abhorred, was his particular favorite.

Later, *Rene* hears a slur cast on his mother's honor by *Verduret*. His actual father happens to be present and becomes involved in the resulting quarrel. A challenge comes between father and son, each unknown to the other. *Helene* is present, horror-stricken at the prospect of a fatal encounter between her beloved son and his real father. A powerful scene follows. The long-suffering husband informs his wife that he has long known her secret; then leaves to confront the man who is the cause of his misery.

The confrontation scene is strong and tautly written. The seducer, unmarried and alone after a life of profligacy, is told that the boy he is about to fight is his own son. He must decline the combat, insists the husband, and apologize at the risk of being looked on as a coward. The lonely man accepts this humiliating situation, longing rather to declare himself to his long-lost son. When *Rene* arrives ready for the duel, his unknown father declines to fight. The boy, thinking him a coward, quits him with words of contempt and scorn. What remains but a duel between the injured husband and the man who had seduced his wife? After a harrowing scene, in which *Helene* doubts which of the two has fallen, the husband, whom she has grown to love, returns unscathed. He accepts *Rene* as his own son, and—honor avenged—the curtain falls.

John Clayton felt that *Helene*'s premarital indiscretion would prove too "delicate" for English audiences. Barry disagreed, pointing out that the denouement hinged on the indiscretion. The manager was adamant. Barry invented a mock marriage to whiten the lady's sin, and Clayton conceded that *Honour* was ready for the stage.

While his play was in production, Barry returned to the haunts of his London years. Friends who remembered Herbert Blyth fell easily into the calling of "Barry," welcoming the hero of Marshall and the author of

Honour with a certain deference to the city of his youth. London did not seem particularly changed to the thirty-one-year-old expatriot, nor had memory cheated him. Publican Nat Langham still held forth at the Mitre, among new faces, to be sure, but some of the old ones remained.

Ned Donnelly, impeccable in frock coat and top hat, was more than ever the Royal Professor. The dream of elevating his beloved sport had been realized. His new rooms in Panton Street stood for the University of British Boxing. His ex-Middleweight Champion exercised daily there, sparring with pupils or "clients," as Donnelly called them, including the aristocracy and many of London's leading lights. Barry was riding one afternoon in Regent Street on the box seat of a 'bus, when the Professor greeted him from the pavement, flourishing the gracious salute reserved for all the young swells who were his intimates.

"Who is that gent?" asked the driver. "Celebrated lawyer, I should think."

"No, you've guessed wrong," Barry replied, "that's Ned Donnelly, the scrapper."

"You don't say!" the driver exclaimed. "Why when 'e was a-riding with me the other day, whenever 'e touched 'is 'at to a gent what was passing, 'e would whisper in me ear, 'That's a client of mine.' Ned Donnelly, is it?"

Paul Potter, a reporter for the London *Times*, was still writing plays, still taking his greatest pleasure from the works of other men. He had kept the rooms off Russell Square which he and Barry had shared, and convinced his old school friend to stay there. Barry's possessions—books, artifacts, clothing—were as he had left them. He had not given them a thought in seven years. Rahj II, fat and complacent, was still in residence. Barry sensed only a glimmer of recognition from his onetime pet.

Familiar friends and haunts intensified the expatriot's realization that he had become irrevocably a man of another place in the years since his departure from Southampton on a "pleasure trip." Perhaps for the first time, the melancholy passing of years struck him. Uncharacteristically, he dwelt upon it, conjuring generations of Englishmen who had ventured out over the seas to become people of other lands. He considered the Blyths and the Chamberlaynes. Even before *Honour* was ready for production, another play was forming. He called it *Homeward Bound*.

Many afternoons were spent researching the new play in the colossal calm of the British Museum Reading Room. He always approached the museum in a flurry of expectation not untouched by reverence. One had to be "over twenty-one" to use the Reading Room, and a jovial, plum-cheeked guard at the wicket gate inevitably put Barry through a mock interrogation. "Come on, lad," he would chivy, "if you're passed the age of consent, I'm Lord Mayor o' London." After the requisite banter, Barry would be admitted into the vast dome of knowledge to take a seat at one of the luxurious leather desks and go about the business of research.

One afternoon, he stopped at a nearby publishing house to arrange for the printing of *Honour*. The proprietor had his thirteen-year-old son helping after school that day. The boy was fascinated by the visitor. "The first actor I remember seeing off the stage," he recalled, "was a dark dashing fellow in a cape-coat, or a cloak, who swung into my father's office one day to see about the printing of a play. He seemed a striking figure to me. That was Maurice Barrymore." (That fleeting vision, perhaps, first inspired George Arliss to seek the theatrical career which he so eminently achieved.)

Squire Bancroft, another denizen of the Mitre, asked the visitor to supper. Seven years before, on the eve of Barry's departure for America, Bancroft had offered him a place in his company at the Prince of Wales's Theatre. Barry, unsure of his future, had refused. At supper, the renowned actor-manager again mentioned employment, this time at Theatre Royal, Haymarket, which he and his wife had recently leased. Barry acknowledged the great compliment, informing Bancroft that two young children in America, and a third due that winter, would prohibit his wife from traveling to England.

At the Bancrofts' table that evening, Maurice Barrymore met a woman, whose impact was immediate, nearly hypnotic. Madame Helena Modjeska was nine years older than he, compelling for temperament more than structured beauty, but distinguished by long blue-black hair and large dark eyes which seemed to reflect the same improbable hue. The love child of a merchant's widow and a Polish prince, she was passionate, unconventional, ambitious, a devout Catholic, and an actress of shattering power.

The lady's reputation was not unknown to Barry. They had journeyed to America in the same year, she to escape political persecution from Germans ruling her native Poland. With her husband Karol, Count Bozenta Chlapowski—the title, some said, was bogus—and a group of compatriots, she had established a Utopian colony on the model of the Brook Farm in California's Anaheim Valley. Residents of nearby Los Angeles were shocked by these Polish litterateurs, artists, actors, and musicians, who shared produce among themselves, and, just as easily, passion. Modjeska, while the Count sputtered, entertained an intense affaire with young Henryk Sienkiewicz, who, "seated at a table in the shade of the pepper trees fitfully writing and smoking cigarettes," began the Roman epic that would be *Quo Vadis?*

But these idealistic Bohemians, accustomed to studios, theaters, libraries, were not farmers. Livestock began to perish from improper feeding; alfalfa died from lack of attention; young fruit trees withered. One day their barn burned to the ground while the colony symphony was "revelling in Bach out in the shade of the oak trees." In June of 1878, the Polish Brook Farm was dissolved, and Modjeska returned to the stage. Despite her pronounced accent, she held audiences "with the spell of an enchantress," quickly gaining an avid following in America and England. She was about to depart on a tour of the English provinces when she met Barry at the Bancrofts'.

Since he courted Georgie Drew, Barry had not wanted another woman. He had not ruled out the possibility. Occasional fascination and its physical fulfillment, he assumed, did not weaken the bonds of marriage. This assumption, as spontaneous as his disregard for conventional society, was first tested by his attraction to Modjeska. She was mutually drawn to the "dark dashing fellow," and shared his liberal views. In fact, Barry found her tendency to intellectualize them her one tiresome characteristic. They were inseparable in the days before her provincial tour began. Count Bozenta, it appeared, was conditioned to such eventualities.

ROYAL COURT THEATRE
SATURDAY, SEPTEMBER 24TH, 1881
AT 8.45
A PLAY IN FOUR ACTS, ENTITLED
HONOUR
FOUNDED ON
L'Honneur De La Maison, OF M. M. LEON BATTU
AND MAURICE DESVIGNES
BY MAURICE H. BARRYMORE

Preceded, punctually at 8, by
To Parents and Guardians
BY TOM TAYLOR

"A large audience assembled to give matters a good start," reported *The Era*, "and to offer encouragement to those whose endeavor it is evident will be to keep up the *prestige* of the house." The brilliant gathering responded enthusiastically to Barry's play, and, in the case of a commercial clerk of seventeen, irrationally. The hapless youth, in a one-shilling gallery seat, "fell over head and ears in love" with Louise Moodie as *Helene*. After the performance, he waited for the beautiful actress in Sloane Square. As she was stepping into her carriage, he ran across the street and threw himself on his knees before her, flourishing a revolver "with the appalling declaration that if she did not favour his burning suit, he would immolate her on the spot." The lady screamed; her servant collared the assailant. "The probable result of his appearance before a Magistrate," predicted *The Era*, "will be his transfer during a couple of years to a House of Correction, his father judging some such punishment necessary to cool his ardour."

The critics were decidedly less demonstrative. *The Theatre* reported that the play "was received with great applause by a crowded house," but no one heralded the advent of a new playwright. "Mr. Barrymore has followed the original pretty closely, his most noticeable departure springing from his desire to accommodate his work to English prudery, and to gloss over the sin of the heroine . . . Nothing is gained by this. Indeed, it appears to us that a great deal has been lost so far as the value of the drama is concerned," *The Era* decided, agreeing with the author. "For two acts *Honour* goes pleasantly along, and there is promise of an interesting play; but subsequently it, so to speak, falls all to pieces. There is plenty of gloom, plenty of sorrow, plenty of tears." Barry took little satisfaction from John Clayton's decision to eliminate the mock marriage and return the play to its original premise.

Before indifferent critical response thoroughly discouraged the playwright, a surprising development diverted him. "There was an almost unanimous prophecy among the theatrical critics of the day that the new play could not probably have a 'run,'" explained the man from *The Theatre*. "It was denounced as 'dreary,' 'disagreeable,' 'repulsive,' and utterly incapable of pleasing a British audience. These prophecies have not as yet been fulfilled. The play does please the public; it actually does 'draw,'" the critic marveled; "and the public, in all parts of the house, from the stalls to the gallery, gives a verdict of 'interesting and exciting,' instead of 'repulsive and dreary.'"

When Barry sailed for America, there was STANDING ROOM ONLY at the Royal Court.

Georgie, five months pregnant, had withdrawn from the cast of *One Hundred Wives*. Without their leading lady, the faltering Gosche-Hopper Company disbanded. "Two seasons of *One Hundred Wives*, despite the support of Georgie Drew Barrymore and a generally excellent cast," conceded DeWolf Hopper, "disposed of what was left of my heritage and I returned to Broadway to look for a job on my own merits." Mrs. Barrymore returned to Philadelphia to await the birth of her third child and the return of her husband.

Barry's exhilaration at the popular acceptance of *Honour* was contagious. The inmates of 119 North Ninth Street rejoiced with their resident playwright. Georgie observed, not without foreboding, the preponderance of Madame Modjeska in Barry's London commentary. She had experienced the impact of the actress when Modjeska played Philadelphia. She could imagine the impact of the woman. Georgie said nothing about it; her husband soon had harassment enough.

Certain English theatrical commentators did not take kindly to London successes, critical or not, by American authors, expatriots or not. A piece to this effect by J. Palgrave Simpson appeared in *The Theatre*, stating that only after rehearsals had begun was it discovered to be a "mere translation." Simpson recounted the "mortification and annoyance of the management" before contradicting himself. "Fortunately the term 'original' had never been used in any advertisement," he wrote; "and on all the bills the play was frankly announced as 'founded on the *Honneur de la Maison.*'" Having assailed Barry's integrity, the critic proceeded to annihilate his creative ability. "The language was considered so weak, that a distinguished dramatic author, known for excellence and strength of his dialogue, was requested to 'write up' the more powerful scenes, and did so with good effect. Another celebrated dramatist undertook to render the ends of Acts I. and III. more dramatically effective, and, cutting away the fifth Act of the original, to invent an entirely new and striking denouement for the conclusion of the play in the fourth. After sundry tribulations with the original adapter," Simpson concluded, "*Honour* appeared before the public on Saturday, the 24th September, was received with great applause by a crowded audience and has since drawn large houses."

Barry did not have to guess at the origins of this contradictory and fanciful piece of slander. As if to verify his assumption, an apologetic letter arrived from John Clayton, stating that Simpson had "misinterpreted certain disclosures in an interview." The Royal Court manager, who had so resented Barry's intrusion, did not mention that he was the critic's adopted son. There was little consolation in Clayton's apology, nor in the defense of American newspapers.

"Barrymore is the hero of another dramatic sensation in London," the *Spirit of the Times* upheld. "*The Theatre* says that John Clayton purchased his new play, *Honor*, as an original work, and was horrified to find it an adaptation of an old French piece. Hold on! There must be some mistake. The same play, *The Legion of Honor*, was done here at the Park, and the *Spirit* pointed out its French original. The subject was widely discussed in the papers, and it was noted then that Barrymore had another version of the piece. At no time did Barrymore represent his adaptation as original." The author did not take it up. Despite the continued success of *Honour*, his debut as a playwright, his return to London had been enough tainted. He remained silent, determined to prove in future, beyond a doubt, that Maurice Barrymore was a playwright.

In New York, soon afterwards, Lester Wallack asked after Lionel. "He is in the best of health," Barry replied, "and I am very proud of him. He is in fact the only thing the newspapers have not accused me of taking from the French."

The disappointed playwright turned to *Homeward Bound*, but the intricate drama confounded him. He discussed the problem with Julian

Magnus, a friend from Wallack's company, whose versatility had impressed Barry. While serving as Lester Wallack's press agent, he moonlighted as music critic for *The Graphic*, acted, played first violin at the Grand Opera House and cornet at the Terrace Garden, all the while writing plays. Magnus contributed much from his varied experience to the discussion of *Homeward Bound*. They decided to collaborate on the project when other commitments allowed. Barry had accepted a lucrative offer as leading man in the touring wing of the Boston Theatre's Double Company, which would present plays simultaneously in Boston and on the road during the 1881–82 season. Whenever there were booking breaks during the New England tour, the actor-author returned to the Lambs' in New York for work with Julian Magnus. During one of these sessions, he was called to Philadelphia.

On February 15, 1882, another son was born to Georgie Drew Barrymore. Mrs. Drew held the infant in her arms just after its appearance. "He looks like little Greengoose," she said, "the pretty lad in the story book." This time, both sides of the family were considered. The child was named John Sidney Blyth Barrymore.

Barry toured again that spring for the Boston Theatre, then returned to New York. In the unlikely atmosphere of the Lambs' Club smoking room, he and Julian continued their labors. Barry loved the Lambs'. The ease of comradeship among his peers stimulated his work and his wit. "Maurice Barrymore was one of the best beloved as well as one of the most brilliant members of the club," noted author Gustav Kobbé. "When he was at his best his speech was so salted with epigrams he never failed to have an admiring audience."

One afternoon, a gift arrived for the new clubhouse from Joseph Jefferson—one of his own paintings. The venerable actor fancied himself a gifted artist in oils, although his work was merely illustrative. Out of respect for the donor, no one would admit this. His picture, a leafy landscape entitled *Summer*, was ceremoniously hung in the lobby of the club, where a group of young actors happened to be lamenting the approach of the hot months and the inevitable lack of work. "Why not save your money in winter," Barry suggested, "and live like a gentleman the rest of the year? You know," he added, pointing to Jefferson's landscape, "summer is not half so bad as it's painted."

He liked best the hour after the theater, about 11:30, when the club filled with players returned from their labors, keyed up, ready to make a night of it. The one bartender always had his hands full at that time, as thirsty actors all at once crowded around. One busy night, Barry was alongside an impatient leading man, who repeatedly demanded a horse's neck. Finally, the harassed bartender approached him. "Now, what was your order, sir?"

"Well, I did want a horse's neck," replied the actor, "but I suppose I shall have to take a piece of the hoof now."

"My dear fellow," interjected Barry, "this is no one-horse club."

Work proceeded amid diversions of the smoker. *Homeward Bound* was entered for copyright on June 28, 1882, "a new play by Maurice H. Barrymore and Julian Magnus." The authors at once sent a copy of the manuscript to Lester Wallack.

Before the summer holiday began, Barry received an offer from John Stetson, Helena Modjeska's manager. Madame would tour America in the fall; she wished to have Mr. Barrymore as her leading man. Barry was flattered by an offer from the illustrious Modjeska, but, considering their London intimacy, was reasonably apprehensive about the situation. He would consent, he told Stetson, only if provision were made for his wife and children to accompany him—at best, a curious strategy.

Documents from John Stetson reached Long Branch later that summer. The pleasure of all Barrymores was requested for the coming season in Modjeska's private railroad car. Barry wished to accept. Georgie had no good reason to object. She cued him in the vast repertoire of leading men that he was expected to know, supervised the packing of trunks, interviewed for a qualified nanny who would care for three children in a cramped touring car. Mrs. Drew, deeply attached to her six-month-old grandson, argued that he was too young for the journey, but Georgie was still nursing him and would not leave him behind. Mrs. Drew was somewhat appeased by her daughter's choice for a nanny: Miss Adelaide Stover, an Englishwoman, who, starched and strait-laced, Georgie said, "was the picture of Mrs. Gilbert doing a 'nanny' at Daly's."

Beyond farewells at West Philadelphia, Nanny quieted the children. Barry was absorbed in the study of *Romeo*. Georgie gazed out of the window.

In Boston, Madame Helena Modjeska waited in her palace car *Poland*.

ACT THIRD

One moment of inspiration is worth all the traditional acting in the world.

MAURICE BARRYMORE

XV

SINCE FIRST SEEING Maurice Barrymore at Daly's six years before, Amy Leslie had become his most ardent and accurate observer. As an impressionable young woman, she nurtured an enduring infatuation for him. As erstwhile drama critic of the Chicago *Daily News*, she nonetheless maintained a certain objectivity. Apropos of the Modjeska tour she noted his utter lack of self-consciousness. "Notwithstanding his own physical beauty, which is exceptional," she wrote, "Maurice Barrymore has so little of the saving grace of vanity that his garb is a Petruchio wedding outfit the year around. He is never aware of his good looks, from which he cannot escape, and even on the stage he is careless about his dress to the point of eccentricity. He cares less about the adulation of feminity, which swamps him all seasons."

Had Barry been vain or more deliberate, he might have suspected the combination of his apprehensive wife, his discarded lover and her defensive husband. As it was, he stood unsuspecting at the center of a potential maelstrom, assuming, since Georgie was with him now, that Modjeska would let the past rest, that Count Bozenta would react, as he had in London, with equanimity. Barry was flattered to be Madame's leading man, and, although playwrighting remained his ultimate goal, was more excited than he had ever been before at the prospect of acting. The dedicated actress, he assumed, saw only his potential as leading man.

It was true that her manager, John Stetson, considered the acquisition of Maurice Barrymore a coup. "Mr. Stetson," Madame noted, "was very proud to have engaged that 'dandy leading man,' as he called him, for me." And the actress, herself, was encouraged to have a partner that would augment her drawing powers with American audiences. Her interest, however, was more than professional, and Madame, it was known in theatrical circles, possessed the will to implement her desires. (Once, dur-

169

ing a performance of "Camille," when annoyed by the chirping of a real canary in a cage, "she coolly took down the cage and threw it, bird and all, out of the window, and then quietly turned to have her heart broken by *Armand*'s father. It looked cruel," noted the New York *Tribune* "but a queen of art must not be interrupted in her fine moods by such a pigmy voice of mere nature as pipes through a canary's throat.")

Six weeks in Boston postponed for a time the intimacy of the palace car. That would come later with overland journeys and one-night stands. For longer engagements, Madame demanded something more suitable than a railroad yard. John Stetson complied with a number of rooms en suite at the Tremont House for his star and her husband, with adjoining rooms for her two maids. Stetson planned to house the Barrymores in comparable luxury. Amelia Fisher had other plans for her favored young man. When she insisted that he and his family stop at 2 Bulfinch Place, Barry, with Georgie concurring, readily accepted. Even Nanny Stover, harboring second thoughts about her theatrical venture, deemed Miss Fisher's establishment most acceptable.

John Stetson, the manager who so catered to Madame and her leading man, was a native Bostonian, self-made, gruff and tender-hearted, an instinctive showman anxious to exhibit his prestigious new stars. The Modjeska-Barrymore combination, he reckoned, would win for his Globe Theatre the elusive patronage of Boston's elite, which he had previously sought by starring his wife, Kate Stokes, an ex-circus rider, in a series of lurid melodramas. Stetson exploited every possible means to advertise his plays and stars. Through his considerable influence, he even had a locally manufactured boot polish named for Modjeska. A dubious honor at best, it also proved confusing and embarrassing when the manager later had playbills posted around the city proclaiming, "MODJESKA at the GLOBE."

Stetson exerted his considerable influence once more to have the boot polish renamed.

The manager's lack of taste was compensated by his respect for those that possessed it. Unschooled in history and literature, he aimed to please those that were. Ever solicitous, he attended all rehearsals so that the stage manager might apply directly if anything were needed. While rehearsing the fifth act of *Adrienne Lecouvreur*, which would open the Boston engagement, Madame noted a discrepancy in the scenery.

"What's the matter?" asked Stetson from the first row.

"The fireplace does not suit the scene," answered his star, "it ought to be Louis Quinze."

"Wait a moment, Madame," replied Stetson. "What did you say— Louie who?"

"Louis Quinze," repeated the actress, whereupon Stetson called the chief carpenter to the footlights.

"Where is this man, Louie Kantz?" he asked. "Bring him to me immediately; I want him to give Madame another fireplace—he must have it ready for the opening." The carpenter turned to the stage manager. The stage manager, biting his lip, turned to Barry. Barry addressed Stetson:

"Louis Quinze is not here, poor man; he died and was buried some time ago."

"Confound it!" replied Stetson. "Never mind, Madame; we may find what you want in other theatres. I'll attend to it directly."

As rehearsals progressed, Barry was swamped by the feats of memory expected of him. To the plays previously announced—*Adrienne Lecouvreur, Lady of the Camellias, Romeo and Juliet, Frou Frou*—were added *As You Like It, Twelfth Night* and *Odette.* Georgie cued him as usual, and "Aunt" Amelia, even Nanny Stover were recruited to assist. Modjeska also helped, though a forgetful leading man was merely one of her worries. "During the rehearsals," she said, "I noticed that my stage manager was doing some guesswork, and that it would be necessary for me to take the direction of plays in my hands. Every scene had to be rehearsed and conducted by me, even the grouping of people, the lights, and scenery." But she faced Barry's difficulty with patience unusual for her, repeating scene after scene until he knew them. Nerves were understandably strained as the opening approached. The last rehearsal of *Adrienne* was suddenly halted when the star and her leading man fell weeping into one another's arms. Barry's tears were of frustration at repeatedly fluffing his lines; Madame's merely tears of sympathy for her tormented leading man.

They were not in vain. "Manager Stetson may congratulate himself upon the auspicious opening of Mme. Modjeska's American Tour," allowed the Boston *Post*, on October 3, 1882, adding that her performance seemed "intensely realistic," particularly in her scenes with *Maurice*, "in which she declares her love for him. These were, perhaps, her best scenes and she enacted them with an earnestness that made the beholder feel that she really loved the man with the whole strength of her nature. Mr. Barrymore made a very manly and graceful *Maurice.*"

The new team was greeted rapturously by commentators and patrons alike. They were strikingly beautiful on stage together, their love-making "natural" and "restrained," eliminating "unnecessary clutching and clawing." As one critic explained it, "She rests upon his bosom in a picturesque way that is pleasing to the eye." Their effect was nearly hypnotic. Forgetting his lines as *Maurice De Saxe*, Barry lapsed unconsciously into *Armand*'s lines from "Camille," requiring Madame to follow suit. So beautifully did they play the wrong scene that the audience, assuming that the actors were demonstrating their artistry, cheered wildly at the finish.

President Chester A. Arthur applauded their *Romeo and Juliet* later that week from a flag-draped stage box, although one reviewer found Madame's imperfect English "wretchedly unfit for *Juliet's* verse." Her *Rosalind*, in *As You Like It*, was better received. The play proved tremendously popular with audiences, mainly because of the "varied, witty and loving scenes" with *Orlando*. That Shakespearean role was deemed the finest portrayal of Barry's career. The worst said of it, by the *Advertiser* critic, was that "Mr. Barrymore's *Orlando* showed such genuine feeling and such lively appreciation of text and situations that its faults of style were easily excused."

When the company boarded palace car *Poland* for New York, the teaming of Modjeska-Barrymore was already considered a theatrical event. John Stetson's acumen was applauded by all; all, that is, except Mrs. Barrymore.

Stetson had furnished a "miniature palace on wheels" for the tour. The exterior of the car was painted a rich wine color; interior woodwork, hangings and frescoing were tasteful, finely finished. The walls of the main lounge were lined with well-stocked bookcases, hung with colorful English landscapes in oils. Large China vases were set about the room, always filled with fresh flowers. Madame's salon and boudoir were separated from the main section by the manager's office, where Mr. Stetson's representative did the company paper work. She attempted to distribute the rest of the company to her own particular specifications. Touring protocol, she announced, required her leading man to sleep in the palace car along with herself, her husband, Stetson's agent, and her maids. Mrs. Barrymore and her three children, their Nanny, and the supporting players were assigned to an adjoining car, along with stagehands, baggage and scenery.

Before the New York state line was crossed, Mrs. Barrymore invoked protocol far more basic. Under no conditions whatsoever, she informed Madame, would she sleep apart from her husband. Provisions were hurriedly made for the Barrymores to be together. It was the first exchange between the two strong-willed women, and, curiously, Georgie came away from it with more than the assurance of her husband's company. From that first encounter, she was drawn to the magnetic forty-two-year-old actress, and Mme. Modjeska, in turn, to the willful Mrs. Barrymore, sixteen years her junior.

The entire company would stay on board during the week at Brooklyn's Park Theatre, settling into their home-on-wheels before arduous touring began. While they were side-railed near Grand Central Terminal, the rigors of railroad yards o' nights became readily apparent. So, too, did the refinements of Madame's life on the road. Thunder of passing trains, banging of switch engines contrasted sharply the gracious formality within. The Bozentas, devoted epicures, had installed a Polish chef for the journey. His culinary specialties were served often and well amid the fine silver and linen of the dining compartment. The Barrymores, Stetson's agent, the two company members next in importance were invited to join the Bozentas daily for luncheon and dinner. They were seated according to their importance in the troupe: Barry at Madame's right; Georgie at the end of the table.

"Mme. Modjeska's engagement at the Park Theatre, Brooklyn," reported the New York *Herald*, "was inaugurated last night with a brilliant performance of *Frou Frou*, before a crowded audience." Critics praised Barry's *de Sartorys*, the unforgiving husband, while patrons expressed disappointment that he had not played *Paul Valreas*, the young lover. Barry had insisted, against Madame's better judgment, upon taking the character part. In future, he would seldom be allowed that luxury.

"Maurice Barrymore was one of those handsome men who also have the rare gift of winning all hearts," observed Madame. "He was much admired by women, but was too intellectual to be a mere matinee idol. He was equally liked by men and women. Sentimental girls used to send him flowers, to his great amusement. They even went so far as to send him white lilies, which were always received with a roar of laughter. His best parts were *Armand, Orlando*, and *Valreas* in *Frou Frou*." Gallery girls must be appeased! At the next performance, as *Dudley*, Barry again clutched Madame picturesquely to his bosom in *Mary Stuart*.

The first leg of the tour included Griswold's Opera House, Troy, New York, for three performances, then the Leland Theatre in Albany, where most of the *Diplomacy* company had taken ill four years before. During two weeks at the Philadelphia Opera House, the Barrymore entourage stopped at North Ninth Street. Mrs. Drew was on a Western tour with Joseph Jefferson, winning further laurels as *Mrs. Malaprop*, but the visitors were kept informed of her progress. Tibby clipped newspaper reports of her stepmother's travels—as she did of the Barrymores' and John Drew's—pasting them neatly into large scrapbooks. "In Galveston," she proudly read to Georgie, "playgoers who had not been out for twenty years braved severe weather with hundreds of others to fill the seats and jam the aisles of the Opera House."

Lionel, Ethel, and the baby reveled in the solicitude of Aunt Tibby and Uncle Googan and the servants. Mrs. Kinloch was confined to her room, but the insistent ringing of her little bell was a constant reminder of her presence. When Georgie considered leaving the children in this environment more suitable than a touring car, objection came from an unexpected source. Madame implored her not leave them behind; whatever her designs on their father might have been, she had developed a strong attachment to the children, particularly three-year-old Ethel. Madame's only daughter had died in infancy twenty years before.

Intact, the entourage departed for Washington, D.C., and a successful week at the National. Four weeks in New York followed. Madame and her party moved with accustomed pomp into the Clarendon House. The Barrymores settled with their brood at Miss Alice Judson's in Gramercy Park.

When they opened *As You Like It* at the Booth, there were some critical reservations about Madame's *Rosalind*. Barry's *Orlando* was a revelation. John Stetson had expected as much. Aware of his leading man's special qualifications, the manager had given particular attention to the play's wrestling scene, providing ropes and stakes for the match, as if it were a prize fight. To play *Charles*, the wrestler, Stetson had hired Lew Brown, a two-hundred-pound professional wrestler and baseball player. The participation of an English champion and an American professional promised verisimilitude, eliciting much comment from the press, and equaling Modjeska-Barrymore love-making as an audience draw. It also became an added concern for Madame, when her dandy leading man and his sparring partner, playing to the house, were carried away by their own athletic prowess. The lighter Barrymore, challenged by his hulking opponent, had used him pretty roughly during the Boston run. Brown determined to have some fun of his own in New York. When Barry made a rush for him on opening night, he was greeted with a grapevine clinch. Brown would not go down. Barrymore would not ask the favor. The audience, aware that they beheld a most realistic interpretation, reacted as they might have in a sports arena. From the wings, Madame watched with extreme anxiety, not knowing where the scene would go. Finally, after several minutes, Barry was forced to his knees, but he was up in an instant. Catching the big man with a sharp turn, he vigorously put him on his back. "The match is uncommonly well acted by Maurice Barrymore, as *Orlando*, and Lew Brown, as *Charles*," noted the *Dramatic News*. "The two men have a Graeco-Roman contest which excites the spectators, and *Charles* is thrown so heavily at the close as to account for his swoon."

Reviewers were enthralled. "Mr. Barrymore has improved so much since his Fifth Avenue *Orlando*," wrote the *Dramatic News*, "as to rank next to Charles Coghlan in his performance of this very difficult part. He looks and dresses the character admirably, and his voice has gained in volume and clearness. On the whole, his *Orlando* was an agreeable surprise to those who have watched his career as an actor, and he fairly shares the honors of the evening with the star."

"Few actors known to modern theatre-goers better realize the hero of Shakespeare's delightful comedy than does Mr. Barrymore," added Edward Fales Coward, dramatic editor of the *World*, in a special column devoted to Barry's performance. "His muscular figure, manly force, and romantic bearing make his *Orlando* an ideal one from a physical standpoint; while his poetical temperament and hearty warmth of manner easily account for the love he inspires in *Rosalind* at first sight . . . There is nothing mawkish in his sentiment; it is honest and manly, and therein lies the secret of his success in this attractive part . . ."

Such praise during the first two weeks at the Booth would have presented a challenge to most actors. Barry did not take it up. Other concerns occupied him in New York that winter, after *Homeward Bound*, his sensitive evocation of his British colonial beginnings, was returned by Lester Wallack. It would have been a noble experiment in good times, the manager said, but the old gentleman was not experiencing them. Compounding his good-natured extravagance and his devotion to old comedy, the current theatrical trend uptown had hurt Wallack's Theatre. He finally made the move uptown that year, building a new theater at Broadway and Thirtieth Street, across from Daly's. He even made an attempt at popular melodrama, but his heart was not in it.

Barry was relieved by the return of *Homeward Bound*, feeling, somehow, that this work was too personal to be handed from agent-to-manager, desk-to-desk. With the approval of Julian Magnus, his collaborator, the author set aside what was undoubtedly his best play, returning to a project less of himself but far more propitious. Modjeska had read *A Bitter Expiation*, Barry's Russian melodrama. It impressed her, she said. With some rewriting, maybe a Polish setting, she told him, it might be a suitable vehicle for herself. Whatever the outcome, Madame reasoned, at least it would keep the author close at hand. Barry needed no further encouragement. Retitling the play, *Nadjezda*, he began fashioning what he determined would be Madame's supreme achievement.

Nadjezda obsessed him. He stopped infrequently at the Lambs' now, spending what little time he took away from his writing at Oscar's, opposite the Academy of Design on Fourth Avenue, where young men struggling in art or literature gathered. Occasionally, Winslow Homer or other established artists on business at the Academy stopped in, but the regulars had yet to make their names: Frank R. Stockton, author of the whimsical "Rudder Grange" stories, still to win fame with "The Lady or the Tiger?"; W. M. Laffan, not yet the magnate he became as J. P. Morgan's colleague and editor of the New York *Sun;* Charles Warren Stoddard, whose "South Sea Idylls" would give contemporary literature a fresh voice; William H. Rideing, of Whitelaw Reid's editorial staff at the New York *Tribune*, who would become one of the best journalists of his time; Brander Matthews, who, at Columbia University, would be America's first professor of dramatic literature. Each of them, and others no less promising, had his own seat at Oscar's round table. They sat good-humoredly, left to themselves by other customers, in clouds of infinite tobacco "with much chaff blowing between us," William Rideing remarked, "and the flapping of the wings of ambitions."

"No one was hailed with more gladness in our symposia at Oscar's than

Maurice Barrymore," Rideing attested. "He would drift in after the play, one of the handsomest fellows in town, well-bred and well-read, captivating in manner, and unspoiled by any of the affectations which cling like paint to so many young actors when they move outside the theatre. His mobile and sensitive face was as pallid as that of Edwin Booth, and, like Booth's, his deep and significant eyes gathered intensity in contrast with its ivory whiteness. He had some repose then, and was not the flighty creature he afterward became through burning his candle at both ends and in the middle, all at once."

Barry joined in the repartee at Oscar's, winning the admiration of this artistic circle. "He was nimble in wit, amiable, courteous, patient under attack, and aglow with enthusiasm," Rideing added. "I say patient under attack. I have seen him bear annoyance as only a strong man can, and shrug his shoulders without other reprisal than a scathing word or two which made the person to whom they applied aware of his own ridiculousness." One Oscarite who persisted in begging the question, muddling it with all sorts of irrelevance, could not be shut up until Barry hit the right definition for him. "The cuddlefish of conversation," he remarked. "It's no use to follow him. If you do he will at once disappear in the cloud of his own exudations."

It was not, however, repartee which drew Barry to Oscar's. William Rideing comprehended the reason for the actor's attraction to the literary round table. "The leading man at the leading theatres, the ideal *jeune premier*, he cared little or nothing for his success as an actor. What he always wanted to do was to write plays: that ambition was ever in his mind, ever on his tongue. In all other things than play-writing he was one of the least vain of men." But when his fellow Oscarites responded, Rideing recalled, "Barry would stay, if you could, till dawn or long after dawn, gaining rather than losing brilliance as the hours passed and the world began to shake its chains. Out would come his latest play, not a manuscript, not even notes, but a rush of turbulent ideas not yet committed to paper. They came and went in and out of his mind like shooting stars, dazzling him with their promise, and then eluding him."

Making a diagram of the stage with matches, ashes, or the tricklings from a glass, he would indicate the action with his finger. His synopsis would be lucid and detailed at first, the characters mentioned by name, but as he warmed up, he would abbreviate, substituting "He" and "She" while action would be described by gesticulations and running commentaries, peppered with sulphurous expletives. "You see! You see!" admonished Barry, at the frenzied climax of a recitation. "He comes in here, R.U.E., the damned blackguard! She's standing at a table, centre, arranging flowers. Sweet as a morning in June. He sneaks toward her. She sees him, and cries 'Ah!' Taken by surprise. Horrified, clutches the back of a chair. He seizes her by the wrist and drags her toward him, and whispers in her ear. She drops to the floor, moaning, paralyzed. Paralyzed! He—the nefarious rotter! grinds his teeth and is alarmed." By now, the narrator was wavering somewhere between total absorption in his roles and horror at the situation. "The scoundrel springs to the doors, locks all of them. Shuts the windows. Pulls down all the shades. Blows out the lamps. You see? Comes back to her. Snarls. He has a knife in his hands, the hoofed and horned lecher, the God-forsaken son-of-a-bitch!"

On that, or something like it, the curtain would fall, and the breathless narrator would light another cigarette "I am writing that little bit for myself," he explained. "I see myself in it. I *feel* myself in it. And Georgie will do the widow."

Discussions of Barry's plays or classical literature or French romances moved at closing time to the lodgings of Edgar Fawcett, prolific author of plays, novels and books of verse. Dawn creeping through closed blinds usually disclosed the symposium proceeding on a floor littered with glasses, ashes of tobacco, and books pulled from their shelves, books of Keats, Shelley, Swinburne, Tennyson, Baudelaire, English and French, opened to the pages that had been quoted through the night.

Occasionally, he still trained with Muldoon, recently crowned Champion Wrestler of the World in the Graeco-Roman style, who had left the police force under the weight of wrestling and coaching obligations. His prize pupil had that year won the heavyweight boxing championship, and England's former middleweight champion was anxious to meet him. John L. Sullivan did not disappoint Barry. The twenty-four-year-old advocate of the rough-and-ready school of bare-knuckle boxing was something of a braggart, but they took straightway to one another, spending hours in heated discussion of the prize ring, occasionally, to the delight of Harry Hill's patrons, illustrating their points in the ring. The hulking "Boston Strong Boy" restrained his style considerably for the gentleman amateur.

Even after such rigorous sessions, Barry usually returned to the Judsons' to write from the wee hours straight through till the following evening, often going directly to the theater without sleep. Georgie, while condemning this unhealthy practice, was nevertheless relieved to have her husband's rambles somewhat curtailed. She kept the Judson household humming, aided, now, by her three audible offspring. Nanny Stover endured. She could not fault the breeding of Miss Alice Judson, but she was somewhat skeptical of the lady's communal ménage. "Theatre folk!" she was given to muttering at times of particular agitation. Georgie would try comforting her with mock solicitations, repressing laughter that the put-upon gentlewoman inspired.

Barry labored through it all, fascinating younger Judsons with his industry in the parlor upstairs. Recalling the now-deceased weasel which he had once brought into their lives, the children harbored the utmost respect for Mr. Barrymore. "We admired his intelligence," Ally, who was ten at the time, later recalled. "That he reciprocated our sentiment in this respect proved our undoing. It all came about through a play which he was writing. Unfortunately of the opinion that my brother and myself were bright, he conceived the original idea of reading his climax to us to test its strength."

"A child is a natural critic," he announced, rolling his eyes in their flattered direction. "In their fearless young faces I shall be able to trace the effect of every line. Where they praise I shall have struck the right note." They disappeared into the upstairs parlor, where the author read *Nadjezda*, vividly acting each part for his excited audience of two.

"Now, sir," said Barry to the brother, "give us your opinion."

"It is well written," replied the precocious nine-year-old, knitting his brows, "and it is terribly interesting. The heroine, too, is perfectly lovely and is as natural as a real girl; but, Mr. Barrymore, I am sorry that you let your hero make that last speech. It was unmanly. No gentleman could have spoken it."

"Fluff! Rot!" snorted Barry. "You are immature. I should have remembered that the man-child is proverbially immature. But the woman-child" —he turned a softened gaze toward Ally—"the woman-child has instincts which are ever in advance of her years. Give me your opinion," he asked gently. "Speak."

"Oh," she gurgled, "the hero is be-yutiful, I think; perfectly be-yutiful! But the girl is such a silly! Really, Mr. Barrymore. Don't let her do what she did. No truly girl would do it. Please change it."

"Go away! Get out! Both of you!" erupted Barry. "You are a pair of —pair of—*idiots* . . ." The children reached the door. "*Japanese* idiots!" he hurled after them as they ran down the hall.

Palace car *Poland* headed West. Twelve weeks on the road lay ahead before the return to New York. They would be together constantly, eating and sleeping on the cars, rehearsing and performing in theaters.

Georgie's admiration of Modjeska increased; Modjeska, in turn, developed a deep, almost maternal affection for the spirited daughter of the Drews. Long philosophical conversations enriched the monotony of train travel as Madame, an ardent Catholic, related legends of her church with theatrical flourish. Georgie, never taken by her mother's stolid brand of Episcopalianism, was intrigued by Madame's relation of Holy Roman scripture. As they talked of the church and many things, Georgie discerned Modjeska's strong mystical strain. It proved contagious.

Georgie marveled also at the poise with which the star played hostess on the journey. It was not easy adjusting to the moods and irritations which came with morning coffee after sleepless nights, or to the forced intimacy of the unusual number of meals per diem, but Madame retained queenly serenity. "I do not always feel pleasant," she confided. "I used to lose my temper very often, so did my husband, but it was not wise for both of us to be excited at once, so we agreed that but one of us should lose his temper on any occasion while the other keeps calm."

"And does it always work?" asked Georgie.

"Perfectly," laughed Madame, "you see Charlie is excited all the time."

Karol Chlapowski, sometimes Count Bozenta, was the average husband of an exceptional wife. His understandable defensiveness was aggravated by his wife's attraction to her leading man, a condition which manifested itself in the Count's chronic agitation, usually vented upon Barry. Undercurrents apart, they made a comical pair. "Mr. Bozenta and my star support were celebrated from Rhode Island to Seal Rock as the two worst dressed men in America," Madame stated. "Bozenta is turned to a pillar of cigarette ashes every day by noon, his neckties are weird and irredeemable, and Barry was positively reckless in the color of vests and license in plaids." Amy Leslie, too, saw humor in the relations of the two men:

"It used to be the loveliest amusement of the season to catch Count Bozenta and Barrymore together when Modjeska petted Barry as her stage lover and faithful devotee everywhere. The count is a Blackstone for argument, and Barrymore, being eloquent, is quite as fond of pro and con." It was Bozenta's habit to blow a storm of cigarette ashes over himself, stop Barry, and, hoping for instant disagreement, hurl both the subject of argument and the answer at him. Aware of Barry's predilection for things British, the Count would rush up, spout such opinions as, "Maurice, wot you think off ze English comedian—he is a hopeless thing toujours, eh?" and dash off again. Once they had a classic squabble over a blackbird. "As obvious and blatant a blackbird as ever stole corn," decided Barry, but Bozenta insisted that it was a robin. The Count brought out tomes of imaginative authority, spouting wholly fictitious reminiscences of Audubon at Barry. And while he glibly quoted, the object of contention flew away.

Besides eight performances a week, fatigue of travel, and unceasing society in the touring car, Barry had *Nadjezda*. "The work was mainly done at night on the cars after everybody else had gone to bed," he explained, "and it was hard work at that." Occasionally, the insomniac Count would come upon the playwright working by gaslight at a small table in the lounge. Popping his head around the side of the entry way, Bozenta would call something contrived to irritate: "Wot you think off Gladstone, Maurice? For me no." While Barry gave an impassioned home rule defense of the grand old man, the count would scurry back to bed.

There were fortunately more congenial companions aboard. Before departure from New York, Lew Brown had left the troupe. It had been short notice to find a replacement with the special qualifications for

Charles, the wrestler, but Barry knew just the man. Billy Muldoon had accepted the job, and now proved a refreshing antidote to the persistent Count. He and Barry added some professional touches to the wrestling scene, working up a fancy-hold match in which Billy made a bridge and Barry jumped on him. But there was hardly room for proper exercise on the cars. About ten miles out of Cleveland, their first stop, the restless sportsmen had the train slow up, jumped off and jogged along the tracks into town, with Billy's beloved mastiff, Crix, at their heels. This became the usual procedure before each destination; once in town, they would seek a gymnasium.

The Euclid Avenue Theatre raised its prices for Modjeska's engagement: General admission, 75 cents and $1.00; reserved seats, $1.00 and $1.50; gallery, 25 cents. The Cleveland *Plain Dealer* chided Stetson for allowing such outrageous prices, but Barry, it turned out, gave them more than their money's worth. He and Billy, having located a gymnasium, followed an afternoon of rigorous exercise with a quantity of ale at a saloon. When they arrived at the theater, Georgie noted that "a funny little devil had hold of Barry." But the performance of *As You Like It* proceeded without incident toward the wrestling match. *Orlando*, as usual, threw *Charles*, fell on him to pin him down. Impulsively, however, Barry stuck his fingers into Billy's ribs, and started tickling him. Billy strained every bit of his will-power to suppress his laughter. "Barry, for God's sake, let up! D'ye want to have me make an ass of myself? Leggo me!" he pleaded in whispers. "Ow-w, won't you quit that?" But Barry went right on tickling. His victim was about to let out a terrific whoop, when the demands of the scene forced Barry to jump up and continue with the performance. "I'll get hunk with you for that, pal; you hear me?" said Muldoon, quietly, when the curtain fell.

"Well, so long as you don't break off a fin, or screw my head on the wrong way, it's up to you," Barry replied good-naturedly, and forgot all about it.

The next performance of *As You Like It*, two days later, progressed smoothly until the bout scene. When the two wrestlers sprang to the center of the ring, Muldoon picked up Barry, clapped him over one knee, spanked him soundly for half a minute "on the spot," according to Billy, "where he most needed it." Then he dropped the chastened *Orlando*, and the scene proceeded. The audience was hysterical. Madame was furious. Lionel, watching from the wings, was terrified. From that moment, the imaginative four-year-old avoided Billy Muldoon.

When the curtain fell, Barry went after his friend raging mad. Billy just looked at him and grinned. Seeing the humor of the thing, Barry let out a guffaw that the boys up in the gallery must have heard.

During a week at Macauley's Theatre, Louisville, Nanny Stover departed. She had simply had her fill of "theatre folk." Georgie again considered returning her progeny to Philadelphia. Madame again intervened. Her maids, Nascia and Hannah, would help tend the children. Jack was nearly a year old; Lionel was almost five, Ethel three and a half. They had adapted completely to the vicissitudes of touring. "The boy was always busy painting ships and railroad trains," Madame observed, "and Ethel was an actress. They composed some improbable dialogues and played them together. Lionel was always 'Pap,' and Ethel was 'Madame.' She could not pronounce all the letters of the alphabet, but she acted with conviction." Ethel adored Modjeska; watching her perform became the little girl's greatest treat. "I often saw her eager eyes," said Madame, "watching me from behind the scenes during the matinees."

When the actress would take the two oldest children to restaurants for special treats, usually the richest cakes with cream on top, Ethel would sit on her lap, talking incessantly, often unintelligibly in her excitement. Lionel was very serious, speaking, when he spoke at all, like an adult, keeping a respectful distance from his hostess. His reserve broke down, however, when Madame gave *chrusciki* parties in the palace car. At the sight of these little Polish cakes twisted into fanciful shapes and sprinkled with powdered sugar, Lionel would forget himself and plow into the appetizing mound.

Influenza struck the company at the Grand Opera House in St. Louis. When one of the child actors fell ill, Lionel was sought to substitute as *2nd Page* in *As You Like It*. Barry consented, but solemnly warned the stage manager, "At your own risk." Georgie patiently cued her son in the two lines and a song which the role required. The four-year-old, three months shy of five, proved a quick study. He entered with unruffled assurance for his debut. Letter perfect in his recitation, he was singing sweetly with *1st Page* when the fierce Muldoon appeared in the wings. The boy stopped the show with a piercing yell, and fled the stage, leaving *1st Page* to finish Shakespeare's ditty.

The Barrymores spent a good part of the following day convincing their first-born that Billy Muldoon was no ogre. He was sufficiently convinced to return to the stage for the matinee, but insisted that his mother accompany him. Since Nascia and Hannah were needed at the theater to dress Madame, and unable to tend the younger children, Georgie was forced to bring them along.

Mrs. Barrymore was pressed into service at the theater. Influenza had felled the actress who played *Celia;* the understudy was filling in elsewhere. Barry took Lionel in hand, helping him into his *Page's* costume. Ethel found a place behind the scenes from which to watch the performance. Jack played among costume bins in the dressing room while his mother prepared. When the callboy knocked at the door, she was ready, but the baby had fallen asleep. Hannah, who was to sit with him during the performance, had not arrived. Georgie wrapped her sleeping son in a shawl, carried him to the wings, where Billy Muldoon happened to be standing. Hearing her cue, she placed the bundle in Billy's arms, and rushed on stage. Clothing or laundry, Billy assumed, and was about to discard the bundle when it moved. Parting the swaddling, he discovered the child. Startled, he began to walk toward Georgie on the stage, stopping just in time to avoid the debut of another Barrymore.

THE RETURN TO CHICAGO OF MODJESKA, was heralded in the local papers, but the star did not monopolize the headlines. MULDOON TO WRESTLE BARRYMORE—proclaimed the *Tribune*, DEBUT OF A YOUTHFUL TRAGEDIAN. "Mr. Muldoon, champion wrestler of the world, is at present with the company in St. Louis, where his 'bout and fall' with Mr. Barrymore won great admiration from the audience, and was very flatteringly commented upon by the press." The *Tribune* predicted that a wrestling scene on stage would prove "a very attractive feature for all lovers of the manly art," hastening to add that "ladies will have an opportunity of seeing an exhibition from which they are debarred because of ordinary disadvantages attending such displays."

McVicker's Theatre was packed for the Chicago opening; silk hats in the orchestra anticipated *Orlando* and *Rosalind*, the gallery boys awaited Muldoon and Barrymore. Neither was disappointed, but the gallery carried the evening. During the wrestling match, at the decisive moment, the rapt silence of the house was broken. "Hey! Billy!" cried a clear voice from above. "Throw 'um up here."

After a week in Milwaukee and one-night stands in Terre Haute and Dayton, Barry presented *Nadjezda* to Madame. During a week in Pittsburgh, she requested the playwright to read his revised work in the privacy of her boudoir. Madame saw great potential in the dual role which Barry had fashioned for her, but she guarded her enthusiasm. Nights on the road, she summoned her leading man to read this act or that scene again. Notwithstanding the presence of Georgie and the children, Madame's attraction to Barry had flourished on tour. She was not a woman of small emotions; the very expansiveness which she lavished on the man's family craved fulfillment in the man himself. The Count sputtered as usual, but Georgie remained relatively calm. She knew how much the play meant to her husband; she assumed that renewed intimacy with Madame was not his concern. Besides, her admired Modjeska would not betray their friendship by pursuing her husband.

Academy of Music, Buffalo: three performances. Madame discerned Barry's exclusive dedication to his creation, but she persisted. Long discussions ensued in her private compartment: Was the play right for her? Would two parts tax her energies? They traveled into Canada. Toronto: three performances; a night in Hamilton. They crossed the border again into New York State. One-night stands: Utica; Syracuse; then Erie, Pennsylvania; and back to Auburn, New York. New York City was imminent, and two weeks at the Fifth Avenue. Madame was aware of the many starring offers Barry had received during the tour. She assumed that others awaited in New York. Nor would he have trouble, she was sure, finding a manager to present his play. Academy of Music, Rochester: two performances.

As they approached New York City, Mme. Helena Modjeska and Maurice H. Barrymore made a gentleman's agreement: *Nadjezda* would be the first play added to the repertoire of the 1882–83 season, on condition that he continue as leading man. Barry, in turn, stipulated that his wife must also be a member of the company. He had fashioned a role for her in *Nadjezda*, he confided, a role that only Georgie could play.

The author was elated; his star merely hopeful. She had yet to achieve her main objective, but she had, at least, guaranteed the presence of her manly *Orlando* for another season on the road.

XVI

THE BARRYMORES FOUND spring in New York when they arrived and green in Gramercy Park. Vitality permeated the city. After thirteen years building, a spectacular granite-towered suspension bridge connected lower Manhattan and Brooklyn, while the city made its way uptown in brownstone, extending the northern limit of fashion to Forty-second Street.

Away from the confining palace car for a few weeks, the visitors seemed gayer than ever to the waiting Judsons. Mrs. Barrymore's dancing eyes foretold new and slightly audacious events; her husband seemed relaxed and ready to participate. Ally and her brother were relieved that no new play in progress would challenge their critical powers. In fact, Mr. Barrymore seemed free of creative preoccupation that April. Upon arrival, he proposed hauling them and Ethel and Lionel off to the circus.

"Take care of them, won't you?" implored Miss Alice Judson.

"The best of care," Barry promised, "the very best."

When they reached the immense enclosure of the circus, Barry demonstrated his style of care to his delighted charges: "Think you can feed the animals without being in yourselves that upon which they make their meal?"

"Yes—oh yes, we can," replied the excited children, whose ages ranged from eleven to three.

"Know how to spend money if you have it?" asked Barry, giving them quantities from his pockets.

"Yes—oh yes," they repeated.

"Then go lose yourselves!" he ordered, before heading for the animal cages to inspect conditions of captivity. Where they seemed wanting, he waged impassioned pleas at startled keepers for better treatment. "It was typical of the gentle simplicity and eternal youth in Maurice Barrymore's contradictory nature," observed Amy Leslie, "that he should look after all sorts of dumb brutes and feathered singers just for the love of them."

The children tore around unattended for three hours. They bought all that they saw, ate all of the tantalizing circus fare that they craved, saw all of the side shows, fell into all of the puddles, talked to everyone who took their fancy. They poked every animal within reach, and examined the hind legs of any that was not caged. Lionel, to the extreme delight of his companions, went so far as to climb into the cage of the trick pigs. He was attempting to ride one of them, when his father arrived. Aware that the pig was getting the best of it, Barry cheered his son on until the afternoon session ended, and closing time had come. Reluctantly, Mr. Barrymore and his small, smeared, exhausted charges returned to Gramercy Park.

"So much did they appreciate this kind of care that they dilated upon its charms when they got home," stated Miss Alice, "with the result that they never knew such rapture a second time." Barry was incredulous when the women reprimanded him. After all, he had promised and given the very best of care.

Just around the corner from the Judsons', near the southwest corner of Irving Place and Seventeenth Street, Oscar Wilde had taken a house. The young leader of London's "aesthetic movement" had invaded America to lecture in his highly aesthetic velvet suit. Although his first play had yet to appear in New York, his much-publicized advent caused a great commotion in the city's literary circles. It caused a greater commotion at the Judsons' when the children ran to the front window on "sunny Oscar Wilde mornings" to watch him posture past, heading for his Fifth Avenue promenades. They had never before seen his like: long locks of hair under a Regency silk hat, coat of sage green velvet, gloves of shocking lavender, white walking stick, boutonniere the size of a peony. "Goodness," exclaimed Ally Judson, "it *is* a peony!"

The Barrymores met this motley phenomenon at the studio of Robert Blum, whose frescoed walls of strutting peacocks provided a perfect backdrop for Wilde's inspired trivia. He chattered exquisitely about nothing: The model posing for Blum, he decided, should wear his favorite colors—"cafe au lait and sage green, with a yellow tea rose"; the painter's "delicious tints," he said, "inspired the sensation of eating a yellow satin dress." The Barrymores watched, appreciating the performance, yet sensing Wilde's own endearing awareness of its artificiality. His monologue paled, however, when he commenced a predictable tirade on "callow America."

"So you see," concluded Oscar Wilde, "America is a most uninteresting place—no antiquities, no curiosities."

"My dear Mr. Wilde," replied Georgie Barrymore, "we shall have the antiquities in time"—she paused to scan him—"and we are already importing the curiosities."

Georgie continued her reign of slang at the Judsons', imparting gems which the children dared not repeat at home but which greatly increased their popularity with schoolfellows. She was a mimic, too, they discovered, delighting with her monkey faces. "She was able to screw her charming countenance into an unmistakable simian caste," Miss Alice shuddered, "and when a little realistic scratching was added to the performance it was real to awfulness."

One day, the youngsters were gathered in the front hall counseling Ally, who was aiming to buy some prizes off a bargain counter. Straw hats, she had read in the morning paper, were marked down to five and ten cents. "If they are good, really good, at five cents," advised Lionel, always practical, "you had better buy two."

"Mama," bawled Ally, "do you think we had better give five cents or ten cents for our hats?" The question was answered, recalled Mrs. Judson, "by a very silvery voice proceeding from a most gorgeously radiant Georgie, as she descended the stairs in full outing finery."

"Give ten cents, if you can, dear," advised Mrs. Barrymore. "It is hard to get a really good one for *less*." As Georgie nodded wisely, tilting the extravagant twenty-dollar article on her own head, Mrs. Judson began to laugh at the obvious contrast. But the children remained serious, looking gravely to their friend for help. Ally was afraid to spend too much, they explained, because the gasman was expected. The only five-dollar bill in the house was being saved to pay him. "If he would only come," they reasoned, "we could use some of the change for more straw hats." Here, on cue, the doorbell rang. Georgie, being nearest the door, opened it. A man, without looking up, thrust a bill into her hand.

"Gas," he announced curtly; "$5.75."

"*God help us!*" moaned Mrs. Barrymore in frenzied grief. Giving her a startled glance, noting her evident despair and elegant trappings, the gasman backed swiftly and silently down the stoop and bothered them no more than day. Georgia shut the door triumphantly, turned to her dumbstruck audience. "Hang the expense," she cried, "and buy a ten-cent one, dear!"

But the Judsons saw another side of Georgie during this visit. "Perhaps the only time she was not funny," Miss Alice said, "was when she used to kneel by the bedsides of her little ones and tell them legends of the Catholic Church." After kissing them good night, she would always leave them with the same promise: "If you are good and say your prayers, angels will come and stand around your beds." The Protestant Judson brood, listening from their own rooms, used to shiver in their beds—not from prejudice but fear. If something white should enter *their* rooms by mistake, how would they tell angels from ghosts?

Under Madame's tutelage, Georgie had converted to Catholicism while in New York. She was also determined to have her three children baptized into the faith. Arrangements were in progress, when business brought Mrs. Drew to the city. Georgie, hardly a fool, would never have mentioned her plans to the pillar of St. Stephen's Episcopal Church, but she was out with the children when her mother arrived. One of the younger Judsons, giving an unsolicited teatime recitation to the visitor, mentioned that she would soon be attending a christening. "How nice," responded Mrs. Drew casually, "and who is the lucky child? Is it one of your little cousins?"

"Oh no, Mrs. Drew," answered the child, "it's your grandchildren. We've never been inside a *Catholic* church before."

Louisa Drew's expression was indescribable. It must suffice to say that in reaction to it the child, who adored her, ran frightened from the room. She wrested further facts from poor Miss Alice, traversing the large drawing room with graduating rage as she listened. "Papists!" she cried. "Papists!" The term became a fearsome epithet as Louisa Drew repeated it.

When the Barrymores returned, Mrs. Drew launched her attack on the assumption that her incorrigible son-in-law had founded this infamy. Presently, to her further horror, she saw that it was her own daughter's doing. Barry, in fact, decidedly light-footed on the path of religion, looked with amused tolerance upon his wife's conversion. Suddenly realizing this, and recalling his Church of England upbringing, Mrs. Drew chose to consider her son-in-law an ally in the fruitless battle with her stubborn daughter. ("For a brief moment," Ethel recalled in later years, "Mummum was under the impression that she and Papa had something important in common—one of her incredibly few errors.") Unable to change Georgie's mind, Mrs. Drew implemented another tactic. When the Barrymores left for the theater that evening, she ordered Jack's necessities packed, and escaped with him to Philadelphia. Since Lionel and Ethel had already received proper Protestant baptism, she reasoned that the waters of Rome could not harm them. Jack, however, had been whisked off on tour before she could make similar arrangements for him.

At seven the next morning, the Reverend Doctor Rudder, rector of St. Stephen's, was awakened by Mrs. Drew's coachman. Shortly after eight o'clock, with Aunt Tibby and Uncle Googan as godparents, John Sidney Blyth Barrymore was welcomed into the Episcopal Church. Proudly, after the ceremony, black skirts swishing, Louisa Drew carried her grandson to the waiting brougham.

In New York that afternoon, Lionel and Ethel were hurried to the nearest Catholic Church. Lionel's godparents were Madame and Count Bozenta. Ethel's were the only other Catholics that Georgie could find on such short notice: Miss Veronica Murray, who ran a local theatrical boardinghouse, and Signor Perugini, an "Italian" tenor born plain John Chatterton in the Michigan backwoods, who, unbeknownst to Georgie, wasn't even Catholic, merely ambitious. He assumed that any association with the Barrymore-Drew clan would advance his career. Later, he married Lillian Russell for the same reason. She left the scoundrel after two months.

Modjeska-Barrymore were playing the Fifth Avenue, where Barry had made his New York debut eight years before under Augustin Daly's management. The elegant old house, which Daly had been forced to vacate, was reduced to playing touring companies, while the Governor had achieved new success at his own uptown theater. As the city spread uptown, Daly's Theatre had become the height of fashion, an American Comédie Française, said his more sophisticated patrons. Once again, Daly openings were brilliant social functions. Patrons, as they entered the richly appointed lobby, received programs from Chinese boys in oriental costume. Those of sufficient prominence—Chauncey Depew or Mark Twain or General Sherman—were greeted by the Governor himself, standing, as he once had at the Fifth Avenue before his failure, proudly by the ticket box at the stroke of eight.

More than elegant furnishings drew the elite. "The Four Hundred," it was remarked, "visit Daly's to learn from Rehan and Drew how they ought to behave." John Drew claimed his birthright. Suave and polished, the best-dressed man in New York, he shone in the Daly brand of comedy. Acknowledged as an upper-class matinee idol, he tended to play the role offstage as well. The Barrymores were amused by John's affectation, which was made more ludicrous by his wife's utter lack of it. Josephine accepted her husband's self-esteem with her usual equanimity; Barry and Georgie fought it with barbs and brickbats. John's sense of humor quickly returned. Self-preservation required it.

It was quite another matter with his stage partner, Ada Rehan. Georgie discovered a curious change in her old friend from the Arch. The carefree accomplice of ten years before seemed high-strung and nervous. Onstage, her "dazzling glee and delicious drollery" had made her Queen of High Comedy. Offstage, she was becoming bitter and distrustful. Retaining some of her intimacy with Georgie, she confided the reason for her extreme change. The reason was Augustin Daly. The Governor ruled her with almost hypnotic powers. "Daly must have been a great actor who could not act," observed Graham Robertson, a London-based painter and friend-of-the-famous. "He was rough and uncouth, with harsh utterance and uncultured accent; a singer without a voice, a musician without an instrument. But in Ada Rehan he found his means of self expression; Ada Rehan with her quaint charm and her gentle nature which he could mould to his will."

Not content with his amorous *Galatea*, nor with his faithful wife, for that matter, Daly also sought the favors of any available young woman in his company "Rehan was jealous to a psychotic degree," wrote Cornelia Otis Skinner, "and in Daly a sadistic streak, equally psychotic, prompted him to parade his conquests in front of her, driving her into near hysterical rages . . ." But he would always return to Ada, and she, each time more bitter, would always take him back.

Delighted audiences saw nothing of this. They saw only the lithe and artful playing of Drew and Rehan. And if they didn't see them, they read about them continually in William Winter's fawning *Tribune* reviews. With Mrs. Gilbert and James Lewis, who had both returned to the Daly fold, they became Broadway's "Big Four."

As palace car *Poland* headed westward, tedious trackside miles were vivified for Barry by his high-spirited progeny. The family was again intact. Before departing, Georgie had delegated her husband to collect their youngest son from Philadelphia. She chose not to accompany him, fearing the wrath of her mother. But, safe in the sanctity of Jack's recent baptism, Mrs. Drew had relinquished her grandson without incident. Heads against the window glass, eyes widened to every second of daylight, Lionel and Ethel—sometimes deigning to hold little Jack between them—swallowed the passing landscape. Indians and antelope and rivers elicited the loudest shouts, but every cow and cactus received its due. When an Indian jumped on the steps of the car for a ride between stops, Lionel had to be restrained from joining him.

The father was exhausted when they finally reached Oakland, the children inexhaustible. When Lionel and Ethel began swinging from the side rail of the ferry, Georgie dispatched their father to threaten them. The children desisted but begged Papa for a demonstration of his own athletic prowess. When the Oakland ferry nosed in at San Francisco, Lionel and Ethel were ecstatic, dockside spectators aghast: Maurice Barrymore was hanging over the side, nonchalantly doing chin-ups on the rail.

Once settled at the Occidental, children and unpacking left to Hannah, the Barrymores strolled out alone over the city's hills. San Francisco was a jumble of architecture—Spanish, Italian, French, mid-Victorian—but from the hill where Barry brought his wife at twilight for her first view of the Western metropolis, its misted landmarks took on a gentle symmetry. Georgie succumbed, as her husband had eight years before, to the luminous city with its rainbow fleet at Fisherman's Wharf, its shacks perched like swallows' nests on Telegraph Hill, its full-rigged barkentines sailing the bay.

Madame was less enchanted by her return to San Francisco. She was irritable, particularly with the Barrymores, perhaps because she seldom had moments alone with her leading man since the matter of *Nadjezda* had been settled. American materialism began to irk her as well, perhaps because her husband had recently begun to personally manage her finances. "It seems to me that your American plays all turn on money," the Count told a reporter. "It is the broker, or the banker, or the fortune on which the action hinges. That is not good."

"Ah, but it is the life," his wife discerned. "There is a very materialistic spirit abroad. How much is he worth? You hear that question everywhere. If an individual is worth a hundred thousand dollars and someone says that his money was made by stealing, the American public will smile and say, 'Smart,' and give the thief his hand."

While bombarded with invitations by local gentry, who considered it a coup to capture visiting Eastern celebrities for display at their soirées, the Bozentas accepted only those from friends in the city's Polish colony, many of whom had settled there after their "Polish Brook Farm" had failed. The Barrymores, equally favored by the city's elite, accepted fewer invitations. Society folk still rankled the Commissioner's son. For both couples, however, there was one notable exception during their four weeks at the Baldwin Theatre—the Bohemian Club. Financial or social standing was not enough to ensure membership in this colorful confederation: talent or appreciation was required; business and shoptalk were taboo. "Weaving spiders, come not here," a line from *A Midsummer Night's Dream*, was the club motto. A reciprocal arrangement with the Lambs' gave Barry access to those "whole-souled clever men," as he called them, and their handsome rooms above a Pine Street fish market.

Beyond San Francisco, the company played one-night stands at San Jose and Sacramento. *Adrienne Lecouvreur* "was greeted by an overflowing house," reported the San Jose *Daily News*, and Barry's *Maurice de Saxe* was praised extravagantly. In Sacramento, the following evening, he was soundly panned in the same role, but the *Union* review mentioned that Mrs. Barrymore was along on the tour with "Lionel, Ethel, and John, all very young."

Oscar Wilde had preceded them to Salt Lake City on his lecture tour. "The Opera House at Salt Lake," he explained, "is about the size of Covent Garden, and holds with ease fourteen families. The President, a nice old man, sat with five wives in the stage box." *As You Like It* and *Twelfth Night* proved unqualified successes with the theater-loving Mormons.

At Denver, Count Bozenta, playing manager, met H. A. W. Tabor, playing impresario. "Haw," as he was called thereabouts, was a Vermont stonecutter who had become the richest man in Colorado. He had spent $800,000 of his mining fortune on the Tabor Grand Opera House, and demanded approval of "Miss Modjesky's repertore."

"Well," said the Count, "there is *Mary Stuart*."

"Who wrote it?" asked Tabor.

"Schiller."

"Is he a first-class dramatist?"

"Surely, surely," replied the Count. "He is most illustrious."

"Humph! Never heard of him," Tabor grumbled. "What else does she do?"

"*As You Like It . . .*"

"Who wrote it?" demanded the backwoods impresario.

"Shakespeare."

"How's he? Good writer?"

"Oh, excellent," the Count attested, miraculously holding his temper; "excellent."

"Well," Tabor announced, "those fellas may be awright as authors, but they ain't well enough known to suit the folks out here. What we want is somethin' popular—somethin' everybody's heard of. I tell you what you do. You get her to give us somethin' of Hoyt's." The Texas-flavored farces of Charles Hale Hoyt, Madame decided, were not just right for herself and her dandy leading man. "Haw" notwithstanding, Schiller and Shakespeare more than suited the folks out there for a week at the Tabor Grand.

"Stupid, it is, this life of mine, frightfully," Madame despaired. "Devouring me, and reducing me to the ranks of vegetables, not living beings." After nine months on the road, her frustration was shared by most of the company. "I am so tired and worn out that I can no longer even weep for myself, and it seems to me that is the way I shall always be. This is the last week of the season." Thus, on June 16, 1883, ended the first Modjeska-Barrymore tour. The Bozentas returned to their farm in California. The Barrymores headed for Philadelphia ". . . ten weeks' rest now that it's over," concluded Madame, "and then, on the nineteenth of September, a new tour of America."

A different house awaited the Barrymores in Philadelphia. Intending to curb the nomadic lives of her three grandchildren, Mrs. Drew had taken 140 North Twelfth Street, a house large enough to accommodate her growing family and its army of retainers. It seemed enormous and wonderful to the Barrymore children after months on the cars. Ethel noted large rooms, cavernous halls, and the most alarming echoes. Alarming but eloquent echoes, for, in addition to Mummum, Aunt Tibby and Uncle Googan, they found Uncle Jack and Aunt Dodo in residence after his season at Daly's. Their fifteen-year-old uncle delighted in chiding his elegant half brother, and the two were constantly bickering. Inspired by their running battle, and by an artisan who cut headstones across the street, Georgie christened the house "The Tomb of the Capulets."

"On the second floor," recalled Ethel, "there was a sitting room, then the bathroom, and then the annex, which was our playroom. Then there was the big front bedroom which was a little frightening to pass, for in it dwelt my great-grandmother, who was ninety-five. There was nothing on earth to be frightened about—perhaps it was the deference and attention Mummum paid her, and Aunt Tibby flying to answer her bell. Grandma Kinloch was very nice to us in a vague, unaware sort of way, but I always felt a little terror."

Terror also visited her youngest brother, who at sixteen months miraculously spouted full sentences. The attic above the third floor had been converted into bedrooms—one for Uncle Googan, one for the Barrymore boys. At bedtime, Jack waited for Lionel before braving the dark stairway to their room. Holding tightly to his older brother's hand, he would admonish the darkness. "You can't hurt me," whispered the little boy. "I have a wonderful power!"

In that attic room, Barry began to be a hero to his sons. When Mrs. Drew was at the theater or in bed, he paid them surreptitious visits, bearing food and stories. Calling Sidney to join them, Barry would jump into bed with his sons, and while they munched smuggled delicacies, regale them with highly colored tales of India. Backgrounds of his childhood— Fort Govindgarh, the bazaar, the Native 59th—embroidered a glorious epic of the Indian Mutiny, which had been quelled, the boys were sure, by young Herbert Blyth and his trusty dog, Rahj. During one of these sessions, climaxed by the 81st Foot Brigade's triumphal entrance into Amritsar, the cheers of the boys awakened Mrs. Drew. In nightcap and gown, she followed the commotion to the attic.

"Well, you," she addressed her son-in-law, "is four o'clock in the morning the best time to scare the children?"

"I was only giving them a touch of India, ma'am," replied the contrite storyteller, "a soothing battle scene."

"I'll give you a touch of something," said Mrs. Drew, "a touch of intelligence perhaps." She sent Sidney back to his room and turned to Lionel and Jack, who crouched together sheepishly on the bed. As Mummum pulled the blankets over her grandsons, she noted the reason for their uncomfortable expressions. "In future," she asked, turning sharply to Barry, "could you manage to avoid such decisive battles until after the season of tropical rains?"

After this episode, Mummum introduced the threat of the "green slipper" into the lives of her grandsons. The object, merely an old slipper of soft Russian leather, became a most fearsome weapon to the imaginative boys.

At more respectable hours, Lionel and Jack would burst into their parents' room to wake Papa. The spectacle of his awakening enhanced their heroic image of him. Proper Uncle Jack, they knew, slept in long, custom-tailored nightshirts, which always seemed as immaculate in the morning as they had upon retiring. Papa, on the other hand, without benefit of underdrawers, wore the short, striped jersey of the West London Rowing Club. The supply had been replenished in London two years before, but, sagging and torn, the garments were as one. From stretched loopholes, tufts of hair protruded "like the wings of St. Michael," said Georgie.

"Papa's extreme hairiness impressed his sons," wrote Gene Fowler of those morning visits. "What a brave apparition he seemed as he rose from tousled sleep! He would gulp some water, shudder, snort, as if returning to mortality, sit on the edge of the bed, scratch his tonsorial upholstery, then rise to stride up and down the room like a Roman senator in a half toga." The yellow-and-blue-striped jersey invariably inspired the same questions from the boys. And Papa would repeat, each time embellishing, tales of his rowing days on the Thames.

Ethel seldom joined in these sessions. She was a shy little mortal, devoted to her mother, with large blue eyes usually cast down when others were about. At such times, Barry would call gently to his daughter, "Look up, Pauline!" a line from *The Lady of Lyons*. It became another family wheeze. "Everything was a quotation in our house," recalled Ethel. "At the table it seemed as if we could never get away from famous lines. If we had to go to bed, it was, 'Stand not upon the order of your going, but go at once!' If we hurried through our meals, we were admonished to eat 'wisely and slow.' Our manners were shaped in terms of theater dialogue." When other children might be promised candy, the Barrymores were quoted an old wheeze from the rural districts, "Speak your piece good and you'll get a big red apple."

News from the firm of Grover and Humphreys in London reached Barry that summer. "Be it known," Edward Humphreys quoted from the Principal Registry, "that Sarah Blyth died on the 28th day of March, 1883, at No. 10 Gensing Gardens, Saint Leonard-on-Sea, in the county of Sussex, a widow without child or parent brother or sister uncle or aunt nephew or niece cousin german or any known relation." Most of the estate left by Sarah Blyth, £4,252″ 19s.″ 3d., over $20,000, was in trust for Barry's brother, Will, and his sister, Evelin, whose husband, George Edward Wace, had become a lieutenant colonel in the Indian Army at Lahore. The Commissioner had stipulated this; his widow had been unable to change it.

Barry's right to Wharncliff, the New Zealand estate left him by his father, had been groundlessly contested by Sarah Blyth. Now, it became solely his. The land adjoined Blythsdale and Kikurangi Hill, which his brother owned. Enclosed with Humphrey's letter was a rather formal note from Will, addressed: "H. A. Blyth, Esq." Carefully avoiding mention of Barry's acting career, Will offered $12,500 for Wharncliff. Any transfer of money, he added, must await probate of Sarah Blyth's will. The prodigal posted acceptance of his brother's offer.

Barry was little touched by the death of the woman who had been both stepmother and godmother to him. She died, he observed, as she had lived: alone and vindictively contesting the Commissioner's will, her own considerable holdings lost through ill-advised Indian stock investments. In her last years, she had become a recluse, obsessed by the estate of which, during her lifetime, she was sole executrix. That she was unable to break the trust became her greatest frustration. Unjustified hate for her step-children flourished. She died determined to deprive them, at least, of what little was legally hers.

Her own estate, valued at £195"4s."0, less than a thousand dollars, was enough to win Sarah Hunter Blyth a final vindictive triumph:

> Administration of the Rest of the Personal Estate of Sarah Blyth was granted to the Solicitor for the Affairs of Her Majesty's Treasury, and his Successors in that Office, for the use of Her Majesty. The next of kin of the said deceased, if any, having been first duly cited, but no one having in anywise appeared.

XVII

Madame summoned the Barrymores to Chicago at the end of August. They arrived for the 1883–84 season buoyant and hopeful. Georgie would be a member of the company; *Nadjezda*, Madame had promised, would be the first play added to the repertoire. The author reached Chicago expecting to begin rehearsals.

A changed management greeted them. John Stetson was no longer company manager. The Bozentas, with Frederick Stinson, previously Madame's stage manager, were in charge. The Count, wearing the cap of authority safely behind the petticoats of his wife, informed Barry that *Cymbeline* was to be rehearsed: "We do your play . . . what you call it, Maurice, we do that later, eh?"

Madame soothed her infuriated leading man, assuring him that *Nadjezda* would be given proper production later in the tour. Twenty-six grueling weeks lay ahead, one-night stands and split weeks, throughout the West and South. *Nadjezda*, she promised, would be presented before they reached New York. Taking the lady at her word, Barry turned to *Cymbeline*.

The managing triumvirate had scheduled Shakespeare's difficult tragedy to open the tour at Chicago's Grand Opera House, giving the Barrymores less than a week to prepare. Fortunately, Georgie was a quick study. Having already put to memory her lines and business for all the previous plays, she learned her new role, cued Barry in his. "The house was a large and brilliant one," reported the Chicago *Tribune* of the September third opening. Yet "beautiful and attractive as Mme. Modjeska was, she failed to impersonate this character,—to rise to the height of this lofty womanhood." *Imogen* never even approached *Rosalind* in Madame's repertoire, but "Mr. Barrymore's *Posthumus* is even better than his

Orlando, and he gives just the right emphasis to the simplicity and lack of stability of the character of *Imogen's* husband."

Before they left Chicago, Frederick Stinson abruptly resigned from the company. "He had trouble with Count Bozenta," the Muskegon *Chronicle* tersely assumed on September 18, as the troupe began two weeks of arduous one-night stands through Michigan, Ohio, Indiana, West Virginia.

The previous season on the road had been quite enough to exhaust Madame's patience: Her ardor for Barry lost its genteel veneer; her manner toward Georgie cooled perceptibly. She dangled *Nadjezda* like a sweetmeat before her leading man, while the Count, aiming to undermine his wife's infatuation, was patronizing and vague about the production. Barry saw none of this. He looked to the future, trusting in Madame's word. Mrs. Barrymore observed her honored friend's behavior, hoping that it was merely a Platonic expression of a passionate nature. Not quite wary, but certainly aware, she waited for Madame to show her hand.

Six uneasy weeks through Pennsylvania, New York, Michigan, Indiana, Wisconsin, and Illinois culminated at St. Paul, Minnesota, with a proclamation from the manager-count. Rehearsals would begin straightway for *A Doll's House*, to be presented three weeks hence at Louisville, Kentucky. Since Henrik Ibsen's play offered the same brand of stark drama as did *Nadjezda*, the Count's strategy was obvious. "I felt annoyed by their action," confessed Barry, "because if *Doll's House* was a hit, it naturally meant the shelving of my play. And shelving it meant to a large extent its ruin because I had written it to fit Mme. Modjeska, and it isn't any use to exhibit silks and satins in a grocer's window." Unless the agreement concerning his play was honored, Barry advised, he would consider his contract as leading man worthless.

Madame was nearly distraught. Had the Count consulted her about the Ibsen play, she would have urged prior production of *Nadjezda*. She had decided that to satisfy Barrymore in regard to his play would be the only way to regain his favors. But now she was in the position of either humiliating her husband before the company or losing her leading man. "So after that we came right down to business," said Barry without enthusiasm, "and what had been purely a work of friendly feeling became at once a matter of self-interest on both sides." Georgie urged that lawyers be called in to make proper contracts. Barry refused. A gentleman's agreement would suffice, he told her.

After their final performance in St. Paul, the Bozentas and the Barrymores met amicably enough in the palace car. In unlikely communion around the small walnut table in the gaslit lounge, they reached a compromise. *Nadjezda* would be mounted for production before they reached New York, whether or not *A Doll's House* succeeded. If his play were produced six or more times in a week, Barry's royalty would be $300;

fewer performances would bring him $50 each. Barry still owed his wife money lent to cover *Diplomacy* debts; he stipulated that all royalties be paid to her. Fearing further claims by alleged *Diplomacy* creditors if the new play succeeded, Georgie advised Barry to copyright *Nadjezda* in her name, thereby averting any such claims. Business done, the residents of palace car *Poland* proceeded in relative peace through Ohio and Missouri.

Playbills at Louisville announced the first production of *A Doll's House* for December 7. Early that week children accompanied by their nurses began purchasing tickets; the sidewalk outside Macauley's Theatre was lined with perambulators. The title of the play was changed to *Thora*, and NOT FOR CHILDREN pasted over the bills. The play proved not for adults either. Madame's *Nora* and Barry's *Torwald* were well received, but patrons and critics were repulsed by Ibsen's stark realism. "The people didn't like it," she admitted. "They didn't like the idea of a woman leaving her husband." Regretfully, after one performance, Modjeska withdrew *A Doll's House* from her repertoire, and preparations for *Nadjezda* began in earnest.

Aware that her leading man would not tolerate further incident, Madame beseeched her husband to desist. She arranged the most elaborate production, sending to New York for the finest costumes and scenery to be ready in eight weeks for a Richmond, Virginia, première. The mounting of his play absorbed Maurice Barrymore. Petty dramas of the touring car—the uneasy silence of Count Bozenta, the strained relations of Madame and his wife—escaped him. Endless invitations on the road were refused, yet, surprisingly, always acknowledged by the preoccupied playwright. From the Maxwell House in Nashville, Tennessee, he declined accordingly on December 21:

> *Mr. Barrymore presents his compliments to Mrs. Demoville and regrets exceedingly that her letter arrived when he was out and did not receive it until too late to accept her very kind invitation. Mrs. Barrymore joins me in returning very many thanks for the delightful egg nogg. Unhappily our room is full of thirsty members of the company who all find it so delicious that my own chances of eating disappear if I do not expedite my gratitude to you.*

They were booked into the New Memphis Theatre on Christmas Eve. That afternoon, a tree was set up in the palace car, and the entire company contributed to its trimming. Lionel and Ethel—Mrs. Drew had managed to keep little Jack in Philadelphia this time—were the center of attention: presents piled up for them under the tree; Madame ordered the chef to prepare *chrusciki*, their favorite little powdered cakes. *Oplatek* were also distributed to the company, holy wafers traditionally broken on Christmas Eve as a symbol of friendship. The Count and the leading man broke one together, Madame and Mrs. Barrymore broke another—not without second thoughts all around.

The first two weeks of 1884 were spent in New Orleans, a thriving, graceful emporium served by five railroad lines; then four exhausting weeks through Texas, Alabama, Georgia, South Carolina, all the while rehearsing *Nadjezda*. The author was directing—with the astute assistance of his star and his wife; even gratuitous interference by the Count was greeted magnanimously. Barry was anxious to weigh every possibility for the best presentation of his work. As Richmond and the première approached, tensions mounted, heightened by minor disasters. When the palace car could not fit the gauge of the railroad leading into Raleigh, North Carolina, the engagement was canceled. Richmond theatergoers were also destined for disappointment. The scheduled opening of *Nadjezda* had created quite a stir, but, at the last minute, it was postponed. ". . . to rehearse too tough," explained Count Bozenta.

At this juncture, Frederick Stinson rejoined the company. Madame had contacted her ex-manager at the risk of offending her husband, aware that his incompetence was endangering the tour.

On Friday, the eighth of February, 1884, a brilliant audience, augmented by special correspondents from New York, Chicago and Boston, packed Baltimore's Academy of Music. The much-heralded production which drew them there was not a disappointment. Word of a singular theatrical event went abroad from Baltimore to the cities of America. REMARKABLE RENDITION OF A THRILLING SOCIALISTIC DRAMA IN THE MONUMENTAL CITY, headlined the New York *Morning Journal*. "When Modjeska appeared upon the stage the building trembled with the tremendous applause, while during the exciting incidents of the prologue the immense house seemed empty, so still was the silence occasioned by the rapt attention of the audience. The conclusion of every act saw double encores, and at the completion of the third act where she succeeds in detaining *Prince Zabouroff* and thus saves her adorer from the crime he contemplates, the house went nearly wild." Modjeska received several handsome floral tributes, "while Mr. Barrymore, the young author, as *Paul Devereaux*, the lover, was not forgotten for his splendid acting. He was presented, at the close of the same act, with a handsome wreath."

The Boston *Herald* ran a front-page report from its special Baltimore correspondent, observing that "*Nadjezda* is not written with gloved hands; it goes straight to the fountainhead of human emotions, and, with audacity, and, at the same time, delicacy, it lays bare those feelings which alone can inspire great acting." Some "unnecessary realism," such as the dressing of a wounded Nihilist's arm on the stage, was deemed displeasing to a sensitive audience, but the piece conceded that the author "has accomplished a delicate task with singular discretion," concluding that "Mr. Barrymore has conquered the position of a dramatist by this unquestionably successful production . . ."

A four-week booking would follow at the Star Theatre, New York. *Nadjezda*, Madame announced, would be played for the entire engagement. Theatrical circles were lively with talk of the new play. Anticipation ran high, lines formed at the Star box office at Broadway and Thirteenth Street. Barry knew the old house well. He had been in the company there when it was Wallack's Theatre, before the manager sold out and moved uptown. Another move affected the Barrymores' New York advent. For the first time since their marriage, they could not stop with the Judsons. Under financial stress, Miss Alice had sold the family mansion and retired with most of her relations to the suburbs. Barry moved his family into the Union Square Hotel.

[SPECIAL DISPATCH TO THE BOSTON *HERALD*]

New York, Feb. 11, 1884. *Nadjezda*, the new play by Maurice Barrymore, which was produced tonight by the Modjeska company, is a pronounced success, and unquestionably the strongest of all the pieces your correspondent has seen in half a dozen years . . . Modjeska was called before the curtain nine times. Barrymore also received a well deserved call. Modjeska remains four weeks and might undoubtedly stay as many months with profit to herself.

New York critics welcomed *Nadjezda*—even the *Tribune*'s William Winter, who had never forgiven Barry's disruption of his literary "at home" eight years before. The dean of New York critics allowed that the play "was received with favor, and indeed at some points, with admiration," adding that "It is a dark subject that Mr. Barrymore has chosen for the basis of his play: but life is full of dark and sad subjects, and they, among the rest are entitled to a suitable consideration . . . Mr. Barrymore appears to have thought that a dramatic treatment of this dark theme would elicit from it striking theatrical situations and a vigorous and impressive display of the passions, under circumstances of a terribly tragical character. The result of his thoughtful and careful labor has shown the correctness of his judgement."

Whatever the feelings about the subject matter, critics and public agreed that a new playwright had emerged. "The theatre was full," attested the New York *Times*, "and those who were in the house offered applause and admiration to Mr. Barrymore's work as dramatist." The dramatist himself, however, was not satisfied. He worked constantly during the New York engagement to perfect his work. The character he had written for himself was of Russian birth and English education—a paradox based possibly on his own Indian-English experience. During the first part of the play, the character adhered to his British training, but in the last act, when he fell in love, the native ferocity of the Slavonic race broke through, and he seized the woman he loved by the throat. "I acted on the old maxim of 'Scratch a Russian and you will find a Tartar,'" stated the author. "The characterization was too subtle for dramatic purposes. The audiences did not understand the change from English suavity to Russian brutality in the character, and it rather repelled them. After the play had been running a few nights I came to recognize this fact, and, on Friday evening, just before the last act, I said to Madame Modjeska that I would change the business and speeches, and asked her to be prepared. I told her that the cues and speeches for her would, however, remain the same. Well, I changed nearly all my speeches, writing them on stage during the act. This, at least, had the merit of novelty, as I have never heard of a similar case during my entire experience."

Such dramatic subtleties did not impair the playwright's acceptance in New York. The silver tray in the foyer of Barry's suite held a daily stack of calling cards from local reporters and out-of-town correspondents. The elated author greeted interviewers in the parlor from morning until show time, sitting erect and unusually businesslike, drawing incessantly on his specially rolled Virginia cigarettes, absorbed completely by the subject at hand.

"If you have read the press notices on the production of 'Nadjezda' in New York," Barry said to the Boston *Globe* correspondent, "you must have remarked that, while the critics were for the most part unanimous in praising the play itself as a play, its construction, characterization and workmanship generally, a good many of them fell foul of the subject. They declared it to be 'immoral,' 'unhealthy,' 'repulsive.' In the case of *Nadjezda*, however, I believe, for my own part, that the one worthy thing about it is this very subject of which they disapprove, and I respectfully submit that from every standpoint it is elementally moral.

"When I cast about me for a theme that would at once supply Mme. Modjeska with a vehicle for the display of her marked talents and at the same time treat, or attempt to treat, some great social question—morally, bien entendu, logically, and, above all, with infinite respect, and that, after all, should unquestionably be the highest mission of the stage—it struck me that Socialism, with its comparative Communism and superlative Nihilism, was the greatest factor in the sum of our modern life."

"Certainly your view is timely," interjected the man from Boston. "The journals are filled with reports of Socialist troubles, of riots and demonstrations in Austria and Germany, Russia, even England."

200

"More particularly in Europe, perhaps," Barry continued, "but even here exerting an influence that has been graphically set forth in that remarkable book *The Bread-Winners*. Why not then base my play on Socialism. Or, at least, that phase of it where two wrongs are made to make a right? Obviously moral, so far, eh? You see, then, I had a sort of lay sermon in mind rather than a mere play, as we with our English limitations are taught to understand the work.

"Now for the text." Barry stood up, addressing his interviewer with the concentration of a university lecturer. "One wrong does not right another wrong. We are taught that in a church. Why not try to teach it in a theatre? They say that my prologue is strong, too strong; it had to be. I was arguing a case, and my opponent had no right of reply; the prologue was to be his case. I had in honesty to make it strong. Socialism is the outcome of oppression. The wrong, I granted, must be cruel enough, and, in all conscience, I have made it so. The critics say too cruel. Well, all right, but fair play is a jewel, and it had to be. A woman, obviously more sympathetic in her helplessness than a man, pure, tender, loving, under the heel of merciless oppression sacrifices her honor to save her husband's life. She is cheated, after all, and her husband sent back to her dead, with a bullet in his heart. In an agony of shame and despair, she dedicates her child to the work of vengeance, and, too self-abased to live, kills herself. She is oppressed, a guiltless sinner, and she dies, but who shall cast the first stone at her? Does my opponent, the socialist, want a stronger case than this? I have been loyal to him, I think. By George, sir, there is not a Nihilist among them all who has a stronger cue for passion than that poor devil. Through the play that follows—my case, in fact—the child grown up to womanhood with her heritage of hate, is hurried by the hand of a destiny as inexorable as that of a Greek tragedy step by step to the very vengeance that is to be her own undoing, until, with fateful irony, she dies exactly as her mother did. Moral. 'Vengeance is mine.' Lesson: We leave our vengeance in His hands.

"There you are," said Barry, catching his breath and smiling at the reporter for the first time; "that is the story in a nutshell. Is it immoral? Do you see why in sarcasm I called it *Nadjezda* ('Hope') when there is not a ray of hope to be found from first to last? And so it is with Nihilism—no hope, 'nothing but hate,' impotent hate." Barry continued his oration, dissecting the critics' reaction to his play's "brutal frankness," lauding Madame's "infinite variety of heart" in the roles of *Nadjezda* and her daughter, *Nadine*, until it was time to leave for the theater.

While her husband's play preoccupied New York, Georgie was hailed as a comedienne. "As an American girl, *Eureka Grubb*," said William Winter in the *Tribune*, "Mrs. Georgie Drew Barrymore is in her element. The 'slang' is a little startling to the audience, and when she says,

'Did I win? Did I hit the ceiling?' the house gives a gasp and then a long, loud roar of merriment." *Eureka Grubb* was something previously unheard of in a stage ingénue—a *nouveau riche* miner's daughter, witty, with a smattering of slang, warmhearted and aware of the possibility of rewarding sexual exchanges between ladies and gentlemen. "How about your intentions," she asks *Lord Alsager*, "honorable or dishonorable?

"Well," he replies, "am I to understand, Mademoiselle, that I have a choice?

"Ha! bravo! shake!" exclaims *Eureka*, extending her hand. "You can't be an Englishman, you were changed at birth.

"And are you a typical American?" wonders the peer.

"Oh, no; I *was*, but like the rest of us, I came to 'Yurup' and became a caricature."

Nadjezda played to full houses during its first two weeks at the Star, but, as Georgie had foreseen, success brought forth strange little men, furtive and short of breath, claiming that Barrymore owed money to them from the *Diplomacy* tour. In a proceeding brought by these alleged creditors, Barry testified that the claims were wholly unfounded, and, in any case, that the play belonged to his wife. The judge agreed, dismissing the case after fifteen minutes.

Internal frustrations also erupted. The reception of Barry's play left Count Bozenta torn between gratification as manager, resentment as husband. The more basic emotion won. He convinced his wife that, success or not, she must rest from Barrymore's exhausting drama. Not that Madame needed convincing. Gratitude to her mentor for the success of his play had not increased Barry's ardor. She was aggravated by this setback; winning her leading man became an obsession. Now, with the inadvertent help of her husband, she would try another tactic. On Saturday, the twenty-third, Barry was informed that *Twelfth Night* would replace *Nadjezda* at the evening performance. Patrons were disappointed, the author distraught.

"I felt troubled," Barry told a *Times* reporter, "that they should not have played my drama through the whole New York engagement, as had been promised after its original hit, because that gave the wholly false impression that it was not a financial success." He relented, however, sympathetic to Madame's honey-coated claims of exhaustion.

"Then they took to performing it on the worst days of the week," he said, "using it to make the business for the repertoire." Again Barry hesitated to bring lawyers into it, but he secured a promise from Madame. In future, his play would be given only at certain agreed performances—Monday, Thursday, Friday evenings, Saturday matinees or evenings—preserving, he hoped, Madame's health and *Nadjezda*'s reputation.

The Bozentas were not satisfied. Without consulting the author, they

BARRYMORE & DREW

NEW YORK

Ordered by Augustin Daly for publicity purposes during the Barrymore-Drew courtship, the above photograph was expressive of much more.

MRS. JNO. DREW.

Entered according to Act of Congress in the year 1865,
in the Clerk's Office of the District Court of the United
States for the Eastern District of Pennsylvania, by
JOS. D. MURPHY, Arch St. Theatre.

John Drew, Sr., at left as *Tim O'Brian* in *The Irish Emigrant,* one of his famous Irish characterizations. Above is his wife, Louisa Lane Drew, during her early years as manageress of Philadelphia's Arch Street Theatre.

facing page: Josephine Baker *(top, left),* daughter of Mrs. Drew's closest friend, became the wife of the younger John Drew. At right, Mrs. Drew's "adopted" son, Sidney, bearing unmistakable Drew family features. Below, Georgie Drew, during her tenure at the Arch, seems to be characteristically teasing her imperturbable mother.

Mr. and Mrs. Maurice Barrymore at the time of their marriage on New Year's Eve, 1876.

facing page: (top), Big Jim Currie (left) sat proudly for a local photographer in the Marshall jail, while awaiting trial for the wounding of Barry and the killing of Ben Porter *(below, left, as Jacques in The Two Orphans)*. Another accused murderer, Abe Rothschild, is at Currie's left.

Joseph Jefferson *(right)*, Mrs. Drew's friend and colleague, as *Bob Acres* in *The Rivals*.

Barry as *Captain Absolute*, Mrs.
Drew as *Mrs. Malaprop*, her most
famous role, during their tour with
Jefferson in 1880.

Joseph Jefferson *(right)*, Mrs. Drew's friend and
colleague, as *Bob Acres* in *The Rivals*.

Barry as *Captain Absolute*, Mrs. Drew as *Mrs. Malaprop*, her most famous role, during their tour with Jefferson in 1880.

Helena Modjeska *(left)*, the great Polish actress, costumed as *Nadjezda* for Barry's tragedy of that name. During the volatile Modjeska-Barrymore tour, wrestling champion Billy Muldoon *(below, left,* with his mastiff, Crix) played *Charles,* the wrestler, to Barry's much-praised *Orlando (below)* in *As You Like It.*

In 1885, Mr. and Mrs. Bancroft, England's foremost acting couple, invited Barry to participate in their farewell season at London's Theatre Royal, Haymarket.

Emily Rigl, as *Nadine*, and Herbert Beerbohm Tree, as the lecherous *Count Zabouroff (above)*, in the London production of *Nadjezda*.

canceled the fourth week of the New York engagement under continued pleas of exhaustion. Exhaustion, however, did not prevent more congenial activities. On Sunday, the *Herald* announced that Madame's plans for her week of rest included "a reception at the Clarendon Hotel tomorrow night which will probably be a brilliant affair," noting that she would not continue her season that week because "It is represented that she is too much exhausted with the strain made upon her by Mr. Barrymore's new play, and that she must have a brief rest." The piece added, however, that she would appear at a Thursday-afternoon benefit in aid of St. Stanislaw's, a Polish school run by nuns. Madame expected that her entire company would contribute their services to the project. Notwithstanding their shabby treatment from the Bozentas, the Barrymores complied. Barry continued to restrain his usually volatile temper, convinced that the future of his play depended on the patronage of his star. Georgie, not wishing to further tax her husband's patience, did not mention her own numerous slights from the tempestuous couple. Mrs. Barrymore rose above them, giving splendid afternoons and musicales in their hotel parlor, even taking a stage box for the St. Stanislaw's benefit, inviting assorted Judsons in from the suburbs to fill it.

A large audience assembled at the Madison Square Theatre for the 1:30 performance of *Adrienne Lecouvreur*. The attentive house hushed as the harrowing climactic scene approached. Modjeska, the persecuted heroine, passionately denounces Georgie, her wicked adversary. The silence was awesome as the heroine ended her tirade with the words ". . . and sits with brow insensible to shame."

"Choked with anguish we gazed at our shrinking Georgie," recounted Miss Alice Judson, "only to see her, from behind the insufficient screen of a gauze fan, make a monkey-face in our direction and give herself a slight but indubitable scratch. To the accident of tumbling backward instead of forward do the children owe the fact that they have never appeared upon the stage."

Madame's respite was followed by a week at the Park Theatre, Brooklyn. *Nadjezda* was announced for Monday, Thursday, Saturday, evenings specified in the previous agreement. But when *Frou Frou* failed to draw on Tuesday, *Nadjezda*, the Count decided, would be given instead at the Wednesday matinee. The Barrymores objected to this obvious sabotage. Not only would it break their agreement, but, as Georgie pointed out, it would degrade the play. The weakest productions of a company's repertoire were traditionally given at Wednesday matinees, marking them second-rate in the theatrical profession. Georgie urged her husband to withdraw the play completely. It would become so thoroughly identified with Modjeska, she reasoned, that it would lose its drawing attraction without her. Barry sent his wife back to the hotel. He would settle the matter once and for all with Madame.

The Count, who had instigated the trouble, urged his wife to let Barrymore have his play if he asked for its return. Madame sent her husband back to their hotel, wishing, she said, to settle the matter peaceably with Mr. Barrymore.

Nadjezda was played instead of *Frou Frou* at the Wednesday matinee. Count Bozenta did not gloat over his victory. And Georgie suspected that Madame had employed more than business sense to win her point. Barry's exaggerated spousal attentiveness, contradicted by Madame's smugness toward her, confirmed Georgie's suspicions. They proceeded tensely through Connecticut—one-night stands at New Haven, Meriden, Hartford. *Nadjezda* was performed only once during the week, at Tow's Opera House, Providence, Rhode Island, where the *Journal* reported its success, comparing it favorably to "the savage dramas of the early Elizabethan dramatists," adding that the author "displayed great power in tragic emotion, and natural and graceful humor in the part of *Devereaux*."

Of Modjeska's performance, the Providence critic was less sure: "The dual characters of *Nadjezda* and *Nadine*, assumed by Madame Modjeska, require the strongest powers of tragic force to adequately display, and she does not possess them. They are the attributes of a personality more powerful than her delicate frame, and a fierce vigor of passion beyond her grasp." There had been similar critical insinuations since *Nadjezda's* première, but Madame's artistry and charm had transcended them. Stated bluntly for the first time, they disturbed her. Although the play was her most popular that season, she seriously considered its value to her career. For the present, she could do nothing. *Nadjezda* was promised for the imminent Boston engagement, and it still remained her primary weapon in the quest for her leading man.

On March 16, Boston papers had announced *Nadjezda* for Monday, Tuesday, and Wednesday of the following week. Without consulting Barry, Georgie accosted the Bozentas, informing them that if their previous agreement as to days of performance were not honored, she would seek legal counsel. On March 23, Boston papers announced that "Mr. Barrymore's new play would be seen on Monday, Thursday, and Saturday evenings." Georgie had won a round, but Madame continued to ply Barry with affectionate solicitude—obviously exaggerated for Georgie's benefit, no less disturbing for that.

The frangible troupe reached Boston, where their touring days had begun. Once, Georgie had approached the city questioning the potential impact of Mme. Helena Modjeska. After two years, she no longer questioned. Mrs. Barrymore was girt for battle.

Boston was primed for *Nadjezda*. Since its première, the play, its star, and particularly its author had been given full and enthusiastic coverage by the local press. Reports of excessive realism and passionate execution titillated potential patrons; the novelty of a favorite actor turned playwright inspired their interest. The time was propitious for the achievement of Barry's overriding goal. In an interview with the playwright on February 29, the *Globe*'s special New York correspondent had observed that the dearth of good European plays decidedly increased the prospects of American dramatists: "It will be an easy matter, I dare say, for such men as Maurice Barrymore to get an opening anywhere. The reception of *Nadjezda* has started that author-actor on the high road of prosperity as a dramatist."

After the Boston opening on March 24, local commentators reiterated such predictions. "For a first attempt at playwright's work, Mr. Barrymore has, in truth, accomplished results that are very noteworthy indeed, and they give promise of even finer achievements," stated the *Herald*. "Such virile strength, such straightforwardness of method, such evident purpose to avoid prudishness and Miss Nancyism in stage dialogue and 'business,' such endeavor to attain the unconventional in effect as Mr. Barrymore's drama displays, would make amends for shortcomings far more serious, and much more numerous than are to be noted with a critic's eye in *Nadjezda*."

"The piece has many merits," concurred the *Post* critic, "and among them are those of freshness and novelty. It is Byronic in sentiment and its keynote is revenge."

"At last, thank heaven, a play without a moral lesson!" exclaimed the *Transcript*. "Virtue is not triumphant in it; neither is vice, for that matter. It ends in the extinction of the heroine, which, as Schopenhauer has remarked, is the soul of tragedy . . ."

"It really seems as if Mr. Barrymore has a great gift for playwrighting," reckoned the *Daily Advertiser*, "and that if he made judicious use of the curb, the bit, the pruning-knife, besides his native genius, he would produce something of extraordinary value and significance, as well as exceptional intensity."

Local commentators, however, were unaware of tension within the company building to a climax. Days of the week that *Nadjezda* was performed became an excuse for the expression of grievances by Mrs. Barrymore and the Bozentas. On Tuesday, the Count informed Georgie that *Nadjezda* would play Wednesday afternoon instead of Friday evening. He had waited until she was alone—Barry had taken the children to call on William Warren and Amelia Fisher at Bulfinch Place—but Georgie coolly informed the sputtering Count that such a performance would violate their agreement. "If the play is performed on Wednesday," she threatened, "I shall forbid its further production."

"The play belongs to me," shouted the Count, "and I will play it whenever I damned please!" John Stetson was called into the fray, no longer as company manager, but as owner of the Globe Theatre where they were playing. The showman sided with the Bozentas, informing

Mrs. Barrymore that no one would tell him what to do in his own theater.

"I see," replied Georgie, surprisingly calm; "then the matter is obviously out of my hands." The Count was disappointed by Mrs. Barrymore's ready acquiescence; but she was far from surrender. She went immediately to the offices of Phillips and Johnson, attorneys at law.

That evening, during "Camille," Georgie mustered her considerable stage prowess to undermine Mme. Modjeska's performance. The subtle maneuver was effective—imperceptible to the audience, but highly distracting to Madame. During the *Nadjezda* matinee next day, Madame sought revenge—at least it appeared so to the Barrymores. "An amusing mishap greatly injured the tragic effect of the final scene of *Nadjezda* Wednesday afternoon," the *Herald* reported. "Mme. Modjeska, as the heroine, died too near the footlights, and, with Mr. Barrymore, was shut out by the falling curtain. As the gentleman was lifting the curtain to draw the actors back under it, it was run up a dozen feet, and before he could accomplish his design it was suddenly dropped, leaving them as badly situated as before. The audience ceased weeping to laugh, and gave the unlucky pair a hearty round of applause."

Sabotage, Barry assumed, barely smiling over clenched teeth during numerous curtain calls, bowing curtly as he accepted a wreath of calla lilies. Shaking in an attempt to hold his anger, he waited backstage for Madame's final bow. "You are aware, Madame," he admonished, "that *Nadjezda* belongs to Mrs. Barrymore. But for me she would have removed it in Brooklyn last week."

"You may take the play away whenever you like, for all I care," replied Mme. Modjeska.

"Then you shall not perform it on Saturday," and Barry went to his dressing room.

Four-year-old Ethel had been watching the play from the wings that afternoon, oblivious to any tension. Enchanted as usual by her adored Madame, she decided that a present was in order. When the curtain fell, the little girl tiptoed onto the darkened stage to retrieve the beautiful lilies Papa had dropped there. She carried them proudly to Madame's dressing room, unaware that the superstitious actress considered white lilies a harbinger of doom. Ethel, excitedly mumbling how wonderful the performance had been, presented the wreath. Gazing at the lilies, the actress suddenly stood up from her dressing table, cast the flowers to the floor. She swept, eyes blazing, out of the room, leaving the startled child crying in her wake.

"How dare you," she cried, storming Barry's dressing room, "to send the child to play such a trick! You know I abhor those wretched flowers."

"I assure you, Madame, I . . ."

"Mr. Barrymore! Mr. Barrymore!" she continued. "You are insulting, you are ungrateful. You owe everything to me. I have given you your position. I have made you!"

"Made *me*, Madame?" repeated Barry, not the least fazed. "Why I was well-known here when Modjeska was merely a boot-polish!"

Georgie remained perfectly calm when Barry recounted his exchange with Madame. Her attorneys should by now have notified the Bozentas in writing that she was reclaiming the play, revoking their right to produce it. She presumed that the Count would disregard the notice, thereby giving her grounds for legal action. Barry was in full agreement with his wife's actions until a messenger arrived with a note from Mme. Modjeska:

Dear Mr. Barrymore:

> *Forgive me for what I said. I was mad at the time. Pray do with the play what you think best. I only produced it to give it a start. Believe me always your friend.*

> *Modjeska*

Madame's diplomacy was calculated. She knew that the chance to shed the burden of *Nadjezda* was at hand, but, first, announced Boston performances must be honored, and her "dandy" leading man assuaged. Barry, touched by the note, wondered if legal action were really necessary. Georgie was adamant, even more irritated by the mock impersonality of the apology. "'. . . your *friend*. Modjeska,'" she repeated pointedly. Barry smiled rather sheepishly, telling his wife to do whatever she thought best.

As You Like It was played that evening, exceedingly well, until Georgie decided to improve Shakespeare and reprove Modjeska. As if to atone for her harsh words, *Rosalind* was being overly demonstrative toward her manly *Orlando*. Georgie, playing *Celia*, grew more furious with each scene. Act IV, Scene 1, ends with a dialogue between the women:

Rosalind: No; that same wicked bastard of Venus that was begot of thought, conceiv'd of spleen, and born of madness, that blind rascally boy that abuses every one's eyes because his own are out—let him be judge how deep I am in love. I'll tell thee, Aliena, I cannot be out of sight of Orlando. I'll go find a shadow and sigh till he come.

Celia: And I'll sleep.

Celia's reply was the exit line, but as Madame started offstage, Georgie took the star's arm, holding her there while she spoke words of her own invention: "Be sure 'tis but sighing you do, Madame, else it lead to deeper things."

Modjeska was outraged. She sought manager Stinson, insisting, while the *Forester* sang his song on stage, that Mrs. Barrymore be punished. Stinson complied, replacing Georgie in the casts of *Cymbeline* and *Twelfth Night*, to be done respectively Friday evening and Saturday afternoon. He did not remove Mrs. Barrymore from the cast of her husband's play, scheduled for Thursday and Saturday evenings. Stinson hadn't the stomach to endure the consequences.

Barry was raging at this insult to his wife; Georgie begged him not to interfere. As she had anticipated, the management disregarded the notice from her lawyers. "Notwithstanding Mrs. Barrymore's threat of legal proceedings," reported the *Herald*, "*Nadjezda* was presented last evening to a crowded audience." Early Friday morning, Georgie returned to the offices of Phillips and Johnson, seeking to enjoin the production of *Nadjezda* on Saturday evening.

The case was set for Saturday morning in the United States Circuit Court. On the eve of the hearing, Frederick Stinson, interviewed by a *Herald* reporter, gave management's side. "I have nothing further to say in regard to the matter," stated Madame's manager before saying a great deal. "The whole story is told in the legal papers. It is true that I did take her out of the casts of two plays for misconduct on the stage. She annoyed Mme. Modjeska, and that lady complained to me, and I substituted another actress for Mrs. Barrymore. This I had a perfect right to do. I don't care to state the reason why I considered the change necessary. I have no desire to injure Mrs. Barrymore, and only intend to protect my rights. Her cause of action is trivial and not worth a moment's serious consideration. You may be pretty certain we believe we have a strong defence when I tell you that we have summoned Mr. Barrymore himself. His testimony, if honestly given, will benefit us. We don't believe he ever conveyed the play to his wife legally, and he certainly could not legally make her a present of it, leaving other creditors unsatisfied. Even if the court should grant an injunction, which is not likely, the play will be produced Saturday night as advertised, since Mr. Stetson is ready to give bonds in a sum sufficient to guarantee the satisfaction of any damage the plaintiff may be considered to have sustained."

The Modjeska-Barrymore hearing was news in Boston. The team which had won first fame there in romantic drama two years before, now played a courtroom scene to standing room only. The *Globe* gave front-page coverage to the event: "Madame Modjeska's company was represented in United States Circuit Court this morning by some of its most distinguished members. The occasion of their appearance in this unwonted place was the hearing to be held before Judge Lowell with reference to the injunction prayed for by Georgiana Drew Barrymore . . ."

There was twittering from ladies in attendance when Maurice Barrymore was called to the stand. Judge Lowell reminded them that they were not in a theater. Augustus Russ, attorney for John Stetson and the Bozentas, began questioning with reference to the performing agreement. "The first conversation regarding times of the performance of the play took place in New York," Barry answered, "and at that time it was expressly stipulated by Mr. Stinson that the play was to be produced only on the days specified. As soon as I found out that the play was to be produced on other nights, I told Mr. Stinson that I would not permit the change to be made. At the times of these conversations I was acting as agent for Mrs. Barrymore."

"Was title to the play lawfully transferred to your wife?" asked Russ.

"The transfer of the play to Mrs. Barrymore took place in writing," the witness replied, "and the substance of the written document was that in consideration of a certain sum of money that I owed Mrs. Barrymore I transferred to her all my American right in the play, although I retained the foreign interests." He testified that the injury to himself and his wife from the change of dates was due to the fact that Wednesday was theatrically known to be a bad performing day. When Russ questioned the witness as to his compensation for the play, Barry said fifty dollars a night under all circumstances, stating further that in a conversation with Mme. Modjeska, he had told her that if it had not been for him, Mrs. Barrymore would have taken the play away in Brooklyn. Madame, he said, replied that he could take it away whenever he liked, for all she cared. Subsequently the lady had written a note of apology. That note was offered as evidence to the court.

"Just before the reading of the letter," reported the *Globe*, "Mme. Modjeska entered the court accompanied by her husband. She was dressed in black, and as usual looked charming." Had it not been for the sobering presence of Judge Lowell, the house would certainly have applauded her sweeping progress down the center aisle. During the reading of the letter, Georgie noted, Madame's reaction qualified her for *Joan of Arc*, a role which she had not previously attempted. "She took a lively interest in the proceedings," observed the *Globe*.

Mr. Russ concluded his interrogation with a direct question: "Why have you brought this action Mr. Barrymore?"

Barry paused a moment, thoughtfully, then softly gave his answer. "Sir, the report has gone abroad that Mme. Modjeska intends to give up the play because it is a failure." Barry winced perceptibly at the thought. "I want the injunction so that the reputation of my play should not suffer."

"At the conclusion of his testimony," observed the *Globe* reporter, "Mr. Barrymore stepped over to Modjeska and talked to her pleasantly for a few moments, the great actress gesticulating and smiling all the while." Again it was necessary for Judge Lowell to warn the ladies against twittering.

No twitters, but an expectant hush accompanied Mrs. Barrymore to the witness chair. Russ asked right off if she would be willing to cancel all contracts with Modjeska's company. "Yes, sir, I would. Decidedly."

"Your own engagement and all?"

"Oh! no," said Georgie with a laugh, "by no means. Make no mistake on that point."

"Who gave this notice on Wednesday to have the play stopped?"

"I did."

"Did you go yourself?"

"I went to my lawyer's office, and told him to serve the notice."

"This was after you were removed from the cast by Mr. Stinson, wasn't it?"

"That hasn't anything at all to do with the case," replied Georgie, sharply.

"Answer my question, please."

"Yes, it was."

"Was there ever any contract as to the play?"

"No, sir, nothing but an informal agreement."

"Now will you tell how you have been injured by the production of this play?"

"Well, I want to make a good deal of money out of it next year, and managers will say: 'Oh! They produced it on off days last year.'"

"Now tell me, please, if you don't think Mr. Stetson would suffer a heavy loss if the play is not produced tonight?"

"What do I care about Mr. Stetson?"

"What rights have you in the play?"

"Why my husband gave it to me. Before anything was written my husband said, 'Now I owe you a good deal of money, and if this play succeeds you shall have all the money that comes from it.'" She then stated again that it stamped a play as second-rate to have it produced on Wednesday afternoon.

"Well, it seems to me," said Mr. Russ, "that the plays of tolerably good authors, William Shakespeare for instance, are often produced on that day."

"Perhaps they are," replied the witness, "but they are already established."

Frank Robinson, stage manager of the company, was next called for the prosecution. "His testimony was not of much importance," decided the *Globe* reporter. This closed the evidence in the case, and Mr. Russ argued briefly against the granting of a temporary injunction. The statutes of the United States, he claimed, provide for such a measure only when it appears that irreparable injury might be done if it were not granted. He offered to postpone any performance of the play after that evening for any reasonable time, or to cancel the contract entirely.

Judge Lowell was of the opinion that there was no call for a temporary injunction against the performance that evening. *Nadjezda*, as announced, would close the Boston engagement. But Mr. Phillips insisted upon being heard. He again stated the grounds of the case, reminding the court that Mrs. Barrymore's rights of ownership must be established. The court decided to continue the case for one week, defendants furnishing security to answer again on April 5. It was ruled that the play would not be performed after that evening until matters were settled. "The hearing closed at 12:30," concluded the *Globe*, "and all the members of the company hastened away to prepare for the afternoon performance."

"Mme. Modjeska took her farewell of Boston in Mr. Barrymore's powerful play *Nadjezda*," reported the *Herald*. "The theatre was crowded in every part, every seat being occupied, while many people watched the performance through the lobby doors and over the rail in the balcony." Judge Lowell shared a box with Augustus Russ and Messrs. Phillips and Johnson, the opposing attorneys, presumably in the spirit of good-fellowship.

The hearing seemed to ease tension within the company. They proceeded to a one-night stand at Springfield, Massachusetts, in the condition of unresolved amnesty. Georgie had made her point, at least, and the Bozentas were all solicitude for the present. Barry perceived the harm done *Nadjezda* by the vicissitudes of the women. He did not express it. He was pleasant and unassuming toward Madame, more attentive than ever to his wife and children. Aware that his play was now inextricably identified with Modjeska, that presenting it in America with another actress would provoke inevitable comparisons and rekindle memories of legal proceedings past, Barry did not relinquish hope for its future.

After Springfield, they played Tuesday and Wednesday at Albany, New York, finishing the week at the Academy of Music, Montreal, Canada. To no one's surprise, Judge Lowell ruled on April 5 that American rights to *Nadjezda* were Mrs. Barrymore's to do with as she pleased. Georgie accepted her victory without pleasure. Out of the heat of the battle, she had the smarting realization that her husband's masterwork had been irreparably harmed. But the harm had been done. Pride and deep disappointment forbade a change of course.

Madame, too, had second thoughts. Shedding the exhausting roles, ones that some critics had questioned her ability to play, left a curious sense of regret. Not merely for the season's biggest draw and most prestigious success but for the challenge of playing it, and for the hope of recapturing the joy of that London interlude with Barry four years before. At the core of Madame's ill-conceived pursuit of Maurice Barrymore had been that persistent memory. She considered the harm done to his play. Pride and the resentful Count precluded apologies.

When the troupe arrived for a week of rest in New York, reporters rushed the Barrymore suite at the Union Square Hotel not to ask about the play this time but "concerning his misunderstanding with Mme. Modjeska in regard to the play." Barry minimized the situation, taking responsibility for it without mention of the ladies. "The matter has been satisfactorily settled," he told a *Times* reporter on April 10, "and the reports of the difficulty which found their way into the newspapers were, I regret to say, extremely incorrect. It was purely a business matter, and I brought the suit because a member of the management had said my play belonged to him and he would play it when and where he d——d pleased. Under my protest he went around bragging as to what he could do to me and my play, and I simply wanted to settle the matter once and for all time. As I had written memorandum with him agreeing to play it on certain days of the week, I proposed to see who was running the play, and I did it. Since then good feeling has prevailed, and there are no hard sentiments among us."

But it was not business matters that preoccupied the press. Reports merely elaborated Judge Lowell's decision and made vivid insinuations. John Bradford, Boston's foremost drama critic, was one of the few who revaluated the author's achievement:

Mr. Barrymore has distanced all competitors, and at one bound taken the first place among American dramatists. And the place is so utterly and highly removed that there is no second and no third. The rest—I mean all—are bunched indistinguishably a long ways below. *Nadjezda* is, so far as my knowledge goes, the most powerful play written in English during the present generation. And even more than this might be said, since to get a drama of an equal and terrible intensity of plot, and barehanded—I had almost said reckless audacity of treatment—one must go back to the titanic tragedies of Ford and Webster. In the plays of Shakespeare there is always a certain restraint, a decorum either of taste or of policy, not to be found in *The White Devil* and *The Broken Heart*.

Nadjezda is a genuine tragedy from first to last . . . At the end of the tremendous prologue I was irresistibly reminded of *The Duchess of Malfi*. This is not through any similarity of plot or situation, but simply from the vague but none the less valid and awful kinship of blood and agony. I might have said tears, but the emotions of the scene are too deep for tears, and can only find vent in the wretched wife's maniacal laughter. Some critics have called *Nadjezda* a red-blood play, but it is a misnomer. It is written in blood, to be sure, but it is heart's blood turned into gall with a bitterness beyond the bitterness of death. It is a play that begins at the rise of the curtain (a rare merit), and once launched upon its destined course it never halts but hurries on with the force of the tropic typhoon to its appointed culmination in desolation, ruin and death . . .

Such praise, running three columns in the *Courier*, should have contributed to the play's continued success. It proved to be its American epitaph. *Nadjezda* was not played again that season. The work which should have placed M. H. Barrymore in the front rank of American dramatists was obscured by the machinations of an apprehensive wife, a discarded lover and her defensive husband.

XVIII

Wary of further conflict with Madame, Georgie accepted another engagement in New York. The managers, Maubury and Overton, were reputable; the play, *The Wages of Sin,* had been successful in London; the role offered the chance for a good comedy characterization. Still, it was not an easy choice for Mrs. Barrymore. Her family would be scattered again, the children with Mrs. Drew, Barry committed to touring with Modjeska until the end of the season. Though perfectly aware that separation would intensify her jealousy, she had resolved never again to interfere with her husband's work.

"Between Modjeska and Barrymore it was evidently a case of 'all passion spent,'" wrote Marion Coleman, Madame's biographer. And even the blustering Count seemed chastened, plying the leading man with something approaching courtesy as the tour continued. When *East Lynne* entered the repertoire in Philadelphia, Barry was far from "letter perfect." Afterward, as the forgetful leading man was making his ablutions, Count Bozenta entered his dressing room.

"Maurice," said the Count, in gentle reproach, "you did not speak your lines tonight, eh?"

"Oh, yes I did," replied Barry, "*my* lines." Bozenta merely smiled, patted the shoulder of his wife's leading man, departed. Barry stared after him incredulously. Never before had the contentious Count allowed him the last word.

Before leaving Philadelphia, Barry received an offer which he considered the most flattering of his acting career. Squire Bancroft and his wife, after twenty years as London's foremost theatrical managers, had decided to retire. In the past, when the Bancrofts had invited Barry to join their company, first at the Prince of Wales's Theatre, then at the Haymarket, he had been unable to accept. This would be his last chance. The

Bancrofts were planning, the following autumn, a gala farewell season of revivals of their greatest successes. "The first of them being *Diplomacy*," Bancroft wrote to Barry, "which has not been acted in London since we first produced it at the Prince of Wales's seven years ago. I have decided, with many a sigh, to give up my favourite *Orloff* to you, Mr. Barrymore, if you so choose, thinking that on the whole I should best serve the general effect as *Henry Beauclerc*." Flattery apart, the offer struck Barry as propitious: a chance to arrange a London production of *Nadjezda*, while introducing Georgie and the children in style to his old city. Besides a generous $200 a week offered by Bancroft, Barry had $12,500 coming from his brother in payment for Wharncliff. He wrote Grover and Humphreys to deposit the money in a London bank, and, bursting with his good fortune, invited Mrs. Drew, Sidney and Tibby to come along. It would be a full-fledged family party, since John Drew was performing in England that summer with the entire Daly aggregation. Mr. Barrymore booked passage on the same ship, the Guion Line's S.S. *Alaska*, sailing July 5 from New York.

Exultant with summer prospects, the Barrymores fulfilled their previous commitments: Barry to Toronto with Modjeska; Georgie to New York and rehearsals for *The Wages of Sin*. On May 12, he was playing the Park Theatre, Hannibal, Missouri, when Georgie's play opened at the Fourteenth Street, New York. "She stepped into the stunning costume of the debutante," reported the *Dramatic Mirror* "and lighted up the house with a few flashes of her admirable comedy."

A fellow player, C. P. Flockton, who had introduced Barry to acting at the Windsor Theatre Royal, noted what a revelation she had been. "She electrified New York," said the veteran actor-manager, "and showed what a great advantage it is to be well trained for the profession one follows." Georgie left *The Wages of Sin* company after four weeks, returning to Philadelphia and preparations for the impending journey.

Barry was waiting there, having finally ended the eight-month odyssey with Modjeska, galvanized by a new project. He had completed another play, *The Don*, during the last few weeks on the road. "Barrymore writes with fierce speed," observed Amy Leslie, "a mental precocity which burns with an exalted light and races away from suspected possibilities in himself. He has woven plays of fascinating intensity, and plunged into themes upon scientific phenomena and social economics." The new play was another powerful essay on injustice and retribution, the story of a wronged aristocrat whom dissipation drags to the slums where his comrades of the gutter name him *The Don*. His adventures, from the shabby heart of London to a convict prison in Australia, culminating in his regeneration, formed the substance of Barry's Dickensian conception.

At the Press Club in Chicago after the theater one night, the author had been describing his newly finished play to some interested actors and journalists. Among them was Henry Lee, whom Barry had previously met at the Lambs' while Lee was winning New York as villain to James O'Neill's *Monte Cristo*. Now, at the Press Club, Lee urged the author to let him produce and star in a Chicago production of his new play. Committed to a season in London, Barry agreed to give him rights to *The Don*.

Frantic preparation permeated the Tomb of the Capulets for the voyage only three weeks away. Mrs. Drew had regretfully decided against traveling to England with her daughter and son-in-law. Arch Street business needed attending, and a daughter, Louise, had been born to John and Josephine Drew. The new grandchild would stay at North Twelfth Street while Josephine accompanied John and the Daly Company to England. Barry implored his mother-in-law to allow Sidney and Tibby, at least, to come along. She decided that her favored Sidney, much to the disappointment of the sixteen-year-old hellion, would stay at home. Although the children would not have Uncle Googan to spice the voyage, Barry's persistence won release for timid Adine Stephens, their beloved Aunt Tibby.

Packing proceeded frenetically, Georgie and the servants filling, emptying, refilling twenty-odd pieces of luggage—steamer trunks, Saratogas, sundry handbags. Only Aunt Tibby went methodically and peacefully about her business. She, who had never been farther than New York City, had read a circular from the Guion Line. "A steamer trunk that could be slipped under the berths seems the most advisable thing," she imparted to Barry, and he watched with a deep smile as she scientifically filled it: warm flannel wrapper, extra clothing for cold days at sea, dress for special occasions, toilet articles, a notebook and a Cross fountain pen, just such accessories as were absolutely necessary.

Much less scientifically, much more elaborately the rest of the party was miraculously packed and ready for departure. Mrs. Drew, Sidney, and Alexina Fisher Baker accompanied the voyagers to New York. As they drove down in carriages to the wharf, they saw a stir of people already gathered on the deck of the steamer. Union Square and the Lambs' Club seemed to have moved to the docks that bright summer morning to bid the Daly troupe and the Barrymore clan bon voyage. Mr. Barrymore and party climbed over the gangplank, down into the saloon, still further down, into First Class outside staterooms—one for Georgie and Barry, with two others adjoining for Aunt Tibby and Ethel, Lionel and Jack. Their steward and stewardess, immaculately uniformed, and a French governess, obtained for the voyage through the Guion Line, introduced themselves with crisp formality.

Leaving more mundane matters to this obviously capable trio, the voyagers returned to bustle and commotion on deck. They exchanged reluctant good-bys with Mrs. Drew and Sidney and Mrs. Baker, embracing after last call, watching, waving as they hurried down the gangplank. The children rushed to find places at the rail. Held tightly by their parents, with Aunt Tibby, Uncle Jack and Aunt Dodo nearby, they searched for Mummum on the crowded wharf below. It was not difficult to find her. She and Mrs. Baker, in perpetual widow's weeds, made a small black island in a sea of waving arms.

At last the order was given, the plank withdrawn. As the great engine began to throb, the motion of the vessel was just perceptible. Gradually the distance widened, friends on shore sent up last calls of good speed and bon voyage, handkerchiefs fluttered, sending signals and wiping tears. Lionel, Ethel, little Jack strained to catch a parting glimpse of their grandmother as the wharf receded out of sight. They turned from boatside to look into the faces of their parents, whose tears, like their own, were not yet dried. Suddenly they began to laugh, Mr. and Mrs. Barrymore, their three children, as S.S. *Alaska* took the open sea.

Guided by their solicitous French governess, the Barrymore children donned appropriate sea garments, and found their steamer chairs, rapturously climbing into them, pulling rugs nearly to their eyes, watching as the stream of fellow passengers passed on deck against the swelling sea. Papa took them on an exploratory tour of the *Alaska*, two-and-a-half-year-old Jack all the while insisting, as they penetrated the palatial labyrinth, that they couldn't possibly be on a boat. At the sound of the half-hour dinner bell, Mademoiselle whisked her charges off to change for their early meal in the children's saloon. Afterward, Georgie, arrayed in exquisite dinner clothes, escorted her three progeny out on deck to watch the sun set over the waves, till, sleepy and tired with the day's excitements, they were taken below.

Mr. and Mrs. Barrymore, Augustin Daly and William Winter were seated among distinguished nontheatrical guests at the captain's table. Winter, erstwhile New York *Tribune* critic and Daly partisan, had come along at the Governor's invitation to witness what would be the first performance of an American company in England. Although eight years had passed since Barry's facetious disruption of a sacrosanct Winter "at home," the critic had not forgotten it. Initial pique had ripened into a lingering skepticism concerning Barry's devotion to his profession, now somewhat mitigated by *Nadjezda* and the young actor's forthcoming engagement with the Bancrofts. But Winter was pleasant toward him during the voyage, when not fretting with the Governor over the Daly Company's potential reception in England.

The voyage proceeded over smooth sea, the shipboard routine enhanced by the speeches, songs and readings of talented passengers in the evening. During a benefit for the children of disabled seamen, performed by the Barrymores and some of the Daly company, a new and suggestive motion of the ship became evident. The performers grasped at near stationary objects, attempting to maintain their balance, while swaying lights and movable objects became increasingly apparent. The Barrymores persevered with their scene from *As You Like It*, until a wave more impertinent or more aspiring than its predecessors dashed through an open porthole, drenching Aunt Tibby. She was speedily rescued, and, with no more harm done than if she had taken a voluntary salt-water bath, changed and returned for the closing scene.

After the performance, the Barrymores made their way to the outer deck. Holding onto the stair railing, then clinging to one another, they observed the awesome spectacle of a storm at sea, as the steamer glided up and down with the strain and creak of timber and rope. Returning to their staterooms to check on the children, Georgie found Mademoiselle calmly knitting as the three little ones lay fast asleep, "literally," observed Mrs. Barrymore, "rocked in the cradle of the deep."

Bulletins were issued each day announcing how many miles had been made, but the anxious children asked the captain over and over again, "When shall we get to Liverpool?" Lionel Barrymore, articulate for his six years, related the response. "Captain Roberts is gracious to us," he told Papa, "but keeps his own counsel and we can only hope soon to see land once more." Then, one clear morning, they saw the red coast of Ireland, with spots of green so well defined that Georgie likened it to "a piece of patchwork."

Next day, Mamma awakened them early, calling cheerily, "We shall be there now, kids." Lionel jumped up to the porthole; the view was not encouraging, just fog and mewing sea gulls.

"Can't see land at all now," he announced.

"What," said Ethel; "why we saw it all yesterday."

"Yes," her older brother repeated impatiently, "but you can't see any now."

At three o'clock, the fog lifted. A steam tug approached. The Barrymore party assembled on deck as the plank was pushed out and a slow procession of men with baggage filed across. After bidding farewell to Mademoiselle, they passed over the *Alaska*'s side, across the plank, into the tug. The children scrambled aboard without a backward glance, clamoring for Papa to lift them for a view of Liverpool.

An estate agent, hired at Barry's request by Grover and Humphreys, greeted the Liverpool train at London's Euston Station. Marshaling Barrymores and baggage into a waiting carriage, he escorted them to the house which had been leased in St. John's Wood, a fashionable London suburb, where modern Britain, ancient Rome, and medieval Holland clashed architecturally. Barry had advised his solicitors to spare no ex-

2 1 8

pense, so the Barrymores' first house of their own was impressive, placed as it was in a row of handsome town houses with wide back gardens protected by high brick walls. From the third-floor nursery at the back of the house could be seen the venerable cupolas of Lord's, the shrine of English cricket. The children, tantalized mornings by the 11:20 pavilion bell, attempted to watch the matches from their window with Papa's field glasses. Barry promised to take them to the Eton-Harrow match in July.

Rehearsals for the Bancroft engagement would not commence until autumn, so, for the first time, the Barrymores were a family unhampered by theatrical obligations. Georgie reveled in the role of wife and mother in this idyllic setting, while Barry played man of the house with new gusto, freely spending the $12,500 which had arrived from his brother in payment for Wharncliff. "Those London days are clear and shiny in my mind," Ethel recalled. "Everything about those two years was magical."

Free of Mrs. Drew's stern opposition, Barry promptly filled the new house with pets. Five or six dogs of various species were soon romping in the garden, and large cages were installed for birds and monkeys. Papa's numerous pets were rough playfellows, but the Barrymore children, particularly the two oldest, managed to excel them. Although fiercely protective of her younger brother, Ethel frequently quarreled with the older. Their disagreements seldom ended in mere words, but, when adults were not about, often came to blows, usually fought to a draw. "My brother was a stout youth," Ethel explained, "and from the outcome of the battles I fancy I was a stout maiden."

Georgie found a congenial young nanny, Polly, with crinkly red hair, whom Papa said looked like the beautiful actress Mary Anderson, only more beautiful. She introduced her impressionable charges to the wonders of London—including the Chamber of Horrors at Madame Tussaud's, which gave Ethel vivid, audible nightmares for some time to come. "In future," Mamma admonished Polly, "the British Museum might be more restful."

Soon after their arrival, the Barrymores were invited to tea by Henry and Elizabeth Wace. The brother-in-law of Barry's sister, Evelin, was now Principal of King's College and Honorary Chaplain to Queen Victoria. Recalling Wace's narrow disapproval of his acting, Barry approached the house in Portland Place, a relic of his old Oxford days, with misgivings but not without curiosity. They were greeted with staunch cordiality by the Waces, although Barry noted that not the slightest allusion was made to his theatrical career. To Henry Wace, this young man was Herbert Blyth of the upstanding colonial family into which his brother had married; the years intervening, the accomplishments therein, simply ceased to be. Much was made of Will Blyth's sheep in New Zealand—"a gentleman's proclivity," judged Harry—and the promotion of Evelin's husband to Commissioner at Lahore.

Georgie had urged the children to display their best manners during this visit, and their behavior was exemplary until tea was served. Lionel, after his first sip, suddenly looked up at Mrs. Wace. "Ma'am," offered the six-year-old, "this tea is damn hot." The Waces exchanged pointed glances. A shocked silence was broken only by Georgie's stifled laughter.

"Georgiana," said Barry, looking sternly at his wife, "haven't I warned you not to let the children stray into the coachman's quarters, where they hear such language?" The Barrymores and the Waces, by unspoken mutual consent, seldom met afterward.

Theatrical London proved more welcoming than the Waces had been. Neighbors in St. John's Wood were the Volkes Family of actors, the current theatrical rage, which included Rosina Volkes, who had wed a solicitor, Cecil Clay, scion of a titled clan. While their frequent parties were amusing, the conscious mixture of theater and society still displeased the son of the Blyths. The attempts of society figures to ape the Bohemianism of actors chafed nearly as much as the attempts of actors to imitate society. This latter affliction ran rampant in the theatrical circles to which Mr. and Mrs. Barrymore were introduced by the Bancrofts. But friends were found among them, including Henry Irving and Ellen Terry; Lillie Langtry and Mrs. Bernard-Beere, society women turned actresses; and particularly William Kendal and his wife Madge—the twenty-second child of a provincial actor-manager, and sister of dramatist T. W. Robertson—who as Mr. and Mrs. Kendal held a place second only to the Bancrofts in the English theater.

Usually, however, Barry and Georgie gravitated to the more Bohemian dramatical and musical circle which gathered around two young men of means and theatrical aspirations. Percy Anderson, a promising artist and theatrical designer, shared a suite of rooms, artistically furnished, in Queen Anne's Gate, with William Fullerton, the son of a noted American judge. Anderson, immaculate and saucer-eyed, with a red handlebar mustache, and Fullerton, of aristocratic bearing, fair and delicate, had formed a devoted alliance when the latter arrived in London after studying music in Leipzig. The Barrymores, John and Josephine Drew, Tibby Stephens joined the artistic assortment of theatrical aspirants, established personages, and forgotten greats drawn together by these talented young men: Hayden Coffin, about to make his debut in *The Lady of the Locket*, the first Fullerton-Anderson collaboration for the theater; George Grossmith, Jr., of Savoy Theatre fame; Henry Kemble, Arthur Cecil, who had played in *Honour;* Mrs. Godfrey Pearse, charming daughter of Carlotta Grisi, the legendary ballerina.

Barry thrived in this atmosphere, and began discussing an *opéra bouffe* idea with Willy Fullerton. Delighted by Barry's concept, Willy suggested that they begin an earnest collaboration in March after *The Lady of the Locket* opened. It would be an exclusive production of the

Queen Anne's Gate group—libretto, music, costumes by Barrymore, Fullerton, Anderson, respectively, and starring Hayden Coffin. Barry once more frequented the British Museum Reading Room to research the new work, which he called, *Waldemar, or The Robber of the Rhine.*

The Barrymores were usually "at home" Sunday afternoons, and the house in St. John's Wood, observed the New York *Tribune*, "was noted as a social, literary and artistic centre." High tea was ceremoniously served—tea and cakes, bread and butter, elaborate French pastries, and, for the heartier guests, coffee, claret or sherry. Repartee flourished at these gatherings, generated by the host and hostess, sustained by new friends, and old ones like Paul Potter, still struggling to break into the theater, and Ned Donnelly, who regaled Barry's boys with monologues on the art of self-defense, sometimes, to their extreme delight, illustrating points with Papa in the garden. The illiterate "Royal Professor" was then enjoying new fame as a result of his recent book, *The Art of Self-Defense,* which he had dictated to a collaborator. Ned proudly "read" from his published treatise to the amused Barrymore children, inadvertently holding the book upside down.

When tea was served, Ethel was usually assigned the passing of cakes, which she performed with her eyes cast shyly down. "Look up, Pauline!" Mamma called one afternoon. Her daughter obeyed, gazing into the singular face of a gentleman guest. She stared for an instant, let go a shattering shriek, dropped the plate, and ran from the drawing room. "Oscar Wilde was the bogie-man of my babyhood," Ethel explained. "He was so tall that it seemed he would never quite get up to his real height, and he had such a great head! I was fond of the other clever people who came to my father's house, but I always feared and disliked him." Nevertheless, Wilde was a particular friend of her parents, and she had offended him. Unlike Lionel's comment at the Waces', which had amused Papa, Ethel's rudeness infuriated him. A London equivalent of Mummum's "green slipper" was located, and Barry thrashed his daughter for the first and only time. "I don't remember ever being so severely punished for anything," Ethel said years later.

On the evening of July 19, 1884, the first American company to play in England made its debut—not without apprehension. "To a city whose theatres held records of celebrated runs and noted actors, a city bristling with tradition and insularity," remarked Otis Skinner, a newcomer to the Daly fold, "the challenge of a troupe of American comedians smacked of the audacious. What right had we to take the bread out of English actors' mouths? The reflection that English actors have for years been filling their mouths with American bread in our country did not, perhaps, occur to them."

Toole's Theatre in Chandus Street, small and somewhat shabby, was filled on opening night. The stalls, fortunately, held a majority of vacationing Americans, but just behind them were the merciless local pittites, ready to hiss and boo if displeased. The Barrymores, with Josephine, Tibby, and Mrs. James Lewis in the back row of the stalls, separated only by a rail from the front row of the pit, heard derisive remarks from that quarter long before the curtain rose. "Well, 'ere's 'alf a crown thrown away!" shouted one burly chap as he took his seat.

As the performance progressed, hostility gradually lessened. Daly had astutely chosen to open the engagement with *Seven-Twenty-Eight*, an adaptation of his from the German, unknown in England, thus discouraging critical comparison. The only hissing was in defiance of aggressively friendly demonstrations by American patrons, but soon that subsided, and the Britons ultimately approved the interlopers. Press notices were what might be called conservative, lightened by grudging praise for the players. When Daly dared to end his London season with an old English comedy, *She Would and She Would Not*, it was paradoxically greeted with greater, if guarded, enthusiasm by press and public. But the Governor's venture was considered an unequivocal triumph by his countrymen. The company was given tumultuous welcome upon its return in September. Even Lester Wallack, Daly's long-time rival, called it "the pluckiest thing ever done."

London's attitude toward Mr. and Mrs. Bancroft's impending Farewell Season was decidedly different. For twenty years as husband and wife, and for a decade before that as Squire Bancroft and Marie Wilton, they had lavished vitality, dignity and reform upon the English stage. Drawing-room comedy and modern drama were popularized by the Bancrofts; the advent of naturalistic acting, functional stage setting and décor were perfected during their respective managements of the Prince of Wales's Theatre and the Theatre Royal, Haymarket. As a student at Wren's, Barry had cheered their comedies at the Prince of Wales's, along with most of London's theater-going public. They had won affection from their patrons, the respect of their peers, the acceptance of society. Even royalty was in their debt after Lillie Langtry, at the behest of her friend, the Prince of Wales, made her debut at the Haymarket under the Bancrofts.

As husband and wife, as well as business partners, the Bancrofts were perfectly matched. He, tall, spare, distinguished, was the perfectionist, a man who had to do it all by himself; she, short, round, jovial, was an inspiration to him, a loyal helper, who optimistically trusted that it would all come right in the end. In policy and business, he was the leader, but in art she excelled. Squire Bancroft was a good, sound, distinguished performer; Marie Wilton Bancroft had genius.

For all their accomplishments, they remained generous and unassuming, always searching out new talent, not merely to enhance their own positions—they often took secondary roles in their own productions—but to create a perfect company for the benefit of players and patrons alike. The announcement of their retirement from management, soon after the twentieth anniversary of the opening of the Prince of Wales's, precipitated regret in theatrical circles, much comment and lead articles in the newspapers, and a rush on the Haymarket box office. The Bancrofts, their sterling company, their jewel-like theater were touched with a special light that season.

Maurice Barrymore would make his London debut in Bancroft's favorite role during this celebrated Farewell Season, an honor which struck Barry only insomuch as his liking and respect for Squire and Marie Bancroft touched him. As previously, in similar associations with Edwin Booth and Joseph Jefferson, he faced rehearsals enthusiastically, with dedication.

On the evening of November 28, 1884, the most brilliant theatrical audience within memory crowded between Corinthian columns into the tawny marble and gleaming mahogany precinct of the Theatre Royal, Haymarket. At the stage door, professional beggars lurked, assuming good-naturedly the guise of a super or stagehand out of work. District flower girls, led by a blue-eyed, Greuze-like creature named Polly, had risen to the occasion, sporting fantastic picture hats laden with ostrich plumes and paper roses, their noses tilted in a vain attempt to walk like their beloved Princess Alexandra. "'Ave a flar, dee'?" they called to passing playgoers.

Inside, amid classical frescoes of gamboling youths and maidens, the mumbling mass filled canopied baroque stage boxes, crowded velvet-covered stalls, overspilled the second circle installed by Bancroft in lieu of the pit which he had abolished. It quieted to an expectant hush as Mrs. Bancroft's ivory-colored satin curtain rose on the first act of *Diplomacy*.

The ovation at the close of the performance held "a genuine ring of heartfelt admiration and encouragement," observed *The Theatre*, and, after double honors had been paid to the principals, Mr. Bancroft came alone onstage to break his long-held precedent and gave a moving "first-night speech."

Despite the emotion of the evening, the critics were not disposed to "giving" the performance to the Bancrofts and their company. Their evaluations were objective and acute. There was little to fault in the production itself, but not all of the players, among England's best, were praised. Mr. Barrymore, re-creating one of Squire Bancroft's most successful roles, and from America besides, might well have incurred critical wrath. "Mr. Maurice Barrymore," began *The Era* critic, "an actor well known in America, made his first appearance in London in the character of *Count Orloff*. Rumour had whispered that he was possessed of many qualifications likely to secure him high favour with London playgoers, and rumour for once had adhered to the truth. Mr. Barrymore has a handsome appearance, an expressive face, a good voice, and an easy gentlemanly style. He received no cheer of welcome, but he went about his work in a way that soon made a good impression, and when the curtain fell upon the second act he had scored a great triumph, and had won the enthusiastic expressions of the house . . . the whole house was ready to admit that an actor of more than ordinary intelligence and skill has come amongst us in the person of Mr. Barrymore."

The dailies concurred, and *The Theatre*, which four years before had bitterly questioned Barry's authorship of *Honour*, stated that "By merely expressing the different feelings aroused in the spectator's mind from the respective performances of Mr. Bancroft as *Henry Beauclerc* and Mr. Barrymore as *Count Orloff*, one would scarcely give an adequate idea of the finished polish of style and manner so eminently characterizing the work of these gentlemen . . . If, on the other hand, enthusiastic applause may be accepted as a worthy tribute of well-deserved success in the truest and best sense of the word, then must Mr. Barrymore rest fully assured of the favourable impression made by him from first to last upon his audience." Such acclaim brought with it honors and irritations during *Diplomacy*'s exceptional three-month run: respect from his peers, which he appreciated; stage-door crushes and fluttering matinee ladies, which he detested. One tattered youth became a fixture outside the Haymarket stage door after performances, day and night waiting to gaze at his idol and follow him, running behind his cab, all the way to St. John's Wood.

One night, Barry left the theater with Charles Brookfield to find the city wrapped in a devastating fog that locals proudly called a "London particular." Unable to find a cab, the two actors began a walk to St. John's Wood. Behind them as they went, they heard footsteps. It was a night for thieves and cutthroats, so when they reached the Barrymore house, Barry pushed his friend through the gate, while he awaited the intruder. Discerning a slight silhouette through the fog, he jumped out and grabbed it by the collar.

"Here's the young beggar that's been following me for six weeks," he called to Brookfield. "What d'ye want?" Overcome by the proximity of his idol, the youth could not answer. Seeing that he was frightened and harmless, his captor released him to run back down the fogbound street. "That," said Barry, pointing to the vanishing apparition, "is my public."

After his auspicious debut, Barry, as usual, turned to other pursuits. Afternoons were frequently passed with Ned Donnelly at the School of Arms, with Lionel and Jack occasionally in tow. Nights were more diversified. The visitor received cards to predominantly theatrical and sporting clubs, the Regency, Green Room, and Savage clubs, attended smoking concerts, and graced Henry Irving's entertainments at the Beefsteak Room. His most frequent retreat, however, was offered by another visitor from America.

"When I wished to picture a real stage hero," recalled James T. Powers, "I always thought of Maurice Barrymore, whom I first met in London. I often think of him and the happy hours I spent with him there." Powers, a young American comedian, who resembled an altruistic gargoyle, had made his first big hit that season in Offenbach's *Chilperic* at the New Empire Theatre. His rooms in Panton Street were directly opposite Stone's wine-and-chop house, and around the corner from the Haymarket. Barry, Charley Brookfield, and Johnston Forbes-Robertson ("Forbie") often supped at Stone's after the play, and, when it closed, usually ended up across the street at "The Jimmie Club," as Barry dubbed it, with the likes of Marius, the French actor, his wife, Florence St. John, English leading man Herbert Standing, music hall comedian Albert Chevalier, and Phil May, the sketch artist. As they made merry with reminiscences, stories, song, Barry inevitably asked Jimmie to sing "Paddy Stole the Rope." One night, while the tenor was hitting his favorite high C, a bobby knocked at the door.

"Please, sir, a little less noise, sir," the officer asked; then, to Barry's urging, replied, "Thank you, sir; I don't mind if I do take a nip, sir." He took several nips, and commenced a comic song of his own, until a voice from without interrupted him.

"Less noise, please," called the lodger next door, "or I'll speak to the bobby on the beat."

When work began with Will Fullerton on *Robber of the Rhine*, Barry took a furnished flat in the circle place at the end of Store Street. The house in St. John's Wood, brimming with children, retainers and pets, was distracting for a working writer, particularly for one who seldom slept, and, therefore, lacked patience. Although Lionel had been enrolled at the Gilmore School in Warrington Crescent, the remaining inmates more than compensated. In Store Street, during the day, there was much peace for working, and, at night, after the play, "there was much—too much—good-fellowship," recalled journalist Harry St. Maur. "Barry had the kind of geniality that catches its glow from surroundings; he had to do what was being done to avoid what would have seemed to him unkindness."

Georgie, at first wary of her husband's new residence, soon had reason to appreciate it. After Saturday evening performances at the Haymarket, Barry would frequently whisk his wife away from St. John's Wood. Free from the distractions of home, they would spend intimate weekends together in Store Street until Monday evenings came, and Barry returned to the Haymarket, Georgie to St. John's Wood.

Thus relieved, Mrs. Barrymore became reconciled to her husband's erratic domesticity. For a time, he would be a doting husband and father, beguiling Georgie, engaging the children in games and frolics, treating them to the Drury Lane pantomime, *Whittington and his Cat,* or mornings at Ned Donnelly's and afternoons in Hyde Park, visiting the zoo and rowing on the Serpentine. Then, for weeks, involved with writing or roistering, he would hardly see them. Though he neither premeditated nor analyzed such behavior, Georgie viewed it as the result of his constant need to divert an overactive mind.

"While he was with you he was indivisibly yours," explained William Rideing, his crony from Oscar's in New York, "and the rest of the world had to wait for him; but when the rest of the world captured him in its turn you became a negligible quantity. His engagements were recorded in air. He meant to keep them, no doubt; he was contrite when he failed, but his clock stopped, and time had no measurements as he abandoned himself to any society that interested him. So amiable was he, so diverting, so original, that his companions never willingly let him go, and they were as much to blame, if not more, for his delinquencies."

Rideing met Barry in the Strand one morning, and took him off to his club, where they spent the whole afternoon in absorbing discussion of the Irish question. As in his student days, English politics preoccupied Barry. He became a passionate spokesman for the Prime Minister, Mr. Gladstone, and Irish Home Rule. Rideing, in London for the New York *Tribune,* had achieved a journalistic coup by getting Gladstone and his archopponent, Mr. Balfour, to debate the explosive Home Rule issue.

It was already dark when Barry interrupted their discussion to say that he really must go. Rideing urged him to stay for dinner; Barry insisted that he had a pressing engagement. "At what hour?" Rideing asked.

"At one o'clock," Barry replied, and it was then nearly seven.

As the libretto for *Waldemar, or The Robber of the Rhine* progressed, *Masks and Faces,* then *Ours* joined the Bancrofts' farewell repertoire. In the first, *The Era* noted, "Mr. Barrymore strengthened the good opinion we have already expressed respecting his histrionic capabilities." In the latter, as *Angus M'Alister,* he disappointed the same critic: "This part we thought would fit this actor like the proverbial glove; but from first to last he was tame and spiritless, and failed to awaken the smallest amount of interest among his audience. Remembering how excellent was Mr. Barrymore's acting in *Diplomacy,* we could only arrive at the conclusion that he was dissatisfied with his task, and took little interest in his performance."

He was not dissatisfied with the role—he had even mastered a Scottish dialect to play it—nor had his admiration for the Bancrofts diminished. But it was true that he took little interest in his performance, for society

226

sapped him, and *The Robber of the Rhine* preoccupied him. He frequented the British Museum Reading Room, seeking information of Germanic gypsies and brigands, of their argot and their names. His fanciful adaptation of German and French names, in fact, lightened many a work session, as he and Will Fullerton went about the exacting business of fitting libretto to music. The *opéra bouffe*, conceived along spectacular lines, inspired extraordinary sketches for costumes and scenes from Percy Anderson. "Through all the years that followed," observed Hayden Coffin, "that wonderful artist never designed anything more striking than his costume for *Waldemar* and I was keenly looking forward to taking the title-role."

Ours played successfully into the summer, until the time came to set the date for the Bancrofts' last performance. "We were much honoured by the Prince of Wales suggesting the date," stated Squire Bancroft, "in order that he might, with the Princess of Wales, be present." Monday, July 20, 1885, was duly set for the last performance. "From the day that our farewell was announced," Mr. Bancroft continued, "the booking-office was besieged by applications, made in every possible way, to secure seats for the last night of our management, and it became a very difficult matter to deal with them, as no building that I know anything about would have held the many thousands who honoured us with a wish to be present."

There was a crush outside the Haymarket on the evening of July 20. Those who had obtained seats attempted to reach them through the less fortunate throng surrounding the entrance in hopes of glimpsing Their Royal Highnesses. "In front of the footlights had assembled a crowded audience, representative of literature, art, science, and 'society'," gushed *The Era*, "while behind them there was another crowd made up of the cream of dramatic talent . . ."

The Bancrofts and their present company did not appear in the first two offerings, excerpts from *Money* and *London Assurance*. These were acted entirely by past members of their companies, who had volunteered this compliment to their former managers. No greater tribute to the Bancrofts could have been proffered than this "host of the shining lights of the London stage," as *The Era* put it, who had, for the most part, been nurtured under Bancroft regimes at the Prince of Wales's and the Haymarket. Such venerable artists as Mrs. Stirling, Mrs. John Wood, Mr. and Mrs. Kendal, Charles Wyndham, and playwright-actor Arthur Wing Pinero had merely enhanced their careers by appearances with the Bancrofts. But the others, including William Terriss, John Hare, Ellen Terry, Lillie Langtry, had inaugurated or substantially furthered their careers by the association.

"Expectation rose to its greatest height," as time approached for the Bancrofts' appearance in the last two acts of *Masks and Faces*, Charles Reade and Tom Taylor's play of eighteenth-century theatrical life. Barry's determination to give his best London performance that evening as *Ernest Vane*, to be worthy of such exalted associates, was heightened by the knowledge that between Georgie and Tibby in the audience sat his fastidious mother-in-law. He had arranged passage for Mrs. Drew and Sidney, and, affairs at the Arch concluded for the summer, they had arrived that week in London. Louisa Lane Drew was touched and excited by this return to the homeland from which she had departed sixty years before. But those emotions did not surpass her unspoken pride in the achievement of her son-in-law.

"How I managed to dress for my part, I know not," recalled Mrs. Bancroft. "I can only remember floral offerings of every conceivable design being brought to me, until there were so many that they had to be taken to a larger room. When I walked on to the stage in the second act of *Masks and Faces*, among *Ernest Vane*'s other guests, my reception was so overpowering, and the 'Good-bye' in my throat so big, that I nearly gave way." Barry, discerning the lady's condition, gently but firmly took her arm. "Mr. Barrymore whispered to me, 'Bear up,' and that brought me to myself," continued Mrs. Bancroft. "I gathered up all the strength at my command, and conquered the almost uncontrollable desire to cry."

At the end of the third act, when Mrs. Bancroft spoke *Peg Woffington*'s farewell to the *Vanes*, more eyes than her own in that elegant house were wet with tears:

> Good-bye. When hereafter you hear harsh sentence passed on us— whose lot was admiration, rarely love; triumph, but seldom tranquility —think sometimes of us and say, Stage *Masks* may cover honest *Faces*, and hearts beat true beneath a tinselled robe.

After an unprecedented demonstration, cheering that must have reached the bronze ears of Lord Nelson in Trafalgar Square, Henry Irving made his way through banked floral tributes to read critic Clement Scott's "Valedictory Ode" for the departing couple; the celebrated comedian J. L. Toole offered a stirring tribute; Mr. Bancroft, painfully agitated, made a moving last farewell; and the audience rose as one to sing "Auld Lang Syne." The Princess of Wales then sent for Mrs. Bancroft, and after gracious words of sympathy, presented her with the bouquet which she was carrying. But none proved more fitting than Mrs. Bancroft's recitation of *Peg Woffington*'s words. They might also have served as a glorious finish to Maurice Barrymore's London sojourn. It was not to be.

Squire Bancroft had granted an underlease of the Haymarket Theatre to Edward Russell and G. F. Bashford, his former business managers, who would reopen in September with the benefit of the Bancrofts' advice. "The new management is already in treaty for several important novelties," announced *The Era*. "It is probable that the opening play will be Mr. Barrymore's *Nadjezda*, which not long since was successfully produced in America, with Madame Modjeska in the title-role."

XIX

THE BARRYMORES, GUESTS and pets in tow, withdrew for the summer to Weybridge, Surrey, where Barry had taken a cottage. In the relative calm following the August departure of Mrs. Drew, Sidney and Tibby for America, amid country pleasures, the author prepared for *Nadjezda*'s London opening. The play was ready for presentation when they returned to St. John's Wood, but the exacting author had been unable to find an English actress suitable for the title role. After much deliberation with Russell and Bashford, from which Georgie pointedly abstained, he decided to offer the role once more to Modjeska. Madame's return cable, regretting that an impending tour prohibited her participation, urged Barry to return as her leading man. But *Nadjezda* was uppermost in his mind, and because of it he was committed to another season at the Haymarket under the new management.

Undaunted by Madame's refusal, Barry sought a comparable replacement. Sarah Bernhardt's manager expressed his client's interest in a Paris production of the play. As Bernhardt performed in French, however, she would not do for the imminent London presentation. The author recalled another actress whose power had once impressed him as equal to the demands of his play: Emily Rigl, his consort at Daly's and his leading lady at Wallack's, accepted Barry's transatlantic offer, advising him that commitments in America would delay her arrival. Another play, therefore, was hastily sought to open the Haymarket season. *Dark Days*, a powerful drama by Hugh Conway and Comyns Carr, was chosen, and Barry cast in one of the leading parts.

The new management achieved a notable success on Saturday, September 26, 1885. The house was crowded by a representative first-night audience, which included Mr. and Mrs. Bancroft, whose appearance in a stage box signaled general cheering. Barry personally liked the new managers but had joined their company, a decided anticlimax to the previous season, only because of the opportunity to present *Nadjezda*. Nevertheless, his playing in *Dark Days* did not suffer. "Mr. Maurice Barrymore as *Dr. Basil North* acted with gentlemanly ease and with appropriate earnestness," attested *The Era*. "We liked the manner of his love-making in the first act, and his determined method in the scenes with *Ferrand* in the second and third delighted the whole house . . . He gave us an impersonation of rare excellence."

Readers of *The Era*, London's leading theatrical journal, were concurrently apprised of other professional pursuits of this protean young actor-author from America: "Mr. Maurice Barrymore, it is said, has put the finishing touches on *The Don*, a new and romantic melodrama, and the manuscript is now in the hands of Mr. Henry Lee, who will produce the play in the early autumn in Chicago in the most elaborate manner as regards scenery and costumes. The play is on the *Romany Rye* order, and is said to be very strong."

Eager anticipation was voiced by Chicago papers before the scheduled opening of Barry's play. "On Sunday evening Mr. Maurice Barrymore's romantic drama, *The Don*, will be presented at the Chicago opera house for the first time on any stage," announced the *Evening News*. "Mr. Barrymore is not only an admirable actor, but he is one of the few actors who possesses literary talent. His play *Nadjezda* was a wonderfully powerful piece of work, and its dialogue was not only effective from a merely theatrical standpoint, but really finely written. Whether *The Don* is a worthy successor of *Nadjezda* cannot yet be determined, but it is said to be a strong and original drama . . ." The author had given Henry Lee carte blanche, specifying only that Charley Vandenhoff be given a role in the production. His cantankerous old friend, Barry had recently learned, was again at liberty, having alienated yet another manager. Besides Charley, Lee had assembled a well-known cast. His preparations for the production had been careful and extensive; the scenic artists for the opera house had been working on the scenery for several weeks.

A. C. Wheeler, the "Nym Crinkle" of the New York *World*, ventured to Chicago for a rehearsal of the new play. "I was amazed at the good work in *The Don*," wrote the critic before the opening, "the cleverness of invention, the play of motive, the contrast of character, the quick transition from pathos to humor, and the abounding evidence of stage effect struck me as being remarkable, and I could not help saying to myself as I recalled *Nadjezda*, 'This young man certainly has the gift that we have been looking for.'"

The Don opened on October 5, a day later than originally announced, "owing," said an advertisement, "to the elaborate character of the production." First-nighters were nonetheless enthusiastic, the *Evening News* reported: "In view of the unusual attractions at the other theatres, it was not to be expected that the Chicago opera house would be filled to overflowing upon the occasion of the first production of *The Don*, but the audience was large and, it may be added, appreciative. There has been such a dearth of everything of a serious dramatic sort in Chicago for the past few months that it is an eminent satisfaction to sit down to a real play, and especially to one with whose production so much care has evidently been taken." This of a play which ran, without particularly long intermissions, three and a half hours!

The scope and scenes of the complex melodrama were admired, from the beautiful house and grounds in Scotland, to a London garret with rickety streets lined by grogshops and gas-flickering street lamps, to the exercising yard of Hobart Town Prison in Australia. "The author shows a Dickensy felicity of hitting off the humors of the slums," observed the *Tribune*, finding several of the characters reminiscent of *David Copperfield*. The performers were generally praised, especially Charley Vandenhoff, "playing the villain in a gentlemanly way—as villains in drama should always be played."

"As for Mr. Barrymore's play," the *Tribune* decided, "it is not a revelation, but it shows him to be clever and prolific in invention . . . is brilliant in spots, pleasing in its phases of humorous portraiture, quick and spirit-stirring . . . but he has not handled his material to the very best advantage, and it will bear revision." Charles Morton Payne in the *Evening News* was not so charitable: "The play needs to be both simplified and strengthened at the critical points before it can pass muster as a creditable piece of dramatic construction. It also needs to be pruned of a large share of the but slightly relevant matter which so confuses its general outline."

Nevertheless, after the close of its remunerative Chicago engagement, *The Don* embarked on a successful Midwestern tour, the author, still hopeful for its salvation, cabling revisions as it went.

With *The Don* streamlined and surviving on the road, *Dark Days* settled in for a long run at the Haymarket, and Emily Rigl's arrival some weeks off, Barry again turned to *The Robber of the Rhine*. He had completed the libretto, but recurring illness compelled Will Fullerton to work sporadically on the score. They would work together when they could in the Queen's Gate flat which Will shared with Percy Anderson, but sessions were curtailed when Percy detected the least sign of fatigue, and hurried his friend off to bed. When Will's health seemed to improve, as it did periodically, work would accelerate, and his and Anderson's Bohemian gatherings would resume. Barry met a young writer there, whose recent novel had been brought to his attention by Ned Donnelly. The Royal Professor had been read installments of the work in *To-day*, a monthly magazine of scientific socialism, and was struck by amazing similarities between the protagonist of the piece and one Herbert Blyth. *Cashel Byron's Profession*, a realistic exposure of pugilism with socialist overtones was far too romantic to be, as some claimed, an indictment of the sport. The book, though well written and socially incisive, was hardly an indictment of anything except, unintentionally, the current school of popular fiction.

Although a few years later, the author, George Bernard Shaw, affected displeasure at anyone who praised his novel for its sporting content, in the winter of 1885 the impecunious young writer was receptive to any interest in his work. And Barry's interest was immediate and overwhelming, for, indeed, *Cashel Byron*, who escapes the middle-class pressures of school and family to become a champion boxer, seemed an incarnation of Herbert Blyth. The twenty-nine-year-old Shaw, whose literary earnings had amounted to six pounds during his previous nine years in London, was gratified by Barry's request to make a play from *Cashel Byron's Profession*. The book, his fifth in five years, had achieved some artistic attention—Robert Louis Stevenson had admired it, and W. E. Henley had considered, then discarded, the idea of making a play out of it—but little popular success had followed. Barry wished to accommodate this seedy apparition, who trimmed his cuffs to the quick with scissors, and wore a tall black hat and black coat green with decay, but with so many other projects pending—completing *Robber of the Rhine*, preparing *Nadjezda*, attempting transatlantic revisions of *The Don*, acting nightly at the Haymarket—he could only hope to adapt *Cashel Byron's Profession* sometime in the future. Nevertheless, he treated the hungry author to countless suppers, where they pursued such fiery topics as Home Rule, on which they agreed, and socialism, of which Shaw was an avid disciple, Barry a staunch foe.

With the advent of Emily Rigl, all unrelated things paled for Maurice Barrymore in *Nadjezda*'s light. Harry St. Maur, himself an actor, dramatist, and contributor to the New York *Telegraph*, observed his friend's condition during those days before *Nadjezda* opened at the Haymarket. "To know a real author at all is a privilege," said St. Maur, "but to be near such a steel-brained, stirring man as Maurice Barrymore was, thrilling with the hope, the reasonable certainty, of producing a great play successfully in a historic London theater—that was something to remember!"

Barry guided his cast through rehearsals, concentrating on the crucial dual characterizations of *Nadjezda* and *Nadine*. Emily Rigl, tall, svelte, sinuous, with luminous, inky eyes, long dark hair and compelling features, gave all of her considerable Germanic will and strength to the creation of these nearly superhuman characters. The author and his wife fit easily into their original roles. Georgie was delighted to be working closely again with her husband, particularly keen to win London audi-

233

ences, since she and Barry had been considering permanent residence in England. The impressive English cast included seasoned professionals Lydia Foote and Robert Pateman, and Herbert Beerbohm Tree, a promising young actor. Little Minnie Terry, Ellen Terry's niece, was engaged to play the child *Nadine* in the prologue. So terrified was she by Emily Rigl's performance that the child fled screaming into the wings during a rehearsal, vowing never again to appear on stage. She was fortunately coaxed out of that state of mind by her persuasive aunt in time for the opening.

Despite a severe snowstorm, the first-night audience at the Haymarket on January 2, 1886, was distinguished and zealous. Overzealous in the case of Barry's many friends in the stalls and balcony. Their gratuitous applause and cheering chaffed the transplanted pittites in the upper regions, "who were quite ready to cheer when cheering was called for by the good work done," attested *The Era*, "but who were equally ready to hiss when they found applause born of friendliness, and of that only."

"What a whirlwind was the *Nadjezda* prologue," remembered Harry St. Maur, who was in the audience that evening. "Can you bring yourself to conceive any kind of woman that was a woman under such conditions? Barry demanded something supreme and Emily Rigl depicted her with a force and fidelity that has sometimes, no doubt, been equalled, but it is hard to believe could be surpassed. She gave in spite of a German accent, such a realization of frightful, frantic, revengeful anger that the cold, calm English audience was moved as never before nor since has it been my lot to see sedate, gentle folks stirred." Seven distinct curtain calls were demanded of Emily Rigl.

As the audience returned expectant to its seats for Act One, "Saint" felt apprehension: "When the curtain had been up long enough for the heroine to reappear in the first act the cause of my anxiety was promptly apparent. Emily Rigl had acted herself out in the prologue . . . Imagine any struggle that is for dear, dear life—that was the poor lady's fight act after act through Barry's great play . . . if she could have fooled with fake force as Bernhardt does, in early acts, and kept the ultimate fury of her power for the last act, there would be a great star actress on the theatrical roster today—Emily Rigl—and an American dramatic author with all the footlight valor of a Sardou and twice his heart and sincerity, whose name would be Maurice Barrymore."

Refinements of performance evident to Barry's friend escaped the pittites. They sensed weakness, attributed the cause to the actress's foreign accent, and began to jeer during her scenes. Where encouragement from the house might have helped Emily Rigl to regain her strength, jeering only drained it further. Audible contention grew among the spectators when Barry's well-meaning claque attempted to counteract the jeering

234

with renewed applause and cheering, arousing angry opposition among impartial patrons, fury from pittites. The latter began hissing, whistling and singing. And what of the author? He had to stand there and act. "He went along step by step, act by act, a fine actor assisting his own authoral damnation," said his friend. "For, can you who only knew Barry, the motive power of ringing laughter, realize that he stood up that night and carried along a load of despair that would have defeated a lesser man."

Nothing could redeem that first performance of *Nadjezda*, not the fine supporting cast, not the inherent power of the piece. "With the fall of the curtain it culminated in hoots and hisses that brought a curious expression to the face of the author," observed *The Era*, "and that led the principal actress to burst into a flood of tears which we hope caused the malcontents to leave the theatre with a feeling of shame at their hearts." The Barrymores comforted their exhausted, distraught leading lady, while across the footlights, came the battle sounds of cheering claque and hooting pittites. After seeing that Emily was escorted to her hotel, and thanking cast and crew, the author and his wife walked silently through the snow to Store Street.

When he heard newsboys calling, Barry went out for the morning papers. Although the *Times* advocated "whistling, cat-calls, singing" as a valid system of judgment, all of the other papers agreed with *The Era* that it had been "the worst exhibition of rowdyism that the reconstructed Haymarket Theatre has known." Barry was relieved that Emily Rigl's performance was generally vindicated, apologies proffered by most of the reviewers. But the author was distressed by the critical response to his wife's performance. They condemned not the actress so much as the role which had been so carefully tailored to her measure. "Miss Drew," decided *The Theatre*, "played an American lady in a fashion which seemed to be unacceptable, but which under other conditions would have seemed original enough, and amusing." *The Era* was less ambiguous, stating that the American belle's "vulgarity and shockingly suggestive wit showed nothing so much as that Mr. Barrymore had made a terrible mistake in gauging the tastes of an English audience."

The play itself garnered some praise amid generally unfavorable notices. "Here it will be seen," the *Times* pointed out, "is indeed a morbid story, crude in places, and with motives not too clearly defined, but undeniably powerful, and such as, under more favourable circumstances, should have commanded strong interest and much approval." But the author was beyond satisfaction from such mixed critical appraisals as this, or even *The Era*'s admission that "nothing stronger, nothing more absorbing, than the prologue of this play has been seen upon the London stage for many a long day." His play, hailed in America as a masterpiece, had been reworked and strengthened for this London presentation. Now, as conflict with the Bozentas had obscured the value of his creation in America, the tumult of its first night obscured it in England.

The Barrymores did not sleep that night. They turned to a revaluation of *Nadjezda*, concentrating on a simplification of Emily Rigl's taxing role, and a revision of Georgie's role in light of the delicate "tastes of an English audience."

Next morning, soon after 10, Harry St. Maur knocked at Barry's door. He passed the servant without a word. Going upstairs, he met Georgie in the corridor. "Good morning, Saint," she said, taking his hand for a moment. "Barry's been working all night, but he'll be glad to see you." She indicated that he go right in. Saint turned the handle softly, slowly pushing the door open and looking inside. Barry was at a small table with breakfast dishes before him; evidently he had managed to eat. Seeing his friend, he rose, extending his hand.

"Come in, old fellow," he said. Saint crossed the room and grasped the proffered hand, watching intently the face of his friend. "The same wonderful smile lit up the handsome features," the relieved visitor observed. "He dropped my hand, turned his back to the fire, standing and smiling a second or two. Then his hands curled round behind him to catch the warmth as he quietly remarked: 'Pretty rough luck, wasn't it?'

"Our talk that morning is not to be produced in words, but its tenor will never die. How full of fineness the gentleman was, hardly any one, even his own children, could realize, for they never heard him talk of *Nadjezda* immediately after that momentous first performance. He was full of regrets for the good actress whose powers had failed her at so crucial a time, and relieved that the reviewers had appreciated her true ability. He said little or nothing of the play, the acting, the audience. The fact that a strength that had meant so much to him had failed was so strange, so unfortunate, so sad, but he made no allusion to the wrecking of his play, to the paralysis of his writing hopes, no reproaches. A sad accident had wrecked the craft, but there was no blame for the crew, no speculation how the ship would have sailed if the accident had not happened. He indicated clearly that *Nadjezda* had died at its English birth.

"I said little, but his touch convinced me he understood and appreciated all I felt. Nor was my visit long, for my self-control was as imperfect as his was perfect. His au revoir was: 'Good-by, Saint. Devilish good of you to have come in.' The same hand grip, the same smile, but a look in the eyes that I can see now, as the pencil is moving, as plainly as then— a disappointment, prostrating, crushing, to kill.

"—dear Barry never entirely recovered from *Nadjezda*. He couldn't care much ever, and after that—he cared not at all."

Nadjezda's London career was far from finished. Controversy raged in the papers, culminating with W. S. Gilbert's letter to the *Times*. The final word on "hissing in the theatres" was given to that respected dramatist of the '70s, whose latest creation, *The Mikado*, was eighth in a series of popular light operas written with composer Arthur Sullivan: "Sir,—I deeply regret to find that your drama critic is an advocate of the system of judgement described by himself as 'whistling, cat-calls, singing, and other demonstrations that go to the "guying" of a performer.' I had hoped that the brutal uproar with which the efforts of a most courageous and capable actress were judged on Saturday night would have been as roundly condemned by him as it has been by his brethren of the press." Gilbert's protest ran a column in the *Times*, praising Emily Rigl's performance, denouncing the "coarse, light-hearted fellows," who were becoming "the dictators of the modern stage."

Such controversy merely served to further humiliate the author by repetition of the harrowing events of his play's first night. It also contributed to the filling of Haymarket coffers. "Since Saturday night we understand certain judicious alterations have been made in the text," noted *The Era*, "and we are pleased to hear that Miss Emily Rigl on Monday was received with enthusiasm, and was honoured with several calls before the curtain. We shall not be at all surprised to find that *Nadjezda* works up into a success, and certainly we shall recommend our readers to make the acquaintance of one of the most graceful and powerful actresses who in recent years have been seen upon the London boards." *Nadjezda* became the play to see that winter, and after the Prince of Wales's visit on January 12, another mild sensation increased its popularity.

Alexandra, Princess of Wales, did not accompany her husband to the Haymarket that evening. The Prince sat unfettered in the royal box, held by the unfolding horrors of the prologue, afterward sending his equerry for the leading lady. "Miss Emily Rigl, whose performance in *Nadjezda* has excited so much interest, had the honour of being presented to the Prince of Wales during the performance of the play on Tuesday last, when his Royal Highness complimented her on her rendering of the difficult role of the heroine." Quite a bit more must have been said, for the curtain was held fifteen minutes while the heir apparent and the leading lady chatted in German. The Prince had a predilection for things German—the heir to the British throne still carried obvious traces of the German accents of his father and his tutors—and a partiality for actresses. As the forty-five-year-old heir of a long-lived Queen, "Bertie," a touching blend of pomposity and bonhomie, encouraged such affairs less for romance than reputation. He was devoted to his beautiful wife, and she tolerant of his need to play the roué. His mother, Queen Victoria, was shocked by such carryings-on, his peers amused, his future subjects caught between disapproval and titillation. All eyes were upon His Royal Highness and the actress as they chatted in the royal box that evening.

Note was taken of the meeting in *The Era*, and talk of it quickly spread from theatrical to social circles. It was observed that the Prince's carriage called for Emily Rigl after the play a few nights later. Rumor reached such proportion that on February 2, three weeks after his first visit, "Their Royal Highnesses the Prince and Princess of Wales and suite visited the Haymarket Theatre on Tuesday evening to witness the performance of *Nadjezda*." This time the leading lady and the author were both summoned to the royal box, where "Bertie" left the dispensing of compliments to his regal wife.

But the London production of his play no longer obsessed the author. Other developments diverted him somewhat, without rekindling his former intensity. An Australian tour was projected with a company including Tyrone Power (grandson of the late Irish comedian, who would father another noted actor of that name), and *The Era* reported that Barry had received "no fewer than five offers of collaboration with a view to the production of the piece upon the Paris boards." Sarah Bernhardt, unable to perform *Nadjezda* in English, also had renewed interest in the play after seeing a minute description of its plot in the Paris *Figaro* that January. She had requested her agent, Henry Jarrett, to obtain a French translation of the piece. When Jarrett relayed his client's wish, Barry himself began a translation. He had, after all, won Blackheath's special French Award.

When *Nadjezda* closed after a profitable six-week run, Barry was relieved. There had been certain satisfactions: Emily Rigl had turned her first-night fiasco into a triumph by the end of the run; Herbert Beerbohm Tree's resounding hit as the perfumed and powdered, be-furred old libertine, *Prince Zabouroff*, ignited a career which ultimately led to the actor-managership of Her Majesty's Theatre and knighthood. For the most part, however, it had been disappointment and humiliation for the author. There were the Australian tour and the possibility of a Paris production, and he worked diligently at the translation, but the success of his creation ceased to be a vital goal. *The Don* also lost his interest after its Midwestern tour. And *The Robber of the Rhine* was abandoned when Will Fullerton, so young and talented, died. Barry presented Will's unfinished score to the bereft Percy Anderson, shelving the libretto wrought of friendship and conviviality.

Toward the end of March, Sarah Bernhardt descended upon London, playing Sardou's *Fédora* at Her Majesty's Theatre. Henry E. Abbey, who managed her American tours, was also in town. A friend of Barry's, he arranged a supper party at which the author and the celebrated tragedienne might meet and discuss his completed translation.

Against the candlelit gilt and velvet of the Grand Café Royal, Georgie Barrymore was vibrant in a cream silk gown embroidered with mimosa sprays of green and yellow. Her preparations had been extensive, for Mr. Abbey's table in the private dining room that evening would also be graced by Sarah Bernhardt and Lillie Langtry. Georgie's efforts were not in vain: the reigning beauties of England and France did not outshine the daughter of the Drews. They tried.

Mrs. Langtry, no longer the Prince of Wales's favorite, had been introduced to Barry by the Bancrofts. She had taken a fancy to him. It was obvious from the moment that Mme. Sarah met him at the Café Royal that she concurred. Georgie, preoccupied with the chatty young Oscar Wilde on her right, expressed unfrightened amusement as the English beauty vied with the French actress for the attentions of her husband. The genteel Jersey Lily, however, was no match for the Divine Sarah's "feline charm, of which she alone possesses the secret." Mostly in French, she engaged her quarry in badinage, and when the evening was nearing an end without victory imminent, La Bernhardt, "who was more subject to such caprices then than she has been in later years," observed the New York *Sun*, "began to direct the somewhat shafts of her Gallic wit at Barrymore, who received the barbs with the greatest good nature. He made it a point not to tilt with women unless absolutely driven to it, and, moreover, he used to declare that he had never been able in the least degree to understand women."

Barry allowed himself to be the butt of Mme. Sarah's "somewhat shafts," making no effort to retaliate until "she sent him some sort of dart bearing upon her belief in his over appreciation of his personal pulchritude, a thing of which Barrymore was never guilty." This brought a noticeable flush to Barry's cheeks, but he waited his moment. Finally, Mme. Sarah turned to Georgie. "You know," she offered, "my son is of the same name as your distinguished and so very beautiful Monsieur Barrymore—my son Maurice." Barry, thirty-six at the time, knew that the boy was twenty years his junior, and that Mme. Sarah was just past forty, and extremely sensitive about it.

"Yes," he put in solemnly, addressing the gathering, "we are of an age, and were playmates at Harrow when he was getting his boy schooling in England. He is well, madame, I venture to hope?" Sarah Bernhardt was excessively amiable toward Monsieur Barrymore for the remainder of the evening, reminding him, as she took her leave, to send his translated play. Barry handed the French *Nadjezda* to Henry Abbey, who sent it by messenger to Mme. Sarah in the morning.

At the Haymarket, on April 3, Russell and Bashford presented *Jim the Penman*, "An Entirely Original Play in Four Acts, by Sir Charles L. Young, Bart." The managers achieved their first unmitigated triumph. The play, in fact, became one of the most popular dramas of its decade, and Barry, apparently rallying for his final contractual commitment, received notices equaling those which he had won as *Count Orloff*. "Mr. Maurice Barrymore, who now takes the part of *Louis Percival*, is the right man in the right place," reported *The Theatre*, "He gives both dignity and earnestness to the character." *The Era* said, "A simple, straight forward part this, but one which gains immensely by being played, as Barrymore plays it, in a manly vivid manner. *Percival* is, we may suppose, a matured man of the world and of business, and the chivalry and generosity of his nature are all the more striking if contrasted with a virile bearing and style."

Although Barry's unqualified acceptance as an actor in London brought with it numerous and appealing professional offers, he had discarded any idea of living permanently in England. Such decisions with him were not arranged or articulated, but Georgie comprehended that America would soon be their home again. For the most part she was relieved. As satisfying as housekeeping and society had been in England, the daughter of the Drews missed her calling. Theater was ingrained, after all, bringing not only satisfaction in the accomplishment but also equal footing with her husband. She had long ago realized that Barry's requirements could not be fulfilled merely by slippers and pipe and healthy progeny. Her London debut had been a disaster, with many of the critics condemning her "Americanness." Mrs. Barrymore was inclined toward her husband's accepting any advantageous offer from the United States. Many had come after his success with the Bancrofts; none had tempted him. They were mostly offers to star, as befitting Maurice Barrymore's newly achieved professional stature. They were neither considered nor discussed by the recipient. Starring implied a responsibility which he was not willing to accept.

During Barry's seasons at the Haymarket, Helena Modjeska had toured the United States under the management of Daniel Frohman, a burgeoning young impresario. As usual, her acting was acclaimed, but her public had not been completely satisfied. "Audiences who had enjoyed the antics of Barrymore, and the way Modjeska handled these," wrote Marion Coleman, "missed their favorite, and could not be satisfied with the substitute." Even critics noticed the loss of spontaneity in the love-making of Madame and her new leading man. And some of them, like Joseph Bradford in the Boston *Courier*, lamented *Nadjezda*. "When she played *Nadjezda*," he wrote, comparing it to a less inspiring role, "she showed herself capable of pure tragedy. For *Nadjezda*, barring the fact that it is not written in blank verse, is tragedy genuine and unadulterated." Mindful of these things, and hopeful that the stormy past would be forgotten, Madame wired Barry in London that spring, inviting him to rejoin her company as leading man for the approaching summer season, and for the following year, offering to double his previous salary and give him unprecedented "star support" billing equal to hers. He refused.

Madame rather desperately replied, reiterating her previous offer, adding that, if the author so desired, *Nadjezda* might open their San Francisco engagement on July 12. Besides *Nadjezda*, which she reckoned the ultimate bait, Madame proffered some additional incentives. She invited Mrs. Barrymore to rejoin the company, and requested Mr. Barrymore to translate from the French and adapt Balzac's novel, *Le Dernier Chouan*, which would join her repertoire that season. *Nadjezda* was no longer lure enough for the author, nor did he care for the time being to work on another play. But Madame's obvious attempts to mollify him suggested other possibilities. The Balzac adaptation would be an appropriate debut for his bookish school friend, Paul Potter, who longed to be a dramatist. Barry also wanted to arrange an engagement for Charley Vandenhoff, cantankerous at the best of times, who had fallen into an unrelieved state of surly depression after the public revival of his father's senile animosity toward him. ("Charles Vandenhoff, the well-known leading man, does not, I believe, claim relationship with this family," assumed a *Dramatic Mirror* reporter after interviewing Charley's father. "From the manner in which George Vandenhoff avoided all mention of him and his refusal to account for the similarity of the younger's name, it seemed as if there were some mystery attached to the case. Some say that Charles, because of Mr. Vandenhoff's tyrannical temper, had quarrelled with and left him in boyhood. But this is mere supposition. If there was a secret Mr. Vandenhoff preserved it to the last, and Charles has not seen fit to satisfy the curious.")

Husband approached wife with the various benefits of accepting Madame's offer. Georgie stated that she would never again act in Modjeska's company, but, aware that her husband's fascination for the actress had faded, agreed that the offer was acceptable if his demands were met. Barry responded accordingly.

While the Barrymores were arranging their exit, the Daly forces were again grouping to enter London. The fanfare accorded their visit, this time to William Terriss's sumptuous Strand Theatre, was in marked contrast to the supercilious announcements of 1884. Local theatrical commentators may have whiffed grapeshot, for the Governor was not planning another season of safe German translations. He would face English critics and patrons squarely with the Bard. After warming up with a few of his own homespun comedies, Daly announced *The Taming of the Shrew*. "Until it occurred to Mr. Daly to attempt a resuscitation of the piece in the shape in which it left Shakespeare's hands," confessed the London *Times*, "it seemed as if this comedy were fated to rank as the most despised and rejected of the poet's productions . . . it has received but scant justice from the professional interpreters—so at least it would now appear—in view of this splendid revival of the comedy, which, sumptuously mounted and acted with admirable spirit and point, keeps the house throughout its five acts in a state of continuous merriment."

With the advent of Daly's company, John and Josephine Drew and their daughter, Louise, replenished the St. John's Wood household. When women and children retired to the Surrey cottage for the warmer months, Barry and John would join them on weekends. With no time to spare after their respective performances, the brothers-in-law would speed in cabs to King's Cross for the late train to Weybridge. Nearly missing it one night, they jumped onto a moving car, landing in a compartment with three other men. Once settled, Barry attempted to start conversation. "We're actors broken down by overwork," he said, "seeking a bit of health and rest in the country."

"I'm a business man," replied one of the others, "also going to the country for a vacation."

"And I'm an engineer," added the second man, "going to the country for the same reason." The third man, turning away, did not speak.

"And you, sir," Barry asked, "are you in the same boat with us?"

"No, I am not," he answered brusquely. "I am going to the country for pleasure. I do not work; I am a gentleman."

"And plainly on vacation," Barry added.

The arrival of the Drews and many of their old friends in the Daly company intensified the Barrymores' desire to return home. Despite their London social success, Barry and Georgie felt an underlying formality, a rigid conformity to tradition and class structure, even in theatrical circles. Congenial and stimulating they might be, but lacking, somehow, spontaneity. The obligatory courting of favor from the aristocracy, even by such established professionals as the Bancrofts, rankled Barry. When Modjeska's reply arrived, meeting all of his demands, he wired formal acceptance of her offer. "Mr. Maurice Barrymore has made arrangements to leave England on the 23rd of June," reported *The Era*. "He is to join Madame Modjeska, and is under engagement to support her during the next twelve months."

On June 19, "Handsome Jack" Barnes, a colleague from Scarborough days, replaced Barry in *Jim the Penman*, freeing him for three days of farewell fetes, heightened by Sarah Bernhardt's assurance that she had read an act of *Nadjezda* and found it "striking to a degree." Hopeful once more for his play's future, Barry departed with his entourage for Liverpool. Five Barrymores, Polly, the red-haired nanny, Paul Potter, giddy with his playwrighting prospects, three dogs, two monkeys, several cages filled with rare birds made bountiful cargo on a small steam launch bound for the waiting liner.

XX

With only a hurried half day in New York before heading cross-country, Georgie and the children visited with Mrs. Drew and Sidney, who were waiting when they docked. Barry dashed around the city seeking quarter for dogs, birds, monkeys, finally entrusting them to the care of the Lambs' doorman, who could usually be counted on to handle such matters. A large group of well-wishers joined the voyagers on the ferry to Jersey City that afternoon. They gathered boisterously around the train, cheering and calling farewells, as their friends began so soon another journey.

The Barrymores anticipated their impending Baldwin Theatre engagement for the return to San Francisco, the city of mists which had enchanted them three years before. They proceeded without trepidation. The Bozentas, Madame and her bumbling Count, ceased to be threats now that *Nadjezda* no longer obsessed Barry. Although the Count had replaced Daniel Frohman as his wife's nominal impresario, Fred Stinson was along as company manager to disentangle inevitable snarls and ease tensions during a season in which Madame would add three new plays to her repertoire. Even before *Nadjezda* opened, she began long, painstaking sessions with Paul Potter to prepare Balzac's novel of Brittany, *Le Dernier Chouan*, for production. Having decided that this moody tale of revolution, of freedom fought for and won, would be the realization of her dream of "ideal theatre," the actress worked closely with Barry's bookish but inspired school friend in her Palace Hotel suite, translating and adapting the French novel for American audiences.

Nadjezda opened on July 12 to "a large and fashionable audience," reported the San Francisco *Bulletin*. "Although *Nadjezda* is full of strong dramatic situations, cleverly handled, it is too bloody in its motif to inspire enthusiasm." The reviews, though not unfavorable, did nothing to

243

bolster the playwright's morale. At the end of its scheduled week, Barry was not averse to a change of bill. His performances were sporadic. "Maurice Barrymore was a good *Armand*," noted the *Bulletin*, "and that is about all that can be said of him." But at a huge benefit for the Native Sons of the Golden West, Barry excelled in his best role. "Mr. Barrymore infuses a good deal of life and vigor into the part of *Orlando*," allowed the *Bulletin*, "and his breezy, dashing manner in the lighter scenes contrasts with the temper shown in the more somber scenes."

During the wrestling scene, Barry's heel accidentally struck the chin of his latest stage adversary, a burly Philadelphia prize fighter named Kelly. Barry apologized after the performance, but the fighter refused to be appeased. They agreed to settle the matter after everyone else had left the theater. "That suited the prize fighter down to the ground," reported the Pittsburgh *Post* correspondent, "and about an hour later, when all was still, Kelly came upon the stage in full fighting regalia. Barrymore followed in shirt, trousers and boots, and there was a fine fight between the men. It ended in the permanent dissolution of partnership between Mr. Kelly and his front teeth, and in the undying conviction upon the part of that pugilist that Barrymore was the greatest man on earth."

Revels of the Bohemian Club diverted Barry during the run, beginning with its ritual of burning in effigy man's enemy, "Care," culminating in midsummer weekend outings to the verdurous Russian River country. Georgie and the children accompanied him on these excursions, memorable for copious refreshment and gay abandon, not to mention Ambrose Bierce's inevitable derby hat, and Charles Warren Stoddard's gentle word-pictures of a California that was fast disappearing. But after three weeks in San Francisco, Georgie decided to return with the children to Philadelphia. Mrs. Barrymore preferred to avoid the hazards of the touring car.

The Modjeska company, now billed MODJESKA supported by Her Own Company and MAURICE BARRYMORE, proceeded to its acclaimed debut at the new Grand Opera House in Los Angeles, a sleepy white city with one business street. They continued on the road for a short season, stopping at three pretentious Colorado opera houses: the Tabor Grand, Denver, where *Nadjezda* won approval from "Haw" Tabor and his "Baby Doe"; The Tabor, Leadville, pride of the Carbonate Camp; and the Greeley, in the co-operative colony inspired by and named for the New York *Tribune* editor who had urged, "Go west, young man!" In Cheyenne, Wyoming, a local theatergoer thought "Modjesky mighty clever as a fellow by the name of *Rosylind* in a piece called *How D'ye Like It*."

The company disbanded until October. The Bozentas and Paul Potter headed for the Hotel Clarendon in New York to complete *The Chouans*.

244

Barry returned to the Tomb of the Capulets. He found Georgie contentedly housekeeping and child-rearing, since red-haired Polly had married the liveryman from the stable where Mrs. Drew kept her brougham. Displeased by his wife's household preoccupation, Barry began commuting regularly to New York, at first, to appear in various benefits for which he was always in demand, in which he never refused to appear. Then, ostensibly, to work with Paul Potter on *The Chouans*. Georgie suspected this second excuse, and reports duly confirmed that he was indeed spending most of his time in the Tenderloin, the wide open district under the elevated railroad, where Broadway intersected Sixth Avenue. She was informed that her husband had become a regular at the brothel run by Georgiana Hastings, where politicians, judges, millionaires gathered, and police dared not enter.

Mrs. Barrymore was offended by the implication, furious at being left to housekeeping while her spouse gallivanted. She nevertheless suppressed her anger until Barry departed for New York one Friday for the afternoon, and returned early Sunday morning. Wearing disheveled evening clothes, he steered a course up the front steps, trying to guide his latchkey into its proper place. Suddenly the door swung open, and there stood his demurely dressed wife with Bible in hand, evidently on her way to church. ("She was made up for the part perfectly and had a prompt book with her," Barry observed later.) Mrs. Barrymore bowed haughtily, and was about to pass, when Barry attempted to engage her in the obsequious manner of an errant spouse. "Why, Georgiana," he began, "aren't you going to speak to your husband?" She wasn't. She continued down the stairs. "Oh, by the way, Georgie, dear," he went on, "I was with Geoff Hawley last night." Georgie hesitated a moment.

"Indeed," she observed, "I thought Geoff Hawley was a man." Stung, Barry tried once more to appease his wife as she walked off toward Logan Square.

"Where are you bound for, dearie?" he called after her.

"*I'm* going to mass," she replied without turning; "*you* go to hell."

Soon afterward, the contrite husband asked his wife to accompany him to New York, where the Modjeska troupe would play four weeks before starting its tour. Torn between children and husband, Mrs. Barrymore again chose the latter. But she did so on her own terms. Eben Plympton, a crony of Barry's, who had played with Georgie in *The Wages of Sin*, was mounting a New York production of *Jack, or Life in Bohemia*. He wanted Georgie as leading lady, and she accepted. She could be with her husband without being dependent upon him.

Succumbing to her mother's insistence that the children stay in Philadelphia rather than being "dragged like urchins" to New York, Georgie engaged in battle over their schooling. Mrs. Drew advocated Episcopal schools for Lionel and Ethel, while Georgie insisted on Catholic educations. Jack, not yet of school age, was left out of the dispute. Finally, a compromise was reached, Mrs. Drew's bargaining point being that if the children were to have a normal home it would be with her, and, therefore, her wishes should be respected. Lionel was duly enrolled at Episcopal Academy; Ethel at the Catholic Academy of Notre Dame. Polly fortuitously returned to the fold before the Barrymores left for New York. Her husband, it seemed, got drunk every Saturday night and beat her. "She might as well have stayed at home!" said Georgie, adding a monkey face for emphasis.

After their two years in England, the Barrymores' official return to New York was triumphal. Together and individually they were sought after and feted by the friends who had mourned the absence of this convivial couple. Both tall, striking and individual, the Barrymores made an extraordinary impact when they appeared together. "Georgie was blonde, a devout Roman Catholic, and the gentlest of mothers to her pretty children," observed Amy Leslie; "Barry, dark as night, a bohemian of the wildest popularity, who believed in his wife and approved of her enthusiastically." He told and retold with relish the tale of their early morning meeting on the Twelfth Street steps, and that, among other Barrymore exchanges, passed into theatrical legend. Georgie was a brilliant match for her husband; "made perfect havoc of his witticisms," said Madge Kendal.

They were seen everywhere together before rehearsals started. When A. M. Palmer gave an author's matinee at his Madison Square Theatre, the theatrical profession turned out in force to see *Elaine*, adapted from *Idylls of the King*, performed by Annie Russell, Alexander Salvini and C. P. Flockton. The Barrymores attended with Richard Mansfield and his wife, Beatrice Cameron, another popular acting couple. Between the acts, William H. Crane, the celebrated comedian, invited Georgie to join his company, and manager A. M. Palmer wondered if Barry might be interested in joining his Madison Square company. "How that glamorous afternoon comes back to me, bit by bit, like some glorious, broken-up rainbow," wrote Mrs. Thomas Whiffen, a veteran character actress. "The guests were a fair representation of all the noted figures in the theatre at that time . . . way down front were the radiant Mr. and Mrs. Maurice Barrymore." That glittering matinee re-established contact between Barry and C. P. Flockton, the English actor-manager who had introduced him to acting at the Windsor Theatre Royal.

On Seventh Avenue, a block above its intersection with Broadway, stood a dull-colored brick apartment house with unoccupied storerooms on the street floor enclosed with shabby wooden shutters and paper shades. Through the gloomy street door, over which the pretentious sounding name, BEAUFORT, was painted, past the dark corridor, up three flights of steep wooden steps was Flockton's flat, where the impres-

246

sion of an average New York tenement gave way to the atmosphere of a bizarre English country house. He had borrowed the services of Palmer's scene painter to give plaster the appearance of brick and garnish ordinary ceilings with simulated oak beams. What matter if they were merely pasteboard? The effect was enhanced by a profusion of Turkish carpets, fur rugs, Indian blankets, leopard skins, couches of bark-covered logs and bamboo; a steaming kettle on a fireplace crane held ingredients for the host's famous hot punch, a zither, his prize possession, stood ready in a corner. Georgie and Barry, curled up together on a roughhewn couch, listened for hours of rainy afternoons while Flockton, in rough coat and tam-o'-shanter, made his soothing music. "Those who know Mr. Flockton," observed journalist Max Eliot, "look upon him as being a little eccentric in his opinions, and accept him as they do his hospitality—with a right good will and pleasure." He had always been just Barry's sort.

Charley Vandenhoff appeared at Flockton's, excited by his forthcoming engagement with Modjeska, unaware that his friend had arranged it, since Barry had asked Madame not to mention his intervention. Pleased to be working together again, the old friends did not mention their recent estrangement. Charley, in fact, gave a splendid supper party at Delmonico's for the Barrymores, taking care to be especially cordial toward Mrs. Barrymore. But she knew, and Charley knew, that, beyond cordiality, he could never quite forgive the woman who had won his valued friend.

Although Georgie accepted the inevitability of Barry's eventual return to club life, it was tacitly understood between them that Georgiana Hastings' establishment would not be included. Barry continued playing the solicitous husband, however, taking for himself and Georgie an elegant residential suite at the Sturdevant House, on the east side of Broadway between Twenty-eighth and Twenty-ninth streets, where he aimed to be worthy of the sedate surroundings. When a slight disagreement arose with the management over some cats, a beaver, and a pair of snow white rabbits, he agreed that the Sturdevant House was not a proper place for pets. Seeking once more the aid of the Lambs' doorman, who had placed Barry's English pets with a farmer on Staten Island, he was duly presented with a bill for their keep, and informed that other arrangements must soon be made. The resident farmer, it appeared, wanted to sell the place. As soon as a buyer was found, the animals would have to be removed.

Barry, cats, beaver, snow white rabbits in tow, ventured over to Staten Island on the ferry to appraise the situation. He found, near Garrettson's, a tumble-down farmhouse, a sagging barn, several ruined outhouses surrounded by fallow fields and scrubby woodlands, where his English dogs and birds and monkeys were flourishing. On the precariously sloping front porch, the grizzled landlord was sleeping in a rocking chair. To

Barry it was a living Arden. Then and there, lock, stock and rocker, he purchased the place, adding a monthly stipend for the old farmer, who was to continue living there, as he always had, to care for the pets. "He is a rather irrational and eccentric lover of animals," observed Amy Leslie, "and when his dogs, birds, beavers, cats, rabbits, and weird furry cubs of various paternity accumulated beyond endurance of his housemates he bought a farm and kept his menagerie there."

When rehearsals began for the 1886–87 season, Barry was apprehensive about the meeting of Charles Vandenhoff and Helena Modjeska. Charley, who could not afford to lose another engagement, had a knack for irritating employers, while Madame was at that time particularly susceptible to irritation. She had invested heavily of money and time in *The Chouans—* costumes alone had cost a fortune, being executed to Madame's specifications in London, Paris, and, to insure the authenticity of native costumes, in Brittany. In the midst of such preparation, the undersized, often cocky, occasionally arrogant Mr. Vandenhoff might have alienated her straightway. Instead, to Barry's relief, their first meeting led to abiding mutual respect and friendship. "Charles Vandenhoff was one of those men who were bitterly disliked by some but dearly loved by others," Modjeska stated. "He was the best friend I had in the profession, and both my husband and myself were very fond of him . . . What a grateful generous nature he had! What pains he took to correct my English and instruct me in the meaning of obscure passages in Shakespeare!"

The Modjeska-Barrymore reunion in general, *The Chouans* opening in particular, created a rush on the Union Square box office before the October 25 opening. "Mme. Modjeska's season, which opens next week, is expected to be marked by unusual brilliancy," heralded the *Dramatic Mirror*. "Not only is this distinguished woman in the prime of her beauty and genius, but she has gathered together her famous company of three years ago . . . Mr. Maurice Barrymore, brilliant both as actor and author, heads the list once more, as fiery, as dashing, as merry as of old . . ."

The good feeling which had prevailed between the Bozentas and the Barrymores in San Francisco continued. Although Georgie refused to become a member of the company, she and Madame resumed to a degree the intimacy which *Nadjezda* had strained three years before, while Barry and the subdued Count were, in their fashion, fast friends again. The Count, who, even in best humor, did not particularly stimulate Barry, was eclipsed by a delightful company, including, besides Charley, the wise and witty Mary Shaw, who would become over the years a notable carrier of Barrymore humor, and the beautiful and worldly Grace Henderson, who would become something more.

The Chouans was not prepared to open the New York engagement as planned. Helena Modjeska and Paul Potter, equally fastidious, would not hurry their offering to "ideal theatre" for a deadline. The replacement brought no complaints from playgoers or reviewers. *As You Like It* captivated New York, might have attracted audiences for several months, but after two weeks, the première of *The Chouans* was announced for Tuesday, November 9. The Union Square Theatre was closed on Monday so that Madame's masterpiece might be set. Tuesday came and went. The anticipated première was postponed until the following evening. Finally, on Wednesday, the work which encompassed the hopes and ideals of Mme. Modjeska was offered to the public. The large and distinguished audience included "Diamond Jim" Brady, playing host that evening to the delegation sent from France for the unveiling of the Statue of Liberty.

"Modjeska's acting last night was little short of perfection," reported the *Times*. Barry was "graceful and fervent," Charley "neat, subdued, and suggestive." The settings were "complete and commendable," costumes "rich and tasteful." The play itself was deemed an utter failure. Only the spectacle and, as in their previous seasons together, the Modjeska-Barrymore love scenes endeared it to the public. "A love scene early in the play's progress," said the *Times*, "has not been rivalled in delicacy and artistic charm in any other recent play." If nothing else, Madame's reinstatement of her "dandy leading man" was vindicated. But she was crushed by the general apathy toward what was to have been her supreme achievement, infuriated by suggestions that the strength of her own part had blinded her to the weakness of the play.

After the performance, Barry adjourned to Browne's chophouse with Paul Potter, determined to cheer his friend after the cool reception of his first play. But Paul was admirably resilient under the circumstances. Following years of unproduced attempts, it had been enough, no matter what the critical reaction, merely to see his work upon the stage. Madame was not so easily satisfied. She took *The Chouans* off after three weeks of dwindling returns, played a popular week of *Twelfth Night*, then presented her second new play of the season, *Daniela*. It proved to be another disappointment for Madame, not redeemed by the critics' contention that Messrs. Barrymore and Vandenhoff carried the piece.

But Modjeska did not leave New York in disgrace at the end of her eight-week engagement. Perhaps at no time in her career had she so touched press and public. ". . . the power, the depth, the beauty, and the polish of her acting in a repertory as extensive as that of any player of recent years," eulogized the *Times*, "have gained the recognition of the public, and she has a lasting place in their esteem."

Georgie, meanwhile, after rehearsing *Jack, or Life in Bohemia*, played a trial matinee at Wallack's and a week on the New England circuit before opening at the Park Theatre in Boston. The play's theme of man's friendship repaid by man's ingratitude was taken by most critics as a delightful little morality tale, and Georgie was given much of the credit. As the ethereal heroine, "Our Idol," she was variously called by Boston reviewers "graceful and pleasing," "sweet and womanly," "winsome and delightfully tender," "charmingly attractive in her simplicity and directness," "admirable," and "perfect." "As the gentle and loving character, *Madge Heskitt*," reported the *Journal*, "her intelligence, naivete and personal graces, combined with the power of clear musical utterance, took a strong hold on popular appreciation." Georgie would have preferred a robust comedy role. As the *Evening Traveller* noted, "Miss Barrymore was at her best in scenes requiring vigorous work."

When *Jack* ended its Boston run before Christmas, the Modjeska company was enjoying a short holiday respite. Mr. and Mrs. Barrymore returned to the Tomb of the Capulets, where the gaiety of Christmas preparations belied, as Mrs. Drew intended that they should, the heaviness of her burdens. Omnipresent concern with the dwindling fortunes of the Arch was transcended now by the dying pains of her mother and the illness of her closest friend. Mrs. Kinloch had fallen into a childish state, inarticulately reviewing the passing of her ninety-eight years, spouting rambling recitations of roles and experiences, distressing, despite her advanced years, to the daughter who had always looked to her for strength and continuity. Concurrently, Alexina Fisher Baker, Mrs. Drew's oldest friend and exact contemporary, the mother of John's wife, had fallen critically ill. She was with John and Josephine in New York, responding poorly to the best of medical care.

Barry left Philadelphia on Christmas Eve to meet Modjeska's touring car in New York. The company was scheduled for two performances in New Haven on Christmas Day before opening in Boston two days later. Madame had invited Georgie to accompany them, but she refused, giving, as an excuse, a week of *Jack, or Life in Bohemia* scheduled for New York in February. Actually, Georgie's reason was more basic. She felt that she was needed by her mother and children. Her husband would have to proceed without chaperon.

Boston patrons were no more enthusiastic about Madame's new plays than New York's had been. Her leading man's reception was appreciative, but reviewers, generally fond of him in Boston, where he had begun his American career twelve years before, discerned that bad habits might be forming. Seeing in his great popularity and reliance on natural gifts the seeds of his professional undoing, their observations were offered as warning rather than condemnation. Barry did not see them. Since *Nadjezda*'s final reckoning in London, he seldom read journalistic evaluations of his work as actor or dramatist.

Beyond Boston, a week of one-night stands through Rhode Island, New Jersey, upstate New York culminated in Philadelphia with two weeks at the Arch. Barry, presenting a most fatherly countenance, received a hero's welcome from his three children. Georgie, too, was welcoming, gauging her husband's loyalty by the fervor of his requirements.

Mrs. Drew carefully maintained an air of cheerfulness for the benefit of her grandchildren. Whatever her personal sorrows, Mrs. Drew would not have her grandchildren dismayed by them. She became sharp and demanding toward the servants, but the three young Barrymores were indulged. Kitty Garrett, the cook's simpering daughter-in-law, who filled in when Polly periodically returned to her liveryman, usually bore the brunt of Mummum's wrath. "Mr. Lionel was very naughty, Mrs. Drew," Kitty complained.

"Well, what did he do?" asked her impatient employer.

"He kicked me, Mrs. Drew. He kicked me in the shins."

"Shins, woman!" cried Mummum. "What are shins? Leave the room!"

But Lionel, who would be nine in April, was seldom so demonstrative. He preferred to spend his time sketching seascapes, building ship models, or stalking Iroquois in the shrubbery surrounding the nearby Academy of Art.

Five-year-old Jack, home all day and overindulged, had the run of the house. On the top floor, he had discovered a hidden closet which became a cache for things that he stole. Lily Garrett, the cook's daughter and Mummum's dresser, was always searching the house for hand props and bits of stage jewelry which the boy had spirited away. Once, after some particularly valuable stage jewels disappeared, Lily summoned the police. They arrived, began questioning and searching, until Mummum noticed painful guilt upon the face of her youngest grandson. Dismissing the policemen hurriedly, explaining that she must have misplaced the jewelry herself, she resorted to the "green slipper."

Still shy at seven, Ethel was tortured by the thought of standing up to recite in English class. "The ease with which so many of the children rattled off Shakespeare was a constant source of wonderment to me," she said. "The confidence of the amateur was not mine." But she excelled in music at the convent, and the sisters advised Mrs. Drew that with study her granddaughter might well qualify as a concert pianist. Papa was exceedingly proud when informed of this, but another aspect of Ethel disturbed him. "In those days I wore heavy bangs—and how he disliked them," she recalled. "He used to push my hair back and say it should be like *Alice*'s with a round comb. This made me burst into tears because I didn't want to be different from the other girls. I won the argument—but how right he was!"

On occasional Saturdays, the three Barrymore children, like the three Drew children before them, were allowed to attend matinees at the Arch. They were awed by Mummum's theater, its façade like the Parthenon's, its red velvet and gold fixings inside. They sat in the box marked "D," for which only Mummum held a key. While Papa was playing in town, they were allowed the special treat of seeing him and Madame Modjeska in three consecutive matinees. Although such refinements of performance were beyond them, they would be seeing their father and Madame at their best. Modjeska, like most theater folk who played Mrs. Drew's theater, was awed by the manageress, while Barry, intimidated by his ubiquitous mother-in-law, was subdued and letter-perfect upon her stage.

Before her grandchildren attended their first Modjeska-Barrymore matinee, Mrs. Drew cautioned, "Whenever any member of the family appears upon the stage you are never to applaud. Never!" she emphasized. "It just isn't done, neither when they come on the stage nor at the end of the performance. To do so would be to break one of the firmest family rules of etiquette." The children did not applaud Papa, sorely tempted as they were to join less privileged patrons when he entered for *The Chouans*. There was no rule against imitation, however. For weeks afterward, Lionel and Jack dueled up and down the Tomb of the Capulets with the only weapons allowed them—fly swatters. Ethel, captivated again by Madame after a "Camille" matinee, merely swooned and coughed continually, until Mummum exclaimed, "Something must be done about that child. She's started to bark like a dog!"

Following a week of *Jack, or Life in Bohemia* at the Fifth Avenue, Georgie was immediately enlisted by her mother. The redoubtable Mrs. Drew had decided to accept offers from two New York theaters to play two weeks in April. She was mounting her own production of *The Rivals*, aiming for added income between all-star tours with Joseph Jefferson. Georgie was cast as *Lydia Languish*, while eighteen-year-old Sidney, heretofore notable only for his pool-shooting prowess, assumed Jefferson's role of *Bob Acres*. The surprising success of the novice, enhanced by his sister's delightful *Lydia*, and crowned by his mother's incomparable *Mrs. Malaprop*, filled the Bowery People's Theatre and the Brooklyn Theatre for the two weeks allotted.

During their New York engagements, Mrs. Drew and her daughter were among the honored guests at Augustin Daly's supper marking his company's hundredth performance of *The Taming of the Shrew*. Seated at a huge round table on Daly's stage, across a bed of yellow roses, jonquils and tulips, Louisa Drew saw her eldest son, the erstwhile *Petruchio*, toasted by General Sherman and Mark Twain, Lester Wallack and William Winter.

While champagne was consumed amid the jonquils on Daly's stage, the Modjeska-Barrymore troupe was in transit from the Grand Opera House, Peoria, Illinois, to Chatterton's Opera House in Springfield. As the five-month tour progressed, Barry's restlessness was matched by that of Grace Henderson, the beautiful wife of David Henderson, manager of the

Chicago Opera House. Mutually attracted, and equally open-minded in such matters, they employed the obvious method to relieve boredom. Barry considered dalliance between fellow travelers, if he stopped to consider it at all, merely a professional courtesy, certainly not a threat to his marriage or his devotion to Georgie. The road was long and arduous. Georgie, too, inspired her fair share of admirers—Eben Plympton for one —while touring. She never succumbed to such attentions, but they did not displease her.

The Barrymore-Henderson alliance may have relieved the participants; others were aggravated beyond endurance. Madame's appetence for her "dandy leading man," understandably renewed by his attentions to Grace Henderson, spurred, in turn, the Count's jealousy. Fearing that her leading man might break the contract which bound him for another season if provoked by her volatile husband, Madame stopped short of placing personal before professional considerations. Her onstage association with Mr. Barrymore was more advantageous than ever, intensified, it seemed, by vicissitudes of the touring car. Critics caviled about Barry's enunciation and Madame's new plays—she canceled the third one—but the public clamored for the "perfect lovers."

When they reached Chicago toward the end of the tour, the Count's continued harassment had Barry close to quitting. Madame invoked the old lure of *Nadjezda*, playing it for five performances at Dave Henderson's opera house. But, as Amy Leslie observed, Barry had reached the end of his patience: "These daily wrangles always ended by Barry's deliberately calling the count a prevaricator, and the count instantly discharging Barry, or the count calling Barrymore an inventor of fabrications, and Barrymore formally but indignantly delivering his resignation. About four times a week these interchanges of decisive courtesies took place, and the adorable Modjeska was expected to accomplish the very easy task of reconciliation." Ultimately, even Madame's powers of persuasion failed. "One night it suited Barrymore to accept the release from his contract, and he took a train for New York, though they are still fast friends."

Barry returned to a house of mourning at the end of June. Eliza Lane Kinloch, sweet singer of ballads, had died peacefully in her sleep a few weeks shy of her ninety-ninth birthday. No less touching for its inevitability, the death of her mother removed the one constant presence in Louisa Drew's long, mutable existence. Alexina Fisher Baker's death followed soon after, taking the woman who had been her closest friend since their meeting in a Philadelphia boardinghouse fifty years before. Mrs. Drew did not falter. The Arch was hardly breaking even, so, at sixty-seven, tours with Joseph Jefferson and additional tours of her own became annual necessities for the upkeep of her household and her theater. When Barry tried to contribute, reminding Mrs. Drew of the added expense of keeping his three children, she sharply reprimanded him. "*My* grandchildren," she corrected. "I consider such an offer presumptuous."

Mrs. Drew had given up her summer house at Long Branch, but Barry had an inspiration for the hot months. He, Georgie and the children, Mrs. Drew, Tibby and Uncle Googan—would retire to his farm at Staten Island. He painted an irresistible picture of a bucolic paradise, the charming farmhouse, the solicitous caretaker. Mrs. Drew was dubious, not to say apprehensive, but she needed a holiday.

Crowded into the only cab available at the ferry stop, with their mountain of baggage following in a farm wagon, the vacationers heard disquieting news. The old "caretaker" had died a week before; his body, discovered a few days after the fact in the rocking chair on the porch, had been removed, and local police had been feeding the animals. Other surprises greeted the party at Barry's bucolic paradise: the precarious house, the sloping porch, the barn roof sagging nearly to the ground, animals everywhere overrunning their congenial environs. "You!" was all that the usually articulate Mrs. Drew could manage.

"Ah, the simple life of the farm," Barry sighed, genuinely impressed, as he and his sons surveyed his tumbledown domain. Lionel and Jack, thinking the place absolutely wonderful, were crushed when Mummum made them get back into the cab and ordered it to Fort Wadsworth, leaving Papa joyously surrounded by his welcoming pets in the midst of his Arden.

At Fort Wadsworth, fortuitously dwelt Mme. Bourquin, an ex-actress who kept a boardinghouse catering to theater folk. Flattered by the unexpected advent of the renowned Mrs. John Drew and her party, she made room for them in her already crowded establishment. Barry strolled over for dinner that evening, unable to understand their sudden departure, but sympathetic to Georgie's request that he sleep with her at Mme. Bourquin's for the time being.

Next morning, conversing with the waiter at breakfast, Barry was impressed by his forceful personality. Before the meal was finished, much to Mme. Bourquin's displeasure, Barry had a new caretaker for his farm. And, so, Edward Briggs came into the lives of the Barrymores. Because of his powerful voice and regal bearing, Barry described him as a black De Reszke, dubbing him the "Black Prince." The boys loved him and spent many hours with him and Papa at the farm, helping to make paradise livable.

Ethel, who would be eight that August, was concerned with other matters. Apart from swimming with Mamma and Papa and her brothers, all of whom she excelled, she had booked the barn behind Mme. Bourquin's for a special Fourth of July performance of "Camille." As

254

producer-director-star, she assigned the two other roles to her brothers, engaging Uncle Googan to do the adaptation—a feat of memory which would have been a revelation to Dumas fils. "The first that Lionel and I knew about 'Camille,'" said Jack, "was when Ethel produced a sheaf of pages covered with pencil scrawls, and told us that here were our parts. Lionel and I looked upon it as good fun. To Ethel it was the beginning of a career."

With Ethel, of course, taking the title role, she cast Lionel as *Armand*, Jack as the *Count de Varville*. Friction arose. "Lionel wanted to play my part because I wore an imposing, droopy black mustache," Jack explained, "but I wouldn't give up the part or the mustache, which I loved. He complained bitterly because as *Armand* he had to play a lover, but finally went through with it." Ethel's singular memory of Modjeska's "Camille" was her magnificent cough, so her basic preparation for the part was locking herself in the one bathroom at Mme. Bourquin's to do simply that—cough. One evening, Mummum noticed an unusually long line of boarders waiting in robes and slippers to use the bathroom. Hearing the curious noises inside, and recognizing her granddaughter's sound, she cried, "My God, she's got a bone in her throat!" and hammered on the door.

Word of the bathroom incident spread among the boarders, serving as splendid publicity for the forthcoming performance. Seats were one cent each—"Entirely too much," protested Mummum—and "The Three Barrymores in 'Camille'" played to a full barn, netting a profit of thirty-seven cents. Lionel and Jack were each paid a dime for their services; Ethel kept the rest. "Ethel produced a number of shows that summer," Jack claimed. "Lionel and I liked acting because whenever we were in a show it was a festive occasion and we were allowed to stay up late and eat ice cream . . . Lionel and I were in the theater mostly because of the ice cream."

Another member of the family, however, was inspired by his participation in Ethel's theatricals. Uncle Googan, who had recently forsaken the pool parlors of Philadelphia for the theaters of suburban New York, decided to become a playwright. He indicated as much to his mother and brother-in-law, announcing that his first work was in progress.

"Does someone in your play get killed with a billiard ball?" asked his mother.

"I have been working on my melodrama secretly," Sidney continued, "laboring over it for days. How do you like this title, Barry? I call my play *Odd, To Say the Least of It*."

"I think that you have been wise to work in the greatest secrecy," Barry replied. "And I earnestly recommend you continue in the same way."

As that summer of swimming and the farm, of Mme. Bourquin and the Black Prince dwindled, Georgie considered not only her mother's losses during the past year but the facts of her own situation. Her husband, a $250-a-week leading man, top pay in that category, was always in demand. But now that inheritances were spent, she considered his utter lack of financial responsibility. Not that he hadn't met his familial obligations. He had. But he was generous in the extreme, indiscriminately so, and extravagant, whether buying a pair of monkeys or treating a friend to an ocean voyage. Now, with only a set salary to draw on, his pockets might be empty before obligations were met. To change him, she knew, would be impossible, to try, cruel. There was a logical alternative: Georgie Drew Barrymore would return full time to her calling. Acting would no longer be merely a stimulating diversion when she felt the need, or a method of keeping pace with Barry. It would be the means by which she maintained her three children and her childlike spouse.

With both parents acting that coming season, and Mrs. Drew touring, it was decided to place the children in boarding schools. Lionel would attend St. Aloysius Academy on the Hudson, "from which every one usually goes into the priesthood or into the Eastern League," he later observed. Ethel would return to the Academy of Notre Dame as a boarding student allowed to return home on weekends. But rather than see little Jack sent away, Mrs. Drew agreed to sending him to the Catholic day school affiliated with Ethel's, where he could spend mornings at the end of the convent garden pampered by round-faced Sister Vincent, returning in the afternoon to the attentions of the Drew household.

The Drew-Barrymore party left reluctantly the glories of Staten Island to meet the various commitments of schools, theaters, touring cars. The children would never forget the elemental pleasures of that golden summer of 1887: "How wonderful it was to see Mamma diving through great breakers and then run laughing so gaily to us along the beach, calling, 'Come along, Kids—lunch!' It was lovely to hear her say 'Kids.'" (Ethel wrote those words nearly seventy years later.)

The Barrymores returned to the Sturdevant House, she to seek a suitable engagement, he to begin rehearsals at Niblo's, the historic theater at the corner of Broadway and Prince Street, where Georgie's grandfather had been treasurer fifty years before. Offered $300-a-week by Imre Kiralfy to star in *Lagardère, or, the Hunchback of Paris*, Barry had accepted the remuneration, but not the elevation to "star." He still dreaded that responsibility. The play was a new version of the old melodrama, *The Duke's Motto*, which offered ample character opportunities; Barry would, in fact, assume three full-blooded roles—a Regency swordsman, a predatory armorer, a wily hunchback. At rehearsals, however, it became apparent that Kiralfy, manager-designer-stager, had not rewritten the piece for character but merely to repeat the success of his previous musical extravaganzas. Barry nevertheless persevered, avoiding conflict with the temperamental Kiralfy, lavishing paternal attention upon the daughter of an old friend, who had been cast at his suggestion.

Twenty-three-year-old Mamie Floyd, youngest daughter of the late Billy Floyd, had worshiped her father's friend since childhood. Mr. Barrymore, when he had visited the family house at 110 Fourth Avenue, or at Long Branch, where the Floyds and Drews had been summer neighbors, was always her special beau. At Niblo's, he looked after his protégée with fatherly concern. Mamie looked to her protector with large calf-eyes, sparked by her enduring infatuation.

Barry may have refused star billing, but New York playgoers anticipated his performance in what appeared to be a star vehicle, "and a full house was present to see with what spirit Mr. Maurice Barrymore in the title role would present the stirring action of the well remembered drama." They were not disappointed. "As is invariably the case with first night performances of spectacular plays," continued the *Times*, "there was some delay, but this only went to prove the relish with which the audience received the piece, but very few seats being vacant past midnight, when there was still a ballet and a last act to be seen. Mr. Barrymore as *Lagardère* was full of life and dash, and in his other parts of *Henriquez*, the Armorer, and *Esop*, the Hunchback, he was thoroughly effective." But he soon lost interest in the proceedings. The usually cavalier actor simply felt that he was not earning his generous salary.

"In the original play, as you know, *Lagardère* is a strong part," he told an interviewer from the *Dramatic Mirror*. "I found that at Niblo's the part had been practically boiled down to the catch line 'I am here.' Now I am not very particular about the length of any role entrusted to me, as I am a very bad study. But what I did object to was having to come on and say 'I am,' then there would be a ballet, after which I was supposed to say 'here.'"

"Ergo, you were neither here nor there," offered the interviewer.

"Anyhow, I wasn't there very long, as I threw up the engagement."

He was at liberty less than a week, when Lillie Langtry beckoned. About to begin a much-heralded engagement in America, she signed Barry as her leading man at fifty dollars less than his Kiralfy salary. He would earn his keep, at least, with the "Jersey Lily."

No longer the Prince of Wales's favorite, the "professional beauty," daughter of an Isle of Jersey clergyman, had long since parlayed the affaire into celebrity. She had become as fashionable as the Prince's trouser cuffs. Duels were fought in her name; reputations tarnished. Lord Lonsdale and Sir George Chetwynd climbed down from their horses in

Hyde Park to blacken each other's eyes after Sir George had roared out, "What do you mean by meddling with my Lillie?" Meanwhile, the cuckolded Mr. Langtry was, according to his wife, "doing well, keeping an inn, or shop, or something of the sort, over in Holland."

Lillie inspired no less devotion in New York than in London. What American swains may have lacked in breeding they made up for in cash. Mr. Fred Gebhard, the scion of a wealthy New York family, had boasted that he could win Lillie's favor. After three years of transatlantic courtship, that boast had cost him two million dollars and a good deal more besides. The ardent Freddy had taken a mansion for her at 361–3 West Twenty-third Street, where curious New Yorkers thronged to glimpse the legendary Lillie. "When she emerged on the arm of her protector, Freddy Gebhard," reported the New York *Sun*, "glittering with diamonds and glowing with gay colors, hundreds would cheer the radiant one as she was ushered into her carriage." But, for her "protector," the adulation of Lillie's public was tainted by the resentment of his peers. "Freddy is only good enough to sail in the Jersey lily's wake," stated a fellow Union Club member, voicing the consensus; "he hasn't the pluck of a mouse, and the members generally know it." Having paid dearly for the favors of Lillie Langtry, Freddy was aggressively covetous of the prize.

As Through a Looking Glass became another Langtry social triumph, filling the Fifth Avenue Theatre for her six-week engagement, becoming the most popular play in her repertoire. Barry, as the déclassé heroine's wicked accomplice, was "often forcible, and worked with evident purpose in view," yet he found it difficult to take his role or his leading lady seriously. Lillie demanded admiration from the men in her life whether circumstances were professional or otherwise. She had little faith in her acting ability, expecting little of it but box-office returns, but she would not tolerate indifference to her more celebrated attractions. Barry and Robert Hilliard, her second leading man, were expected to pay proper homage to their star. The two actors were cronies from the Lambs', sharing a penchant for wit and a talent for boxing, although Hilliard's extreme vanity made him eager to prove his superiority in both. Barry, in fact, had good-naturedly refused repeated suggestions for a boxing match, aware that his friend lacked experience. In the matter of their demanding star-employer, however, the two actors stood united. They could but parody her grandiose expectations.

Lillie had been attracted to the Bohemian Mr. Barrymore when first meeting him in England. He became more attractive to her at close quarters, but so did Robert Hilliard, with his middle-parted hair slicked down, neatly trimmed mustache turned up, his impeccably tailored suits, matching fedoras, and small gardens of posies in his buttonholes. Chagrined by Lillie's demands for obeisance, and amused by Freddy Gebhard's *opéra bouffe* jealousy, the two actors nourished both, exaggerating their onstage love scenes with the star, while their offstage solicitations became overpowering. On his way to the stage before each performance, Barry entered Lillie's dressing room, fell to his knees, and with expressions of undying devotion, kissed the tips of her silken slippers. Not to be outdone, Rob Hilliard would enter after Barry's departure, and kiss the hem of her gown. This ritual, enhanced by Freddy's rage, caused a stir during the New York engagement.

"Now when the American reporter is engaged in 'writing-up' personal and private matters," began Lillie's diluted version of the situation, "nothing daunts him, so, grasping this golden opportunity, he interviewed even my theatrical dresser, from whom he learned that one of the two actors was in the habit of kissing my shoes every evening on his way to the stage. He thereupon published such columns of nonsense that it gave rise to a topical song, with the refrain, 'He kissed the popular actress's shoes/ But it wouldn't agree with me.'" Lillie, who thought it perfectly natural that her slippers should be kissed, missed the joke but welcomed the publicity. Poor Freddy, humiliated again, merely fussed and fumed. Nothing could have amused the pranksters more.

Barrymore-Langtry relations rapidly deteriorated. Barry became increasingly irritated by the star's attentions to distinguished patrons during performances. This professional courtesy of Mrs. Langtry's, displayed without warning, proved distracting to her fellow players, making acting with her precarious. One evening, when her flirting with a gentleman in a stage box became unbearable, Barry retaliated during their love scene. "Barrymore, inspired by a sense of mischief," reported the *Sun*, "far overstepped the limit of his bestowal of this kiss. He not only deprived it of the remotest semblance of the conventional stage kiss, but kept his lips glued to the actress's for an unconscionably long time, until the audience rocked with laughter, the actress's eyes blazing with anger while he held her in his relentless grasp."

The next afternoon during his daily stroll along the Rialto, Barry met Abe Hummel, a noted lawyer. "Barry," Hummel remarked, "you clung to that caress last night for a deuced long time. What was the idea?"

"I was seeking reputation at the cannon's mouth," replied Barry. "Instead I lost it. You should have heard her when the curtain fell."

From New York, the Langtry company headed to Montreal's Academy of Music in Lillie's luxurious, seventy-five-foot-long private car, appropriately christened *Lalee*—Indian for flirt. Montreal responded to Lillie Langtry. Critics noted that she had taken "immense strides in her profession" since last appearing there three years before, and that Mr. Maurice Barrymore "does very good work." Word of the company's acceptance appeared in New York theatrical journals, overshadowed by an item which even the *Times* deemed fit to print:

MONTREAL, CAN., Nov. 8—Maurice Barrymore, of Mrs. Langtry's Co., in a fight at a restaurant on Sunday morning at three o'clock, in which a party of lacrosse men and swells were engaged, got two of his ankle bones dislocated by a severe kick.

Those who knew Barry smiled knowingly, while theatrical journals condemned him for "revelling in what might be described as a 'pot-house'," and "desecrating the sanctity of the holy day," and undermining "the dignity of the actor's art." *The Theatre* offered a stern lecture: "When Mr. Barrymore's numerous friends and admirers learn through the public prints that he permits his animal spirits to get the better of his discretion, they cannot avoid such a feeling of mortification as might come to a pure girl who sees her lover in his 'cups.' Mr. Barrymore is not so young as he once was, and really cannot afford a notoriety which might gratify a professional bruiser, but must jeopardize one's claims to good manners. In all kindness *The Theatre* suggests to Mr. Barrymore that he should make this Montreal incident the last of its kind, and in future expend his superfluous but enviable vitality on some pursuit worthy of his name, his fame and his breeding."

If Barry read the rebukes, he did not take the suggestions. After a tiring journey in the *Lalee* from Montreal to Boston, during which his bones presumably mended, he satisfied Rob Hilliard's persistent request for a boxing match. The contest was set for the afternoon of the Boston opening, in the alley beside the Globe Theatre, witnessed only by the stage doorman, who, proclaimed the confident Hilliard, would be witness enough to his victory. The challenger never struck a blow.

Robert Hilliard's understudy played the Boston opening that evening. But the victor did not go unpunished; he suffered Lillie's fury until it was considerably assuaged by the resulting publicity.

While Boston critics attributed two sold-out weeks to everything from Lillie's "English social prestige," to the "sweeping natural lines of her figure," her leading man was not overlooked. "Mr. Barrymore leads with *Capt. Jack Fortinbras* the adventurer, which he plays with admirable spirit, sang-froid ease and effective gentlemanly blackguardism," the *Post* remarked, the *Herald* adding that "the talented author and actor is about as different a personality from the disagreeable character, as a thoroughbred horse is different from a worn-out plug."

During the last week in Boston, the specter of *Nadjezda* rose again. On November 24, the day of the Langtry company's opening in Boston, a new play, *La Tosca*, by Victorien Sardou, opened in Paris. The title role had been written for Sarah Bernhardt, and most of Paris's playgoers crowded the Théâtre de la Porte St. Martin to see what their master of melodrama had given their great tragedienne to play. At the close of the performance, opinions of the play were diverse. The audience agreed on one thing only. "Bernhardt! Bernhardt! Vive Sarah!" they shouted wildly.

Barry read cabled reports of Bernhardt's triumph, wondering what had become of *Nadjezda*. After the French reviews appeared, a disturbing answer was forthcoming. *Le Figaro*, in Paris, noted a startling resemblance between *La Tosca* and *Nadjezda*. *The Theatre*, in New York, reported that "*La Tosca* is in part a plagiarism of Maurice Barrymore's play." Barry, at first incredulous, proceeded cautiously.

"As Mme. Bernhardt had been approached and the story and subject of *Nadjezda* submitted to her two years ago; as she had actually in her possession for some months a French translation of the same; and as, moreover, I had placed the greatest store upon her appearance in the title role, I confess I was not a little alarmed." Barry was talking to a reporter from *The Theatre*, who had come to Boston especially for an interview. "I expressed my uneasiness on a certain occasion, and also my intention to beg an explanation of M. Sardou in, of course, the politest and most good-natured terms. But alas for the fallibility of human propositions! The next day the affair was the public property of the press. The cables were put into requisition, and in a few brief hours, to my intense astonishment, I found myself reviled in the choicest French, English and Bernhardtese."

The "Divine Sarah" mustered her indignant best to refute the claims of a mere mortal. *Le Figaro* printed one of her more controlled refutations. "An idea sometimes is suggested to a dramatist by an obscure source," she maintained. "Sardou is a master; the man who accuses him insignificant." The New York *Mirror* reported the "master's" reaction: "When Sardou first heard of the former's claims he naively inquired, 'who is this Monsieur Barrymore?' and the question is likely to puzzle him for some little time to come."

"Inasmuch as I had not personally seen the play," Barry stated, "I had no real grounds for reply." There, for the time being, the matter rested.

With her husband's return to the Sturdevant House, Georgie discerned a general dissatisfaction in his demeanor, obviously aggravated by the unresolved *Nadjezda* controversy. His much-publicized altercations on the road were not isolated events: belligerence underlay his usually carefree mien. During the two-week Langtry engagement at the Grand Opera House, several incidents confirmed Georgie's perception. He did not speak of them; when friends did, he was always cast as cavalier. "He is essentially a combatant and a chivalrous man," revealed a profile in the Chicago *Tribune*. "He loves a fight, intellectual or physical, for its own sake." But recurrent newspaper reports distressed Mrs. Barrymore.

"At Delmonico's a few days ago," *The Spirit of the Times* reported, "he knocked down a young man with true Sullivanistic energy, because, as it is alleged, the youth had ogled a lady." The young man, it turned out, was the son of a noted jurist. Rising from Delmonico's richly carpeted floor, he addressed his adversary: "May I ask who you are?"

"You may. I am Maurice Barrymore."

"Oh, well," replied the youth. "In that case, this is no disgrace."

A New York correspondent for the Pittsburgh *Post* witnessed another skirmish, when a stalwart young New Yorker named Van Brunt, "who had cleaned out a Fourteenth street saloon, and believed himself a bad man from Bitter Creek," picked a row with Barry in a Twenty-sixth Street chophouse. "Barrymore sitting down doesn't look a very powerful man. He has a rather small head, a boyish face and a slender neck. Most people would regard him as easy game for a fight," the correspondent noted. "Mr. Van Brunt fell into that error, said some unpleasant things to Barrymore, and the pair adjourned to the sidewalk. Mr. Van Brunt received a terrible thrashing, but took it so pluckily that after it was over Barrymore shook his hand, took him back into the chophouse and bandaged his wounds."

A few days after the chophouse brawl, an intoxicated Negro got on a Thirty-fourth Street cross-town car at Lexington Avenue, and handed the conductor a club check for a transfer ticket. When the conductor would not accept it, the man poured forth a stream of oaths that shocked the women on the car. The conductor ordered him off, but, refusing to go, he continued his vile tirade. "A broad-shouldered passenger grabbed the Negro by the coat and slammed him against the side of the car in a way that made his teeth rattle, but did not subdue his pugnacity," the *Times* rather graphically submitted. "Policeman Monday was called and, after a short struggle, dragged the Negro from the car and took him to Yorkville Court. The broad-shouldered man, who was Maurice Barrymore, the actor, went along to court, accompanied by Lester Wallack, who was with him in the car." After they told Magistrate Meade what had occurred, the prisoner, who said he was Thomas Payne, a waiter at the Union League Club, was locked up in default of a five-dollar fine.

Barry's intentions might have been interpreted as honorable enough in each incident, but Georgie beheld an ominous pattern. She did nothing, however, until her husband perpetrated a crowning match.

After the last Friday performance of the New York engagement, before the tour resumed, Barry and Rob Hilliard stood Freddy Gebhard drinks at the Lambs'. It was the least that they could do to repay the pleasure derived from the poor fellow. Freddy was not so good-natured. After one drink, he contrived to put down his hosts decisively by asserting his privileges. "Well," he said for all at the bar to hear, "I'm going home to lovely Lillie." He faced his two adversaries with a vivid leer.

"That's not a gentlemanly remark," countered Barry, "and I must ask you to retract and apologize at once." When Freddy refused, Barry was forced to fight for the honor of his employer. He made a quick job of it, taking care not to hurt his opponent severely.

Before the matinee next day, the object of his chivalry accosted him in a rage. "Mr. Barrymore," she demanded, "have you never known what it is to be associated with ladies?"

"Yes," he answered, "I was born and I am married."

"I said ladies, sir! *Ladies!*" Barry's face turned red with anger, but he controlled his reply.

"Oh, dear me, yes. I understand. You mean the demi-monde. Yes," he said, pointedly, "I know *them* also." The Jersey Lily had no rejoinder.

By mutual agreement, Barry's contract was terminated after the evening performance. "This is poetic justice," he told Hilliard. "I should never have gilded this lily."

Georgie took action. Aware that the core of her husband's dissatisfaction lay in his frustrations as a playwright and his basic dislike for acting, she presented an alternative: reject the numerous acting jobs offered and try serious writing, exclusively. The children's schooling was paid for; she had saved money of her own, plus part of his salaries from Kiralfy and Langtry, and she had been engaged by Henry Abbey for a new play opening in two weeks. So obvious a course had never occurred to Barry. Often termed profligate, he had not been idle for a season in twelve years. Presented so logically by his wife, a sabbatical season did appeal to him, but burdening Georgie with financial responsibility did not.

When *L'Abbé Constantin* opened at Wallack's Theatre on January 20, 1888, "The clever Georgie Drew Barrymore, specially engaged," recorded George C. D. Odell, "made a hit as the *Countess de Lavardens*." She was surrounded by the aristocracy of Wallack's company, John Gilbert, Harry Edwards, Mme. Ponisi, with whom Barry had played ten years before, but Lester Wallack guided their destinies no more. Fighting desperately against constantly increasing competition, already an old man, Wallack had commissioned David Belasco to write a suitable vehicle for him, "which, he pathetically declared," Belasco told Barry, "would probably be the last role he would ever memorize." It was not a success. The convivial dean of actor-managers had been forced to lease his theater during the past few seasons. He had even been obliged to borrow the theater of his rival, Augustin Daly, to present the last performances of his venerable company. "When the curtain fell for the last time on the Wallack company in New York on May 28, 1887," wrote Daly's brother, "it closed a stage record which for thirty-five years had been identified with the social life of New York and which had rendered great service to art and to the public welfare."

The new management at Wallack's, however, achieved success. The popular reception of *L'Abbé Constantin*, and its expected long run, decided Barry to accept Georgie's generous proposal. Gratified to see her husband planning a regimen of writing and reading, Mrs. Barrymore envisioned halcyon days ahead.

XXI

WHILE MRS. BARRYMORE and her colleagues filled Wallack's Theatre once more with genteel laughter, her husband courted authorship. Wary of playwriting after the latest and as yet unresolved skirmish with *Nadjezda*, he turned their Sturdevant House sitting room into his idea of an author's study to begin a romantic novella called *Homeward Bound*, after his most personal play. He augmented the family income with weekly contributions to the *Dramatic News*. His essays, witty and alive with anecdote, derived from his varied theatrical experiences, became a popular feature of that theatrical journal, repeated and remarked upon in the places where theater folk gathered.

In the winter of 1888, as Barry resumed his Broadway rambles, Madison Square, smart and modern, with its plunger fountain and Saint-Gaudens bronze of Farragut, had just won from Union Square, nine streets farther south, the title of theatrical center. From the Sturdevant House when Georgie was in town, from the Lambs' when she wasn't, Barry would head in that direction on his daily promenade. "He turned night into day," *Vanity Fair* noted, "drank with the best of them and stayed sober, and came out the next noon as though he had taken the best care of himself all his life." When others went home to sleep, Barry shaved and continued his activities in the open air. Strolling over to Delmonico's, he would peer through the big plate-glass window of the men's café, and if friends were there—Steele MacKaye, Richard Mansfield or Kyrle Bellew, possibly—he would join them for breakfast.

Three blocks down from Delmonico's, where Fifth Avenue and Broadway wedged sharply to form Madison Square, Barry continued his stroll, joined at Twenty-fifth Street by a tide of other easy promenaders. Every clement day, other than matinee days, from ten until three, members of the theatrical profession moved with almost small-town neighborliness through throngs of nonprofessionals who knew them by sight. Fashionable New Yorkers passed in private rigs with liveried coachmen, while workaday denizens passed in omnibuses drawn by slow-plodding horses. Only the members of Daly's company were absent: their contracts with the Governor forbade them to show themselves on Broadway.

Barry was at liberty. While many of his peers were brokers on the curb, fixing contracts with printers, appointments with authors, railroad rates with hustling agents, sometimes simultaneously, Barry merely made conversation. He was "a tall man, dark and pale," wrote actress Virginia Tracy of the promenading Barrymore, "with cool Northern grey eyes that saw everything everywhere and never did anything about it except understand it. He was lightly built, but of round-muscled, strong-shouldered powerful lightness. Dazzlingly handsome, of course, and witty, with the most enchantingly light, lazy manners in the world, he had an habitual expression of deferential considerateness, combined with an indifference to appearances so profound that while strolling up Broadway in moccasins, eating a piece of pie, he thought of himself as rather a conventional and conservative person, and would occasionally point out the folly of a rash or extreme deportment."

Barry's contempt for the tag of matinee idol—which he never admitted himself to be—manifested itself by careless attire and a new shaggy mustache, provoking consternation among his more fastidious colleagues. One of them, noted for his classical acting, impeccable wardrobe and pomposity, stopped him on Broadway. "Ah, Barrymore," began the distinguished interpreter of Shakespeare, "here you are in a disgraceful suit of clothes, as usual. This one, however, is even more shocking than its predecessors. Wearing it on a bet, old man?"

"Yes," Barry replied.

"You must have given the other man long odds."

"I did," he confessed. "I wagered him that of all the readers of blank verse now upon the stage you were not the most mediocre."

Wilton Lackaye stopped Barry on the Rialto to introduce a critic who had recently written a scathing piece condemning the Barrymore sloppiness and its reflection upon the acting profession. "Oh, Barry," called the mischievous Lackaye, "I want to introduce you to Mr. Jenkins, of the *Northern Mail*."

"I should be delighted," he replied without appearing to take more than ordinary interest. "How do you do?" The critic responded timidly, uncomfortable at meeting face to face the object of his virulent attack. Lackaye, wishing a confrontation, emphasized the critic's name.

"But this is Jenkins, Barry, of the *Northern Mail*."

"Yes," said Barry, "I know it is Mr. Jenkins," and, shaking the fellow's hand, he added, "Now I see you, all resentment ceases."

"Oh, you read my paper then?" the critic blurted out.

266

"Of course," Barry assured him, "I never get to the newsstand until four in the afternoon, and by then it is the only morning paper left."

When critic "Alan Dale," nee Alfred J. Cohen, observed in the *World* that a suit of Barry's "looked as though he had got it for $4.57 marked down from $8.00," someone asked Barry what he was going to do about the insult. "I can't dispute the estimate with him," he answered. "His name is Cohen."

Barry's vigorous rambles somewhat undermined Georgie's vision of halcyon days. But second thoughts about the arrangement which she had suggested were infrequent and humorously expressed. On the Rialto with Madge Kendal, who was touring with Mr. Kendal in America, Georgie encountered her sauntering husband. After extending Mrs. Kendal a courtly greeting, Mr. Barrymore turned to his wife. "And you, mademoiselle," he suggested with a leer, "have I not had the pleasure of your acquaintance?"

"I hardly think so, sir," she protested. "I am a woman with three children."

"And one husband, I trust?"

"A husband, yes," countered Mrs. Barrymore, "but not one I trust."

But Georgie was generally pleased with their life in New York. His work progressed, and, although friends diverted him, she knew that other women were not involved. He was affectionate and attentive, usually returning to the Sturdevant House by three to spend afternoons with her before she left for the theater. Then he would write for a few hours before meeting her for supper after the performance. They would return home together, and after she had fallen asleep, he would write and read through the night, sleep for a few hours, if it occurred to him, or return to the Lambs' or to any of the other places where friends might still be gathered.

"Nobody ever knows when Barrymore does his reading," wrote A. C. Wheeler ("Nym Crinkle") in *The Theatre*. "But he must do it. It is equally impossible to tell when he does his thinking. But there it is, don't you know, all the same. Among the younger actors of the day Barrymore passes for a brainy man. I believe he has tried every human means to correct the impression. But he cannot fight public opinion, although he will at a moment's notice fight anything else. This quality of brains flows out in all directions, discursive, spontaneous, erratic. It shapes itself into romance, sketches, weird conceits, and sometimees bubbles till three o'clock in the morning in a cascade of café wit and humor."

Barry was generous with his gifts but not indiscriminate. His companions of an evening might be theatrical colleagues, artists, writers, sporting and newspaper men, a prize fighter or a safe-blower, but he avoided the company of bores and, with few exceptions, members of and pretenders to the four hundred. When he was taken to the Union Club by Herman

Oelrichs, one of the exceptions, he found a gathering of "commercial men," as Mrs. Drew called them. He was greeted effusively, and, as he accepted the invitation to join them, a stranger slapped him familiarly on the back, crying, "Barry, speak us a piece."

"We've all heard that you're a great entertainer," added another, and a chorus joined in. "Yes, get funny, old man, cut up . . ." Barry glared around at them for a moment.

"I'll do a handspring for you, gentlemen," he said quietly, "but I can't speak a piece." Picking up his hat, he walked past silent clubmen to the door.

Since his school days in London, Barry had declined the honor of being society's resident Bohemian. Occasionally in New York, however, it was unavoidable. At a supper party one evening, reported the *Sun*, an adoring society woman leaned across the table to ask Barry "if the tips of his ears were furry, and then most inconsiderately gazed at his feet, possibly expecting the faun hoofs."

Such pretensions were not suffered gladly at the Lambs', although a few bores made the membership rolls. Two of them, after having their appendixes removed, spent much of their convalescence at the club, accepting anyone's hospitality, reciprocating with unceasing talk and pointless questions. When Barry unwittingly stumbled upon them, they pounced. "Come here, Barry!" one of them called. "We are discussing a very important matter, and we want your opinion. What part of a man's anatomy retains consciousness longest? Is it the brain, the heart or the lungs that dies last?"

"In short," added the other, "just where do you think a man's soul is located?" Barry looked them over from head to foot before he answered

"Judging by what I now see before me, gentlemen, I do not hesitate an instant in saying that the soul is located in the vermiform appendix."

But snobs and bores seldom displaced compatible comrades and good talk at the Lambs', where a table d'hôte dinner was served for fifty cents at a large communal table, and men were like members of a large family. And in that whole-souled, democratic atmosphere, Barry thrived. "We actors are not the most self-effacing of mankind," admitted DeWolf Hopper, "but we put aside most of our airs in our club. The motto of The Lambs is *Floreant Agni*, which translated from the Sanscrit, means 'You may be all the world to your public, but you're only an actor to us.' "

Barry's peers as raconteurs at the club were Wilton Lackaye and Steele MacKaye. Lackaye, blunt and burly but refined offstage and on, was a master of incisive repartee and inventive humor. "But there is this gentle difference in favor of Maurice Barrymore," observed Amy Leslie; "his most artful and subtle point is rose-blown with pleasantness and the welcome lack of harm. Lackaye is bitter, intensely cynical and caustic, with-

out a touch of the Barrymore sweetness to allay his severely unapproach-
able wit. Lackaye's steel-cold eyes, big and penetrating, go with his
vitriolic shafts of humor, and Barry's beautiful, soft, gipsy orbs carry
mischievous apologies for every unkind thing he may be whirled into
slipping from his storehouse of fun. Together these irrepressible humor-
ists are dangerous enjoyments."

One denizen of the Lambs', Marshall Wilder, a dwarf, whose magnetic
smile and amiable acceptance of his lot contributed to his great popularity as comedian and comrade, was proverbially tightfisted with a dollar,
never offering to treat, but always willing to be treated. He inevitably
joined Barrymore and Lackaye at the club bar, knowing that they would
stand him drinks. "I am writing an autobiography," he announced, one
afternoon, "and you two will figure decoratively."

"An auto-buy-ography?" inquired Lackaye. "With the accent on the
buy?"

"No," corrected Barry, "with the accent on the ought-to."

Wilder's book, *The People I've Smiled With*, was published soon afterward, and Barry did indeed figure decoratively. "Maurice Barrymore is a
splendid fellow to smile with," Wilder wrote; "he always seems good-natured . . . He never slumbers or sleeps, unless while his eyes are open and
he is busy talking and telling stories. He has no chestnuts, but any story
he tells reaches the dignity of a chestnut in a very short time, it is
repeated so industriously." It was an indication of the varying effects of
Barrymore and Lackaye that the latter was not even mentioned in
Wilder's book.

Steele MacKaye was more amiable. "Of all the boon companionships in
my father's club life," wrote Percy MacKaye, "his friendship with
Maurice Barrymore was probably the most spirited and congenial. During a comradely intimacy of many years, their mutual traits of eloquence
and effervescing imagination exulted in continual jousts of playful badinage and of earnest philosophizings." Their fellow-Lambs called them the
"twins of the fold." And Henry Irving regretted that the club had no
"official 'Boswell' to fence their casual gambollings." In *The Theatre*,
"Nym Crinkle" described the subtle contrast between them: "You get
the theme from MacKaye and you are drinking Falerian out of an Etrus-
can flagon. You get the same theme from Barrymore and it is poured out
of a Flemish beer mug."

The versatile MacKaye, splendid actor and excellent reader, had
authored *Hazel Kirke* and *Rose Michel*, among the most popular plays of
the day. At a Lambs' dinner, calling forth all of these talents, he rendered
a scene from a piece which he had written and played with great success.
At the finish, Barry seemed the most enthusiastic man at the table, leading
the ovation, clanking his knife against his plate. "Bravo! A hundred times
bravo!" he shouted. "MacKaye, you ought to be an actor."

There were frequent allusions in the press to their rosy fellowship. "After some first night of interest," reported the *Sun*, "you may often see Steele MacKaye and Maurice Barrymore, with other choice spirits, in some well-known café, discussing drama and more soothing refreshments, with keen acumen." With Barry's London crony, comedian Jimmie Powers, the twins founded the Five A's Club (American Actors Amateur Athletic Association), which met at Browne's chophouse. The members seldom exercised more than their tongues, although the drinking arm was occasionally tested with some Indian-wrestling. In the café of the Union Square Hotel, a great round table was reserved for the twins and their cohorts, Lester Wallack, dean of American actor-managers and Shepherd of the Lambs, Geoffrey Hawley, a brilliant young actor who later drank himself to death, Sheridan Shook, manager of the Union Square Theatre, and Cazauran, a wild-eyed, would-be playwright. Gathered around a plateau of motley bottles and tall glasses, they sent bright volleys of shafts and jabs through blue clouds of Havana-cigar smoke, punctuated by MacKaye's pounding fist, general raucous laughter, and Barry's cries of "the drinks are on me; and what are you guzzling sons of laughter-hags going to have?"

That laughter dwindled for Lester Wallack. Soon afterward, an all-star benefit was held for the destitute dean of actor-managers, highlighted by Edwin Booth's *Hamlet* played with an unprecedented supporting cast of stars: Modjeska as *Ophelia;* Frank Mayo, the *King;* John Gilbert, *Polonius;* Lawrence Barrett, the *Ghost;* Rose Coghlan, the *Player Queen;* Joseph Jefferson and William Florence, the *Gravediggers;* Eben Plympton, *Laertes;* and Maurice Barrymore, *Osric*. Minnie Maddern Fiske, May Robson, E. L. Davenport and Ferdinand Gottschalk, stars in their own right, consented to be supers. In an age of gala theatrical benefits, New York had never before seen its like. Over ten thousand dollars was realized for the beloved spendthrift—to no avail. Lester Wallack, at sixty-eight, died before he could enjoy any of it, leaving an unchallenged legacy of excellence and genteel laughter.

At the end of February, Georgie went to play *L'Abbé Constantin* in Boston, leaving her husband free to enjoy, besides a newly acquired mongoose, a most unexpected companion. Shivering and covered with soot, a startling apparition appeared at the Sturdevant House one cold February evening: Master Lionel Barrymore had run away from school. Having walked from St. Aloysius Academy through the tunnel into Grand Central Terminal—monstrous trains without flashlights bearing down on him in the dark—the nine-year-old found his way into the great, turreted station, then out onto Fourth Avenue, and down to his parents' hotel. Barry was impressed by his son's ingenuity, touched by his boarding-school grievances. Recalling his own unhappy days at Harrow, he acted unpredictably, at least for most fathers, when the inevitable wire arrived from the school. "They say that Lionel Barrymore has run away," he informed his son. "I hope they find him." Barry telegraphed the good fathers that the boy was with him and would remain with him for a short period of stern paternal guidance.

No son ever had more singular paternal guidance than did Lionel Barrymore during his stay in New York. He became Papa's boon companion, strolling with him by day along Broadway, rounding with him at night and into the morning. Barry's colleagues were impressed by the matter-of-fact demeanor of the boy, who, as the days progressed, became by far the more sensible of the two, even managing to get his father to sleep occasionally. Lionel was impressed in turn by Papa's friends, particularly John L. Sullivan, surprising the Boston Strong Boy, and Papa as well, with his knowledge of the prize ring. But he was unusually reticent with another friend at the Hoffman House one evening, when the bushy gentleman stopped at their table to chat.

"This is Mr. Clemens," Barry announced. "My son, Lionel." But the boy was unimpressed, interested only in the gentleman's request to the waiter for a "hot apple toddy." Lionel asked, and Mr. Clemens explained that it consisted of an apple, hot water, cinnamon, and a bottle of applejack from which one poured as much spirits as seemed to suit the occasion; whereupon, he poured a suitable amount and sipped the aromatic concoction. The boy fell into a bored silence as the two men talked. Lionel noticed Mr. Clemens' laughing eyes as Papa described the inadvertent fight of his pet mongoose and an alley cat: "All you saw was an acrobatic cat and a halo of mongoose." And his nod of approval after asking for a description of someone mentioned: "I'll tell you," Barry said, "he looks like a man who might play the piano."

At length, Barry turned to his son. "Haven't you anything to say to Mr. Clemens?" Lionel shrugged doltishly. Mystified at the boy's indifference, he covered with small talk, then made a final effort to include him. "This is Mr. Clemens, Lionel, but I expect you know him better as Mark Twain."

Lionel's transformation was miraculous. The boy looked Mark Twain rapturously in the eye, commencing a relentless recitation: "I began to tell him his own story, the part about Nigger Jim, and I gave it to him verbatim, mostly whole paragraphs at a time, except for some interpolations of my own which seemed to improve the tale. My father moved to fetch me a kick under the table and tried to stop me from this impertinence of reciting Mark Twain's own story back to him, but Mr. Clemens laid a hand on his arm and gave me his whole attention. At the end of my recital there were tears in his eyes. He beckoned to a waiter and bought me an apple with spice and hot water, omitting, of course, the brandy."

The idyll of father and son reached an abrupt end when Georgie returned. Horrified at what she found, Mrs. Barrymore ordered her husband to return their son to school, and, while he was at it, his mongoose to Staten Island. So Papa and Lionel made a reluctant ferry trip to the farm, left the mongoose with the Black Prince, and then headed for St. Aloysius Academy. So impressed were the good fathers by Mr. Barrymore's self-professed piety and traditional theories of child-rearing that Lionel was allowed to return without punishment.

Confused by his wife's reaction to his fatherly interlude, Barry nonetheless took care to be particularly solicitous. Georgie was at liberty for a while, so his usually solitary pursuits were curtailed somewhat. The Barrymores again appeared strikingly together at the places which gentlemen frequented with their ladies, and Georgie was often "at home" to their wide circle of acquaintances. Barry even spent a long, lazy March day snuggled with his wife by their sitting-room hearth. Of course, it took the historic blizzard of 1888 to accomplish it.

New Yorkers had awakened that morning to a scene of arctic desolation; snowdrifts imprisoned people in their houses, traffic and railroads stopped, food supplies could not be delivered, telegraph and telephone connections were cut off, many citizens died from cold and exposure. Only Augustin Daly's company and those indefatigable Britons, Henry Irving and Ellen Terry, at the Star, played that evening. There were more people onstage than in the audience at Daly's, but the house was sold out for performances to come, so the Governor would not cancel. John Drew walked to the theater under the tracks of the Sixth Avenue Elevated; Otis Skinner fought his way through the drifts from Washington Square; Ada Rehan's carriage took three hours from South Brooklyn. *A Midsummer Night's Dream* was presented to a handful of devotees.

Late in the evening, the Barrymores decided to brave the few blocks to the Lambs', open, because of the calamity, to ladies. They found food, warmth, and snowbound companions there. Barry returned with Georgie to their suite, but, still awake after she had fallen asleep, he dressed and went back to the Lambs'. The storm had kept William H. Crane there long after his usual hour of departure. Living way uptown, he had decided to stay at the nearby St. James Hotel in order to keep a morning appointment. Barry caught the conservative comedian as he was leaving, convincing him that, since it was only one o'clock, a few games of pool were in order. Barry was a very good player, but in trying to score on a relatively easy shot, he missed the first ball entirely. His ball went around the table three or four cushions, finally scoring a fluke so extraordinary that a spectator jumped up, crying, "Holy God!"

"No, not wholly," said Barry; "I am partially responsible."

It was six o'clock when Crane finally attempted to leave for the St. James to sleep a few hours before his ten-thirty appointment. Barry stopped him: "Don't be foolish, old man, you come along to my place. I will provide a bed, breakfast at ten and have a cab waiting for you at ten-fifteen."

"He could guarantee all this," observed Crane, "because he was not going to bed for some time." They trudged through the whirling snow to the Sturdevant House, and up to the Barrymore suite. In order to reach the guest bedroom, they had to cross a corner of Georgie's room. They tiptoed, but a floor board creaked, awakening Mrs. Barrymore. Light coming in from the side of a window curtain illuminated the spectacle of her husband and a cohort, covered with snow, sneaking through her bedroom. Georgie was not in the least surprised until she recognized the usually staid comedian.

"Great heavens, Mr. Crane," she cried, "has he got you at last?"

Halcyon days ended jarringly in March: Fanny Davenport opened an English version of *La Tosca*. Barry had previously stated that without seeing the play he could not ascertain plagiarism. "Tonight, however, I had the opportunity, and I state categorically that the fourth act of *La Tosca* and the fourth act of my play are identical. The motive, the action to the smallest detail are stolen bodily—and not the less so because they are vulgarized, brutalized and enfeebled almost out of all knowledge. Now, sir, I claim that the happiest and most inspirational quality in a play is the germ from which the play springs; the finest and best quality in the dramatist, the imagination that conceives that germ. Your cane is none the less your property because the thief that steals it builds an umbrella on it, and in this case, to continue the metaphor, the theft was all the more heinous, it seems to me, inasmuch as it was my host who stole it out of his own hallway, where I had myself confidingly deposited it."

He had attended the performance of *La Tosca* with Abe Hummel, "the smartest lawyer in New York," whose diminutive body supported a huge, bald, raptorial head, and whose clients included seventy-four New York brothel owners; Mother Mandelbaum, the city's leading fence; the Sheeny mob, a national syndicate of pickpockets; and such theatrical elite as Henry Irving, Edwin Booth, Lester Wallack, and Lillie Langtry. Hummel, apprising a clear-cut case of plagiarism, decided to begin a suit to ascertain as much, and to determine whether his client could obtain "pecuniary relief" on account of the alleged piracy. "To brutalize, vulgarize and enfeeble another man's work cannot justify the claim of creation," Barry reiterated. "Sardou, aided and abetted by Sarah Bernhardt, has boldly taken scenes, situations and in some instances the language of the plot and play created by me, and I propose to force the issue immediately, in the courts, to learn whether such proceedings can continue."

Instituting the suit in equity, Barry named Fanny Davenport a defendant in addition to Sardou and Bernhardt, alleging that Bernhardt's attention had first been called to *Nadjezda* by Henry Jarrett, her agent, after a minute description of the plot appeared in the Paris *Figaro* in January 1886; that, in April, a translation of the play had been furnished Mme. Bernhardt in London at the request of Henry E. Abbey; that, in June, the French actress told him that she had read one act and found it "striking to a degree." From that day, he had heard nothing of his play, and the translation was still in the actress's possession. Then, in November 1887, less than two years after the publication of *Nadjezda*'s plot in Paris, Sardou produced *La Tosca*, claiming to have written it at the request of Bernhardt.

The direct charge stated that "Sardou obtained *Nadjezda* from Sarah Bernhardt, and, after making slight alterations, recopied certain scenes, incidents, plot, and cast of characters, entitled the copy *La Tosca* and then delivered it to Miss Davenport." The continued performances of *La Tosca* at the Broadway Theatre, the complaint alleged, were depriving Barrymore of the benefit of his own play, and causing him irreparable injury. Hummel's first move was to seek an injunction and an accounting of benefits received from *La Tosca*'s production.

"In regard to *La Tosca*," added Barry, "the first and second acts had nothing to do with the play, told no story and advanced no action, and might artistically be regarded as nonexistent; the third act really began the play, but it was from the fourth and fifth that the play sprung and from which the rest was inversely evolved, and these two acts are mine pure and simple." The order to show cause why an injunction should not be granted was set down for argument on Tuesday, April 3. Ex-Judge Dittenhoefer, appearing for the defendants, asked for an adjournment until April 25, in order to present affidavits from Sardou and Bernhardt. This was readily granted by Judge Barrett of the New York Supreme Court, and the case was adjourned without the defense showing its hand.

Abe Hummel assured Barry that the ultimate decision would be in his favor. The journals, whether they agreed or not, made the case the talk of the Rialto. Barry's own affidavit was backed up by several friends or interested observers. Dramatist Clay M. Greene, actor T. W. Robertson, son of the late English playwright, and actress Selina Dolaro were colleagues who supported him, while several prominent New York legislators were quick to submit affidavits, as well. The issue was roundly debated in the papers, and, although they generally sided with Barry, he began to have second thoughts about continuing the suit.

Nadjezda, as in Boston with Modjeska, and in London with Emily Rigl, had again become a *cause célèbre*, not for its intrinsic value, but for related sensational matter. Sensitive still to the reception of his masterpiece, he observed the furor with growing consternation. When the *Mirror* suggested that Miss Dolaro, among others, "Polonius like, will readily grant a resemblance to anything that anybody suggests," Barry was furious that friends should be taken to task on his account. The reactions of other so-called friends disgusted him. Henry E. Abbey, for instance, who had himself given *Nadjezda* to Bernhardt in London, maintained a recreant silence rather than jeopardize his profitable management of her American tours. Then, too, the controversy was creating an avid public for *La Tosca*, which initially had been neither a critical nor a commercial success.

Petty irritations were added when ferrets started working. Laura Daintrey, author of such maidenly fiction as *Miss Varian in New York*, informed the *Mirror* that "there exists a poem of John Pomfret's, 'Cruelty and Lust,' developing the same idea as *Nadjezda* and *La Tosca*, contained in *The works of the English Poets* (Volume 17) prefaced by Dr. Samuel Johnson and published in 1790." As if such startling erudition were not enough, someone else discovered a French play, *Severo Torelli*, with a similar theme, although the obscure work had been published in Paris a year after *Nadjezda*'s first performance.

Nearly as offended by the aftermath as he had been by Sardou, Barry was nevertheless ameliorated for the time being: Abe Hummel reassured him that they would win the suit, while the theatrical communities of two continents rallied behind him, anticipating a long-overdue reckoning for the prolific French hijacker. "Sardou is naturally indignant," reported the *Spirit of the Times*, "though he has little time to devote to Mr. Barrymore, as he is using most of it at present to denounce newspapers that find his play dull or that accuse him of various plagiarisms. It should be said for Barrymore that *Nadjezda* is really a strong drama, the strongest drama in which Mme. Modjeska has been seen, whereas *La Tosca* is said to be a failure." A Parisian *chroniqueur*, Albert Millaud, concurrently printed a satirical piece about the author, concluding that "M. Sardou was born a plagiarist, and a plagiarist he will die."

On the eve of his scheduled hearing, Barry instructed Abe Hummel to withdraw the suit. But the persuasive lawyer and his partner, William F. Howe, who was to plead the case, urged him to do otherwise, again predicting victory. While lawyers and client dickered, the *Times* noted that Fanny Davenport appeared in court for the April 25 hearing "arrayed in a 'stunning' costume and escorted by her counsel, ex-Judge Dittenhoefer." Howe & Hummel said that they were not ready; Dittenhoefer, who had Bernhardt's and Sardou's depositions from Paris, wanted to proceed, saying that the lawsuit was a hardship on his client and should be dismissed as soon as possible. The hearing was nevertheless postponed until the following day. Having given the opposition an edge, Barry reluctantly allowed his lawyers to present the application for an injunction, stipulating, however, that he would not appear in court.

When William F. Howe entered the courtroom without his client on the morning of April 27, the *Times* was still preoccupied with the defendant's toilette: "Miss Davenport was present arrayed in great splendor, and with her hair as blonde as blonde could be." Mrs. E. L. Davenport, her mother, and Harry, her brother, sat beside her. Many theatrical people were present, and the courtroom, crowded with spectators, had a first-night aura about it, as Howe read Barry's affidavit and others supporting his allegations. Dittenhoefer said that he would present good reasons to the contrary and read counteraffidavits. "Victorien Sardou says in his affidavit," quoted the *Tribune* "that 'he has never received from Sarah Bernhardt or any other person the manuscript of a certain piece called *Nadjezda*.' From what he has heard he believes it has been copied from Shakespeare." Sarah Bernhardt swore that "she had never seen Barrymore; he had never shown her the manuscript of *Nadjezda*, and that consequently she had never told Sardou anything about it."

"Miss Davenport put a good deal of feminine spite into her affidavit," observed the *Times*. "She asserts that she paid Sardou 100,000 f. for the right to produce *La Tosca* in this country and 10,000 f. for incidentals; that it cost her $38,000 to put 'La Tosca' on the stage of the Broadway Theatre. She charged that Barrymore's claim is only one of the claims which 'obscure authors are in the habit of making; that Sardou has plagiarized from them in order to get notoriety.' She says that Barrymore has testified under oath that he did not own *Nadjezda*, having transferred that honor to his wife, Georgie Drew Barrymore, to pay her for money which she had given him with which to support the family; that *Nadjezda* had been a notorious failure, Modjeska and everybody else having had to drop it; that Barrymore was notoriously insolvent, whereas she was pecunious to an eminent degree."

No doubt seduced by the virtues of solvency, presiding Judge Barrett promptly decided that Fanny Davenport ought not to be enjoined from producing *La Tosca*. "Miss Davenport has expended a great deal of money in bringing out *La Tosca*," imparted the learned judge; "she is perfectly responsible, and if Mr. Barrymore is entitled to any damages he can eventually collect them of Miss Davenport."

"Fanny Davenport smiled sweetly at Judge Barrett when he gave his decision," concluded the *Times*, "and, taking ex-Judge Dittenhoefer's arm, sailed out with great majesty."

Howe & Hummel suggested an appeal. Barry refused. Newspapers and magazines, upholding the defeated author and his plagiarized play, attacked *La Tosca*. "It is a pity, all the same," remarked the Boston *Transcript*, "that this disgusting sensational play cannot be driven from the stage by some means." Barry did not read them. He seldom spoke of his beleaguered masterpiece. After a particularly supportive column appeared in *The Police Gazette*, the Bible of every American barbershop, he met its writer on Broadway:

"Did you see our piece on *Nadjezda* this week, Barry?"

"Sorry, old man," he replied. "I shave myself."

Ten years later, during an interview for the *Dramatic Mirror*, he was questioned about the old controversy: "Hasn't it been claimed that *La Tosca* was stolen from *Nadjezda?*"

"Well," Barry began, aiming for equanimity, "there is no doubt that both plays bear such a strong resemblance to each other that either *La Tosca* was stolen from *Nadjezda*, or *Nadjezda* was a dead steal from *La Tosca*." But the old memory smarted. "Now, barring the fact that my play has the priority of production in its favor, I can prove that at the insistence of Henry E. Abbey I supplied him with a French translation, which Sarah Bernhardt had in her possession for a whole year, and during the very time that *La Tosca* was being written for her by Sardou. So you can draw your own conclusions as to whether my claim is sound or not." Neither had his faith in the strength and originality of the play diminished. "At all events, *Nadjezda* is the pioneer of the strong plays of its kind, and was followed by the production of numerous plays based on a similar thesis."

Nor did faith in his masterwork die with him. "Later, Puccini wrote the music for the opera *La Tosca*, from a plot based on the play by Sardou—whose inspiration was plainly *Nadjezda*." So wrote Lionel Barrymore some fifty years after his father's death. Barry's son had once met Puccini in the Knickerbocker Hotel, while the composer was dining with David Belasco: "I approached, and as I did I could hear Belasco whisper to Puccini: 'Watch out, here he comes!' But I merely bowed and said: 'Might it be that I could shake the hand of the maestro?' And I was allowed to shake the hand of the maestro.

"Still, whenever I hear *La Tosca* played," Lionel confessed, "I experience venal emotions. I believe that I should get a rake-off for my father's plot."

XXII

BARRY'S NOVELLA, *Homeward Bound,* described by *The Theatre* as "a powerful romance," was accepted by *Lippincott's Magazine* in May. Heartened by such response to his literary efforts, he once more considered playwrighting. Cautiously, at first, he contemplated finding another composer to complete *The Robber of the Rhine,* the *opéra bouffe* started in London. Other play ideas were fermenting as well—one of them, his first comedy, he titled *Blood Will Tell,* but he resisted the actual writing for the time being.

Georgie had played another young widow, made another big hit in *A Fair Bohemian* at the Madison Square. Then, with the approach of summer, she arranged for the children to join them. John Drew was again going to England with the Daly company, taking his wife and daughter along, so the Barrymores decided to sublet his apartment. From that charming walk-up on Sixth Avenue near Fifty-third Street, the delights of a New York summer unfolded for the children, augmented by trips to the farm on Staten Island and various summer resorts. Papa, under Georgie's strict surveillance, offered only proper diversions to his progeny. They enlivened his promenades, inspiring admiration from the passing parade. "Fine family, Barry!" exclaimed John L. Sullivan, as he passed them on the Rialto. "Fine family!"

In the Central Park Zoo, Papa would lead them from cage to cage, gathering a crowd of listeners as he lectured authoritatively on the various inmates. "The llama is a domesticated variety of the guanaco," he commenced before the appropriate enclosure, "and spits in your eye if he doesn't like you. The first dramatic critic was a llama. The great-grandfather of William Winter was one . . ." Jack, his attention drawn to a nearby aviary, kept tugging at this father's sleeve.

"Tell us about the birds, Papa," he urged. "Look at 'em!"

"Presently," Barry replied. "You must learn about the llama first. Would you believe it? He is of the same family as the camel?"

"Please, Papa," persisted Jack, pointing to the aviary. "What kind of birds are they?" Barry turned toward the huge cage. It was filthy, spattered gray-white with droppings.

"Presumably," Papa answered, "they are birds of passage."

To celebrate Ethel's ninth birthday on August 15, Georgie suggested that Barry spend the day with her. She had noticed a certain uneasiness in the father-daughter relationship, caused partly by Barry's formality toward Ethel as opposed to his easy exchanges with the boys. But Georgie mostly blamed herself for the prevailing condition. ("It is strange to think of the difference in behavior of my father, coming from the sort of family he did, and the family into which he married," mused Ethel in later years. "He was, of course, intensely emotional and what is now called uninhibited. So, in a way, are we. But such is the powerful and lingering influence of my grandmother, our deepest feelings are not disclosed.") As buoyant and gay as Georgie was, she was no exception to this rule of Drew reticence. She shared her deepest concerns, those involving her husband and their marriage, only with her adoring daughter. She feared, however, that such confidences had left Ethel resenting her father.

Papa was charmed by the idea of a day with his daughter. And what would be more appropriate to celebrate a little girl's birthday, he reckoned, than a trip to the Polo Grounds? Baseball, in general, the Giants, in particular, had become Barry's latest passion. "Well, this day the Giants lost," Ethel recorded, "and my father couldn't have been more agonized. He walked violently up and down the platform, throwing his arms to heaven, saying, 'God! how could you do this to me, how could you?' I slipped into another car in the train, pretending I didn't know that eccentric Englishman—and I can't tell you how English he sounded in the shadow of Coogan's Bluff. I had no idea where to get off the elevated train, so I was eventually removed to a police station and returned rather in style to my parents and the green slipper. It was later that I learned to love baseball, but I never, never had a favorite team!"

In September, Ethel and Jack returned to school in Philadelphia, while Lionel was sent to Seton Hall Academy in East Orange, New Jersey, another Catholic school, but less parochial than St. Aloysius. Georgie opened the season as leading lady of the Union Square Theatre Company, playing *Violet Mendoza*, "who smiles at fate," in Sydney Rosenfeld's *A Possible Case*. Barry was still unable to realize his new comedy, and, in spite of numerous contracts for magazine and novel writing, was far from satisfied with the results of his sabbatical. Besieged during the past six months by attractive acting offers, he finally capitulated to the urging of a friend.

A. M. Palmer was mounting a two-week revival of *Held by the Enemy*, actor-author William Gillette's popular war melodrama. Palmer, a man of taste and education, of regular features, intellectual expression, large, pale eyes, and full gray side whiskers, had long sought Barry's services. He had challenged the supremacy of Augustin Daly and the late Lester Wallack during his successive managements of the Union Square and Madison Square theatres. Recently, with the brashness of Daly—he had leased Wallack's Theatre and changed its name to Palmer's—and the good fellowship of Wallack—he was one of Barry's nocturnal confederates—Palmer had reached the pinnacle of New York managers. With the acceptance of Palmer's offer, Maurice Barrymore would accomplish the feat of being employed, in turn, by the three unquestioned autocrats of the American theater.

Barry and William Gillette had previously been mere acquaintances. During rehearsals for *Held by the Enemy*, they became warm friends. Gillette, a tall, ruggedly handsome matinee idol, a scholarly, solitary man, who had achieved the playwrighting success which Barry sought, did not share Barry's Bohemian tastes. Their friendship was based on intellect rather than café humor. His play offered exceptional roles for both of them, and Barry's playing reflected the satisfaction of their association. "William Gillette's *Thomas Henry Bean* was as amusing as ever, perhaps more so," reported the *Times*, "and Maurice Barrymore gave the best portrayal of *Col. Prescott* that character has ever had." But their successful fortnight's engagement was, for Maurice Barrymore, merely a prelude.

On the afternoon of June 20, 1888, at London's Haymarket Theatre, Herbert Beerbohm Tree had produced an experimental performance of *Captain Swift*. Immediately after that initial presentation, A. M. Palmer had secured the American rights. From the first, the astute manager saw in Haddon Chambers' four-act drama more than ordinary potential. If he achieved the correct theatrical blend, *Captain Swift* could well become his greatest success. The key ingredients would be his excellent company, his usual impeccable production, and the singular services of Maurice Barrymore. The first two were foreclosed. The third took considerable urging.

Barry had begun writing his comedy and was then considering potential composers for his *opéra bouffe*. Palmer was persuasive. When he stated that Dion Boucicault would rework the play to Barry's specifications, the reluctant actor finally consented, convinced that a reunion with Boucicault would be propitious. The prolific Irishman had written *London Assurance*, in which H. A. Blyth had made his acting debut at Windsor, and *The Shaughraun*, in which M. H. Barrymore had made his American debut in Boston. A friendship had developed and continued when Maurice Barrymore appeared with the author-actor in more of his plays at Wallack's in New York. Boucicault accepted Palmer's offer to doctor *Captain Swift*, without program credit, for a less auspicious reason: Boucicault was broke. The most prolific playwright of his time, a popular actor as well, he had probably earned more money at those pursuits over the past forty years than any contemporary. But always a man of uneasy temperament, he had become increasingly eccentric. Three years before, at the age of sixty-three, he had deserted his wife, Agnes Robertson, one of the theater's best-loved, most-respected women, and eloped to Australia with a young actress. Returning penniless to New York, he became Palmer's resident playwright at the Madison Square Theatre and head of its School of Acting.

Rehearsals for *Captain Swift*, overseen by Palmer and Boucicault, magicians of stagecraft, taskmasters supreme, lasted three weeks. Barry was equal to their example, his commitment, as usual, reflecting the congeniality of his colleagues. Not only were Palmer and Boucicault his friends but the company held J. H. Stoddart, E. M. Holland and Frederic Robinson, three of his particular Lambs' cronies. Good humor and playful badinage lightened the strenuous rehearsal period, eased first-night tensions, as the actors prepared in their dressing rooms. Holland's was to the left of Barry's, Robinson's to the right, facilitating rapid volleys.

"Hey, Holland!" Robinson shouted. "What time is it?"

"Quarter past 8."

"Sure?"

"Cert!" replied Holland. "I've had this watch sixteen years, and it has never once gone wrong."

"Don't be too sure, my boy," Barry called out. "*I* went wrong at 16."

The Madison Square Theatre overflowed capacity for *Captain Swift*'s opening on December 4, 1888. "Mr. Maurice Barrymore had been especially engaged for the part of *Mr. Wilding*, the adventurer from Queensland," noted the *Dramatic News*, "and it was evident that his friends were in force." As usual, Barry's comrades formed a demonstrative claque not, however, out of keeping with the general response that evening. Mrs. Barrymore, "ravishing in ice-blue décolleté, looking the proud wife," and her sister-in-law, Josephine Drew, "a yet young woman, who long since abandoned the stage," sat with Mrs. A. M. Palmer in her stage box. The traitorous Henry E. Abbey, the bigamous Dion Boucicault and his young wife occupied boxes, while the Booth family was represented in the orchestra chairs by the younger son of Agnes Booth, witnessing his famous mother's return to the stage after a long hiatus.

Palmer gave a sumptuous supper in Delmonico's Blue Room after the opening. The reaction of the "fashionable and discriminating first-night audience" had left the participants in a heightened state of excitement, optimistically anticipating the reviews of the morning papers. Barry, involved in storytelling with John Drew and E. M. Holland, affected indifference as the first reviews were read. But later, at the Sturdevant House, he had Georgie reread them, reacting to the raves with childlike glee.

Critical opinion was epitomized by Edward Fales Coward, dramatic editor of the *World*, in his first Barrymore essay since *Orlando* in 1882: "The parts best associated with his reputation are *Orlando* and, now, *Captain Swift*. These two impersonations are performances of great strength and beauty; and, had he done nothing else, they would still entitle him to a high place in histrionic ranks . . . Of course due praise must be given to Mr. Chambers for the masterly way in which he sketched the role of *Swift*; but it was the genius of a true artist that made it real and human, and that Mr. Barrymore certainly did. It was throughout a most evenly balanced delineation of character, strong in color, perfect in poise, and sustained in its power and beauty."

When Barry entered the Hoffman House bar on the afternoon following the opening, he was greeted with cheers from his comrades and colleagues. Only one among them expressed reservations. "Oh, Barry," said Steele MacKaye, "I saw you act last night. Rather good."

Barry gave a wary, "Thanks."

"But to be really great, a brilliant actor," MacKaye continued patronizingly, "you should have had some great suffering, an abiding sorrow."

"Well, Steele," Barry offered, "you write me a play, and then I'll have both."

MacKaye's was the exceptional view of Barry's gallant Australian highwayman trying to break with his criminal past. As Coward said of the Barrymore interpretation, "One pardoned his rascalities because one felt that they were the natural outcome of an impulsive nature . . . no matter how mean the act might have been, it was surely accomplished with a courteousness and grace that made it rather an honor to be singled out by such a dashing knight of the road." Barry himself said, "I don't consider *Captain Swift* a villain. He was the natural result of the circumstances that shaped him. When a child is thrown out to die if he must or live if he can, and struggle up to manhood feeling the world against him, it's hardly to be expected that he will become a member of the Young Men's Christian Association on his twenty-first birthday . . . I think I like *Swift* better than any character I've played of late years."

Reviews and sketches in weekly and monthly publications agreed, reaffirming the verdict of the dailies. "Barrymore has cared little of late years for acting," the *Dramatic News* remarked. "He has no liking for travel, and has established himself in New York for literary work in preference to acting. But it is probable that the success of *Captain Swift* will keep him before the public for many months on the stage. In the meanwhile he will have his hands full of magazine work and novel writing that have been arranged for." Nor did *The Theatre* equivocate: "Mr. Maurice Barrymore, the best leading man on the American stage and a brilliant fellow in every way, played the part of *Mr. Wilding*, alias *Captain Swift*, with a dash, nonchalant and devil-take-you air that was simply superb. He is altogether a splendid specimen of manly grace."

The actor was pointed out and admired with new respect on his daily promenades. Stationers' and jewelers' windows along the Rialto displayed silver frames containing his photographs in the impeccable dress suit of *Captain Swift* (the Stationery Department of Brentano's Literary Emporium, 30 Union Square, was sold out of *Swift* portraits a week after the opening). His dressing room at the Madison Square became a rendezvous for the leading wits, poets, playwrights, and players of the day. If his chin was held perceptibly higher, his smile a touch complacent as he swaggered along the Rialto, if considerations of the future were more remote than ever, the celebrant was forgiven. What greater balm for an actor, even an actor whose ambitions lay in the direction of authorship, than a Broadway triumph? At the age of thirty-nine, at a time when he had finally decided to devote himself exclusively to writing, the reluctant actor had achieved a Pyrrhic victory.

During the first rush of *Swift* commentary, the *Spirit of the Times* had predicted that "When Manager Palmer has had enough of the play, Mr. Barrymore can take it and star in it and make as much money as James O'Neill with *Monte Cristo* or Fanny Davenport with *Fedora*." As it was, the $250-a-week leading man might have substantially increased that figure. Lucrative starring offers came rapidly—from Daniel Frohman, whose elegant Lyceum Theatre company was challenging those of Daly and Palmer, from Daniel's younger brother, Charles, a burgeoning new presence in the New York theater, who offered Barry the lead in *Shenandoah*, Bronson Howard's latest play. He refused. Wilton Lackaye subsequently made his greatest hit in the part.

Manager Field of the Boston Museum also had a little correspondence with Barry. "He got on his Boston dignity, did Manager Field," reported the *Courier*, "and with his *de haut en bas* style he wrote the actor that he had long watched his progress with interest, and would be pleased to add him to his fold." Field confided that the Museum paid the smallest salaries of any theater in the country, but that the financial department should be glad to compliment Mr. Barrymore by making an exception of him and offering $75-a-week. With the document still in hand, Barry rushed to the nearest telegraph office:

MY DEAR, MY VERY DEAR FIELD: LETTER RECEIVED. GOOD JOKE–DASHED GOOD JOKE! HAVE SENT IT TO *PUCK*. THANKS.

Typically, however, that comic-paper offer was hardly less remunerative than the summer engagement which he did accept. Charles Matthews and William G. Smythe, fledgling managers and Lambs' acquaintances, approached the possibility of his starring in *The Burglar*. The first four-act play by Augustus Thomas depended on a "name" to secure its production. Thomas's only previous work for the theater had been *Editha's Burglar*, a one-act version of the same play, based on a short story by Frances Hodgson Burnett. Barry had not read the play when he agreed to meet the young author during the spring of *Captain Swift*'s run.

Augustus Thomas's bright red hair, fresh pink cheeks, and searching blue eyes belied his thirty-two years and varied experience as everything from a page in the House of Representatives to a reporter on the St. Louis *Post-Dispatch*. But experience did not mitigate his nervousness when he met Barry rather inauspiciously in the converted dwelling where Smythe and Matthews had desk room. He knew that the production of his play depended on Barrymore's decision, and he assumed that the decision depended on their meeting. "Barrymore at that time was not only the matinee idol," Thomas noted, "but was the favorite leading man of most of the theatre-going men in New York."

Sensing the younger man's anxiety, Barry smiled, shook hands with him, and, looking him up and down, said, "Somewhat of a husky, eh?" Still holding his right hand, he jabbed playfully at his ribs with the left. When Gus instinctively stopped him, Barry added: "Know something about that, do you?"

More than Maurice Barrymore's participation in *The Burglar* was accomplished with that disarming, juvenile exchange. "That meeting characterized the intercourse between us that covered the next twelve years or more–the last of his active life," Gus Thomas testified. "He had an army of friends, but that during that final period I was the nearest to him I believe none informed will dispute."

While preparations for *The Burglar* commenced, *Captain Swift* continued its run easily past the New Year and into spring of '89, remaining the season's most popular play, gaining the approval of society and the profit of its frequent theater parties. But, with New Yorkers still clamoring for seats, Palmer packed his production after the May 4 performance, and headed with the original cast for three weeks in Boston and Philadelphia. Barry's much-praised performance had improved, gaining greater strength and subtlety by the time of the Boston opening. Even such former adversaries as columnist "A. Harlequin" capitulated: "Barrymore has always been a most annoying actor to me. Nature has been so uncommonly kind to him that I never could help resenting his indifference, and his carelessness, which he never took the least pains to conceal from the public gaze. His acting has in the past more often than not been an insult to those who paid to see him. At last this part may almost be said to explain why Barrymore was born."

Barry performed a sorrowful duty during the Boston run. William Warren, the veteran comedian who had befriended him after his arrival from England, had died. When he called at 2 Bulfinch Place to offer condolences, his first American home was shuttered and empty. Miss Amelia Fisher, bereft after Warren's death, had gone to live in the country with a married sister. The benign maiden lady did not long outlive her honored friend.

Palmer's touring company proceeded to the Arch. Mrs. Drew, accompanied by Georgie, sat watchful and proud in the family box as her son-in-law won the approbation of her constituents. "Turning from the consideration of the play as a whole to the acting in detail the first place must be accorded Mr. Maurice Barrymore," decided the Philadelphia *Times*. "His *Wilding* is by all odds the best thing he has ever done . . . He not only gives the part a virility that is extraordinary, but he captures the sympathy of his audience at the outset and holds them until the end of the play by the simple magnetism of the character he embodies."

Georgie, a lady of leisure for the time being, had come to Philadelphia when Barry's tour began. The Tomb of the Capulets, revived by the brief return of the Barrymores, had lost most of its regular residents. Mrs. Drew had sustained another unexpected loss earlier that year when Adine Stephens, beloved Aunt Tibby, had died, as her namesake had died twenty years before, of a heart ailment. This gentle daughter of John Drew, Sr., and Georgiana Kinlock, whom Mrs. Drew had raised as her own, left a deep void in the dwindling household.

Sidney Drew, forsaking pool and playwriting, was touring in William Gillette's *A Legal Wreck*, making a "decided hit," while John Drew continued his reign at Daly's. Lionel was away at Seton Hall. Ethel, boarding at the Academy of Notre Dame, came home for weekends. Only Jack returned to North Twelfth Street after school each day.

Like his older brother, Jack was becoming something of an artist, specializing in drawings rather macabre for a seven-year-old. When he misbehaved at school—which was often—Sister Vincent would punish him by putting him in a corner with an oversized copy of Dante's *Inferno* illustrated by Doré. The book was supposed to frighten the boy, show him the error of his ways. Instead, it fascinated him, inspiring imitation. Papa was impressed by the artwork of his younger son, amused by the cause of his most recent punishment. "I got into a fight with a school-mate, and threw a hard-boiled egg at him," Jack confessed. "I hit him right in the ear. It lodged there for some time." Papa was quick to reprimand his son.

"You might be an actor someday," he admonished, "and have an egg thrown at you."

Ethel and Jack saw the Saturday matinee of *Captain Swift*. Papa returned the call on Sunday, when Ethel took part in a piano recital at school. "There was never a time during my school days when I did not build air castles about becoming a great musician," Ethel wrote. "My voice was not strong enough for any vocal attainments, but I determined to be a wonderful pianist. My ambition would hear of nothing less than my being a kind of female Paderewski. I worked hard at the piano, though perhaps at nothing else. I practised five hours a day. Those were quiet, beautiful years." Her music teacher, Sister Aloysius, considered the ten-year-old a prodigy. "In a general way my father knew what his daughter was 'taking' at the convent, but how well it was taking did not dawn on him until that Sunday afternoon."

The Barrymores and Mrs. Drew sat on folding chairs close to the piano in the small classroom, while Ethel played Beethoven's Sonata No. 13. Barry was transfixed. ". . . as I looked up when I had finished," Ethel remembered, "I could see that that there were tears in his eyes."

"Vienna, Leschetizky—she must go—" cried Barry, naming the great music instructor. Ethel won a silver medal that afternoon, but it hardly equaled the thrill of her father's pronouncement. As the child dreamed of Vienna, Barry returned to New York, raving at the Lambs' about his prodigious daughter.

"I was thrilled," said Ethel, "and never heard of it again." But Georgie did not forget. She consented to tour that summer as William H. Crane's leading lady, determined to earn the money to make good her husband's offer.

When school ended for the summer, the children visited their parents in New York for what would be only a week. There was a zoo visit, a Giants game—this time, to Ethel's relief, Papa's team won—and an extraordinary treat for Lionel and Jack: A morning visit to the gymnasium where John L. Sullivan was training for his fight with Jake Kilrain. The boys were puffed beyond words when Papa was invited into the ring for a little relaxed sparring with the Champion of Champions.

For the last afternoon of the children's visit, Georgie planned a special excursion to Manhattan Beach at the far eastern shore of Coney Island. There was a steamboat ride from the Battery with the gay party Mamma had assembled: Gus Thomas and his wife, E. J. "Ted" Henley, an actor friend from England, and Mr. and Mrs. Thomas Patten, Sr., with her daughter Mamie Floyd. Patten, a prominent banker, had been deemed worthy of Barrymore patronage after his marriage to Ernestine, the widow of Barry's old friend Billy Floyd. Mamie, no longer a child, flirted outrageously with Barry, her childhood cavalier; Georgie was amused by his flustered response.

The festive party changed and ventured decorously from an ornate bathing pavilion into the surf. After changing again into suitable evening wear, they withdrew to the vast, flag-festooned Manhattan Beach Hotel, its wide piazzas overlooking well-tended lawns and blazing red borders of salvia. They dined that warm windy evening to the music of Patrick S. Gilmore's band, highlighted by the cornet solos of Barry's friend, Jules Levy, climaxed by Payn's patriotic fireworks display.

The June night had grown chilly when they boarded the launch for Manhattan. Ethel and Jack dozed off, her head in Mamma's lap, his in Papa's, while Lionel fought sleep between them. In the morning, the children would return to Philadelphia, while Georgie railed west with the Crane company, Barry sailed to Boston and *The Burglar*. As they steamed down the harbor toward the Battery, the last of Payn's fireworks sputtered behind them, a fitting valedictory to summers *en famille*.

Passage to Boston on the palatial *Plymouth* had been booked as a matter of economy. Smythe and Matthews, new to managing, could not afford the expense of train travel, which was faster but hardly more comfortable. Amid Corinthian columns and red-carpeted corridors, the newest addition to the Fall River Line slept 1,200. "She is lighted with 1000 incandescent electric lights, aggregating 12,000 candles," assured a company brochure, "and Mr. Edison has exhausted his inventive facilities in fitting up this magnificent vessel."

Nobody in the company was making important money—largest on the list was Barry's $200—but it was a splendid aggregation, the managers having included the choices of Thomas and Barrymore. William Seymour, an experienced director, had been engaged to rehearse the first-rate cast. Sidney Drew, just twenty-one and already a popular comedian, had joined his brother-in-law, along with John T. Sullivan, a prominent leading man. Leading lady Emma V. Sheridan was chaperoned by her father, General George Sheridan, known as "Silver-tongued George." Ingénue Gladys Rankin, the comely daughter of actor-manager McKee Rankin, was pursued by a love-struck Sidney Drew.

Chosen for congeniality as much as talent, the *Burglar* troupe sat down like a family group to its first shipboard dinner: Barry at the head of the table; the others strung along down the sides. When a pretended dispute arose over the honor of ordering dinner for Miss Sheridan, Sidney said, "We'll toss for it." Barry marked a sugar cube on its six sides like a die, handing it to his brother-in-law for the first throw. No stranger to pool halls and crap shooting, Mrs. Drew's wayward boy hunched over the table, shaking the cube in his hand, shouting, "High man out!" as he threw.

"Must I remind you," admonished Barry with mock propriety, "that the stake is the honor of ordering dinner for a lady?" But Sidney had set the pace. With back-alley shouts and gestures, the others in turn tossed the "die." Their rowdy gaiety attracted attention in the formal dining saloon. Joseph Holland, on board with another Boston-bound troupe, appeared as the last man threw, wondering what they were gambling for. Sidney, who had lost, saw his chance.

"It's dinner for the whole party," he lied.

"A large stake," Barry added.

"Joe threw and lost," recalled Gus Thomas, "and after the order was given, being also in an actor's summer, made a tour among the members of his own company, borrowing for the prospective bill. When the checks came Barrymore paid for all the dinners."

The sense of purpose and camaraderie, which withstood four weeks of grueling rehearsals, was not lost on the first-night audience. The calls were encouraging, applause, laughter, and deeper emotions abounding. A delegation of actors and managers from New York, and Joseph Grismer, a successful West Coast actor-manager, had journeyed to Boston for the opening. Grismer held an option on the play's Western rights, but when he failed to come backstage after the performance, Smythe and Matthews assumed that he had changed his mind. The managers retired to their rooms ominously without a word. The deflated dramatist returned to Clark's Hotel with Barry and Sidney to sit up for the morning papers.

The reviews were decidedly mixed as to the play's merits. Although most of the critics agreed with the *Globe* that Barry gave "a really fine portrayal of the burglar," he was unconcerned with his own reception or the starring potential of his role. He considered Gus Thomas, whom the tepid reviews had disheartened. "Barrymore's indignation and revolt were magnificent," Gus recalled. "He consigned all the critics to the bow-wows, and disposed to send the audience with them." As daylight broke through the windows of Clark's Hotel, Barry slapped his distraught friend on the shoulder, offering a parting consolation.

"Boston, my boy!" he exclaimed. "Why pay any attention to it? What is it? A city of Malvolios." Sidney broke in with his own attempt at encouragement.

"Now, Gus," offered the novice, "I've been in too many first nights—"

"You have, Mr. Drew, you have," interjected his brother-in-law, pushing him from the conversation.

"Well, I'm a wonder," Sidney replied with his comedy smile.

"You do yourself an injustice," said Barry, "you're a freak."

The following day, Joseph Grismer announced that he still wanted the Western rights, and business during the two-week Boston engagement proved encouraging. But the continued pessimism of Smythe and Matthews distracted the author and irritated the leading man. After the final matinee, A. M. Palmer proposed that *The Burglar* be brought to New York for as long as it would hold up that summer. His terms were for the theater to take the first $2,000 each week. If less than that were taken, of course, Smythe and Matthews would be responsible for that sum, as well as salaries and advertising. The apprehensive managers hesitated. "Take it!" Barry demanded. "If the money doesn't come in you'll owe me nothing, and I think I can answer for most of the company." With this guarantee, the timid managers accepted Palmer's offer. When they attempted to thank Barry, he interrupted them. "I'm not doing it on your account," he said. "This is for Thomas."

"The Madison Square was crowded, on Monday night, with a professional audience," the *Spirit of the Times* reported. "All the actors and actresses in town were there, and many had come back to town to see whether Mr. Barrymore had secured a play in which to star. He has not. *The Burglar* is in every respect inferior to *Captain Swift*, which offered him some genuine dramatic opportunities." The play did eventually achieve some popularity on the road with a different cast and became a stock-company staple, but Gus realized little profit from it. He had ill-advisedly agreed to a royalty of forty dollars a week, rather than a percentage, and, in need of money after the New York opening, he sold out even those rights for $2,500.

The Burglar proved also to be a mixed blessing for the Barrymore career. His performance, as the *Dramatic Mirror* revealed, "made a most favorable impression by his artistic realism. His pathos in the third and fourth acts was not only sympathetic but wonderfully true to nature. The suffering depicted in his features was not so much the result of facial stimulation as the genuine portrayal of strong emotion. The absence of conventional methods made his impersonation all the more heart-stirring." But *The Burglar* failed to accomplish the necessary step forward for the acclaimed *Captain Swift*. By refusing more promising offers after the *Swift* run, he had let the propitious moment pass. He signed as a regular member of A. M. Palmer's stock company to re-create his most famous role at the end of August.

With Georgie touring, Barry settled into a room at the Lambs', finding that congenial atmosphere hardly conducive to writing. Nearby, in Mrs. Higgins' boardinghouse, he maintained a little hall bedroom with washstand and iron bedstead. He didn't sleep there, but kept five trunks of valuable costumes there, ready, if needed, at a moment's notice. He often donated the premises to needy acquaintances and gave it as his address to people that he wished to avoid. Mrs. Higgins was instructed to say always that Mr. Barrymore had just gone out.

Barry was still seeking perfect writer's atmosphere when he dined one evening with Gus Thomas. Gus was living frugally on what remained of his $2,500 payment, most of which had been sent to his wife in St. Louis, whom he could not yet afford to bring permanently to New York. He had taken quarters, for three dollars a week, at 205 West Twenty-fifth Street, a fine room for the money, nearly twenty-five feet square, with three large windows at the front. Its only drawbacks were humble furnishings and rich, permeating cooking odors from an Italian restaurant below. Gus brought Barry there for the table d'hôte dinner—thirty-five cents with a pint of red wine thrown in. "Wasn't that a fine offering for the money?" the host asked.

"Great!" Barry answered. "Let's have another!"

After seeing Gus's room upstairs, Barry declared that his haven was found. "Anyone ought to be able to write in such rich and redolent quarters, away from all distractions and calls!" he exclaimed, inhaling the perfume from below. When the rear room on Gus's floor became vacant, Barry rented it at the same price.

"On his first day as a tenant," Gus recalled, "he brought in two reams of soft printing paper, typewriter size, and two dozen plain wood pencils already sharpened and made of a grade of plumbago suggesting stove polish. They had retailed at ten cents a dozen. He declared his intention of starting in the next morning to write a play. But he didn't come that morning or any other morning." Having met a new friend, Barry decided to establish another residence conducive to writing.

Colonel Edward Alfriend appeared in New York that summer, an archetypal Kentucky colonel from Richmond, Virginia. He was sixty years of age, extremely tall, and suddenly portly at the middle. Prominent features were punctuated by a white walrus mustache, which he stroked conspicuously to hold the floor during rare pauses in his discourse. His ambition was to be a dramatist. His most prominent friend in the theater, he was quick to circulate, was A. M. Palmer. The Colonel spent many hours in Palmer's office, though Palmer was obviously not insisting on it. "I am very close to A. M. Palmer," his oft-repeated declaration, became a theatrical joke. When one of Barry's female devotees wished to embroider a sofa pillow, she asked Gus Thomas to draw profiles of herself and her idol on a square of silk. After drawing hers, he asked, "How close to that do you want the profile of Barry?"

"About as close as Alfriend is to Palmer," the lady answered.

Barry held the old man in great affection, insisting that his other friends share his enthusiasm, and that Gus, in particular, share his quarters. He had found a furnished fourth-floor flat for himself, Alfriend and Thomas on Thirty-fourth Street between Seventh and Eighth avenues—

three bedrooms, a little parlor, dining room, kitchen—for forty dollars a month. The services of Sarah, black, plump and motherly, the custodian of the building, were included for housework and cooking. "I don't remember a happier period," Gus Thomas admitted.

The flat predictably became a gathering place for Barry's wide range of friends, literally from morning till night. When fish were running thick in the North River, and a five-pound shad with roe could be had for thirty-five cents, General George Sheridan, having alerted Sarah the night before, would appear in time for breakfast with the delicacy in brown paper. After preparing the fish to the bearer's specifications, Sarah would place it on the table where "Silver-tongued George" discoursed eloquently upon the scientific way to separate fiber from bone.

Barry accomplished little work in the Thirty-fourth Street flat. Gus wrote two plays there. The Colonel wrote several. Adapted from works of the vintage of the "Deserted Village," his plays were pitiably short, consisting of nothing but long soliloquies written for Barry. "Barrymore listening to one of these, and looking to me for help," said Gus, "would have been an inspiring subject for 'When a Feller Needs a Friend'; but with his diplomatic skill he always protested himself an unworthy exponent." It soon became apparent, however, that Barry's enthusiasm for the Colonel and the flat had subsided. He and Gus were walking on Broadway one afternoon when a menacing Wilton Lackaye approached. "See here," he cried angrily, "what do you fellows mean by sticking the Colonel onto me?"

When the run of *The Burglar* ended, Barry sent for his children. Mrs. Drew had previous plans for Ethel. Not without trepidation, she put Lionel and Jack on the train for New York, where Papa was involved again with *Captain Swift*. "We used to hang around backstage during Papa's rehearsals," Lionel recalled. When rehearsal ran late, Barry would give the boys fifty cents each to buy their lunches. One day, they invaded Delmonico's elegant establishment, where their parents had sometimes taken them. Spotting French pastry on the menu for a quarter, they deemed it a worthy meal. The waiter brought a silver tray laden with éclairs, napoleons, and sundry ornamented delicacies which the boys gleefully consumed, marveling at the amount of food for the price. The bill rudely awakened them. Pastries were a quarter *apiece*. They had gobbled five dollars' worth, but the youngest Barrymore was unperturbed. "So Jack called the maître d'hôtel over, and, leaving me in hock," Lionel confessed, "went out, got the old man, and had him come over and redeem me."

Ethel, meanwhile, digested the more sedate pleasures of Cape Cod with Mummum and Joseph Jefferson. Jefferson's new summer estate, Crow's Nest, was set on a hill overlooking the upper waters of Buzzards Bay. All carved mahogany and Jefferson landscapes, the main house was rather forbidding to the ten-year-old visitor. But there was the warm bay for swimming, the stable with riding ponies, and Jefferson's youngest son for companionship.

Evenings after dinner, they sat on a wide stone piazza overlooking the bay. The children sang popular songs. Mrs. Drew and the Jeffersons conversed softly. When Mr. Jefferson ended a sentence with, "don't you think so, Louisa?" Ethel heard Mummum say, "You know, Joseph, you are the only one left who calls me Louisa." It seemed so sad to Ethel that she burst into tears. Mummum was about to reprimand her for such an outward show of emotion, when the voice of a neighbor came floating across the bay:

"Coming fishing in the morning, Joseph?"

"No, Grover. Mrs. Drew is spending a few days with me."

"Oh! My respects, madame," the gentleman responded.

"Who was that fat man in the boat, Mummum?" Ethel wondered, and she was sent promptly to bed. One did not so characterize people, particularly the President of the United States.

"In the late 'eighties, though the standard of acting in Europe was unusually high, the American Stage, then in its greatest period, gave place neither to England, France, nor Germany." So wrote Seymour Hicks, the "Admirable Crichton" of the British theater, a dramatist and actor-manager, knighted for his services by George V. "Those were the days of the mighty Edwin Booth and Joseph Jefferson, Lawrence Barrett, Coghlan, Barrymore, Richard Mansfield, and a host of minor giants . . . I had the pleasure of meeting Maurice Barrymore, but being a boy I was only an open-eyed listener and cannot say, of course, that I met him on terms of anything like equality. I am glad I saw him act, as he was one of the finest actors America ever produced, and in private life certainly one of the wittiest." Hicks had seen it all firsthand, visiting America as the boy-actor of Mr. and Mrs. Kendal's company, during *Captain Swift*'s return.

> The re-opening for the season of the Grand Opera House, on Monday night, was made a notable event by the presentation of *Captain Swift*, with the original cast and scenery, by A. M. Palmer's home company. The principals in the cast were warmly received when they made their first entrance, Maurice Barrymore and Agnes Booth received numerous curtain calls in the third act, and the entire performance was fully appreciated by a discriminating audience.

After two weeks at the Grand Opera House, the *Dramatic Mirror*'s sentiments were affirmed and amplified throughout an early autumn tour of the boroughs. Acclaim for Barry's performance continued, more matinee hearts were trammeled, and the play took on the aura of a classic.

Georgie arrived in New York during a fortnight's break in her tour to spend a week with her husband. After another week in Philadelphia with the children, she rejoined the Crane company in Chicago, opening, on September 16, as William H. Crane's leading lady in *The Senator*. "She was charming and delightful in the role," Crane attested. "It suited her, and she made the most of it." The play, the star, the leading lady made resounding hits, playing long engagements in Chicago and Boston before the scheduled January opening in New York. "Wherever we went," said Crane, "she was always the life of the party with her buoyant spirits."

Georgie, away all but a week of summer, and scheduled to be away for another four months, left her husband susceptible to intermediate liaison. The opportunity arose when Grace Henderson, who had considerably lightened the burden of his last Modjeska tour, arrived in town to rehearse a new play for Daniel Frohman. Mr. Henderson was managing his Chicago opera house. Mrs. Henderson was lonely in her New York flat. Mr. Barrymore's quest was short and sweet. The affaire, unbeknownst to the participants, became a favorite topic in theatrical circles.

The scheduled opener of Palmer's regular season was a short comedy, *Aunt Jack*, with suitable parts for all the principal company members but Barrymore. Palmer had been searching for a one-acter which would open the bill and supply Barry with an appropriate chaser to the heady *Captain Swift*. After several possibilities were submitted to and rejected by the leading man, he brought Palmer a dramatic sketch by Gus Thomas. The manager was enthusiastic about the piece: *A Man of the World* headed the opening bill on October 30.

"Those who were not present while Mr. Barrymore restored peace to the disturbed Willard household last night, and read a kindly lesson on the danger of platonic courtship to *Mrs. Willard*'s romantic young suitor, *Ellis*, missed a very finished and graceful bit of acting," the *Herald* remarked. "Mr. Barrymore was wonderfully 'discreet' and natural in the part of the 'Man of the World' as he lectured the husband on the folly of imperilling his domestic happiness by letting business calls neglect his amorous duty."

"The burden of the work falls on Maurice Barrymore," reported the *World*, "and he may be congratulated upon doing one of the cleverest bits of acting he has ever attempted." Barry reveled undaunted in the playing of this "tired old soldier" with powdered wig and faded dressing gown. The role proved a worthy successor to *Captain Swift*, matching its popularity, placing Barry once again at the pinnacle of American leading men. For Gus Thomas, it was another step toward playwrighting success; for A. M. Palmer, another box-office hit—in the words of an opening-night patron, "At last another theatre-party play."

Only Barry's old adversary, William Winter, dissented, his customary needling in the *Daily Tribune* strengthened by the personal implications of the new role. "Barrymore managed to preserve his gravity while uttering an admonition to neglectful husbands and the intrusive lovers of married women," observed America's foremost theatrical moralist. "The value of this production is not a dramatic value, but its morality is unimpeachable. It would be improved by the omission of its allusions to red noses and brandy and soda. It would be more impressive, likewise, if its preceptor were able to carry conviction. Sincerity of voice, in these cases, is equally to be desired with gravity of manner." The theatrical community was aware of the critic's intent: Mr. Winter was condemning the Barrymore-Henderson alliance.

Neither Winter's warning nor the wisdom of the "tired old soldier" enlightened the actor. While his play ran at the Madison Square, Grace Henderson opened in *The Charity Ball* at the Lyceum. The new play by David Belasco and Henry C. DeMille was an immediate hit, insuring Grace's presence in New York. Rumors of the affaire increased, the most extravagant being that Grace Henderson was carrying Maurice Barrymore's child.

During the run of *A Man of the World*, starring offers recurred. He was considering one of them, an offer to star under the management of J. M. Hill, because it included Gus Thomas. "I was casting about in an effort to devise for him a play that would show to best advantage the Barrymore qualities," said Gus. "My association with him and the little circle about him at this time put a decidedly new twist into my way of thinking of the theatre." A newspaper item struck the playwright: two Southerners had fought a duel by drawing lots from a hat, with the understanding that the man who drew the marked card was to suicide. This, combined with other incidents equally bizarre, inspired a treatment, which Gus submitted to Barrymore and Hill with the notion of developing a play.

Hill was enthusiastic. Barry, still reluctant to star, was noncommittal. "Thomas has presented me with a terrible dilemma," he told a mutual friend. "He's got a play he wants me to 'star' in, and I'm averse to starring at present." When Barry ultimately gave approval, Gus retired to the Twenty-fifth Street room, where, wafted from below, he wrote *Reckless Temple*.

Before his wife's scheduled return to New York, Mr. Barrymore stopped seeing Grace Henderson. The affaire had been dwindling for some time, and, though displeased to lose her dashing lover, the beautiful Mrs. Henderson was not without understudies for the position. Assuming that his recent past would rest, Barry engaged the usual suite at the Sturdevant House, his fourth current residence in New York. He met his wife's train with a bouquet of roses, whisking her back to the privacy of their rooms. A homecoming so rapturous, a husband so attentive left Mrs. Barrymore incredulous.

At luncheon with Ada Rehan a few days later, her suspicions were confirmed and eclipsed. Georgie had learned to accept the inevitability of her husband's romantic peccadilloes when they were apart, but the intimation of his fathering a child by another woman devastated her. She stood bolt upright from her chair in Delmonico's. Without a word to her companion, she rushed through the palm-shrouded dining room out into Fifth Avenue.

Mrs. Henderson, the maid announced, was not at home. Mrs. Barrymore would wait. Sitting in the impeccable parlor, attempting to overcome her obvious trembling, Georgie spotted an ornately framed photograph of her husband, a particularly complacent study from *Captain Swift*, in dress suit, holding in his hands a saucer and demitasse from which his attention had just been distracted. To clinch matters, it was inscribed, "From Barry—to his little Gracie." As repulsed as she was infuriated, Georgie swept the picture to the floor along with the table's other ornaments. Then, as the maid watched dumbstruck, "she wrecked the apartments as effectually as only a cyclone or an angry woman could," reported the *American*. "On top of a mountain heap of debris that had been her rival's furniture, she left her card."

Mrs. Barrymore repaired directly to the law offices of Howe & Hummel, then to the Twenty-third Street Ferry Station. Ethel was arriving from Philadelphia for the weekend. They returned to the Sturdevant House, where the agitated mother, with deletions appropriate to the sensibilities of her ten-year-old daughter, unburdened herself.

When Barry arrived from the theater that evening, the chain was on the door. "Your daughter and I wish to be alone," Georgie explained through the crack, and the perplexed husband retreated to the nearby Lambs' Club.

By a fire blazing to warm the cold January night, he fell into deep conversation with Steele MacKaye. Another club member remembered that evening: "I was alone at four-in-the-morning in the deserted clubhouse, —alone, that is, with two others, who had been sitting at a small table, talking like mad since midnight . . . God, Man and the Devil, Socrates, Swedenborg, Christ, art and atheism . . .

"At last the clock rang out 'four,' and the club watchman came in, 'hemmed' his throat, stood round a bit and then coughed out, 'Excuse me, Mr. Barrymore. —Ahem!' But the steady storm of speech rolled on— oblivious. 'Beg pardon, sir, Mr. MacKaye, but its after four, and orders is to close down. Here's your hats and coats, gentlemen. And I fetched along an umbrella. Sorry there's only one in the rack, sir. It's startin' to snow outdoors. No wind, sir, so I guess this will cover for two, till you find a cab.'

"I was lodging in the club that night, but not feeling sleepy yet I took up a magazine and settled myself in an armchair to read . . . the next stroke of the clock I heard was 'six.' Then I rose, stretched, and started for bed. First, though, I thought I'd take a snuff of air to turn in on; so I went to the front door, unlocked it and stepped out on the sidewalk.

"The snow now was falling thick and quiet, and a pale dawn was commencing. Through the swarming flakes, the light from a corner lamppost burned cloudily, and lit the dim-white cover of snow on the sidewalk—all except one, round, dark spot whence a low stream of sound was rising in a steady rhythm. Over that dark, round spot, motionless, hung a raised umbrella; and under that umbrella stood Barrymore and MacKaye—still talking madly . . . Around them, the fires of philosophy and friendship had thawed a 'faery-ring' in the dawn-bright snow."

The two friends finally bid farewell in the light of dawn. Handing the umbrella to MacKaye, Barry trudged through the snow over to his room on West Twenty-fifth Street. When he struck a match to light the gas, he noticed a stranger in his bed. He went next door and woke Gus Thomas. "What's all this in there?" asked Barry.

"That's a little philanthropy of mine." Aware that Barry never used his room, Gus had given it to a youth, who, shivering, had asked in the street for a dime to get a bed.

"Well, where am I to sleep?" questioned the rightful tenant.

"What's the matter with the Thirty-fourth Street flat?" Alfriend had guests for the weekend. "What about the Sturdevant House and Georgie?"

"Ethel is over from Philadelphia to visit her mother, and I've been turned out."

"What about the room at Mrs. Higgins'?"

"King Hall has that this week." ("I couldn't help laughing," Gus wrote afterward, "at the picture of America's favorite and best-paid actor, with four apartments for which he was paying rent and no place to sleep.")

"I don't know what you're going to do, old man," said Thomas.

"I do," answered Barry. He threw off his wet clothes and jumped into Gus's bed.

After a few hours sleep, Barry returned to the Sturdevant House. Again, Georgie peered at him through the crack of the chained door. "See Abe Hummel," she said. He caught a glimpse of his daughter's reproachful blue eyes before the door was closed. He played the matinee as usual at the Madison Square; then followed his wife's terse suggestion.

"Barry, my friend," said Abe Hummel directly, "Georgie wants a divorce . . ." The lawyer went on to explain. Barry froze; all color drained from his face. For once, he had no rejoinder. He found himself walking down Broadway, without forethought, to his little bedroom at Mrs. Higgins', which King Hall had that day vacated. Hunched awkwardly on the tiny iron-steaded bed, he stared at nothing. The possibility of losing Georgie was presumably beyond his comprehension.

At the Madison Square that evening, the crisis of Barry's absence was met by Gus Thomas. Knowing the lines, at least, the author went on for his friend in *A Man of the World*. After the performance, he went searching, stopping first at the Sturdevant House. Georgie, distraught by then, confided the obvious cause of her husband's disappearance. Gus made a round of Barry's numerous retreats. He found the outcast toward midnight at Mrs. Higgins', hunched trance-like on the small bed. "Tell her . . . tell her—" He broke off, looking at his friend for the first time. "Well, goddamn it, Gus, you're a writer; you know what to tell her." He returned to his staring.

Perhaps no other of Augustus Thomas's many creative feats equaled his recitation to Georgie Barrymore that morning. The heart-rending description of the contrite husband hunched on the undersized iron bed in the trunk-filled hall bedroom would have won interests less vested than Mrs. Barrymore's. Gus left her weeping at 3 A.M.

Sunday morning, after putting Ethel on a train for Philadelphia, Georgie ventured to Mrs. Higgins'. She found her husband, exactly as described, irresistible. Amid successive tearful promises of reform and forgiveness, the Barrymores reconciled.

Chief among Barry's resolutions was the relinquishing of his nomadic ways to take a proper family apartment for the first time in New York. Held by such sweet prospects, and pleasures more immediate, they made do with the crowded hall bedroom until Barry reported back to the Madison Square on Monday.

Any of Georgie's remaining doubts concerning the fruits of Barry's affaire were soon dispelled. David Henderson sued "little Gracie" for divorce, naming George A. Ballantine, son of the Newark brewer, as the other man in the case. (But rumors of a Barrymore-Henderson offspring persisted. When Grace was acting for D. W. Griffith at Biograph around 1910, Blanche Sweet recalls her visiting a New Jersey sanitarium each week to see a reputedly "mad or retarded" son. Studio gossip had it that the child was fathered by Maurice Barrymore.)

XXIII

ON MONDAY, JANUARY 13, 1890, the Star Theatre playbill announced a comedy of political life in Washington, by David Lloyd and Sydney Rosenfeld. *The Senator* was a Broadway triumph for all concerned. "Think of an original American comedy with quotable lines! Such a phenomenon has not been known before in this generation," exclaimed the *Spirit of the Times*, proceeding to the play's crowning adornment: "The daughter of Mr. and Mrs. John Drew; the sister of John and Sidney, and the wife of Maurice Barrymore—in short, the clever member of a clever family—Georgie Drew has, for several seasons, been promising to take the lead as a comedienne. Now, she has taken it. As handsome as a picture, exquisitely dressed, brimming over with fun and an actress to the tips of her fingers, she captured the audience at once and kept them in roars of laughter and applause, fairly dividing the honors with Mr. Crane, who seemed as proud of her success as his own."

While their hits ran simultaneously in New York, the Barrymores searched for an apartment, deciding to settle beyond the temptations of the Rialto. The city had been building north and west, creating new dwellings for its one and a half million inhabitants, but Fifth Avenue, bordering the park's east side, was still considered the center of fashion. Although trade had recently reached Forty-second Street, it was certain not to progress farther, for there the great houses of the rich flourished. With astonishing regularity, Manhattan millionaires began building architectural variations of European châteaux and palazzi. Fontainebleau rose within a few blocks of Azay-le-Rideau. William Waldorf Astor's cream-colored Touraine château, on the northwest corner of Fifty-sixth Street, vied with Collis P. Huntington's gray-stone palazzo, on the southwest corner of Fifty-seventh. And so on up the avenue—Vanderbilt, Morgan, Gerry, Whitney, Central Park on one side, a wooded stretch of farms and small-town vignettes on the other, and the cobblestone, ailanthus-lined streets of "the overgrown village of Harlem."

On Fifty-ninth Street, one block east of the "millionaires' colony," the Barrymores found a bright six-room flat with wide windows facing Fifth Avenue and the low, red-brick Plaza Hotel. Barry gave up his other residences, keeping only the trunk room at Mrs. Higgins', and Georgie, for the first time, went about the business of furnishing a home. Most of the furniture was purchased new, although Mrs. Drew sent some family pieces along with Barry's precious trunk of books and manuscripts from her Twelfth Street attic. The money which Georgie had saved expressly for Ethel's musical education went into the apartment. With the success of *The Senator,* however, she planned to earn enough to replace it. By the end of February, the flat was ready for occupancy.

The Barrymores took exuberant pride in their first New York home. The children visited frequently on weekends and school holidays, rejoicing at the presence of Papa and Mamma, and the added pleasure of Polly, their red-haired English governess. Escaping her brutal livery stableman, she returned as cook, occasional governess, and maid-of-all-work.

Free from the restrictions of his mother-in-law, Barry introduced another resident to the cheerful household: Belle of Clyde, a pedigreed Clydesdale terrier, whose silky ears and large, wide-apart eyes, expressive of great intelligence, recalled Rahj, his childhood pet. When Barry purchased the two-year-old for $200 from Clifford A. Shinn of Philadelphia, she had already won prizes in Westminster and Rochester bench shows. "Belle's well-bred but democratic," stated her master, and the dog became the family mascot, Barry's companion everywhere.

In the flat presided over by his sociable wife, Barry became nearly a homebody, forsaking his after-theater rendezvous for home-based entertainments. With *The Senator* playing to crowded houses, and her frequent participation in benefits, Georgie nevertheless found time to arrange large Sunday-afternoon "at homes," or more intimate little suppers after the theater. Old friends were recovered, like the Judsons, whose gay association with the Drews and Barrymores had been somewhat curtailed by their move from Gramercy Park to the suburbs. "When she had afternoons and musicales and things of swelldom in her new flat," recalled Ally Judson, "she invariably requested 'the pleasure of our company.'"

Georgie's suppers were always theatrical in flavor, beginning after the theater, lasting until three or four in the morning. "After the performance one night," recalled James T. Powers, "I attended a party given by Maurice Barrymore and his wife, Georgie Drew. We had a wonderful time!" Other guests that evening included John and Josephine Drew, Mr. and Mrs. James Lewis, Mrs. Gilbert, all of Daly's company, and John Mason, another actor friend of the Barrymores, individuals noted for high spirits and good humor. John Drew told entertaining Celtic anecdotes which, between sips, gained a thoroughly Scotch flavor. Jimmie Powers sang his irrepressible comic songs. Mrs. Gilbert told tales of the senior Booths and Drews, of the theater long before. None eclipsed the hostess.

"Georgie Drew Barrymore was always the life of the party," observed Powers, "and her husband, with all his cleverness, was like the straight man in vaudeville with Georgie overtopping all his sallies." At the host's behest, Powers sang "Paddy Stole the Rope," a favorite of Barry's at the "Jimmie Club" during their London days. His encore was an Italian love song ending on a spectacular high C.

"Don't sing the second verse, Jimmie," admonished Mrs. Barrymore, "my three little shooting stars are asleep in the back bedroom and I don't want them to include grand opera in their repertoire—they are noisy enough as it is. I want them to be missionaries."

"Wonderful idea!" her husband agreed. "Then I can get some sleep in the morning. On second thought, it would be of no use, Georgie, for I could hear them even in Africa. Let them go on the stage and I'll be a missionary."

"If you should, Barry," answered his wife, "the ghost of John Howard Payne would sit up in his grave and scribble another verse for 'Home, Sweet Home.'"

"In her charming little flat in East Fifty-ninth Street," wrote critic "Alan Dale," "she is one of the most accomplished hostesses imaginable. It is at her home that she prefers to be seen." When "Dale," nee Cohen, requested an interview, Georgie had replied characteristically:

My dear Mr. Cohen,

Will you come up to our flat some night after the theatre, and take supper with Mr. Barrymore and myself? I think it will be so much easier to talk, and you can do more in half-an-hour at that stage of the game with me than in s'teen interviews.

"Mrs. Barrymore is as amusing in private life as she is upon the stage," Cohen observed afterward. "She is a typical American, vivacious, entertaining and irresistible." As for her husband: "Barrymore is a delightful fellow to meet. He is an Englishman with a very thorough education. He can talk on any subject, and he isn't a bit shoppy. He and his wife are on terms of complete good-fellowship."

Alfred J. Cohen, of the *World* and later the *Journal,* was leader of a new school of critics rebelling against the professorial William Winter and his colleagues. Rather than scholarship and traditional theatrical ideals, they invoked the first person singular, striving to be sensational, clever, and, above all, amusing. Barry welcomed their challenge to the "fuddy-duddies"—their label for the Winter school—but they had failed, so far as he was concerned, to grasp the essential problem: "The cowardly conspiracy," Barry called it, "to measure men of the theatre by the standards of dealers in dry goods." The Bohemian Barrymores played a singular game with such critics during interviews. They satirically affected the quintessence of middle-class respectability.

"The Barrymores have three lovely children, of whom they are intensely proud," Cohen continued. "These children have been the tie that long separations and the distractions of vigorous stage life have been powerless to dissolve. If all husbands and wives, seeking livelihoods upon the stage, had the same souvenirs of early married life, a pretty home like that possessed by the Barrymores would be less unusual among dramatic couples." The critic had succumbed to the charade. "I would like to bet that the three little Barrymores will never be seen upon the stage," he predicted in closing. "I know nothing at all about it, but I am convinced that Papa Maurice would have a fit at the idea, while Mamma Georgie would indulge in the feminine equivalent—a nice swoon."

Georgie was forced to leave the cast of *The Senator* for a few days in May. A difficulty in breathing which had hindered her performance was diagnosed as a touch of bronchitis. Her doctor prescribed rest. The daughter of the Drews was not so inclined. After an inadequate respite on May 1 and 2, she resumed her part on Saturday, the third. Barry did not hear of his wife's indisposition. He was playing in Boston with the Palmer company, where *A Man of the World* repeated its New York success. But other disheartening news did reach him there: Charley Vandenhoff was dead.

Despite his rapport with Modjeska, Charley had left her employ that season after repeated disagreements with her irascible husband to tour in Steele MacKaye's *Paul Kauvar* as leading man and stage manager. When they played Seattle on April 23, Charley felt ill after the performance and went directly to his room at the Rainier Hotel. As the troupe was about to leave town, he appeared alarmingly worse. Doctors at Providence Hospital diagnosed typhoid pneumonia. "The parting words of his fellow actors were full of cheer," reported the *Dramatic Mirror*, "but hardly had they left him to the tender care of the sisters when delirium set in and death ensued."

Helena Modjeska, on a celebrated starring tour with Edwin Booth, was told in Wheeling, West Virginia, before the third act of *The Merchant of Venice*. "I went through the third act with my face flooded with tears," Madame remembered. "It was dreadful to think that he, with all the refinement he possessed, all the delicate tastes, should die in a hospital in Washington Territory—a half-civilized country where the word 'comfort' is almost unknown. Poor, dear man! I did not even write to him lately; it is hard to think of the duties which we have not accomplished, and which we cannot accomplish because it is too late!"

Barry's self-recrimination was greater. Though they had finally reconciled, relations between him and his oldest friend had been strained since his marriage. He did not match Madame's eloquence when the news reached him at the Tremont Theatre. He said nothing. After the performance that evening, he walked until dawn the streets of the city to which he and Charley had sailed from England fifteen years before.

When *The Senator* ended its five-month run in New York on May 10, Georgie returned to Philadelphia before beginning a summer tour. She had managed to be there when school let out: her mother was touring.

In her unceasing efforts to balance Arch Street losses, Mrs. Drew had mounted an exquisite production of Buckstone's old comedy, *Married Life*, with a cast of exceptional quality, not the least of which were Mr. and Mrs. Sidney Drew, so billed for the first time. With relentless courting after *The Burglar* trip, Uncle Googan had won McKee Rankin's beautiful daughter, Gladys. Mrs. Drew approved the merger wholeheartedly: the girl's father was not only a good friend but a good actor.

"Most complimentary to Mrs. Drew was the audience at McVicker's last evening," reported Chicago's *Inter-Ocean* on June 17, "in all parts of the well-filled theatre being persons whose patronage is more desirable than easily secured. The estimable actress could hope no more agreeable evidence of her popularity here, especially as her reappearance was made in a play of which this generation of play-goers knows little or nothing." The *Inter-Ocean* critic, along with his Chicago brethren, marveled at Mrs. Drew, a legend, who, at seventy, continued to grow as an actress: "Her work is quiet, undemonstrative, and aside from a certain primness of dress to heighten the comic effect, her entire success is in the tones of her voice and in the expressions of her face. But it is a success so emphatic and enjoyable that one concludes it was a lucky chance, after all, that decided her to make use of this long-neglected play."

Acclaim continued, but the tour was not a great financial success. Like those who called her "Louisa," the refined patrons of Mrs. Drew's brand of theater were fast disappearing.

The journey across the continent with Palmer's congenial company relieved Barry's lingering depression. Unlike numerous other managers, A. M. Palmer offered equal treatment to all in his employ. "We always had our own private car," recalled James Stoddart, "and the humblest person employed was treated, as far as comforts of travel were concerned, in the same manner as were the principals." This made for a relaxed, democratic atmosphere in which Barry and his traveling companion, Belle of Clyde, thrived. "Our party, too, this season was an exceptionally jolly one," said Stoddart. "Barrymore, Holland, and Harris could usually banish dull care under almost any circumstances, but on this particular trip they seemed to outdo themselves in pleasantry."

After years of resisting starring offers, Barry was excited by the autumn prospect of Gus Thomas's *Reckless Temple*. "Barry read it on the cars to Stoddart," remarked Amy Leslie. "They were both wrought up to fevered excitement by the absolutely indisputable elements of success bristling out in every situation. It was pronounced the masterpiece of the young playwright by a select corps of actor-critics." Charlie Harris was so enthused, in fact, that he decided to leave Palmer at the end of the summer tour to support Barry in his first starring venture.

San Francisco's friendly air permeated the theatrical community. Palmer's company was hailed; *Captain Swift* and *A Man of the World* were held beyond their allotted weeks. There was easy camaraderie between companies visiting San Francisco and local players. When Nick Long, a local stock actor, broke his leg, a benefit was arranged by the two touring companies then in town. Russell's Comedians, including William Collier, May and Flora Irwin and Charley Reed, joined forces with Palmer to facilitate an extravaganza, highlighted by an all-star burlesque of "Camille." Chubby May Irwin was perfectly miscast in the title role, with Collier and Reed burlesquing *Gaston* and *Armand*. Barrymore, the perfect *Armand*, was to be the villainous *Count*, but he suggested that some popular San Franciscan, for local color, should replace him. He offered the part to a youthful bank teller, handsome, courtly, Irish, who largely through amateur performances in the boxing ring was already "Frisco's Pride."

"Feeling quite thrilled," recalled James J. Corbett, "I did my best at rehearsals, and one night I went to Barrymore's dressing room and asked for some suggestions as to my make-up."

"Have you ever been on stage before?" asked Barry, scrutinizing the strapping boxer.

"No," Corbett answered, "I've never been on stage in my life."

"H'm—let me think . . ." offered the actor, looking very serious, stroking his mustache. "Yes, that's it! All the others will have on burlesque make-up, you see, so you go out in full evening dress and play the Count just as I would if I were playing with Modjeska. Be very serious. Stalk out on stage and *try* to act, and you'll be so rotten you'll be the hit of the show!" ("I was!" admitted "Gentleman Jim" afterward.)

The Palmer troupe returned to New York via Chicago and two weeks at Hooley's Theatre. Barry's undiminished playing in *A Man of the World* occasioned a two-column *Inter-Ocean* testimonial, which noted that "so little of his familiar mannerisms is to be detected in the nonchalant bearing of a really earnest soldier that, but for the unmistakable shape of the head and the undisguisable voice one might doubt the actor being Barrymore . . ." The testimonial aura was enhanced at French's during a dinner of the Forty Club, a congenial and diverse group of men, including clergy and journalists. A. M. Palmer stood to offer a toast: "Maurice Barrymore, the clever actor and polished gentleman, severs his connection with A. M. Palmer's company after tonight's performance," announced the manager, "and goes direct to New York to put into rehearsal his new play, *Reckless Temple* in which he expresses unbounded faith. It is by Gus Thomas, who wrote *Editha's Burglar* and *A Man of the World*, and Barrymore believes him to be the coming playwright. Those who know Barry will wish him success as a star, for he is a royal good fellow and a splendid actor."

After four weeks of rehearsal in New York, manager J. M. Hill took his *Reckless Temple* company to Portland, Maine, for its première. A Boston *Herald* correspondent reported the event:

RECKLESS TEMPLE IN PORTLAND

PORTLAND, ME., OCT. 20.—(Special)—Thomas's new play, *Reckless Temple*, was given its first representation in this city last evening by Mr. J. M. Hill's company, and it met with great favor. It is a society drama of more than common strength, full of action, but a little too long drawn out. Maurice Barrymore and Mrs. Herbert Kelsey have the leading parts, and play them well; and, with only one or two exceptions, the cast may be called strong. The audience was enthusiastic.

The strategy of opening so far from New York was plain: The company faced Broadway optimistically, while potential patrons digested out-of-town enthusiasms. New York's Standard Theatre was consequently filled by a large audience on opening night, many of them Barry's friends, hopeful for his starring debut, aiming to demonstrate appreciation. At the end of the third act, the *Dramatic Mirror* critic asked an English acquaintance of Barry's for his opinion. "Barry's a dear old chap," he replied, "but really, you know, I cawn't grawsp it."

"Which described the audience's frame of mind completely," added the critic: "*Reckless Temple* is not a drama, properly speaking. It is merely the idealization of Maurice Barrymore, whose lot is cast, for the nonce, among several more or less unreal personages, and into whose mouth are placed speeches and sentiments that glitter, but do not ring. *Temple* is a Ouidaesque individual, whose dissipation, impulsive recklessness, and mock heroism are likely to enshrine him in the hearts of impressionable schoolgirls that have not got beyond the period when

304

artificial romanticism is attractive . . . But here compliment must pause. His reading is exceedingly bad. Early faults have crystallized. He delivers his lines without meaning, much less expression. His method is to explode the first word or two of a speech like a bomb, and then glide to the end of a sentence with a *diminuendo* that shrouds the final words in the mystery of inaudibility. He lacks passion and power. But he poses industriously and picturesquely. So much for this reckless personation."

The *Mirror* did not go uncontested. "In spite of the utter absurdity of the medium in which he makes his first appearance as a star," said *The Theatre*, "Mr. Barrymore acts bravely and well throughout . . ." This review, appearing five days after the opening, reported that "So far the drama has played to good business; but its prosperity is entirely due to the large popularity of Mr. Maurice Barrymore."

As much for Gus Thomas as for himself, the star was dismayed by the play's critical reception. He rounded little after the opening, preferring the company of his wife and the comforts of their flat. He and Belle of Clyde would leave for the theater early each evening, long before his customary hour, when the world of canvas and limelight was emerging from chaos. Wedged between a liquor shop and a laundry, the Standard stage door opened onto a narrow, brick-walled passage with a back view of the stage just beyond it. After his preliminary chat with the doorman, who spouted vernacular in a battered hat, Barry walked to his dressing room. Stagehands were pulling at ropes, like men aboard a man-o'-war. The rosy painted ceiling was flapping down into place. The dismantled stage was gradually assuming the appearance of a modern drawing room. For the first time in his career, Barry took comfort from this backstage atmosphere.

Puffing on a Virginia cigarette, stroking Belle of Clyde, "Mr. Barrymore lounged in amiable negligence," noted a Providence *Telegram* correspondent upon entering the spacious star dressing room. "He was ready for the last act of the play and waiting for his cue. The New York stage has plenty of Apollos, but for delicacy of outline and play of expression his face is easily first. In *Captain Swift*, he looked himself. In *A Man of the World* he was a middle aged philosopher, viewing the battle complacently after he 'had been through it all,' and in *Reckless Temple* he is young, with his hair whitened prematurely by a great shock. The effect of his frost above the brilliancy of his eyes is so striking, that it is surprising he does not try to cultivate a great sorrow merely for the chastening effect upon his hair. I hardly think he is of the emotional sort though."

After its scheduled two weeks in New York, *Reckless Temple* set out on a sixteen-week tour. The Barrymore name proved to be no antidote for poor reviews. The star forwent his salary in an attempt to keep the show running, but to no avail. They closed, less than ten weeks out, in Kansas City. Barry purchased a rare polar bear cub from a local animal dealer, and headed for New York.

On December 20, the eve of her fourteenth wedding anniversary, Georgie was again required to leave the cast of *The Senator*, which had been revived by popular demand. Bronchial complications were diagnosed as before. Her doctor urged rest in a southern clime. She agreed reluctantly to rest, but a change of temperature was out of the question: the children had come to Fifty-ninth Street for their Christmas holidays. With *The Senator* running successfully, Mrs. Barrymore had been extravagant with their presents and pleasures. Now, her weekly income had stopped. Financial crisis was imminent, when a wire arrived announcing that her husband was on his way.

"We were waiting for Papa to return from a Western tour," recalled Jack. "It was always a festive occasion when he arrived, and this was the greatest of all, for he brought home a roly-poly bear cub that he had bought from an animal dealer in Kansas City. We kids were delighted. But Mamma cried—though why, we children didn't understand at all. It wasn't until some time later that we learned that my whimsical father had arrived without a cent in his pockets. He had spent all his money for the bear cub." The cub went directly to Staten Island; Papa went to work.

Concerned by Georgie's illness, Barry accepted the first position offered. But the humiliation of his failure as a star, though unspoken, did not escape him; nor did the consequences. The $250-a-week leading man re-signed with A. M. Palmer for $200.

Barry began 1891 with Palmer's company in Boston. The manager had wisely chosen *Captain Swift* to rehabilitate the reputation of his leading man. Two years had not dimmed the luster of the actor's favorite role. "The *Wilding* of Barrymore is even and good, as a matter of course," reported the *Herald* critic, in concert with his colleagues.

When the company returned to the Madison Square, he originated roles in two of Palmer's English importations, *Sunlight and Shadow* and *The Pharisee*, in which, the *Spirit of the Times* noted, "Mr. Barrymore did some of the best acting of his career." But the plays were not hits. Palmer still sought his season's success.

Content and seemingly improved in the Fifty-ninth Street flat that winter, Georgie rejected her husband's suggestion of a cruise in southern waters. While she minimized her indisposition, he fretted about it, hastening each evening after the performance to his wife and their cozy flat. He restricted his social activities to special events at the Lambs'—on March 3, he appeared in the first Gambol, *Shenandoah, Jr.*, a burlesque of the popular Bronson Howard play—and to occasional afternoons in the men's café of the Plaza Hotel, a block from their flat. Lionel was introduced to that convivial precinct during his spring holiday from Seton Hall.

"I had been bidden to go to the veterinarian's one afternoon to fetch Belle of Clyde, who had come down with an ailment, and to meet Maurice Barrymore at the old Plaza Hotel, then a red brick building," recalled Barry's elder son. "Belle and I naturally found our way to the gentlemen's café for our rendezvous with Maurice, and there we met a friend of my father's, a doctor."

"What are you boys doing here?" asked the doctor. "Step up to the bar and have a drink."

"So Belle and I stepped up to the bar and had a gingerale on the doctor. Presently a gentleman enveloped in a beard and a fur coat entered, greeted the doctor, had a drink with him, and the two of them spoke together for some minutes in an odd language that I could not understand. I was presented but did not get the name of the furry gentleman . . ." When Barry arrived, again introducing his son, the conversation switched to French, as unintelligible to the boy as the previous language had been. But the furry gentleman began to illustrate his words with extravagant action. He whacked Papa on the back, and hugged him heartily. Taking two squizzle-sticks from the bar, he waved them sweepingly, while Barry and the doctor roared with laughter.

"What was that man doing back there?" asked Lionel, as he and Papa walked home.

"He was showing us what Andrew Carnegie did at a dinner party last night. Carnegie imitated him as he looks on the conductor's box. He came over from Russia to conduct at the opening of Carnegie's new concert hall."

"Andrew Carnegie did?" wondered Lionel.

"No," said Papa impatiently, "Tchaikowsky. Don't you ever listen to introductions, my boy?"

On the strength of *Editha's Burglar* and *A Man of the World*, and at Barry's urging, Gus Thomas had been named Palmer's dramatist extraordinary, replacing the prolific, impetuous Dion Boucicault, who had recently died at sixty-eight. But Gus lost considerable ground after the New York failures of *The Burglar, Reckless Temple* and *A Woman of the World*. (The last, written for Georgie as a companion piece to *A Man of the World*, never approached the success of Barry's vehicle. As the *Spirit of the Times* observed: "The only thing in it is Mrs. Georgie Drew Barrymore. She carries the trifle on her shoulders and uncovers them to do it. They are superb and the audience were delighted.") Faith in theatrical circles extended only as far as one's last success. Following the reading of his new play, *Alabama*, written specifically to the measure of Palmer's leading players, Agnes Booth whispered, "Rotten, thank you!" and declined to play the part written for her. When his English productions failed to capture the public, however, Palmer reluctantly decided to present Gus's play on April 1, 1891.

"Manager Palmer, with his usual tact, brought out the play without any preliminary puffery," presumed the *Spirit of the Times*, "and the audience—many of whom had painful previous experiences of Mr. Thomas in *The Burglar* and *Reckless Temple*—were taken by surprise, agreeably disappointed and thoroughly delighted. The cast is perfect; the scenery charming; the play has every possible advantage, and we confidently predict that it will be one of the greatest successes of this theatre of dramatic miracles." The *Spirit of the Times* was merely echoing cries of triumph from the dailies. "The acclaim with which Mr. Thomas' new play *Alabama* was greeted," added the *Dramatic Mirror*, "would seem to point to the speedy realization of Mr. Howell's prediction that the future American drama will be 'a prolongation of character sketches.' Its success at the initial performance last Wednesday evening was pronounced; the critical verdict was unanimous in its favor and the piece will enjoy a long lease of life and prosperity, beyond question."

Padded to blunt his youthful frame, bearded graying black, Barry triumphed as *Captain Davenport*, the character role fashioned expressly for him by the author. "Mr. Maurice Barrymore, the best leading actor in America," raved the Chicago *Inter-Ocean* correspondent, "has a role unlike any in which the public has seen him, that of a mature man, a father, in which nobility of character and deep, strong sentiment are well balanced. He presents the character admirably, and with a tenderness that is at times singularly affecting. He proves himself master of gentle emotions as well as of passionate, aggressive force."

After only three weeks in New York, the Palmer company embarked on a tour arranged prematurely by the apprehensive manager before the New York opening. It broke attendance records and shattered critical reserve everywhere. Almost everywhere, that is. "I confess to being unable to understand why *Alabama* does not achieve popularity in Pittsburgh," declared a baffled local critic. "It must be that we Pittsburghers don't want *Alabama*. If that be the case it would be interesting to know why?" Despite Pittsburghers, Augustus Thomas's idyll of the far South— the sectional prejudice, the ceremonious courtesy, the narrow views of small communities, the jasmine-scented decay following the overthrow of ante-bellum institutions—was already on its way to becoming one of the decade's sustaining hits.

Before heading west with *Alabama*, Palmer's company returned to New York, where the erstwhile manager was to helm a charity gala. An alfresco performance would be given on June 16 at the palatial residence of Mrs. E. A. Stevens, Castle Point, Hoboken. *As You Like It* would be the play. Maurice Barrymore would be the *Orlando* to the *Rosalind* of Rose Coghlan—ideal lovers amid great spreading elms and wide greensward of the patrimonial twenty-acre estate with its venerable castle on a bluff. "The noise of New York penetrates but faintly to this place," noted the *Dramatic Mirror*. "The performance will take about two hours and a half, and will be over before the tremendous salvo from ten thousand six-o'clock whistles pierces the silence."

No more perfect surroundings could be imagined for the re-creation of Shakespeare's rustic idyll set "Under the greenwood tree . . ." The lawn was cut the day before the performance, drying grass raked into haycocks to enhance the rural scene. So careful was attention to detail that even the nails driven for *Orlando* to hang his odes upon were painted green to simulate twigs with leaves on them. An amphitheater, shaded by oak and maple trees, was erected of unpainted pine, chairs placed on its steps for a thousand spectators. Only a thousand tickets, at five dollars each, were issued. "Nearly all of these are sold," announced the *Mirror* a week before the performance, "but a few are still to be had at Hazard's drug store under the Fifth Avenue Hotel."

At each gate, on Tuesday afternoon, ticket takers and Hoboken policemen awaited the throng: personages of the theater, the arts, and society. Mrs. Barrymore and her three children crossed on the same ferry with the likes of Mrs. Chauncey M. Depew, Brigadier General Van Vliet, Mrs. Frances Delafield, Mrs. W. C. Whitney, and the Marquise de Talleyrand Perigord. "*We*," declared the imperious Mrs. William Astor, speaking, presumably, for her self-appointed four hundred, "anticipate with pleasure the performance of Mr. Barrymore."

"*We*," replied Georgie, just as imperiously, with only her husband and, possibly, her clinging progeny to represent, "most surely thank you."

They strolled up the low rolling hill to the Stevens estate, through the old stone gateway, along the elm-lined avenue to the amphitheater. It was oppressively hot. By 3 P.M., men's collars had wilted, women's face powder had disappeared in little rivulets. Great trees overhead were tremulous in a faint breeze, filtering the intense sunlight of the hottest day of the year, making golden shafts and glistening fragments. *Orlando* awaited his cue behind a rippling cedar hedge.

"Suddenly the blare of a trumpet sounded, a call such as in stage language heralds the approach of a king," recounted a Boston *Herald* dispatch. "And almost instantly there appeared the *Orlando* of the day in the person of the man who has been called the best *Orlando* of his time— Mr. Barrymore." A ripple of refreshing applause greeted him as he emerged from the trees, and the play began. "Mr. C. W. Couldock, the veteran actor, as *Adam*, was with him, and the effect was strange when the handsome young noble and the gray-haired servant began to talk together . . . Those who saw Maurice Barrymore playing his part on the grass and under the trees at Castle Point, Hoboken, today, saw what they are not likely to forget, however long the last of them may live."

So compelling had the first act been that ominous clouds gathered unnoticed. Between the acts, Mrs. Stevens, indicating the blackened sky, proposed a postponement. "No, madam," said Barry, turning his face to the menacing clouds, "God will not permit a charity like this to be ruined by rain." No sooner had he spoken than his cheek was rudely struck by a raindrop. "This is the way infidels are created," he observed plaintively; but the second act proceeded as scheduled.

Parasols dotted the bleaching boards. Those who hadn't brought umbrellas held camp chairs over their heads. The accurate and natural costumes of seventy-five lords, ladies, hunters, and halberdiers, purchased by Palmer from the immaculate wardrobe of the late Lester Wallack, were wilted in the downpour. *Orlando* and *Rosalind* made sprightly love in waterproofs. Action of the play raced action of the clouds. Peals of thunder punctuated Shakespeare's sentimental lines. Lightning distorted verdant scenes. The remaining spectators left their seats, flanking the dampened stage, Rock's coats and Worth's gowns making sodden communion with jerkins and leggings. "In spite of the adverse circumstances," concluded the *Mirror*, "all said they had a capital time. And so they had, but it was the same kind of a good time that picnickers have when the grass and the bugs get into their plates. It was a novelty, and Americans love a novelty." The actors had worked without pay. Mrs. Stevens had covered the other expenses. Five thousand dollars was raised for charity.

While Barry toured west with *Alabama*, Georgie and the children commuted rather festively between New York, Philadelphia and Staten Island. Most of July was spent at Mme. Bourquin's with Mrs. Drew. The boys delighted their grandmother by taking healthy daily walks around the island. So they said. Unbeknownst to Mummum, they were merely visiting the Black Prince and Papa's forbidden menagerie. Relaxation and the warmth of summer improved Georgie's health. Still determined to facilitate Ethel's musical aspirations, she began to consider acting offers again. The most lucrative came from a young, apple-cheeked theatrical adventurer.

Charles Frohman was the son of a German immigrant—a dry-goods peddler in the Hudson Valley, who became a Rialto tobacconist. The boy had seen his first play, *The Black Crook*, at Niblo's Garden in the '60s. "I have seen a play," he told his brother, Daniel. "It's *wonderful!*" The round, beaming face, the popping-bright eyes inspired by that event never left Charles Frohman where the theater was concerned. His personal life meshed totally with the professional. Theater became living reality to him.

While brother Daniel was securing his popular management of the

Lyceum Theatre, Charles had graduated rapidly from advance agent for plays and minstrel shows to management in his own right. After his first success, *Shenandoah*, for which he had unsuccessfully sought Barry's services, he had inaugurated a profitable stock season at Proctor's Twenty-third Street Theatre. He had offered the position of leading lady to Georgie, but she was playing with Crane at the time. Frohman, with a penchant for Drews and Barrymores, persisted.

When he formed a second company, Charles Frohman's Comedians, Georgie accepted his lucrative offer. Her first appearance under his auspices, *Mr. Wilkinson's Widows*, a new comedy by William Gillette, opened at Proctor's on August 27. The *Dramatic Mirror* placed the leading lady's picture on its coveted first page and devoted an editorial to her: "It is one thing for an actor to be popular with audiences; quite another to be popular with his, or her, brother and sister professionals, and when the actor is popular both before and behind the curtain, he, or she, is indeed lucky. Georgie Drew Barrymore is on this account, at least, lucky. There may be hundreds of 'Georgies' in the dramatic profession, but the mention of the name at once causes the mind to any one familiar with the stage to fill in a mental blank—Drew Barrymore. It calls to mind a tall woman, with a fine figure, who dresses gorgeously and in the fashion; a woman with a voice that is thin, and that breaks, and that reminds one a little of the chirps of a canary bird; a woman with a fund of animal spirits and *fin de siècle* repartee . . ."

Mrs. Drew visited Proctor's. She saw the performance out, applauded at the end, and departed without breaking her rule against dressing-room calls. The next evening, Charles Frohman, awed by the mere mention of Mrs. John Drew, asked the leading lady what her mother had said about the performance. "She didn't say much," Georgie replied thoughtfully. "She never does. She squeezed my hand and kissed me on the cheek, and I interpreted that as meaning she approved of me."

"But what did she say?" persisted the young manager.

"She didn't say anything," Georgie reiterated. "I suppose she was afraid that if she did I'd be sending congratulatory telegrams to myself."

A few days later, Mrs. Drew set out on a 27,000-mile tour with Joseph Jefferson. To their staple offering of *The Rivals* was added *The Heir-in-Law*, in which, as Louisa Lane, sixty years before, she had played *Dr. Pangloss* to the *Zekial Homespun* of Jefferson's grandfather.

A letter from her youngest grandson reached Mrs. Drew as she toured. "I was attacked by this huge fellow and without cause," wrote Jack, who had joined his brother at Seton Hall. "And, as the great brute advanced toward my desk, I tried to placate him; but he struck me a blow which felled me to the ground." With Georgie also on tour, the horrified grandmother was obliged to forward the letter to her son-in-law in New York. She admonished him to make haste to Seton Hall. "My father's on his way to beat seven kinds of hell out of the entire faculty," Jack promised his schoolfellows.

Barry arrived for his appointment with Father Marshall, the headmaster, and was duly informed of the genesis of his son's complaint: While reprimanding Jack for reading *Buffalo Bill's Adventures* behind an open textbook, an assistant instructor had placed an admonishing hand upon the boy's head. That evening, the imaginative nine-year-old had written to his grandmother. Barry was impressed by his son's creativity, and delighted by the conversation of Father Marshall, "a priest so honest that Diogenes would have put away his lamp," he observed, "and so learned that Plato would have kicked Socrates in the behind." They fell into discussion of the currently controversial case of Carlyle Harris, a medical student convicted on toxological evidence of murdering his young wife. After a lengthy debate as to Harris's innocence or guilt, they strolled arm in arm, chatting amiably, to the visitor's waiting carriage. They shook hands warmly; Barry said, "Tell the boy to look out and behave himself," and departed for New York.

Jack watched from protective shrubbery, jeered by schoolfellows. "My disappointment was very bitter," he recalled, "for I had let it be known that my father, who had been amateur middleweight champion of England, was coming down to beat up the entire school. I had promised that there would be great ructions. It was an awful anti-climax."

Barry had returned to New York from his Western tour with Palmer only a few days before Georgie departed on a tour with Frohman's Comedians. *Alabama*, by popular demand, opened Palmer's home season, and Barry returned to night life, without, somehow, his usual fervor. The recently formed Players' Club at No. 16 Gramercy Park became a frequent resort. Unlike the Lambs', which cherished nothing so much as its reputation as a "good time" club, the Players' was founded on dignity and tradition. Among the incorporators, besides Edwin Booth, who had presented the stately clubhouse to his fellows, were Joseph Jefferson, Augustin Daly, John Drew, Samuel L. Clemens and General Sherman—the last two illustrating that, despite its name, the club was not limited to theater folk. Although this allowed for the inclusion of certain social hangers-on, Barry had joined, prompted by the presence of his brother-in-law, and by his admiration for Edwin Booth. That admiration was shared by his fellow members, who often carried it too far.

Hung as it was with portraits of Booth in every conceivable role, the Players' might easily have become a shrine rather than a clubhouse, hardly what the unassuming donor had intended. One evening a group began discussing, in reverent tones, Booth's courage in recently doubling the top price of theater tickets to an unprecedented three dollars. During a prolonged dissection of this topic, the bored Barrymore noticed a regal

312

portrait of Booth as *Richelieu,* raising his right arm, three fingers extended, invoking the curse of Rome.

"Hello!" Barry exclaimed within earshot of Booth, "there's the 'old man' raising the price to $3!" There was a moment's awkward pause. Then Edwin Booth began to laugh, the others following suit. None was more relieved than the "old man."

As usual, Barry supplemented regular performances at Palmer's with numerous benefits for colleagues and Sunday-night "Sacred Concerts" for charity—so called to circumnavigate Sabbath performing restrictions. After the December 2nd performance of *Alabama,* he boarded the late train to Boston for the Fourteenth Annual Benefit of the Benevolent and Protective Order of the Elks in aid of the Boston Lodge's charity fund. A cause close to the hearts of theater folk, the Elks had been formed in New York in 1867, when actors were still generally treated as social outcasts. "Born of brotherly love," stated the preface to the club bylaws, "it is designed to offer to the actor the certainty of warm hearts and welcome hearths in the various cities to which his nomadic profession summons him. Courted by the public, yet ostracized by society, known to thousands, yet stranger to all, one can well realize his sincere satisfaction in finding in each strange city a little circle of kindred minds . . ." Whenever their schedules allowed it over the years, the Drews and Barrymores —Barry was a member of the Executive Committee—contributed their talents to this worthy organization, whose charity fund aided needy actors.

Georgie was playing *Mr. Wilkinson's Widows* at the Columbia, when Barry landed in Boston for the benefit. He was a startling but welcome apparition that morning in her Hotel Plaza room. By ten o'clock, he was at the Hollis Street Theatre, guiding his supporting cast through a quick rehearsal of *A Man of the World.* At noon, they opened the bill with a splendid rendition of the curtain raiser. Afterward, *Captain Bradley*'s powdered hair and dressing gown intact, Barry was whisked by cab to the one-o'clock train for New York.

Six hours later, with the co-operation of the Boston & Albany and the New York, New Haven & Hartford, he reached Grand Central, and, shortly thereafter, Palmer's Theatre, in time to apply the hirsute accessories of *Captain Davenport.*

A singular dissatisfaction had come upon Maurice Barrymore. The urge to write had struck decisively. The act of writing was not forthcoming. He again tried to force work on his new play, the comedy of scientific phenomena called *Blood Will Tell,* and again considered the unfinished *Robber of the Rhine.* He spent less time with fellow actors, seeking, instead, the company of writers and journalists. He found some of his former literary cronies at Oscar's, and at the Silver Grill, on Sixth

Avenue and Thirteenth Street, frequently joined the reporters' round table. "Among the newspaper men were Blakely Hall, Leander Richardson, Charlie Bryne, and Arthur Brisbane," recalled Jimmie Powers, "each with his chin resting on his hands, gazing into Barrymore's twinkling eyes, absorbing his delightful essays." Amusing these attentive young men, who would become America's foremost newspaper editors, did not satisfy the frustrated dramatist.

On December 15, 1891, his literary disappointments weighing heavy, Barry attended a supper at the Lotos Club tendered by Bronson Howard to Charles Gayler, America's dramatist emeritus. Apart from honoring Gayler, whose major work antedated the Civil War, Howard's supper was prompted by another motive. "I was talking with a number of the younger playwrights not long ago at the Lambs' Club," he had written to the old man, "and they all expressed their interest in meeting you as the senior of our guild. We have at last become a body of dramatists with a promising future; and it seems to us that there is no way to emphasize the fact so well as to gather around our oldest member, who bore for us the early and hardest part of our struggle."

Besides Howard and the guest of honor, Barry was among thirty-two other dramatists of the day, including Steele MacKaye, Henry C. DeMille, Augustus Pitou, Sydney Rosenfeld, Clay M. Greene, David Belasco. Two men whose careers Barry had considerably influenced, Paul M. Potter and Augustus Thomas, were included, and, at Barry's particular request to the host, would-be author Colonel Edward M. Alfriend. Out of this prestigious gathering grew the Society of American Dramatists and Composers, then the only institution of its kind in the world, the first to activate the amending of copyright laws to make play piracy a misdemeanor punishable by imprisonment.

Maurice H. Barrymore was a charter member of the Society, a prime mover in establishing its prerogatives. That evening made a more personal impact as well. Inclusion in this august body had touched him fundamentally, inspiring an immediate desire to validate such an honor.

Three days later, Charles Puerner, composer of such operettas as *A Royal Tramp* and *The Trumpeter of Amsterdam,* agreed to write a new score for *The Robber of the Rhine.*

XXIV

ABANDONED AFTER WILL FULLERTON'S untimely death in
London, *The Robber of the Rhine* came abruptly back to life when
Charles Puerner agreed to compose a new score. The elusive ingredients
of theatrical production, responding to the author's boundless energy, materialized. H. C. Miner contracted to have the elaborate production open
his New Fifth Avenue Theatre on Twenty-eighth Street. Fire had leveled
the original house, where Barry had made his New York debut, but
Miner's crimson and cream replacement was splendid. At Barry's behest,
the original costumes by Percy Anderson, Fullerton's friend, were to be
utilized, and Hayden Coffin, originally set for the lead in London, was
engaged. "I was very pleased at last to have this chance of appearing as
Waldemar," Hayden wrote, "and took over at request, to the states, the
wonderful costume which had been especially made from the designs of
Percy Anderson, but my disappointment can be hardly imagined when I
found that the music of my dear friend Fullerton was not being used, but
that of Charles Puerner, who was a stranger to me."

Without Fullerton, the enthusiasm of those initial working days at
Queen Anne's Gate was never quite recaptured. Barry worked tirelessly,
however, to revive it. Richard Barker was chosen to direct the play. A
fine musical cast was assembled to vivify such *opéra comique* denizens as
*Baron Von Piffleseltzer, La Comtesse de Foie Gras, Dr. Hyacinth, The
Grafin Hildegarde,* and the brigand quintette: *Kaspar, Klootz, Schpoof,
Schweip,* and *Schplitz.* A young actress from Canada was to make her
New York debut as *Cunigonde,* the brigand heroine. "I was a friend of
the friend of the man who was putting up the money," recalled Marie
Dressler. "No sooner had I presented myself for rehearsals than I realized
I was the right person in the wrong pew. Nobody wanted me in the cast,
and everybody did everything they could to get rid of me. I pretended

that I was a rhinoceros and laughed gaily at barbed darts." Only Barry befriended the buoyant newcomer, helping her through "long, miserable weeks of rehearsal and discord," hiding his own growing concern as they faced the ordeal of opening night. She recalled many warm chats during that hectic period: "It was Maurice Barrymore who first fathomed my secret ambition to play tragedy and warned me against it."

"You were born to make people laugh, Marie," he advised gently. "Don't fly in the face of fate!" Words that Marie Dressler remembered and profited by.

On that evening of May 28, 1892, Barry's well-wishers were in force at the New Fifth Avenue Theatre. "Mr. Barrymore was expected to justify his personal reputation as a wit in his new departure," reported the *Dramatic Mirror*. "It was thought that *The Robber of the Rhine* would scintillate with bright thoughts and fairly bubble with merry quips." Even his most avid supporters, however, found little to amuse them in the first act. When the curtain fell, the *World* noted, the audience, "denied a laugh in the operetta, called for the author, feeling that 'Barry,' in *propria persona*, would be good for at least one quip." In response to repeated calls, the curtain was raised, revealing a "super" trailing across the stage in tattered hose and a cap with broken plume. The crowd roared at the supposed mishap, as the bedraggled fellow came forward.

"Ladies and gentlemen," said Maurice Barrymore, "I thank you for the first hearty, spontaneous laughter of the evening."

Nothing else in the three acts remaining inspired heartier audience response. The actors were not at their best. "I prompted everybody in the cast," recalled Marie Dressler, "because I seemed to be the only one who hadn't lost his head in the excitement." It was not the cast, though, that was blamed for the play's shortcomings. "Mr. Barrymore has chosen an unconventional story for his book," said the New York *Times* review, "but has treated it with less flexibility of style than might have been expected from one of his experience in stagecraft. The fault of the book appeared last night to be a fondness on the part of the author for his own dialogue which led him to write more of it than was necessary for the achievement of his designs. If Mr. Barrymore will apply the pruning knife with a stern hand and—as they say in the profession—cut everything down to the bone, he will probably find that the effects which were missed last night will be achieved."

"The dialogue proved to be poor stuff, utterly lacking in humor and ponderously dull when the intent was to be playful," added the *Dramatic Mirror*. "The lyrics—most of them, at least—lacked the singing quality. Sometimes the clumsiness of the syllabification caused singers something akin to distress. The plot is stale. The old materials were put together with no evidence of inventive skill. The fact cannot be concealed that Mr. Barrymore sadly disappointed his friends and bored the public." The

Times, at least, marked the introduction of "a very good operetta company." And Barry gained some satisfaction from critical response to the players. If nothing else, *The Robber of the Rhine* introduced Hayden Coffin, Marie Dressler, and designer Percy Anderson to Broadway, heralding three extraordinary careers.

The play kept the stage for five weeks, playing to dwindling houses, but the author still harbored some hopes for it. As *The Theatre* had reported before the opening, Thomas H. Pratt planned to send the operetta on the road in September. And Wm. A. Pond & Co. published some of the words and music, including "Hast Thou Forgot?" the main love song, with Barry's lyric evocation of "serenades," and "ritourelles," and "lattic'd dim tourelles." Puerner's lilting waltz, Barrymore's sweet libretto joined the repertoires of roof gardens and cafés, concert halls and bandstands. Its popularity that summer proved to be the author's only consolation in the wake of diverse humiliations.

"Alas, the opera was not a success," lamented Hayden Coffin, who had previously signed to tour with Lillian Russell. "It was a serious handicap to appear in a failure in America before the Lillian Russell tour started, and a very material handicap too, for it led Henry French to reduce considerably my engagement on the financial side, an arrangement which I was not in a position to refuse." Influenced by similar considerations, Thomas H. Pratt withdrew his offer to send the operetta on the road.

"Poor Maurice!" declared Marie Dressler. "It practically broke his heart."

While *The Robber of the Rhine* distracted Barry, his mother-in-law faced new challenges in Philadelphia. When Mrs. Drew lost her eldest child, Louisa Mendum, early that year, sorrow compounded business pressures, forcing a crucial decision. "To return to the subject of the Arch Street Theatre," she wrote: "when I returned there in 1892, at the close of *The Rivals* tour, I found the business of the season had been so very poor; and as the outlook for the next season was no better, I concluded to give it up (if the stockholders would permit me to do so), and I wrote to the Board of Agents to that effect, and they agreed to my wish." Philadelphia responded with a series of receptions and testimonials. One of them, a largely attended reception at the Art Club, tendered by the foremost ladies of Main Line society, was an unprecedented gesture toward an actress in the City of Brotherly Love.

It was a time of superlatives. "No woman has ever before rounded off thirty-one years of successful management," stated *The Theatre*. "It is unprecedented in theatrical annals." Louisa Drew had begun her management by playing, during the first three seasons alone, ninety-two different parts. Characteristically, she chose to end her unbroken run in a new role—the *Widow Green*, in Sheridan Knowles's old-time comedy,

The Love Chase. "Few actresses and fewer actors learn new parts in their 70's," noted the Philadelphia *Times*'s "Man in the Lobby." "I cannot now recall any American actress who has paralleled Mrs. Drew's achievement."

Loyal survivors of her passing constituency, groups of her old friends gathered nightly during her farewell week. On Saturday, when the curtain fell after her last performance as manageress of the Arch, the audience made no attempt to leave. "It was not a very large audience," reported the local *Times*—she had not chosen to publicize her departure; and her regular following was limited of late by age and taste—"but it had been very appreciative and enthusiastic during the play, and now it remained seated and applauded with the greatest earnestness." They refused to leave the theater. They encored until their beloved citizen would recognize their tribute with a speech.

The curtain rose, revealing the erect figure of Louisa Drew in the eighteenth-century finery of *Widow Green.* She did not hesitate: "The time has come for me to say farewell." She spoke slowly, simply, with gentleness and emotion. "We meet now for the last time as auditor and manager. This is much worse for me than it is for you. It is a wrench for me; I confess it. After a most successful thirty-one years in this dear old theatre . . ." Her voice trembled, and she paused, unable for some time to regain control of it. "I don't know exactly what to say. This week has been a very happy one for me. The only drawback was, it was the last. To hear these walls resound with applause for simply acting and nothing more, the acting of an old comedy, merely acting, is something to make an actor's heart almost burst with joy." This inspired prolonged applause. "I thank you sincerely, you representing the public, for your attendance and for your appreciation. I must also thank the entire press of this city. Their notices and criticisms of this play have been more than generous. I should feel proud if I deserve half that the press has said of me. And now let me add the undying gratitude which I feel for the owners of this theatre for thirty-one years of unswerving courtesy and substantial kindness, which I can never repay, but which I am glad of the opportunity to acknowledge publicly now. There is nothing more, I think, to say"—again her voice faltered—"but farewell, and as Dickens's Tiny Tim says, 'God bless us, every one.'"

No acting in the Arch Street Theatre ever touched an audience more. "The actress bowed her head, her eyes glistened with tears, the audience applauded and slowly rose to depart," elegized the *Times*, "and the green curtain descended and hid from view the most remarkable and memorable figure in the history of Philadelphia theatrical management." The venerable inscription—MRS. JOHN DREW, SOLE LESSEE—disappeared from the playbill of the Arch.

A week following Mrs. Drew's farewell, a testimonial was initiated by

Joseph Jefferson, William H. Crane, and Mr. and Mrs. Kendal. The matter was placed in charge of a committee of prominent Philadelphians, the event set for the Academy of Music. "The advance sale of seats has been something phenomenal," gushed the *Enquirer*, "and although the season is practically at an end, there will be such an audience as hardly has been seen in a Philadelphia theatre in a generation. Many citizens have deferred their departure for summer homes to be able to assist at the affair, and others will come to town especially for the occasion."

The program included William H. Crane and his company in an act of *The Senator*. Georgie, touring with Frohman's Comedians, was regrettably unable to take her original part. But the bill concluded with its unquestioned highlight—the second act of *The Rivals*, with Mrs. Drew and Joseph Jefferson in their famous roles, aided by Maurice Barrymore, in his popular rendition of *Captain Absolute*. "It was a memorable night for me," Louisa Drew noted with typical understatement.

Honor and tribute notwithstanding, the living legend could not rest on her laurels. Nor would she accept the willing charity of her children. "The next thing was, what was I to do with myself! I couldn't live in Philadelphia in the manner in which I had always lived; couldn't afford it. So I moved to New York, after nearly forty years of housekeeping in Philadelphia. It was a terrible wrench! To look about for 'something to do' at seventy-two years of age! But I was still in possession of splendid health, good spirits, and the love of my remaining children."

Mrs. Barrymore returned from touring in June to find husband, children, and mother in residence at Fifty-ninth Street. Georgie, tired but cheerful, worried about her mother, who seemed lost without the responsibilities of management. Such concern was short-lived. Offers of employment began coming immediately for the indomitable veteran.

Sidney and Gladys, who, as Mr. and Mrs. Sidney Drew, had emerged as stars in *That Girl from Mexico* the previous December, undertook to make a five-week summer engagement supporting his mother. They played with great success in Philadelphia, Brooklyn and Harlem. "What a pleasure it would be to see some of our tragedians play with the artistic finish of Mrs. John Drew!" declared *The Clipper*.

Barry had rejected offers for summer tours, preferring, while *The Robber of the Rhine* was at least yielding weekly income, to spend those months with Georgie. He had already contracted for an autumn engagement with Mrs. Bernard-Beere, a colleague in the Bancrofts' company, who was making her American debut that November. Meanwhile, a tranquil summer of family and friends beckoned.

A bicycle craze had struck New York. The whole city on wheels, it seemed, was swarming avenues and paths. "You cannot serve God and skylark on a bicycle," ranted the Reverend Asa D. Blackburn, but bicycling schools and clubs abounded. One afternoon, Lionel and Jack were astounded by the spectacle of Papa and Richard Mansfield riding tandem down Fifth Avenue. They were used to Papa's cycling—they often accompanied him—but this day something decidedly different had been added. The two eminent actors were dressed as antic twins in black tights, fur jerkins, Zouave sashes, and astrakhan hats. Mansfield, the theater's *Beau Brummell*, had designed the costume to amply display his athletic build. He had insisted, perhaps for protection, upon presenting an identical one to his friend. Together they rode the avenues, according to Gene Fowler, "like a pair of variety acrobats." Papa waved nonchalantly to his sons, as they disappeared into Central Park.

The antic twins only sartorial competition on the avenues was another theatrical team, referred to as "Beauty and the Beastie." None other than Lillian Russell and Marie Dressler, who, taking Barry's advice, was to be La Russell's comedy support in the forthcoming *Princess Nicotine*. "Even in those far-off days when curves were curves and no apologies to anybody," Marie recalled, "Lillian was afraid of getting fat. Bicycles were modish and she hit upon this new toy of the fashionables as a means of keeping us both in trim. Every morning, rain or shine, we would climb on our wheels and bending low over our handlebars give an imitation of two plump girls going somewhere in a hurry."

As Lillian lived at Seventy-sixth Street and Fifth Avenue, the girls dashed into the nearby park for a turn around the reservoir. They frequently encountered Barrymore and Mansfield. After an amiable chat, the foursome would again split into segregated couples to continue their exercise. Once out of earshot, Mansfield would begin ridiculing Marie's recent fad for wearing a large chrysanthemum over each ear. "Well, it will never be pronounced the correct thing in society," Barry laughed, "but it's funny just the same." Marie's posies were merely a prelude to Mansfield's abiding grievance—La Russell's blatant lack of taste. Her white serge cycling costume with leg-of-mutton sleeves did not offend him so much as her vehicle. Presented by her friend, "Diamond Jim" Brady, the conveyance was entirely gold plated, its hubs and spokes set with precious stones, its mother-of-pearl handle bars monogrammed L.R. with diamonds and emeralds. Richard Mansfield could not bear to be upstaged.

Early in August, all of the Drews happened to converge in New York. A Sunday-evening dinner party was arranged by Georgie to commemorate the event at the Claremont Inn, an elegant open-air restaurant overlooking the Hudson River from a wooded plateau below Grant's Tomb. In the spirit of a breezy summer evening, Mrs. Drew, John and Josephine, Sidney and Gladys, and the Barrymores rode in open carriages along the new Riverside Drive. The two oldest Barrymore children—

Lionel was fourteen; Ethel would soon turn thirteen—had been given special permission to join the party.

Glowing Japanese lanterns were strung through the trees over white-topped tables. Varicolored bicycle lamps flashed like fireflies along Riverside Drive. Liveried waiters served cold lobster and champagne to the festive party. The band played music for a soft summer evening. When the bandmaster dedicated "Hast Thou Forgot?" to Mrs. Barrymore, she and Barry stood up and waltzed to the lilting melody of his song. Other patrons, in silent deference, moved to the edges of the floor, making room for Mrs. Barrymore's shifting yellow silk against the tall, sure steps of her stalwart husband. The resident soprano sang Barry's sentimental lyrics:

> *The air was still and passion fraught the night*
> *Athwart the flags, the ghostly shadows lay*
> *Thy face look'd down, so pale in wan moon-light,*
> *'Thou are my love, my all' it seemed to say . . .*

Ethel remembered that Lionel was preoccupied with an elaborate ice-cream concoction, while she, eyes filled with tears, watched her parents whirl with easy grace beneath the trees.

Reunions, always rare for the peripatetic brood, nearly disappeared altogether with the advent of a pop-eyed, pint-sized, burgeoning impresario. To Charles Frohman, the Drews had always symbolized theatrical tradition and excellence. His ambition to guide their professional destinies, besides being shrewd business, would validate his own recently won position in the theater. By end of summer, 1892, the Hudson River peddler's son was becoming practically manager extraordinary to the Drew family.

He had already won Georgie. On August 8, she began her second season with Frohman's Comedians, following *The Robber of the Rhine* into the New Fifth Avenue. *Settled out of Court*, a new comedy adapted by William Gillette from Alexandre Bisson's Paris success, "would have been dull," reported the *Spirit of the Times*, "had it not been capitally acted by Joseph Holland as *Harriman*, and Georgie Drew Barrymore as the mother-in-law." But the play proved popular, plaudits for Georgie "full of the quaint, fetching abruptness of gesture and speech which belong to her alone," continuing in New York and on tour.

Meanwhile, Frohman realized another long-cherished ambition: Mrs. Drew came under his management for a three-week engagement at the Standard Theatre. In another new role, a theatrical mother-in-law, appropriately enough, in *An Arabian Night*, she captivated new audiences. But Charles Frohman's greatest family acquisition had yet to materialize.

"At the time I was not much interested in other theatrical managers," stated John Drew. "Ada Rehan, Lewis and the rest of us at Daly's felt that these newer managers were intruders. Daly never thought what happened outside of his theatre was of any importance, and this spirit of his prejudiced us." But Frohman envisioned a galaxy of stars under his command, with John Drew as the first. Over a period of three years, the little round manager had courted Daly's leading man—subtly, through mutual friends, at first, waiting for the propitious moment.

Daly had instituted a semiproprietary arrangement with his "Big Four," giving them a share in season's profits apart from their regular salaries. But after one season, John said, "Daly wrote us that 'in view of certain contingencies' he had decided that it was inexpedient to continue this arrangement. He proposed that we take increased salaries in place of the percentage. A small increase in salary went into effect, but a season or two afterwards, when I asked Daly for more money, he declined to give it to me." After sixteen years with the Governor, John Drew had become one of the most celebrated and popular actors in America and England, but, technically, he was still not a star in his own right. He remained one of the "Big Four," with Ada Rehan, James Lewis, Mrs. G. H. Gilbert, a leading player of the Daly company. Of late, the Governor had become increasingly preoccupied with the career of Ada Rehan, choosing plays to suit the mercurial talents of his leading lady, often to the detriment of his leading man. Also, while the emergence of his younger half brother as a star the previous December had gratified John Drew, it had rankled somewhat, as well.

Aware that his opportunity had come, Frohman asked actor Henry Miller, a mutual friend, to bring Drew to his rooms at the Hoffman House for a Sunday-evening card game. "When Drew and I reached the hotel," recalled Miller, "we were ushered, not to the modest Frohman quarters, but into the finest private suite the house possessed. My manager, remembering the gossip about the decline of Daly's prosperity, wished to impress Drew with his own apparent wealth. This suite, of course, was merely a 'one-night stand.'" When they sat down to play cards that evening, it became apparent that Frohman would go to greater lengths to gain his objective.

"We played poker for a while," the honored guest noted, "and I felt, as subsequent events developed, that I had been allowed to win and had not won through my own cleverness or prowess with the cards. I do not know whether I was right about this, but I do know that Frohman was a very good player . . ." Whatever the means, John Drew was susceptible. The manager won the actor's friendship, ultimately offering him $500 a week to star under his aegis. Upon hearing of the offer, Augustin Daly cried, "What is this wicked world coming to?" and locked himself in his office.

322

The intensity of Georgie Drew Barrymore's brood, Ethel, Lionel, John, captured by Broadway photographer B. J. Falk in 1890, already indicated extraordinary destinies.

For thirty years, New York *Tribune* critic William Winter carped over Barry's performances on and off the stage.

Chicago *Daily News* critic Amy Leslie assiduously adored and observed Barry during his years on the stage.

Sardonic Wilton Lackaye was Barry's chief competitor for the title of club wit at the Lambs'.

Augustus Thomas became Barry's closest friend and America's foremost dramatist.

GEORGIE DREW BARRYMORE

The photograph as *Captain Swift (above)*, Barry's most popular characterization, decorated stationers' and jewelers' windows along the Rialto. The souvenir cigarette card of Georgie, at left, was responsible for Lionel's expulsion from Seton Hall.

Grace Henderson (*above*) lightened Barry's months of touring and nearly shattered his marriage. Mrs. Leslie Carter *(right)* shocked society and became a star.

Lillie Langtry fired Barry.

Sarah Bernhardt swindled him.

During his zoological *Aristocracy* tour, Barry posed in San Francisco with Belle of Clyde (on stool), while Miller Kent held Barry's recently acquired Japanese spaniels, black chow puppy, and Huskies, Kimo and Rita, on a special chain harness devised by the master of them all. The fox terrier (center) belonged to Kent.

As a tattered youth, William Faversham *(left)* followed Barry through the streets of London; later toured with him in *Aristocracy*. Virginia Tracy, who adoringly documented that tour and the exploits of its leading man, later wrote epic film scenarios for William Fox.

Mamie Floyd, who had worshipped Barry since her childhood, courted and won him after Georgie's death.

William Gillette *(above, left)* wrote *Secret Service* for Barry, but manager Charles Frohman *(above, right)* cheated him out of the role. Frohman, long Barry's adversary, paradoxically brought Ethel, Lionel and John to stardom.

Richard Mansfield, the theatre's *Beau Brummell,* made a bizarre bicycling partner for Barry when the two-wheeler craze hit New York.

B. F. KEITH'S
NEW UNION SQUARE THEATRE.

PERFORMANCE CONTINUOUS FROM 12.30 to 10.45 P. M.

159TH WEEK OF THE SEASON
—OF—

REFINED AND HIGH-CLASS VAUDEVILLE.

COMMENCING MONDAY, MARCH 29, 1897.

SEE STAGE CARDS FOR EXACT ORDER OF PROGRAMME.

First Appearance in Vaudeville of the Distinguished Actor,

MR. MAURICE BARRYMORE,
In Mr. AUGUSTUS THOMAS' Petite Comedy,

A MAN OF THE WORLD.

THE CAST.

CAPTAIN BRADLEY.........................Mr. MAURICE BARRYMORE
Clay Willard...Joseph A. Reilly
George Ellis...Moyan E. Coman
Mrs. Willard..Miss Marie Floyd

Eleventh Week of the

AMERICAN BIOGRAPH.

Owned and Controlled by the American Mutoscope Co., New York.
Invention of HERMAN CASLER.

In a Series of American Views, viz. :

1. Yale Football Game.
2. The Dancing Darkies.
3. Ten-Inch Disappearing Gun.
4. The Monkey's Feast.
5. "Boys Will Be Boys."
6. Scaling a Wall.
7. Why Papa Can't Sleep.
8. Caught in the Act.
9. Marching through Sallyport.
10. Inaugural Parade, 71st Regiment, Washington.
11. Governor of Ohio and Staff at Inaugural Parade.
12. Troop A, of Cleveland, at Inaugural Parade.
13. A Hard Wash.
14. Empire State Express.

THE RUSSELL BROTHERS,
In their Ever-Welcome Celtic Comedy Sketch.

THE ABBOTT SISTERS,
As "The Waifs" (farewell week in America this season).

WILLIAM J. ROMAIN and BERTIE ROBISON,
In "After the Masked Ball" (first time in Vaudeville).

THE TWO BOSTONS,
Eccentric Comedy Pair.

ALBURTUS and BARTRAM, Club Experts.
THE SA VANS, Equilibrists Par Excellence.
MARY NORMAN, in Society Caricatures.
THE MORELLOS, with their Funny Trick Dog, "Bob."
LOUISE HAMILTON, Soubrette (Late Star of "Coon Hollow").
MARIE MATHER and ANITA CLUSS, Song and Harp Solos.
THE MARIANS, Burlesque Aerialists.
GEORGE GRAHAM, Monologue Comedian.
THE ÆOLIAN TRIO, Artistic Singers.
"KID" ST ONGE, "Dusty Roads Cyclist."
EDWARD J. BOYLE, the Blind Marvel.

Programme continued on second page following.

Barry shocked the legitimate establishment when he became its first star to enter vaudeville.

At that time, gossip of his decline notwithstanding, Daly was the most powerful of managers, Frohman the weakest. Not having a theater of his own for John Drew's starring debut, he was obliged to rent one. He chose Palmer's, directly across from Daly's. The irony was not accidental. The peddler's son had been ousted by the Governor years before from his first offices in the Daly theater building. "He found not a little humor in pre-empting the services of the Daly leading man as a sort of reciprocal stroke," Frohman's brother admitted.

On October 3, a noteworthy audience, the sort coveted by Charles Frohman, crowded Palmer's Theatre for the opening of *The Masked Ball*, a French farcical comedy adapted by Clyde Fitch. That representative audience had not been drawn by the play. They had come to see John Drew flourish or fail as a star. Barry escorted three Drew women: his wife, his mother-in-law, and John's wife, Josephine. They sat still and hopeful through Act One.

Between the acts, reporter Hillary Bell crossed the street to Daly's Theatre. He found the Governor standing in a dark corner of the house, remote and melancholy. "Well?" Daly wondered. "Is it well with him?"

"It is well," replied the reporter.

"The house?"

"Crowded."

"His greeting?"

"Cordial."

"Ah! the public has forgotten." Daly sighed heavily, ending with a half-convulsive, "My boy! My boy!"

"But he has a new leading woman who is making considerable stir—that thin, little girl who used to be with Hoyt."

"I remember—Maude Adams. I have no interest in her." He gazed once more toward Palmer's Theatre. "My boy! My boy!" the Governor murmured, retreating into the darkness of his own theater.

When the final curtain fell at Palmer's, the ovation penetrated the bosom of Daly's darkened house. The play, the company, the leading lady received the ready calls of that notable assemblage. (The incessant query—"Where will John Drew find an actress who can and will stand up for comparison with Ada Rehan?"—was answered that evening. "It is difficult to see," said *Harper's Weekly*, "just who is going to prevent Miss Adams from becoming the leading exponent of light comedy in America.")

The star of the evening was not eclipsed. John Drew received a unanimous benediction. They called him, as a star, before the curtain to speak. Characteristically, he did the graceful thing. Brief thanks for their generous reception was merely a prelude. ". . . all these plaudits and this great greeting might not have been mine but for one who has taught me how to merit and deserve them," he continued with quiet sincerity. "He who from the beginning of my career has watched and guided my steps, smoothing the way to success for me and encouraging me in times of trial and discouragement; in fine, striving to make me worthy of this great honor tonight. I feel, too, that this poor and halting tribute of the heart is little to offer for the many years of care and trouble he has bestowed upon me, but it is from my heart, and I wish to offer it and am glad, too, to be able to offer it before you, his friends as well as mine. Whatsoever things are of good report in me I owe to his splendid direction and friendly guidance. I need not mention the name of my friend and preceptor, Augustin Daly."

The effect upon the audience was tremendous. The building fairly shook with applause—all the more because, both before and behind stage, the words had been totally unexpected. Daly read Drew's tribute in the morning papers. It helped a bit to ease the keen regret of parting with his leading man, but the damage was irreparable. The Governor never again approached the perfection and popularity of his Big Four.

The magnitude of the Drew-Frohman triumph was reflected in the *Dramatic Mirror*. "John Drew has achieved one of the most distinguished successes in the history of the American stage," began the lengthy editorial. "The New York papers have fairly teemed with delightful expressions in regard to every point in Mr. Drew's personality and his career, and he has received within one week a degree of complimentary newspaper notice that few of the greatest actors have ever achieved in a lifetime." His wife, his sister and brother-in-law were also effusive with heartfelt praise. His mother merely kissed his cheek. Her verdict, the crucial one for John, reached him secondhand. "Mrs. Drew's delight in her son's success is very touching," noted *The Clipper*. "It seems to be like renewing her own old triumphs."

Georgie was heading west with Frohman's Comedians when Barry and Mrs. Bernard-Beere opened the new Manhattan Opera House on November 14.

Oscar Hammerstein, owner of Harlem's Opera House and Columbus Theatre, aspired to leave the ailanthus-fringed suburb to become New York's impresario of German opera. To this end, he built the titanic Manhattan Opera House on Thirty-fourth Street. All of the would-be impresario's resources went into this 2,600-seat monument to his own ambition, leaving grand opera beyond his means. Obliged to open with a straight play, he still aimed to win the patronage of the elite audience hitherto loyal only to the Metropolitan. Concurrently in London, Mrs. Bernard-Beere had been making a resounding hit in the West End. A respected society woman turned successful actress, she embodied the qualities essential to Oscar Hammerstein. She accepted the manager's generous offer to star, stipulating that Maurice Barrymore must be her leading man. Barry, keeping a promise that he had given in London, accepted. He admired this warm, attractive woman, a particular friend of his and Georgie's during their English sojourn.

Lena Despard, Mrs. Beere's London hit, opened the engagement. The drama was not new to American audiences. Lillie Langtry had already presented an unauthorized version of the same play, retitled *As in a Looking Glass*, when Barry was also her leading man. Comparisons did not smooth the way for Mrs. Beere. She was much the finer actress, but had not enjoyed the Jersey Lily's notoriety. "Remember," admonished one of P. T. Barnum's preceptors, "all we need to insure success is *notoriety*."

"The new theatre is a dream," reported the *Herald*, "a something dazzling, pleasing, yet scarcely understood; a harmonious mingling of blues with delicate tints of pink and cream and gold; a rhapsody of odd stairways, unique balconys, inviting ottomans and electric lamps." But the vast house, "obviously designed for grand opera," observed the *Times*, swallowed the performers and the play. "Maurice Barrymore managed to hold attention as *Captain Jack Fortinbras*," concluded the *Herald*, "and to do better work than the star, better, insofar that he was uniformly strong and consistent." Mrs. Bernard-Beere and her largely English company failed to capture New York.

Barry entered the Lambs' the following afternoon evidently much distressed. Nat Goodwin wondered why. "I am terribly annoyed and excessively angry at the brutal treatment of Mrs. Bernard-Beere by the press of New York," Barry told him.

"Brutal!" cried Wilton Lackaye. "It was thoroughly deserved! I was there and I never saw such an immoral play in my life before a civilized community!"

"Granted, but why censure the lady personally, a foreigner as well?" Barry asked. "We can at least be courteous. Only the offensive theme of the play was dwelt on; no attention was paid to her finesse and subtle art. That was all lost, due to the huge playhouse in which we were forced to appear. Hammerstein's was never intended to house acting that requires such subtle treatment; it should be devoted to opera or the circus. Nothing ever gets beyond the third row."

"Which is most fortunate," countered Lackaye. "You punish the musicians, and save the remaining rows the suffering endured by those closer to the actors. I am no prude, but I felt the blush of shame mounting to my cheeks as the terrible and unwholesome dialogue came over in chunks." Barry moved to end the dialogue before his relentless friend provoked him.

"But you fail to realize, my dear Lackaye, that Hammerstein's is a theatre where one may be obscene and not heard."

The discussion dissolved good-naturedly, but Nat Goodwin perceived his friend's anger at the reflections cast upon the lady. He asked later why the famous Barrymore fists had not come into play. "Every blow struck in defense of a woman is a dent in her reputation," was Barry's reply—a theory apparently gleaned from his contretemps with Lillie Langtry.

Ariane replaced *Lena Despard* for Mrs. Beere's second week at Hammerstein's. "Even stupider than its predecessor," said the *Times,* and not helped by Barry's inability to learn the lines of a new part. As a dissolute husband, whose wife leaves him, taking along their little daughter, Barry abases himself, begging the child to intercede for him, bursting into tears. The daughter asks, "Why do you cry, papa?" building to a strong climax in his sob-broken reply.

"One night Barrymore came on as usual in this scene," recounted Guy Standing, of Mrs. Beere's company, "but he was plainly all at sea. He started his long speech, 'dried up' in his linen, and took the first way out by bursting into tears two minutes too soon. The child stood there, first on one foot and then on another, very angry at being thrown out of her best scene. A stage child is very easily offended, you should know. At last she put her hand on Barrymore's knee and asked, 'Why do you cry, papa?' It was all she could do and she wanted to save the scene if she could. Barrymore raised his head, and, shaking with sobs, blurted out, 'Why do I cry? boo hoo! I cry because—boo hoo—because I've forgotten my lines!' The rest of us sneaked off the stage as best we could, and the house simply roared. The child wouldn't speak to him for weeks."

On December 10, Hammerstein abruptly terminated the English-woman's contract. She sued. The manager maintained that the actress, booked to fill his theater, had not done so, thereby obviating any further obligation on his part. The court agreed. The case attracted public attention, making Hammerstein something of a Broadway character, a reputation which he nourished and eventually parlayed into the fulfillment of his grand-operatic aspirations. Returning to England, Mrs. Bernard-Beere was reclaimed by society and her adoring public. Barry, his theatrical stock fallen, was at liberty.

In San Francisco with Frohman's Comedians, Georgie captivated local theatergoers. In *The Sportsman,* she "made a most decided hit," reported the *Chronicle,* playing with "a spirit, a life and a breeziness and a perfection of farce acting which brought the curtain down upon an outburst of applause, which at once sealed the fate of the comedy." The *Argonaut* added that "Mrs. Barrymore, who has hereditary claims to dramatic genius—the daugher of Mrs. John Drew takes rank by virtue of her birth —is always correct, lady-like, and superbly dressed, as well as animated and vivacious."

L. R. Stockwell, owner and manager of the local Stockwell Theatre, offered Georgie "a fabulous sum," reported the *Argonaut*, to star in a series of matinees which would not interfere with her regular engagement. She was tempted, but her contract with Frohman prohibited outside performances. On the nothing venture, nothing win theory, however, Georgie telegraphed her manager in New York. She ended a detailed statement of the offer with, "Will you release me?" The manager's answer was prompt and concise:

Mrs. Georgie Drew Barrymore
Palace Hotel
San Francisco

NO.

CHARLES FROHMAN

Her reply was equally swift and characteristic:

Mr. Charles Frohman
1127 Broadway
New York City

OH!

GEORGIE DREW BARRYMORE

Georgie was plagued by the return of bronchial congestion during the San Francisco run. Fits of coughing which struck offstage she managed to control while performing. Frequent loss of breath was not so easily managed. Concerned for her health, the company manager suggested a few days' rest. She refused, dismissing the malady as slight. Worried, he wired Frohman. Frohman contacted Barry. Barry wired money to his wife, imploring her to quit the company and take a restful sea voyage. But Georgie continued acting until her health utterly failed, and, forced to heed her husband's advice, she sailed for New York by way of Panama.

Barry, frightened, somewhat bewildered by his wife's recurring illness, uncharacteristically sought work as an antidote, steady income as insurance. A. M. Palmer was quick to re-engage his departed leading man, so at the end of December, he undertook a revival tour of the New York boroughs with the original cast of *Alabama*. Afterward, he indirectly joined his various relatives under Charles Frohman's banner, since Palmer was producing *Lady Windermere's Fan* by arrangement with the ubiquitous Frohman, who had procured the American rights. Palmer assigned to Barry a part in Oscar Wilde's new comedy by special request of the author. As *Lord Darlington*, the epigram-tossing, would-be lover, Wilde had envisioned his London friend.

Palmer premièred the play at Boston's Columbia Theatre, on January 23, 1893, to a "large, brilliant and exceedingly enthusiastic company of spectators." In Boston, and to a lesser degree at Palmer's in New York, the play won the critics. A few Broadway arbiters agreed with the *Herald*'s assertion that "unfortunately, epigram and neatly pointed moral may adorn a tale and yet fall far short of making a play." All agreed, however, that Maurice Barrymore stole the show. "He delivered precious lines with an unction truly remarkable," said George C. D. Odell: such lines as "I can resist any thing but temptation"; and "Experience is the name a man usually gives to his mistakes"; and "Scandal is gossip made tedious by morality."

There was some question as to the play's potential popularity. "One thought occurs in connection with Maurice Barrymore's performance as *Lord Darlington*, the cynic and would-be betrayer," mused the *Times*. "A singular feature of the great success of *Aristocracy* in Palmer's was the fact that it attracted the very people whom it chiefly arraigned and scored. They enjoyed the play apparently, but one wonders how they will like to see the real article scorched—the objects of their admiration held up to ridicule by a man who speaks with authority. Mr. Barrymore may mitigate their feelings of anger." Mr. Barrymore did. Society flocked to Palmer's to see themselves ridiculed, reviving the reputation of the leading man and gratifying the author, who cabled the manager "sincere thanks for the admirable company of actors you have secured for the presentation of 'Lady Windermere's Fan' in America and for the artistic care and taste with which you have put my play on the stage."

Mrs. Barrymore returned tanned and gay from her sea voyage, seemingly healthy. Against her husband's wishes, she rejoined Frohman's Comedians when they opened at the Standard on February 14. The first New York production of W. Lestocq's *The Sportsman*, the play in which Georgie had won San Francisco, brought her further acclaim. To *Post, Herald, Recorder*, respectively, she was "infectious and irresistible," "breezy and piquant," and possessed "inimitable tact, spirit, grace and finish."

"Georgie Drew Barrymore," concluded the *Journal*, "could draw humor from the heart of a stone."

Early in March, Georgie began falling ill again, and her understudy was frequently summoned to take her place. Barry prevailed upon his stubborn wife to leave the cast entirely, arranging consultations with a battery of physicians. Their diagnoses were inconclusive, but the learned gentlemen agreed that an excursion to southern climes would be therapeutic. Recalling what Mark Twain had once said about Bermuda—"The deep peace and quiet of the country sink into one's body and bones and give his conscience a rest, and chloroform the legion of invisible small devils that are always trying to whitewash his hair."—Barry found the local offices of Bermuda's Hamilton Hotel. He made arrangements for his wife and their maid, even wiring the hotel's manager, William A. Barron, whom he had met through Charles Delmonico, to insure Georgie's welcome and subsequent comforts.

At Sanderson & Sons, 22 State Street, agents of the Royal Mail Steamship Company, he booked passage for the second Wednesday in April, delivering his wife to Pier 50, North River, on the morning of departure. While Polly scurried about, seeing to the luggage, the Barrymores made their farewells. "Maurice was weeping," wrote Gene Fowler. "Georgie held his hand."

She explored lily fields and limestone hills on a bicycle hired for eight dollars a month. She swam benign waters. She dined in the elegant, latticed environs of the Hamilton Hotel at the table of William Barron and his charming wife. Georgie succumbed to the "deep peace and quiet" of the Bermudas.

While his wife sought recovery in the sun, Barry held the stage at Palmer's. The successful run of *Lady Windermere's Fan* was followed by *Mercedes*, a two-act drama by Thomas Bailey Aldrich, which Barry vivified in his role of a dashing chasseur.

Mrs. Drew, meanwhile, undertaking a spring tour with Julia Marlowe in *The Love Chase*, was astounding critics and playgoers. "As she was seen at the Adams House one day the past week," noted the Boston *Herald*, "wearing a stylish walking gown of green cloth and silk, which fitted her still neat figure prettily, with her brown hair slightly streaked with grey—and bearing witness to the flight of time more by its thinness than its color—carrying herself erect with the easy dignity of one accustomed to being observed, it was almost impossible to believe that her stage career had covered 65 years of active work in this country."

At the close of Palmer's 20th Regular Season, at the end of *The Love Chase* tour, Maurice Barrymore and Mrs. John Drew joined forces in *The Rivals*. The family rallied in an attempt to raise money to pay the last of debts incurred during the Arch's losing years. Having used her own money to keep the theater going during those last years, Mrs. Drew was without funds. An all-family, all-star tour of the New York boroughs, it was assumed, would recoup her dwindled fortunes, with Mrs. Drew and her son-in-law re-creating their popular roles of *Mrs. Malaprop* and *Captain Absolute*, Sidney Drew again essaying Joseph Jefferson's role of *Bob Acres*, and Gladys, his wife, playing *Lydia Languish*. Completing the family picture, Mr. and Mrs. McKee Rankin, Gladys's parents, appeared as *Sir Lucius O'Trigger* and *Lucy*. To the surprise of no one, audiences responded heartily to this unprecedented aggregation.

While her family was winning the boroughs, Georgie returned to New

York apparently nourished by six weeks in Bermuda. She was cheerful and optimistic. But her coughing fits resumed. Mild, at first, they became progressively more violent, more frequent. For the first time, buoyancy deserted her. "With her health," noted the *Dramatic Mirror*, "she lost her wonderful spirits and the fund of humor that so endeared her to all who know her."

Fear was not a familiar emotion to Maurice Barrymore. Now, he experienced terror. Night rambles terminated. He left Georgie only for the theater, returning to her immediately afterward, no matter which of the boroughs he was playing. He and his mother-in-law acted together each evening, avoiding discussion of the subject which painfully preoccupied them. Mrs. Drew's unspoken concern was somewhat assuaged by her son-in-law's efforts to procure the best possible medical attention for her daughter.

The few invitations accepted by Barry, in hopes of diverting and soothing his wife, were quiet gatherings of close friends. One afternoon, they attended the first reading of *In Mizzoura*, a new play that Gus Thomas had written for Nat C. Goodwin. It was still light and fair when the reading ended. Georgie wanted to walk home along the Rialto. When Nat Goodwin hailed them near Delmonico's, Barry mentioned the reading. Goodwin, who had commissioned the work, had no idea that it was completed. He understandably wondered about its content.

"Well, I like it immensely," said Barry, "but I don't know how it will strike you, my boy. It is out of the common and most original. All the parts are exceptionally well placed." Georgie was unusually silent. Barry kept glancing toward her as he spoke.

"What kind of part is mine?" asked Goodwin.

"You play a Missouri sheriff," Barry replied, glancing protectively at his wife. Goodwin's questions continued, but Barry had ceased to answer them. What formerly might have led to an all-night session at the Lambs' was terminated with a polite, "Go and hear Gus read it." Mrs. Barrymore was holding on to her husband's right arm. He placed his free hand upon hers, as if to reinforce her hold, and they continued up Broadway.

Georgie's illness prompted Barry to serious second thoughts about money. Previously, he had been content to spend as fancy led him, paying for rent and the children's schooling, allowing his wife to assume many of the incidental expenses of housekeeping and child-rearing. He was not intentionally remiss. He simply did not consider such things, and she had preferred not to pester him. Her savings for Ethel's musical education had gone toward the Bermuda trip. Now, without her own income, they were dependent upon his weekly salary, ample usually, but at the moment minimal. In deference to Mrs. Drew's needs, his engagement in her support was gratis.

Fortunately, *The Rivals* tour was a financial success. When physicians again diagnosed acute bronchitis, suggesting treatment by a specialist in Santa Barbara, California, Mrs. Drew contributed a share of her profits for the journey. Barry hastened to make necessary arrangements, suggesting the hiring of a nurse to accompany his wife. She refused, reasoning that a stranger would require social exertion. Mrs. Barrymore wished only the companionship of her thirteen-year-old daughter.

Two weeks before summer vacation would have begun, Ethel was taken from the convent and sent to New York. *The Rivals* company was about to begin a week at the Harlem Opera House when Georgie and her daughter departed. "We were to go by boat down to the Isthmus of Panama, across it in a train, then up the Pacific to Santa Barbara, where Mamma was to get well," Ethel wrote. Lionel and Jack came in from Seton Hall to see their mother and sister off. It seemed a festive occasion to the boys, with Papa, Mummum, Aunt Gladys and Uncle Googan, Aunt Dodo, and cousin Louise there in force. Gus Thomas arrived with a china teapot filled with chocolate creams for Georgie. "It was all very exciting," remembered Ethel, "and I kept hoping I would be all right and not too shy or scared."

As farewells were said, and the boys devoured Mamma's chocolates, Ethel felt a keen foreboding: Mummum stood stark white and silent beside her daughter; Uncle Googan's gaiety seemed forced; Papa was weeping. "It was bad just before the boat sailed when Mamma was saying good-by to Papa and begging him not to forget her."

XXV

Accommodations on the sea voyage were not the most luxurious. Mrs. Barrymore and her daughter made the best of them, delighting in each other's company. "She always seemed young for her age," Ethel said of her mother, "and I was old for mine, so that brought us close together in tastes and habits." They spent most of their waking hours together, and all of their sleeping ones, since they shared a very small cabin. Georgie attempted a gay exterior. Her daughter saw beneath it. "My mother was very quiet, and I realized for the first time how ill she was."

As the voyage progressed, Ethel was made more poignantly aware of her mother's condition. "I slept in the upper berth of that little cabin and one night I woke up to hear Mamma crying and saying over and over, 'What's going to happen to my three kids!' I felt a sort of terror, but also felt I mustn't let her know I had heard. Then she coughed and coughed— not loud, rather gently—and then she fell asleep."

Each attempting to hide the truth from the other, they continued on. Their journey was broken by changes from sea to land to sea again, diverted by the consequent scenic variety. "I stood on the back platform of the train crossing Panama," Ethel wrote to her envious, school-pent brothers, "fascinated by the great deserted machines of the de Lesseps attempt sinking into the ground . . . then the other boat, stopping at several Mexican ports . . . and then Santa Barbara."

Their first night was spent at the Arlington Hotel. Next morning, they moved into the house which Barry had arranged for in New York, a "lovely little house covered with roses even all over the roof and pouring into my window," Ethel recalled, where a Chinese cook greeted "Missis" and "little Missy."

A letter from Georgie's New York doctor was duly presented to the local medical specialist, a great, tall man with a bright red beard. He listened to the patient's chest, heard her cough. "Yes," he observed slowly, "and who is taking care of you, Mrs. Barrymore?"

"My little girl," she answered. The doctor pulled gingerly at his bright red beard, looking very grave.

"You have no nurse?"

"Oh, no, I don't want a nurse," Georgie laughed. "Just my little girl."

"Yes," the doctor reiterated, turning toward Ethel, "she will take good care of you."

Ethel set about the business of housekeeping, with the help of their Chinese cook, who became a kind and willing man-of-all-work. "Mamma had brought all her clothes with her and I spent some happy hours upstairs in a big room with huge cupboards unpacking them. Lovely brocade evening dresses and brocade evening shoes . . . I really think she had brought all the possessions she had in the world."

Santa Barbara was a theater-loving community, welcoming to actors who played there. Clara Morris called it "God's own spot." James Stoddart had given Georgie several letters of introduction to local residents. "The situation of the place and the climate," he had remarked, "together with the character and refinement of the people, tend to make it an ideal resort." Georgie found it to be so: The clearness of the sky and the mildness of the air, the unmolested seascape, the courteous, friendly citizens, the solicitous doctor hastened her recovery during the first two weeks of their stay.

L. R. Stockwell traveled all the way from San Francisco to negotiate an autumn starring engagement at his theater. Mrs. Barrymore optimistically accepted. "The eternal sunshine of Southern California has revived her old-time girlish spirits," reported the local paper. "She lives out of doors all day, inhaling the soft air from the Pacific Ocean. She talks of her plans for next season. She even laughs sometimes at her little daughter's whimsicalities." Georgie wired her husband to that effect.

Elated, Barry replied that he had signed a lucrative contract with Charles Frohman to head a Western tour of *Aristocracy* later that summer. He had officially joined the Frohman fold, after refusing several previous offers, to facilitate a visit to Santa Barbara. The manager, anxious to accommodate him, had agreed to Barry's contractual stipulation that Lionel and Jack should travel with the company in order to visit their mother. Delighted by the news, mother and daughter prepared the little house for the advent of their men.

Georgie seemed her old self again, readily accepting an invitation for a Sunday drive with the Mayor of Santa Barbara and his family. Her daughter had other plans. "When I brought in her breakfast that morning," Ethel recalled, "she was very gay and said how well she felt and that I must run off to mass, as she knew how much I wanted to, so I did."

333

The twelfth of July was warm and breezy. The mayor, his wife and daughter called for Mrs. Barrymore in an open carriage. She was still noticeably pale, but her cheeks were cleverly rouged. Her eyes shone. Her fair hair ruffled in the breeze. She was dressed all in blue. A matching parasol shielded her gracefully from the sun, as they proceeded to an antiquated monastery.

Set high on a bluff, the picturesque old building was still inhabited by an order of monks. They wore long gray gowns and cowls, beads and sandals. The mayor's party stood by a cliff overlooking the sea, talking with the abbot, an ascetic old man of generous humor. As he related a lively history of the establishment, Georgie's light laughter filled that ancient precinct. On the way back in the open carriage, she began to cough violently.

Ethel did not hurry back after mass. "I was walking slowly home in the middle of the road, kicking stones and every now and then doing a little dance, when I saw a girl running toward me. It was Mabel, the mayor's daughter."

"Ethel! Hurry home," she called, "your mother has had a hemorrhage."

Ethel ran as fast as she could. Faster. "I got home just before she died. She didn't know me." But the mayor's wife remembered Georgie's last words.

"Oh, my poor kids," she had cried out, "what will ever become of them?"

"It was only then that we knew she had consumption," Ethel lamented. "Perhaps if the doctors had told us we might have saved her . . . I suppose I was in a state of shock because I didn't cry very much until I began packing all the lovely clothes and all the lovely shoes. Then I cried and cried, and our dear Chinaman brought me a cup of tea and patted my shoulder and went away . . ."

There was no time for any of the family to come to her, but the mayor and his wife, and some friends of James Stoddart's, the Dibblees, helped her through the following days. She wired her father and Uncle Googan to tell Mummum and the boys. She ordered a black dress—"a grown-up dress," she said—and put up her hair. Determined that Mamma should be returned to Philadelphia, she made all of the necessary arrangements with the undertaker and the railroad.

Most of Santa Barbara's population was at the station to see Ethel off. Helena Modjeska and her husband journeyed from their farm in Anaheim to comfort Georgie's daughter between trains at Los Angeles. Ethel only vaguely remembered her childhood idol, but their thoughtfulness was no less appreciated. Madame tried, for the child's sake, to stop crying. She did not succeed. It was the child who did the comforting.

334

"But they were very kind," Ethel remembered, "and gave me courage for the long, lonely journey."

Passengers on the southern route from California noticed a pale, sorrowful-eyed child, wearing a loose black cloak, traveling alone in the Pullman car. "It is Georgie Drew Barrymore's little girl," the conductor whispered. "She is taking the remains home to be buried." If the train stopped for any length of time, Ethel hurried out of the Pullman to the baggage car, looking at its brown side and shining roof as though they hid something precious from her.

"I did not cry," she declared. "I knew that the strangers on the car knew and cared nothing about my trouble. I read four or five books a day, turning over the leaves but not knowing what I read."

She avoided newspapers. Bereaved tributes were already appearing in publications across the country, epitomized by the last lines of the *Dramatic Mirror*'s lengthy eulogy: "Several actresses have, from time to time, attempted to imitate Mrs. Barrymore's charm of manner and her dash; but they have succeeded only indifferently, and the death of the comedienne leaves vacant a place in the American theatre that will not be easily filled."

Barry was rehearsing *Aristocracy* at Palmer's Theatre when Gus Thomas walked over from the Lambs' with the wire. He read his daughter's message, looked up at Gus, his face drained of color, expressionless. "It was beyond his comprehension," his friend said. "He gazed at me in numb bewilderment." Mumbling something about the ferry, he left the theater, heading in the direction of Twenty-third Street. Gus followed, running to keep up with him, imploring him to wait at the Lambs' while someone went to Fifty-ninth Street to pack a bag. Barry gave dumb assent.

He sat silent in the Lambs' foyer, while Gus made arrangements for the journey. Sidney Drew found him there. He had also received a wire. He told his brother-in-law that he was on the way to tell Mrs. Drew and the boys, who were at Madame Bourquin's on Staten Island. Barry nodded uncomprehendingly. Sidney departed.

After the ticket had been purchased, Gus sent a wire to Ethel, saying that she would be met by her father in Chicago. There would be a long wait for the train. Gus suggested that they stay at the club. Barry insisted that they go immediately to Jersey City.

He sat stiffly on a wooden bench in the ferry station until train time, his friend beside him. "It was nearly a two-hour wait," Gus recalled. "Barry never uttered a single word."

When he met Ethel in Chicago, her burden was not lessened. It was increased. He was, by that time, completely devastated, comprehending, but unable to accept the fact of Georgie's death. Ethel made all of the arrangements for the continued journey to Philadelphia. "Together they watched the baggagemen carrying a long box to another train," observed the *American*. "And the man and child followed, weeping."

Ethel composed herself once inside the Pullman again. Barry sat beside her, pathetically holding her hand, quiet, still weeping. He remained so for the rest of the journey. She watched her father, pity tempering whatever other feelings she might have held toward him. "Next month I'll be fourteen," she remembered thinking.

At the Broad Street Station, Ethel was relieved of duty. Mummum was waiting. "The keenest sorrow of my life came to me in '93," wrote Mrs. Drew, "when my dearest daughter, Georgie, died in California, whither she had gone in search of health, and only found death." Ethel noticed the ashen face, the unfathomable sadness in her eyes: "My grandmother was never the same afterward. She never got over it."

Erect and steady, nevertheless, Louisa Drew took command. No longer a Philadelphia resident, she had taken rooms at The Stenton. Unable to submit to a Catholic burial, she had made appropriate arrangements at St. Stephen's Episcopal Church. She had been a member there during her forty years of residence in the city. Georgie had been baptized there. Even in death, she would not accept her daughter's willful conversion.

Relatives and friends gathered in Philadelphia. Of the immediate family, only John Drew was absent. He and his wife and daughter were in London that summer. When the cable arrived, informing him of his younger sister's death, Graham Robertson was with him. "It came to him as a great and unexpected blow," said Robertson, "but characteristically he found time to remember the shock it would be to Ada Rehan." She was also playing in London at the time. They seldom met after John departed Daly's, the Governor forbade it, but always kept in touch through mutual friends. Robertson, a noted portraitist, was their London emissary.

"I wish you would go and tell Ada," John asked. "Don't let her read of it first in the newspaper or hear of it casually."

Robertson went to Ada's hotel that afternoon, finding Daly's star in good spirits, ready for a chat. Before the messenger broached the subject which had brought him, there was a strange sound in the room, like the snapping of a violin string. "Hush," cautioned Ada, holding up her hand. "Did you hear that?" Robertson nodded. She rose, walked to the window, gazed out for a moment, returned to her chair. "Who is dead?" she asked. "You have come to tell me that someone is dead."

"John's sister—Georgie Barrymore." They sat silent for a moment.

"An old friend," murmured the actress. "I knew that it was an old friend. I have heard that sound several times and always it has been fol-

336

lowed by the news of an old friend's death. It is a sign for me," she said with a tragic sigh. "I always recognize it."

St. Stephen's was thronged on the morning of the funeral. The service opened with the hymn "Almighty God I Call to Thee," followed by the anthem "Lord, Let Me Know Mine End and the Number of My Days." "Many tears fell as the 'De Profundis' was chanted," noted the Philadelphia *Times*. Three of the bearers, Eben Plympton, Joseph Holland, Paul Arthur, had been her colleagues. They were joined by McKee Rankin, dramatist Clay M. Greene, and Dr. J. N. Mitchell, who had delivered her and her three children. They bore a polished wooden box draped with a dark-blue velvet pall. Her husband had supplied its only adornment, a wreath of laurel entwined with blue immortelles.

Barry, his eyes fixed on some distant object, followed with Ethel poised at his side. Lionel escorted Aunt Gladys. Mrs. Drew, straight and firm, held nonetheless tightly to Sidney's arm. Jack, his dark eyes bewildered under straight black bangs, walked just behind them with a number of Drew relatives and friends. Miss Alice Judson and her grandniece, Ally, were among them. Days were not forgotten of frolic with Georgie in their house on Gramercy Park. "When the news came to us of her lonely death in a far-away California town," said Ally Judson, "we felt sorrow as true and deep as though our years had been treble what they were, and our rebellious young hearts dared to question the wisdom of the reaper—that he should take one so joyous, so loving, so fond of life, and so beloved, when there were many left who seemed more ready to go." Miss Alice Judson, then in her eighty-third year, must have nodded deep assent to the words of her grandniece.

Lionel rode to Glenwood Cemetery with his father and Eben Plympton. "My father seemed unable to believe that Mamma was gone," his elder son observed. "He kept trembling and denying the tragic fact." On the way to the cemetery, he pulled incessantly at his high, stiff collar, staring absently toward the floor of the carriage.

"Why don't you have a cigarette, Barry?" Plympton asked. "It might settle your nerves a little."

"But would it be the right thing to do?"

"Of course," Plympton assured him, placing a cigarette in his friend's mouth, providing a light. Barry continued staring at the floor.

"It's not true," he kept repeating. "It's not true." Lionel noticed that the cigarette went out.

ACT
FOURTH

The thorns which I have reap'd are of the tree
I planted,—they have torn me,—and I bleed;
I should have known what fruit would
    spring from such a seed.

GEORGE GORDON, LORD BYRON*
(Childe Harold's Pilgrimage)

* Last of three quotations chosen by Maurice Barrymore
to introduce his play *Nadjezda*.

XXVI

THE BUSINESS REPRESENTATIVE of the Frohman office held the platform beside the *Aristocracy* car, checking off company members as they arrived. The actors had reached Jersey City in plenty of time for their departure, bursting with importance and self-consciousness. Not only had a private car been supplied for the leading players, but they would make an unusual move for those days. They would steam clear across the continent to San Francisco without performing along the way to break expenses.

All of the company waited excitedly on the car, all, that is, except the leading man. No one was surprised. It was like Barry, they decided, to be on the last ferry from New York. But when the last boat arrived, there was no sign of him. "The stagehands, who adored him, climbed down from the baggage car, the trainhands came for instructions," recounted Virginia Tracy, a young actress in the company. "Eleven o'clock struck; the conductor said 'Well, I'll give him two minutes.' We were up in the very front, the platform seemed to stretch back for blocks into the dark of the ferryhouse. The two minutes passed. Then, out of those dim distant shadows, unconsciously arresting the signal to start, a calm figure emerged."

Barry sauntered along the platform, looking nonchalantly about him. His hat perched rakishly on the back of his head. His right hand held a palm-leaf fan. His left hand clutched the end of a long string, at the other end of which ambled Belle of Clyde. The conductor shouted; the train hands ran back to their places. The engine whistled, and the actors all waved and called in unison: "Barry, you're late! The conductor won't wait any longer! Time's up, Barry!"

In the midst of this uproar, there remained two serene figures—

Maurice Barrymore and Belle of Clyde. "Quite so," drawled the object of concern, as he lifted Belle and headed for the baggage car.

"No, Barry!" cried the chorus. "Don't waste time—private car—keep Belle with you—quick—get on!"

"Oh, private car. Really?" He smiled and handed Belle up to actors hanging down from the vestibule. Others leaned out to catch Barry's shoulders, heaving him aboard as the car lunged forward.

As they steamed westward on the first leg of the journey, Barry was withdrawn, aloof from the festivities of the car, preoccupied with Belle and managerial injustice. During his touring days with Daly or Modjeska or Palmer, the entire company had received the benefit of private cars. Charles Frohman limited those benefits to principal players, his manager or agent, and the necessary crew. Lesser members were required to pay an exorbitant price for berths, which they seldom could afford. "The result was great hardship for them," Barry declared. "They were waked up at all impossible hours for the trains, sometimes they even had to change trains in the middle of the night . . . No one can expect a good performance from a sleepy actor."

He wired as much to A. M. Palmer. But Barry's past employer, once New York's leading manager, was powerless to facilitate changes. Although he was Charles Frohman's partner in the present venture, all policy decisions were firmly in the hands of the peddler's son. *Aristocracy* had followed John Drew's starring debut upon the proliferating list of Frohman successes, clinching his bid for the carriage trade, placing him at the forefront of American theatrical managers. The touring hardships of subsidiary players were a mere intimation of the ruthless Theatrical Trust that would emerge from Charles Frohman's ubiquitous regime.

Those aboard, who had known a more convivial Barrymore, discerned the deeper reason for their friend's unaccustomed withdrawal. "It was just after his wife died," William Faversham understated. "He was distracted about it." Faversham's past association with Georgie in Frohman's Comedians afforded singular perspective, as well as immediate entree to Barry. Any friend of Georgie's, the bereaved husband touchingly reasoned, was a friend of his. Faversham, a fledgling matinee idol from London, was quick to point out another common denominator.

"Do you recall, Barry," he wondered, "when you played the Haymarket in London, a poor boy who used to follow you every night from the theatre to your house? Cold and in tatters, he'd wait outside the stage door until you would come out, then run behind you all the way to St. John's Wood."

"I do, indeed," Barry replied. "But how did you come to hear of it?"

"I was that boy!" Faversham exclaimed. Barry appraised the tall, aristocratic young man that stood before him.

"My boy," he reflected, "I almost skinned you alive."

Though never quite regaining its former luster, Barry's disposition was lightened by the efforts of his colleagues in the car. At Chicago, while the private car was aligned for the westward haul, he hustled some of them off for a look at the much-heralded World's Columbian Exposition of 1893. The spectacle of buildings and lagoons sculpted along the lake shore only moderately impressed Barry. A small circus within the fair grounds, however, made an unforgettable impression. There, amid its motley menagerie, he was hopelessly smitten by a pair of full-plumed, full-lyred skunks. "I must have the little darlings," he told his friends; whereupon, he made an irresistible offer to their owner. Naming them Molly Bawn and Minnehaha, placing one in each of his overcoat pockets, the new owner proudly repaired to a Turkish bath, where male company members had arranged a rendezvous.

There was not quite a stampede for the steam-room exit when Maurice Barrymore appeared, stripped, with two skunks. Several strangers departed. His colleagues, warily, remained. Barry appeased them with repeated assurances that the creatures had been "duly arranged for civilization." Not that he approved such a measure. "Presumptuous tampering with nature," he called it.

Barry found Amy Leslie of the Chicago *Daily News* waiting for an interview back in the private car. He greeted enthusiastically the erstwhile keeper of Drew-Barrymore chronicles, mentioning that he had that day received a scolding letter from his mother-in-law. Mrs. Drew, also touring that summer, had taken Ethel along. Of necessity, however, with trepidation, she had left the boys in their father's care. Having recently learned that this care consisted of leaving them at his ramshackle Staten Island farm with Edward Briggs, she informed her son-in-law that such an arrangement was "unsuitable, a disgrace." Barry, baffled by Mrs. Drew's displeasure, told Amy Leslie that he would contact his sons immediately to see if it was a disgrace.

Amy considered the contradictory nature which allowed him to lavish paternal devotion on dogs and skunks, while leaving the care of his children unconcernedly to others: "He is the most charming bundle of contradictions ever created. He has not even profited by his wonderful good looks, and a handsome man sometimes makes capital of that. He is as tender and gentle and sympathetic as a little mother, and he even wastes that. While his magnificent children were growing up he rarely asked about them, but would burst into tears of repentance and joy at hearing of them through an affectionate mediator. He has not an insincere bone in his perfect constitution, but he is made up of unfulfilled expectations of his friends and unfulfilled promises to himself."

He spoke of Georgie to the critic that had been her admirer as well as his, professing that, since her death, he had embraced Christian Science.

He commenced a diatribe on that religion, no less vehement for its lack of documentation.

"I suppose, Barry," Amy speculated, paraphrasing *Macbeth*, "you would throw physic to the dogs?"

"Not good dogs," he returned gravely.

He grew meditative, confiding that he had signed originally with Frohman, and arranged to have his boys accompany him, in order to visit Georgie in California. Now, he intimated, the *Aristocracy* tour was merely a painful obligation. "He mourns her always now that she is gone," Amy Leslie concluded, "speaks of her as 'my Georgie,' and loves to talk about her."

When the westward journey resumed that evening, Barry retired to his berth with Belle, and Molly Bawn and Minnehaha. The night passed quietly, aside from one sally made by the skunks into a neighboring berth.

"The trip was a horror of dirt, and heat, and alkali," complained Virginia Tracy. "There weren't even train window-screens in those days. Crossing the desert, everybody's skin got discolored and sandpapered with alkali—the suit I wore on the train smelled so of it that it had to be thrown away. There was one member of the company, however, whose toilet was always carefully made. This was Belle Barrymore." Every morning, while the rest of the company was still asleep, or, at best, yawning and tossing paper breakfast dishes out of the windows, a table was brought out by a steward, and set up in front of Barry. Placing the long, low Belle upon it, her master would begin the painstaking process of restoring her coat, matted and snarled by the elements, to its original luster. No less than an hour each day was required to achieve the desired texture of glossy, perfectly straight, silvery blue spun glass. "There was never anything like the patience of it," Virginia said, "the infinite subtlety of little careful strokes."

Most of Barry's colleagues approved of his pets, to the point, even, of befriending the skunks—at least, trying to befriend them. Molly Bawn and Minnehaha would have nothing to do with anyone but their master. Others would call them, cajole them, try to pet them. Only when Barry called their names would they show the least interest. Moved, perhaps, by these rebuffs, William Faversham sent for his wife to bring on his two prize-winning bull terriers. Not to be outdone, Miller Kent, a Barrymore crony from the Lambs', sent for his wife to bring on his fox terrier.

One company member dissented. Old Montgomery, who had once supported all the leading Shakespearean actors and was now playing the butler, cursed the Barrymore menagerie. "Highly unprofessional," he railed. "Leading man, indeed!"

Old Montgomery, it developed, was no model of propriety himself. He displayed what was other than paternal interest in Mary Hampton, the "baby" of the troupe. Not yet twenty, the beautiful ingénue was pampered and beloved by her colleagues. In the guise of protector, old Montgomery deplored these innocent attentions, while plying Mary with lecherous petting and hand-holding. "Now, dearie," the old goat admonished, squeezing her hand, "don't you pay any attention to any of these handsome young men. You are going to take me, aren't you?"

"What as?" Barry interjected. "An emetic?"

The *Aristocracy* company was booked into the Golden Gate Hotel in San Francisco. Despite the manager's obvious disapproval, the leading man was allowed quarter with the silky Belle, Molly Bawn and Minnehaha. The arrangement was short-lived. The morning after his arrival, Barry visited the wharves where ships from Japan unloaded. He returned to the hotel with seven Japanese spaniels, very rare, and a black chow puppy, the first of the breed that any of his colleagues had seen. The Golden Gate manager was not impressed.

The evicted menagerie settled into Barry's dressing room under the stage of the Baldwin Theatre, while their master sought more suitable accommodations. No landlord would house the entire congregation. But, finally, he located separate quarters for the two-week San Francisco stay. For Belle and the skunks, he hired a room in one boardinghouse; for the spaniels and the chow, a less expensive room in another. Barry would alternate between the two, ministering to the needs of his pets.

On the first evening, he went out to buy some roast beef sandwiches for the new dogs, neglecting to take down the address of their boardinghouse. A door-to-door search was initiated. "Have you seen seven Japanese spaniels and a black chow who might need some roast beef sandwiches?" Barry inquired, casually, at each door. It took six tries before he found the right house. ("There are probably six families in San Francisco," wrote Nathaniel Benchley, "who still flinch every time the doorbell rings.")

When the company headed for Los Angeles, Mrs. Faversham and Mrs. Kent had joined them with three more dogs. Miller Kent had also purchased two Japanese spaniels for himself, while Bruce McRae, with years of cowpunching experience just behind him, had been understandably won by two prairie dogs. The young actor's attachment to a pair of Japanese mice was somewhat less clear. The pervading influence of the company's leading man was not: McRae named the mice Waldemar and Hildegarde, after the principals in Barry's *Robber of the Rhine*. "I don't know what you're going to do with all of them," grumbled old Montgomery to the leading man.

"Why, bless their hearts," smiled Barry ingenuously, "just make every one of them happy." It was no longer possible to share a berth with nine dogs and two skunks, but, between towns, he rode with them in the baggage car.

They passed through San Francisco again, on their way up to Portland, Oregon. Pet dealers, naturally assuming that Mr. Barrymore would be interested, sent word that another boat had come in. Mr. Barrymore was interested. He acquired, this time, a five-foot cage filled with thirty-five tiny, twittering, strawberry birds with red heads. "He tried to buy an anteater," recalled Virginia Tracy, "but his money ran out, and hardhearted persons who wanted room in the baggage car for baggage refused to lend him the necessary forty dollars."

The road to Portland was littered with opportunity. People were waiting at every depot with animals to sell to Mr. Barrymore. But the collector was broke and his colleagues were adamant. Barry's pleading grew particularly inspired when a man appeared at one stop with a chimpanzee. But no money was forthcoming. Eventually, the most susceptible of the actors gave way at the Seattle depot. Miller Kent, as taken with a huge pair of Huskies as Barry was, agreed to make a loan. Others of the company, bound to dissuade the benefactor, partially succeeded. The Portland trip was resumed with the addition of only one Husky—Kimo, the male of the pair.

By the time Portland was reached, Kimo's pining for his lost mate had touched his new master. Fortified by another week's pay, he wired back to Seattle. A few trains later Rita, Kimo's mate, arrived.

Huskies were hardly a novelty to Maurice Barrymore, as a letter from Staten Island must have reminded him. Written by Jack, but obviously dictated by Edward Briggs to allay Mrs. Drew's fears, the message enumerated the bucolic pleasures and wholesome pursuits of two boys, eleven and fifteen, indulged by Edward and engulfed by their father's original menagerie. Commander Robert E. Peary had given Barry four of the Huskies which had carried him on his 1891 polar expedition. As a result of intramural activities and neighborhood sallies, they had multiplied to thirty-five. "Practically an acre of dogs," Jack wrote, "and they swarm through the house, sharing our beds, chasing cats, and yelping at the moon." Often there was not enough to eat—money from Papa arrived sporadically—but the forceful Edward managed to wangle enough for subsistence from local grocery stores. Occasionally, someone would offer as much as five dollars for a dog. But Lionel and Jack were their father's sons. No matter how hungry the boys might have been, they would not part with any one of them. "And, as for Edward Briggs," Jack's letter concluded, "he is a noble fellow and I love him."

"Maurice naturally detected the imposture," Lionel later attested. "Also, naturally, he laughed like hell, showed the letter to his friends, and let us stay on the farm with the Black Prince." Barry was aware that the letter, dictated or not, was true. Edward was devoted to the boys, and they to him. "There grew up between us an attachment not unlike that between *Huckleberry Finn* and the Negro *Jim* in Mark Twain's great book," Jack remembered. "*Huckleberry Finn* is my favorite of all books and I read it at least once a year, and, in reading it, live over with real affection that summer with Edward, the Black Prince."

Despite a reassuring wire from Barry, Mrs. Drew had continued to fret over her grandsons' situation. When her tour had ended, she wrote to them from Long Branch, New Jersey. Once, Louisa Drew had kept a home brimming with family and friends at that seaside resort; now, she had returned there alone to a theatrical boardinghouse. The boys, excitedly misreading her letter, assumed that Mummum was coming to visit. They prepared industriously with Edward, scrubbing floors, making beds, bathing innumerable pets. On the appointed day, Lionel and Jack, in their best clothes, waited on the lopsided porch, watching the road from the station. Mummum never came.

Next day, she sent a telegram, wondering why they hadn't come to Long Branch. Jack replied, explaining their mistake, adding that, in any case, they hadn't the money to get there. A few days later, a ticket was sent to bring Jack to his grandmother. She did not send one for Lionel. Louisa Drew could only spare enough money for one of them that summer, and Jack was her favorite. "I remember that as I was driven away in the hack I looked back," Jack wrote, "and Lionel and the Black Prince were standing on the porch waving at me. There was a big lump in my throat and I wanted to cry. It seemed unfair—as if I were being taken away from Lionel forever. It was a cruel thing to do to Lionel, who was only fifteen and sensitive; a cruel thing to do to both of us, for, although I returned to our ramshackle house a few days later, it was a long time before I got back to Lionel. My grandmother's favoritism had built a wall between us. It was years before he forgot."

Barry continued to lavish attention upon his animals, as the *Aristocracy* tour progressed. His first concern, when reaching a new town, was their comfort. By this time, of course, proper hotels were out of the question. So, loading the portable zoo miraculously upon a carriage, he would search out a boardinghouse with an understanding landlord and a back yard for the length of the play's engagement. Next, he visited a lumber yard to purchase materials for a shed, always building it himself to be sure that various species were properly partitioned. Then, on a special oil stove purchased in San Francisco, he brewed an elaborate concoction with a rice base for the daily nourishment of his pets. During the two-week stay in Seattle, he managed to rent space in a boardinghouse where some of his colleagues had also taken rooms. Virginia Tracy watched as he performed his painstaking ritual. "I remember seeing him from my window, late one warm September afternoon," she wrote, "coming away from his hired yard, all love's labor done, covered with straw and bits of stick, his hat on the back of his head, occasionally raising an arm to wipe his red and perspiring face. In one hand he carried an empty tin can, and in the other two beer bottles, now also empty. As he grinned up at me in passing, I can remember the thrill of realizing that he was the handsomest man I had ever seen or was ever likely to."

William Faversham and Miller Kent stopped by the boardinghouse one afternoon, expecting to find Barry with his animals. They were disappointed. "He's been gone since morning," the landlord told them, "investigating a traveling circus, pitched a few miles out of town, near Lake Washington." The two actors set out to find their friend, trudging along the hot, dusty highway.

Suddenly, in the middle of the road, appeared an enormous brown bear. On a rock close by, sat a tramp. The actors saw him take a bottle from his coat pocket, and throw it to the bear. The bear caught it, tore out the cork, and drained the contents. "Barry ought to catch this chap," said Miller Kent, as he and Faversham moved closer.

"By George!" cried Faversham. "It *is* Barry!"

Barry saw his incredulous friends approaching. "Bought Bruno for $10 from a circus man who has several of them. Watch him, boys!" Barry stood, hitched up his suspenderless trousers before they fell, and turned to the bear. "Come to papa, you ruffian," he cajoled, adoringly; "come here to me!" The hulking bruin submissively rolled toward his new master, stood up, embraced him. He was rewarded with another bottle, which, the actors noted, was filled with beer. Bruno drained it with one swallow. The game of toss 'n' swig continued as the bizarre foursome headed home.

There was some difficulty convincing the landlord to admit a bear. Barry applied his most persuasive means. Finally, the gentleman of obviously Promethean patience allowed the new boarder into the back-yard zoo. Barry was not satisfied. He wanted more private accommodations for his bear. An afternoon of beer-drinking, it seemed, had caught up with Bruno. He was drunk as the proverbial skunk, of which Barry already had two, anyway. When the landlord departed, he spirited the drunken bear up to his bedroom. Bruno promptly passed out at the foot of the bed.

Next morning, early, some of the company gathered to view their leading man's latest acquisition. All was peaceful. Japanese spaniels and black chow were tied out on the porch. Molly Bawn and Minnehaha, Kimo and Rita were secured in the back-yard shed. The strawberry birds were twittering in the sitting room. Barry and Belle were upstairs asleep, with Bruno tied to the foot of their bed. When Barry's anxious colleagues stormed the bedchamber to rouse him, only Bruno stirred. The great bear

348

pressed his front paws against his temples, moaned, plaintively, and eyed the intruders, suspiciously. Bruno was in no mood for company. He dragged the bed to the middle of the room, taking swipes at anyone within reach. The actors dodged and ran. Barry, in only his bedraggled West London Rowing Club jersey, jumped out of the relocated bed and attempted to calm his disgruntled bruin with tender entreaties. This time, far from embracing his master, the bear lunged at him, making a deep gash in his shoulder.

Barry swerved, handed Belle to a cowering actor, pushed them out of the room. Just in time. Bruno, still tied to the iron bedstead, had commenced a destructive rampage, dragging the bed behind him. One by one the room's objects were smashed or overturned. Barry edged up companionably against his pet, whispering gentle promises. Bruno would have none of them. Roaring with rage and distrust, he locked powerful arms around his master. Hardly, Barry was forced to admit, a loving embrace. He managed to squirm free and shot through the open door.

Outside, on the landing, Barry plied his quaking colleagues with paternal excuses for his pet. Inside, Bruno continued his roaring rampage.

Then, there was a lull. "There you are, old chap, all quiet," Barry assured the cursing landlord. He poked his head confidently through the open door. At the sight of his master, Bruno resumed his rounds, running up a damage bill in excess of a hundred dollars.

Friends prevailed upon the disheartened Barrymore to send for the bear's previous owner. The circus man arrived, easily restoring the beast to his former placid condition. Reluctantly, Barry agreed to send Bruno back to the circus. "Melancholy sat upon the Greek-god countenance of Mr. Barrymore," wrote Amy Leslie, after the bear's departure, "and if somebody had not eased the suicidal pressure of failure upon Barry's sensitive heart by promising to send him two wise beavers in a peripatetic mud-bath he would have probably retired to a monastery or taken to vaudeville many years too soon."

Bound for Tacoma, Washington, the animal lovers decided against the train. They hired, instead, a fair-sized motorboat, loaded their pets aboard, and made Tacoma pleasantly by water. There was some trepidation when Barry spotted a sea lion in Puget Sound. "But he hadn't really set his heart on that," conceded Faversham; "he had just wondered if it was possible to get hold of a sea lion."

The boat had not been hired merely for pleasure. Train hands were refusing to make the unscheduled stops necessary to service the animals. Consequently, scenery and baggagemen, who were devoted to Barry, were nevertheless growing tired of seeing their part of the train clawed, chewed, and littered. Audiences, too, began voicing objections. When the leading man came onstage, a perceptible animal odor wafted out across the footlights. "The first night in Tacoma the audience fell into coughing so that the lines were obscured," attested Faversham, "and the legend of Barrymore's attractiveness was questioned in several quarters." Frohman's business manager wired as much to the home office.

Aristocracy was scheduled for a six-week stretch of one-night stands. In an attempt to dislodge the offensive menagerie, management telegraphed that the baggage car would be eliminated. During the grueling wilderness trek, local scenery would be used and the actors would not see their hotel trunks for six weeks. "The owner of the eleven dogs, of the countless birds, of Molly Bawn and Minnehaha, however, was not perturbed at all," recalled Virginia Tracy. "He simply telegraphed in his two weeks' notice. It was manifestly impossible, he said, that he should go where he could not carry his animals. It did not take the management very long to telegraph back that the car would be carried." Charles Frohman could not afford to lose his leading man for the time being. Animals and odors notwithstanding, Maurice Barrymore was a drawing card.

When *Aristocracy* arrived for one-night stands, locals naturally assumed that the circus had come to town. The actors, it appeared, were merely escorting trained skunks and trick dogs. Barry encouraged this misconception, drawing many trusting persons to the theater who cared little about Bronson Howard's society drama. Even in towns too small for a single performance, where the train paused to take on coal or water for the engine, citizens would get a show at the depot. The leading man, in his shirt-sleeves and tilted bowler, would saunter from private car to baggage car to release his pent-up charges for exercise and nourishment. Only Belle of Clyde was exempt from this ritual. She would watch, aloof, from a window of the private car, as her master supervised a promenade of lesser beasts along the platform. Following this smash opening, amid the cheers of townsfolk, Barry would set up his oil stove and begin the rice mash boiling. He then pulled out a baggage truck and a station bench, placing animals along the truck, pans for food, bowls for milk along the bench in front of them. As he dashed up and down, dishing out the meal, delighted spectators would shout questions.

"Do they show with ye, tonight?" someone asked.

"Does they do tricks?" wondered another.

"Surely," answered Barry, describing their acts as he kept pace with their hungry mouths.

"Look at him, I ask you!" muttered old Montgomery from the train. "Does he look like a leading man? What a head to a company! I ask you!" No one replied. All eyes were on the show.

"What does the skunks do, mister?" shouted a small boy in overalls.

But the days of the touring menagerie were numbered. Charles Frohman and A. M. Palmer were in cahoots. Not only partners in the *Aristocracy* tour, but, previously, in the American production of *Lady Windermere's Fan*, they were planning a revival of that Oscar Wilde comedy and wanted Maurice Barrymore to repeat his much-praised characterization of *Lord Darlington*. This was feasible, since Wilton Lackaye, who had originated Barry's *Aristocracy* role in New York, was currently able to join the touring company. Besides giving each production a strong leading man, Frohman reasoned, the switch would alleviate the mounting problems of the animals, and eliminate the corps of freeloading supers and small-parts actors being kept by Barry on the private car. The wily Frohman had even arranged to make the change without disclosing Barry's importance to the Wilde revival; thereby excluding the probability of a raise. Since Barry preferred not to employ an agent, he was easy prey to such manipulations.

Frohman's second telegram regarding the removal of the baggage car elicited the desired response. The leading man again sent in his two weeks' notice. This time, it was accepted. "At some junction in the western desert he climbed off the train, took all of his animals with him and waved the train out of sight," remembered William Faversham. "No one knows how long he stood there at the grade crossing, surrounded by forty-odd assorted animals, but almost two weeks later we learned that he had them all on his farm on Staten Island."

Wilton Lackaye, smelling only of expensive cologne, joined the *Aristocracy* tour in Kansas City. Wistful, if not fragrant, memories of the departed leading man and his menagerie were nevertheless harbored, heightened by the belated delivery to the Coates Theatre of a crate addressed to M. H. Barrymore. The precious cargo, sent from Wisconsin, was the promised pair of beavers. The company baggageman forwarded the splendid specimens East, with waybills calling for food and care made out "Two in a box," the shipping bill adding, "Beavers."

At a stop midway to New York, the receiving agent planned to give the cramped beavers some exercise and a proper meal. He pried open the crate. Out jumped two scrawny, scared cats. Somewhere, on the journey from Kansas City, a change had been accomplished. The agent fed the hungry pair, anyway, charged it up on his waybill, and sent them along with a fitting epitaph for Barry's *Aristocracy* tour: "Two in box," he wrote. "Is cats."

Frohman and Palmer submitted their offer before Barry reached New York. The suggested salary, $200 a week, offended him. He telegraphed Palmer that he would not accept less than $250. "Impossible to pay so much," Palmer replied, confident that Frohman's ploy had reduced Barry's market value.

Autumn had come, bringing with it the burden of boarding-school tuitions. In deference to his late wife's wishes, Barry had returned Lionel and Jack to Seton Hall, Ethel to the Academy of Notre Dame. He accepted Palmer's terms, making a final demand to ease his injured pride.

By way of compromise, he demanded "the full amount that my notice to the *Aristocracy* concern called for." Frohman's and Palmer's agent, Dave Hayman, agreed. The revival of *Lady Windermere's Fan* was set to open in Boston on October 2.

Critics deemed Maurice Barrymore's acting "generally excellent." Although many of those who had previously chided him for flamboyance found his performance unusually subdued. "He might perhaps lay his colors on a thought more boldly without doing his part any harm," the *Globe* reviewer speculated. "But his quiet style is in good taste and calls for no downright criticism." Offstage matters required a bolder approach. The two weeks' salary still due him from the *Aristocracy* tour had not been paid. He submitted a formal request to A. M. Palmer, his onetime comrade, acknowledging that "the whole matter was obviously a deal between Messrs. Hayman & Frohman and yourself . . ." Palmer complied, on condition that his leading man continue with *Lady Windermere's Fan* in New York. Humiliated by the belittling means required to achieve his rights, resentful of Frohman's methods, suspicious of what he foresaw would end in a ruthless theatrical trust, Barry reluctantly proceeded with the play to New York.

He would not set foot in the Fifty-ninth Street flat which had been his and Georgie's. He gave the furnishings to Gus Thomas, whose wife had recently joined him from St. Louis, had his trunks removed for storage to Mrs. Higgins' boardinghouse, and took a room for himself at the Lambs'. Fellow members indulged the subdued cavalier when they had the opportunity. He seldom socialized at the club, preferring less hectic evenings at the Players' or with old friends.

He was a frequent guest of Thomas G. Patten and his wife, Ernestine. In the stately Patten mansion on West Eighteenth Street, the detached visitor received the ardent attentions of Ernestine's twenty-eight-year-old daughter. Fair-haired, doe-eyed Mamie Floyd had worshiped the family friend since childhood. Barry continued to treat her, as he always had, with paternal solicitude. Mamie encouraged him, playing the ingénue, aspiring toward better things. Barry delighted in her seeming naïveté. When he presented a bottle of absinthe to her stepfather, wide-eyed Mamie insisted upon tasting it. "It is like something I had when I was a child," she said, wrinkling her nose. "I mean, it's just like paregoric."

"You are quite right," Barry laughed. "Absinthe is the paregoric of second childhood."

Barry's own children had benefited from parental solicitude at least to the extent of their schooling. He had enrolled them at the institutions of Georgie's choosing, and left them to fend for themselves—until a telegram summoned him to Seton Hall. He was ushered into the office of a stern Father Marshall, the headmaster, who had previously been so congenial. Lionel was sent for. "Even if he dies," was the boy's greeting, "he never should have said my mother was disgusting."

Barry turned, astonished, to Father Marshall. The headmaster explained. "Yesterday," he began, "some of the baseball team were having an illegal smoke in the locker room after practice." Lionel and Jack had been in full participation, when the shortstop opened a fresh box of Sweet Caporals. Each box, besides the forbidden cigarettes, held a premium, a miniature photograph of some noted athlete or stage personality. This one yielded the likeness of a beautiful lady in an evening gown.

"It's Mamma!" Jack exclaimed. "Look, everybody!"

"It's Mamma, all right," Lionel verified. "What an honor!" He grabbed the picture, proudly displaying it to his gathered comrades. "Isn't she wonderful? She's my mother."

"I think it's disgusting!" announced a condescending teammate. Lionel promptly punched the offending fellow's jaw. His head struck the edge of a locker as he fell. He landed, unconscious, on the floor. The school doctor had feared the worst. But, finally, the boy recovered.

Barry, sympathizing with his son's action, found it difficult to reprimand him. Father Marshall sympathized also, but regretted that Lionel must be expelled. Barry complied, further stating that it might be best if Jack went along. The headmaster offered to make arrangements for the two boys at other schools. "Just for Jack, if you would," Barry answered. The words surprised him no less than they did Father Marshall. When he turned to his gratified elder son, however, he understood. Lionel, like his father after Blackheath, had taken all that he ever would from schooling.

Jack remained at Seton Hall while arrangements were made for him to enter Georgetown Preparatory School, established, since 1789, on ninety-two acres near Washington, D.C. Lionel returned with Papa to the Lambs'. ("I left Seton Hall at fifteen," Lionel wrote, sixty years later, "never again to return to the formal halls of learning. I had learned, of course, to read. I mean to read books, and somewhere along the line, perhaps not in school, I learned to listen when my betters speak wisdom. And that encompasses all my knowledge about anything.")

Lionel spent most of his time in New York, as Papa did, at the Patten mansion. Although Mamie Floyd was nonplussed by the proximity of her hero's son, her mother and stepfather were kind to the boy. He was no trouble. Quiet and withdrawn, he spent hours studying their numerous paintings—Arabs and sunsets, mainly, which were then fashionable, and a few Corots, probably spurious. Lionel was nevertheless fascinated. He made painstaking copies of them, then attempted his own versions. The Pattens' player piano also impressed him. "I heard Bach's fugues for the first time," he recalled. "I discovered that I could make shift to imitate

353

playing certain simpler passages by placing my fingers on the keyboard and going along with the mechanism."

Music and painting had become Lionel's absorbing interests, when Mummum, about to begin a cross-country tour, came to town. If schooling were to be discarded, Mrs. Drew announced, then a livelihood must be considered: Acting, of course.

Barry had no objections to his son's touring with Mrs. Drew. Concurrently involved with rehearsals for the first American presentation of *A Woman of No Importance*, he was gratified to have the boy looked after. Barry was essaying his second dissolute lord in his second Oscar Wilde play at the request of Rose Coghlan. The formidable comedienne had called in Barry at the last minute to replace her brother, Charles, who had once been Barry's chief competitor in Augustin Daly's company. Charles had recently scandalized society by eloping with a fifteen-year-old girl. As producer and star of the Wilde play, Rose deemed it expedient to let the furor simmer down before her brother resumed acting. Barry had only a few days to learn the glittering epigrams of *Lord Illingworth*.

"Even though Mr. Barrymore jumbled and fumbled line after line," stated the *Dramatic Mirror*, "the merit of *Illingworth's* speeches was noted. Nearly all the remarks and epigrams of this bold, bad lord are nasty; but they are witty, too; and when Mr. Barrymore remembered them and his cue, he reeled them off in excellent style."

Lionel enjoyed touring. Although his freedom under Papa's relaxed surveillance had been curtailed, he liked being close to his grandmother. In hotels along the route, he was given small rooms adjoining hers. Every night before bedtime, wherever they might be, he shared cheese and crackers with her, as she sipped a dram of rye whiskey. The fifteen-year-old was not entrusted with acting assignments right away, but Uncle Googan, who was tour manager for his mother, gave him various chores. Foremost among them was mixing the manhattan cocktails which his uncle consumed with astounding regularity.

Lionel had no particular ambition to act. He was content to putter around backstage with scenery painters and stagehands. But as the tour proceeded, he could not help but be impressed by the example of his invincible grandmother. From San Francisco to Chicago, the seventy-three-year-old actress was the marvel of every observer. Her vitality, her youthful mien impressed as much as her celebrated talent. Her face, gentle, frank, strong, was amazingly unlined. "Mrs. Drew impresses as being a refined, well-dressed woman of about 60 years," noted the San Francisco *Chronicle*. Devoid of affectation and conceit, she conveyed without effort her position as the oldest and most honored English-speaking actress still before the public. "Mrs. John Drew!" the Chicago *Tribune* exclaimed. "'Tis a name that shall be found in the list of the marvels of the stage generations hence."

Such tribute did not galvanize the box office. Mrs. Drew's public had dwindled, current tastes had by-passed her own specialty, old comedy. The tour, so far, had been a personal triumph but a financial disaster. Much of the blame, she was soon forced to face, was due to the mismanagement of her favorite son. "It is an open secret that Mrs. Drew has had financial troubles of late," noted the Chicago *Daily News*, "due to her motherly devotion to the theatrical interests of her son Sidney." After the close of her two-week engagement at the Schiller Theatre, she was abruptly apprised of her financial situation. There was not enough money to take her company out of Chicago. The honored veteran applied to various theatrical managers for a loan. Not one of them would help.

Barry's friend John L. Sullivan happened to be giving a matinee performance in Chicago at the time. The world's champion had been having great success with dramatic performances built around boxing exhibitions. When he heard of Mrs. Drew's plight, he immediately contacted her. "Why, Mrs. Drew," he consoled, "don't ya worry 'bout a thing like that. I'll pull ya through. How much did ya say? Where's my manager and my checkbook? We are all members of the same profession and must hold to one another." Louisa Drew may have winced, but she appreciated the forthright generosity of the champion.

She proceeded to New York with her company, stopping at Philadelphia to deliver Christmas gifts to Ethel and Jack. Unable to gather her scattered brood, Mrs. Drew had arranged for Jack to spend the holidays with his sister at the Academy of Notre Dame. Ethel, at fourteen, was equal to the responsibility. She had made a paragon of her late mother, and her attempt to emulate Georgie in every way included playing surrogate mother to Jack. This entailed one decision that would have horrified Mummum. Ethel waited until her grandmother was safely on the way to New York before implementing it.

Georgie had been a devout convert to Catholicism. Her daughter, therefore, embraced the faith with the zeal of Joan of Arc. When she discovered, during the holidays, that her little brother had not been baptized a Catholic, assuming that their mother would have wished him to be, she made immediate arrangements. Ethel, naturally, would be godmother. Sam McGargle, a student of Sister Vincent's school across the convent garden, was pressed into serving as godfather. He looked old for twelve. After the singular juvenile ceremony took place at St. Patrick's Church, Jack departed, a proper Catholic, for his first term at Georgetown Prep.

Success in New York was crucial for Mrs. Drew. She had been forced to reduce her company, managing to retain a minimum staff, in some cases, because of individual loyalty to her, in others, because Sullivan's loan facilitated a payroll. Whatever their reasons, everyone pitched in.

Even her grandson assumed a small acting part. "I wanted to paint," insisted the recruit, "but I had to go to work."

Lionel Barrymore made his Broadway debut on Christmas night, 1893, at the Fourteenth Street Theatre. His father could not attend. Having finally mastered *Lord Illingworth*'s epigrams, he was concurrently drawing full houses to *A Woman of No Importance*. As it turned out, there was little of his son to see. Reviewers took no notice of Lionel as the wordless footman in *The Road to Ruin*. He was hardly noticed by anyone. Papa's friend, Billy Muldoon, attended the performance at Lionel's invitation. "See here, Lionel," he fumed afterward. "What do you mean by telling me you were going to become an actor and getting me to sit through a play in which you never appeared?"

"I beg your pardon, sir," Lionel replied, "but I did appear. Why, man alive, I made my debut that night! You could not have seen the whole performance."

"Yes, I saw the whole show," Billy affirmed. "I saw the whole blooming thing. I was there when the curtain went up and I was there when the lights went out. But I didn't see you on the stage."

"It's queer," mused the debutant. "If you were there throughout the performance and didn't see me, there's only one explanation. You must have blinked just as I made my entrance."

Lionel was not offended. Only one aspect of the production received any particular notice—the vehicle, Thomas Holcroft's seldom performed old comedy, was considered outmoded; Mr. and Mrs. Sidney Drew, as players and producers, were mentioned merely in passing—"Mrs. John Drew, however," reported the *Times*, "is the only one of the actors thoroughly at home in old comedy. Her impersonation of the designing and artful, yet woefully simple-minded widow, is delightful in every scene . . . She is still remarkably active and as graceful as ever. When she danced, to express her joy at the seeming success of her scheming, she roused the audience to enthusiasm."

New York audiences responded to Mrs. Drew's artful widow and, even more so, to her famous *Mrs. Malaprop*, when *The Rivals* was added to the repertoire. Lionel was given a small speaking part in the Sheridan classic. His footman in *The Road to Ruin* had been small enough to overlook. His coachman in the front scene of *The Rivals* was painfully apparent. He returned to the Union Square Hotel after the performance to find a note propped up on his bureau:

My Dear Lionel:

   You must forgive your Uncle Sidney and me for not realizing that when Sheridan wrote the part of Thomas *he had a much older actor in mind. We feel that we were very remiss in not taking cognizance of this—although we are both happy that you are not at the advanced age you would have to be in order to be good in this part.*

We think, therefore, that the play as a whole would be bettered by the elimination of the front scene and have decided to do without it after this evening's performance. Sincerely and with deep affection, your Grandmother,

Mrs. Drew

Sacked by his own grandmother, Lionel was nevertheless elated. He called at her room, as usual, that night to gobble cheese and crackers, while she sipped her dram of rye whiskey. "She looked up at me with brimming eyes and opened her arms," he remembered. "And then her expression changed. She saw I was almost laughing."

"This is odd, sir," said Mummum. "I find the occasion rather distressing, but here you arrive garlanded in smiles."

"Oh, well, you see, Mummum, it's just that I agree with you so completely. You and Uncle Googan are quite right. Entirely right. The play will be much better without the front scene. You mustn't mind me at all."

"So," she considered. "Well, dear boy, what would you like to do then?"

"Perhaps I could paint scenery. Or would you rather send me home?" His grandmother reflected. There was no longer a home where he could be sent.

"We'll keep you around," she replied. "Perhaps something will come of this after all. I am forced to remember that your father was not so distinguished an actor either when he first started out."

Success in New York brought enough money to repay John L. Sullivan and continue the tour. Lionel remained with his grandmother's company. He did not act. He painted scenery, observed stagehands and actors, and mixed manhattan cocktails for Uncle Googan.

Charles Coghlan's elopement scandal subsided by the first of the year. He returned to New York with his child bride to assume, as previously arranged, Barry's role of *Lord Illingworth.* Barry was amenable, anxious to begin another project. He would not, after his skirmish with Frohman and Palmer, consider any offers from the Broadway establishment. He was intrigued and flattered, however, by lucrative overtures from an independent Broadway newcomer—Mr. "Buffalo Bill" Cody.

The dime-novel Western hero, with his fortune from Wild West Shows, was determined to make a star of his mistress, Katherine Clemmons, a former circus rider. Sparing no expense to facilitate the legitimate debut of his beloved, Buffalo Bill hired the venerable Fifth Avenue Theatre and unearthed *A Lady of Venice,* a forgotten blank-verse tragedy, "with modern improvements and a happy ending," whose author had the sense to remain anonymous. Miss Clemmons' basic dramatic qualifications, apart from riding horseback, were a beautiful face, a large quantity of pale yellow hair, a sort of heavy grace, and a large mouth generally wide open to display a full set of handsome teeth. Much of Buffalo Bill's investment went toward the promotion of these endowments. Consequently, much of the newspaper press had been "worked" for over a year in her behalf. Her genius, her beauty, her wardrobe were persistently proclaimed. Titillating news items were regularly planted: She was the cause of well-publicized duels that were never fought; fictitious swains were forever threatening suicide when she rejected them. Buffalo Bill's big, bawdy paramour merely laughed at all of this calculated attention. At heart, she remained a circus girl.

Barry reveled in carnival atmosphere as they rehearsed the ostentatious production. No wonder. He was being paid $500 a week, double his usual salary, for the privilege. But more than that, as usual for Barry, it was the congenial company that delighted him. He returned to the night places of New York for the first time since Georgie's death, buoyed by the robust companionship of the frontiersman who had scalped Chief Yellow Hand.

Public and press responded good-naturedly to the debut of the obviously unschooled Miss Clemmons. "Her performance was not ridiculous," conceded the *Post,* "but the floral tributes to her made it appear so." Buffalo Bill had procured the contents of several flower shops to commemorate the occasion. The *Times* noted that Barry always looked well in costume: "He was a handsome figure as the crafty villain *Spinola,* but he acted in a manner midway between that of a modern comedy and that of a romantic drama. He can do better when he tries. Indeed, few can do as well as he can." The actor considered the manner appropriate to the occasion. He continued in the unhampered enjoyment of his surroundings and salary, until a distressing news story broke on February 19. That evening, Barry invited some members of the press to his dressing room at the Fifth Avenue.

"Maurice Barrymore denied last night that he was married two months ago to Miss Mamie Floyd," the New York *Sun* reported, "and said that he did not know what had given rise to the report, except that he had been a friend of Miss Floyd's family for years." Unknown to Barry, what had given rise to the report was girlishly secure within the Patten mansion on West Eightieth Street. "It was said at her home last evening," concluded the *Sun,* "that Miss Floyd was too ill to be seen."

Barry had immediately denied the false report, fearing that his children might hear of it and be upset. Marrying again had not occurred to him. Now that the doe-eyed Mamie had cleverly planted the notion, she intended to nurture it. (Her infatuation had been a family joke since childhood. Her late father, William R. Floyd, stage manager and actor at Wallack's Theatre, had been one of Barry's first friends in New York. Her mother, Ernestine, was from the theatrical Chanfrau family, with whom the Drews had been friendly. After Billy Floyd's death, Ernestine had married banker Thomas G. Patten, later New York's Postmaster General, brother-in-law of William Horton, founder of the Horton & Company brokerage firm.)

Friendship notwithstanding, Mrs. Patten, Sr., tried to discourage her youngest daughter's obvious pursuit. Barry was fifteen years older than Mamie. His deficiency as a family man was proverbial. Mamie would not be dissuaded. She continued to ply him with solicitude, all the more winning because, as the Chicago *Daily News* observed, she was "a very beautiful blonde, highly accomplished and of lovely personal characteristics." The man that many had found "cynical and indifferent" since Georgie died responded.

The event which had been prematurely reported in February transpired early in July, one year after Georgie's death. Gus Thomas attended his friend at a small private ceremony in the home of the senior Pattens. Mamie was attended by her two sisters. "The courtship and marriage of this handsome and talented pair have been subjects of much discreet controversy," noted the Chicago *Daily News*. "There was an atmosphere of romance about it all which lent particular interest to the quiet affair. The betrothal of Mr. Barrymore and Miss Floyd took place so closely following upon the death of Georgie Drew Barrymore that respect for the memory of that charming woman led both Maurice and Miss Floyd to a request for as little publicity as possible." Neither the Barrymore children nor any of the Drews attended the nuptials. Fearing that his remarriage would upset them, the sheepish bridegroom had simply not informed them. It proved to be an unfortunate tactic.

At the convent school in Philadelphia, Ethel was summoned by the Superior. "My father was married again, and she had not wanted me to hear of it from one of the day scholars," Georgie's daughter related. "I do not want to dwell too much on this, but it was years, really years, before I could take it in stride."

XXVII

The second marriage of Maurice Barrymore was not officially announced until the newlyweds reached Chicago two weeks later. Requisite tabloid reportage ensued, purple prose from romantically inclined commentators, Amy Leslie among them, or rather dark dispatches from the moralists. But Barry was there to assume a role in *New Blood*, Gus Thomas's latest play. The controversial nature of the new work quickly eclipsed the actor's personal vicissitudes.

That summer of 1894, traditionally opposed forces of labor and management collided in the town of Pullman, Illinois, near Chicago. Differences between the Pullman Company and workers in their car shops assumed national importance, when Eugene Debs, the labor spokesman, called a strike of the American railroad unions to obstruct trains carrying Pullman's cars. When, consequently, United States mail trains were stopped, President Cleveland entered the fray. The dispute had become a major disaster, when the *New Blood* troupe reached Chicago at the end of July. Their train approached the depot through miles of burning freight cars. The city was under martial rule, field artillery strung along the lake front. When local police had been unable to quell agitated mobs, the militia had been called out. Further incensed by militiamen, citizens chased them through the streets and pelted them from rooftops. A company of regulars, faces the color of mahogany, regimentals faded and worn, was brought by forced march from the plains. They advanced upon the rioters with fixed bayonets, scattering them like so many sheep. Uneasy peace was restored to the turbulent city.

With uncanny foresight, Gus Thomas had based his new play on a similar confrontation, casting labor in heroic light against the dark forces of management and the trusts. "The people who came at night to see our Chicago performance," Gus recalled, "were obliged to show tickets to soldiers at intersecting corners and establish the peaceable character of their errands. Of course, in that *milieu*, with that subject and that excellent company, the management thought we had the greatest American play that could be written."

Critics and patrons did not quite agree. Nor did they agree with one another. The Chicago *Tribune* decided that "It was imprudent in the author to introduce so burning a question as that of labor and management." The *Herald* complained that the author had not come to terms with the issue: "It seems rather like a fashionable fad, such as slumming or teaching Chinese Sunday schools, which rich people engage in now and then out of curiosity or as a sort of amusing penance." Conservatives denounced the play's "dangerous socialistic tendencies," holding veteran manager J. H. McVicker responsible for allowing its presentation in his theater. Liberals cheered the play as an exposé of the rich, praising McVicker's courage. The rich, bound to be entertained, according to Amy Leslie in the *Daily News*, "have taken *New Blood* as a comedy, taking its preachments as so many blemishes." She illustrated her point with the singular reaction of a local dowager: "Mrs. Hobart Chatfield-Taylor was a wrapt listener to the golden eloquence of Barrymore's entertaining confessions—but when she glanced at the pearl-gray trousers encasing Barry's matchless legs she gasped to behold snuffy bronze gaiters capping his aristocratic instep and then she wanted to go home right away."

As *Barstow Adams*, a Chicago millionaire by whom the play's Trust versus Labor thesis is rather artificially resolved, Barry was deemed "most seductive" and "extremely diverting, with the keen humor of a good-hearted cynic." Gus Thomas had tailored the role to his friend's contradictory talents. Amy Leslie noted that he "easily commands the sympathy and gentler emotions of the pleased auditors." The *Tribune* concluded that, although his role was unreal as written, "as the character of Barrymore it is thoroughly enjoyable."

New Blood audiences grew nightly, while a condition of quiet unrest prevailed in Chicago. Manager McVicker received menacing notes from local zealots, their affiliations less clear than their threats. The theater was kept under guard, players warned to keep off the streets.

The Barrymores, meanwhile, in the wake of their wedding announcement, were besieged with invitations. Not disposed usually to making formal social commitments on the road, Barry deferred to his bride, subjecting himself to repetitive teas and luncheons proffered by society friends of the Floyds and the Pattens. On August 28, en route to luncheon at Mrs. J. C. Anderson's Highland Park home, he was subjected to far more. Front-page headlines blazoned the news:

MIGHT HAVE BEEN KILLED

Iron Bolt Hurled Through a Car Window Hits Actor Maurice Barrymore

A Very Painful Injury is Inflicted

"The missile flew close to Mr. Barrymore's head and dug violently into his wrist," reported the *Daily News*. "Had it been directed or swerved a shade nearer his head the accident might have proved fatal. As it is, an ugly wound gashes his arm, and, though he is not inclined to acknowledge the fact, Mr. Barrymore is still suffering from considerable shock."

There was conjecture that the incident was perpetrated by union or management forces, although the offending side was unclear. But, as the *Daily News* subheadline indicated, Chicago newspapers had grown tired of labor-trust disputes:

HIS BRIDE SUFFERS FROM NERVOUS SHOCK

Romance of Actor's Recent Marriage

Mr. Barrymore's recent marriage has not been generally talked about out here, and it may be interesting to learn that his bride accompanies him and was completely prostrated by the accident . . . Mrs. Barrymore did not faint when the missile struck her husband, but is still suffering from the effects of so great a threat to her happiness.

Barry was probably relieved to avoid another luncheon. In any case, the accident did not disrupt performances of *New Blood*. He played *Barstow Adams* with his arm, according to the inimitable Amy Leslie, "in a becoming plaster."

A. M. Palmer braved zealots and field artillery to attend a Chicago performance of *New Blood*. He made immediate arrangements to present the timely production, becoming plaster and all, in New York after its six-week run at McVicker's. At the urging of Gus Thomas, Barry agreed to continue his role under Palmer's banner, past grievances somewhat assuaged by the manager's offer of $300 a week and the undeniable benefit of playing a part already memorized.

Ethel Barrymore stayed on at school after the start of summer vacation, until Mrs. Drew summoned her to Montreal. It was the last that she would see of the Academy of Notre Dame. At fourteen, Ethel was to go upon the stage. Uncle Googan forwarded forty dollars to pay the fare from Philadelphia and buy some cheap material for a stage dress. "I had thought I was going to be a great pianist, with fine dreams of Vienna and Leschetizky. But suddenly there was no money, no Arch Street Theatre, no house, and I must earn a living. No one talked about it," she said, "no one talked about it at all, ever."

Ethel joined her grandmother, Uncle Googan and Aunt Gladys in their touring production of *The Rivals*. Lionel was around, too, but not on-stage. He was content backstage, still painting scenery and serving man-hattan cocktails to Uncle Googan. For Ethel's debut, Mrs. Drew restored the small part of *Julia Melville*, which had been omitted from the Jeffer-son version. The girl was told simply to learn the part. No help in the playing of it was forthcoming from her seasoned relatives. Once, she asked her grandmother something about acting. "You should know that without being told," replied Louisa Drew.

To get into the spirit of the play, Mrs. Drew sat upon the set stage for ten minutes before each performance. On the evening of her debut, Ethel, trembling, joined her there. Her grandmother's face was rigid, but the girl noticed tears in her eyes. Ethel's eyes filled, too, and, suddenly re-alizing the importance of what lay ahead, she mumbled something about hoping that she could get through with it. "Get through with it!" echoed Mrs. Drew. "Get through with it! Of course, you'll get through with it. Have you forgotten what blood flows in your veins!" Ethel got through with it.

After three weeks in Montreal, Mrs. Drew left the company to fulfill an engagement at Saratoga, New York. Lionel accompanied her, travel-ing on to New York City, where he was to join his father. Ethel contin-ued touring with her uncle and aunt, with Mrs. McKee Rankin, Aunt Gladys's mother, replacing Mrs. Drew. The company did not prosper. Mrs. Rankin, the former Kitty Blanchard, one of the original *Two Orphans*, was no match at the box office for Mrs. Drew. In St. John, New Brunswick, the company stayed in the darkened theater till after midnight, and, leaving their luggage at the hotel, took the milk train out of town. "I remember Aunt Gladys leaving the theater that night looking very proud and grand, also rather fat," Ethel observed. "She had on five dresses."

Mrs. John Drew, meanwhile, captivated Saratoga, the Queen of Spas, as *Dame Quickly* in *Merry Wives of Windsor*. The alfresco performance in the court of the Grand Union Hotel preceded the annual August races of the Saratoga Association for the Improvement of the Breed of Horses. A high-sounding name for a series of horse races. But, then, it was America's foremost turf event. Representatives of the nation's social elite commingled with racing enthusiasts, gamblers and touts on the wide ve-randa of the elegant, four-hundred-room hostelry. The Shakespearean offering, with an all-star cast, was a highlight of the brilliant season. Those in attendance, however, from Edward Everett Hale, the Boston author, to Pat Sheedy, the Saratoga gambler, gave the performance to Mrs. Drew. Sheedy, in fact, offered to back the company for a summer engagement at the Metropolitan Opera House, stipulating only that "the old woman play *Dame Quickly*."

Lionel Barrymore surprised his father at the Lambs' Club bar. After nervous greeting, Barry led his eldest son outside, hailed a cab, ordered the driver to an uptown address. As they rode up Broadway, Papa commenced a barrage of small talk, pointing out evidences of a West Side building boom, remarking, as they passed Fifty-ninth Street, that Broadway had been renamed Western Boulevard from that point. Talk stopped abruptly with the carriage at 161 West Ninety-seventh Street.

Lionel would learn presently that this imposing cream-brick row house was his father's new residence, wedged, at Mamie's request, between the similar dwellings of her two married sisters, not far from the house of her mother and stepfather. But Barry was not inclined to divulge such information, as he nervously led the way up curving stairs to a salon, where the new Mrs. Barrymore was ensconced. Lionel would be the first of his children to confront this new arrangement—Ethel was still touring with the Sidney Drews in Canada; Jack was summering with the John Drews in Westhampton, Long Island. The father dreaded the confrontation. The son was less apprehensive. He had already been informed of the marriage by his grandmother. "Marriage is a man's own business," she had told him, "only your father is no business man." Besides, Lionel had known Mamie Floyd and her family for most of his life. Papa nevertheless attempted to formally introduce his son and his bride.

"Miss Floyd. My son. My good friend, Miss Mamie Floyd. May I present my older son, Lionel? Miss Floyd's people have been wonderful to me, Lionel, simply splendid . . . Mamie . . . that is, Miss Floyd . . . well, Mamie this is my son, Lionel, as I believe I have said . . ." Barry floundered. Lionel did not know what to say to help him. Mamie, secure in her elegant salon, saw no reason to say anything. Abruptly, Barry left the room. He returned with a pail. "Lionel, get some beer," he ordered, handing the pail to his son. "Mamie and I are married. Hurry back."

Barry expected his son to join them in the house on Ninety-seventh Street. Mamie, without any particular enthusiasm, accepted the young man. It was only fair. The house was usually brimming with her own protective mother and stepfather, her older sisters and their husbands—Henrietta had wed her stepbrother, Thomas G. Patten, Jr.; Ernestine had wed George C. Boniface, Jr., scion of a prominent theatrical family. The sisters, both former actresses, had become archetypal gentlewomen since their marriages, a development which amused and rather riled Mamie's husband. "An actress gone 'society'," he observed, "presents a spectacle only slightly less tawdry than a society woman gone theatrical."

Lionel seemed immune to the preponderance of Floyds, Pattens and Bonifaces. Taking the marriage less personally than Ethel had, he main-

364

tained a cool but polite relationship with his father's wife. Mamie, on her part, made no effort to be a proper stepmother. It was probably just as well. Any attempt by the bride to replace Georgie would have inevitably caused resentment. In any case, the young man was diverted, nearly obsessed, by an ambition to paint. Convincing Papa that his destiny lay therein, he was duly enrolled at the Art Students League. His studies began fortuitously under John Twachtman and Kenyon Cox, alongside future artists Clarence F. Underwood and Ferdinand Pinney Earle.

Ethel did not return to her father's house after the tour. She could have joined Lionel there, but the girl would not face her father and his new wife. Instead, she was moved "like a pawn," she recalled, from the Canadian tour to the Sherman Square Hotel in New York, and told to ask for Uncle Jack's apartment. Finding her grandmother already residing at the substantial hotel on Seventy-first and Broadway, Ethel was installed in a small, dark cubicle, she called it a "friar's cell," next to Mummum's room.

The morning after her arrival at the Sherman Square, the fifteen-year-old began looking for work. She left the hotel early and spent the day perched hopefully in a straight-backed chair of one agency or trudging back and forth between agencies. This became ritual, repeated for months *ad nauseam*. She could describe in minute detail the mundane waiting rooms of Mrs. Fernandez or Simmons & Brown. (Years later, Ethel Barrymore gave advice culled from those early years. "To be a successful actress," she admonished, "one should think like a man, act like a woman, look like a girl, and work like a dog.") But Ethel, at fifteen, had not even the ambition to be a successful actress. She still dreamed of a career as a concert pianist. "I went on the stage because I did not know how to do anything but act," she said, "and I did not know how to do that." Ambitious or not, the refrain of "Nothing today!" did not deter the girl. She trudged from agency to agency, from morning till night, her determination strengthened by the necessity of earning a living and a growing concern for her grandmother.

"Mummum was unhappy at being dependent for the first time in her life, although it was on her own son," Ethel observed, "and she was bewildered by my not getting a job—all very tragic for her because she had been such a commanding person with everyone's life in her hands for so many years. But instead of drooping, her back seemed straighter and straighter as she gazed out over the sinister rooftops of New York. I felt so sad because I couldn't help.

New Blood opened at Palmer's Theatre on September 17. "Maurice Barrymore's part suits him admirably," noted the New York *Times*. Most of the critics agreed, William Winter, backhandedly, among them. "Mr. Barrymore is rather negative," he said in his *Tribune* review, "which perhaps may have something to do with his satisfactory personation." Gus

Thomas's topical play, while not duplicating its Chicago success, had a good run, giving Barry a chance to promote projects and future plans that autumn in New York. Foremost among them was the production of his recently completed comedy, *Blood Will Tell.* He sought independent backing for the play, hoping to star jointly in it that winter with his friend E. J. Henley. The package was an attractive one: Barrymore and Henley were audience favorites; the play was perhaps Barry's best. Not only was the Barrymore wit suited for farcical comedy, but for the first time he had set a play in New York, peopled it with variations of characters that he had known, and hinged its action on the exposure of the kinds of human hypocrisy that he had long observed and abhorred. His dialogue, realistic and smooth, avoided the pedantry of his previous works. His plotting was less cluttered. In bringing much of the play's crucial action on stage only through subsequent dialogue, he presaged Anton Chekhov's more notable use of that method in Russia one year later.

Barry's long-overdue recognition as a dramatist seemed imminent. New York's foremost managers vied for the property. But the author remained adamant. No matter how much acceptance as a playwright meant to him, and it meant a great deal, he refused to concert with the Broadway establishment. The production of his play would be expensive. Few independent managers could raise the necessary capital. "Buffalo Bill" Cody read it, liked it, but had been burned by his *Lady of Venice* disaster. Barry persevered, his faith in the play unshaken.

The pivot of *Blood Will Tell* is a lifesaving transfusion, something of a scientific phenomenon at the time, which results in an exchange of personalities between a self-righteous philanthropist, *Ptolomey Boppinger*, and his drunken cousin, *Binks*. The philanthropist, who declared that "No clime has been too remote for my far-reaching benevolence. At this very moment my flannel petticoats are teaching the beautiful lesson of maiden modesty to the dusky daughters of ocean-girt Owyhee!" assumes the character of the drunk, who prides himself on "waking up with the lark in the—hic—afternoon." Into the consequent confusion comes a stageful of Barrymore characters. *Milly* is a variation on the "Georgie" character from *Nadjezda*, a slang-tossing, insouciant young woman, who continually shocks the proprietary mother-in-law of the piece. "There, there, mamma, don't be too hard upon Milly," consoles the heroine. "Remember her disadvantages, poor child, being as she is, just fresh from the giddy whirlpool of a fashionable boarding school." There is also a character reminiscent of Ned Donnelly, whose presence occasions some inside jokes for Barrymore devotees. "The man's a pugilist," exclaims *Boppinger* before his transfusion. "What a horrible position!"

The author, still fancying himself a Christian Scientist, took frequent swipes at medical quackery. "I've treated him for every disease from

366

whooping cough to Hades," complains *Clarence Starke, M.D.* "The man's a drug store if he only knew it—everything from Cockle's pills to dynamite. But devil take him, he won't even blow up, and give me a chance to swear it was spontaneous combustion." Nor was the clergy spared. A caricatured Englishman, the *Bishop of Soda and Bee,* a euphemism for brandy and soda, dotters about the stage with a notebook, delightedly recording the American slang of *Virginia Bright,* "the Queen of Serio-Comedy."

While playing at Palmer's and trying to arrange production of his comedy, Barry partook vigorously of New York's night life. His previous resorts were augmented by Kirk's, at the corner of Broadway and Twenty-seventh Street, which his presence made a rendezvous for expatriate English cronies like E. J. Henley, John Glendinning, and Tyrone Power, who had toured Australia in *Nadjezda.* Ted Henley, brother of noted British poet W. E. Henley, was one of Barry's closest friends. A fine actor and lively companion, he was given to excessive drinking and chronic apologies for the infirmity that it caused. "Staggering is a sign of strength," Barry assured him. "Weak men are carried home." But Ted's thirst eventually necessitated taking the "Cure" at a New Jersey sanitarium, dashing Barry's plans to star with him in *Blood Will Tell.*

The patronage of Barrymore, John L. Sullivan, and James J. Corbett also made Jake Wolff's Casino Bar fashionable ground for actors and sportsmen that season. But Barry's presence did not do quite that for various Bowery "free and easies." Although noted representatives from every walk of life commingled there, those seedy nocturnal haunts could hardly be called fashionable.

"The Devil surely must have had his central office on the Bowery," decided Jimmie Powers, who accompanied Barry on many a slumming jaunt through that liveliest, most notorious street in New York. McGurk's Suicide Hall, noted for the ever new, very young girls in its upstairs brothel, was a favorite Barrymore resort, as was Owney Geoghegan's free and easy, which had replaced English Harry Hill's as the gathering place for prize fighters, second-story men, and slumming swells. At dawn, he could usually be found among politicians and police officials, pickpockets and brothel keepers at Lyons' restaurant, where the previous night's residue of garlic, onions, stale beer, and corned beef and cabbage mixed with the odors of frying breakfast food and the cheap perfume of high-corseted street ladies.

Barry's early morning greetings at West Ninety-seventh Street grew progressively strained. Not at all what Mamie had envisioned from her childhood cavalier, such behavior dashed her romantic illusions. Georgie had faced Barry's vicissitudes with wit and understanding. Mamie was incapable of either. She pouted and sulked. When this method failed to gain the desired response from her errant husband, she resorted to high-pitched tantrums. Bewildered by what seemed to him unreasonable behavior, and frustrated by his failure to find independent financing for *Blood Will Tell,* he was relieved when a prolonged tour was proposed.

Marcus Mayer, an independent manager, was presenting the first American tour of Olga Nethersole, who had recently won great success in London. He offered Barry $300 a week to be leading man, aware that the Barrymore name and popularity would bolster the draw of his twenty-five-year-old English import. At Wallack's Theatre, on October 15, the unique Nethersole astonished and mystified the critics, defying their attempts to classify her. New York arbiters were unsure where to place her as an artist, but, to a man, they acknowledged her right to a niche in the temple. The opening play, A. W. Gattie's *The Transgressor,* was not so fortunate. On October 29, "Camille" replaced it. "She gave an admirable performance of this well-known part," noted "Handsome Jack" Barnes, Barry's Scarborough friend. "Barrymore played *Armand Duval* excellently, and I was extraordinarily fortunate as *Duval* père."

The critics agreed with neither Barnes nor one another in the matter of Barry's New York performances. The general reaction, however, was disappointment. It was becoming Maurice Barrymore's lot, as if to punish him for possessing an abundance of mortal attributes, to be always measured by his potential. No matter how good his best was, it was never good enough. No matter how bad his worst was, it never eliminated expectations of something better. "It seems to be the fate of that actor to be highly esteemed in New York, when he is absent from it," noted the *Times* critic, "and often to be neglected when he is at hand."

Perhaps his recent loss of Georgie and the expected tempering of character by great sadness had prepared theatrical commentators for a professionally chastened Barrymore. Perhaps it was the concurrent twentieth anniversary of his American debut. Whatever the reason, during that New York engagement with Olga Nethersole in the autumn of 1894, a raft of editorial comment ensued, epitomized by the *Dramatic Mirror*'s lengthy, poignant appraisal of Barry's career: "Not many years ago—and yet stage reputations have since been won and lost—the town resounded with praise and prophecy of the handsome fellow whose face appears in the corner . . . This gifted, accomplished, and popular actor appears now occasionally as an originator of character in notable productions; but, like a promissory note many times renewed, his greatest professional pledge is still in futurity."

When *Romeo and Juliet* was added to the Nethersole repertoire in Philadelphia, local critics were inclined to praise Barry's lovelorn *Romeo.* Not that the pleas of New York commentators seemed to have been responsible for the improvement. On the surface, he appeared to be less concerned with his profession and more than ever the old Barrymore, preoccupied with the needs of the omnipresent Belle of Clyde, wholeheartedly participating in the festivities of the road. A Philadelphia Press Club fete in his honor was among the most festive occasions, until an inebriated English guest began making odious comparisons between his country and America. Assuming that anyone of similar origins would be in full agreement, the offensive fellow addressed his countryman. "Why, hang it, Barry," he cried, "they can't even spell in this country, can they? They spell honour h-o-n-o-r, and labour l-a-b-o-r, don't they?"

"Of course, old man," Barry agreed, "when they are talking about labor and honor they leave *you* out of the question."

Despite his surface gaiety, Barry had been touched by the New York critics, by the truth of their words and their notable lack of malice in expressing them. But, as in the past, the dramatist, not the actor, responded to the challenge. Playwriting still inspired his respect and fired his ambition, while selling his plays continued to frustrate him. Unable to find an independent American manager with the means to mount his new comedy, he considered an English production. When Jack Barnes left the Nethersole company after its Pittsburgh engagement to return to England and a new career as playbroker, he carried with him the manuscript of *Blood Will Tell*.

Barry returned to New York with Nethersole for two weeks at Hammerstein's Harlem Opera House. He received enthusiastic welcome at West Ninety-seventh Street. Mamie had missed her touring husband and was herself about to embark on her first trip abroad. She and her mother were scheduled to sail a few days after Barry's opening. With another separation imminent, Mr. and Mrs. Barrymore faced the approach of their first wedding anniversary in the traditional spirit. That spirit, unfortunately, was severely tested on Hammerstein's stage.

For all the critical carpings, Barry remained his public's darling, one of those rare celebrities whose professional and personal activities equally fascinate their followers. The chief components of his fascination, particularly for matinee ladies, were his apparently romantic marriage to Georgie Drew, their three children, and her tragic death. The second Mrs. Barrymore was constantly reminded of this, but never before quite so poignantly as in her husband's quavering delivery of a particular line at the opening of *Frou-Frou*: "The *Sartorys* of Mr. Barrymore was big and handsome," explained the *Times*. "His pathetic promise to 'dine with Georgie' was worth going further than Harlem to hear."

On the road again with the Nethersole troupe, Barry traveled from Indianapolis to Chicago, while Ted Henley happened to be traveling with another company from Chicago to Indianapolis. Henley had overslept that morning at Mrs. Stewart's theatrical boardinghouse in Chicago. He had awakened with a hangover and had barely enough time to throw his clothes in a bag, hail a cab, and catch the train for Indianapolis. Halfway to his destination, it occurred to the actor that he had forgotten a pair of trousers under the mattress at Mrs. Stewart's. It further occurred to him that his salary was in a pocket of those trousers. He urgently wired the information to Mrs. Stewart.

Barry, meanwhile, having arrived at Mrs. Stewart's, was shown to the same room that his friend had occupied. He immediately fell into bed, went to sleep. The good boardinghouse keeper awakened him that afternoon to present Henley's telegram. Turning over the mattress, Barry found the trousers and the money. Removing a ten-dollar bill, he sent the rest along with a receipted voucher:

From E. J. Henley

To Maurice Barrymore:
To pressing one pair of trousers . . . $10.

"Not the least of Miss Nethersole's claims to admiration is the circumstance that she seems almost likely to make an actor of Maurice Barrymore," jabbed the Chicago *Evening Journal.* "His *Armand* was a revelation of unsuspected force and grace." Ironically, the same paper had made a similar observation ten years before, when Barry had played the role with Modjeska. "Barrymore, it is true, still speaks his lines for the most part as though he had no comprehension of their meaning, but let it be known that more than once as *Armand* he indicates unmistakable feeling."

Reviewers were less sarcastic during a subsequent round of one-night stands and split weeks, but the leading man was obviously getting bored. "Mr. Maurice Barrymore was a strong, manly and generally satisfactory *Armand Duval,*" remarked the Detroit *Free Press.* "He belongs to the order of men of whom women like to make heroes and he can act with force and delicacy, too, whenever he happens to be so minded." He was less inclined to be so minded, as the company proceeded to Olga Nethersole's much-heralded Boston debut.

Boston critics were not disappointed by the actress. But, in a city where critics knew his weaknesses and cherished his strengths, Barry's *Armand* was roundly panned. "Mr. Barrymore did not appear to particular advantage for an actor of his ability," opined the *Globe,* while the *Courier* allowed that "only occasionally does he have a moment worthy of his reputation or of what talent he possesses." The *Beacon* complained that his "flying coat-tail rantings carried Miss Nethersole to more sensational heights than one would wish for her own safety."

At the week's final performance, however, an astounding transformation took place. Barry's *Armand* was likened to his romantic playing of the role with Modjeska a decade before. Critical reaction was not responsible for the sudden improvement. Maurice Barrymore had a much more poignant reason for tidying up his stagecraft: His daughter was in the audience.

After months of fruitlessly hounding the Broadway agencies, Ethel had swallowed her independence and joined Uncle Jack's company for some general understudying and tray-carrying. Her social career had progressed more rapidly. During her time of professional frustration, she had met the group of young men who used to call on her uncle, well-born young men making names for themselves in the realms of literature and art. Richard Harding Davis and Charles Dana Gibson, leaders of this lively circle, made Ethel a charter member. She traveled in a drawing room to Richmond, Virginia, with Davis's sister for the fabulous wedding of Gibson and Irene, one of the beautiful Langhorne sisters. She attended the Yale Prom. Her dress was homemade, but her escort, Bruce Clark, was from the best of families. The press began to make much of this social daughter of Barrymores and Drews. "She is a great favorite with her friends because of her unaffected manners and frank unconventionality, which is refreshing without being bizarre," explained the Boston *Beacon*.

Charles Frohman, her uncle's clever manager, took note. He decided to give Drew's niece a try. Before a Wednesday matinee, toward the end of the New York run of John Drew's current vehicle, *The Bauble Shop*, Elsie DeWolfe became too ill to appear. Without time for rehearsal, Ethel was recruited to replace her as the worldly *Lady Kate Fennell*.

"I had heard of Georgie Drew's daughter, of course," attested J. E. Dodson, of John Drew's Empire Theatre company, "and had counted myself among the most ardent admirers of the girl's brilliant mother; but this daughter's aspirations had never even been hinted at in my presence, and the public was certainly not prepared for it." Every member of that seasoned company was visibly nervous before the performance, everyone but Ethel Barrymore. "This girl, who had never faced a New York audience before, walked on the stage with as much assurance as if she were about to recite her geography lesson in school. She went through the performance so neatly that one could hardly avoid the notion that she had been acting since she was a baby of five."

Soon after Ethel's New York debut, her cousin Louise, Uncle Jack's daughter, had been sent abroad to attend school at Versailles. Aunt Dodo had accompanied their daughter, taking Mummum along for a much-needed holiday. With the ladies gone, and his annual spring tour about to begin, Uncle Jack preferred not to leave his niece alone in New York. He had consulted Charles Frohman, and the manager agreed to let the girl tour as *Lady Kate*. The success of her recent matinee performance, coupled with the publicity surrounding her social activities, Frohman reasoned, would not hurt the box office on the road.

John Drew always began his spring tour in Boston. Arriving for rehearsals a few days before the scheduled opening, Ethel was able to see her father perform at the Boston Museum.

After viewing *The Lady of the Camellias*, Ethel was taken by her father to Olga Nethersole's dressing room, where, the girl recalled, "she terrified me by asking me to recite something for her." The following Monday, however, with her unruly yellow hair pulled up in an insecure French twist, that same girl made her Boston debut as *Lady Kate Fennell*, English society leader, age thirty-two, whose chief requirements were dignity of carriage, easy delivery of social patter, and the wearing of smart frocks. "I didn't even look fifteen," she complained. "I looked about eight. Like some dreadful child 'playing lady' in her mother's clothes." The *Beacon* reviewer, albeit diplomatically, agreed: "Miss Barrymore is tall, and strongly resembles her mother in figure. At present she is handsomer off the stage than on." But he and every other Boston critic joined Boston audiences in giving her the performance by virtue of precocious "beauty and charm."

Barry, playing concurrently, was unable to witness his daughter's performance. But her appreciative notices, according to Olga Nethersole, moved him to tears. He was moved, also, to more practical paternal expressions. For the first time since his second marriage, father and daughter kept company. On days when they had no matinees, he proudly escorted her, Belle of Clyde always in attendance, to the city's finest restaurants. Occasionally, John Drew, whom he had also sheepishly avoided since remarrying, would be included. These *soigné* luncheons never took place at Barry's hotel, of course, because, as Ethel observed, "he always lived in terrible ones," ones that would accept his inevitable traveling companions. During the Nethersole tour, he had somehow managed to acquire a mongoose, a raccoon, some monkeys and several birds.

That brief filial interlude in Boston would remain precious to Barry and his girl. Always rather intimidated by the responsibility of a daughter, Barry had behaved with great formality toward her. Their strained relationship, nurtured long before Georgie's death, intensified afterward, had broken when he remarried. They had purposely avoided meeting since that event—Ethel unable to face what she considered the ultimate betrayal of her mother; Barry avoiding what he accurately assumed would be his daughter's reaction. But if the girl irritated dormant guilt, valid or not, for his treatment of Georgie, she also embodied warm memories of her. If the supposed ill-treatment of her mother haunted Ethel, Papa himself restored happier days of summers *en famille*, the sojourn in England, the protection of Mamma and home. Whatever strain remained between them, beneath it persisted the basic needs of daughter for father, father for daughter.

"I have always regretted that I saw so little of him," Ethel lamented. "I remember his superlative beauty and how engaging and gay he was, but I heard all the amusing anecdotes about him and his stabbing wit only from other people." Even in Boston, during that period of implicit truce, Barry retained a scrupulous formality with his daughter.

When the Nethersole tour ended, Barry considered joining Mamie in France. He reconsidered when Charles Frohman beckoned. The manager was producing a new Civil War play, *The Secret Service*, by William Gillette, which, five weeks into rehearsals, seemed destined for failure. Having previously scored two tremendous hits with military plays, one of them Gillette's own *Held by the Enemy*, Frohman remained optimistic about the new play. He determined that the actors and actresses were responsible for its faults, and decided to make some changes. Gillette convinced Frohman that Maurice Barrymore was the only actor who could vivify the dashing Union spy, *Captain Challoner*.

If the success of a play depended upon it, C.F., as the mananger had come to be called, would agree to anything. He invited Barry to his stately offices on the third floor of his new Empire Theatre building. Barry accepted the invitation only to accommodate William Gillette, whom he admired as actor and author and counted as a friend. Frohman proffered drink and cigars. Barry refused. Frohman launched into an apology for any offense caused by his actions during the *Aristocracy* tour. Barry nodded curtly. Emboldened by this meager response, the wily manager attacked the issue at hand. If Barry would forget past differences and join the cast of *The Secret Service*, C.F. cajoled, he would receive star billing and $300 a week plus expenses starting immediately and including the period of rehearsals. Barry made no reply.

"*Captain Challoner* is a part that only you could play," Frohman flattered. "You *are* Challoner. You must do it. I will have no one else but you. The actor now rehearsing the part hasn't the faintest conception of it." He stood for emphasis behind his manuscript-laden desk, focusing sharp, bulging eyes upon his quarry, insinuating that no other actor in the whole theatrical firmament could possibly understand the part. The object of all this attention knew Frohman and his methods. But he was disarmed by the spectacle of the rotund little manager, nearly a foot shorter than he, craning his neck above the piled manuscripts, dashing to and fro. Perhaps this lent a necessary helplessness to the volatile plea. In any case, Barry smiled. "Besides," Frohman concluded, aware that he had already won, "he has a Northern accent which will not become Southern. We have tried and tried. It is no use. You must help me out or the play is ruined."

The problem of an English accent becoming Southern in a week did not seem to bother Frohman. It bothered his new star. But with the help of his Southern leading lady, Odette Tyler, he mastered the accent in time for the May 13th opening in Philadelphia. Learning the lines, as usual, was more of a problem. But Barry also found first-rate assistance in that area. Having deposited his latest menagerie at the farm, he had chosen more suitable traveling companions for himself and the ubiquitous Belle. Lionel had accompanied his father from New York, and Jack joined them at the Stenton Hotel for a weekend away from the scholastic rigors of Georgetown. The rigors of cueing Papa proved greater. The boys persevered, tossing lines at him as he paced their rooms clad only in his tattered boating-club jersey, alternately scratching his sides, puffing Virginia cigarettes, sipping English ale.

"Just before the curtain went up," Odette Tyler remembered of opening night, "Maurice Barrymore and I were walking nervously up and down the stage. That was a habit of ours." Barry sought to reassure his distraught partner, who had already taken three doses of ammonia to steady her nerves.

"If you forget your lines," he advised, "say anything you want to and I will do the same. We must keep the conversation moving. Don't let it drag. Fill up as best you can." Evidently his method worked. The performances of Maurice Barrymore and Odette Tyler proved to be the highlights of *The Secret Service* in Philadelphia. The New York *Times* correspondent wired to his paper that they had made "great popular hits." All of the critics agreed that Barry had finally found the role to establish him as a star. "Maurice Barrymore's *Captain Challoner* was full of warmth and passion, and yet subdued force," noted the Philadelphia *Enquirer*, "all of which made it romantic and stirring. No detail was wanting in the characterization to give it naturalness and vitality."

Seeds of greatness were discerned in the play itself, but they were generally deemed dormant. Desiring to nurture them properly, Gillette and Frohman decided to withdraw the work for revision. C.F. assured Barry that he would again be *Captain Challoner* when the revised play was presented in New York in September. They signed a contract, giving the manager exclusive right to the actor's services during the forthcoming autumn season.

Mamie had written repeatedly to her husband, urging him to join her on the Continent that summer. Barry again considered doing so, but he was experiencing an unwonted resurgence of interest in his profession. When L. R. Stockwell invited him to be leading man of his Columbia Theatre stock company in San Francisco, he accepted, presumably foreseeing a summer in repertory more agreeable than traveling with his wife and her mother.

His Western departure was delayed in order to enter Belle of Clyde in a New York bench show. Amy Leslie, aware that her theatrical hero's prize Clydesdale was sure to carry off a medal, came in from Chicago for the event. She searched in vain, however, for Belle and her master. "The third day I saw, creeping listlessly about the show, Barry, unshaven, miserable, hollow-eyed, and distrait," she recounted. "I made my way to him, and he clasped my hand in a desperately tragic way, and then in a torrent of tears he told me that some miscreant at Staten Island had set his farmhouses on fire and burned up his entire collection of vertebrae, ornithological and mammal."

Edward Briggs, fortunately, and some birds, cats, and Huskies had escaped; otherwise, the place was in total ruin, all of his other beloved creatures lost. Barry was inconsolable. He had wandered around the smoldering ruins in a daze, clinging pathetically to Belle of Clyde, vowing wildly to Edward that he would work until he had earned enough money to rebuild every shed and outbuilding on the place. His resolve to do so, more than the pleading of friends and the restatement of contractual obligations by L. R. Stockwell, decided the disheartened actor to proceed to San Francisco.

He was less rational in regard to another crucial matter before he departed. No amount of urging could move him to reconsider his violent reaction to a letter and a large check from Jack Barnes in London. *Blood Will Tell* had been optioned by actor-manager W. S. Penley for production at the Globe Theatre. Penley saw in Barry's farce a likely sequel to his resounding success in *Charley's Aunt,* which had recently set a London record of 1,466 performances. Barnes's letter related what he considered an amusing, merely incidental occurrence. When Penley had submitted the play for licensing, Barnes wrote, the Lord Chamberlain had stipulated that it would be granted only if certain changes were facilitated. These stipulations were recorded in the Lord Chamberlain's ledger on June 21, 1895:

> *Words and Passages to be omitted in Representation* omit in representation the title of character 'The Bishop of Soda and Bee' and no offensive 'make up' as a Bishop. Note The Examiner of Plays has been informed by W. Penley, Lessee of the theatre that the character will be eliminated in representation and he trusts this will be done.

What Barnes found amusing, and Penley found easily fixed, the author found untenable. Furious that Penley had given a performance of the play for copyright purposes with the *Bishop* character deleted, Barry obdurately returned the check, withdrawing permission to produce the altered play. Penley dropped his option. Messrs. Greet and Englebach picked it up. But after continued opposition from the Lord Chamberlain, and consequently from the author, they also dropped it. Reluctantly, with no other choice, Jack Barnes withdrew the play from circulation in London, returned it to his friend.

A short time later, a *Dramatic Mirror* interviewer asked Barry if he had written any new plays.

"Yes," he replied tersely; "W. S. Penley bought a play from me recently called *Blood Will Tell*, which he produced for copyright purposes in England. I am at work at present on a play of English life, which I hope to finish shortly."

The implication was obvious. Another work had succeeded *Blood Will Tell* as the ultimate vehicle of Maurice Barrymore's literary ascent. As for his ambitious comedy of scientific phenomenon, the author never mentioned it again.

XXVIII

San Francisco worked its singular spell upon Maurice Barrymore. He had arrived there visibly shaken and withdrawn. Not because another chance for recognition as a playwright had been lost but because of the Staten Island holocaust. The lethal fire had left him abstracted, immoderately preoccupied with the welfare of Belle. His solicitude, touching as it was, struck many observers as too zealous, disturbing. Amy Leslie knew that he was merely compensating for the loss of his beloved menagerie. "The Belle of Clyde was saved," she explained, "and she is always with her owner, under his chair and occasionally on the stage, as intelligent as a whole lot of actors."

But the city of mists seduced him, as it had since his first visit with Daly's company twenty years before. He had tried its singsong girls and reveled in the easy camaraderie of its Bohemian Club. He had climbed its twilight hills with Georgie in the early days of their marriage, and later, after her death, had discovered its bustling wharves, where precious cargo from the Orient disclosed Japanese spaniels and strawberry birds.

As Barry responded to San Francisco, local theatergoers, in turn, responded to him. He rewarded them that summer in the Columbia Theatre repertory, mastering plays new to him, *Nance Oldfield* and *The Critic*, reviving some of his popular vehicles, *Twelfth Night* and *A Man of the World*, and concluding the engagement triumphantly with the first local presentation of *A Woman of No Importance*.

Lionel Barrymore, between semesters at the Art Students League, was earning his keep on a "summer snap" through the Middle West. Aunt Gladys's father, McKee Rankin, was head of the company, and his repertoire tried the newcomer in everything from *Magda*, a turgid German melodrama, to *Oliver Twist*. The troupe was a small one, requiring everyone to undertake two or three parts in each play. *Ingomar*, an old tragedy, tested Lionel's versatility with six different characters.

While their brother plied the family trade, Ethel and Jack spent the summer with Uncle Jack and Aunt Dodo at Westhampton, Long Island. The brimming cottage by the sea, shared with the James Lewises and the Henry Millers, also held cousin Louise and Mummum. Aunt Dodo made her home, wherever it might be, a home for her mother-in-law and her niece and nephews. Her kindness and consideration were proverbial. While Uncle Jack compensated somewhat for the Barrymore children's errant father, Aunt Dodo, as Mummum grew old, was the only person who came close to replacing their mother.

Maurice Barrymore found his professional services much in demand when he returned to New York from San Francisco. But his hopes, that autumn of 1895, lay in the revised *Secret Service*, scheduled for an October opening. Charles Frohman summarily informed him otherwise. The role originated by Barry in Philadelphia, which critics had deemed a potential vehicle for his long-delayed ascent to stardom, had been assigned to William Gillette, the play's author. Barry's contract with Frohman, the manager's lawyers informed him, did not specify that he would necessarily appear in *Secret Service*, only that he was indentured to the wily manager for the autumn season. Frohman, to avoid investing money in a friend's forthcoming production, had given Barry's services instead. The disappointment of losing that promising role and the humiliation of being once more outsmarted by Charles Frohman were somewhat mitigated by the nature of his new assignment. He was to perform in aid of a friend from early San Francisco days, David Belasco, and Belasco's infamous protégée.

Belasco, a barber's son, had started his career as callboy at San Francisco's Baldwin Theatre, later winning Broadway success with a series of plays written in collaboration with Henry C. DeMille. Of late, however, he had become obsessed by another goal: the theatrical advancement and education of Mrs. Leslie Carter, a surpassingly beautiful castoff from Chicago society. Mrs. Carter, during her much-publicized divorce case in 1889, had become America's most infamous gentlewoman. After bald accusations of infidelity and promiscuity left her shunned by society, deprived of her child and her income, she had approached Belasco in hopes of being trained for the stage. "I am a horsewoman," she announced. "I wish to make my first entrance on a horse, leaping over a hurdle." Belasco dismissed her.

The lady relentlessly pursued him. "She told me much of the story of her domestic tragedy—and a heart-breaking story it is—and, as she told it and I listened, I began to see the possibilities in her—if *only* she could act, on the stage, with the same force and pathos she used in telling her story."

378

The tall, fiery, red-haired society divorcee, impeccable in dress and manner, and the short, deep-eyed, bush-headed man of the theater, always adorned with clerical collar and full stage make-up, had devoted five years to achieving that end. All of Belasco's playwriting profits were sacrificed to the training of Mrs. Carter. They persevered, dining in cheap East Side restaurants—her mother, as a belated nod to propriety, always in attendance. During that period, Mrs. Carter rehearsed no fewer than fifty-eight plays with her mentor, not for production, for stage experience.

The Heart of Maryland opened at the Herald Square Theatre on October 22. "Do you hear that?" cried Belasco to Mrs. Carter, as the cheering first-night audience called their names. "Do you know what that means? It means that never—never—never again will we have to eat in a Third Avenue restaurant." The critics were not so confident. Many of them panned the play for its obvious melodrama, the star for everything from her morals and acting to her bright red hair. But Belasco's lady and his picture of neutral Maryland during the Civil War, essence of lilac and sniffs of gunpowder, enthralled the public to the extent that even critical dissenters reconsidered. "The remarkable and unquestioned success that *The Heart of Maryland* has achieved is a double triumph for Mr. Belasco," the initially negative *Herald* admitted, two weeks after the opening. "It has proved that he was right both in his estimate of the play and of Mrs. Leslie Carter as an emotional actress." (Belasco had indeed been right. Those first-night cheers, echoing for years on Broadway and the road, heralded one of the decade's greatest hits, one of the most popular plays of its time. David Belasco and his protégée never ate in a Third Avenue restaurant again.)

Mrs. Leslie Carter, after five years of rigorous training, was deemed an instant star. She triumphed as *Maryland Calvert*, a part requiring more than merely emotional powers. At the end of the third act, a bell is about to be rung to warn prison guards of the escape of *Maryland*'s lover. The loyal lady climbs winding stairs to the belfry loft, clings to the great bell's giant tongue as the rope is pulled from below, and, swinging violently back and forth, prevents the alarm from sounding. Mrs. Carter's gymnastics never failed to bring cheers and shouts and standing ovations. As *Colonel Alan Kendrick*, 9th Cavalry, U.S.A., the object of such rabid devotion, Barry was found worthy by the critics. He also had his share of audience-rousers. When he shoots a Southern spy, another character cries, "What have you done?"

"Saved Charlesville and the United States!" exclaims *Colonel Kendrick*, to patriotic cheers from the house.

Barry took little satisfaction from continued cheers and critical praise. "Maurice Barrymore never appeared to better advantage and never had less to say and do," noted the *Spirit of the Times*. "He is the handsome excuse for the heroics of Mrs. Carter." Such appraisals had irked him since his debut at the Windsor Theatre Royal nearly twenty-five years before. His distaste for making love and false heroics in support of temperamental tragediennes, imported debutantes, beloved mistresses, and ambitious amateurs was irritated by a critic in the Herald Square gallery. During a scene in which the wrist-bound *Kendrick* is viciously beaten, he dares the blackguards to untie him and try the same.

"Why don't ya kick 'em on the shins, Barry?" yelled the gallery critic. "Your feet ain't tied." From that moment, the leading man cursed *Colonel Kendrick* and *The Heart of Maryland*. But his bondage was not without compensations.

"Maurice Barrymore, the hero of our most successful drama this season, receives $250 a week," reported the New York *Press*. "Roughly calculated, he earns about $5 every minute he is on the stage. Allowing an hour in the dressing room, he remains four hours in the theatre every night. Thus he has twenty hours of leisure every day." The reporter was contrasting an actor's "easy lot" to the "hard work" of a newspaperman. "In Barrymore's case," he conceded, "this period of freedom from duty is employed to good advantage, for he is writing a drama which is soon to be produced at Palmer's."

This rare nod to Barrymore industry did not mention that he was also investing time and most of his salary to rebuild the Staten Island farm. His dedication to both projects was admirable. His writing, however, took precedence, augmented by another goal after the opening of *Secret Service*. William Gillette was hailed as an author, while his playing of the role originated by Barry in Philadelphia elevated him to stardom. Negotiated out of that opportunity by Charles Frohman, Barry was determined to emerge, once and for all, not only as an author but as a star. The vehicle for the achievement of such heady aspirations? His play of English life, *Roaring Dick & Co.*

The Heart of Maryland's run seemed interminable. Going into the sixth month, Barry was no closer to achieving his goals. A. M. Palmer had offered his theater for the presentation of the new play, but he could not afford to finance it. Financial pressures and the burgeoning syndicate had forced the venerable manager to disband his stock company and concentrate on managing the career of but one star—Richard Mansfield. As Barry's search for backers continued, however, his spirits seemed higher than at any time since Georgie's death. So it appeared, at least, to a man from the *Dramatic Mirror*, who stopped at his Herald Square dressing room to ask him to be the subject of an interview.

"I read your interview with Clara Morris in the last *Mirror* with great interest. She is, indeed, a great actress," Barry said of his onetime cohort at Daly's. "Actresses who really possess the divine afflatus are few and far between. Clara Morris is one of them. Eleanora Duse is another. One moment of inspiration is worth all the traditional acting in the world."

"I quite agree with you," the reporter assured him, "but I want you to talk about yourself, not about others."

"That's rather an egotistical undertaking," replied the prospective subject; "but if you'll come up to my home in Ninety-seventh Street tomorrow afternoon I'll try to dig up the milestones of my career—if that's what you're after. There's my cue. *Au revoir*."

"You've kept our appointment, I see," Barry said, as he and Belle greeted the reporter. Mrs. Barrymore, recently returned from the Continent, was next door at her sister's. The host led his guest through a wide reception room, up curving stairs, past Mamie's salon, a music room, a dining room, to a small back parlor. This secluded chamber, book-strewn and cluttered, was obviously the master's study. Barry sat at a huge desk piled high with hand-written manuscript pages. "Make yourself comfortable," he offered. The reporter sat down; a servant brought refreshments. "Now put me on the stand and cross-question me as much as you like."

The comprehensive interview covered the career of Maurice Barrymore from birth in India to *The Heart of Maryland*. Barry's replies in regard to his plays and performances were accurate but terse. More speculative questions inspired more imaginative answers. Stroking Belle, who was sprawled before him on the desk, he launched an attack on the conglomerates which were currently driving independents like A. M. Palmer out of the field. "Here in America there has been a strong tendency since the combination system gained a firm foothold to run theatres on the business methods that obtain in a large dry goods house. What has been the result? Until very recently even the prominent dramatic authors of this country found it difficult to market their plays, as the commercial gentlemen engaged in conducting metropolitan houses wouldn't give a play much consideration unless it bore the hall mark of Castle Garden. In other words the majority of New York managers only dealt in London and Paris successes.

"I am glad to see that latterly the American dramatist is getting some sort of chance because American audiences are beginning to assert themselves, and haven't hesitated to call down in a single night plays that don't interest them, and that were imported just because they had been gigantic successes abroad. The star of the American playwright is in the ascendant," he concluded optimistically, "and plays with American human interest will be in large demand."

Barry augmented his marathon run in Belasco's play with appearances at numerous benefits as he continued the search for backers. On March 17, *A Man of the World* opened the Grand Benefit Matinee at Palmer's Theatre in aid of the Fresh Air Fund. This performance of Gus

Thomas's popular curtain raiser created particular audience interest, because, for the first time, Maurice Barrymore was supported by his elder son. Critics, apparently, were not so interested. The most that could be said of Lionel's performance was that it must have been inconspicuous enough to escape critical comment.

As *The Heart of Maryland* passed its two hundredth performance, Barry found William A. Brady, a young entrepreneur, who, by his own admission, was "playing the theatre like a roulette wheel." From his first boyhood theatrical enterprise, hawking defunct groceries outside of the Bowery Theatre ("Here y'are, gents, fruit, vegetables and rare old eggs to throw at the actors!") to the exclusive management of James J. Corbett's considerable boxing and theatrical interests, Bill Brady had prospered enough to support his brand of roulette. He had also met Maurice Barrymore. "I'd got to know him well through his close friendship with Corbett—that arose out of Barrymore's being a fine amateur boxer as well as a brilliant actor. He was good," Brady attested; "he really could stand up and spar with Corbett and come off very prettily so long as Jim remembered not to put on too much pressure."

Loafing along the Rialto with Corbett and Brady one Sunday in May, Barry bemoaned his inability to find backing for his new play. When his companions expressed interest in the work, the author hauled them up to Ninety-seventh Street for a reading. He escorted his guests to his cluttered study, seated them in comfortable chairs, sat himself at his desk behind the looming manuscript of *Roaring Dick & Co.* He didn't sit for long. "Barrymore read it in a fashion that threatened to tear down the lighting fixtures and rip up the boards in the floor—a performance that got me mesmerized in no time," Brady admitted. "During the third act he cried so hard that you could hardly hear the words—great big, fat tears." Brady found the virtuoso performance irresistible: "Well, thought I, if just reading it through makes this veteran actor blubber like this, what will it do to an audience?" He bought *Roaring Dick & Co.* on the spot, promising to prepare it for autumn production.

With the production of his play assured, Barry accepted Belasco's offer to tour with Mrs. Carter. One of his stipulations, besides a fifty-dollar raise, was the inclusion of his elder son in the cast. Lionel Barrymore—disguised, onstage, as a Confederate soldier, offstage as a man of the world—became Papa's good and constant companion during that summer of *The Heart of Maryland.*

Others of the family also took to the road. John Drew, with his niece again in support, commenced a spring tour in his latest Frohman success, *The Squire of Dames.* Drew's annual tours were anticipated certainties. His mother's concurrent departure was an unexpected pleasure.

Mrs. John Drew, Sr., in her seventy-sixth year, had signed with Joseph

Jefferson for an unprecedented all-star tour of *The Rivals*. A series of thirty one-night stands and matinees had been booked in nearly as many cities during the month of May. A special train of Pullman cars stood ready to carry the illustrious company on its incredible route: May 4th, Springfield; 5th, Hartford; 6th, New Haven; 7th, New York, matinee; 7th, Brooklyn, night; 8th, Philadelphia; 9th, Baltimore, afternoon; 9th, Washington, night; 11th, Pittsburgh; 12th, Louisville; 13th, Cincinnati, matinee and night; 14th, St. Louis; 15th and 16th, Chicago, two nights and matinee; 18th, Milwaukee; 19th, Indianapolis; 20th, Grand Rapids, Mich.; 21st, Toledo, Ohio, afternoon; 21st, Detroit, night; 22nd, Columbus, Ohio, afternoon; 23rd, Cleveland; 25th, Buffalo; 26th, Rochester; 27th, Syracuse, afternoon; 27th, Utica, night; 28th, Albany; 29th, Boston, afternoon; 29th, Worcester, night; 30th, New York.

Mrs. Drew traveled from New York to Springfield with Nat C. Goodwin, Francis Wilson, Fanny Rice, Edward and Joseph Holland. Awaiting them in the Pullman cars, sidetracked by the river, were Joseph Jefferson, Robert Taber and Julia Marlowe-Taber, and William S. Crane. "If the beloved interpreters brought together in this happy play were to join hands and sing 'ring-a-roundy-rosy,'" Amy Leslie speculated, "all the public would sit in rapture and pay colossal figures for the privilege."

As it was, the public was being charged the unheard of sum of five dollars a ticket for the privilege of seeing *The Rivals*. They paid it. The only house not sold out on the entire route was in Grand Rapids, where a few seats remained empty in the back rows. The only customer complaint was not that prices were too high but that performances in each city were too few. Jefferson had considered it prudent to limit them. "It is better," he said, "to underrate than to overrate." He had widely underrated.

While others were "thoroughly tired, nervously so," with anticipation and dread, Mrs. Drew and Mr. Jefferson, nine years her junior, seemed indefatigable. Early the next morning, they commanded the heads of a long table in their Pullman dining room, their colleagues strung along the sides between them for the first of many breakfasts together. "As these two royal representatives of the drama sat talking," Francis Wilson observed, "and I contrasted their simple, unaffected manner, both of speech and action, with that of some pretentious members of the players' profession, I was reminded of the remark of a gifted artist who, when his attention was called to some students whose long hair and conspicuous dress obviously proclaimed their artistic ambitions, said: 'Oh, if they only knew that art does not consist of *that!*'"

Joseph Jefferson never had enough of his erstwhile stage partner and her *Mrs. Malaprop*. During one performance, while Francis Wilson was crossing behind the scenes, he spotted Jefferson looking through a crack

in the center doors of the set. He assumed that the old gentleman was siz-
ing up the house. "That's a sight worth seeing," Wilson commented.

"I was not thinking of the audience," Jefferson replied. "Stay a moment and watch this laughing exit of Mrs. Drew's." Wilson stood behind
him, peering over his shoulder, to see *Mrs. Malaprop* finish her scene. Afterward, they walked around to make their joint entrance, as Mrs.
Drew bowed and bowed and bowed to a seemingly endless ovation. "I
have had the honor of playing with that lady hundreds of times," Jefferson said, "and I have never failed to watch that scene."

John Drew was playing *The Squire of Dames* in Chicago when *The
Rivals* company arrived. On Sunday night, before the all-stars left for
Milwaukee, he gave a dinner for his mother and her colleagues at the
Annex. It was a festive gathering, sparked by the witty reminiscences of
Mr. Jefferson and Mrs. Drew, and the singing of Ethel Barrymore. "I
remember how enchantingly embarrassed she was," said Francis Wilson,
"when I expressed delight at having, at last, heard a singing voice worse
than my own."

Despite her brief success as *Lady Kate* the previous spring, Ethel had
been reduced to playing a smaller, more appropriate part in *The Squire
of Dames* company. She didn't mind. The sixteen-year-old was uncertain
about the pursuit of acting. Her sights were still aimed at a musical career
of some sort. "From something she and her grandmother had said," Wilson assumed, "I thought it might be along the broad way of light opera.
She was already a capable musician, 'soothing her young heart with
catches and glees,' and, notwithstanding my jest at our respective voices,
sang with taste and intelligence." Wilson nevertheless expressed to Lewis
Baker, Aunt Dodo's brother, doubt as to whether Ethel had inherited the
family talent.

"My dear Francis," replied Uncle Lulu, as the Barrymore children
fittingly called him, "why be in doubt? In the family, Ethel's ability has
long been a matter of hilarious jest." A public impressed with the young
lady's beauty and social successes did not agree. In Chicago that same
week, she made a much-noted social debut at a ball given by Mrs. Arthur
Caton (later Mrs. Marshall Field). Her progress, social and otherwise,
was not going unobserved in influential areas. Charles Frohman saw her
perform on the road that summer.

"He looked at her sharply," noted his brother Daniel, "but said nothing."

At Columbus, Ohio, toward the end of *The Rivals* tour, a commemo-
rative flashlight photograph was to be taken. After the performance, the
all-stars " 'lined up,' as in football," Mrs. Drew noted. The photograph
was taken. The blinding glare was followed by a mock officious command from Jefferson's young son: "Now wash up!"

384

"Why, he talks to us as if we were minstrels," Mrs. Drew jested.

In a warm rush of humor and reminiscence, and the more heated acclaim of cross-country audiences, the all-star *Rivals* neared the end of its brief existence. "The tour has ended," Wilson elegized in New York. "We have shaken hands all around; inscribed final names on final programs and photographs; told each other how much we have enjoyed the social and professional participation, how much we hope for another such coalition—a hope, likely, never to be realized."

Mrs. Drew stopped at the Bevan House in Larchmont for a week of rest, or, perhaps, for just one more week of independence, before rejoining her son and daughter-in-law at Westhampton.

Ethel and Jack also spent another summer with the Drews, but the holiday, for John Drew and his niece, at least, was curtailed by early August rehearsals of *Rosemary*. Drew plays had become seasonal events. Frohman's star was called "the young Henry Irving of America," deemed worthy of the weekly $600 that his manager paid him. His popularity reached its zenith when he opened as the *Squire of Ingle* on August 31. The "gay and pretty" *Rosemary* ("That's for remembrance.") proved to be a landmark, also, for two other Frohman players.

Maude Adams' tremendous hit as *Dorothy* decided Frohman to star her during the following season. (Her consequent performance as *Lady Babbie*, in J. M. Barrie's *The Little Minister*, began one of the most illustrious starring careers in the history of the American theater.)

Ethel Barrymore originated the small role of Priscilla, a rustic maid. "She had a dress and shoes which might have made another young girl seem grotesque," said her uncle. "However, in spite of this most unbecoming attire, her beauty made a great impression." "Alan Dale" noted that "Miss Ethel Barrymore scored an unexpected hit." Unexpected to him, perhaps, since he had predicted five years before that the Barrymore children would never appear on the stage. Other critics were less surprised, more effusive. A *Dramatic Mirror* writer was even inspired to publish a poem entitled, "Miss Barrymore in *Rosemary*":

> *No wonder dear* Dorothy *kindled a fire*
> *In the lonely old heart of the bachelor squire;*
> *But how in the world could he live and die single*
> *With a girl like delicious* Priscilla *at Ingle?*

Audiences noticed that the girl tossed out lines in the same delightful way as her mother had done. Her delivery of one line in particular—"Your words r-oll and r-oll and r-oll."—delighted patrons, and was often repeated by the most ardent of them to illustrate her unique drawl. After Mrs. Drew attended a performance of *Rosemary*, her granddaughter, flushed with success, questioned her: "Please tell me how I did, Mummum?"

"You would have done very well," replied Louisa Drew, "if it had been possible to understand a word you said."

After its New York run of one hundred nights, *Rosemary* went on tour. Play and star, leading lady and rustic maid duplicated their Broadway successes in every city. "The most interesting member of Mr. Drew's company was his niece, Ethel Barrymore," Maude Adams remembered of their tour. "A lovely girl. One always thought of Meredith's line: 'Beautiful she looks, like a tall garden lily.' She had the most charming ways, and a delightful seriousness about her work. Mr. Drew was very proud of her." It was not merely the pride of a doting uncle. Others were capitulating.

"There is going to be a big development in one of my companies before long," predicted Charles Frohman. "There's a daughter of Barry who gets a big reception wherever she goes. She has got the real stuff in her."

Papa was no slouch, either, that autumn of 1896:

MR. BARRYMORE'S SUCCESS

WASHINGTON, Nov. 9—The National Theatre was crowded to its fullest capacity tonight to witness the first performance of *Roaring Dick & Co.*, the new play by Maurice Barrymore, in which the author himself played the leading role, that of *Roaring Dick*. The play was a decided success. Mr. Barrymore has a part which fits him admirably.

The highlight of the performance, a festival at the end of the third act, disclosed two hundred mischievous youngsters devouring fruit and sweetmeats at long tables under a huge marquee. Their gaiety and natural laughter, jolly beyond mere acting, was infectious. "Just how the mob of youngsters is enthused to such a degree is a secret of stage direction that should be made public," decided one reviewer. The method was not complex. Barry had borrowed two hundred children from local orphanages, and simply given them a real party onstage. The audience, including President and Mrs. Cleveland, Secretary and Mrs. Carlisle, Secretary of the Interior Francis, stood and cheered. The author-star was called before the curtain.

"The performance suggested imperfect preparation and the advisability of 'chopping,'" cautioned a New York *Times* dispatch, "which was promised by Mr. Barrymore, when, in response to demands for a speech, he returned his thanks for the kind reception extended to his play, and asked indulgence from the critical who could not know the disadvantages under which it had been produced." The author's apology and allusion to rehearsal difficulties were unnecessary. The serious illness of Barry's old friend, Leslie Allen, which had forced him to leave the cast, and the chronic, gratuitous meddling of Bill Brady left no shadow upon the first-night proceedings. Washington critics were unanimous in their praise of the play, its presentation, and Barry's performance in the title role. *Roaring Dick*, after all, was that old stage acquaintance, the prodigal son, thrown out upon the world by a heartless father at nineteen, returned ten years later, hardened and desperate, to secure his share of the parental wealth by fair means or foul. It was a variation on a theme long close to Barry, paralleling, somewhat, his own relationship with the Commissioner, reflected in his play, *The Don*, his affinity for Shaw's *Cashel Byron*, his playing of *Captain Swift* and *Reckless Temple*.

Like all of the aforementioned characters, *Roaring Dick* is kindness personified. His heart is a perfect reservoir of delicate and noble impulses, temporarily dormant, but ready to flow in a generous stream for everybody's benefit at the slightest provocation. Having cajoled his old father, by means of lies and liquor, into giving him control of the family fortune, and, incidentally, saving the old curmudgeon from murder and robbery, he proceeds to illustrate his natural benevolence by raising salaries, condoning felonies, feeding the poor, entertaining school children, and, finally, after clearing himself of suspicion laid by a discarded accomplice, marries the heroine and settles down to prosperity and respectability.

Short on novelty, the plot was made palatable by the author's dashing portrayal and excellent supporting company, by his strong dialogue, effective dramatic touches, and social comment. "No play in years has advanced such liberal and enlightened views as to the proper compensation of the employed," stated the Washington *Post*, "or has so emphatically expressed the universal opinion of the working man on the subject of wages. Mr. Barrymore's perseverance, energy and love of justice enter largely into his play of *Roaring Dick & Co.*"

The author worked tirelessly to cut and strengthen his play before the New York opening. Bolstered by *Roaring Dick*'s reception in Washington, he envisioned a Broadway success long overdue. New York awaited Barrymore & Co. with inevitable skepticism. "I have always believed," the *Journal* critic averred, "that Barrymore chuckled in his sleeve at the gullibility of the public and made no bids for lasting favors, being satisfied with temporary bread and butter. What he will do in *Roaring Dick & Co.* will be interesting to watch, and what the public will do will be even more interesting. He may simply say, 'I'm going to give you the Maurice Barrymore you have always liked, and if you are sick of him, well—*place aux autres.*'"

The large and demonstrative audience crowding Palmer's Theatre on the evening of November 16 hailed Maurice Barrymore as a star, his play as a triumph. When he and Bill Brady were called before the curtain,

Barry, visibly touched by this indication that his goals had been finally achieved, briefly expressed his gratitude. Brady, in the costume of a supernumerary, dwelt upon his upper-Broadway advent, making magnanimous promises to a new clientele secured by the apparent success of his first uptown venture.

William Winter, in the *Tribune*, conceded that the first-night audience had been "amiably animated by personal good will." Barry's erstwhile adversary conceded little else. "*Roaring Dick & Co.* is rubbish," he began unequivocally, "and the success of it—if success with such stuff were possible,—would only reflect additional discredit upon a public taste which has already been degraded to the lowest level of folly. It is melancholy, therefore, to find such an actor as Mr. Barrymore associated with such platitude." Then Mr. Winter sounded the old refrain in a lower key. "There was a time when, in the field of intellectual culture and artistic achievement, much was confidently anticipated of this actor; but that time is past, and, evidently, it may as well be forgotten."

Winter's critical brethren, while not recording a triumph, did not bury the author-star. "Mr. Barrymore, the actor, has not much to complain of in the work of Mr. Barrymore, the playwright," noted the *Post*, explaining that he "has a special gift for depicting upon the stage an amiable outlaw brought by fortuitous circumstances into contact with good society." The *Dramatic Mirror* felt that "taken as a whole the piece proved decidedly creditable to Mr. Barrymore's ability as a dramatist," while the *Times* commended his "realistic dialogue" and "frequent touches of humor."

The exacting *Spirit of the Times* critic, long a Barrymore partisan, implored the author to take stock and say to himself: " 'I will rewrite the play properly if I have to stay away from the Lambs' Club for a month; I will put all my clever things into it, instead of saying them to other people; I will act with all my heart. This is my chance to be a Boucicault with all the modern improvements, and I will make the most of it for my own sake and the children's.' Mr. Barrymore has all this in him, and more, and we hope to see him bring it out and do himself justice."

Barry, far from discouraged, heeded this admonition, although his desire for quality might easily have been undermined by developments at Palmer's box office. "*Roaring Dick & Co.* is a success in spite of the critics," noted *The Stage* two weeks after the opening. "Drawn to the theatre by Barrymore's name, the public has decided to overlook crude construction and commonplace dialogue for the sake of the bold sketching in of some strong stituations and of unwonted stage spectacle. Maurice Barrymore is a *Roaring Dick*, every inch of the many he can boast."

Brady, who Winter complained "deals with plays and acting as a grocer deals with butter and pickles," urged Barry to leave well enough alone. The manager was pleased with the play's profits during its scheduled four-week New York engagement, heartened by predictions of great popular success on the road. But the author continued rewriting until the tour's Boston opening, determined to win that city's critical delegation.

"Maurice Barrymore has a legion of friends and a goodly number of them helped to crowd the Boston Theatre last evening," reported the *Globe* of the December 14 opening. Hearty plaudits greeted Barry's entrance in the first act, and throughout the performance there came enthusiastic evidence of good will toward the actor and his play. After the third act, he was called before the curtain half-a-dozen times. A huge floral tribute was passed over the footlights, accompanied by more applause and demands for a speech.

"As he stood," observed the *Herald*, "a handsome figure, against the curtain, waiting for the applause to die out, after the sixth raising of the curtain on that children-packed third act, he was suddenly overcome by one of those chokes in the throat and tight pressures behind the eyes that will come unexpectedly even to strong men." He began bravely enough.

"Ladies and gentlemen, I don't know how to thank you for all your kindnesses. Twenty years ago—" He became inaudible. A look of intense agony crossed his face. After a moment, with visible effort, he regained control of himself. Words came slowly, one by one, through sheer force of will. "It was twenty years ago on this very stage that I first appeared in America, and I am glad to find that I have friends in Boston that still hold me in esteem. I hope to always deserve your good will." He mentioned that C. Leslie Allen, at whose benefit he had made that first appearance, had played with the *Roaring Dick* company in Washington. He regretted that illness had prevented his friend from continuing with the troupe to his home city.

"There was no questioning the fact that the big, manly fellow was simply 'broken up,' and suffered in collecting himself," concluded the *Herald*. "But his house liked him all the better, and the little sob-broken speech received the heartiest applause of the evening."

Local critics offered little more encouragement to the dramatist than their New York colleagues had. Nor did Boston theatergoers respond after the heartening first night. Business was only fair during the first week, until a streetcar strike diminished even that. On Wednesday of the second week, the city was further incapacitated by a blizzard. Receipts that evening were forty-three dollars, the least taken in thirty-three years at the Boston Theatre.

Barry remained in the dim theater after the performance. His fellow actors had trudged through the snow to their nearby hotel. Some of the local stagehands, who lived farther away, were spending the night in the theater. As Barry gazed out over the empty house, he noticed for the first time that the cut-glass chandelier, which had shone like a great, glowing jewel over his Boston debut, had been replaced by eight small electric clusters. The splendid fixture, a stagehand told him, had been removed by a new manager to avoid accident, "a danger more apparent than real," he added. No buyer could be found for the chandelier, which had originally cost thousands of dollars. No one would even remove it for the value of its materials. It had been dismantled and stored above the dome of the theater, a few feet from the site of its former glory.

Barry went to the small stage door, which opened onto Mason Street. Outside, a narrow path had been cleared. He walked its length, snow towering above him on both sides. He turned and stared at the portal through which he had passed to make his first American success, and, twenty years later, his worst failure.

Barry urged Bill Brady to end the *Roaring Dick* tour in Boston. Despite further predictions of success in the hinterlands, Brady relented. The author-star was clearly far too disheartened to continue.

Within the week, he was in New York again, sitting with counterfeit cheer at the Lambs'. His more perceptive friends surmised the injury inflicted by his latest failure. Others, as Barry preferred, embraced the popular view. "Troubles run off him like drops of water from a sea gull's back," presumed an observer from *Vanity Fair*. "He is the personification of good cheer and generosity and high impulse, an ideal Bohemian such as we often hear tell of but rarely see."

Henry Bagge, late of the *Roaring Dick* company, happened to be at the club that evening, obviously very drunk. He garrulously approached Barry, only to be received with a curt nod. "You shouldn't mind me, old chap," Bagge cajoled. "I've always been your friend. I was with you in *Roaring Dick*."

"For that I love you, Bagge," replied Barry. "For that I regard you as one of my best friends."

"Why are you so fond of me because I was with you in *Roaring Dick*?" the actor wondered.

"Because, old man," said Barry, "you're my only excuse."

XXIX

Six weeks after *Roaring Dick*'s demise, Barry accepted the featured role of *Manoel Clavajal,* a swarthy Cuban adventurer, in *Spiritisme.* "Mr. Barrymore," noted the *Post,* "acted well in the unthankful part of the lover." But the latest product of M. Sardou's theatrical sleight-of-hand managed only a brief run at the Knickerbocker. That suited Mr. Barrymore just fine. He was merely biding his time before giving a tweak to the Broadway establishment.

Although vaudeville had won the hoi polloi by 1897, its brand of variety entertainment was disdained by legitimate purveyors and their patrons. J. Austin Fynes, manager of B. F. Keith's New Union Square Theatre, sought to remedy that discrepancy by adding "dignity" acts to top-hat his variety bills. A few lesser legitimate performers had succumbed to the lure of big money and less work. As yet, however, Fynes had not won a player of sufficient stature and popularity to render vaudeville respectable—a player like Maurice Barrymore.

When *Roaring Dick* failed, Fynes reasoned that Barrymore himself might consent to do the pioneering. The vaudeville manager approached Broadway's foremost leading man with an irresistible offer—$750 a week and complete autonomy in the selection, casting, and staging of a dramatic sketch. Fynes made proud publicity of the New Union Square bill for the week beginning Monday, March 29, 1897:

REFINED AND HIGH-CLASS VAUDEVILLE
First Appearance in Vaudeville of the Distinguished Actor,
MR. MAURICE BARRYMORE
In Mr. Augustus Thomas' Petite Comedy,
A MAN OF THE WORLD

"When Maurice Barrymore had carried his point in *A Man of the World* at Keith's yesterday," reported the *Morning Telegraph*, "and the young husband had taken his wife in his arms, he turned away and, with a groan of relief said, 'Oh, that's all right,' with an indescribable stress on the 'that's.' There was the point of the play, and nobody but a first rate actor could say it with real feeling. The audience suddenly and spontaneously applauded Mr. Barrymore, and indeed they gave all evidence of enjoying hugely this excursion of his into the continuous theatre."

With an old one-acter and a curt ad libitum phrase, Maurice Barrymore had legitimatized the vaudeville.

The *Morning Telegraph*, which had headlined its report of Barry's variety debut, was devoted to covering sporting and theatrical events, with a recent emphasis on vaudeville. The more staid publications joined most of the legitimate community in silence. Aghast at Barry's professional audacity, few of them cursed the inevitable. Some of them even cheered it. Mamie Barrymore, for one, who had been pouting over her husband's prolonged absences of late, particularly during his engagement with the infamous Mrs. Carter. Billed by her real name, Marie Floyd, presumably to avoid confusion with Georgie Drew Barrymore, she became her husband's leading lady in Gus Thomas's four-character sketch. (Actually, in the new Barrymore version, the one-acter had five characters. The ubiquitous Belle of Clyde was prominently at her master's feet during every performance.) Other legitimate artists showed their approval with astonishing celerity. True to manager Fynes's prediction, as Barry's engagement at Keith's grew from one week to eight, he was followed into vaudeville by Agnes Booth, Robert Hilliard, John Mason and Marion Manola, Marshall Wilder, Mr. and Mrs. Sidney Drew.

One legitimate arbiter, appalled by the "stampede," cursed Barry for its initiation. While Boss Croker's Tammany Hall candidates swept city elections by promising "To Hell with Reform," William Winter was still upholding what he supposed should be the morality of the American stage. In a vitriolic *Herald* piece, he attacked not Barry's acting but his morals, his Bohemian life, his defection to the vaudeville stage.

Winter's attack found an unusually vulnerable target. The day before its appearance, Belle of Clyde had suddenly died, leaving her master of seven years utterly bereft. He had commenced a marathon bender with James Huneker, a congenial young drama critic, whose father had been Mrs. Drew's painter at the Arch. "We had been on the loose since the afternoon before," Huneker recalled, "though not off the list of the living by a long shot."

At the Arena bar, Barry read Winter's attack. He called for paper and pen. "I don't see what my doings off the boards have to do with my capabilities as an actor," he muttered, as he scribbed a reply:

Sir, in your column of the Tribune *this morning you allude to me as an immoral actor who should not be allowed to blister the gaze of the theatre-going public. Sir, I never kissed your daughter.*

Maurice Barrymore

"But Barry," Huneker remonstrated, "people don't write such letters."

"But they do, Huney," Barry rejoined with a swift dagger glance, "they not only write them but they mail them." As they proceeded to Mould's on University Place, he did mail the letter. Afterward, he turned to Huneker and winked: "Of course, you know the old hedgehog has no daughter. I shouldn't have written it if he had."

Barry never mentioned Belle during that two-day binge. His grief manifested itself cryptically. Conceiving the notion that a glass dog was following him, he found an imaginary glass chain with which to lead the fragile creature about. At Mould's, he explained the dog's invisibility by the fact that "light passes through it and casts no shadow." One patron was bluntly skeptical. After fighting the unfortunate fellow to a finish, Barry pulled him by the scruff of the neck to the bar, bought him a drink. "Now, next time you'll know a glass dog when you see one!" he suggested. The skeptic readily agreed.

Barry confidently resumed his tour, leading the invisible canine and the congenial critic to the new Lambs' clubhouse at 70 West Thirty-sixth Street. Huneker paused on the front steps, aware that dramatic critics were not admitted into that actors' precinct. "Oh, come in, come in," Barry urged, "you are no dramatic critic." So they went in, the dog tinkling after them on crystal paws, and, finding Victor Herbert and Victor Harris at the bar, didn't go home till daybreak.

Following his highly successful variety debut, Barry traveled on the Keith Circuit, its best-paid, most popular star. "Maurice Barrymore, sandwiched in between Charlie Abbe and the biograph at Keith's, sacrifices none of his numerous and familiar inducements thereby," attested the Boston *Herald*. The difference between vaudeville and legitimate audiences was even more pronounced in Boston than in New York. Barry realized the necessity of having to win patrons, who, for the most part, had never seen an actual theatrical performance. In a strictly "variety" house, he could not rest upon his past reputation. The Boston *Herald* discerned the subtle transformation worked by actor upon patrons:

There was not much applause for Mr. Barrymore when he made his entree, but it was pleasing to note how those hardened continuous performancers warmed up to him. There was the usual houseful of people who do not patronize Keith's for thinking purposes, but the clever

393

actor made them think. They followed the splendidly human story with breathless interest, except when Mr. Barrymore made one of the few subtle comedy points of the piece, when they laughed as one man, but were instantly all attention again. It was evident that some in the audience were receiving their original introduction to this species of dramatic art, and were a little dazed at the outset, but at the end they were undeniably enthusiastic, and kept up their applause until the curtain had lifted three times to enable the newcomers to bow their pleased acknowledgments—and there was no doubt that Mr. Barrymore was pleased, for he looked it."

At the end of his column, the *Herald* reviewer implied that Maurice Barrymore's defection was not the only recent challenge to legitimate theater on the bill. "The new pictures in the biograph were all that had been promised, and were as heartily applauded as any act on the programme." Herman Casler's invention, owned by the American Mutoscope Company, had been introduced at Keith's New York theater in January. "The comedy hits in this wonderful motion-picture are equal to many of those taken part in by 'the real artists,' as nothing much funnier than the pillow fight between the four small girls can be imagined."

While Barry's engagement broke house records at Keith's, his rooms at the Hotel Plaza on Columbus Avenue were deluged with unsolicited manuscripts. Most of them were one-acters aimed at variety presentation by unknown writers. The recipient nevertheless took pains to answer every one of them.

> *My dear Sir,*
>
> *I have read the little play & think it very powerful & interesting, but my intention at present is only to play in the Vaudeville Theatres for the few weeks that remain of this season—next year I shall be playing the regular theatre and am afraid would not have the opportunity to utilize a 1 act play. I am glad however to have read the play and testify to its merits.*
>
> > *I remain*
> > *Yours faithfully*
> >
> > *Maurice Barrymore*

Apart from the thoughtfulness of such replies, written on Hotel Plaza stationery, or that of other hotels in other cities on the Keith Circuit, they carried another implication. The weekly $750, three times his usual salary, and unquestioned stardom in continuous performance, had not vitiated Barry's legitimate concerns. He had already agreed to return in the fall to "regular theatre."

While in New York between Keith's bookings, Barry heard of his daughter's recent progress. When the *Rosemary* tour had reached St. Louis that spring, John Drew had handed his niece a wire from Charles Frohman: WOULD ETHEL LIKE TO GO TO LONDON WITH GILLETTE IN SECRET SERVICE? Since the idyllic family interlude in St. John's Wood, returning to London was Ethel's abiding dream. Frohman's offer would facilitate this return to the city of childhood memories. Moreover, she would be traveling in the company of William Gillette, her particular theatrical hero of the moment.

Barry, who had not seen his daughter since their Boston meeting two years before, was demonstrably excited about her good fortune. He boasted unceasingly to friends, and planned to give her a proper send-off. "My father heard about my leaving and promised to come down to the dock to see me off," Ethel remembered. "As he was a great friend of Gillette, he said he would introduce me to him, but knowing his genius for irresponsibility, I wasn't disappointed when he didn't turn up." Armed with her ticket, a carpet bag holding all of her possessions, and letters from Richard Harding Davis to Bernard Shaw and the Sidney Webbs, Ethel boarded the boat for England without benefit of Papa's patronage.

"In one evening," reported the London *Mail*, "*Secret Service* scored a victory and swept away all traditions." The Prince of Wales summoned William Gillette and Charles Frohman to the Adelphi royal box after the May 21st performance. His Royal Highness complimented Gillette upon the acting of his part—the part that Barry had originated in Philadelphia. Ethel's beauty drew comment in the role of *Miss Kittridge* ("Sewing for the Hospitals"), which consisted of walking on with some surgical bandages, saying a line or two, and retiring. It was hardly the young lady's stage career which won English and titillated American observers that season in London.

"No tendency of the time is more gratifying to friends of art in the best sense of the word than encouragement of closer relations existing between society and the stage. A very pleasant instance of this fact is the recent social success in London of Miss Ethel Barrymore." So wrote the New York *Journal* in one of the endless accounts and evaluations of Ethel's social triumphs in the year of Queen Victoria's Diamond Jubilee. Americans devoured reports of her attendance at the Duchess of Devonshire's fancy-dress ball, her standing invitation to the American Embassy every Thursday to pour tea with Ambassador Hay's daughters, her presentation to the Duke of York at Mrs. Cavendish-Bentinck's reception. "The young gentleman, who," sighed one reporter, "if he outlives his father, the Prince of Wales, will in time be the King of England, honored her with a ten or fifteen minutes conversation, evidently enjoying her comments on people and things."

The rest of the theatrical community, it was reported, noted with "awe" that she was the one actress honored with an invitation to the Queen's Jubilee garden party. She viewed the Jubilee parade from the privileged vantage of a Piccadilly town house. "It was a terrific spectacle, more magnificent, I think than any of the coronation parades that followed it," Ethel remarked. "I shall never forget the Indian princes, dripping from chin to waist with fabulous jewels, unbelievable strings of pearls, diamonds and rubies." Impressive, indeed, to a seventeen-year-old, who had conquered London society with live-oak leaves, in lieu of tiaras, twined in her hair, and one evening gown—a tight, homemade velvet affair that burst a seam while she danced with the Prince of Wales one evening.

"Don't you find when you go out to dinner in London," Helen Hay, the ambassador's daughter, asked Ethel, "that you have to take with you everything you ever knew or read to be able to cope with the brilliant young men?" Ethel had much to bring, coping not only with young men, who courted her relentlessly, but with the creative likes of Anthony Hope, Henry Irving, E. V. Lucas, Whistler, and Henry James. Although, in later years, she liked to remember herself as a "shy little mortal," Ethel Barrymore was anything but that. "Actually, the sweet young thing was a damosel of keen biting intellect, a sharp Irish mind, and a razor-sharp Irish tongue," attested Percy Burton, Henry Irving's business manager. "The roles she played were saccharine, the books she read were of the Nietzsche-Voltaire school." (Ethel's inveterate reading, "eating books," she called it, was a pastime shared by her brothers. "None of us had schooling that rates now with the education of a high school graduate," Jack Barrymore confessed. "Fortunately, however, we inherited from my father, a man of the highest English culture, a tremendous love for books. No matter where we were, there were good books to read, and we devoured everything within reach.")

On the evening of June 9, Ethel's social standing was briefly enhanced by professional accomplishment, when she was suddenly called upon to replace the ailing leading lady. Her appearance surprised most of the audience. The loud applause usually greeting the leading lady's entrance was absent that evening. "But the news of Miss Tyler's unfortunate illness had reached several of Miss Barrymore's personal friends," noted *The Era*, "and they were on hand, among the 'Standing Room Only' contingent, to welcome her with a little rattle of the palms." That rattle became an ovation at the end of the performance. The *Tribune*'s London correspondent wired a special dispatch to New York. "True to her pedigree," it began, "Miss Barrymore went straight at this difficult fence, and cleared it beautifully." When C.F. returned her to "Sewing for the Hospitals," Ethel, unaware that her manager was saving her for better things, was heartbroken. She determined to remain in London and succeed on her own.

William Gillette and his American company were returning to New York in August, relinquishing *Secret Service* to an English cast. With the day of departure approaching, Ethel had been unable to obtain another engagement. "Uncle John Drew was in London and might have helped her," brother Jack speculated, "but even when she was forced to admit she was licked, that she had to go back to New York or starve, Ethel wouldn't ask favors."

Henry Irving and Ellen Terry occupied an Adelphi box during the last London performance of Gillette's *Secret Service* company. Afterward, Miss Terry left a note for Ethel, asking her not to think of leaving London without saying good-by. Ethel, accordingly, ran over to the Lyceum before sailing, to see England's foremost actress, whose fifty years were belied by the fluffy, fine blond hair and deep turquoise eyes illuminating her girl-child face. Loving the young, loved by them in return, she was ageless. Ethel was her "Bullfinch," because, the actress said, she resembled that tiny bird. "Well, little Bullfinch," she tested, "I suppose you are glad to be going back to America?"

"Not at all," Ethel replied. "I have been a trifle anxious to see my grandmother upon the other side of the water, but I really don't care to leave London just yet."

"Well, my child, you need not go if you don't want to."

"And why? I can't find anything to do."

"Why, Sir Henry, I am sure, will employ you if you care to remain with us." Ethel's eyes widened.

"I should be delighted," she answered incredulously, "but I'm afraid there will be nothing that I could do in the Lyceum company."

"We will see about that," the actress said. It was known in theatrical circles that Henry Irving seldom refused Ellen Terry anything, and next day he sent a note offering Ethel a place in his company. She hurried over to the Lyceum to thank Sir Henry, once more expressing her fear that there would be nothing in any of his plays that she could undertake. The imperious Irving features, befitting the first actor to be honored by knighthood, softened.

"Oh, yes," he said, "I think there is a part that will suit you to a nicety in my son Laurence's new play, *Peter the Great*. I saw your acting the other evening, in company with Miss Terry, and we both feel that a triumph awaits you in the character we have chosen."

"And now, are you satisfied?" wondered Ellen Terry.

"Yes," said Ethel, "but—"

"But what? You are not getting homesick again?"

"Not exactly, but I would just like to run over to New York and tell my grandmother good-by."

"Well, my child, you can," Miss Terry countered. "There is yet nearly two months, perhaps more, before we do this play and you will have ample time to go to America and back before even rehearsals begin."

"Yes," repeated Ethel hesitantly, "but—"

"Oh," interrupted Sir Henry, "I see." He stepped over to his desk, wrote out a check, presented it to the girl. "There now, you can go, go with me, let us say, tell your grandmother all about it, bid her good-by and run back in a week or so to begin work with us in right down good fashion."

Mrs. John Drew reached her seventy-seventh year on the road, touring in the title role of *The Sporting Duchess*. There were complications. A recent heart ailment combined with a recurrent kidney complaint hindered her playing of the lengthy star part. Mrs. Drew made no mention of these afflictions, but for the first time in her long career, she made her excuses. "She had only played the part a few nights," said Frank Perley, the company manager, "when she sent me word she would have to resign. There were too many changes of costume for one of her years, and then, too, she was afraid of the horses." Seventy years after being thrown by a horse and nearly killed on the stage of Cooke's amphitheatre, Liverpool, Louisa Lane Drew retired, or, rather, as she was quick to correct, "rested" from the stage. "To the last minute, it never occurred to her that she had retired," said her grandson, Lionel. "She was confident that she would be on stage again next year." And so it seemed.

On February 26, when the Professional Women's League held its annual reception at the Waldorf, Mrs. Drew, charter member and vice-president, participated, playing with "characteristic cleverness." She was also among the stars in attendance when J. H. Stoddart received a loving cup commemorating his sixty years as an actor. Many great stars formed a line on the stage of the Academy of Music to honor Mr. Stoddart. Mrs. Drew and C. W. Couldock, being the oldest, were brought chairs. Mrs. Drew sat down. Couldock did not. The lady wanted to know why. "I don't want them to think I'm too old to stand," answered the gentleman.

"Neither do I," replied Mrs. Drew, quickly standing up. And Couldock could not persuade her to sit down again.

Mrs. Drew's ailments were aggravated by the coming of hot weather. She retired to the Bevan House in May, where absence of any immediate family emphasized the consequences of an actor's lot. Her elder son was touring the Pacific coast in *Rosemary*. His wife, Josephine, had returned to France, while Louise completed her schooling there. Sidney and

Gladys Drew were in England, making a great hit in the music halls. Ethel was also performing in England. Lionel, having left art school to earn his living, was on tour in the Middle West. Jack was still at school in Georgetown.

The solitary matriarch made the best of her situation at Larchmont. The long latticed porch of the Bevan House overlooked Long Island Sound. Seated in a stiff wicker chair, a small writing table before her, she worked on the memoirs which one day would be published posthumously. Mr. and Mrs. Bevan, proprietors of the hotel, were old friends. She soon made new friends among the others. They all showed proprietary concern for Mrs. Drew, inquiring each day as to her health and comfort, ministering to her needs as she worked on the veranda. She was visited by columnist "Penn." of the Philadelphia *Times:* "Her memory of what she had done or seen in the course of nearly eighty years seemed to be copious and accurate, but her conversation was colored with the sense of sorrow that she was living in what, artistically, she thought to be a dissolute and degenerate age. I doubt whether she ever felt happy after the doors of the old Arch had closed upon her for the last time."

When school let out early in June, Jack Barrymore joined his grandmother at the Bevan House. "Penn." described him as "a manly fellow of fifteen," bearing a striking physical resemblance to his father. But he was shy, devoted to his grandmother, fiercely possessive of her devotion to him. "She was fond of me, fonder, I think I may say, than of any of her grandchildren," Jack stated proudly. "Lionel always was a steady citizen and never did outrageous things. Ethel behaved herself perfectly. I was always getting into trouble, as Sidney Drew had done. Yet I was Grandmother Drew's favorite grandchild, and it was family tradition that she had always favored Sidney over John Drew."

Jack attended to the needs and amusement of his ailing grandmother at the Bevan House. Escorting her to a cotillion in the clubhouse of the hotel, he did not dance. He stood dutifully by her side, as she watched young ladies in white summer dresses whirl by. The beauty of that youthful scene impressed Mrs. Drew. She spoke of it often that summer. She spoke of many things to her grandson that summer, but as weeks passed, her memory seemed to fade. "She would break into the middle of a topic as though we had left it but a minute before," Jack recalled. "Mostly, she spoke of other times and other manners in the world of the theater." He would listen attentively to his grandmother's ramblings. When she tired, he would help her upstairs, fetch basins of hot water and bathe her swollen feet and ankles, before putting her to bed.

Lionel visited Larchmont between tours. He found Mummum sitting in a rocking chair on the long veranda, gazing out toward the Sound, while Jack perched close by on the railing, sketching seascapes. "My grandmother regarded illness as a kind of gaucherie," Lionel observed, "as a combination of social and professional error which no well brought up Drew would permit. But on this visit I found her in grave pain, although she gallantly and lightly denied it." They talked, instead, of Ethel's recent adventures in London, of Lionel's reluctant acting career.

"An actor," admonished Mrs. Drew, "should play his part as carefully as if he knew that everyone in the house is watching him with a prompt book in their hands." Offended by her grandson's consideration of acting as merely a profitable alternative to painting, she reminded him of the constant study and discipline necessary to achieve theatrical excellence. "I was intensely enthusiastic in my feeling for my profession, as, indeed, I am yet. I applied myself to studying it with great zeal, and was extremely anxious that the audiences and everybody should like me. To these feelings I attribute most of my early success."

"How did you find time to go to school, Mummum?" Lionel wondered.

"How did I find time to go to school?" she repeated. "Bless you! I never went to school. I studied my profession, as I say, but that was about all my school days consisted of—just one quarter in London when I was a very little girl and a few months of attendance at a school in Baltimore. Aside from that I have absorbed what general information I possess. I have learned my lessons from experience and the open book of life. And, then, acquaintance and friendship with the great number of extremely clever and talented people I have known is a liberal education in itself."

Mrs. Drew repeated as much to Ethel when her granddaughter arrived from England to spend ten days at the Bevan House. She added more, besides, in an effort to bequeath, if not worldly goods, of which she had few, at least the wealth of experience. An inordinate amount of newspaper space heralding Ethel's return to America had convinced her grandmother that firm guidance was in order. The New York *Tribune* had even presumed to credit Ethel's social success to her distinguished Drew lineage. As Jack read this to her, Mrs. Drew humbugged such presumptions. While being pleased for her granddaughter, and somewhat flattered herself, she feared that the girl might mistake social success and celebrity for professional achievement.

She attempted small talk when Ethel first arrived—about the hotel and its patrons, about the engagement with Henry Irving, which seemed to please her, although her only direct comment upon the subject was, "Can you always understand what he says?" Small talk gave way suddenly to more essential concerns. "You must be intensely fond of your profession," she told Ethel, "and apply yourself to the study and practice of it with utmost diligence, leaving nothing undone to constantly improve." She spoke of earlier days, of stardom earned, not managed. "There were not many stars in those days. Managers put all their strength into their companies; a company often comprised thirty or forty people, every one first-class in his or her respective line. All the people strove to do their best," she emphasized. "The utility men took just as much pains with a part of eight or ten lines as the leading man did with the principal part."

When Ethel sailed for England on the *Paris*, the New York *Journal* explained that "though her stay has been brief, she has had a great deal of attention paid her in a social way, so that she can make no invidious comparisons between her reception at home and abroad." She had not returned for society. Her memory of that visit would remain singular. "I saw a great deal of Mrs. Drew then," she recalled, "and I can't remember the time when I did not want to be a woman like her, as dignified and great-hearted and generous."

Mrs. Drew had rallied for the visits of Lionel and Ethel. Afterward, she seemed to wilt. Jack would carry her downstairs to the porch every morning, where she would sit rocking all day. "She had innumerable paper-backed books, and there was always one in her hands, but she seldom read." Jack remembered. "She sat gazing across the Sound, but she was really gazing at old half-forgotten things, things that had once seemed important and which were now becoming confused in her mind."

On Saturday, August 29, she felt well enough to play cards with her nieces, Mrs. J. C. Stewald and Mrs. C. T. Hitchings, nonprofessional relatives of her late husband.

On Sunday, her condition worsened. Dr. C. W. Jackson, who had been in regular attendance, called in Dr. W. E. Bullard for consultation. They decided to summon the immediate family at once. John Drew made arrangements to leave his company at Salt Lake City. Mrs. Stewald and Mrs. Hitchings arrived from New York.

On Monday, Mrs. Drew rallied. Her son postponed his departure from Salt Lake City until Tuesday night, in order to complete the engagement there.

She seemed in good spirits on Tuesday morning during a long and pleasant talk with her grandson. He left her bedside, smiling, telling concerned residents of the Bevan House that she appeared much improved. She chatted for a few minutes with Mrs. Bevan, recalling the beauty of the scene in the clubhouse on cotillion evening. She called for Jack again, reached over and touched his arm, and fell into what was hoped would be natural sleep. After examining her, however, Dr. Jackson disclosed that she was not likely to revive.

Reporters were clamoring on the front lawn. Jack composed himself, went down to make a statement. "You know her age," he said, "there is very little vitality. Her heart is very weak, and I think the greatest immediate danger lies there." He returned to his grandmother's bedside to keep vigil with Mrs. Stewald and Mrs. Hitchings, Mrs. Bevan and the doctor.

Louisa Drew lay unconscious until seven minutes before three, when she was taken with a slight convulsion. The end came at three o'clock.

Across the nation which she had so assiduously trouped, newspapers invoked that oft-used phrase, accurately, for once, the end of an era. "Mrs. Drew is dead," declared the *Dramatic Mirror*, "but she will live long in memory, and in the nineteenth century records of the American stage hers will ever remain a prominent and representative name. She was an excellent actress, and was more than this. In the field of theatrical management she was eminently successful, and she lent additional honor to the name of mother."

Headline reports and tributes emphasized the professionalism and longevity of the actress, while telegrams and statements from friends and colleagues recalled the woman. "I have known Mrs. Drew nearly half a century," recalled C. W. Couldock. "We played together in Albany away back in 1850, and she was then regarded as one of the foremost actresses on the American stage. Mr. Drew was a member of the same company, and she married him at the end of the season. To me she was always one of the most charming women of my acquaintance and an accomplished and a versatile actress. She was always so bright and happy" —the old actor's voice caught for a moment—"that age seemed to have no effect on her, and I can scarcely realize now that she's dead and gone."

Despite John Drew's wish to keep services for his mother as private as possible, a throng filled St. Stephen's Episcopal Church. The number of family, friends, and colleagues, an honor roll of the American theater, whose careers Louisa Lane Drew had touched upon as actress and manageress, was augmented by hundreds of strangers. They displayed none of the morbid curiosity peculiar to those usually drawn to a celebrity's funeral. They seemed, rather, a group of representative patrons dutifully attending a farewell performance, for, as the local *Times* explained, "In thousands of Philadelphia homes there has been felt toward her by the old or has been inherited by the young something like a spirit of kinship."

The coffin rested in front of the altar amid mounds of flowers. From London, Sidney Drew sent a pillow of roses and asters with the words, MOTHER, FROM SIDNEY, in blue immortelles. There was a large wreath of white roses and wild flowers from John Drew; a great heart of autumn leaves from Joseph Jefferson; splendid offerings from, among others, Charles Frohman, Ada Rehan, Augustin Daly, A. M. Palmer, the Elks, the Twelfth Night Club, the Professional Women's League. Overlooked amid more elaborate offerings was a small bouquet from Maurice Barrymore.

As their carriage negotiated the crowd from church to railroad station, Joseph Jefferson addressed Francis Wilson. "I doubt," he said, "if the death of any lady in Philadelphia would awaken such interest or draw together such a number of people." The old actor had managed excellent control during the church service. But his head was bowed on the way to the station, his lips were trembling. A great throng had gone to Glenwood Cemetery in trolley cars and carriages. Joseph Jefferson was not among them. His excellent control would not have withstood the burial of his honored friend.

Others who had come from New York left on a later afternoon train. John Drew made connections to rejoin his company in Salt Lake City. Jack Barrymore, alone and bewildered, boarded the train that would return him to school in Georgetown. ("When my masters, the psychologists, the psychiatrists, and the learned reporters who attempt to explain everything about everybody from the dream-books, apply their techniques to John Barrymore," his brother observed, "I make the simple suggestion that they remember that his grandmother who reared him and adored him died when he was fifteen. Jack never felt safe anywhere after that.")

Ethel received the cable at her London lodgings, as she was about to leave for her first rehearsal with the Lyceum Theatre company. "Oh, Missie, you're late!" admonished the stage doorman when she finally arrived. The company was standing about, waiting. Sir Henry Irving, at his imperious best, sat alone stage center, staring coldly from under his formidable eyebrows at the latecomer.

"Sir Henry," she sputtered, "I'm terribly sorry to be late, but something terrible has happened." He continued staring. Nothing could excuse lateness to a Lyceum rehearsal. "I just got a cable that my grandmother has died." Irving raised his eyebrows.

"Mrs. John Drew?" he asked. When Ethel nodded, his face suddenly softened. "She was the finest actress in her line that I have ever seen." The great man was whispering. "Go home, my dear," he said. "No rehearsal for you today."

Barry had been out West on the Keith Circuit when Mrs. Drew died. A month later he was making another bid for legitimate success as *Jean Lafitte* in *A Ward of France*. The play was given its first tryout performance in Scranton, Pennsylvania, on October 14. It moved to the Walnut Street Theatre in Philadelphia four days later. He reached the city of his first wife's forebears on a clear and sunny afternoon. Clemency fortified his resolve to pay last respects to Mrs. Drew.

He had not visited Glenwood Cemetery since Georgie was buried there nearly five years before, but he easily found the family plot. Mrs. Drew had been placed between her last husband and her younger daughter, near her mother, her half sisters, Adine and Georgiana Kinlock, her stepdaughter, Adine Stephens. According to his mother's wishes, John Drew had marked her grave with a simple stone engraved with a stanza from Mrs. Barbauld's poem:

> Life! we've been long together,
> Through pleasant and through cloudy weather;
> 'Tis hard to part when friends are dear;
> Perhaps 'twill cause a sigh, a tear;
> Then steal away, give little warning,
>> Choose thine own time;
>> Say not Good-Night, but in some brighter clime,
>> Bid me Good-Morning.

The visit unnerved Maurice Barrymore. He would not return to that place where Georgie and his past lay buried, until he was brought there finally to join them.

XXX

Barry was duped again by Charles Frohman. Unaware of the ubiquitous manager's involvement, he had agreed to play *Jean Lafitte* in *A Ward of France*. Klaw & Erlanger had signed him, were credited with the production. It soon became apparent, however, who pulled the strings. C.F. had wanted Barrymore as *Lafitte*, and, knowing that the actor would not work for him again, had delegated others to do his bidding. So the independent leading man was involved with a "Trust show," a designation which became volatile during its Boston run. Barry had intimations of a burgeoning theatrical trust while touring for Frohman in *Aristocracy*. Since then, the manager had consolidated his interests, gained powerful allies. He was pitting a streamlined organization against independent managers and actors who refused to capitulate.

Most of the theatrical community had acquiesced at first, appeased by C.F.'s front of well-deserved prestige. For all his wiles, Frohman possessed a genuine love of theater and excellence. But his allies, the ruthless works behind the front, Alf and Dave Hayman, his business manager and treasurer, were prevailing. They began by drastically reducing the terms of such stars as Modjeska and Fanny Davenport, because, according to Alf Hayman, they were getting old and losing their box-office appeal. Incensed by such methods, Francis Wilson chose to play independent theaters rather than renewing his contracts with Frohman & Co. When the Trust began an overt campaign to break the defector, the *Dramatic Mirror*, which maintained a neutral policy, covered both sides of the skirmish. Such objectivity was apparently not enough, or, perhaps, too much, for the Trust. Alf Hayman stormed the offices of Harrison Grey Fiske, the *Mirror*'s editor and publisher.

"Fiske, I order you not to make another mention of the Theatrical Syndicate in your paper!" Hayman commanded. "What the Syndicate does is my private business and no concern of the theatrical profession or the public."

"On the contrary," Fiske replied, "actors and managers have a right to opinions about their profession, and everyone concerned has obligations to the public. The *Dramatic Mirror* will continue to report matters of general interest, without fear or favor."

"You go and do that," cried Hayman, "and I'll kill the *Mirror*, break you, and drive Mrs. Fiske from the stage!"

Fiske announced, soon after Hayman's visit, that the *Mirror* would print a monthly supplement devoted to "fighting the Trust." Syndicate magnates threatened to have him jailed for malicious libel. The Washington *Post* and the New York *World* rallied to his defense. "That this organization is beginning to adopt a high-handed style of dealing with opposition is proved by its treatment of the New York *Dramatic Mirror*," declared the *Post*. "In Philadelphia this paper has been barred from all hotel news-stands that sell tickets to Syndicate theatres, and for some time past the *Mirror* has been forbidden even to mention the firm name of Klaw and Erlanger on penalty of exclusion from the news companies. Moreover, a reputable theatrical manager told the *Post* yesterday that he had been ordered to take his advertisement out of the *Mirror* if he wished to book his attractions in syndicate houses."

At the Boston Theatre, the business manager of Klaw & Erlanger's *Ward of France* company posted a warning:

NOTICE IS HEREBY GIVEN THAT, UNDER PAIN OF DISMISSAL, MEMBERS OF THE CAST ARE FORBIDDEN TO ADVERTISE IN, BUY OR READ THE NEW YORK *DRAMATIC MIRROR*.

Barry read the notice, rushed out, bought a copy of the paper, and dispatched a wire:

HARRISON GREY FISKE
DRAMATIC MIRROR
NEW YORK, N. Y.

HAVE RARELY READ A DRAMATIC NEWSPAPER BUT WILL READ THE MIRROR REGULARLY HEREAFTER

MAURICE BARRYMORE

Anticipating a confrontation, he returned to the Boston Theatre flagrantly displaying his copy of the forbidden journal. He was disappointed. The manager, fearing repercussions from his unlawful threat, had removed the notice. Barry nevertheless continued to denounce the Trust from the unique vantage of one of its own companies. The magnates took no immediate action against the rebel. That would have merely supplied additional ammunition to their opposition. Besides, Maurice Barrymore was drawing patrons to their otherwise unexceptional production of *A Ward of France*.

Barry's swashbuckling portrayal of pirate *Jean Lafitte* was popular in spite of or, perhaps, because of the role's exaggerated heroics. "Mr. Barrymore's *Lafitte* is the conventional brigand of grand opera," noted the Boston *Globe*, "and he is therefore, to be consistent, forced to be as unreal as he can be." His leading lady, Emily Rigl, up to the vigorous standard of her London *Nadjezda*, played a passionate, vindictive fortuneteller. But any critical attention paid to Barry's latest starring attempt was overshadowed, as were most theatrical events during the early months of 1898, by Trust-Independent battles.

When the play reached New York in January, critics took sides and reviewed accordingly. The *Sun*, on the side of the Trust—in its pay, some said—was contradicted by the *Dramatic Mirror*, spokesman for the Independents: "The New York *Sun* says that '*A Ward of France* has met with ready acceptance at Wallack's;' that 'its florid and active blend of creole romance and Louisiana history has been rewarded by enthusiastic audiences;' that 'Maurice Barrymore and Emily Rigl have made the hits of their stage careers;' and that it 'was booked for two weeks, but a third will be added if the coming of *The Salt of the Earth* can be delayed a little.' In point of fact, *A Ward of France* was just put on for a run, and it is to be withdrawn because it is as dire a failure in New York as it was at the Boston Theatre a month ago. It is a 'Trust show.'"

Barry was not concerned with the play's reception. He, too, was preoccupied with the battle, making fiery curtain speeches denouncing the Trust, helping to form the Association for the Promotion and Protection of an Independent Stage in the United States. His allies in that lofty venture included such stalwart advocates of independence as Mr. and Mrs. Fiske, Modjeska, Joseph Jefferson, Augustin Daly, William A. Brady, and John Norris, crusading editor of the *World*, who printed a front-page attack on the Trust's "systematically and persistently practiced fraud and deceit on the public."

Momentum was gathering. James O'Neill blasted the Trust all along the route of his annual *Monte Cristo* tour. Francis Wilson made a triumphal anti-Trust tour of New England, traveling on a special train with the Second Regimental Band. Sarah Bernhardt, rather than submit to syndicate demands, played the United States in a portable circus tent. Such was the power of the Trust as it reached out cold-bloodedly, raiding talent, acquiring theaters. But it seemed that Their High Mightinesses had a full-scale rebellion on their hands. Richard Mansfield, most avid of the independent crusaders, haranguing the opposition while playing its theaters, was elected president of the Association by an overwhelming majority.

On the eve of the Association's incorporation, the heart was cut out of the rebellion. The Trust bought Richard Mansfield. Disheartened independents, one by one, capitulated to syndicate demands or were forced into retirement. The *World* abruptly stopped its attack. Only the Fiskes, Barry, and a few other die-hards continued the active fight. "People lamenting the well-known 'decline of the American theater,'" wrote William A. Brady forty years later, "give you every reason for it, from the introduction of coeducational drinking to the periodic recurrence of sun-spots. As one who saw the syndicate rise and fall and fought it every step of the way, I can tell you that its injection of big business into the theatrical game had more to do with the decline of the American theater than any other ten things you can mention."

The turncoat *World*, apparently, had more immediate theatrical news to report in that crucial January of 1898. As Barry swashbuckled west with *A Ward of France*, reviling his employers as he went, a *World* headline proclaimed:

YANKEE BRIDE FOR IRVING

Son of the Great English Actor Betrothed
to Miss Ethel Barrymore

The announcement, it transpired, was slightly premature. Not for Laurence Irving's lack of trying. He had been infatuated by Ethel since first seeing her in London. In fact, it was he who had asked Ellen Terry to convince his father to hire the young American. Proximity had fanned his ardor, as they toured the English provinces with the Lyceum company, rehearsing his new play, *Peter the Great*. Young Irving's ardor was something to be reckoned with. Since his return from Russia, where he had been the guest-student of Tolstoy, a theatrical sense of Russian gloom pervaded his plays and personality. One of his creations, *Godfroi and Zolande*, began with the stage direction "Enter a chorus of lepers."

Ethel, intrigued by such somber intensity, responded in kind. Back in London after the tour, their romance continued along its morbid path. He proposed marriage half-a-dozen times; Ethel finally gave in. "A curious thing about me at this time—and practically always—" she disclosed, "was that, in spite of the fact that I saw nothing of my father, or, shall I say, he saw nothing of me, I still had a strong urge to belong to someone, and there was no one left but my father. So I cabled him at the Lambs' Club, the only address I knew, telling him of my engagement."

Since Barry was playing St. Louis at the time, the cable did not reach him immediately. But he must have been experiencing strong familial urges of his own. After news of Ethel's engagement broke in the local papers on January 23, a reporter from the St. Louis *Star* found him awaiting confirmation from his daughter. "Maurice Barrymore, the father of Miss Barrymore, is at present playing in *A Ward of France* at the Columbus Theatre," noted the *Star*'s front-page report. "Up to a late hour last night he had not heard from his daughter about the engagement. He had, however, left word at the stage door that any cablegram which might arrive should be brought to him immediately."

Later that night, two cable dispatches were delivered to his hotel. ENGAGED TO LAURENCE IRVING. HAVE BOTH WRITTEN. LOVE ETHEL, read the first. HOPE YOU WILL APPROVE MY ENGAGEMENT TO YOUR DAUGHTER. HAVE WRITTEN. LAURENCE IRVING, added the second.

"My daughter, while less than eighteen years old, is a girl who knows her own mind," Barry assured the *Star* reporter. "I am perfectly satisfied with her choice, and it is especially gratifying to me to recollect the many pleasant things I have heard of young Irving in the days when I had not thought of him as a possible son-in-law. I know him to be a very bright young man, and although he is barely twenty-five he has met splendid success in his writings." The impending marriage of a daughter, it appeared, could make even the most detached parent wax paternal. "I cannot say how pleased I am that my daughter should have selected one of her own profession for a husband. It is manifestly unwise for professional people to intermarry with non-professionals, since the desire for their art is sure to return, which will mean a separation likely to become permanent." He cabled his consent to Laurence, and to Ethel wired simply, CONGRATULATIONS. LOVE. FATHER.

Winning the girl that he loved, coupled with his acceptance as a playwright after *Peter the Great* opened, changed Laurence Irving. "He got all cheerful and hearty," Ethel contended, "and I couldn't bear him." She broke the engagement, and apprehensively cabled the news to her father. His reply was reassuring: CONGRATULATIONS. LOVE. FATHER.

A Ward of France ended its tour in St. Louis. The Trust had survived Barry's relentless needling, but Charles Frohman would never quite regain the unquestioned respect which he had once enjoyed. Nor would Barry ever again work for Frohman or his cohorts.

He returned to vaudeville at Proctor's Theatre in New York. *A Man of the World* was the vehicle, Mamie the leading lady, and, as before, the public responded heartily to the package. During the run, his family feeling was again challenged. Word came from Georgetown Prep that Jack had been expelled for a "serious breach of conduct." The wire did not elaborate. He waited curiously for the Baltimore & Ohio to deliver his son to Pennsylvania Station.

Jack, verging on sixteen, was reticent at first, releasing only strained bits of the story as his father probed. Some older boys, it seemed, had taken him along on a visit to a Washington bawdyhouse. Jack had been in the parlor merely "chatting with a nice lady," when a raid ensued. The other boys had escaped. Jack was captured and taken to the headmaster. A faculty committee had attempted to ascertain the names of his accomplices. When the boy refused to divulge them, he was expelled. "I didn't do anything in that house, Papa," Jack protested. "I mean . . ."

"I know precisely what you mean," Papa interrupted. "Didn't do anything, eh? Why not?" Far from punishing the boy, Papa presented him with a ticket to the Creedon-McCoy fight as a birthday present—all the more unusual because Barry never remembered birthdays—not even his own. As he was playing at Proctor's, and unable to attend himself, Jack was charged with reporting the rounds in detail afterward. "Some time after midnight the lad appeared at the Lambs," recounted the *Herald*, "and from then on till gray dawn the battle was fought over with deepest interest on both sides. Barry declared it was the best report of a fight he had ever had."

When Barry sailed for England early that spring to appear in a West End production of *The Heart of Maryland*, his younger son and his second wife were along. Such fatherly devotion, unusual for Maurice Barrymore, was borne by Mamie with polite indifference. Any chance to travel with her husband was reward enough. And it became apparent, even to Mamie, that Jack needed his father.

Lionel and Ethel had always been fiercely independent—the elder son content to pursue art studies and occasional acting chores with few favors from anyone; the daughter capable of facing world and profession unaided. Jack, pampered by his late grandmother, seemed more vulnerable. Lionel and Ethel resembled their mother in appearance. Jack had his father's voice, physique, agility, and, increasingly, his "epic frailties," as Gene Fowler later observed, "the thoughtless behaviorisms, the capricious tendencies for self-ruination." Barry had always shared terms of good fellowship with his elder son while being somewhat awed by his daughter. The youngest, however, inspired an unfamiliar sense of paternal responsibility.

Jack was enrolled at King's College School, where Henry Wace happened to be headmaster. Not that Barry had consulted the prominent brother of his sister's husband. He still held resentment for the man who had been his mentor during Oxford days, administrator of his allowance, and, later, the Commissioner's spokesman against his boxing and acting proclivities. Lionel Brough, an actor friend from those early London days, after whom Lionel Barrymore had been named, had arranged for Jack's admission to King's. Member of a noted English acting family, Brough had himself attended the school. Barry considered this recommendation more tenable than one from his highly placed relative by marriage.

Coincidentally, Evelin, the sister whose marriage had facilitated the Blyth-Wace tie in the first place, had returned widowed to London. Brother and sister met for the first time since Barry had left their home in Amritsar forty years before. The resemblance of the siblings was startling for more than physical appearance. Northern gray eyes, finely chiseled features were augmented by more subtle similarities of spirit. After her husband, Colonel Edward Wace, died while Commissioner at Lahore, Evelin had taken her inheritance and several children, and toured the Continent for several years. Unconcerned with the formal education of her brood, the Commissioner's daughter had continued on her adventurous way until money ran low, forcing her to settle on her widow's pension in King Henry's Road, Hampstead.

Preferring, perhaps, to leave memories of his Anglo-Indian upbringing dormant, Barry saw little of his older sister during that spring in London. But Ethel and Jack were delighted by the appearance of Aunt "Eva" and their Wace cousins. While they stayed in England, the Hampstead house became a congenial retreat for them.

King's College School had recently been moved, after seventy years, from the Strand to Wimbledon Common. In this bucolic suburb of London, Jack excelled in extracurricular activities. "In appearance and manner, he is very like his father," noted the New York *Tribune*, "and the possession of prize cups won at King's College for running and jumping gives further evidence of the likeness between sire and son. Incidentally, he dearly loves sparring." Scholastic requirements ran a poor second to sports, although he displayed talent for freehand and mechanical drawing offered in the Modern Division of the Upper School. He was also prodigious at inventing excuses for weekend permissions to visit his father in London. He was bothered, however, by the necessity of traveling in third-class compartments on these excursions.

"How is it," he asked his father, "that while all of my friends, sons of fathers of whom no one has ever heard, travel first or second, *I*, the son of the great Maurice Barrymore, have to travel third?"

"You travel third, my son," Papa explained, "because there is no fourth!"

The Heart of Maryland opened on April 8, providing Barry with a triumph comparable to his London debut in *Diplomacy* twelve years before. "None of the artists have any chance of greatly distinguishing themselves in their indifferent parts; but Mr. Maurice Barrymore gave a vigorous and forcible interpretation to the role of *Colonel Alan Kendrick*." *The Era* was not alone in its estimate of Barry's playing, but its tepid response to the play was unique. London reviewers and theatergoers reveled in Belasco's Civil War melodrama and Mrs. Leslie Carter's re-creation of her celebrated role.

The rush on the Royal Adelphi box office for tickets to an American war play was attributed in part to concurrent reports from abroad. Newspapers transmitted America's jingoistic frenzy, which would culminate, one month later, in the Spanish-American War. The various attractions of Mrs. Carter and Mr. Barrymore, however, could not be overlooked. Even the dissenting George Bernard Shaw conceded in London's *Saturday Review* that "*The Heart of Maryland* is not a bad specimen of the American machine-made melodrama. The actors know the gymnastics of their business, and work harder and more smartly, and stick to it better than English actors." The once-impecunious author of *Cashel Byron's Profession* had become, in the dozen years since Barry had befriended him, one of England's most powerful critics and promising playwrights.

Barry was not immune to the praise of a London triumph, nor nonplussed when much of the press considered it his London debut. *The Sketch*, in a three-page *Heart of Maryland* layout, introduced him as "father of Ethel Barrymore, who has become a favourite on this side of the Atlantic." Far from offending him, his designation as Ethel's father made him very proud indeed.

Ethel was delighting Lyceum audiences in Sir Henry's repertory that spring. Her break with Laurence Irving had injured neither her professional nor social standing. With Suzanne Sheldon, another young American in the Lyceum company, she shared a flat over Heinemann's publishing offices, on the fringe of Covent Garden. Across the street lived Ben Webster, also a Lyceum player, and his wife, May Whitty. Since theatrical and social London's younger set ran back and forth between the two flats, Ethel's smaller abode was called the "Left Bank of Bedford Street."

May Whitty decribed Ethel at eighteen—"eager young face and beautiful line of jaw . . . her hair blonde cendrée, swept back in wings . . . low, throaty voice and gurgling laugh . . ." May's daughter, Margaret Webster, later revealed tales of the Left Bank's beautiful inmate and the single evening dress which, by the clever addition of various neckpieces and undersleeves, saw her and Suzanne Sheldon through a sociable season. She also passed on Suzanne's stories of her much-courted roommate—"mischievous stories about the romantic heroine of the hour: how she had woken in the middle of the night, flung her arms to heaven in a gesture of despair, cried out in her famous contralto: 'God! How bored I am!' and instantly gone off to sleep again."

Whatever Ethel did that spring was news: Whether she dined with ardent Anthony Hope, author of *The Prisoner of Zenda*, at his house in Buckingham Street, attended a private viewing at the New Gallery with Mrs. Beerbohm Tree and May Whitty, danced with the Prince of Wales, who would be Edward VII, chatted with the Duke of York, who would be George V, or "starved" on the Thames embankment. This last occurred when she and Constance Collier, a Gaiety Girl, and Cissie Loftus, wonder-child of the Music Halls, decided that they needed "realistic experience," such as starving on the banks of the Thames. "After a good supper at the Carlton and having provided themselves with a bag of buns," wrote actress Lena Ashwell, "they sat through the summer night, enduring pangs of hunger, gazing at the Thames." The three actresses later described their ordeal as "most thrilling."

The second Mrs. Barrymore had expressed little concern for the welfare of her husband's children. She considered Jack's London dependence rather an intrusion, yet developed an uncharacteristic interest in Ethel, repeatedly suggesting to her husband that proper family meetings should be arranged. Far from experiencing maternal pangs, Mamie merely sought to bask in the reflection of her stepdaughter's social triumphs. Barry probably did not comprehend such motivation, but he understood Ethel's resentment of his young wife. Forestalling a confrontation between them, he occasionally called at 21 Bedford Street without Mamie. During these visits to his daughter, which were formal and usually in the presence of others, he impressed both sides of Bedford Street. Ethel's friends marveled at the appearance and manner of her illustrious parent, who, one year short of fifty, had lost none of his magnetism. When Suzanne Sheldon gushed over how attractive he was, Ethel seemed somewhat surprised. "Yes," she murmured, "I suppose he is . . ."

Despite the lack of her stepdaughter's patronage, Mamie was introduced to London's theatrical elite. Her husband's many friends, including the Bancrofts, the Beerbohm Trees, the Kendals, welcomed and entertained her. Comparisons to Georgie were inevitable, but the youth and charm of the second Mrs. Barrymore made a favorable impression. Barry, meanwhile, partook of club life in his old city with English cronies and visiting Americans, leaving a fair share of "Barrymore stories" behind when he and Mamie sailed for America in July.

One evening, it was related, W. S. Gilbert had imperiously approached a hatless fellow outside of the London Lambs' Club, assuming that he was a vagrant. "Here, you," Gilbert commanded, "call me a four-wheeler."

"You are a four-wheeler," replied the assumed vagrant, with a distinguished salute.

"How dare you," sputtered Gilbert.

"Oh, by all means a four-wheeler, my dear sir," the fellow continued; "anybody could see you are not a hansom man."

Mr. and Mrs. Herbert Beerbohm Tree and his half brother, Max Beerbohm, later discussed that confrontation. "Shaw is a mischievous wit," remarked young Beerbohm, who would succeed him as *Saturday Review* drama critic, "plucky and Irish as clover. You know it was Shaw who took such an amusing rise out of Gilbert over the cab order."

"Oh, no," corrected Mrs. Tree, "that was not Shaw, that was Yeats."

"Not a bit of it," Tree interjected. "I had it credited to Barrymore, and that is about as near as wit ever roosts upon its home perch."

The actor's Haymarket triumphs, twelve years past, had been long forgotten. Recent acclaim at the Adelphi faded in the wake of his own personality. His acceptance in the West End, rare at times when Americans were merely tolerated by theatrical London, was overshadowed by more ephemeral products of his wit. It was never the actor, somehow, that was remembered, but the good fellow. His bons mots were repeated in salons, club smokers, theatrical biographies. His plays and performances were neglected in the more durable annals of the English theater.

Jack moved into his sister's flat at 21 Bedford Street for that summer of 1898. Before sailing, Papa had entrusted Ethel with money for his keep and further schooling in the fall. The young man preferred to be close to the source of his income. He did not, however, choose to participate in the festivities of the Left Bank. Jack, at sixteen, was terribly shy. While open and amusing with the sister who was becoming a near substitute for Mrs. Drew, he retreated when she hosted such galas as a tea for the American cast of *The Belle of New York*, including Aunt Gladys's sister, Phyllis Rankin, and her fiancé, Harry Davenport. Jack would not come downstairs to join them. "I said, 'You've got to,' but he wouldn't," recalled Ethel. "He broke out into a cold sweat, and I didn't ask him any more."

Jack was not averse, however, to tagging along with Ethel and Gerald du Maurier on hansom-cab rides to Hampstead Heath, where the three of them played "Red Indian" games. Gerald, actor son of the late author of *Trilby* and *Peter Ibbetson*, was tall, witty, charming, the opposite of Laurence Irving. He called Ethel "Daphne," because she twined oak leaves in her hair, and fell brightly in love with her. Papa had been allowed to give his consent to their engagement before English and American papers exploited it.

At first, Gerald's protective mother, his three doting sisters, his watchful older brother had fretted over the loss of their youngest. (Years later, Daphne du Maurier, Gerald's daughter, who had been named for his first love, reflected the family's reservations: " 'Daphne' was very young and pretty, and undeniably charming, and of course one knew who were her people, and she seemed very talented and all that; but really these things did not mean that she would make Gerald happy, and how could she possibly know her own mind at nineteen? She was very self-willed.") When the protective du Mauriers had finally decided that marriage and "Daphne" were just the thing for their Gerald, and newspapers were filled with reports of the forthcoming wedding, the bride-to-be experienced her own second thoughts. She visited Jackwood

Hall, the Shooters Hill estate of Nat C. Goodwin and his current wife, Maxine Elliott, to debate whether or not to marry Gerald. Still undecided, she agreed, at Gerald's urging, to accompany him and Harry Esmond on a fishing trip to Ireland, where she would once and for all make her decision.

At the Bay View Hotel, Waterville, where they stayed, Ethel captivated everyone. "She played the piano, and was temperamental, and wore her hair in a pigtail with a crimson tam-o'-shanter, and looked elfin, and adorable, and never more than fourteen," wrote Daphne du Maurier. But the swain was suffering. Love of Ethel had changed Laurence Irving from a brooding romantic to a gay Lothario. It changed the witty, sophisticated Gerald du Maurier into a lovesick dolt. Threatening suicide, he ran down to Kerry beach, waded into the water up to his neck, stood white and obdurate waiting for the tide to rise.

"Gerald, Gerald, come back!" implored his "Daphne." Gerald came back. Ethel's love did not. The du Mauriers were informed that the marriage had been postponed for the time being. Mrs. du Maurier was furious. She reviled the heartless girl to her son.

"You mustn't be hard on her, Mummie," the twenty-five-year-old Gerald insisted; "after all, she's very young and hasn't found her level yet. It won't do me any harm, perhaps a little good. I don't bear her any grudge, and you mustn't say unkind things about her before me, because I won't allow it. You must not be intolerant, darling, and, anyway, I haven't given up all thoughts of it yet, whatever she may say." But Ethel's decision was final.

"In spite of all their kindness to me," she explained, "when Mrs. du Maurier began to tell me how to take care of Gerald, what to make him wear in the winter and so on, it all alarmed me so that all I could think of was getting home to the four walls of my dressing room—any dressing room." Ethel had just enough money for passage to America via Canada and the night train to New York. She arranged for Jack to stay with Aunt Eva Wace until school started, left his allowance from Papa to be doled out by the Websters, and asked the Broughs and other friends to watch over him. With her brother well supervised, she departed for Southampton.

Barry was touring in *Shenandoah* when his daughter reached Grand Central. She gave her last quarter to a redcap and grandly ordered her cab to the Waldorf. That hotel, then at Thirty-third and Fifth Avenue, New York's most opulent and expensive, was a curious choice for the penniless traveler. But she hoped to find her uncle in residence. Apprehensively, head held high, she tread the cabbage-rose carpet to the lobby. Four or five clerks rushed toward her with ceremonious greetings. The manager came forward to offer his immediate assistance. News of her

London exploits, glorified in the New York papers, had made Ethel Barrymore a celebrity. "The cab is waiting, Miss Barrymore," said the porter.

"Oh, yes," she drawled, turning to one of the clerks. "Will you pay my cab, please?" Ethel was never slow to assert her prerogatives.

Fortunately, Uncle Jack *was* in residence. Next day, he brought his niece to Charles Frohman's office above the Empire Theatre. C.F. offered her a supporting role consisting mainly of two exquisite gowns, for which, at one hundred dollars each, she was required to pay out of her weekly thirty-five dollars. C.F., well aware of the young lady's potential, considered it best to let the public go on discovering her themselves for the time being. Ethel, relieved to find any work, took an advance on her salary and moved out of the Waldorf into Mrs. Wilson's boardinghouse. She paid nine dollars a week for a hall bedroom and three meals a day in the comfortable house, one of a row of brownstones on Thirty-sixth Street, across from the Lambs', and near the Garrick Theatre, where she would open in *Catherine* on October 24.

Maude Adams and her mother also lived at Mrs. Wilson's. Georgie Mendum, Georgie Drew Barrymore's namesake, soon arrived there. Ethel had not seen her cousin from Boston, Aunt Louisa's daughter, since childhood. They became immediate friends. When Georgie also obtained a small role in *Catherine*, the two girls cued one another. (Over the years, Georgie Mendum was the only person who could cue Ethel in the preparation of her roles.)

Ethel Barrymore's entrance at the first performance of *Catherine* elicited an ovation. "This is awful," she kept saying to herself. "I have nothing to do—just two or three lines in this act and two or three in the next!" Charles Frohman was watching from the audience, a complacent smile on his cherub's face.

Bronson Howard's *Shenandoah*, starring Maurice Barrymore and Mary Hampton, toured the United States with great success following the three-month war with Spain. Producer Jacob Litt, assuming as much, had mounted this revival of the Civil War play to exploit a victorious nation's patriotic fervor. Barry and Miss Hampton shared the stage with two hundred extras, fifty horses, and twenty-five genuine Roosevelt Rough Riders. "*Shenandoah* should be seen by every patriot of our country," proclaimed General William Tecumseh Sherman. "It is the best play I have ever seen," added General Nelson A. Miles.

"During the presentation of *Shenandoah*," reported the Indianapolis *Journal* on September 13, "Mrs. William E. English who occupied her husband's box, was overcome at the sight of the soldiers and the noise of the battle scene and fainted. So intense was the excitement over the realism of the scene that her condition was not noticed, except by her friends in the box." While Union boys are retreating at the battle of Cedar Creek, firing as they flee, a cry goes up—"Here comes the General!" Suddenly *Sheridan* gallops across the stage. Amid wild cries for their general, the men cease their retreat and begin to advance, as the curtain goes down. The Indianapolis audience cheered wildly. The curtain was pulled up six times to reveal, as advertised, two hundred supers cheering and waving flags. Patrons sprang to their feet, one woman shouting to nearby stragglers, "Get up if you have a grain of patriotism!"

Barry's heroic *Colonel Kerchival West* was not overlooked in the melee. "Barrymore is a distinct type of society actory," decided Claude G. Bowers, a distinct type of society commentatory. "He is very graceful, quite handsome, and has that air of abandon which is very attractive to young women. Yet in places, as in the battle scene, he displayed very strong qualities." Bowers found Mary Hampton "just a tiny bit too plump." Barry had no such reservations about his tall, supple, Titian-haired leading lady, whom one journalist described as having "a slender, arched throat, melting eyes and elbows like flowers." *Shenandoah* would tour for ten months. Barry, who had protected Mary from the lecherous old Montgomery on their *Aristocracy* tour, did not resist such inviting attributes as the company proceeded along its arduous route.

When they reached Buffalo in October, the star incurred the wrath of that city's most conservative element. He had begun a new play, an adaptation of Victor Hugo's *Les Misérables*, with the hope of playing *Jean Valjean*. When not inside the theater at Buffalo, he was over at Niagara Falls working on the manuscript. "Buffalo is too gay a place to meet the requirements of authorship," he told a group of native sons, "while at Niagara Falls I can secure the quiet which enables me to do consecutive and satisfactory work." That harmless statement incensed locals, provoking their municipal pride. Barry departed the city in a barrage of sarcastic journalese:

> Maurice Barrymore, actor, at twenty-five, fifty, and seventy-five cents and sometimes $1.50 and $2 a guess; once the idol of strong men, dirty-faced boys and handsome women; dog-fancier, general all-around scrapper, cigarette manipulator and advance agent of 'The Pace That Kills,' left Buffalo yesterday. There was no cheering when Mr. Barrymore stepped aboard the train. There were no handkerchiefs waving in the air, no tears falling to the platform, no 'God-bless-yous,' no hearty handshakes—none of those things. 'There goes the big stiff,' was the best he got, and that from a newsboy. 'He used t' could act, but he can't no more.'

The New York papers, for once, rallied to Barry's defense. "If in the course of his wanderings Mr. Barrymore should run across this 'brilliant' sample of Buffalo newspaper writing," speculated the *Morning Tele-graph*, "it is not entirely impossible that he may consider the advisability of inditing a few words by way of response. When it comes to saying things, Mr. Barrymore is about as bitterly scintillant a customer as one is likely to find in a day's journey." If he ever did see the piece, he did not dignify it with scintillant responses or any other kind. He used them to combat more touching effrontery, after his dramatization of *Les Misérables* had been submitted to and rejected by New York's few remaining independent managers.

"But, Barry," wondered Fred Peel, the *Sheridan* of *Shenandoah*, "will you ever get a New York manager to produce it?"

"Produce it?" the author replied. "I can't get a New York manager to pronounce it!"

Shenandoah, the Academy of Music's Christmas week attraction, was sold out before it opened. "The battle of Cedar Creek was refought as it had never been before," observed the *Dramatic Mirror* of the New York opening, "and the audience went wild, both men and women cheering until they became hoarse." Mamie Barrymore was not among them. She was traveling in the South with her mother and one of her sisters. Since their return from England, the Barrymores had not met. There was talk around the Rialto that all was not well with them.

Crowds and acclaim continued throughout New England, until the *Shenandoah* tour ended early in June. Barry was in New York on June 19, 1899, among the throng filling St. Patrick's Cathedral for the funeral of Augustin Daly.

The man who had introduced Maurice Barrymore to New York audiences twenty-three years before, the last of the great independent managers to remain active, had died at the age of sixty. Unlike most of his managerial predecessors and contemporaries, the Governor died a rich man. He left an estate of $600,000, the bulk of which, after debts and expenses of administration had taken nearly half, would be shared by his widow, his mother, and his brother. He further designated that the operation of Daly's Theatre in London should be continued by his executors, and, not forgetting the members of his once-illustrious Fifth Avenue company, bequeathed shares of its yearly profits to the five that were living and loyal. Of the original Big Four, only Ada Rehan and Mrs. Gilbert were included. James Lewis had died three years before. John Drew had deserted. The lion's share, in any case, would go to Ada, his erstwhile *Galatea*.

After John Drew left him, the Governor had concentrated on the considerable solo talents of Ada Rehan. He never quite regained his managerial pre-eminence, but she became the most beloved actress in America, inspiring in audiences the faithful devotion which she had never quite achieved in her turbulent relationship with Daly. After the Governor's death, she starred successfully in America and England for a while. But without the driving ambition of her mentor, her interest waned. Reclusive and shy, rich and lonely, she soon retired from the stage.

For the first time in his career, to help him avoid the proliferous Trust, Barry hired an agent. He was immediately booked for a summer on the Keith Circuit, again playing *A Man of the World*, again receiving the highest salary of any legitimate player in vaudeville. While he toured, his progeny were making diverse progress of their own.

After five years of road companies and art school, Lionel doubted his ability as an artist in oils. "The only thing that prevented my becoming a good painter was sheer lack of talent," he admitted modestly, but not quite accurately. (His excellent nautical etchings, done in later life, would become among the most popular and often reproduced works of an American artist.) He considered the necessity of making a living, his future as an actor. Gus Thomas facilitated both by offering him a chance to originate a small role in his new play, *Arizona*. The purely American melodrama, the third in Thomas's series of plays named for states, became an instantaneous hit after its first performance on June 12 at Hamlin's Chicago opera house. Lionel's playing of *Lieutenant Young* received little comment, good or bad. It didn't matter. For the time being, at least, he was satisfied just to have steady employment.

His sister's career was proceeding more swiftly. After her role in *Catherine*, she toured as one of Uncle Jack's leading ladies in Henry Arthur Jones's *The Liars*. While Boston critics debated, on the first leg of the spring tour, whether the theater's first gentleman should wear a double-breasted white evening waistcoat or a single-breasted black one, they all agreed that his niece was charming. "It was a small part," reported the *Herald*, "which Miss Barrymore invested with much gentle womanliness." All was going as C.F. had planned for the "daughter of Barry."

All was not going as planned for the younger son of Barry in London. When the routine of King's College School began to bore him, Jack invented a major, supposedly a friend of his father's, who frequently demanded his presence in London. At first, these escapes were merely visits to Aunt Eva Wace's Hampstead house, to Ben and May Webster in Bedford Street, where his allowance was doled out, or to Lionel Brough's house outside of London. "He used to come down to our house on Sunday evenings," wrote Brough's granddaughter, Jean Webster-Brough; "from all accounts, a singularly quiet, and rather dull young man at that period of his life, whose unfailing remark, just as the last train was due to depart, was: 'I must e'en fly!' After which he stayed on another couple of hours."

The young man's visits to family and friends of family soon succumbed, as his father's had twenty-five years before, to the pleasures of

London's sporting world. He became a regular at the School of Arms, where Barry had trained for the Queensberry championships, and traveled with the colorful crowd headed by Tod Sloane, England's foremost jockey. When the Websters received a cable from Ethel, however, announcing the date of her arrival that summer, Jack dutifully hurried off to Southampton to meet her boat. He got as far as the dock, met some sailors, and joined them in a game of billiards. That, at least, was the extent of his explanation to his sister when he finally turned up at Bedford Street, broke and disheveled, two days later.

Ethel and Jack shared a cottage on the Thames that summer with the Websters and others of the Bedford Street group. During an afternoon fishing expedition, Jack went in for a swim, leaving his clothes in the bottom of his boat. As he swam peacefully in the all-together through the cool water, his craft drifted away. Jack was not perturbed. But his nonchalant stroll through Cookham village became legend. Surprising for a young man who, the summer before, had broken out in a cold sweat when his sister asked him to join her guests at a tea party. "This terror of people and gatherings," observed Ethel, "left him at an early age."

Barry ended his vaudeville tour in Toledo, Ohio, after a prosperous trek through the Middle West. While checking into his hotel, he noticed that a famous young actor had registered ahead of him—rather grandly:

Richard Harding Davis & valet.

Barry signed just below:

Maurice Barrymore & valise.

Variety audiences responded to this genuine representative of the legitimate stage, bestowing upon him the bouquets and obsequities befitting a bona fide matinee idol. One month short of his fiftieth birthday, he was inclined to welcome attentions, which, as a younger man, he had deplored. As always, he was quick to give proper acknowledgment of gifts and devoted declarations from young ladies and, occasionally, young men. He wrote from his dressing room at the Toledo Casino to thank one admirer, who had submitted two heroic odes celebrating the Barrymore career:

Dear Mr. Gibson,

I have copied both the poems & wd like to thank you in person—but I have gone to town to wire acceptance of a contract at Proctor's in New York before my agent goes away. I leave photo—will write on it if you will send it to Hotel—Hope to see you again before I go—Pray say goodbye to your friend.

Yours
M. Barrymore

While headlining Proctor's variety bill for a week, far from bouquets and heroic odes, Barry was given the raspberry by local commentators. Except for one successful week of *Shenandoah*, he had not played New York for two years. During that time, he had triumphed in London and on the road. His metropolitan critics, evidently, did not recognize such far-flung achievements. His concurrent performances in *A Man of the World* did not occasion the assaults—such purists would not have deigned to enter a vaudeville house. Perhaps, it was merely an overdue rebuke for his original defection, or the old nagging disappointment with the actor's failure to realize his potential. Whatever the reason, while he nightly won new audiences at the highest salary of his career, Maurice Barrymore's theatrical stock had never been depicted as being so low.

Traditionally, the critical stance had been that Barry simply did not choose to exert his obvious talent. But that position was being supplanted by a less comfortable one. "Barrymore seems to be on the decline as an actor," announced the *Herald*. "He lacks the fire of his early days, and there is always the inclination to forget his lines and extemporize." At the recent Lambs' Gambol, Gus Thomas, as *Maurice Barrymore*, had convulsed the audience, including Maurice Barrymore, by repeatedly pretending to forget his lines. "Barrymore is discouraged by the failure of most of his plays, and because he is not the actor that he believes himself capable of being," the *Herald* concluded.

"His walking gentleman walks Broadway rather than Fifth Avenue," added old reliable William Winter; "his lover woos with a confident swagger rather than an elegant grace; he serenades his lady love with a banjo rather than a mandolin; his man about town is more at ease in a box coat than in evening dress—in short, Mr. Barrymore's acting lacks refinement, tenderness, pathos, elegance."

"Critics declare that he is careless and slouchy," epitomized the *Journal*, "but I am inclined to believe that he invariably does the best he can, and is content to rest beneath the accusation of carelessness and slouchiness, rather than fall beneath heavier and perhaps truer ones. Barrymore is in fact generally disappointing on the stage. Once behind the footlights, and you wonder what has become of his ineffable graces."

Rebuttal from the object of all this conjecture was not readily available. He was in Montreal when it appeared, preparing a new role and an implicit reply for prophets of doom.

XXXI

"He is ineffably lazy by inclination," Amy Leslie determined, "but works if he must, as some indolent men do, with a ferocious ardor inspiring in its vital endurance." Barry validated the Chicago critic's view with his industrious preparation for *Becky Sharp*. This new dramatization of *Vanity Fair* inspired him because of his enduring admiration for Thackeray's works and his desire to play *Rawdon Crawley*, one of his favorite characters. He was also moved by the dedicated participation of Harrison Grey Fiske and his wife, Minnie Maddern Fiske, fellow standard-bearers against the Trust.

Harry Fiske, publisher of the *Dramatic Mirror*, had taken a year to prepare a vehicle worthy to follow his wife's previous success, *Tess of the d'Urbervilles*, and to challenge the ubiquitous Trust. He had spared no expense in mounting the production. He employed forty speaking actors and an army of supernumeraries; scenes included a spectacular war tableau and the Duchess of Richmond's ballroom at Brussels on the eve of Waterloo, which shimmered with gilded, filigreed balconies and stairways and repeated frescoed arches, giving in its magnificence the illusion of being larger than the theater which housed it. Fiske's relentless attention to detail was evidenced by the production's costumes, an improvement of those described by Thackeray. *Vanity Fair*'s author had incorrectly clothed his characters in the dress of 1845, while the period of the novel was circa 1815. Fiske had hired Barry's old friend Percy Anderson, who had done costumes for *The Robber of the Rhine*, to design an authentic wardrobe for *Becky Sharp*. In London, Anderson scrupulously painted colored plates depicting proper dress for each character, down to minute accessories, to be executed by Herrmann & Dazian, Costumers, in New York. The Regency finery and dashing guardsman's uniforms created for Barry were among the finest costumes that he had ever worn on stage.

422

Barry had joined rehearsals late, after completing previous vaudeville contracts. With less than two weeks to prepare, he was miraculously letter-perfect for the September 4th première at the Montreal Academy of Music. Harry Fiske had chosen to launch the play in Montreal, assuming that they would be out of the Trust's reach there, and that Canadian audiences would give enthusiastic welcome to an English classic. As it turned out, he had misjudged both the Canadian taste and the far-reaching power of the Trust.

Maurice Barrymore's playing was praised by the local press. Sets and costumes were admired. Mrs. Fiske and the play were roundly condemned. The Montreal *Herald* printed an editorial vilifying the actress for undertaking the degenerate *Becky*, labeling Thackeray's comedy "a tragic riot of evil." In New York, the pro-Trust *American* avidly picked up the editorial, reprinting it in full. Mrs. Fiske, overwrought from months of grueling preparation, wired the editor: "The malicious and abusive article in the Montreal *Herald*, and its dissemination, can be safely attributed to the industrious mercenaries of the Theatrical Trust . . ." But the damage had been done.

"What are we going to substitute for *Becky?*" asked the Fiskes' company manager. There was no substitute.

"*Becky* isn't dead yet," asserted Harry Fiske. But he approached New York uneasily.

Despite Trust efforts to bar them from a New York theater, the Fiskes leased the independent Fifth Avenue. Its cream and crimson premise was filled for the first night of *Becky Sharp*. "The large and appreciative audience was essentially a literary one," noted the *Herald*, "with its Thackeray at its fingers' end." Few theatrical luminaries risked the wrath of the Trust to attend the September 12th opening, although one Frohman contractee was very much in evidence. Miss Ethel Barrymore, returned from England, eagerly awaited her father's entrance. Neither she nor the literary and social personages crowding the Fifth Avenue that evening were disappointed. There would be the inevitable attacks on the Fiskes by the Trust-friendly papers. Praise for Mrs. Fiske's performance would be tempered by occasional reservations and criticisms. But from the moment of his entrance as *Rawdon Crawley*, looking sleek and barely thirty in Regency finery, Maurice Barrymore took the evening.

"To look upon, to watch, to listen to Maurice Barrymore in a congenial part is to behold nature in her liveliest temper of pleasantness," Amy Leslie observed. "Mr. Barrymore perchance has faults, but they are not of personality nor face nor figure nor intelligence. He is about as near a desirable man to see across the footlights as the stage shall ever grant us." It had seemed recently that Amy was alone in her stubborn appreciation of the actor's talents. After *Becky Sharp* opened, every New York commentator was vying with the Chicago critic for superlatives.

"Unquestionably the greatest individual success was scored by Maurice Barrymore," reported the *Evening Sun*. "As *Rawdon Crawley* he was superb. In looks, speech and manner he might have stepped directly out of Thackeray's pages. His performance was a blending of sterling manliness and the gentlest pathos. Who that heard it will forget his reading of that letter from his little boy? Barrymore, in short, has re-established himself. His *Rawdon Crawley* must rank as the finest performance of his career."

The *Times* stated that Barry's "investiture of *Rawdon Crawley* was as nearly a perfect piece of acting, a living photograph, of the Thackeray creation as could possibly be conceived," while the *Herald* spoke of his "art that justified itself." The Brooklyn *Eagle* noted that he "returns to his form of a dozen years ago, when he was the best leading man in America." The *Daily News* found him "the most artistic, dramatic and fascinating figure on the stage," adding that "it was indeed Mr. Barrymore's masterpiece."

The magnitude of the Barrymore triumph could be gauged by William Winter's *Tribune* review. After twenty-five years of Barrymore-baiting, the conservative dean of critics finally relented in a three-column paean to *Becky Sharp*: "*Rawdon Crawley* lasts till the end of act third, and this part was finely played by Maurice Barrymore, who, indeed, gave an uncommonly touching display of the subduing and softening effect of love upon a raw and rough nature. Mr. Barrymore has not hitherto for a long time done such ample justice to his fine powers. *Rawdon's* goodby to *Becky*, before Waterloo, his reading of the letter from his boy, his weakness in *Becky's* hands, his terrible anger and misery in looking on her disgrace,—in each of these he touched the heart. For Mr. Barrymore this was a night of signal triumph . . ."

First-night ovations anticipated the critics. After *Rawdon's* third-act discovery of *Becky* and *Lord Steyne*, *à deux*, which stage historian Forrest Izard deemed "one of the high water marks in the history of American acting," twelve curtain calls were demanded of the three players. For the hero of the evening, they were transcended by his daughter's appearance among the crush of well-wishers and sycophants in his dressing room. If shame had tinged his relationship with her since Georgie's death, in this moment of triumph, at least, he could face her with unabashed pride. When the crowd had dispersed, refusing more elaborate celebrations, Barry and his daughter shared a quiet supper at Delmonico's. ("He was superb as *Rawdon Crawley*," she wrote fifty years later. It was the only performance of her father's that Ethel Barrymore remembered.)

As the nineteenth century turned into the twentieth, amid tumultuous celebrations and toasts to America's future glory, Barry's "masterpiece" was drawing full houses to the Fifth Avenue. Other New York theaters also greeted 1900 with Drews and Barrymores and their relatives in prosperous display. Sidney and Gladys Drew had returned from England to regale Keith's vaudeville patrons with their own comedietta, *Love Will Find the Way*. Gladys's sister, Phyllis Rankin, was among the all-star cast of a Casino musical, *The Rounders*, which included Harry Davenport. Phyllis had married Harry, son of E. L. Davenport, brother of Fanny, thus allying the Drews and Barrymores with yet another notable theatrical clan. John Drew, "who never has looked, on the stage, as if his income were less than $10,000," was pacing the Empire stage-drawing room in Haddon Chambers's *The Tyranny of Tears*. At a Wednesday matinee, his daughter Louise, not yet seventeen, made her debut in the maid's part usually played by her cousin, Georgie Mendum.

Mornings at the Empire, Charles Frohman was rehearsing the touring company of Captain Robert Marshall's *His Excellency, the Governor*, in which Ethel Barrymore was essaying her first leading role. C.F. sat in the darkened auditorium of his elegant theater, as the dress rehearsal proceeded. The scene is a sumptuous apartment in the Government House of an island in the Indian Ocean. Ethel, as *Stella De Gex*, not exactly an adventuress, but leaning toward that type, entered in a white, flowing garment, declaring, "I desire to call your attention to the fact that my gown, though white, is a tea gown." When the scene had ended, C.F. walked on stage, gave his leading lady's shoulder a pat.

"You're so much like your mother, Ethel," he said. "You're all right."

Lionel, meanwhile, was still touring in the small role which he had originated in *Arizona*. He preceded his father at the Tremont in Boston, but was on the road again when *Becky Sharp* opened there.

Heralded by such critical superlatives as "The Dramatic Sensation of the Season," *Becky Sharp* began touring after four sold-out months in New York. Although Barry once more triumphed, Boston reviewers, perhaps in defiance of the billed and posted encomiums from New York, were guarded in their praise of the play. Patrons had no such reservations. Three weeks of Standing Room Only in Boston merely increased the attraction of play and players as the tour continued.

Ethel, in the white, flowing gown of *Stella De Gex*, followed her father into Boston. "Beautiful Ethel Barrymore won a distinct success," observed the *Herald*, "and Mr. Frohman has again given proof of his keen judgment in placing this young actress in a role which at first would seem beyond her present powers. Her performance last night furnished convincing proof of the fact that she had developed more rapidly in the past two years than any other actress on the American stage. In fascination of manner and charm of personality she greatly resembles her brilliant mother, and has the added advantage of being a singularly beautiful girl." The Barrymore personality was already influencing matinee girls as she toured, leaving in her wake a country full of puny, gushing copies of her style and manner.

Ethel was still wearing the white tea gown when a *Globe* reporter called at her dressing room after a Boston performance of *His Excellency, the Governor.* "I am just as pleased as I can be," she declared, "both at the opportunity of playing this role and the hearty manner in which the public receives me in it. It is my first leading role, and it is a marvelous opportunity for one who has been on the stage only five years. I like the part and I am very grateful to Mr. Frohman for giving it to me."

"Do you want to be a star?"

"Of course, I want to be a star—some time—but not until I am fitted for it. I am still very young, you see," smiled the twenty-year-old, perhaps recalling her grandmother's admonitions. "If I could have five years in good parts—parts that would give me the experience I need—I should be better fitted for such a step." She paused for a moment. "Yes, perhaps ten years would be better. I know I must learn. I will try to do so." But such charming humility was already beside the point. The current play was merely C.F.'s sly test of his embryo star.

Undaunted by the often shabby non-Trust houses that it was obliged to play, the *Becky Sharp* company toured victoriously. Literary monthlies and illustrated weeklies had exalted the production, saturating the American public with play and players, creating a nationwide run on box offices. A majority of critics praised the production; where there was dissent, Barry remained exempt from it. "Barrymore was the only member of the *Becky Sharp* cast who received universal praise," attested Mrs. Fiske's biographer, Archie Binns; "several cities declared that the play was a Barrymore rather than a Fiske triumph, and that the actor, who had seemed to be losing his grip, had come back triumphantly."

Mrs. Fiske remained on congenial terms with her leading man during the four-month tour, and even shared his love of animals. Barry's particular traveling companion, his first pet since Belle died, was a self-contained Maltese cat named Patrick Boniface. Along the route, he acquired two mongrel puppies, naming them Pidgewidge and Dodor. Barry's example activated Mrs. Fiske's concern for animals of all kinds. She began taking in stray cats and dogs, rehabilitating them, and presenting them to friends along the way. In St. Louis, she had a driver arrested for working a pair of harness-galled horses.

The St. Louis engagement began the last leg of the tour. There, also, began the leading man's occasional onstage lapses of memory and difficulties of enunciation. They were infrequent and not surprising, considering Barry's reputation as a poor study. But the Fiskes were concerned, wary. Patrons and critics were oblivious. Amid raves, St. Louis reviewers described him as "looking thirty," the *Star* surmising that he "had drunk deep of the Fountain of Youth." Critical praise continued through Cincinnati and Pittsburgh. The Fiskes were not reassured. Barry was distracted and vague on the cars as they approached Philadelphia, the final stop of the tour. They fretted over him before the opening performance. They needn't have bothered. The American home of Drews and Barrymores hailed *Rawdon Crawley* as the greatest achievement of his career.

Lapses noticeable to his colleagues were invisible to spectators. Barry commenced the second week in Philadelphia apparently in top form. "The performance last night lacked no whit of the brilliancy of the opening night," reported a follow-up piece in the *Telegraph*, "the interest centering naturally in the principals of the main intrigue—*Becky*, *Rawdon Crawley*, and the *Marquis of Steyne*." But toward the end of the week, Barry's condition deteriorated. Reality and illusion became blurred. During the celebrated discovery scene on the last night of the tour, he was carried beyond mere stage frenzy. The curtain had to be lowered while stagehands rescued Tyrone Power, the lecherous *Lord Steyne*.

Fearing that another tour would completely break his health, the Fiskes did not re-engage their leading man for the following season. Barry returned, furious, to New York. He did not seek medical help. He did not acknowledge any need for it. He went to the Lambs' and dashed off a note—perfectly justified under the circumstances, he determined—challenging Harry Fiske to a duel.

(Over the years, for their frequent revivals of *Becky Sharp*, the Fiskes engaged some of the ablest actors in America to play *Rawdon Crawley*. "But in Mrs. Fiske's 'dream theatre,'" attested Binns, "the great guardsman was still played by Maurice Barrymore. To the end of the *Becky* chapter, thirty years later, the gap Barrymore left remained unfilled.")

Seeking boisterous reassurance after the abrupt termination of his greatest triumph, Barry returned to the watering holes of Manhattan. "Notoriously free with his money," observed the *Sun*, "there were always plenty of hangers on to accompany Barrymore when he was in his merry moods. Every time he stopped in a café there was a crowd to hang upon his words and offer flattery which was so dull that Barrymore generally didn't relish it." Such sycophancy hardly reassured the wounded actor. It drove him from the clubs and cafés which had once been his unquestioned domain. The house on West Ninety-seventh Street became a convivial alternative.

Mamie was in Long Branch with her family when her husband returned to New York that summer. He and Patrick Boniface, Pidgewidge and Dodor were not alone for long. When Virginia Tracy, who had toured with him in *Aristocracy*, called at Ninety-seventh Street, she found that the Barrymore residence had become virtually a boardinghouse.

"There were old ladies in that house who had come on a week's visit, before they went to the poorhouse, and stayed literally forever," Miss Tracy avowed. "There was anybody there who was out of luck and who did not kick the dogs." One resident, who posed as a hero because he had been in Florida during a yellow fever epidemic and hadn't the price to escape, was supported by Barry for two years. Glen McDonough, librettist of *Babes in Toyland*, was hiding there from an actor who was trying to subpoena him as a witness in a court case. After many visits to the house, where the host repeatedly denied knowledge of McDonough's whereabouts, the actor had continued his search elsewhere. One of the boarders asked Barry what had become of him.

"Oh, he's engaged in the pursuit of literature," Barry said.

"What!" cried the boarder. "Why, it's all he can do to read the parts entrusted to him."

"Still, what I say is true," Barry insisted, "because he's chasing Glen McDonough."

The Barrymore household was dominated not by the host but by Patrick Boniface, the Maltese cat. To Virginia Tracy, who recalled Barry's devotion to Belle of Clyde, this seemed only fair. "I could not bear, even in the grim procession of time, to see him with dogs without Belle," she confessed. "I did better with Patrick . . . I have known many terrifying cats, but none so consistently a putter-down of the herd as Patrick." The Maltese, it seemed, did not scratch, it struck. Standing on its hind feet, it swung enormous front paws indiscriminately at man or fellow beast with the aim and impact of a prize-fighter. "He kept down Pidgewidge and Dodor, dear Patrick!" Virginia rejoiced. "No other dog ever reigned in Belle's place."

To escape, occasionally, from his charitable ménage, Barry would go over to Staten Island to help Edward Briggs, who was slowly rebuilding the fire-gutted farm complex. Physical labor, coupled with the soothing company of the Black Prince and what remained of his menagerie, relaxed the restless actor. The congenial, if less soothing, company at Ninety-seventh Street delighted him. But halcyon days were interrupted by Mamie's return from Long Branch. Finding her home turned into a commune, she ordered the multitude from the premises. Barry acted quickly. He bought a house in Coytesville, New Jersey, and evacuated Patrick, Pidgewidge, Dodor, cronies, and charity cases across the river. He did not return to Ninety-seventh Street. The town house was left in Mamie's hands, the Barrymore marriage in limbo.

Coytesville was a small farming community three miles north of the Fort Lee ferry landing. Its citizens had never seen an actor close up before, a gap in their experience that would be abruptly filled. Barry's rambling, brown-shingled farmhouse, already holding his regular boarders, was overrun on weekends. Among his more frequent visitors were Rose

Moulton, current Broadway idols Walter Allen and Henry G. Donnelly, and Dorothy Donnelly, who would later play *Madame X* and write librettos for Sigmund Romberg. Rose Moulton's accomplishments were less easily defined. The *Journal*, in fact, mistook the beautiful young actress for Mrs. Barrymore. It was an understandable mistake. Barry and his wife had been seldom together of late, and his numerous and comely replacements proved confusing to the press.

The Barrymore marriage had quietly disintegrated without benefit of publicity. The recent town-house incident was their first overt confrontation. But Mamie had become disillusioned long before with her childhood hero, unable to cope with his eccentricities. As for Barry, a wife that expected more from him than she gave was perplexing. He had been accustomed to Georgie's challenge and independence and sacrifice. When he compared his first and second wives, as he inevitably did, Mamie fell far short.

Coytesville was his escape from such complexities, and he lost no time in winning over his Broadway cronies to its pleasures. "One day he gave a house party," explained the New York *Journal*, "and in the afternoon let his guests sit on the veranda and watch him plough. After that emigration was easy and frequent by the dwellers of Playville." Broadway denizens sailed over on the ferryboat via Fort Lee, buying or renting houses near Barry's, making a theatrical summer colony of the little farming community.

As the population increased, Barry took on the mantle of a founding father concerned for the welfare of his constituents. Donating a hose cart and his services as captain, he recruited all of the theatrical residents as volunteer firemen, and established Coytesville Hose Company No. 1. "We Strive to Conquer and to Save" was the motto that he had painted on the hose reel. But the farmers were nonetheless skeptical.

The first Saturday in August found the Barrymore house brimming with guests. Conviviality had turned to torpor, when a midnight alarm rang for Hose Company No. 1. The chimney of old man Coytes's farmhouse on the hill had caught fire. "It's a landmark, boys. We've got to save it," shouted Captain Barrymore, taking command in a pair of pink pajamas. Walter Allen, Henry Donnelly and a score of other Broadwayites strained at the hose cart ropes as it crawled up the hill. Rose Moulton and Dorothy Donnelly cheered them on from the front porch.

"The fire's out," yelled old man Coytes from his ridgepole as the brigade approached. "I put it out with a bag of salt."

"Salt doesn't go with Hose Company No. 1," shouted Captain Barrymore. "Turn her on!" The mighty stream washed away the last remaining sparks—and half of Coytes's chimney.

After Coytes had cursed Barry, actors, and acting in general, the Captain decided that Hose Company No. 1 was not getting proper respect from the locals. Uniforms, he determined, were the missing ingredient. A benefit performance to raise the money was announced for the following Saturday. He secured the Fort Lee Town Hall and the services of his most celebrated colleagues. For days before the event, crops were supplanted as the chief topic of conversation in Fort Lee and Coytesville. The chance to see Broadway stars perform in their own town hall at a quarter top for reserved seats distracted the locals.

John Drew, who had been considering buying land near his brother-in-law's, was among the scheduled participants. But that same week he bought land in East Hampton, Long Island, part of the ocean-front Mulford property on Lily Pond Road. He was the only actor ever to be admitted to that stronghold of society, a testament to his standing as First Gentleman of the American Theatre. Busy with arrangements for building a cottage on his new property, John Drew did not participate in the Coytesville Benefit on August 11. Numerous others did.

Nan, the Good for Nothing, an antique melodrama, was performed by Captain Barrymore & Co., along with some vaudeville. There had been no scenery in the town hall, but Barry made do with the outfit used by the Coytesville M. E. Church at its last Christmas Pageant—one red-brick chimney, one sleigh with one set of sleigh bells, a large quantity of sheeting, and one imitation reindeer, slightly damaged. It proved to be just the bill to attract the farmers. Proceeds were sufficient for the purchase of boots, red flannel uniform shirts, and helmets with "Hose Company No. 1" tattooed across the front.

Ethel had managed to save enough money from her tour in *His Excellency, the Governor* to finance another summer in England. Arriving in London, she went directly from the boat train to Charles Frohman's rooms at the Savoy Hotel.

"Where are you going to live?" her manager wondered.

"I don't know yet," Ethel replied.

"You had better get a room here."

"I can't afford that."

"Never mind," said C.F., "get a room here. You can't be roaming around." She graced the Savoy as Frohman's guest for one night only.

"You can't live at the Savoy Hotel all by yourself," insisted Millicent, the young Duchess of Sutherland. "Come stay at Stafford House." To the delight of American newspaper correspondents, Ethel Barrymore was introduced to the social and political whirl of the Sutherlands' great town house. And great it was, perhaps the greatest in London—"I come from my house to your palace," Queen Victoria had once said to the third Duchess. The South African War had diminished London's usual gaiety that season, but Stafford House was alive with charity balls and benefits for the war effort and the wounded. Ethel contributed her services.

When she sold programs at an Albert Hall concert given by the Union Jack Club to benefit war widows, American newspapers deemed it worthy of front-page coverage.

Ethel found her eighteen-year-old brother more like Papa than ever, romantically handsome and thoroughly Bohemian, hair long and unruly, clothes careless and unkempt. Having left Kings College School, Jack was completing a year of courses at the Slade School, the art department of London University. His work was greatly influenced by the bizarre illustrative art of Aubrey Beardsley. "I was also fascinated," Jack said, "by the race of this emaciated young artist against death." He discussed Beardsley at length with Max Beerbohm and other members of the artist's circle, emulating his equally bizarre Bohemianism, as well, seldom appearing at Aunt Eva Wace's in Hampstead, where he was ostensibly living. Nights in Bohemia seldom ended till light of dawn dispelled them, and his sister was subjected by acquaintances to some colorful accounts of Jack's nocturnal romantic adventures. Two prominent ladies, it seemed, were in avid pursuit, one, a married lady of rank, the other, an actress much older than he. When the Sutherlands asked Ethel to their ducal estate in Scotland, she used the invitation to lure her brother away from the temptations of London.

Henry James was among the guests at Dunrobin, the Sutherlands' stone-turreted castle overlooking the North Sea. He called Ethel his "Gothic Gargoyle," which offended everyone but the recipient, who swore that she knew exactly what he meant. She loved his Old World manner and the way he talked in long, perfectly constructed paragraphs like those in his novels. Another guest assiduously set out to win Ethel's favor. Twenty-six-year-old Winston Churchill, slight, fair and tenacious, usually achieved his ends. Son of the late Lord Randolph Churchill and his American wife, Jennie Jerome, Winston had recently made a hero's return from the South African front. While serving there as *Morning Post* correspondent, he had been taken prisoner by the Boers. Undaunted, he had made a heroic escape from captivity. His published account of the experience, *London to Ladysmith via Pretoria* was currently popular reading in England.

Ethel was duly impressed by the young man's exploits, but horrified when they fired Jack with the notion of running off to fight the Boer in South Africa. She tried to dissuade her impressionable younger brother with the prospect of returning to America and continuing his art studies. For once, although, for different reasons, Ethel and her father were in complete agreement. Papa had repeatedly communicated concern over his younger son's progress. "I used my time very poorly," Jack explained. "Finally my father became more impressed with my expenses than with my scholastic reports and summoned me home."

When Ethel sailed for America at summer's end, Winston Churchill had not yet gained his objective. But she had gained hers. Jack was safely in tow.

"I didn't become really acquainted with my delightful father until I was eighteen years old," Jack remembered, "when we were together constantly for more than a year." Ethel had been assigned a taxing new role by Charles Frohman when she returned to New York, so Jack was handed over to Papa at Coytesville. The youngest Barrymore had no particular inclination toward acting, although Uncle Jack kept reminding him of his "birthright."

"Birthright has nothing to do with the case," added Papa, when Jack wanted money to enroll at the Art Students League. "Would you rather be an artist and daub, or an actor and have romance?" The question was rhetorical. Barry had already decided to promote his son's entry into the family trade. He arranged for Jack to make his acting debut in *A Man of the World* at another benefit for Hose Company No. 1.

On the night of the benefit, Barry made up as usual for *Captain Bradley*, applying the regulation mustache. Jack was playing the small role of the young seducer, which Lionel also had once played with Papa at a benefit. Having received no instructions for his own make-up, Jack merely imitated his father. He applied enough hirsute flourishes to cover half of his face, making himself, he supposed, "terribly dangerous looking."

As the young seducer entered that evening, his father turned to the audience with a look of utter amazement. John Barrymore's first theatrical entrance was accompanied by the derisive laughter of Coytesville farmers. Undaunted, the debutant commenced a good-natured burlesque of his role. Afterwards, he mentioned to Papa that he would like to change roles with him some night, since an imitation of his illustrious parent would be "a cinch."

"Very well then," Barry countered, "go ahead and reek of turpentine and starvation." Dismissing his first bout with the family trade, Jack gladly accepted enough money to enroll at the Art Students League.

"I didn't take the stage any more seriously in those days than a puppy takes a rubber shoe," he admitted. "Father gave me up as a bad job, professionally speaking, and I returned to my artistic ambitions."

The evening of September 27 found Papa and his younger son in first-night seats at the new Republic Theatre, where Lionel was opening in *Sag Harbor*. James A. Herne's eternal triangle drama held special significance for the twenty-two-year-old actor. It gave him a chance to play an out-and-out heavy. After the performance, at the Lambs' with his father and brother, Lionel traced his preference for character roles to early experiences in McKee Rankin's company. "I was very comfortable in such character parts as *Flash Toby Crackitt* in *Oliver Twist*, and reveled in the funny 'old man' parts that Rankin intrusted to me," he explained, "but when it came to the juvenile-lover business I was exceedingly distressed, and felt like thanking the audience for having spared my life at the end of each such performance. At present I do not hesitate to admit my exceeding failure then to portray passionate attachment and to spout heroics." Barry recalled his own irritation, during early acting days, at being cast as nothing but a "walking codpiece."

Barry and his sons spent the night of Lionel's opening in easy camaraderie. Occasionally, friends and acquaintances, interviewers or presumptuous strangers stopped at their table to enhance or disrupt their enclave. Gus Thomas joined them and chided Barry for not going to see the *Hamlet* of their friend, E. H. Sothern, which was currently running none too successfully at the Garden Theatre. "Why don't you go and witness a performance?" Gus asked. "Go and sit out only one act."

"My boy," Barry explained, "I never encourage vice."

But if Lambs' cronies and hangers-on were expecting the old, epigram-tossing Barry, they were disappointed. He directed attention away from himself toward his sons, making much of Lionel's performance that evening, of Jack's potential as an artist. ("I can suppose, now that I like to think of such things," Lionel recalled years later, "that he was proud of us.")

Barry started writing another play that autumn of 1900—a dramatization of *Cashel Byron's Profession*, the George Bernard Shaw novel which bore such a marked parallel to Herbert Blyth's early experiences. It did not occur to the fervent adapter that he was basing his rights to the book on an invalidated verbal agreement made with Shaw fifteen years before. He proceeded with the long-delayed adaptation, making lucrative forays into vaudeville to maintain himself, his estranged wife, his younger son, and his three current residences. Fortunately, his *Becky Sharp* triumph and insured his top vaudeville salary of $750 a week. *A Man of the World* proved as popular with variety audiences as it had previously been, but the quality of the headliner's performances varied extravagantly. *Cashel Byron's Profession* was not his only distraction. Another matter had become even more pressing.

The most powerful vaudeville managers and theater owners, emulating the legitimate Trust, had recently formed the United Booking Office, incorporating the Keith, Albee, Poli, and Proctor chains. Variety performers, always somewhat exploited by theater men, were placed completely at their mercy by the merger. George Fuller Golden, a poetry-loving prize fighter turned professional hoofer, set out single-handedly to fight the monopolists and defend "My Lady Vaudeville." His first move was to form the Chivalrous Order of White Rats, an American vaudeville actors' union. The eight founding members, including future headliners Montgomery and Stone, elected Golden its first Big Chief, or, as he variously liked to call himself, the "Dromio" or "Fool."

At first, managers took little notice of the new order—their ranks were small, there were no big names among them. Soon, however, their number doubled, trebled, then swelled to hundreds of performers sick of exploitation. The order still lacked spokesmen with sufficient standing to stir complacent managers, until Edwin Milton Royle, an actor-author in both legitimate and variety theaters, who later wrote *The Squaw Man*, enlisted Digby Bell, a Barrymore crony.

"Royle and Bell were both members of the Lambs' Club," explained Big Chief Golden, "and as soon as Bell joined the society he was the means of bringing into the fold several members whose prominence begot an interest in the Order that had not previously been manifested by either press or public." Bell brought in DeWolf Hopper and Maurice Barrymore, and they, in turn, brought in other theatrical stalwarts. Myths concerning the aloofness and affected dignity of legitimate stars toward their variety counterparts were quickly dispelled. "With no possible motive to lure them," attested Golden, "they not only lent their names, but gave their time and money, and exerted their best efforts for the cause of their struggling Vaudeville Brothers."

None entered the fray with more ferocity than Maurice Barrymore, whose hatred of the Trust, legitimate prototype of the United Booking Office, fanned his ardor. "The brilliant wit of Theatrical Bohemia," as Golden called him, "ardent in his enthusiasm, and eloquent of speech," withdrew in protest from Keith's, refusing to play in any house controlled by the U.B.O. He made speeches and wrote circulars condemning monopolists, paid to have them printed on three-sheet bills and posted around the city. He made no exceptions. When Abe Erlanger, a Trust manager, offered him the *Prince of Morocco* in an all-star production of *The Merchant of Venice*, Barry submitted a terse refusal:

> I have received your offer to act the Prince of Morocco and feel myself compelled to decline. It is true that the existing conditions in theatrical management have driven me into vaudeville. But I have not yet gone into negro minstrelsy. I could recommend to you George M. Thacher, Press Eldridge or half a dozen other experienced burnt cork men who would be better in the part than I.

Aside from his blanket refusal to work for the Trust, he was convinced that the offer had been made merely to humiliate him, to undermine his professional standing. The opposite was true. Erlanger, assembling an all-star cast headed by Nat C. Goodwin, had considered Barry a worthy addition to an extraordinary company. Characteristically, however, when a fledgling independent producer offered a far less prestigious engagement, Barry readily accepted.

434

Daniel V. Arthur was mounting his first major production, a dramatization of Gilbert Parker's popular novel *The Battle of the Strong*, to star Marie Burroughs. Barry's engagement as leading man was generally considered a comedown for the triumphant *Rawdon Crawley*. Parker was no Thackeray. Miss Burroughs was no Mrs. Fiske. But she had been Barry's leading lady in *Captain Swift* a dozen years before, and he was fond of her. Stipulating that his part must be improved, its *Sydney Carton*-like characteristics emphasized, Barry had agreed to lend his name to her first starring tour.

As an actress, Marie Burroughs may not have challenged Mrs. Fiske, but as a beauty, she was without peer. Tall, dark, with violet eyes, she moved like a goddess—no mean feat, considering that every day she spent an hour walking with a glass of water on her head to correct a slight stoop. Such imperfections were obviously invisible to the mysterious Mr. Holbrook, who was financing, regardless of cost, Marie's first starring attempt. Gifts for her were always arriving from Mr. Holbrook during rehearsals—checks to cash, extravagant jewelry, boxes of silk lingerie. "I wondered how he always managed to get the right size in these lovely things," mused another actress in the cast.

Marie was unspoiled by Mr. Holbrook's attentions. She was generally good-natured and, since supporting him at Palmer's in *Captain Swift*, a staunch Barrymore admirer. Aware of the value of Barry's name to her first starring tour, she did her best to assuage him during a difficult rehearsal period. Nevertheless, when some of the changes that he had requested were found impracticable by the author, Barry asked for his release. He had completed his dramatization of *Cashel Byron's Profession*, and would just as soon have stayed in New York to arrange its production. "The manager urged the injury my withdrawal would inflict upon his enterprise, my engagement having been extensively announced, and begged me not to leave him in the lurch and to play the part," Barry stated. "This against my better judgment and inclination, I was weak enough to agree to do; but Mr. Arthur had been most kind, straightforward and polite to me and I had not the heart to disappoint him. Good nature, all my life, has been my greatest professional as well as personal stumbling block.

"During rehearsals," he continued, "constant changes in the manuscript were made, which, while they did not in the least improve my opportunities, made the task of committing my lines to memory almost beyond my powers." He could not learn his cues, and had to be repeatedly reminded of his entrances and exits. Unable to remember his lines as written, he interpolated words of his own which had no relevance. Marie Burroughs doggedly defended him, while manager Arthur fretted. Barry assured him that such behavior was customary, that he never did all expected of him until the first public performance: "It is notorious that I have the misfortune to have a very poor study and have been often well-nigh flayed alive for apparent indifference and neglect, when in point of fact I had worked harder and often hopelessly to acquire my lines, and had devoted more time and labor to my task than had the entire company combined." Arthur accepted the explanation, relieved, at least that the scheduled Thanksgiving Day opening in Louisville would not need postponing.

Barry sustained a mortal blow before the company left New York. Dramatist Harrison V. Wolfe announced the opening of another version of *Cashel Byron's Profession*. Barry immediately hired lawyer Abe Hummel to press his claim for legal rights of dramatization. It was hopeless. He had no legal rights. Wolfe had letters to prove payment of $500 to Shaw as a retainer for the rights, with an additional $2,000 if the play succeeded. It didn't. Wolfe's version opened on December 27 at the Herald Square, quickly closed. Its failure did not mitigate Barry's disheartening realization that another of his playwrighting attempts had been annihilated.

Marie Burroughs' first-night anxiety was diverted briefly by the arrival of an eight-carat marquise diamond ring from Mr. Holbrook. Nothing else happened to distract star and company from the impending Louisville opening. With new lines and business being mercilessly inserted, the actors rehearsed right up until curtain time. One scene was particularly elusive. The play's climax, a duel between Barry, the hero, and Holbrook Blinn, the heroine's faithless husband, was tried again and again without success. It was intended to be a swashbuckling, picturesque scene for the hero, as he fights for milady's honor with her son, played by "Little Blanche" Sweet, perched upon his shoulder. But something was lacking in its execution. Barry pondered, decided that realism was the missing ingredient. During the final run-through, without telling his stage adversary, he removed the guard from his foil, and abandoned himself to the passion of the scene. Holbrook Blinn played the Louisville opening with his wounded right arm in a sling.

Blinn's injury was one of several first-night calamities which indicated to critics that *The Battle of the Strong* was not ready to open. Whatever potential it held, they agreed, was hampered by the leading man. "He was not even able to fake his part, a resort of actors with bad memories," noted the *Courier-Journal*. "He is a victim of nervous disorder and his movements are erratic. At times he would stand helpless on the stage, delaying the action of the play, or else make a wrong exit."

The critic was kinder to the play. "Rewriting will be necessary," he admonished. "When this is successfully done the play will not lack in the elements that bring success." Other Louisville commentators were not so optimistic. Most agreed, however, that "Miss Burroughs acted with intel-

436

ligence, imagination and fine dramatic effect," that Mr. Blinn's performance was "finished, clear-cut and incisive," that Mr. Barrymore was "drunk or otherwise impaired." The actor who seldom read his reviews, cared little about them if he did, became uncharacteristically defensive in regard to his purported condition. He even asked Holbrook Blinn to write the *Courier-Journal* and explain that the duel scene was ineffective because of his injury. Convinced that he had not seriously faltered, that the critics were out to destroy him, Barry attempted to justify himself in letters to local editors:

"In consequence of new lines having been given me to speak on the very morning of production, and which in justice to myself I should have declined to attempt to speak, I admit in one little speech my memory faltered, in a way, however, not noticeable, I fancy, to any save the astute theatrical sharp. I was assaulted by a t'upenny h'apenny reporter in terms that could not have been justified by the combination of atrocities worthy of Jack the Ripper. I was sacrificed for the ruination of the play because, forsooth, the sword fight in the last act was not effective, when it should have been apparent to a twenty dollar a week intelligence that the ineffectiveness of the combat was due to the fact that my colleague, Mr. Blinn, who fought against me on the stage, had injured his right hand, it being palpably bandaged, and his sword held in his unaccustomed left. But this was all lost on our Rhadamanthus in his truculent mood. To show the malevolence of this reporter's point of view, when Mr. Blinn kindly wrote and explained the circumstances, the amende made was both curt and offensive." Barry mentioned neither the origin of the injury, nor the fact that Blinn had written at his urging.

"There was nothing, however," he concluded, "to justify the statement that I was either drunk or paretic, a fact which might easily have been verified by a twenty-five cent telegraphic inquiry to the management or to myself." Miss Burroughs and manager Arthur stood staunchly by their leading man, as they departed for a week in Milwaukee.

The *Journal* noted that Gilbert Parker's novel, on which the play was based, had sold three thousand copies "in Milwaukee alone." Such popularity augured well for the play's box office, predicted the paper, with the popularity of Marie Burroughs and Maurice Barrymore in the Cream City as additional lures. "Therefore the play has everything except prestige, perhaps, in its favor." What little prestige was gathered during the week in Milwaukee was not for the play but for Marie Burroughs. As for her leading man, the reaction to his performance ran the critical gamut.

"Maurice Barrymore gave Miss Burroughs excellent support in the character of *Detricand*, the French nobleman who is saved to himself by a woman's loyalty to country, and his own love for her." The *Sentinel*'s verdict was reassuring. "There are times when Mr. Barrymore grows a little too strenuous, but on the whole he was excellent in his rendering of the harum-scarum, tippling young man who in spite of his ways succeeds in endearing himself to everyone and who in the end reforms and saves the day as a hero should." The *Sentinel* was the first paper on the streets after the opening. Later editions were less encouraging. The *Evening Wisconsin*, at least, blamed the play.

"The faults in the construction of the play are possibly more apparent now than they will be later," the reviewer speculated, "because the production is very new and the rough edges have not yet been smoothed. Some excellent actors in the company seem to have no definite ideas of the characters they are called upon to represent and they consequently flounder. Mr. Barrymore is conspicuous in this respect, which is more the fault of the dramatist than his own." Other reviewers were less sympathetic.

"Maurice Barrymore has played many parts and played them well," conceded the *Daily News* critic. "But to say that he is even satisfactory as *Compte de Tournay* would be flattering him. He rants and raves, mumbles his words, shouts in his love passages and roars and bellows in the tenderer scenes. True, *de Tournay* is a swaggering French soldier and adventurer, but we have been led to believe he was a gentleman and courtier as well, if a man addicted to his cups. It was in this last that Mr. Barrymore played the part too well. His acting was realistic—too realistic to be wholly pleasing." Noting that the play was still in "the experimental stage," the *Daily News* at least reserved the right of final judgment on the Barrymore performance. The *Journal* made no such reservation.

"The support rendered Miss Burroughs by Maurice Barrymore was such as to upset the entire plot of the play and to render the efforts of *Guilda* to show her love for him as *Detricand* a positive burlesque. His work last night was atrocious, and that he did not entirely ruin the performance was due to no fault of his. His elocution was at times unintelligible and his stage business was awful. He hesitated in speaking his lines, and after his first few scenes his rambling work almost threw the remainder of the company into a panic. Miss Burroughs' agitation was plainly evident from the first row, and her work as his opposite in the play was magnificent, when it is considered with whom she was playing." The *Journal* critic also noted a preventive measure taken by the management on behalf of Holbrook Blinn and four-year-old Blanche Sweet. "The duel scene in the last act between *Detricand* and *Philip d'Avranche* was opportunely cut out after a reckless stab that Barrymore made, and the scene was brought to a finish as rapidly as possible." Since his injury at Louisville, Blinn had played in fear for himself and "Little Blanche."

Despite the critics, Milwaukee theatergoers responded to *The Battle of the Strong*. The Davidson Theatre was filled on the second night; the advance sale for the rest of the week was heavy. The play, still rehearsing for hours each day, was constantly being changed. Barry worked hard, straining against the accusations which he neither accepted nor understood. The *Daily News,* having reserved its judgment until the second performance, recorded an improvement. "Mr. Barrymore seemed to have taken a new grasp of the character of *Compte de Tournay* and played the part with a nicer discrimination and better results."

The Milwaukee engagement ended with a Souvenir Matinee and a Gala Evening. Both performances were well attended and enthusiastically received. Handsomely mounted posters of Miss Burroughs were presented to the ladies. But the final verdict of the press was not encouraging. "The twelve performances and steady rehearsals the play has received should have placed it on a basis satisfactory to the management and to the public," concluded the *Daily News.* "That this is not the fact is due to the playwright and not to the star or the company." With Barry apparently absolved, and Mr. Holbrook's faith and financing intact, the company headed for a week in Kansas City, Missouri.

BARRYMORE FIRED

Leading Support of Marie Burroughs
Given His Notice

Maurice Barrymore, leading man in *The Battle of the Strong,* which closed here Saturday night, has been given his two weeks' notice by the management. The cause for the act is not stated, but stories of his doings on and off the stage have been very numerous since he came here. It will be remembered that the *Journal* criticism of the play spoke of his work as 'atrocious' while other Milwaukee papers appeared to think he was 'splendid.' To those who 'saw' his performance, it is not surprising that he should be discharged.

This bit of self-indulgence by the *Journal* on December 10 was quickly contradicted by other Milwaukee papers. "Miss Marie Burroughs denies a report that Maurice Barrymore is to leave her company," noted the *Daily News.* "The actress professes to be perfectly satisfied with the acting of her leading man." Barry, in Chicago, on his way to Kansas City, emphatically denied the *Journal* report. He stated that his relations with manager Arthur and other members of the company had been most cordial, and that no differences had arisen between them. "Actor Barrymore believes that the Milwaukee report was originated by an enemy who sought in this manner to bring discredit upon him," explained the *Evening Wisconsin.* "The company will play at Kansas City, Mo., this week and Mr. Barrymore will appear in the leading role as usual."

Barry's performance was judged competent by Kansas City reviewers. His offstage behavior was the cause of some concern. In the café of the Coates Hotel one evening, the conversation turned to history and the Battle of Waterloo. The Grau Opera Company happened to be in town, and the café was filled with its French, German, and Italian members. One of them, a German, credited the Waterloo victory to his country's soldiers. Leaping suddenly to his feet, Barry began abusing the German, Germany, and every country but his own. Their citizens, he proclaimed, were cowards and liars, everything that was mean and low. A simultaneous move to swoop down upon him merely made the orator louder, more fierce and abusive. The others held back, sensing potential danger in his light-eyed ferocity. Confident that he had vindicated British honor, Barry swung gracefully out of the café.

He held his own onstage during the week, giving Kansas City critics a chance to scrutinize the play. They found it wanting. Manager Arthur decided that the company would not perform during the week before Christmas. They would stop in Chicago, at Mr. Holbrook's expense, for a week of revision and rehearsal. This respite gave the relentless Milwaukee *Journal* the excuse for another attack on December 17:

BARRYMORE LEAVES

Maurice Barrymore was compelled to leave the *Battle of the Strong* company at Kansas City and return to New York on account of his health. His memory appears to be gone and his friends are worried greatly over his condition. When Miss Burroughs' company appeared in Milwaukee, Barrymore hampered the production by forgetting his lines. At times he would stand helpless on stage delaying the action of the play.

Aware of Barry's reputation as a poor study, Broadway commentators had dismissed previous reports of a breakdown. Their repetition, however, was gaining attention in the national press. When distressed inquiries from his children reached Chicago, Barry had manager Arthur reply that he was "in good health and certainly not losing his mind." Despite such denials, New York papers picked up the more colorful reports.

"Is Maurice Barrymore in New York and what is the state of his health, mental and physical?" wondered the *Morning Telegraph* on December 18. "Such was the question asked up and down the line last night and in the cafés and clubs where the actor was once a well known and welcome figure. The reports which have come out of the West lead them to fear that despite denials by some of his family, he is on the verge of a breakdown."

Jack Barrymore was interviewed at Mrs. Wilson's boardinghouse, where he was staying with Ethel. "His son declared his father is not here and is not likely to be soon," the *Morning Telegraph* added. "He characterized the stories of the actor's breakdown as without foundation and declared telegrams had been received saying he is in the best of health." At the Lambs' Club, the report continued, "none of the members approached would admit knowledge of a precarious condition of his health. Some declared the stories were without foundation." Front-page conjecture persisted. The *World* had him meandering through the streets of New York in a daze. The *Sun*, on December 20, published what amounted to a premature obituary.

After a thorough reworking in Chicago, *The Battle of the Strong* opened a week's engagement in St. Louis. Barry's first-night performance was praised by local critics. The next day, Christmas Eve, in his dressing room at the Century Theatre, he carefully composed a letter to editors of the offending New York papers:

St. Louis, Mo., Dec. 24, 1900.

Sir:

My attention has been called to a series of absolutely unfounded statements that have appeared in your journal, to the effect that my health and reason were so impaired that I have not only ruined the production of the play in which I am now appearing, but my condition was such that any possible continuance of my career, such as it has been, upon the stage, was out of the question. That this is all entirely and palpably untrue is established by the fact that I am still with The Battle of the Strong *company, and that I was never in better condition, mental or physical, in my life . . .*

He detailed the constant rewriting during rehearsals, and rationalized his notorious inability to commit lines to memory.

Mere memory, however, is not the first or most essential quality of an actor. I played with Mr. Edwin Booth, at the Fifth Avenue Theatre, in New York, when he 'struck' eight times in his first speech of seven lines in the part of Richard III. *after ten years of the profoundest preparation. Mr. Stuart Robson, too, the dean of our profession, the most admired and most beloved member of our trade, has suffered in this regard without decapitation. But, 'what in the Captain's but a choleric word,' etc.—we all know the old quotation . . .*

His anger surfaced as he recounted the responses of "t'upenny, h'appeny" reporters in Louisville and Milwaukee.

In any case, the manager had purposely come to these two little watertank towns confessedly to try it 'on the dog,' as both Louisville and Milwaukee are worthless, financially considered, and their obscure verdicts of little or no importance to the well being of the play. What was his horror, then to find that the little mishaps he cheerfully expected and paid out his good money to discover and inter in these queer little theatrical morgues, were given a publicity and importance worthy of the greatest national issues . . .

He underscored statements made in his letter to Louisville editors at the start of the tour, emphatically denying that he had been "drunk or paretic."

The statements were all utterly untrue, but they have caused the deepest distress to my children, to my friends and to myself. I think you owe it to me, upon whom you have inflicted, unwittingly if you will, a very cruel injury, to do all you can to repair it by publishing as much of this explanation as the justice of my request demands, and your space warrants. I remain yours faithfully,

Maurice Barrymore

The *Morning Telegraph* printed the entire letter in two full columns, with a retraction stating "beyond doubt, that stories published concerning the health of Maurice Barrymore have been exaggerated in a manner not warranted by the facts. Mr. Barrymore's letter makes it self-evident that his intellect has not undergone any change for the worse, and it is a pleasure to this paper to be enabled in this emphatic manner to set at rest all rumors concerning the failing of the actor's mental power." The retraction further explained that "the stories concerning Mr. Barrymore printed in this paper, and to which he alludes, were secured from telegraphic correspondents in the manner usual to all newspapers." The *Sun* and other offending papers, with one exception, printed parts of the letter and full retractions. Only the *World* refused to do so, and Barry wired Abe Hummel to start legal proceedings immediately.

With its leading man's problems apparently settled, *The Battle of the Strong* company faced another crucial matter. The week of revision and rehearsal in Chicago had not improved the play. St. Louis critics had lambasted it. Even the generous Mr. Holbrook was losing faith. It was decided to cancel Washington and New York commitments, to give the production a decent burial in St. Louis.

Barry did some shopping before leaving the city. He arrived penniless in New York with his purchases—twenty-two $14 suits of identical color, cut and fabric.

REMORSE

One of Jack's macabre early paintings.

Student-artist Jack at eighteen (circle); actor-artist Lionel at twenty. Below, Ethel at seventeen, when she made her first hit in *Rosemary*.

Ethel's sensational debut as a star in *Captain Jinks of the Horse Marines* was helped immeasurably by the costumes of her father's friend, Percy Anderson.

Barry, at fifty, reached the pinnacle of his career as *Rawdon Crawley* in *Becky Sharp*, the popular dramatization of Thackeray's *Vanity Fair* with Mrs. Fiske (*above*) in the title role.

"Little Blanche" Sweet (*left*), costumed for *The Battle of the Strong*, was photographed in Louisville at the start of Barry's last tour.

facing page: Dame Ellen Terry (left) and Sir Henry Irving (right) helped Sir Henry's son, Laurence (below), in his courtship of Ethel Barrymore, whose splendid profile helps to explain his interest. Young Irving became the first of that much-courted girl's many fiancés.

In the small part of an Italian organ grinder, without uttering a word of English, Lionel Barrymore stole *The Mummy and the Humming Bird* from its elegant star, his uncle, John Drew, caricatured (*left*) in "fashionable society clothes for the benefit of those for whom he long served as a model."

A TYPE

ANGLO-INDIAN
TYPE

Evelin Nesbit (*below, left*), John Barrymore's professed first love, might well have invoked the caption below in chorus with many other young ladies during Jack's early years as a Manhattan artist (illustrations, *left*) and newspaperman.

"JACK'S THE BOY FOR ME"

Maurice Barrymore sat for his last photograph when *The Battle of the Strong* company stopped in Chicago the week before Christmas, 1900. When compared to his picture as *Rawdon Crawley*, taken only a year earlier, the progress of his insidious disease is already painfully evident.

XXXII

De ferred payments from previous vaudeville tours kept Barry after his sartorial return from St. Louis. He spent the proceeds lavishly, never wisely, according to his critics, wisely, indeed, according to friends, acquaintances and occasional strangers who benefited from his convivial care and feeding. The more perceptive recipients found him somewhat distracted, but not to the extent reported from the West. The good fellow had apparently survived.

The Barrymore name had also managed to survive the progenitor's latest vicissitudes. In St. Louis, it was considerably embellished by his elder son. "The name of Barrymore is a guarantee of excellence in things dramatic," the *Star* reaffirmed, "and Lionel, the son of Maurice Barrymore, who was with Marie Burroughs in *The Battle of the Strong* at the Century last week, makes a straight-forward, manly *Lieut. Denton*. The part of the sorely tried young hero affords excellent opportunities for melodramatic flare-ups—which he avoids. He carries himself as you imagine a brave young fellow would under the circumstances—modestly and without bravado."

When *Sag Harbor* had closed after seventy-six performances in New York, Lionel joined a touring company of Gus Thomas's *Arizona*, advancing from his minor role in its original production to romantic hero on the road. Although he despised playing such roles, this one gained credulity from his quiet interpretation. Praise and family comparisons continued during *Arizona*'s cross-country tour. As one Midwestern commentator put it, "The young man is doing his best to live up to his name and the traditions that encircle it." The company, an excellent one, included Eleanor Robson, who later married millionaire August Belmont. "Lionel took a hand in my education by introducing me to the works of Rudyard Kipling," Mrs. Belmont recalled. "He read aloud the jungle books. As we jolted along, on one-night stands, we forgot the uncomfortable road and reveled in the adventures of Rikki-Tikki-Tavi, the song of the Bandar-log, and loved Wee Willie Winkie and his 'parkle crown.' "

Jack, meanwhile, was not excelling in the art studies subsidized by his father. Barry was informed that his younger son had attended only one class at the Art Students League. "I don't want to know why you skipped classes," Barry told the would-be artist. "The thing that I can't understand is how you happened to go once!"

Papa was nevertheless impressed by Jack's macabre sketching and general appreciation of art. Rembrandt was his favorite old master, he told his father, "because he is honest, direct and strong." Of the moderns, he liked Watts, "because of his poetry, imagination and meaning, suggested rather than expressed." The works he most wanted to illustrate were Heine's *Florentine Nights*, the stories of Edgar Allen Poe, and Flaubert's *Salammbô*. If he could create scenery and costumes for any play, he speculated, it would be *The Hunchback of Notre Dame*.

Jack's recitation of Professor Hegel's philosophy, that part about the beauty of art being "essentially a question, an address to a responding breast, a call to the heart and spirit," was irresistible to Barry. He again financed his son's studies, this time, private lessons with George Bridgman, the renowned painter.

If Barry seemed distracted to his friends that winter, it was, they reasoned, in the best tradition of Barrymore distractions. He was waging battle with the unrepentant *World*—verbally brilliant when the plaintiff carried it to the cafés, laggard in the law offices of Abe Hummel. And another play was brewing. *The Lady and the Burglar*, as he called it, was not up to his usual standard. It was merely another one-act dramatization of Mrs. Burnett's short story, "Editha's Burglar," on which Gus Thomas had already based a one-acter and eventually a full-length play, *The Burglar*, featuring none other than Maurice Barrymore. Barry's new version, which owed much to Gus's original, was to be a vaudeville alternative to *A Man of the World*. When it was finished, he accepted an offer to play the independent Park Theatre in Worcester, Massachusetts. His popularity in that New England mill town had been insured two years before, when he headed its first vaudeville bill. His new one-acter, he assumed, would be welcomed there.

"The principal feature of next week's vaudeville bill at the Park theatre will be one of the most expensive acts ever seen here in the person of the famous actor, Maurice Barrymore, and his own company of four people, presenting his greatest success, *A Man of the World*." The *Evening Gazette* was joined by the other local papers in heralding Barry's arrival. "Maurice Barrymore is one of the most popular and highest salaried lead-

444

ing actors in the country," declared *The Spy*. "Mr. Barrymore is one of the most entertaining actors who has appeared in a sketch at the Front-street house," added the *Daily Telegram*, "and has been in vaudeville several years. He likes vaudeville, and has made a success of it. He has a new sketch which is well spoken of, and it is possible he will give it in Worcester this week, although he will open with the *Man of the World*."

From the moment of his Sunday-afternoon arrival at the Lincoln House, Barry rehearsed his company in *A Man of the World*, while preparing *The Lady and the Burglar* for its first production. He had assembled a fine cast—character men Bert Anderson and Arthur Dighl, and Miss R. Stuart, former leading lady at New York's Murray Hill Theatre. Jack Barrymore, less complacent than he had been during the Hose Company No. 1 benefit, worked diligently along with them to prepare for his professional debut on January 21, 1901.

"Seven strong acts played the Park theatre yesterday," observed the Tuesday *Telegram*, "the principal being Maurice Barrymore, the mere mention of his name being sufficient to draw a large patronage." The critic praised the choice of *A Man of the World*, and offered the first recorded critique of John Barrymore's acting: "Mr. Barrymore is assisted by his son Jack, who is following in the footsteps of his father as a good actor." The *Evening Gazette* did not belabor the obvious. "It was to be expected that Maurice Barrymore would be a success," stated its terse notice. Such unsullied support heartened Barry after the assaults of his recent tour. He announced that *The Lady and the Burglar* would have its première on Thursday afternoon.

The new one-acter made an immediate hit with Worcester patrons. *The Spy* even suggested that it "seems to be a better vehicle for Mr. Barrymore than his *A Man of the World*. There is more possibility for good 'business' in it." *The Lady and the Burglar* was played again on Thursday evening, when another new feature also appeared on the bill. Josephine Gassman, to counteract an injurious rumor, was offering more than her usual "Singing Pickaninnies." "Many of the people who have seen Josephine Gassman at the Park Theatre this week are under the impression that she is a negress. In order to establish proof that she isn't," explained *The Spy*, "this evening, Miss Gassman intends to show how she makes up her face to give herself the complexion of a mulatto."

The Lady and the Burglar continued to please Worcester patrons until the end of the week, convincing Barry that he had written a worthy successor to *A Man of the World*. He was cheerful and spouting plans for a tour of independent vaudeville houses, when a man from *The Spy* visited his dressing room. "Maurice Barrymore, the ideal of the matinee girl, is a pleasant man to meet socially," the reporter attested. "His reminiscences of the stage are intensely interesting, and last night, after his act was over at the Park, he entertained *The Spy* man for more than an hour, telling funny little stories about stage people." Recent problems were also touched upon. "It will be remembered that he has a big libel suit pending against the New York *World*. The article complained of insinuated things that roused the blood of the actor, and he swears that he will make them eat all kinds of fire before he is done with them."

Barry did not return to New York with Jack and the rest of his company. He went to Boston to appear in a Sunday-evening benefit at the Tremont. That theater's publicity man, Ned Perry, a friend from early Boston days, had asked him to recite W. S. Gilbert's ballad of the two men who had never been introduced, a popular Barrymore recitation. The Boston audience gave warm welcome as their old favorite walked on stage. The first verse rolled lightly off his tongue. But halfway through the ballad, he struck and began again. He repeated the first verse half-a-dozen times, straining for the elusive lines. They would not come. He began to mumble, then stood silent, gazing helplessly toward the audience. Ned Perry finally had to come out and lead him off.

While Jack tried vaudeville with Papa, and Lionel toured in *Arizona*, their sister was far from idle. "Ethel, I have a nice part for you at last," Charles Frohman had predicted when she returned from England. The "Little Napoleon of the Theatre" was seldom wrong. The part was *Madame Trentoni*, a young "Italian" prima donna, who is actually *Aurelia Johnson* from Trenton, New Jersey. The play, *Captain Jinks of the Horse Marines*, was the latest endeavor of Clyde Fitch, Broadway's playwright of the hour. The title, taken from a popular music hall jingle of the '70s, perfectly suited this tale of New York life after the Civil War, a period of side-whiskers, the "Grecian bend," and *Godey's Ladies' Book*. Barry's London friend, Percy Anderson, was commissioned to do costumes based on Godey's prints. C.F. stipulated, regardless of expense, that Ethel's gowns should make the matinee ladies swoon.

Frohman was anticipating the addition of another star to his flourishing galaxy. Clyde Fitch was not so confident. The playwright had wanted a more established actress for the role, one that would insure the success of his latest work. He was not an easy man to convince, and Frohman did not wish to offend his most profitable playwright. But finally the persuasive manager had prevailed. Clyde Fitch accepted Ethel Barrymore.

At first, the young actress was intimidated by the effete playwright, who audited rehearsals smoking gold-tipped cigarettes, wearing immaculate high collars, English hats, spats, and never the same suit twice. But beneath the façade of a dandified ass was a lover of beauty, a brilliant writer of plays with a keen knowledge of human nature, an astute man of the theater. He knew every bit of scenery, drapery, furniture in the Frohman storehouse, and wrote around them. He could tell the women

446

how to dress and, on occasion, could even make the frocks and hats himself. He worked tirelessly during *Captain Jinks* rehearsals, rewriting, helping C.F. with the staging, fussing over Ethel's costumes.

Ethel worked equally hard, and Fitch soon became her greatest champion. He even rewrote the play to her measure, basing a "take off" of local press methods on Ethel's own experiences with reporters, who were concurrently attributing at least one headline betrothal a week to her. The leading role was a taxing one. After each rehearsal of a particularly emotional dance scene, the frail young actress would faint. Harry Reeves-Smith, her leading man, was always ready to catch her as she fell into the wings.

WALNUT STREET THEATRE, PHILADELPHIA
WEEK BEGINNING MONDAY, JANUARY 7TH, 1901
CHARLES FROHMAN PRESENTS
A FANTASTIC COMEDY IN THREE ACTS, ENTITLED
CAPTAIN JINKS OF THE HORSE MARINES
BY CLYDE FITCH
WITH
ETHEL BARRYMORE

C.F. had chosen the home of the Drews for the play's première. Ethel's confidence was not bolstered by the choice. She anticipated a half-empty house for her featured debut, a closing notice in the morning. Just as the stage manager was about to signal the rise of the curtain, Ethel cried, "Oh, no; please wait one second." Fearing the outcome of the first performance, she had sent for Frohman's company manager. "I haven't any money," she confessed to him haltingly; "do you think you could let me have five dollars until salary day?"

"Five dollars!" roared Frohman's representative. "Do you know how many people are in the house?" Ethel looked puzzled. "No? Well, look through there." Squinting out through the peephole in the curtain, she saw a house packed from pit to dome—managers, playwrights, society, Philadelphia critics, New York correspondents, and first-night regulars in the gallery ready to approve what they liked, denounce what they didn't.

There was positive applause when Ethel entered. But her opening lines did not register. She was nervous and not quite audible. "Speak up, Ethel," cried someone from the gallery. "You're all right. The Drews is all good actors."

"We loved your grandmother, Ethel," added another, "and we love you."

Ethel spoke up.

"'A charming comedy and a decided success,' was the verdict of the audience," reported the New York *Herald* correspondent. "The play has many witty lines that were received with hearty laughter and applause from an overflowing house." Philadelphia papers were more equivocal about the play, but they agreed with the *Record* on one point: "Ethel Barrymore is very fine. She has developed appreciably, and her comedy work could not be better." After a fortnight's stay in Philadelphia, the company played two weeks of one-night stands—Lancaster, Trenton, Atlantic City, Wilmington, Scranton, Wilkes-Barre, Ithaca, Rochester, Syracuse, Albany, Schenectady. "I congratulate you on the *BIG* success at the Garden!" Fitch wired Frohman. "Of course I was tremendously anxious that *our* piece would go! And Ethel make a hit, which she has!"

Ethel sat at her dressing table before the New York opening, staring at a gift which had just been delivered. Uncle Jack, performing at the Empire that evening, was unable to attend his niece's first night. But recalling the old rural wheeze that had been quoted so often to the Barrymore children—"Speak your piece good and you'll get a big red apple."—he had sent the biggest, reddest apple to be found in New York. The thought was appreciated. Ethel, however, despite success on the road, was beyond comfort. "Why am I doing this?" she kept repeating to herself. "Why didn't I try to do something else?"

The Garrick Theatre was sold out for the February 3rd opening. Most of the glittering assemblage seemed predisposed to giving Ethel the evening. "She is the daughter of her mother, a woman who has never been replaced in the profession in which she was a unique figure," noted the *Journal*. "Many an 'old timer' in the theatre brought with him somewhere under his vest a very friendly feeling for the lovely daughter of Georgie Drew." Jack Barrymore sat in a box with Aunt Dodo and a covey of swells. Barry preferred to be inconspicuous. He and Gus Thomas bought standing room and leaned on the bulkhead at the back of the crowded house.

Ethel made her first entrance from a ship tied up at the landing deck of the Cunard Steamship Company. Reporters from the *Times, Tribune, Herald,* and *Sun* waited at the foot of the gangplank to interview her:

The Newsboy *whistles shrilly through his fingers to attract their attention, and they all turn quickly to look as* Aurelia *appears on the ship. She is quite the most lovely creature that ever came, like Venus Aphrodite, from the sea! Youth and beauty join in making her adorable, and a charming individuality, with a sense of humor bewilderingly attractive, makes her victory over mere man, irrespective of age or station, child's play. Her modish bustle only accentuates the grace of her girlish figure. And even a 'waterfall' only seems to make a friendly background for her perfect brow and finely poised head. She carries in her arms a very small black-and-tan dog; she wears an ermine fur tippet and carries a muff. The* Reporters *quickly draw up to one side. Aurelia stops at the top of the gang-plank for a moment, looking around her and smiling, and then runs gaily down.*

It was a tribute to Ethel Barrymore that she not only achieved Clyde Fitch's stage directions for that entrance but surpassed them. After a spontaneous hush, the audience broke into prolonged applause. "Of course, her friends present were ready-handed to applaud her anyway," noted the *Sun*, "but her performance needed no unearned approval, and the ado made over it soon became wholly sincere." Ethel held her opening line for several minutes.

> *Aurelia.* Hip! hip! hurrah! Here we are at last on American soil—planks—never mind, *soil*—E Pluribus Unum! (*She stands by the foot of the gang-plank. All the* Reporters *raise their hats.*)

Barry's eyes were filled with tears when he turned to Gus Thomas. "My God," he whispered, "isn't she sweet?"

Some others in the audience seemed less susceptible. Between acts, Jack overheard Elisabeth Marbury, the playbroker who had first brought Frohman and Fitch together, tell the playwright that *Captain Jinks* was terrible and wouldn't last a week. Jack fretted through the last act, until "kidglove-bursting applause" and much bouquet-tossing during Ethel's bows reassured him. He joined the crush of admirers gathered around her dressing-room door afterward.

Representatives of the four hundred mingled with friends and family in an effort to congratulate the heroine of the evening. Abandoning the "rogues and vagabonds" view of actors, at least of some actors, New York society had become unusually proprietary toward "their Ethel." Aunt Dodo and Jack, Mr. and Mrs. Richard Harding Davis, the Charles Dana Gibsons were joined by Mrs. Ogden Mills, with the Misses Mills, Mrs. George Gould, formerly Edith Kingdon of the Daly company, the Cornelius Vanderbilts, the Stanley Mortimers, the Clarence Mackays, the Stanford Whites, the N. de R. Whitehouses, and Frederick Gebhard, Lillie Langtry's spurned protector, with his new wife, Marie Wilson, one of the original *Florodora* girls.

Bouquet-proffering scions of New York's first families were also much in evidence. Worthington Whitehouse, Robert L. Gerry, Alphonse Navarro, Frank Bishop, R. H. Russell, Charleses Mathews and Bohlen assiduously vied for attention from the young actress. Her thoughts were elsewhere. "Where's Father?" she asked her brother. "He promised he'd be here." Neither Jack nor anyone else present could answer. But when the throng diminished, Barry appeared from the wings, where, unnoticed, he had stood watching. He kissed his daughter, whispered, "It was wonderful, darling," and disappeared.

"This was too important a moment in his life to share with a crowd in a dressing-room," Jack explained, "and he went home to be alone with his great happiness."

"I sat up all night," Ethel confessed, "because I could not sleep through fear of what the critics might say of me." They said much of her. The *Times*, devoting nearly its whole review to the twenty-one-year-old actress, observed that she "impresses a careful observer as being a young woman who will bear a good deal of watching in the future. She comes of excellent stock, she is handsome, she has 'presence,' she has a sense of humor, she has a good voice, she already has appreciable force. She may yet do wonders . . . The fact must be borne in mind, too," the critic added, "that Miss Barrymore was received last night with all the honors due to a Modjeska or a Cushman."

"Miss Barrymore's acting will carry the play, which will serve its purpose to pass a merry hour or two away," predicted the less-guarded *Herald*. "The triumph scored last night is a personal one for Miss Barrymore, who as *Mrs. Trentoni* acted with taste and spirit and looked refreshingly pretty." The *Sun* observed that "Her inheritance of a gift of comic expression that betrays no effort, her beauty of a type to impart an aspect of refinement to her fun, and her sufficient skill to utilize her natural advantages effectually in serio-comic scenes, make her the full equal of Georgie Drew Barrymore as an exposition of debonair sentiment."

"I have spoken of the darkest time of my life," Ethel told an interviewer, referring to her mother's death and its aftermath. "The brightest was the morning after the opening of *Captain Jinks*. I read the earliest editions of the papers and found that the critics had been good to me. That was the happiest day of my life. I felt that I had done something, even if very little, to divert the newspapers from printing fables twice a week about my engagements, often to men I had never seen. I hoped that I had ceased to be a joke because of those engagement fictions. Hence most of my joy."

Some critics, however, were not so encouraging. William Winter, foremost among them, conceded that "Miss Barrymore presented a pleasing appearance," but found her "a juvenile performer, still in the experimental stage." Such dissent had little effect on the avid public that kept the play sold out after its opening. Uncle Jack, extremely proud of his niece, urged all of his friends to visit the Garrick. Clyde Fitch, with four plays running on Broadway, gave frequent box parties to applaud the personification of his *Aurelia Johnson*. Weber & Fields paid the ultimate compliment by replacing the concurrent show at their Music Hall with a

Captain Jinks burlesque, which achieved one of their biggest hits, while increasing the already enormous popularity of the original.

Success did not turn Ethel's celebrated head, but the weekly salary of $125 allowed her to make a grand move—from the hall bedroom at Mrs. Wilson's to the second floor front. The new room was larger, with an alcove that alternately served as a sitting room, or a sort of "friar's cell" when Jack stayed there. One evening, three weeks into the run of *Captain Jinks*, Jack walked his sister from Mrs. Wilson's on Thirty-sixth Street around the corner to the Garrick on Thirty-fifth. As they approached the theater, the marquee lights seemed different to Ethel. Thinking nothing of it, she continued chatting with Jack. But something compelled her to glance up again. She stopped, held tightly to her brother's arm, and began to cry. Jack looked up at the marquee. Above the title, in huge electric lights, blazed ETHEL BARRYMORE. Jack, too, began crying. His sister was a star.

Next day, Ethel went to Charles Frohman's office above the Empire Theatre. "It was a wonderful thing for you to do," she told him.

"I didn't do it," C.F. replied, pointing through the window to people in the street below. "They did it."

Ethel saw nothing of her father in the weeks following his appearance at the *Captain Jinks* opening. Jack kept in more or less regular contact with him, serving as intermediary between him and Ethel. The youngest Barrymore was again pursuing the artist's life, and an artist needed a studio. Papa complied to the extent of financing an unfurnished hall room at Fourteenth Street and Sixth Avenue. The "studio" was bare, except for a sink and a gas plate, but Papa promised to send the necessary furniture. He did so, only his idea of necessary furniture, it turned out, consisted of four crates of his old books, including the cookery books which had graced Aunt Amelia Blyth's "English" kitchen in Amritsar. Jack soon found new uses for these, as well as for the works of Dickens and Fielding, Thackeray and Trollope. He read them, to be sure, but discovered also a previously neglected benefit of great literature. On cold winter nights, he burrowed himself under the great pile of books to keep warm.

Barry was still devoting himself to *The Burglar and the Lady* and the White Rats. He rewrote the one-acter, held auditions to cast it, then rewrote it again. The more he worked it over, the more it resembled Gus Thomas's original. Barry seemed unaware of any similarity as he read his latest version to Gus, and Gus thought it kinder not to disillusion his friend.

Rewriting had reinstated the child part in Barry's playlet, a part which was perfect for "Little Blanche" Sweet, who had toured with him in *The Battle of the Strong*. He lost no time in locating the rooming house on West Thirty-fourth Street where the child lived with her grandmother,

Cora Alexander. At first, recalling the hazards of Barry's dueling on the road, Mrs. Alexander was apprehensive. But Mr. Barrymore seemed gentle enough, and Blanche was fond of him. "I must have liked him," she remembered, "or I wouldn't have worked with him. I was only four or five at the time, but I wouldn't work with anyone I didn't like. I refused to play with Richard Mansfield that season, no matter how much my grandmother pleaded, because I didn't like his face." Barry became a regular visitor at their third-floor walk-up, rehearsing "Little Blanche" for a vaudeville tour of *The Burglar and the Lady*.

His support of the burgeoning White Rats was more frenetic. Friends noted a compulsive drive in his commitment to the vaudeville union and a conversational fixation upon it. At the Lambs' he indulged in long-winded, repetitive discourses on the topic, until even his most loyal admirers balked. One evening, after a bitter Barrymore harangue against vaudeville managers, Wilton Lackaye gazed pointedly at his friend from across their table and recited Aubrey's epitaph:

> *He walked beneath the moon,*
> *He slept beneath the sun,*
> *He lived a life of going to do,*
> *And died with nothing done.*

Barry was undaunted. When he attended board meetings, presided over by George Fuller Golden, the Big Chief or "Fool" of the White Rats, he became involved and overwrought. When Golden momentarily left a meeting to get some papers from another room, Barry stood and addressed the remaining members.

"You see that fellow?" he began, pointing after Golden. "He is a Fool. I once came through a glacial region where men were made of stone and hearts were made of ice, and those men were all congealed together, till they formed one huge mountain that reached to the sky." His voice became tremulous, increasingly impassioned. "There was no way around at either end, and in front of this mountain of rock and ice stood a Fool glaring at it. Back of him stood his army of Mountebanks. I said to him: 'Whither goest, Fool?' and he answered, 'Through the mountain.' I ran away, shouting, 'Fool! Fool! Fool!' My laugh reverberated all through the valleys of the glacial region. Anon, I returned, and there stood the Fool. His penknife was splintered, his hands were bleeding, but, by all the gods, the mountain was gone! and the Fool and his Army went marching on!"

Barry was shouting by the end of his impromptu parable. The assemblage watched silently, amazed. Even in the light of their fervent crusade, this paean was excessive. "He hated all forms of cant and sophistry," Golden said of Barry, "and woe betide any ill-advised pretender who dared to enter the lists with him! His wit was brilliant, scintillating, pungent, but in his heart he was a poet. However, he was on the wane at this time, and his admiration for the Fool was great."

A few nights later, on the Fort Lee ferry, police impounded a knife that Barry was brandishing. He explained that he was "out to get" Edward F. Albee, head of the United Booking Office.

Friends like William Rideing tried to avoid the obvious, reminding themselves that Barry had always been eccentric. The Barrymore-Rideing friendship, having survived eccentricities and twenty passing years since they had first gathered with the literati at Oscar's, was not about to be shaken by reports of his recent exploits. The faith of Rideing and his wife was rewarded when Barry arrived for a luncheon party not only on time but impeccably attired, and joined them and their other guests in conversation, "making, as it were," Rideing attested, "still water effervesce. Epigrams were easy for him. He was not addicted to long speeches; what he said was crisp and edged with raillery. We talked of books, of pictures, and, be sure, of plays—Shakespeare and the musical glasses. How he found time to read I do not know, but he was a well-read man." When talk turned to religion, Barry fondly recalled Georgie's devoted Catholicism.

"You are not a Roman Catholic, Barry!" his host exclaimed.

"Yes, William, I am," he responded surprisingly, "but I'm afraid God does not know it."

As the afternoon wore on, however, a disheartening transformation took place. "He stayed and stayed, remaining long after the others had gone," Rideing recalled, "and such a rapid change came over him as I had never seen in any human being before and hope never to see again. He became lachrymose, spasmodic, and hysterical. He aged before our eyes as though years were slipping away from him instead of hours. His speech rambled and stumbled, tears fell from his eyes, his handsome face became haggard and senile."

Reacting more to the evident discomfort of his friends than to any understanding of what was happening to him, Barry strained to regain control. "He pulled himself together and laughed before his departure," Rideing concluded. "But the laughter was constrained, and when the door closed, the door that had been opened for him so gladly, I had a too soon verified presentment that we should not meet him again."

Barry was still living at his Coytesville country house tended by a manservant, dominated by Patrick Boniface. The willful Maltese, with paws like velvet-covered bricks, finally forced the master of them all to remove Pidgewidge and Dodor to Staten Island, where they would join the descendants of Commander Peary's Huskies and other survivors of the fire, proliferating under the relaxed supervision of Edward Briggs.

Sailing to the farm with his ostracized mongrels, Barry met Virginia Tracy and her mother on the packed ferry. "He stood in front of the seats which he had quickly found for us," Virginia remembered, "his hands in his pockets, swaying a little to the motion of the boat, talking and telling jokes on himself and his dogs." Virginia, reminded of their *Aristocracy* tour, mentioned his loving care of the black chow, of Kimo and Rita, of seven Japanese spaniels, of twittering strawberry birds. The ferry docked at Staten Island. Barry and the ladies parted with promises of future meetings.

"I was still more or less young," Virginia mused afterward, "and if anyone had told me that I should never see him again I could not have believed it. He, at least, never grew old."

XXXIII

Barry returned to vaudeville with a vengeance on March 25, headlining a White Rats benefit at the Lion Palace Music Hall. "There was a large audience drawn there," reported the *Journal*, "chiefly by the not yet departed vogue of the once great actor and in part by the stories of his ardent advocacy of the cause of the White Rats." Anticipating an incident at the Lion Palace, Broadway denizens journeyed uptown to 110th Street. They were disappointed. Barry's opening-night monologue was impassioned but otherwise uneventful.

Afterward, he repaired to Broadway and Thirty-fourth Street, where his old friend James J. Corbett had recently opened a café. True to his sobriquet, "Gentleman Jim," the retired boxing champion prided himself on running a clean, orderly establishment, catering to theater people, sports figures, and men about town. Barry seemed "his usual cheerful self," Corbett observed, when he appeared there after the Lion Palace opening.

"Hello, Jim!" he called, slapping his friend on the back, before sitting down with him. As they bantered, Corbett remembered something that he had wanted to ask.

"Barry," he wondered, "would you mind giving me a copy of that poem you recite—the one about the clouds?"

"Did you like that?" Barry inquired, rather excitedly.

"Yes, I thought it was beautiful."

"Immediately he stood up and started to recite it with his fine rounded voice and magnificent gestures," Corbett recalled. "It was always a treat to listen to him. But just as he said: 'The big cloud said to the little cloud' (I forget the exact lines, but they were sad) he started to cry." Corbett stood up, pulled his friend down into a chair.

"Barry," he reasoned, "you're too big a man to get up and recite in a place like this before a lot of strangers." Barry ignored him. He stood up again and muddled through to the end of the poem, his rounded voice flattened, his magnificent gestures broken.

"Don't do it," Corbett implored. "There are two newspaper men over there, and it might get in the papers." Such an argument could only incite Maurice Barrymore. He rushed over to the reporters, and began abusing them with a magnificent flow of rhetoric. "He seemed to remember every grievance he had against any paper in this country or England, and was taking it out on these two fellows, and I never heard a man more eloquent." Eloquence notwithstanding, "Gentleman Jim" also considered the reactions of his other patrons. Barry was not confining his attack to the two reporters. He was addressing the crowded café at large. Corbett maneuvered him into another room and again implored him to keep quiet. Wheeling around suddenly, Barry seized the champion's lapels.

"Jim," he cried, "I'm a greater man than Shakespeare!"

Corbett stared incredulously at his old friend, trying to fathom this uncharacteristic outburst. "Now I knew he hadn't been drinking, and that by nature he was one of the most modest men that ever walked the stage. So I felt it must be all up with poor Barry." Jim sent a message over to the Lambs'. Digby Bell, an old Barrymore crony, arrived to escort him back to the club. Barry became docile when Bell appeared, took his proffered hand, and followed him childlike out of Corbett's café.

His condition seemed improved when they reached the Lambs'. He chatted amiably with fellow members, even tossing off some epigrams and rejoinders. He rhapsodized about the charm and beauty of his daughter's *Madame Trentoni*, implying that no actress had ever before possessed these attributes. Digby Bell agreed that Ethel was indeed charming and beautiful. "But Barry," he added. "The old flames!"

"This is the only flame," insisted the proud father. "Those were only matches."

Presently, before the eyes of his astonished cronies, a change came over him. His superlative features contorted, his deep green eyes grew pale and shallow. He raved over injustices committed by managers against the White Rats and himself, "the best actor in the world." When the orator ignored suggestions that he rest in an upstairs room, Gus Thomas was sent for. Barry was no more responsive to the urging of his best friend. Gus finally went across Thirty-sixth Street to consult Ethel and Jack at Mrs. Wilson's. Jack returned with him to the Lambs'. Barry also ignored the entreaties of his younger son. Long the go-between for his father and sister, Jack retreated to Ethel's rooms.

"Papa is nervous and excitable," he reported.

"More than usual?" Ethel asked.

"More than usual," Jack replied. They looked gravely at one another, used to anxiety over their erratic parent.

456

Jack's reports to his sister continued. On Tuesday, it was "bad." Wednesday it was "worse." On Thursday he followed his father to the Lion Palace Music Hall.

A full house, drawn by reports of Barry's recent misadventures, applauded with morbid enthusiasm when he appeared. "Barrymore looked strange in spite of his makeup," reported the *Journal*. "His eyes were large and staring. He looked unkempt and his hands twitched nervously." Stepping to the front of the stage, he did not recite his usual monologue.

"Down with the Trust!" he cried. "Death to the syndicate! Charles Frohman is doomed!" He spoke fast, indistinctly; only those in the front rows understood all of what he said. His meaning, however, was plain. George Fuller Golden and the White Rats were glorified. Frohman, Albee, managers in general were roundly reviled, consigned to the fires of hell.

The stage manager ordered him off. If the orator heard, he did not obey. Tossing his arms above his head, striding from one side of the stage to the other, he aimed bitter invective at Jewish managers, Jews, and, finally, all mankind. Tears coursed uncontrollably down his cheeks. The audience stared incredulously, at first, then began tittering. One woman screamed. The curtain was rung down.

Oblivious to the fiasco of his act, Barry announced backstage that he was going to Browne's chophouse. Once out of the music hall, he changed course, running twenty blocks to the Fort Lee ferry, at the foot of 130th Street. Jack followed. But Barry would not acknowledge the presence of his son. He neither spoke to Jack nor even looked at him. He did, however, try to engage every other passenger waiting in the ferryhouse. Those who would not respond were treated to a blast of Barrymore expletives. Women left the ferryhouse with their escorts, apparently regarding March wind less cutting than Barry's insults. He badgered remaining passengers during the half-hour wait, talking wildly to one couple until they changed seats to avoid him. When he persisted in following them, the man complained to a policeman. Barry was roughly advised to behave himself.

"I'm not used to be ordered about by a policeman," the offender protested, striking a glancing blow to the officer's left cheek. The officer came back with a hard right to Barry's jaw. Jack, with the help of other passengers, managed to separate them. He averted an arrest by assuring the policeman that he would control his father. It was a rather optimistic view, considering that his father, at that moment, was strutting about the ferryhouse, shouting, "I am Maurice Barrymore, the greatest actor this country ever saw. I have been assaulted by a policeman, and tomorrow I will have him removed from the force." He demanded the names of eyewitnesses. They snubbed him. He flung oaths and obscenities at them. Everyone except his son went outside. "That's not Barrymore," he called after them; "that man's divine; he's the Messiah. Why, I'm greater than Lincoln. Mankind will forget Lincoln, Webster, Booth and Barrett, but they'll remember me!"

Jack stood silent beside his father in the emptied ferryhouse. When the boat arrived, they both walked toward it. As they were boarding, Barry turned and shoved his son down the gangplank. He landed on his back on the wooden dock. Other passengers crowded around him. The ferry pulled away.

On the short crossing to Fort Lee, another quarrel ensued after Barry insulted Peter Ryan, an ex-policeman from Englewood. Ryan objected. The offender knocked him down. Bystanders rushed between them, preventing another melee, but Barry was still hurling abuse when the ferry docked on the Jersey side. His manservant, who had driven from Coytesville at the usual hour, tried to dissuade him from quarreling.

"Take your hand off me," his employer shouted. "You are my servant, you dog!" But, finally, the patient fellow prevailed. Barry rode quietly to Coytesville.

Ethel had declined an after-theater supper with Alphonse Navarro that evening. She was waiting at Mrs. Wilson's for her brother. He did not arrive till after two, pale and distraught, with Gus Thomas at his side. As the young man related the evening's events, his persistent sobs interfered. The three sat in council all night, separating at daybreak without a plan of action.

Against Ethel's wishes, Jack returned alone to his studio. He did not sleep. He sat up absently turning the pages of his father's ancient cookbooks. ("He kept these cookbooks until the close of his own life," wrote Gene Fowler forty years later, after insuperable achievement, adoration, and alcohol had ravaged John Barrymore. "And sometimes, when too ill to eat, would create menus based on the old recipes, and grace the lettering with ornate initials, then add the notation: 'See if my lawyer thinks I can afford all this.'")

Ethel did not sleep, either. At ten that morning, she was still sitting in a chair, staring out of the window toward Thirty-sixth Street, when sounds of commotion came from the hall. Pushing past Mrs. Wilson's servant, who was trying to announce him, Barry burst into his daughter's room.

"I'm the greatest theatrical manager in the world!" he proclaimed. "William C. Whitney has promised to build me the biggest theatre in America on Amsterdam Avenue next Fall." He swaggered about the room, face contorted, body taut. "Death to the syndicate!" he cried, clutching his daughter's shoulders, shaking her violently. "Charley Frohman is dead! The White Rats have killed him. Charlie Golden is greater than Christ, and I'm his vice-regent." Ethel did not flinch. She smiled.

"That's true, Papa," she whispered reassuringly.

"The Trust is doomed!" His restless hands grasped her throat. She kept on smiling. Their eyes met.

Suddenly violence abated. Barry's hands dropped to his sides. His face and body relaxed. His voice became soft and unperturbed. He told his daughter about a new comedy that he was going to write, and laughed while recounting one of its situations. Jack, sent for by Mrs. Wilson, arrived. Barry walked to a window. Gazing out, he recognized the Lambs' white façade across the street.

"Great times! Good times!" he exclaimed, turning to his children with what Amy Leslie once called "a glorious light of amusement in his wonderful eyes." He ran from the room, out of the house, and across Thirty-sixth Street to the Lambs'. His son followed.

Barry wandered around the club spouting gigantic schemes and future triumphs, rambling on about building the largest theater in the world, which would fill several city blocks and give power and influence to the White Rats. The city would be covered with huge posters, he promised, announcing that "all the theatrical managers are jealous of Maurice Barrymore, who has brains." He gave an exaggerated account of his fight with the policeman in the Fort Lee ferryhouse, adding proudly that he had "killed a man" for interfering.

"In such affectionate regard was he held in the fold," noted the *Herald*, "that the members would have permitted him to remain there indefinitely had it not been for their belief that he would exercise his great strength in wrecking the furniture." Digby Bell, DeWolf Hopper, Wilton Lackaye, particular Barrymore cronies, who happened to be present, called Jack aside for a conference. They decided to summon Gus Thomas and continue the meeting at Mrs. Wilson's. They discussed the situation for over an hour in Ethel's rooms, agreeing, finally to consult her attorney, William A. Redding, of Redding, Kidder & Greeley. After another hour of discussion, it was decided to obtain a medical opinion.

"I was called to the Lambs' Club by relatives and friends," attested Dr. Robert Stafford Newton, the alienist, "and at a glance saw that Mr. Barrymore needed rest more than anything else. He was very, very tired. I was told he had been under great excitement for some days and his appearance confirmed that statement." Dr. Newton advised the Barrymore children to place their father under temporary restraint for a thorough examination. The best facilities in such cases, he told them were at the new Pavilion for the Insane at Bellevue. It was a public facility, he added; legal commitment papers would be required. Ethel and Jack balked at such an extreme measure. Dr. Newton convinced them of its necessity if a proper examination were to be obtained. The doctor hastily wrote out a statement to the effect that Barry was "dangerously insane," while attorney Redding prepared an accompanying complaint.

Dr. Newton and Mr. Redding waited in a coach outside of the Lambs'

Club. Jack went inside to get his father. He pleaded for half an hour without success, until Digby Bell implemented a plan. He urged Barry to lodge a formal complaint against the policeman with whom he had fought in the ferryhouse. That idea appealed to him. At a little after 3:30, he swept out of the club with Jack at his side. Once inside the waiting carriage, he seemed to forget his mission. He did not acknowledge the presence of Newton or Redding. He sat back, closed his eyes, and rode contentedly to Bellevue.

Dr. George T. Stewart, hospital superintendent, ushered the Barrymore party into the admitting office. Barry remained silent as his pedigree was taken. Jack, seemingly composed, answered the perfunctory questions, until, suddenly, he began to weep. Barry turned, looked with terrible compassion at his youngest child.

"My son has an exaggerated idea about my condition," he said, and proceeded to answer the remaining questions himself, pacing the office with his celebrated stage swagger. His answers were terse: He was Maurice Barrymore, fifty-one years old, born in East India of English parents, residing currently in the Lambs' Club, No. 70 West Thirty-sixth Street. "My real name is not Barrymore," he added. "That is merely a stage name. My own name is Blyth." He wrote a two-page letter, folded it, and handed it to Jack; then Dr. Stewart and two attendants escorted him to the Pavilion for the Insane.

His large room overlooked the East River. It contained a desk, chairs, and two beds—one for himself, one for his attendant, Charles Dumm. "What grand surroundings!" the new inmate exclaimed, sitting on the edge of his bed with an expression of utter relief. "See the water out there, and the boats. The view is very fine. Thank Heaven!" He sprawled out on his bed and fell asleep.

Jack stopped on the hospital steps to read what his father had written. The two-page message was fragmentary, but it seemed to be meant for the public which had once made so much of Maurice Barrymore:

> *My Dear Friend—I, Maurice Barrymore, your old-time friend, knowing full well what I've been up against . . .*

The subsequent paragraphs were indecipherable, except for occasional broken phrases:

> *. . . I have traversed the whole country . . . big audiences . . .*
> *Applause . . .*
> *Think that I should come to this: to be barred . . .*

"The son, weeping," noted the *Journal*, "left his father at the hospital." (In later years, Lionel discerned that their father's ordeal had placed a lingering burden on his younger brother. "I think it is true that Maurice Barrymore's collapse, following Mummum's and his mother's death, had a lasting effect on John Barrymore. I believe that Jack was haunted, in those dark moments which come to all men, by the fear that he too would collapse; and I have been told that it is psychologically sound that the thing you most fear is precisely the thing that is most likely to happen to you.")

Yorkville court was already closed for the day when Jack and attorney Redding arrived. Finding Magistrate Mott still in his private room, Redding presented Dr. Newton's letter and the official complaint. Jack, to avert additional notoriety for his sister, became the complainant:

> John Barrymore, art student, nineteen years old, residing at No. 61 West Thirty-sixth Street, being duly sworn deposes and says that on the 29th day of March, 1901, in the city of New York, county of New York, Maurice Barrymore, now in Bellevue Hospital, was acting in a strange manner to-wit—talking in an incoherent manner and in danger of doing bodily harm to himself and the members of his family.
>
> Deponent verily believes that the said Maurice Barrymore is disordered in his senses and unfit to be at large, and prays that he may be committed to the care and charge of the Commissioner of Public Charities for examination as to his sanity.

"None of the members of the actor's family would talk to-day about his commitment," reported the *Tribune*. But Dr. Newton made a conciliatory statement. "Mr. Barrymore will be kept in the pavilion until Monday. If he shows marked improvement by that time his friends will probably take him to his home in New Jersey. If not, he will probably be sent to a sanitarium. It is too soon yet," the doctor admonished, "to say what course his mental trouble will take. I understand from his friends that he has been under high nervous excitement for six weeks."

The New York press did not heed Dr. Newton's admonition. Between the first and second acts of *Captain Jinks* that evening, shrill newsboy voices could be heard calling extras outside the Garrick Theatre: MAURICE BARRYMORE, INSANE, ATTACKS HIS DAUGHTER ETHEL, ran the *Journal's* front-page headline; HE IS A WRECK, IN BELLEVUE PAVILION.

Ethel did not falter during the performance, although she had confided to Jack that she would surely be overcome. The large audience, every man and woman of which knew what had happened, showed its sympathy by loudly applauding Barry's daughter throughout the play. Her dressing room was deluged with telegrams, flowers, cards, and callers afterward. She would only admit Charles Frohman and Augustus Thomas.

Her manager, the one most severely reviled by Barry in recent weeks, advised his newest star that her salary was to be doubled. He was sailing for England, he told her, but instructions had been left at his business office to advance whatever money she might need, whenever she might need it.

Gus Thomas advised her to make a statement for him to read to reporters inevitably hovering around the stage door. "My father has been in poor health for a year and a half," she wrote, "and my brother Jack and I consulted physicians, and they advised us to have him sent to a hospital, where he would receive the very best care and attention. Our family physician named Bellevue, and he was taken there." She wrote also to Dr. Newton, asking him to make a statement that might tone down hysterical press reports. The doctor complied.

"It is unjust to say that Barrymore is insane," he wrote. "He has broken down from the tremendous work he has been doing lately. All he needs is complete rest. We went before the magistrate merely as a matter of form."

Once again, the newspapers ignored the doctor, preferring to fill afternoon editions with fanciful reports of Barry's behavior. "About 3 a.m. the demented actor awoke the other 21 patients in the insane pavilion," fabricated the *Herald*, "and told them they must take parts in a new play, of which he was the author. After the parts were assigned, Barrymore made them rant and shout, and sing until the whole neighborhood was aroused by the noise." Papers cross-country picked up the story, supplying their own embellishments. MAD BARRYMORE A STAR THO' IN A LUNATIC'S CELL, headlined the Chicago *American*. Reports had him stalking the floor of the pavilion, spouting lines from Shakespeare, drifting from character to character, declaiming speeches from nearly every play that he had ever acted, turning attendants into stagehands. Finally, the *Sun* contradicted these fabrications: "Dr. Stewart says that the story describing the actor as rehearsing plays in the insane pavilion and casting other patients in parts of his dramas is absolutely groundless."

Out West with *Arizona*, denials notwithstanding, Lionel Barrymore saw only the most flamboyant reports. He sent his sister a wire, informing her that he would quit the tour and return straightway to New York. Ethel replied that he must under no condition leave the company on such short notice, that she and Jack could manage. She optimistically assured her distant brother that newspaper reports were exaggerated. Though older by a year, Lionel knew better than to question his sister's judgment. He proceeded on his Western tour, relieved, somewhat, by Ethel's assurances. It became presently evident, however, that truth was even more readable than fiction.

After sleeping about four hours, Barry awoke and asked his attendant, Charles Dumm, for some paper. He wished to write his daughter, who, he confided, was "detained from him." Hunched over the desk, scribbling indecipherably, he cried, "Oh, Ethel, Ethel! Don't talk to your father that way." Returning to his bed, he fell into a troubled sleep.

He woke again at 5 A.M. to find Charles Dumm sleeping on the other bed. "Ha, ha, ha!" he chortled, "there is *Claudius*, the King of Denmark, asleep!" He demanded more paper, and began writing, not resting from his work until ten, when Dr. Schultz, medical inspector for the Department of Charities, called. Barry talked volubly and entertainingly to him of the stage, giving no impression of stress. Later in the day, Dr. Fitch of the Bellevue staff examined him. When the doctor had finished, the patient returned to his writing.

Mamie Barrymore, recently returned from France, visited her estranged husband in the afternoon. "The actor expressed his pleasure on seeing her," reported Charles Dumm, "and they chatted pleasantly together." That evening, Jack and his father's manservant arrived with a bundle of clothing. Never notable for his neatness, Barry became inordinately fastidious at the hospital, insisting on daily changes of linen, and shaves and shoeshines twice a day. He required fastidiousness of his fellow inmates, as well. "Get up here, you lazy loafers," he demanded of anyone sitting dejectedly. "Stir yourselves. Brace up. We'll all be out of here in a few days." He paraded a score or more of them up and down the long ward, ordering, "Now, right about face! Fall in line! March!" The other patients invariably saluted when Barry passed.

Otherwise, he took his second day of confinement resignedly, growing angry only when his supplies of writing paper and ink ran out. "Mr. Barrymore is most docile," Superintendent Stewart told a *Telegraph* reporter. "But one thing troubles him now and that is the report he read in a morning paper that during one of his frenzies he had choked his daughter Ethel. He cried when he read the story and begged me piteously to have it corrected."

On Sunday morning, he went straight to the desk by the window and resumed his writing. Just outside was a splashing fountain. He did not hear it. Beyond was a splendid panorama of the East River and its shipping. He did not seem to notice. "The writing of a tragedy takes up nearly all his time," Dr. Stewart reported, "and while working he never utters a word. The only signs of irrationableness he shows is when at long intervals he imagines that his character the *White Fawn*, as he calls her, and the Greek hero, are in the cell with him, and with them he carries on long conversations. For an hour to-day he sat on a bench and talked and gesticulated with them in arguing over some situation for his play and its development." Occasionally, his creations would flee.

"They are gone!" he cried. "*White Fawn*, where art thou? Let me have your hand again." Holding out his left hand, as if grasping the hand of his imaginary maiden, he continued writing. When Dr. Stewart appeared, he waved his manuscript triumphantly.

"Doctor," he exclaimed, "this is the greatest poem of the age! Homer is outdone! I've combined an American epic with Grecian mythology." Barry handed the doctor six closely written sheets of foolscap, containing about a hundred stanzas. It was, he announced, the first draft of his new verse play, *White Fawn*.

Dr. Stewart read the intricate creation of his patient. The action begins in Athens as war is declared on Turkey, although the author seemed uncertain of the date. A young Greek noble, sailing to join his country's fleet, is caught in a violent storm. His ship is driven across the Atlantic. Land is sighted. They come ashore in the New World, where they are confronted by *Tecumseh* and his warriors. A battle ensues; then, a truce is negotiated, stipulating that the Greek noble must perform great deeds of courage. He accomplishes these, and he and his men are offered the hospitality of the Shawnee nation. Once settled in *Tecumseh*'s village, the young Greek meets *White Fawn*, the chief's favorite daughter. He is struck by her great beauty, and hails her as a reincarnation of Helen of Troy. "The lines describing their first meeting are beyond anything Rostand ever wrote," observed Dr. Stewart. "More beauty of language is given in the scene where the Greek confesses to the old chief his love for the daughter."

Tecumseh spurns the visitor's suit unless he performs what seem to be impossible labors. When every challenge is met, however, the chief consents to the marriage—on condition that the Greeks remain there always, and aid him in a war he is about to make on a neighboring Indian nation. The suitor agrees. A great battle is fought, winning new honors for the Greek, and facilitating a splendid tribal wedding. As months pass, the visitor tires of aboriginal life. He tells his bride of the wonders beyond the sea, and she agrees to flee with him. After countless dangers, they reach an island in the Mediterranean.

Up to that point, the manuscript, written in a legible hand, developed logically enough. "The verses were in a highly florid style," noted the doctor. "Still, they were coherent, and now and then seemed to display genuine flashes of genius." After the escape to Greece, the plot deteriorated into a rambling dissertation on the social evils of New York. Dr. Stewart suggested that the ending might be fixed. The author flew into a rage, grabbing his manuscript from the superintendent. "I never did meet a doctor who had any intelligence," he snapped.

Gus Thomas found Barry an exaggeration of his former self, when he called that afternoon. "He is dictatorial, egotistical to a marked degree," Barry's best friend resignedly wrote to the touring John Drew, "and does not hesitate to express his supreme contempt for everybody." That same afternoon, a policeman from the West Twentieth Street station entered the pavilion with a patient. "The sight of his uniform excited Mr. Barrymore," reported the *Herald*, "who gave one of the nurses orders to have the policeman executed."

At 2 A.M., Barry awoke from troubled sleep, roused Charles Dumm, and announced that he was writing his will.

> *To my friend, Charles Dumm, I will and bequeath the manuscripts of my plays.*
>
> > *Lambs' Club,*
> > *MAURICE BARRYMORE,*
> > > *and everywhere else.*

This invalid document was the only will that Maurice Barrymore ever wrote.

Barry's official examination had been set for Monday afternoon, the first of April. Two carriages drove up to the hospital before the designated hour. Ethel and Jack Barrymore were in the first. Mamie Floyd Barrymore was in the second. Their simultaneous arrivals had been coincidental. Ethel and her stepmother had not met since Barry's second marriage had taken place. The women nodded to one another—gracious but final—without inviting conversation. They did not see the patient before the examination. It was feared that the sight of them might excite him. They waited in Superintendent Stewart's reception room.

Robert Stafford Newton, the family's doctor, and F. Valentine Wildman, the pavilion's presiding physician, performed the examination with Dr. Stewart in attendance. Barry seemed delighted to see them. He stripped to the skin and stood erect as a giant. To show his strength, he seized another patient, an unsuspecting Swede, weighing two hundred pounds, and, with little effort, lifted the man high above his head. "That's the first hold on *Orlando*," he explained. The doctors agreed that he was in fine physical condition.

Other findings were less optimistic. When an ophthalmoscope was put to the patient's eye, Dr. Newton observed great clots on the brain. As the lengthy examination continued, Barry became restless. "But you could tell in four minutes whether I am insane or not," he said.

"Under certain circumstances maybe, yes," replied Dr. Newton.

"When, then, am I to be allowed to go?"

"You will leave here tomorrow," the doctor promised. Barry seemed greatly pleased. He made no demur when Newton added: "But you are to go for a short rest into the country. It will do you good, you know."

His children and his wife were waiting when the examining doctors came out of the ward. "Mr. Barrymore is suffering from incurable mania," Dr. Wildman told them; "it is necessary for him to be deprived of his liberty." The report was not unexpected. But Ethel wondered if her father might not be sent to Billy Muldoon's new health resort, where he would have congenial supervision. "The case is a peculiar one," added Dr. Newton. "Your father has maniacal symptoms, upon a religious basis, that will ultimately develop into paresis." The doctors, as delicately as possible, intimated that Barry's symptoms indicated the last, incurable stage of syphilis. The disease, which he had probably carried for several years, had long since passed the infectious stage, they were quick to add, thus averting contagion for Mamie and her recent stand-ins. He would probably not live more than six months. Under the circumstances, a suitable medical facility must be found for him. Ethel reluctantly signed an application for commitment to the Long Island Home for the Insane at Amityville.

Mamie visited him after the examination. Barry was enthusiastic when his wife was announced, incredulous when she entered. "This is not my wife," he protested. "My wife is Georgie Drew." Dr. Stewart explained that Georgie was dead, that Mamie was his wife. "No . . . not dead," he insisted. "Georgie Drew is my wife." That was the last meeting of Mamie Floyd Barrymore and the man who had been her childhood cavalier. (Eventually, she gained legal possession of the Coytesville place, the lease on their town house, sold them and retreated to Paris, where she lived, as Mrs. Maurice Barrymore, at 16 Rue de St. Cloud. Mamie had never seen, nor was she interested in owning, Barry's ramshackle farm on Staten Island. The Barrymore children presented it and its surviving menagerie to Edward Briggs, the Black Prince, who had been its caretaker. The last of Barry's pets was also exiled to the farm after Jack tried unsuccessfully to adopt him. Patrick Boniface, the self-willed Maltese, would have no master but Barry. Even the Black Prince could not win him. Patrick chose to starve himself to death.)

News that Barry would be committed spread rapidly. But no one, not even the tabloids vying for flamboyant coverage, named his forbidden affliction. Not that naming it would have sufficed. Maurice Barrymore, son, husband, father, comrade, matinee idol, had never been a simple study, nor would a simple explanation of his condition serve. There came as many views of his collapse as there were shades of madness.

"My father has not been well for a year," Ethel hedged. "He has never fully recovered from a severe attack of the grip at Baltimore last year."

"I have seen him during the last two weeks," said DeWolf Hopper at the Lambs', "and have noted that he appeared to be under a severe nervous strain. He has taken a great interest in the 'White Rat' movement, and attended the meetings regularly. It is a sad case. I hope the affliction is only temporary."

"'Alas, poor Yorick!'" quoted William Rideing. "Draw the veil on his frailty, for it was far outweighed by kindness and many other merits. In his character and temperament he was not unlike his own favourite of fiction—Fielding's Tom Jones—a sinner, but a very sweet one."

In her walk-up on Thirty-fourth Street, Cora Alexander had been waiting for Barry to resume rehearsals with her granddaughter, "Little Blanche" Sweet. Anticipation turned to fear when she heard of the actor's breakdown. "I remember my grandmother sitting in a rocking chair, humming to me as she held me in her lap," said Blanche Sweet. "She would drink coffee, dipping a Uneeda biscuit in it, and I never knew until later that she was listening fearfully for Barrymore's light step on the stairs. Grandmother had heard that madmen come back to the last people they see—every time she heard a step, she was afraid."

Amid inevitable tabloid headlines of BARRYMORE CANNOT LIVE MUCH LONGER and MAD BARRYMORE PLAYS HIS ORLANDO IN MADHOUSE came more gentle reminiscences from traveling comrades. Harry St. Maur was in Chicago. "'There is a tide,' etc.," began the friend who had seen Barry through *Nadjezda*'s London debacle. "If Maurice Barrymore had got his deserts with *Nadjezda* his present sad sanctuary would never have known him. With a position in the world he knew belonged to him, his pride would certainly have enabled him to conquer himself, but the feeling with me today is what it has always been —dear Barry never entirely recovered from *Nadjezda*. He couldn't care much ever, and after that—he cared not at all."

At a meeting of the Midnight Club, a fraternity of Chicago journalists, St. Maur broke the news to W. H. Thompson. That venerable character actor, a Lambs' crony of Barry's, "broke down and wept like a child for a few minutes," Saint recalled, "and then, recovering himself, launched forth into a glowing appreciation of the man and of the artist that brought tears to the eyes of the hard headed and unemotional members of the Midnight Club. For eloquence, sympathy and critical justice I have never heard Mr. Thompson's estimate of Maurice Barrymore equaled by any oratorical effort to sum up the wonderful strength and the wonderful weakness of this prince of gentlemen and of players."

William Faversham was touring as a star, when reports reached him in Kansas City. As a tattered street urchin in London, Faversham had made Barry his idol, following him each evening from the Haymarket Theatre to St. John's Wood. Later, he had supported Barry on the zoological *Aristocracy* tour. "It must have been ten years ago that we played *Aristocracy* here," Faversham told a *Star* reporter, "at the old theatre up on the hill—the Coates. Didn't Barry play here? No? Well, it was just after his wife died—I guess that was the reason. He was distracted about it." Faversham attempted to clarify the reporter's assumptions about the breakdown of his friend. "Few people, I imagine, knew Maurice Barrymore better than I did," he said, invoking the past tense, "but it's a mistaken idea that he was a hard drinker. Why, man, three glasses of beer was all he could stand. He never went to bed, that was his trouble—if he took two hours sleep he thought it enough. I've seen him nutty, it's true, but not from liquor. It was dissipation, smoking cigarettes and staying up all night—noble fellow that he was."

Their tense was present, but the more dignified newspaper accounts were eulogistic. The *Dramatic Mirror*'s second page, usually devoted to obituaries, held an affectionate tribute to Barry:

> . . . The experts' decision that Mr. Barrymore is hopelessly insane ends the public career of one of the most accomplished and popular players of the last quarter of the nineteenth century. A capable actor, a brilliant wit and scholar, and a prince of good fellows, 'Barry', professionally, and personally, had a legion of admirers. His conversation sparkled with cleverness, and there was ever a crowd ready to hear him, and quote his sayings. By many of his intimates he was considered the Dr. Johnson of his time. 'Barry's' extreme good fellowship was the main cause of his pathetic fate. Always ready to entertain, he would sit with a crowd of boon companions until the dawn broke. Perhaps for two or three days he would hardly sleep, and then when his exhausted vitality demanded rest, he would take too little. He is of the temperament, the doctors say, that is most liable, if overtaxed, to mental derangement. Nervous, excitable, enthusiastic, strong in his likes and dislikes, he has always been a violent champion of some cause. Twenty years ago his hobby was the wrongs of Ireland; to-day it is the injustice of the theatrical and vaudeville syndicates. It was inevitable that with his irregular life, his ceaseless working of a splendid brain, the human machine should some day break down, and his ardent sympathies become mania, and bring on the utter demoralization of an unusually talented man . . .

The irony of Barry's condition was nowhere more poignantly expressed than in two statements by his best friend. Early in their friendship, Augustus Thomas had observed that "Mentally Barrymore was capable of interest in the most abstruse questions, but as far as I was qualified to judge he did not care to seem profound. He was vastly more amused in surfaces, but to the depth that facts and theories, forces, events and expression in all forms did interest him his was the quickest, most alert, the most articulate, the wittiest, and most graceful intelligence that I ever knew." After the doctors' decision was announced, Gus made another statement to a badgering *Journal* reporter.

"There are breakdowns and breakdowns," he said, his voice quavering.

"Some are little jolts in a rut. Some are like that of the deacon's One-Hoss Shay. There's nothing left to build a new one. That's the way with Barry. Poor Barry. There is very little hope, I am afraid. Poor old Barry!"

On the afternoon of April 2, 1901, Maurice Barrymore was taken by his younger son, Dr. Newton, and two attendants from the insane pavilion at Bellevue Hospital to the Long Island Home at Amityville. "His removal to Amityville was accomplished without trouble," the *Dramatic Mirror* assured its readers, "he being under the delusion that he was going to fill an engagement in Philadelphia."

XXXIV

The Long Island Home occupied eighty-five acres along the Sunrise Highway in Amityville. Its buildings rose discreetly from lawns and fields and predominantly oak woods. Patients were encouraged to make full use of the grounds.

Maurice Barrymore was housed in a gabled, lattice-railed villa near the main building. His ground-floor room, spacious and well furnished, affording views of wooded landscape from two large windows, was the best to be had. "His daughter ordered that his surroundings be as much as possible those of a home," reported the Chicago *American*. "She ordered that no money be spared."

Peaceful atmosphere seemed to soothe Barry; the healthful regime to invigorate him. His mind grew clearer, allowing him to read, and to work on his epic poem. Daily excursions to the gymnasium proved that his still-youthful physique had not been impaired by his affliction. The brawniest attendant that put on gloves to humor him invariably regretted the act of kindness. He enjoyed visits from family and friends, and companionship from the institution's head physician and his wife. "I never thought this would be the end," he once confessed to the doctor. But such sentiments were seldom expressed. Barry appeared to be content, resigned to his situation. Ethel and Jack entertained hopes that their father might one day return to his former life.

Their hopes were short-lived. The affliction was progressive; his hallucinations reappeared. He began feverishly writing new plays, forcing them on attendants and visitors. "I have a new play," he told Gus Thomas. "Run your eye over this." Taking the proffered manuscript, Gus paled at what he saw.

"I think it's fine, Barry," he said, trying to keep his voice even, "perfectly fine." On a hundred foolscap pages, Barry had scrawled one phrase over and over again: "It was a lovely day in June."

The patient, with remarkable skill, constructed a cardboard theater and modeled tiny characters for it. For hours, he would stand behind its miniature proscenium, moving his cardboard players, spouting lines from imagined new plays or repeating snatches from old remembered parts. It was a treat for physicians and attendants to hear Barry's rich baritone reviving the lines of *Captain Swift* or *Rawdon Crawley*. But the recitations soon became incoherent, old and new meshing into garbled monologues.

Several weeks after Barry's commitment, Digby Bell attempted to visit him. He was not admitted. A doctor informed him that only immediate family was allowed. An imprudent orderly explained that the patient had reached the homicidal stage. "Barrymore imagines that Charles Frohman is his bitterest enemy," the orderly divulged, "and he spends considerable time in trying to devise measures by which he may escape from the sanitarium and kill the manager. A few days ago he picked up a table and struck one of the attendants upon the head with it, rendering him insensible, so that several hours of constant effort were necessary in order to restore his consciousness."

Barry still recognized Ethel and Jack when they visited. The haggard face would become handsome again, as he exclaimed, "Oh! Here are my two kids!" As the illness progressed, however, his welcomes became less enthusiastic. He was suspicious of everything Jack said, contentious and cruel toward Ethel. If he mistook his daughter for Georgie, which he increasingly did, he became suddenly tractable, falling into long-lost conversations. "She visited him often," the *American* said, "and when she returned from the visits she was deeply depressed, although none but her most intimate friends would have guessed it."

When Lionel returned from the *Arizona* tour, he assumed his share of filial duties. His weekly visits to Amityville had a quietening effect on the patient, who not only recognized his elder son but even greeted him with a semblance of their former camaraderie.

Despite his successful tour, Lionel's return to New York was not triumphal. Newspapers relentlessly sought new ways to headline Barrymore ironies. But Lionel did not choose to capitalize on them. Ethel and Uncle Jack would have offered easy entree to Charles Frohman. Barry's elder son was fiercely independent and not at all resigned to a theatrical fate. Painting and, more recently, composing interested him. Only to finance musical studies with Mrs. Agnes Morgan did he resort once more to the family trade.

"Barrymore," suggested one of his father's Lambs' cronies, "a couple of newcomers from Syracuse are going to put on a show. Why don't you go over and see them?" Lionel went over and saw the newcomers, three sons of an immigrant peddler named Shubert. Sam, Lee, and Jake, having shown their enterprise with modest stock-company presentations in upper New York state, had promoted backing from a Syracuse haberdasher for their Trust-baiting invasion of New York. The brothers were delighted to enhance their third Broadway managerial attempt with a Barrymore for seventy-five dollars a week.

The Brixton Burglary, a farce in three acts by Frederick W. Sidney, ultimately opened at the Herald Square Theatre on May 20, 1901. It did not set Broadway on fire. It did have a healthy enough run, forty-eight performances, to advance the careers of some of those involved. "Lionel Barrymore, at twenty-two, is one of the best leading juveniles on the stage," decided the *World*, "and gives promise of being a far better actor than his father." As for the brothers Shubert, *The Brixton Burglary* was the modest cornerstone of a lavish theatrical empire. In time, the peddler's sons would accomplish what Maurice Barrymore, the Fiskes, and so many other crusaders had not accomplished. They would devastate the Trust—not for the sake of the theater, for the sake of the Shuberts.

Theatrical success meant one thing to Lionel: increased income for his musical studies. Under the tutelage of composer-conductor Henry Hadley, a Lambs Club acquaintance, he attacked the theory of harmony and composition. To facilitate these studies, he even moved into a Carnegie Hall studio next door to Hadley. Lionel's relative wealth and comfortable new quarters attracted his younger brother. The impecunious artist, having lost his parental subsidy, appeared at odd hours in search of food and lodging. Obtaining drink, however, was no problem for young Jack. Whether at Minnie Hay's boardinghouse on West Thirty-fourth Street, where he consorted with seasoned writers and newspapermen, or at clubs and cafés, where his father's exploits were already becoming legend, indulgent friends were always willing to supply liquid refreshment in exchange for the convivial presence of another Barrymore.

Ethel fretted over her younger brother. "Isn't it a pity that Jack can't get recognition for his work?" she remarked to her friend, Cecilia Loftus.

"What *is* his work?" asked the mystified Miss Loftus. Ethel evidently cleared up the point, for Cissie was instrumental in obtaining Jack's first commission as an artist. She was about to open as E. H. Sothern's leading lady in *If I Were King*, a new play by her husband, Justin Huntley McCarthy, to be produced by C.F.'s brother, Daniel Frohman. Cissie had no trouble, in such friendly territory, arranging for Jack to design the poster for the production. His striking creation, which adorned billboards during the play's long run and subsequent tours, netted the artist five dollars.

Jack's art was beginning to be recognized. "Barrymore may take a place beside Denis, Bernard, Filiger and the ancient, hallucinated William Blake as a mystic," artist-critic Henri Pène DuBois decided in the *Journal*. "He has the anxiety, the disquietude that the Duchess d'Angouleme regarded as an inevitable cause of sadness in all beings well born, and that gives to his work a palpitating interest. The mind that is not disquiet annoys and bores one. Barrymore, sincere, may never have that effect. He is strikingly individual."

Jack's subjects tended toward the macabre, but he maintained a sense of humor in regard to his brooding creations. "I conceived a picture called The Hangman," he related. "It was one of those bright, gay and cheerful little masterpieces of which I was guilty." The drawing was exhibited at the Press Artists' League. "One day I dropped in to find a 'sold' sign on it. Investigation revealed that Andrew Carnegie had paid $10 for the picture of the hangman as he trudged down a dismal road, his shadow making a gallows. Faces of his victims leered down at him from all sides." Not such a curious choice, perhaps, for the twilight years of even the most benevolent of Robber Barons.

A piece in the Sunday *Herald*, AN UNKNOWN BARRYMORE AND HIS ART, took another view of Jack's achievements. Although five of his drawings were reproduced, the copy concentrated on inevitable family comparisons, comparisons whose repetition by commentators seemed to delight the reading public. "Aside from any merit which this work possesses," wrote the *Herald* art critic, "it is interesting as a study of the characteristics which have been transmitted, or rather shifted, from one department of art to another. For example, there has not been on the American stage any woman who had a nicer sense of humor than the mother of this boy, and in the 'chevalier d'industrie', the gaunt 'Anglo-Indian' and other similar studies that maternal influence is clearly shown." Comparisons with his mother, whom he scarcely remembered but ardently idealized, did not displease Jack Barrymore. Capitalizing on his family's accomplishments did.

"I am awfully anxious," he told the *Herald* critic, "to do something so that I won't be known only as 'Ethel Barrymore's little brother.'"

Ethel was experiencing her own impatience with repetitive hereditary comparisons. "It is enough to say," ran a typical piece in *Frank Leslie's Popular Monthly*, "that she inherits from her mother, the late Georgie Drew Barrymore, the graciousness, the eternally feminine quality, the keen sense of humor and the beauty that made that clever actress famous, while from Maurice Barrymore she has derived the wit, quickness, sympathy and courage that made him an idol of thousands." Such evocations were well meant but relentless. When she wearied of would-be family friends telling tales of her girlhood, she threatened to publish a volume, *Knees I Have Sat Upon.*

Benign evocations of her background inspired Ethel to humor. Occasionally, however, she was cowed by the limitations imposed upon a daughter of Drews and Barrymores. "Why, I have been acting for seven years," she protested. "At fourteen I played with my grandmother in Canada. We slept on trunks. That, you know, isn't an unusual experience with barnstormers. And yet every time I appear they set me down as a beginner and talk about my personality. I am discouraged." A veteran Lamb, who had gamboled with her father, heard the remark.

"Don't do that, Ethel," he admonished. "That is the way poor Barry used to talk when he couldn't pull off the plays he wrote." Hereditary comparisons grew more ominous. One tabloid even headlined THE BARRYMORE CURSE.

Whatever frustrations she may have felt regarding her heritage and the extent of her acceptance as an actress, she remained America's reigning "glamour girl"—in fact, its original "glamour girl," since the term was coined in an attempt to define her unprecedented status. Newspapers strained to feature "The Barrymore." When a passenger liner sank in New York Harbor while Ethel happened to be sailing on a nearby yacht, the *Morning Telegraph* headlined its report of the disaster: MISS BARRYMORE SEES VESSEL SINK.

Every stratum of society, it seemed, found in Ethel something to admire. "In her audiences," *Smith's Magazine* told its far-flung readership, "this worthy daughter of a long line of players inspires an affection that makes her one of the most popular actresses on the American stage. Matinee girls gush over her, stage-door sycophants adore her, elderly heads of distinguished families long to give her a paternal hug, and white-haired mamas declare that she is sweet and lovely." The public had always had its theatrical idols, the four hundred its sacred cows. Seldom did the two choose the same object for admiration. Ethel Barrymore, for the public-at-large, represented the unattainable glamour of theater and society. For descendants of the original four hundred, second and third generations growing comfortable with their fortunes, she represented a lineage equal, if not superior, to their own. "At a dinner a gentleman sitting beside a debutante should congratulate her upon her debut," advised Francis Crowninshield, "and in a few well-chosen words, should discuss the usual debutante topics—i.e., platonic love, banting, Ethel Barrymore, French dressmakers, John Drew, the relative merits of Harvard and Yale, love at first sight, the football match and the matter of her great personal beauty and charm."

The object of all this approval did not seem inordinately impressed by it. "Did you enjoy the afternoon?" asked a supporting actress, when Ethel returned to the Garrick after a reception in Mrs. Astor's Fifth Avenue palace.

"Yes," she allowed, "but I like my own crowd the best."

474

"Isn't it nice, Miss Barrymore," her support observed.

"What is nice?" wondered the star.

"That you should go out so much with the '400'."

"Perhaps," replied Ethel in her uniquely languid, husky voice, "but it is well that my father doesn't hear of it. He is very particular about the company I keep."

Perhaps none were more awed by Ethel's celebrity status than her two brothers. They avoided capitalizing on it. They benefited enormously from it. "Miss Barrymore's devotion to her brothers is a beautiful example of sisterly affection," *Smith's Magazine* effused. "Her income has always been their income—when they required it—hers has been the encouragement that has aroused in them an ambition to make a name on their individual accounts rather than be contented to reflect ancestral glory."

Jack's ambition, still artistic, landed him a job illustrating Arthur Brisbane's editorials in the *Evening Journal*. "Brisbane thought so highly of the drawings that he paid Jack $50 a week," Ethel noted with pride and, possibly, relief.

There was still her older brother to consider. The would-be artist, fledgling composer, reluctant actor was floundering after the close of the Shubert show, wallowing in his running aversion to the family trade. Such self-indulgence, however, was not condoned by his sister in New York in Lionel's twenty-third year. "Ethel is an adorable Drew," Jack observed, making his own hereditary comparisons. "She looks exactly like the pictures of our mother, and has her brilliant wit and charm. Like my Grandmother Drew, she is an executive as well as an artist. When Ethel wants something—whether it is a powder puff or a great play—she gets it or, zowie! there's an earthquake."

During her English sojourn that summer, Ethel went over to Paris with Charles Frohman. Entranced by her introduction to the City of Light, she did not forget that she wanted something. She sat patiently across a little table from the rotund impresario at Armenonville in the Bois, while he devoured an astounding assortment of napoleons, éclairs and tarts. When he looked up beaming from his empty dish, she pounced: "What are you going to do about Lionel?"

Seduced by the Bois and the pastry and the charm of his most recent asset, C.F. assumed that there was something to be done about Lionel. "So," he responded, "I will give him something to do. I will put him in a play."

Lionel Barrymore always maintained that he was made a Frohman actor "principally so that Charles Frohman could keep Ethel quiet and have a pleasant evening eating in the Bois."

Lionel's first Frohman play, Robert Marshall's *The Second in Command*, opened at the Empire on September 2, 1901. It did not prove to be a milestone in the young actor's career. As another lovelorn lieutenant, in support of Uncle Jack, he received little attention from the critics. "I was acceptable," he said, "and they let it go at that." Lack of critical response, however, was more than compensated by lessons learned from his uncle. "He was like the urbane captain of a ship," Lionel said. "He had a certain type of scholastic humor and irony in him off stage, but before an audience he preferred workmanship. His point of view was that from the time the curtain goes up until the time it goes down is the time you are out there making your living."

With Lionel ensconced at the Empire, Ethel reopened *Captain Jinks* at the Garrick that autumn. Having demanded as much, her public responded with tribute on opening night. The stage manager made use of it in the scene showing *Madame Trentoni*'s flower-laden Brevoort suite after her operatic debut. "A pretty feature of the performance was the display on the stage of the floral tributes sent to Miss Barrymore by her numerous friends in the audience," noted the *Tribune*. "Usually these are 'property' flowers, but last night they were all real, and their freshness and fragrance enhanced the realism of the scene remarkably." That aura of sweet success pervaded the season's proceedings at the Garrick, and continued throughout a spring tour.

The new star's triumphal began in Boston, where she was "received with uproarious demonstrations of delight," according to Henry Austin Clapp in the *Advertiser*, arousing her auditors, the *Globe* added, "to a high pitch of enthusiasm." Harvard's Hasty Pudding Club gave her a dinner, while the undergraduate population pressed invitations to proms and dawn teas. Front-runners in the race for her attentions were Robert Goelet, Jr., who was said to have one and a half millions for each of his twenty-one years, and Ogden L. Mills, Jr., no pauper himself. The smitten millionaires vied for the honor of driving Ethel to her April 17th opening at the Providence Opera House. Unable to choose between them, she accepted both.

On the morning of her scheduled opening, Ethel, her maid, Goelet, Mills, and a chauffeur headed for Providence on the "mobe." Outside Pawtucket, Goelet's Paris-made machine broke down. The zeal of the two suitors and the skill of one chauffeur did not prevail. The star reached Providence in a farmer's carryall, late, but in time to soothe an irritated audience. Goelet arrived later, in time to facilitate another engagement rumor for a public preoccupied with the touring adventures of "The Barrymore."

Jack was becoming a Broadway personality in his own right that spring. A new mustache, which he liked to stroke extravagantly in the manner of his father, added substance to his claim of twenty-two years. Twenty, he felt, was no age for a serious man about town, and Jack had certainly become that. His entire salary from the *Evening Journal,* plus handouts from Ethel, was spent squiring young ladies of the chorus to the more fashionable Broadway rendezvous. It could not have been spent on a wardrobe suitable for such activities. He cared less about clothes than his father had. "It is related of John Barrymore," wrote critic George Jean Nathan, "at any rate in the days when the handsome dog was known as Jack, that he at one time wore the same suit, along with the same underwear, for so unduly protracted a stretch that his loving and solicitous sister Ethel was mercifully constrained one night to sneak into his room, steal it, and have it burned."

For special occasions, of course, he could help himself to Uncle Jack's magnificent wardrobe. Such occasions were architect Stanford White's gatherings in his voluptuous Tower Room atop Madison Square Garden, where he entertained denizens of Bohemia and ladies of the chorus. Heavily curtained exclusivity was enhanced by priceless medieval tapestries, carved stone pillars, great green velvet divans, tiger and leopard skins, illuminated by the roseate glow of electrified glass oranges nestled in artificial orange trees. This heady hunting ground could hardly fail to entice even the most stoic visitor. Jack Barrymore was no stoic. His youthful ardor and romantic nature, his roving eye found an object for concentration—the host's own "protégée," seventeen-year-old Evelyn Nesbit.

White had first seen Evelyn in *Florodora* the previous year. Rich, prominent, married, he had approached the beautiful sixteen-year-old with paternal solicitude, wooed her, deflowered her, grown fiercely protective of her. Perhaps the little dancer inspired Jack to similar ends. He was, in any case, smitten when he first met her in the Tower Room. He kept pinching his mustache and tossing covert but pointed glances at her, until White left the room for a moment. "Quick! Your address and telephone number," he whispered, scribbling them on his shirt cuff. That evening he sent her violets and a note illustrated with tiny sketches.

"The girls think he's good-looking to-day, adore his famous profile," Evelyn wrote, thirty years later. "They should have seen him then— when he was about twenty-two! He possessed an effervescent originality and a Villonesque charm that was like nothing and nobody else. He would order a glass of milk, set a rose leaf on its surface, and say: 'that is your mouth.'" Such tactics would have won hearts less susceptible than Evelyn Nesbit's.

When her protective mentor left New York for two weeks, Jack closed in. Calling for Evelyn each evening at the Knickerbocker Theatre, where she was dancing in *The Wild Rose,* he took her to supper at Rector's. Young and beautiful, presumably in love, they created a sensation. "We laughed so much together," Evelyn recalled, "that people at nearby tables stared at us enviously." Tabloids also took note. "We knew that

Jack Barrymore had fallen head over heels in love with Evelyn Nesbit," announced the *Morning Telegraph*, "but we did not know that she had affected his mind to this extent: Says Barrymore: 'She is a quivering pink poppy in a golden wind-swept space.'"

"Hey, there, quivering pink poppy," teased the ladies of the Knickerbocker chorus.

"Barrymore's robbing the roost," declared friends of Stanford White, ominously.

When White returned to the city, the young lovers attempted secret trysts. Rector's gave way to less conspicuous restaurants for after-theater tête-à-têtes. After supper at a little Italian restaurant one evening, Jack suggested that they return to his nearby studio. At the time, he was sharing a flat with Herbert Bayard Swope, a reporter on the *World*. But he had kept the room which his father had furnished for him primarily with cookbooks. Lack of furniture did not hamper young love. Jack spread a cloak on the floor, telling Evelyn that his father had worn it as *Romeo*.

"I stretched out on the floor and fell sound asleep," Evelyn claimed, giving a highly unlikely version of what must have transpired. "Jack parked himself somewhere and did likewise. We both slept the heavy, dreamless sleep of youth. Many hours passed. I awoke at eleven the next morning and roused Jack." He brought Evelyn home. Her mother, preferring the easy luxuries of a "protector" to the uncertainties of impecunious young love, summoned Stanford White.

"Come along, Evelyn," White ordered, taking her firmly by the arm and transporting her to the home of his physician. Locked in a small room all day without food or water, she was interrogated, examined, treated, until, presumably, any Barrymore influence had been exorcised.

Jack might have dwelled poetically on love's loss had not more prosaic matters interfered. During his fervent courtship, work at the *Evening Journal* had become a tiresome necessity. Arriving at the office, when he arrived at all, late and usually suffering aftereffects of an evening's frolic, he hastily illustrated Arthur Brisbane's pieces "with my strange little beasts, which were labeled, to back up the preachings of the editorials, Greed, Lust, Hate, Treachery, and all the other vices." When his hurried efforts repeatedly failed to enhance the great Brisbane's eloquence, Jack was summoned.

"Tell me," Brisbane asked, "your family has distinguished itself on the stage?" The question was rhetorical. The editor had been one of the admiring young reporters that gathered around Barry at the Silver Grill in the '80s.

"Yes, Mr. Brisbane," Jack replied.

"Don't you think perhaps you could be an actor?"

"Yes, Mr. Brisbane."

"I think you are a very wise young man," concluded the editor. "Good luck."

The unemployed artist sought out his elder brother, currently in funds as the run of *The Second in Command* continued. They went to a frequent rendezvous of theirs, the Café Boulevard on Second Avenue, where Jack devoured Hungarian food and red wine, and related the tale of his polite sacking. Alternatives to the one glaring alternative were proposed and discarded, until Jack faced the inevitable. "It begins to look as though I'll have to succumb to the family curse, acting," he conceded.

"I know how you feel," Lionel commiserated. "There is no escape for us. We are in the cul-de-sac of tradition."

Ethel had reached the same conclusion concerning her younger brother's career. She implemented it immediately. *Captain Jinks* was playing a return engagement in Philadelphia at the time. When one of the company was called away for a few days, Ethel arranged for Jack to replace him—"before I could conceive an alibi," the recruit bemoaned.

"I went to the theater as nonchalantly as if I were going to a dinner," he confessed. "I seemed to have had no sense of inherited responsibility. My sister was nervous and anxious about how I'd get along, but I wasn't a bit. I put on my uniform and went on as gayly as if I'd been doing it a thousand nights, and just as sure of myself. And then, when my cue came my memory just fell into a bottomless hole. I didn't remember a word of my lines. Not a letter!" He should have been cold with fright. It seemed merely a huge joke to him. When some of the audience began to titter, he fixed them with an expression of utter scorn.

"Have a heart," he called across the footlights. "I have only two hours to make a fool of myself—you have the rest of the night."

Ethel, wavering between rage and laughter, managed to cover for him until the middle of his big scene in the first act, when he turned to her and cried, "Well, I've blown up! Where do we go from here?" Ethel was scarcely able to speak a line after that. If she tried, her laughter interfered, and one of her skilled support would say: "Oh—don't you mean so-and-so?" and finish her speech.

Miraculously, the audience seemed to relish the performance. At the end of the second act, they clamored for the star to lead the various players out to the footlights for their curtain calls. Instead, when the curtain was raised, Jack left the line of other players, swaggered up to the footlights, and bowed low and alone to the cheering house. "It was the silliest thing I have ever seen done," recalled his indulgent sister, "and, at the next curtain call, all of us were laughing hysterically at him. But he was not to be outdone; he graciously came forward, led me by the hand, bowed to me, and then to the audience, as if he were introducing a shy debutante."

More miraculous, even, than the reaction of the audience was that of

Charles Frohman. Ethel's demanding manager, coincidentally viewing the play that evening, rushed backstage after the performance. He headed for Jack not with rage but with the glow of discovery on his round, pink face. "With a better memory," C.F. predicted, "I think you might make a comedian some day." Someday had not yet come. When the original actor returned to *Captain Jinks* after three nights, his replacement was speeded back to New York with, Jack said, "unflattering demonstrations of joy." The youngest Barrymore, having outmaneuvered the family fate, was ecstatic. With income from Ethel and Lionel, free access to Uncle Jack's wardrobe and baronial "cottage" at East Hampton, he returned to what he romantically described as "another period of bankrupt bohemianism."

Ethel headed for another summer in England when her triumphant tour ended, trailing a string of engagement rumors. The honor roll of fiancés, besides legitimate casualties Laurence Irving and Gerald du Maurier, included several unofficial entries, some of whom, Ethel protested, she had never even met: the Duke of Manchester; the Earl of Ava; Sir Robert Peel; Anthony Hope; brothers Richard Harding and Charles Belmont Davis; Indian potentate Prince Ranjitsinji, whom she called 'Prince Ragtime'; publisher Herbert Stone; architect and cotillion leader Charles Delavan Wetmore. Presumably to clear the field for any summer liaison, the *Morning Telegraph* announced ACTRESS GOES TO EUROPE WITHOUT MATRIMONIAL DESIGNS UPON ANY RICH AMERICAN YOUNGSTER, implying, rather indelicately, that Jrs. Goelet and Mills had joined the casualty list. Having set the stage for a new romance, the press missed it when it happened.

Since their meeting at Dunrobin, the Sutherland castle in Scotland, Winston Churchill had pursued Ethel. The twenty-eight-year-old Conservative Member of Parliament from Oldham, one of an outspoken group called "the Hooligans," was smitten and moved to poetry. He called her "my harp with the golden sling," showered her with attentions and favors, even enlisted the aid of his mother in the pursuit. Winston's mother, formerly Jennie Jerome, daughter of a New York speculator, widow of Lord Randolph Churchill, advocated her son's romance. Ethel was invited to spend the weekend of July 12, 1902, at Blenheim Palace, the Marlborough-Churchill family seat.

After tea with his mother, his grandmother, the Dowager Duchess of Marlborough, and various other family members, Winston conducted a private tour for Ethel—hall to hall, little drawing room to east drawing room to state drawing room, treasure to treasure. She browsed in the magnificent library, marveling at the finest works of Rubens which hung there. Winston saw only his companion, slim and graceful in white pleated afternoon frock, picture hat, and feather boa, outshining the plump creations of the master. The tour proceeded past Corinthian porticoes, tended gardens, a small zoo, woods, to a vale not far from the palace. Ethel sat beside a man-made lake, while Winston paced behind her. All afternoon, she had noticed her guide becoming progressively nervous, oversolicitous, fumbling.

Abruptly, continuing to pace, the son of Churchills and Jeromes proposed marriage. Sweetly but quickly, the daughter of Blyths and Drews refused.

Ethel was fond of Winston Churchill. She admired him, but felt personally, as Lord Balfour did politically, that the young man carried "heavy but not very mobile guns." She had been concerned of late with her theatrical heritage. Her father's breakdown had somehow emphasized its importance to her, its uniqueness, its tenacity in the face of personal upheaval. Winston understood. His own father, at the height of a brilliant political career, was felled by the same disease, gradually losing his mind, dying a hopeless paretic. Just as Winston sought to expiate his father through his own brilliant career, so Ethel used the theater. She knew that "yes" to this suitor would mean an end to that career. He would not be as pliable as Laurence Irving and Gerald du Maurier, or most of the others on her casualty list. ("When I asked why she hadn't married him," Churchill's son related years later, "she said she didn't think she could live up to that sort of world. Her world was the theatre, and she didn't think she could adjust herself to my father's world.")

Winston did not accept rejection easily. He continued his pursuit, escorting her to the festivities surrounding the coronation of Edward VII that summer. To see if she wouldn't like to share a politician's life, after all, he gave a dinner for her, inviting only Neville Chamberlain, Lloyd George and Lord Rosebery, three of England's foremost statesmen. Ethel listened to their talk, participated brilliantly, did not change her mind. "Ooooh!" Winston lamented. "I was *so* in love with her! And she wouldn't pay any attention to me at all!"

Ethel returned to New York on the S.S. *Philadelphia*. Newsmen waited on the pier, as they had for *Madame Trentoni*, with inevitable questions about her summer romances. "I saw Richard Strauss at a party in London," she confessed. "He was sitting there just like an ordinary man listening to what was going on. But I felt as if I were in the presence of a divinity." She did not mention Winston Churchill. (Ethel and Winston remained lifelong friends, keeping what had happened beside the man-made lake at Blenheim Palace their secret. In fact, the proposal was not made public until Churchills's son did so sixty-five years later, after Winston and his "harp with the golden sling" were dead.)

Lionel, again thanks to Ethel's intervention with C.F., was to play a small part in Uncle Jack's seasonal offering, *The Mummy and the Hum-*

ming Bird. Frohman had been dubious about the young man's ability to do the pivotal role of *Giuseppe*, a Sicilian organ grinder, who speaks Italian, with only a smattering of English. Ethel persevered, offering even to forfeit her previous season's bonus if her brother were given the role. Her manager eventually relented without accepting that sacrifice from his star.

Giuseppe was the kind of character part that Lionel, the most private of the Barrymore siblings, relished. While Ethel and, increasingly, Jack were branded, as their father had been, with personality status, Lionel learned early to apply the protective cover of character make-up. He was always scrupulous in his approach, and for *Giuseppe*, he consulted George Barnum, who had played Ethel's Italian guardian in *Captain Jinks.* Barnum called in Ralph Delmore, nee Donnarmo, another skilled character actor. They worked every day for three weeks on the characterization, eventually bringing in a real Italian organ grinder to observe. Bit by bit, Lionel meticulously built his character.

The usual elegant John Drew audience flocked to the Empire on September 4. Ethel attended with a party including a Roman count. After her brother's scene had garnered a tumultuous ovation, she turned to the visitor: "What did you think of the Italian?"

"He is *not* Italian," replied the count indignantly. "He is Sicilian!"

> Lionel Barrymore scored a real hit in Isaac Henderson's *The Mummy and the Humming Bird* at the Empire last night. Nothing that he has ever done before could be mentioned in the same class as this performance for cleverness, and without in the least depreciating Mr. Drew's work it can be honestly said that Mr. Barrymore's was the solitary marked success of the night.

That opening paragraph of the *Times* notice was an indication of the unanimous praise from New York's critics. Lionel had arrived. Uncle Jack was astonished but delighted, exceedingly proud of his nephew. He took him everywhere, introducing him graciously. "My nephew," he would announce, "in whose production I am playing quite a minor part."

No one took more pleasure in Lionel's success than his younger brother. Apart from requisite fraternal pride, it meant solvency to Jack. Lionel was making a nightly hit at the Empire, receiving a substantial weekly salary from C.F., ensuring Jack's food and lodging while he reveled and painted in New York.

Evelyn Nesbit was no longer in the city. To keep her out of young Barrymore's reach, Stanford White had enrolled her at the DeMille School in Pompton, New Jersey. He assumed that its remote location, coupled with the strict supervision of Mrs. Henry C. DeMille, widow of the noted playwright, would protect his protégée. But Jack's ardor had not entirely abated. He found his way to Pompton to rescue his "quivering pink poppy." Fearing the wrath of her protector, she declined to see him. The young son of the headmistress saw him. "Barrymore left ardent notes addressed to her on the tennis court and at various places around the property," wrote Cecil B. DeMille, "which must have made exciting reading for the girls who found them."

Jack returned, disheartened, to the city. But the pain of lost love was quickly dissipated by other romantic involvements. It was just as well. (Four years later, the White-Nesbit affaire ended in tragedy. Evelyn married Harry K. Thaw, the eccentric, insanely jealous son of a millionaire. One evening at the Madison Square Roof Garden, Thaw shot Stanford White. The celebrated architect fell dead, fittingly enough, in the shadow of his infamous Tower Room.)

Ethel's New York season opened in January, following a three-month tour. *Munsey's Magazine* noted her success: "And now, with *A Country Mouse* and a touching curtain raiser from the French, *Carrots*, Miss Barrymore has made another ten strike. *Carrots*, a study in family life, gives Miss Barrymore her first opportunity to appear in man's attire. She impersonates a boy of fifteen, misunderstood by both father and mother." In the bright red wig and tattered togs of the shy country boy, it was generally conceded that Ethel was irresistible. But, more satisfying to the new star, her characterization could not be attributed merely to charm.

"In the double bill Charles Frohman has found his first really strong card of the theatrical year," concluded *Munsey*'s review, "and there seems little reason to doubt that Miss Barrymore can remain at the Savoy throughout the season." According to box-office receipts, she could have. Ethel, however, decided otherwise. She demanded that her season be curtailed, and, not wishing to displease his star, C.F. complied.

Some observers felt that her action was that predictable manifestation of early stardom—temperament. It was true that she had considered audiences and critics not properly appreciative of *A Country Mouse*. But the consensus was that exhaustion from her frenetic pace had been responsible. Returning from the professional and social rigors of the road, she had straightway opened her taxing double bill at the Savoy, played society's darling offstage, and furnished her first New York apartment—on West Fifty-ninth Street, overlooking Central Park. After filling the new residence with favorite books, music and works of art, her pace did not slacken. She proceeded to fill it with people. "She does not retire until there is none left at whom to direct her running fire of repartee and anecdotes," claimed the *Metropolitan* magazine. Her guests often feigned drowsiness in hopes of getting her to sleep. Her cousin and confidante, Georgie Mendum, sometimes tampered with the clock. "Even after withdrawing to her boudoir," Georgie said, "she has been known to start a new story over the transom."

After prematurely closing her successful double bill, Ethel went to a resort in Lakewood, New Jersey, to rest. The newspapers suspected a story. John Drew was questioned. "She'd be all right if she would only rest," he lamented, "but she doesn't seem to know how to rest." Uncle Jack was baffled by his niece and her brothers. "They are strange children, those," he said. That was enough for the tabloids.

IS THE ILL-FORTUNE WHICH HANGS OVER THE BAR-RYMORES JUST THROWING ITS THREATENING SHADOW ABOUT THE LOVELY LITTLE GIRL WHO HAS CHARMED SOCIETY HERE AND ABROAD? wondered the *American*, in a five-line head spread across its front page. "To her friends physicians explain that they have grave fears of consumption," fabricated the subsequent article, "which caused the early death of her brilliant mother, or of nervous prostration, which from time to time afflicted her unfortunate father, who is slowly dying at a sanitarium at Flushing, L.I., or a most unfortunate and piteous combination of both."

Barry was still at Amityville, but the *American*'s mistake was minor compared to those of other tabloids. Two of them had reported him dead, and many of his friends presumed them correct. The autobiography of his Haymarket colleague, Charles Brookfield, was published that year. The actor devoted a fond and evocative chapter to his old friend. "One of the pleasantest companions I ever met in a theatre was Maurice Barrymore," he began, "now, I am afraid, no longer with us." Such misconceptions were understandable. Only Barry's children were allowed to visit him, and they had forbidden the sanitarium to issue any information.

Occasional newspaper pieces appeared, recalling Barrymore witticisms, which were still being circulated by such diverse emissaries as Gus Thomas and His Eminence Cardinal William Post. "Some of the quips that have made Maurice Barrymore famous will live for many a long day after the gifted actor is forgotten," the *Morning Telegraph* accurately observed. "While many of them have been told again and again, his friends daily recall other sayings that have not become public property." But, after two years of confinement, the public memory of Maurice Barrymore was usually evoked only when one or another of the tabloids reported him dead or dwindling, or fabricated melodramatic comparisons between the father and his progeny. "It seems pitiful that the gifted creatures who flutter down into the gray working-day world, touching days with the color of their own brightness, should be so quickly forgotten!" lamented the *Telegraph* piece. "But this is what it comes to as far as the world's concerned. Poor Maurice Barrymore!"

The inmate was not able to read such premature eulogies, nor would he

484

have been capable of harboring such painful concepts if he had. Only once after his first months at Amityville did he express awareness of what might still be. During a visit from his sons, he surreptitiously brought a manuscript out from under his mattress. Swearing the boys to secrecy, he attempted, in guarded, none too articulate whispers, to explain its origin. It was a dramatization of George du Maurier's *Peter Ibbetson*, which had been, the boys knew, one of their father's favorite novels. The manuscript had been forwarded from the Lambs', where its adapter, Mme. Rankey, had sent it in hopes of reaching Maurice Barrymore. Obviously unaware of his present condition, she wondered if he would consider starring in a Broadway production of the play. Clutching the manuscript to his chest, glaring defiantly with wild, lightened eyes at his sons, Barry vowed that he would return in glory in the title role. He never did. (Fifteen years later, Jack did, co-starring with Lionel rather gloriously, in another dramatization of the same book. "My father was crazy to play it," Jack recalled at the time, "but he died before he could put it on. I've always wanted to play it myself. And now I am carrying out his ambition and mine.")

Barry did not again refer to *Peter Ibbetson*, to Broadway, or to glory. He was quietened with drugs most of the time. He would seldom eat, and his once splendid constitution began to give way. When his children visited, rationality was approximated only by aspersing what he imagined to be their current activities. Otherwise, his existence was carefree, childlike. He could no longer read nor write. He would play with his cardboard theater, and walk, hand-held by attendants, the grounds of his oak-shrouded sanctuary.

XXXV

THE 1903–4 BROADWAY SEASON saw the emergence of a Barrymore triumvirate. (Wherever their diverse paths led over the next fifty years, however great their individual fame, the three children of Maurice Barrymore would always be considered a set. "The flying Barrymores— 3, count 'em 3," Ethel gibed, "and we are very happy over it." Their ultimate achievements, coupled with the legacy of their forebears, would create a "Royal Family of the American Show World," shedding glory upon the name adopted arbitrarily by Herbert Blyth in an English railway coach. Even after Ethel, the last of the three siblings, died in 1959, "Barrymore" remained colloquial for actor.)

Ethel and Lionel were simultaneously presented in two Frohman productions on October 19. Ethel's first nights had become theatrical events, and this time she was opening the new Hudson Theatre, built expressly for her by C.F. Her play, another hand-picked London hit, was Hubert Henry Davies' quiet but clever comedy, *Cousin Kate*. Ethel's growing cult applauded her depiction of another eccentric young lady; reviewers praised her "charm" and "personality"; the young star longed for meatier roles throughout a prosperous run.

Lionel's opening, at the old Academy of Music, may have been less auspicious than his sister's, but *The Best of Friends* offered him another impressive character part. Disguised as a veteran Boer general, he once more astounded the critics and, incidentally, his younger brother. "He seems to check his personality like an overcoat whenever he goes into a part," Jack marveled. Lionel's acting redeemed an indifferent play, carrying it for sixty-five performances.

Jack left behind any admiration of his brother's acting, of acting in general, when C.F. sent him to Chicago for some practical experience before his Broadway debut. He was to play juvenile roles, just as Lionel had, under McKee Rankin's management. Aunt Gladys's father found Jack far less purposeful than Lionel had been, but assigned him the same role for his Chicago debut. Before the October 31st opening, Jack met actor-playwright Edgar Selwyn in the lobby of the Auditorium Hotel.

"Hello, Jack," Selwyn began, "What are you doing here?"

"Going to become an actor," Jack assured him. "Tonight's the night and *Magda*'s the piece. Better come around and watch the sport."

"But, man," wondered Selwyn, "isn't *Magda* a pretty stiff proposition for you to tackle, especially if you've never been on the stage?"

"I don't see how it can be so very stiff," the novice replied; "Lionel played it and wasn't roasted."

Jack's confidence was premature. Even his father's long-time champion could not avoid the newcomer's incompetence. "The part of *Max* was essayed by a young actor who calls himself Mr. John Barrymore," wrote Amy Leslie in the *Daily News*. "He walked about the stage as if he had been all dressed up and forgotten."

His confidence survived critics and the Rankin repertoire. His small salary did not survive women and drink, Chicago's night life. When C.F. summoned him to New York for rehearsals, Jack did not have the train fare. Undaunted, he headed for a Western Union office. FOR CHRIST'S SAKE, he jotted on a wire to his sister, SEND FIFTY DOLLARS. Such profanity, the clerk advised, could not be transmitted. Jack felt that nothing less emphatic would do. "But I am an actor in the employ of one George W. Christ, whose company is stranded in Chicago," he extrapolated. "The wire is being sent in his behalf." The message was transmitted unchanged. The money was sent. The youngest Barrymore reached New York in time to prepare for his Broadway debut.

Jack rehearsed *Glad of It*, Clyde Fitch's new comedy, while Lionel was rehearsing *The Other Girl*, written for him by Gus Thomas. Frohman, grooming another Barrymore for stardom, had the new play waiting when *The Best of Friends* closed. Without even a weekend off between productions, Lionel began to develop his characterization of pugilist *Kid Garvey*. C.F. had originally commissioned Thomas to write a play for John Drew, including a suitable part for his nephew. As the play developed, however, Lionel's part took precedence, and the manager decided to find something more suitable for Uncle Jack.

However good his part might be, Lionel would make it better. "In the theatre his happiness is delineating character," Thomas maintained, "and he goes at each new subject with the technical interest of an artist interested in surfaces and in the face behind them." When cast for *Kid Garvey*, Lionel began developing an interpretation from memories of his father's sporting friends, the likes of John L. Sullivan, Jim Corbett, Billy Muldoon. Though already well suited for the role—as Wilton Lackaye observed, Barry had separated two principal characteristics in transmitting his traits: "The teacup quality he bequeathed to Jack and the prize-fighting excellence went to Lionel."—he nevertheless sought perfection. Kid McCoy, champion middleweight of the world, became his inseparable comrade during rehearsals for *The Other Girl*. He gleaned refinements of his characterization from the champion, even down to McCoy's curly locks. Before every performance, Lionel would have his hair curled artificially to lend verisimilitude to his playing.

John Barrymore was introduced to Broadway on the evening of December 28, 1903. Ethel, who ceased being *Cousin Kate* at 10:30, reached the Savoy Theatre in time for the last act of *Glad of It*. Although her brother did not appear in that act, she witnessed the ovation given him during curtain calls. She did not join in. She had been taught by Mummum at Arch Street matinees long ago never to applaud her own.

ANOTHER BARRYMORE TREADS THE BOARDS, headlined the next day's *Journal*. "He was only in one act, the second," complained the *Dramatic Mirror*, "when he could advantageously to himself and Mr. Fitch have been in all four." Despite the size of his role as *Corley*, the press agent, a bright future as a comedian was generally predicted. "His resemblance in voice and manner to his father of twenty years ago, walk and gesture, smile and look," the *Mirror* noted, "was startling."

The next evening, *The Other Girl* opened at the Criterion, with Lionel given featured billing. Critics were unanimous in their praise of "Mr. Lionel Barrymore, who, as it seems," summed up the *Times*, "has got the trick of genius in character parts." Inevitable comparisons to Kid McCoy were admiringly made, while a more apt comparison was missed. Tall, lean, muscular, attired in pugilistic finery, Lionel was a dead ringer for another champion. But none that visited the Criterion during *The Other Girl*'s long run had witnessed Queensberry Cup championships, Lilliebridge, West Brompton, thirty years before.

Three nights after its première, Ethel hurried over to the Criterion for the last of her brother's play. As she approached the theater, tears came to her eyes. LIONEL BARRYMORE had been raised above the title.

The simultaneous advent of three Barrymores had Broadway commentators and their readership aflutter. For Lionel, Ethel, and Jack, it occasioned their first substantial reunion since the death of their mother. For New York hostesses, it became a challenge to display all three Barrymores at once at their soirees. The objects of such attention, enjoying the first flush of treble success, responded. They even worked up a skit, a parody of a music hall trio—Ethel at the piano, Lionel and Jack doing a soft-shoe routine, and a grand finale with all three joining hands for an "exit clogging." After achieving considerable drawing-room success, Ethel decided that it would be enjoyable and charitable to offer the skit at an Actors' Fund benefit. She asked C.F. for permission.

488

"I am sure you would enjoy it," chided her manager, "but would the audience?" The Flying Barrymores returned to the drawing-room circuit.

On matinee days, they sought more private communion. They met in Ethel's suite at the Hotel Algonquin, just the three of them, for luncheon and talk between performances. Lest his star suffer the journey from the Hudson Theatre on Forty-fourth Street, east of Broadway, to her West Fifty-ninth Street flat, C.F. had provided this convenient alternative. In her comfortable sitting room, enjoying rare hours of privacy, conversation inevitably turned to the family trade. Not that the boys had acknowledged complete surrender. Jack, while relishing his newly won celebrity, had yet to consider acting his calling. As for Lionel, another aspect of *The Other Girl*'s success pleased him far more than the stardom achieved. "Between the 2nd and 3rd Acts," the program announced, "the Orchestra will render Caprice 'Twilight' by Mr. Lionel Barrymore." While acting became a practical alternative, the more successful he became at it, the more he indulged dreams of painting and composing. (All of his life, the eldest Barrymore would wage that solitary war of independence, deserting the stage at the height of his fame for the déclassé silent screen, refusing to play romantic roles, becoming, in spite of himself, Hollywood's *père noble*, maintaining all the while, until his death at seventy-six, that he was not an actor at all, but, depending on his project of the moment, an artist or a composer.)

Prompted by critical and popular reaction to Jack's playing in *Glad of It*, C.F. gave him a bigger part in the play. But Clyde Fitch's latest comedy had little to recommend it beyond the performance of the youngest Barrymore. C.F. transferred the production to Chicago, where the fire of 1904, followed by driving blizzards, discouraged whatever audiences it might have drawn. Frohman did not allow his latest Barrymore to languish. On April 4, after Lionel and the long-running *Other Girl* had been moved to the Empire, Jack opened at the Criterion in *The Dictator*. Richard Harding Davis's farce in three acts was a vehicle for William Collier, another Frohman star, but Jack shone in a supporting role. As *Charley Hyne*, tippling wireless operator for the Red C Line, he won every critic. More than acceptance, he gained experience. During a long run and subsequent tours, under the cover of good fellowship, Collier imparted valuable lessons in comedic art to the cavalier newcomer.

Assuming, apparently, that two Barrymores could hold Broadway, C.F. concentrated his considerable energies on arranging a West End starring debut for Ethel. Despite her social celebrity in London, she had not appeared there professionally since her season with Sir Henry Irving. C.F. announced that *Cynthia*, a new play by Hubert Henry Davies, *Cousin Kate*'s author, would introduce Ethel Barrymore to London audiences supported by her former fiancé, Gerald du Maurier. It was about time. Many of her English friends were curious as to just what the charming young American did. On the evening of May 16, 1904, at Wyndham's Theatre, they found out. "It is a triumph for Miss Barrymore that she has succeeded despite the shortcomings of her play," wrote the New York *Times*'s London correspondent. "Her charming personality caught the sympathy of the audience from the first." Max Beerbohm, who had become quite a personality himself among London's critical brethren, decided that she was "the modern *Pierrot* woman."

Repeated critical cries of "personality" and "charm" irritated the actress. Her "absolute naturalness," was observed, her "kittenlike playfulness," her "remarkable beauty of face and form," her "peculiar breathlessness of delivery and a way of clipping her words," as if they had nothing whatever to do with the art of acting.

"Maybe it's intended to be complimentary," she speculated, "but I can't see it in that way. Never mind, though. I'll make them believe that there's something besides personality in what I do. I've plenty of time." She was already badgering C.F. to let her try Ibsen and other substantial dramatists. For the time being, however, Frohman decreed froth for his popular star.

Society and, specifically, suitors continued to vie for the attentions of this much-publicized young lady. Clarence Jones of New York followed her to London, honored her with the season's costliest dinner party. He paid $1,500 for the privilege of entertaining Ethel and ten other guests in a private dining room at the Carlton. Gold chains were presented to the gentlemen, hand-painted fans to the ladies. The room was filled with hundreds of American Beauty roses—a pointed tribute to the guest of honor. Jones did not gain his objective.

Winston Churchill sent flowers to her dressing room each evening, and always went to Claridges for supper, knowing that Ethel usually dined there after the theater. She remained fond of Winston, but he could not rekindle even a semblance of romantic response from her. Another Englishman was considerably more fortunate.

Captain Harry Graham, second son of Sir Henry Graham, K.C.B., had begun his career in the Coldstream Guards, served for five years on the staff of Lord Minto, Governor General of Canada, and earned the prestigious post of private secretary to former Prime Minister Lord Rosebery. Winston Churchill's lineage and political accomplishments were more impressive. Clarence Jones was richer. Harry Graham possessed one qualification which Ethel found irresistible. He was a poet. His witty volume of verse, *Misrepresentative Men*, published that year, was "gratefully dedicated" to her.

Despite his accomplishments, Harry, at twenty-nine, was good-humored and unaffected. He proved it during tea in Ethel's Charles Street flat, when Aunt Evelin Wace's son, Edgar, stopped by. On his way to a Civil Service post in Egypt, young Wace wished to say good-by to his cousin. Edgar had not only followed Grandfather Blyth's profession, he had inherited other traits of the Commissioner's, as well. His dress, manner, speech, counterfeits of the aristocracy, would have impressed his grandfather. To the literary men and peers of the realm gathered in his cousin's flat, they seemed merely strained and rather funny. Edgar, having also inherited the Blyth pomposity, assumed that he was cutting a fine figure as he chattered away in the clipped, exaggerated style of a musical-comedy Englishman. After he had gone, Captain Harry Graham, D.S.O., turned smiling toward his hostess. "That, I suppose," he speculated, "is what would be called an English accent." Those present, including two duchesses, a Member of Parliament, and Henry James, laughed. Ethel laughed with them. But the celebrated daughter of the black sheep of the proper Blyths could not have fully appreciated the irony.

Cynthia, scheduled for a six-week run, closed after four. "The vogue of that work, short as it was," explained *The Era*, "was solely due to the captivating personality of that actress." Ethel wanted to spend the summer in England. C.F. had other plans. She returned immediately to New York to begin a nationwide tour of *Cousin Kate*. Her arrival was accompanied by the usual engagement reports. This time they were not denied. Before leaving England, she had consented to marry Harry Graham.

Newspapers had a field day. One of them, the *American*, in a full-page story headed, "YES," SAYS LITTLE ETHEL BARRYMORE AT LAST, underscored the evanescence of fame. Ethel was identified as the daughter of "the late Lawrence Barrymore."

While the journals rhapsodized over "Little Ethel's" latest engagement, Lionel had quietly married. The lack of fanfare surrounding the event was characteristic of the eldest Barrymore, who refused to live his private life in the public eye. His bride was Doris Rankin, whose family had been allied for years with the Drews onstage, in friendship and marriage. Her parents, McKee Rankin and Kitty Blanchard, had long been friends of Mrs. Drew's. Her older sister, Gladys, had married Sidney Drew.

Lionel had first seen Doris while traveling with the Rankin troupe. He had been fifteen at the time, she four or five years old. They had not met for many years, when Harry Davenport, who had married Phyllis, another Rankin daughter, invited Lionel to his upstate New York farm. "I suppose that I had not taken a good look at Doris until she became sixteen," Lionel observed with his usual reticence. "Let us say: we fell in love."

Their June wedding took place in New York at St. Xavier's Catholic Church on Sixteenth Street. Ethel was still in London. Uncle Jack was on tour. But Jack was his brother's best man, and those of the Drews and Rankins who were in town were in attendance. "This I remember precisely," admitted the twenty-six-year-old bridegroom, "before the ceremony was over, it occurred to me bleakly that this nice girl, only sixteen, hadn't the slightest idea what she was getting into, taking on a partner such as I."

The youngest of the Rankin girls was more than merely sweet and pretty. Although she had yet to embrace the family trade, the rigors of a touring childhood had inured her to the hardships of theatrical life. She not only adjusted to the necessary separations from her husband but fiercely protected his privacy and fostered his artistic ambitions.

"I think I should quit the stage and go to the Art Students League again," Lionel would say.

"Why go there?" Doris would counter. "Go after the real thing. You've been to the Art Students League. Go to Paris." (Two years later, that idea, subsidized by Ethel, became a reality.)

As *Cousin Kate* toured that summer, Ethel had been simultaneously rehearsing *Sunday*, her play for the autumn season of 1904. The strain of such a schedule was heightened by disquieting rumors: Her father was dying. No such report had reached her from Amityville. But rumors persisted, reaching a crescendo during *Sunday*'s first tryout week in Syracuse. "Reports have it that Barrymore is dying," stated the New York *Journal* on November 5. "He is having strange hallucinations of the stage and fancies that he was once again the actor who won applause as *Rawdon Crawford* [*sic*], and as *Mr. Wilding* in *Captain Swift*. Periodically he becomes violent and at such times his attendants are fearful that the end is near."

Similar reports had periodically appeared since Barry's confinement. Their persistence, this time, alarmed his daughter. After the last Syracuse performance on Saturday, a special train carried her to New York, and would wait there until she was ready to leave for her next engagement in Buffalo. "Will she go over to Amityville to visit her father?" a reporter asked one of the company.

"Miss Barrymore has not said so," was the reply. "She seldom does mention matters of that sort."

Ethel did go over to Amityville. The rumors had not been true. It might have been preferable if they had. Death seemed no more imminent than it had been at any time during the last three and a half years. But Barry had completely lost his physical strength. He was a hopeless invalid, his once-perfect features ravaged by the insidious disease. He did not revile his daughter, nor mistake her for her mother. Ethel wasn't sure if he recognized her at all.

On November 15, Ethel opened her New York season at the Hudson, hoping to convince the critics that she was an actress. *Sunday*, written by four English actors under the nom de plume, "Thomas Raceward," gave her a part unlike any she had previously attempted. From the moment that she stumbled onstage shouting "Damn!" with a Southwestern drawl, wearing an ill-fitting gingham dress of angry red, her hair braided double and tied tight in an uncoquettish red bow knot, Ethel's *Miss Sunday* of Silver Creek captivated the public and elicited the kind of critical consideration for which she had been striving. It even managed to eclipse the announcement that she had broken her engagement to the dashing guardsman-poet. (Ethel did not marry until four years later, when Russell Griswold Colt, son of the president of the United States Rubber Company, finally managed to get her to the altar. They had three children, but after fourteen stormy years as "Mr. and Mrs. Barrymore," they were divorced. True to her mother's Catholicism, she never remarried.)

Her performance as a clumsy mining-camp orphan preoccupied reviewers. The play, mentioned incidentally in most of the notices, was found wanting. Her public didn't care. "It's so big it makes me sick to think of it," said one ticket speculator of the advance sale. "If I had just a little piece of the ownership of the American rights to *Sunday*, I'd be a rich man at the end of the season, an' the only time you'd be able to get a glimpse of me would be when I was bearin' down on you in my 60-horsepower." It was reported that Ethel received an average of twenty-five applications per week for interviews during *Sunday's* run.

A line which she had inserted to fill an awkward pause in the play—"That's all there is. There isn't any more."—became world famous, gaining meaning far beyond its original intent. She used the line to quell applause after repeated curtain calls, until, over the years, repetition by devotees and chroniclers made it inextricably hers. Elsie Janis, a young vaudevillian from Columbus, Ohio, used the line in her Barrymore impersonation. When Ethel brought Jack to see the Janis performance, he was astounded by the similarities between his sister and her impersonator.

"Ethel," he wondered, "did Papa ever play Columbus?"

A huge furniture van stood before the house at 94 Park Avenue, as burly men moved mahogany pieces, crates of books, paintings, and artifacts through the front door. Ethel Barrymore was moving into New York's fashionable Murray Hill section. An interviewer from the *Daily Mail*, arriving to record the event, made his way through the hall amid sounds of scraping, bumping, crashing. One unmistakable sound took precedence. Ethel stood at the head of the stairs, laughing. "Would you call this courage or mere nerve," she called down in her husky Barrymore drawl, "being interviewed on moving day, when a woman has a right to be in bad humor?"

Lionel and Doris had arrived that day from Boston, where he had contracted pneumonia while playing in *The Other Girl*. Still weak after three weeks of acting while ill, he was on his way to recuperate at Harry and Phyllis Davenport's upstate farm. "Everything is at sixes and sevens— mostly sevens!" Ethel exclaimed, seeming to enjoy the novelty of domestic confusion. "This is my house. At least, it is mine for a year. I have rented it, notwithstanding the expense, and for the first time in a long time I feel I have a home."

Lionel and Doris left after a few days for the Davenport farm, where he was to rest and regain his strength. He needed it. C.F. had scheduled a Western tour of *The Other Girl* to begin in January. For the first time, Lionel would face the hinterlands as a star. Two weeks of country air and his wife's solicitude prepared him for the journey. Before departing, he went to see his father at Amityville.

Barry's condition had somewhat improved. He was able, at least, to recognize his elder son, and to be suspicious of him. "He regarded me with the baleful doubt of a man who thinks another man is setting out to engage in shady card games or in the robbing of orphanages," Lionel recalled. When he mentioned the imminent Western tour, his father assumed a mistrustful leer.

"Where did you say you were going?" he asked.

"West, and then to San Francisco."

"You are a God-damned liar, Lionel," Papa snarled. "Everyone knows that San Francisco has been destroyed by earthquake and fire." He did not speak again, nor seem to hear. Lionel said good-by and departed, saddened by his father's senseless ramblings. (One year later, San Francisco *was* destroyed by earthquake and fire. Lionel was not there at the time. But Jack was.)

Ethel took *Sunday* on the road that spring of 1905. On March 24, while playing the Garrick in Philadelphia, she ran up to New York to appear at a matinee benefit for Joseph Holland, who had been her parents' close friend and colleague. Afterward, she hurried back to Philadelphia for her Friday-evening performance, unaware that her father's condition had become critical.

Perhaps fearing another false alarm, or merely from negligence, the sanitarium authorities had not informed the Barrymores of their father's decline. A week before Ethel's hurried trip to New York, he had fallen into semiconsciousness. A decisive change for the worse came at ten o'clock on Friday night. Nurses were assigned to stay with him around the clock.

At 3:55 on Saturday morning, he opened his eyes, turned toward the nurse, and smiled, nearly transcending his disease-ravaged features. "Our trade falls heavily upon these feeble folk," he said, clearly, before closing his eyes again.

At four o'clock, he died.

The appropriateness of that closing line was remarked in obituaries and savored by friends. But no one, neither critics, who recalled his performances, nor commentators, who rehashed his excesses, nor comrades, who celebrated his wit, not even his children, remembered its origin. It was a line from his failed masterpiece, *Nadjezda*.

Epilogue

The curtain falls, the play is played;
The beggar packs beside the beau;
The monarch troops and troops the maid;
The thunder huddles with the snow.
Where are the revelers high and low?
The dashing swords? The lover's call?
The dancers gleaming row on row?
Into the night go one and all.

W. E. HENLEY*

* Among Maurice Barrymore's favorite lines of verse.

A WIRE FROM the Frohman office was delivered to Horace McVickar, Ethel's manager, before the Saturday matinee began. Ethel was standing beside him in the wings when it arrived. Seeing his face sadden as he read the message, she asked what the trouble was. "Nothing," he lied; "it is a business matter."

The wire cautioned McVickar to keep the news from Ethel, to intercept any telegrams, until the business manager of the Frohman enterprises could get there from New York. She played her matinee as usual, and found Alf Hayman waiting in her dressing room after the last act. Although the worst had been expected for some time, it was a shock. Ethel fainted. Restoratives were hastily administered, but after recovering consciousness, she fainted again. Company members gathered at the door, offering help. Hayman advised that nothing could be done for the time being. Notice was given that there would be no evening performance.

After the initial shock, Ethel recovered and took charge, as she had after her mother's death, twelve years before. She sent wires to her brothers, made arrangements to leave immediately for New York. News of Barry's death had spread rapidly. Scores of Philadelphians had already surrounded the stage door, waiting to see "their Ethel" come out. A cab drove up and was stationed nearby. Two reserve policemen arrived to keep the crowd at a distance. Fifteen minutes later, Horace McVickar appeared, whispered to the cabman, the policemen, and walked down Broad Street. The cabman drove at a trot around to the Garrick's Chestnut Street entrance, out of sight of the unsuspecting onlookers. Ethel, on Alf Hayman's arm, entered the cab unnoticed and drove to Broad Street Station. She changed trains at New York for Amityville.

Lionel was between shows in San Francisco when word reached him. Leaving his starring role to an understudy, he started at once for New

York. The New York *Tribune* promulgated a more colorful version: "Lionel Barrymore learned of the death of his father while in the Juarez bull ring to-night. He went on in his part as usual."

Jack was in Buffalo, playing *The Dictator* with William Collier. He was so shaken by the news that only with Collier's help did he manage to board the New York train. Ethel had friends meet him at Grand Central to accompany him to her home. She joined him there, after leaving their father's body at the Stephen Merritt Burial Company.

"Though four years have gone by since Barrymore was a figure along Broadway," eulogized the Sunday *Telegraph*, "the announcement of his death evoked a general expression of positive grief. At the Lambs', where Barrymore in his prime was 'facile princeps' in a noted coterie of wits, the club was plunged in mourning." It had been late Saturday before news reached the clubhouse, so a special meeting was called for Sunday afternoon. Although no concerted action would be taken until the children were consulted, it was assumed that the Lambs', in conjunction with the Actors' Fund and the Elks, would have charge of funeral arrangements. As it turned out, Barry's fellow clubmen were permitted only to draft appropriate resolutions. Ethel, considering her father's ravaged condition, decided on a private ceremony.

In response to the clamoring press, Jack made a statement from his sister's house. The family, he announced, was agreed upon holding the funeral in strict privacy, and orders had been given that no callers would be allowed to view the body. Hundreds of Barry's friends and followers were turned away from the undertaking rooms on Tuesday. Ethel telegraphed Uncle Jack for permission to bury her father in the Drew family plot in Philadelphia. He wired immediate approval.

John Drew had heard of Barry's death from C.F. after his Saturday-evening performance at the Tulane Theatre in New Orleans. Frohman had been at the theater when Lin Bonner, a fledgling reporter, arrived in hopes of getting some quotes from Drew concerning his late brother-in-law.

"Barry dead?" asked C.F.

"Yes," Bonner assured him, "Mr. Barrymore is dead, and they want me to get a statement from Mr. Drew about it."

"This is tragic," said Barry's old adversary, "but a blessing for Barry— he has been mad, you know." This was news to the young reporter. In fact, Maurice Barrymore was news to him. "Please do not ask me to break the news to Mr. Drew now," C.F. continued, "but if you will come to the St. Charles Hotel at eleven tonight—after I have broken the news to him—I promise that you shall have an interview."

At the appointed hour, Bonner found John Drew seated on a divan with Frohman in the St. Charles lobby.

"Poor Barry! He's at peace finally," John Drew began, pausing as if to take strength for what was expected of him. "Barry, you know, probably was the greatest wit we ever have had in this country. I could tell you dozens of tales about him, but here is one which will give you a better view of his mental agility than any other." A pensive smile appeared, apparently recalling lost pleasures, as he told the story. "When Ethel, Lionel and John were little babies it was their custom to come each night to their mother's knee and say their prayers. Barry, usually, would be reading a book, a play or a newspaper. The children would say their 'Now I lay me down to sleep, etc.,' and Georgie, their mother and my sister, would prompt them in the benedictions of 'God bless Mama, God bless Papa,' and, invariably, if I were present, Barry would break in with 'and God help Uncle Jack to be a better actor.'"

Concurrent newspaper eulogies, while no less affectionate, were products of prosaic men. A protean saga begun in Victoria's India fifty-five years before was reduced to a melodrama of professional opportunities lost. "He will be remembered with many a smile, at the quips and cranks in which he rejoiced and which made his comrades glad," conceded the indefatigable William Winter, "and with perhaps many a sigh, that Fate, which is another word for character, should have ordained him to a life of almost fruitless activity, closing, prematurely, in the haunted gloom of intellectual decay."

The funeral was held at ten o'clock on Wednesday morning in the chapel of the Stephen Merritt Burial Company. The closed casket held a pillow of orchids and gardenias from his daughter. The short Episcopal service was read by the Reverend Doctor George C. Houghton, rector of The Little Church Around the Corner. Uncle Jack had returned from New Orleans to join his niece and nephew and their few invited guests: Lionel's wife, Doris, Augustus Thomas, William Gillette, Benjamin J. Fagin, secretary of the New York Lodge of Elks, and Alf Hayman, representing the Frohman office. Hayman, ironically, who had brought Ethel the news of her father's death, one of the few invited to mourn Barry, had been an object of his fierce attacks during battles with the Trust. And among numerous floral offerings around the bier, none was more imposing than that of Charles Frohman.

Other tributes brought gentler memories. Boston Lodge, No. 10, B.P.O. Elks, in whose annual benefits Barry had participated for twenty years, sent a stand of lilies and carnations bearing a streamer inscribed CHARITY, JUSTICE, BROTHERLY LOVE, FIDELITY. There was a wreath of roses from Freddie Gebhard, who had afforded Barry such good sport during his tour with Lillie Langtry. There were countless little unsigned clusters of violets, lilies of the valley, loose-cut roses sent by onetime matinee girls paying a last, loving tribute to youthful afternoons with *Orlando* and *Captain Swift* and *Reckless Temple*.

After the brief service, those present accompanied the body to Philadelphia in a special car banked with flowers. Mr. and Mrs. Sidney Drew, Mrs. John Drew, Horace McVickar, and J. C. Hyde, Ethel's agent, met them at the station. They drove immediately to Glenwood Cemetery.

Despite efforts to insure privacy, several hundred persons gathered near the Drew plot. Most of them were curiosity seekers. Some, Kitty and Lily Garrett, who had been nurse and dresser in Mrs. Drew's household, were honoring the past. Others, Ethel's maid, Nanette Watson, the stagehands from the Garrick, were merely dutiful. The crowd shifted, as spectators positioned for better views. Ethel and Jack were still. Maurice Barrymore was lowered to his place beside Georgie Drew.

The two Barrymores did not speak until their carriage stopped at the stage door of the Garrick. Jack got out, helped his sister down. "We could go over your lines, if you like," Ethel offered. She had arranged for her brother to join the cast of *Sunday*.

"I think I have them down," he said. "I'll go to the hotel." She walked toward the stage door, calling back to him as he climbed into the cab.

"You will be back in time to ready yourself?" Jack said that he would, before driving away.

In her dressing room that afternoon, Ethel slept fitfully for an hour or so, until Nanette Watson arrived to prepare her for the performance.

Jack did not go back to the hotel. He changed his mind, ordering the driver, instead, to 140 North Twelfth Street. "It had seemed such a wonderful place to me," he recalled, "and the rooms had been so big; but now it was all drab and dreary. I do not know of what substance those conventional white Philadelphia steps are made, but they were being washed by a slatternly woman, and they did not seem to get much cleaner in the process. Those three steps that Ethel, Lionel and I had jumped up and down in our countless trips in and out of that house. John Drew had crossed them to see his mother. Grandmother, with her stately dignity, had left them to go to the theater. Jefferson, in his calls upon her, had walked there. It was perhaps on the second step that my mother stood one Sunday morning when she met my father as he was returning from an all-night party.

" 'Where are you bound for, dearie?' he asked.

" 'I'm going to church. You go to hell.' "

When Ethel Barrymore made her entrance at the Garrick that evening, the audience stood as one to applaud. In the second act, after her line—"That's all there is. There isn't any more."—there was an awed hush from the house that few actors ever achieve. They stood again when the curtain fell, this time, cheering. Ethel brought her brother forward to

502

share the ovation. This was, they both knew, a final tribute to the man left that afternoon at Glenwood Cemetery.

There was a wire waiting afterward in Ethel's dressing room:

STARTED AT ONCE FOR NEW YORK. TRAIN SO LATE COULD NOT POSSIBLY MAKE CONNECTIONS. TURNED BACK AT CHICAGO FOR THE WEST. DEAR OLD DAD—BUT THANK GOD IT IS OVER. HE IS BETTER OFF.

LIONEL

Ethel and Jack removed their make-up, changed into street clothes, then waited for the last of the stage-door mourners to disperse. To avoid stragglers, the doorman ordered their cab to the Chestnut Street entrance.

They did not go directly back to their hotel. Ethel asked the cabby to just drive for a while, and Jack recounted his visit to North Twelfth Street. "I went into the house and looked at the old rooms where I had played, and of which I had such deathless memories. They were cramped and fusty." (Ethel said nothing, but years later expressed the frustration which had followed upon her father's death. "This ended a chapter in my life that has always seemed tragically incomplete," she wrote. "I shall always wish that I might have seen him oftener and known him better.")

They rode silent, lulled by clattering hoofs and wheels on cobblestone, until Jack resumed the account of his visit to their childhood home. "I saw the place on the top floor which was a cache for the things I stole." He paused. An astonished smile appeared. "I was really glad to leave and that I had a nicer place to go to—a theater, where there was room to move about."

—CURTAIN—

Bibliography and Acknowledgments

I was originally tempted to supply footnotes. But being an obsessive reader of them myself, and finding them usually an intrusion, I resisted the temptation. Instead, quotes from newspapers and periodicals are credited in the text, while those from books are attributed to their authors. The latter are listed below, categorically and alphabetically, for the benefit of readers wishing further consultation:

General References:

Barnhart, Clarence L. (ed.), *The American College Dictionary*. New York: Random House, 1953.
Clarence, Reginald, *"The Stage" Cyclopaedia of Plays*. London: *The Stage,* 1909.
Fowler, H. W. and F. G. (eds.), *The Concise Oxford Dictionary of Current English* (5th ed.). Oxford: Clarendon Press, 1964.
Hartnoll, Phyllis (ed.), *The Oxford Companion to the Theatre*. London: Oxford University Press, 1957.
Haydn, Hiram, and Edmund Fuller (eds.), *Thesaurus of Book Digests*. New York: Crown Publishers, 1954.
Odell, George C. D., *Annals of the New York Stage*. New York: Columbia University Press, 1940.
Parker, John (ed.), *Who's Who in the Theatre* (10th ed.) London: Pitman & Sons, Ltd., 1947.
Webster's Dictionary of Synonyms. Springfield, Mass.: G. & C. Merriam Co., 1951.
Yust, Walter (ed.), *Encyclopaedia Britannica*. Chicago: William Benton, 1959.

Plays and Novels (The British Museum Manuscripts Library allowed access to the Lord Chamberlain's Register of Plays, where every play by Maurice Barrymore produced or copyrighted in England was scrupulously preserved. Unfortunately, the same cannot be said of those in America. A Library of Congress employee informed me that because of storage problems many plays of that era had been burned . . .):

Barrymore, Maurice H., *Blood Will Tell*. London: Lord Chamberlain's Office, No. 194, 1895.
——, *Honour*. London: Lord Chamberlain's Office, No. 163, 1881.
——, *Nadjezda*. London: Lord Chamberlain's Office, No. 244, 1885.
——, and Charles Puerner, "Hast Thou Forgot" (from *The Robber of the Rhine*). New York: Wm. A. Pond & Co., 1892.
Fitch, Clyde, *Captain Jinks of the Horse Marines*. New York: Doubleday, Page & Co., 1902.
Graham, Harry ("Col. D. Streamer"), *Misrepresentative Men*. New York: Fox, Duffield & Co., 1904.
Shakespeare, *As You Like It*. New Haven: Yale University Press, 1954.
Shaw, G. Bernard, *Cashel Byron's Profession*. New York: Brentano's, 1899.
Sheridan, Richard Brinsley, *The Rivals*. London: J. M. Dent & Sons, Ltd., 1910.
Thackeray, William Makepeace, *Vanity Fair* (*Becky Sharp* ed.). New York: Harper & Bros., 1899.

Family Sources (From its inception, this book has benefited from the enthusiastic participation of Maurice Barrymore's granddaughter, Ethel Barrymore Colt—Mrs. Romeo Miglietta. Her brother, Samuel Pomeroy Colt, also offered his interest and memories, while Barry's grandnephew, E. Pat Wace of London, contributed invaluable family records and photographs, and led me to his cousin, Mrs. E. B. Gordon of New Zealand, who shared rare Blyth reminiscences and letters):

Alpert, Hollis, *The Barrymores*. New York: Dial Press, 1964.
Barrymore, Ethel, *Memories*. New York: Harper & Bros., 1955.
——, "My Stage Life Up To Date." *Metropolitan Magazine*, June 1901.
——, "My Reminiscences." *The Delineator*.
Barrymore, John, *Confessions of an Actor*. Indianapolis: Bobbs-Merrill Co., 1926.
——, *We Three*. New York: Saalfield Publishing Co., 1935.
Barrymore, Lionel (as told to Cameron Shipp), *We Barrymores*. New York: Appleton-Century-Crofts, Inc., 1951.
Dithmar, Edward A., *John Drew*, New York: Frederick A. Stokes Co., 1900.
Drew, John, *My Years on the Stage*. New York: E. P. Dutton & Co., 1922.
Drew, Mrs. John, *Autobiographical Sketch*. New York: Charles Scribner's Sons, 1899.
Eaton, Walter Prichard, "The New Ethel Barrymore." *The American Magazine*, 1911.
Ford, James L., "The Ethel Barrymore Following." *Appleton's Magazine*, November 1908.
Fowler, Gene, *Good Night, Sweet Prince, The Life & Times of John Barrymore*. New York: Viking Press, 1944.
Fyles, Vanderheyden, "The Degree of L.L.D." (Leading Lady to Drew). *The Green Book Magazine*.
Halbert, Delancey M., "Ethel Barrymore, A Sketch." *Frank Leslie's Popular Monthly*, May 1903.
Judson, Alice, "A Child's Recollection of the Drews." *Metropolitan Magazine*, January 1901.
McKay, Frederic E., and C. E. L. Wingate (eds.), *Famous American Actors*

of Today. New York, Boston: T. Y. Crowell & Co., 1896. ("Maurice Barrymore" by Edward Fales Coward; "Mrs. John Drew" by Colonel T. Allston Brown; "John Drew" by James S. Metcalfe.)

"Pearson's Talks with Players—Ethel Barrymore." *Pearson's Magazine*, 1904.

Power-Waters, Alma, *John Barrymore, The Legend and the Man*. New York: Julian Messner, Inc., 1941.

Skinner, Cornelia Otis, "The Radiant Ethel Barrymore." *McCall's*, March 1950.

Tracy, Virginia, "The First of the Barrymores." *The New Yorker*, October 11, 1930.

Wace, Alfred A., *Wace Memoirs*. Privately printed, 1932.

Wace, Brigadier General E. G., *The History of the Wace Family*. Privately printed.

White, Matthew, Jr., "Ethel Barrymore." *Munsey's Magazine*, November 1905.

Wolf, Rennold. "Ethel Barrymore." *Smith's Magazine*, November 1907.

India (In London, John Wallford and Commander Godfrey of the Public Records Office, and Miss Towler of Orbit House, the India Office Library, led me to countless Bengal Army Lists, Descriptive Long Rolls, Casualty, Marriage, Baptism Lists, as well as New Calcutta Directories, Bengal Revenue Consultations, Bengal Almanacks, and Punjab Gazetteers on the search for Blyth-Blake-Barrymore antecedents):

Bhanu, Dharma, *History of Administration of the North-Western Provinces*, 1803–58. Agra: Shiva Lal Agarwala, 1957.

Cotton, Sir Evan, *East Indiamen*. London: Batchworth Press, 1949.

Dutt, R., *Economic History of India Under Early British Rule*. 1906.

Hickey, William, *Memoirs*. New York: AMS Press, 1925.

Imperial Gazetteer of India, Provincial Series (vols. 2, 8). Calcutta: Superintendent of Government Printing, 1808–9.

Kincaid, Dennis C., *British Social Life in India, 1608–1937*. London: Routledge, 1939.

Lees, N. W., *The Drain of Silver to the East and the Currency of India*. 1864.

Phillimore, *Historical Records of the Survey of India*. Dehra Dun, India.

Roberts, Paul E., *History of British India* (3rd ed.). London: Oxford University Press, 1952.

Smith, V. A., et al. *The Oxford History of India* (3rd ed.). 1958.

Thompson, Edward, and G. T. Garratt. *Rise and Fulfilment of British Rule in India*. Allahabad: Central Book Depot, 1958.

England (Nowhere were professionalism and congeniality better blended than in the staffs of London's borough libraries: the Central Research Library, St. Martin's Street, Westminster, and its Theatre Collection; Plumstead Library, Greenwich, S.E. 18, and its Boxing Collection; The Manor House, Lee, S.E. 13, where Miss I. M. Dyer and Mr. R. A. Manser located the discarded records of Blackheath Proprietary School. Fruitful guidance was also lent by the staffs of the British Museum Reading Room and its Newspaper Library at Colindale, N.W. 9; Somerset House, London's General Register Office; Scarborough Library; the Royal Naval College Library, Dartmouth;

the Harrow School; Lincoln College, Oxford; London's Amateur Rowing and Boxing Associations. London booksellers, Andrew Block of Barter Street, and David Drummond of Cecil Court, turned up a wealth of material. Researcher Miss V. A. Ledger led me to the Blyth wills. The late Margaret Webster shared her bibliography and notes and the diaries of her mother, Dame May Whitty—rare views of the London exploits and courtships of Ethel Barrymore—while the late Randolph Churchill gave valuable insight to the courting of Ethel by his father. J. W. Thomas, vicar of St. Michael's, Kirby-Le-Soken, allowed me to examine church records, and led to Sneating Hall, where the present owner, Derek Allen, had estate records dating back to the time of Squire William Edward Blyth. On the walls of an old stone stable, Mr. Allen and I even discovered boyhood inscriptions of the squire's sons):

Abell, H. F., *School Memories of Old Blackheath*. Privately printed.

Arliss, George, *Up the Years from Bloomsbury*. Boston: Little, Brown & Co., 1927.

Ashwell, Lena, *Myself a Player*. London: Michael Joseph, Ltd., 1936.

Baedeker, Karl, *London and Its Environs*. London: Dulau & Co., 1894.

Bancroft, Mr. & Mrs., *On and off the Stage*. London: Richard Bentley & Son, 1889.

Barnes, J. H., *Forty Years on the Stage*. London: Chapman & Hall, Ltd., 1914.

Betjeman, John, *Victorian and Edwardian London from Old Photographs*. London: B. T. Batsford, Ltd., 1969.

Bettinson, A. F. and B., *The Home of Boxing*. London: Odhams Press, Ltd.

Brookfield, Charles H. E., *Random Reminiscences*. London: Edward Arnold, 1902.

Burton, Percy (as told to Lowell Thomas), *Adventures Among Immortals*. London: Hutchinson & Co., Ltd., 1938.

Cochran, Charles B., *Showman Looks On*. London: J. M. Dent & Sons, Ltd., 1945.

Coffin, Hayden, *Hayden Coffin's Book*. London: Alston Rivers, Ltd., 1930.

Collier, Constance, *Harlequinade*. London: Bodley Head, Ltd., 1929.

Collins, J. S., *Shaw*. New York: Alfred A. Knopf, Inc.

Cook, Mrs. E. T., *Highways and Byways in London*. London: MacMillan & Co., Ltd., 1902.

Cooper, Gladys, *Gladys Cooper*. London: Hutchinson & Co., Ltd., 1931.

Craig, Edith, and Christopher St. John (eds.), *Ellen Terry's Memoirs*. New York: G. P. Putnam's Sons, 1932.

Disher, Maurice Willson, *The Lost Romantic* (Sir John Martin-Harvey). London: Hutchinson & Co., Ltd.

Donnelly, Ned, *Self-Defence; or, The Art of Boxing*. London: Weldon & Co., 1887.

Doré, Gustave, and Blanchard Jerrold, *London—A Pilgrimage*. New York: Harper & Bros., 1890.

du Maurier, Daphne, *Gerald, A Portrait*. New York: Doubleday, Doran & Co., Inc., 1934.

"Dunrobin Castle." *Country Life* (vol. L).

Ervine, St. John, "Life of George Bernard Shaw." *Seven Famous Reprints*. New York: Encyclopaedia Britannica, Inc., 1926.

Fishman, Jack, *My Darling Clementine*, The Story of Lady Churchill. New York: Avon Book, 1963.

Forbes-Robertson, Diana, *Maxine*. London: Hamish-Hamilton, 1964.

Goddard, Arthur, *Players of the Period*. London: Dean & Son, 1891.

Henderson, Archibald, *George Bernard Shaw, His Life and Works*. Cincinnati: Stewart & Kidd, 1911.

Hope-Hawkins, Anthony, *Memories and Notes*. London: Hutchinson & Co., Ltd., 1927.

Irving, Laurence, *Henry Irving*. London: Faber & Faber.

Irving, Laurence, *The Successors*. London: Rupert Hart-Davis, 1967.

Kirby, J. W., *History of the Blackheath Proprietary School*. Blackheath: The Blackheath Press, 1933.

Knebworth, Viscount, *Boxing*. London: Seeley, Service & Co., Ltd., 1931.

Lehmann, R. C., *The Complete Oarsman*. London: Methuen & Co., 1908.

Leverton, W. H. (with J. B. Booth), *Through the Box-Office Window*. London: T. Werner Laurie, Ltd., 1932.

Leyson, Peter, *London Theatres*. London: Apollo Publications, 1970.

MacQueen-Pope, W., *Haymarket: Theatre of Perfection*. London: W. H. Allen, 1948.

Margetson, Stella, *Fifty Years of Victorian London from the Great Exhibition to the Queen's Death*. London: MacDonald & Co., Ltd., 1969.

Martin, Ralph G., *Jennie* (vol. II). New York: New American Library, 1972.

Martin-Harvey, Sir John, *Autobiography*. London: Sampson Low, Marston & Co., Ltd., 1933.

McCall, Dorothy, *When That I Was*. London: Faber & Faber.

McCarthy, Justin, *Portraits of the Sixties*. New York: Harper Bros., 1903.

Mitchell, R. J., and M. D. R. Leys, *A History of London Life*. Penguin Books, Ltd., 1958.

Nicholson, Robert, *London Guide*. London: Nicholson Publications, 1968.

Pennell, Joseph and Elizabeth, *The Stream of Pleasure*. London: T. Fisher Unwin, 1891.

"Pugnus," *History of the Prize Ring*. London: 1876.

Robertson, Graham W., *Time Was*. London: Hamish Hamilton, 1931.

Rosebery, Lord, *Lord Randolph Churchill*. London: Arthur L. Humphreys, 1906.

Rowell, George, *The Victorian Theatre*. Oxford: Clarendon Press, 1956.

Saintsbury and Palmer (eds.), *We Saw Him Act* (Henry Irving). London: Hurst & Blackett, 1939.

Scott, Clement, *Ellen Terry*. New York: Frederick A. Stokes Co., 1900.

Scott, Mrs. Clement, *Old Days in Bohemian London*. London: Hutchinson & Co.

Steen, Marguerite, *A Pride of Terrys*. London: Longmans, 1962.

Thompson, David, *England in the Nineteenth Century, 1815–1914*. Penguin Books, 1950.

Trevelyan, G. M., *English Social History*. London: Longmans, Green & Co., 1942.

——, *A Shortened History of England*. Penguin Books, 1959.

Webster, Margaret, *The Same Only Different*. New York: Alfred A. Knopf, 1969.

Webster-Brough, Jean, *Prompt Copy*. London: Hutchinson & Co., Ltd., 1952.

White, James Dillon, *Born to Star, The Lupino Lane Story*. London: Heinemann, 1957.

Wren, Walter, "A Letter to the Right Honourable The Earl of Kimberley,

on the Regulations Now in Force for Selection and Training of Candidates for the India Civil Service" (pamphlet). London: Waters, 1883.
———, "What Is Education?" (pamphlet). London.

America (The greatest single source of information was the superb Theatre Collection of the Harvard College Library, where curator Jeanne Newlin and her assistant, Martha Mahard, offered expert guidance, interest and enthusiasm far beyond the call of duty. Access was also given to the vast resources of the New York Public Library at Forty-second Street and its Theatre Collection at Lincoln Center; the Museum of the City of New York; the Boston Public Library's newspaper files; the Chicago Public Library's Theatre Collection; Chicago's Newberry Library; the Milwaukee Public Library; the Worcester Public Library; and the music section of the Library of Congress. Librarians Robert L. Rose of San Francisco's Bohemian Club, Beatrice Peterson of the American Kennel Club, and, particularly, Louis A. Rachow of New York's Players' Club, and Virginia Doane and Martha Stone of Brooks Free Library, Harwich, Mass., were of great assistance, as were John Herron and Charles Campbell of the Worcester Historical Society, and writer Michael H. Drew of the Milwaukee *Journal*. I am in the debt of the good people of Marshall, Texas, the local *News Messenger*, and the Harrison County Historical Society; of Eileen Flood, legal secretary to the late Robert J. Riddle, who allowed me to see the will of Mamie Floyd Barrymore's mother, and Administrator Cornelia F. Cassidy of South Oaks Hospital, The Long Island Home, Ltd., Amityville, who checked for records and allowed me to walk the grounds that Maurice Barrymore walked. Valuable material was uncovered on Cape Cod at Parnassus Book Service, Yarmouthport; Steve Willins' Book Store, Wellfleet; Don Hall's Old Curiosity Shop, Harwich Center; and Ben Thatcher's Old Sound, West Harwich; in Boston, at the Brattle Book Shop; in Cambridge, at the Starr Book Shop, Pangloss Bookshop, and Bryn Mawr Book Service; in Ithaca, Smith's Book House, and in New York City, the Memory Shop, The Gotham Book Mart, Milt Wyatt's former Cornelia St. shop, and Anna Sosenko's shop; in Chicago, at Thomas Tomc's Fly by Nite Antiques. Special thanks is due Blanche Sweet, one of the first "movie stars," for vividly sharing her childhood memories of Maurice Barrymore, particularly since she is to my knowledge, and this indelicacy amuses her, the only living person who knew him):

Ayres, Alfred, *Acting and Actors*. New York: D. Appleton & Co., 1894.
Bacon, Louisa Crowninshield, *Reminiscences*. Boston: 1922.
Beehn, Ruth Merritt, "Stories from the Files of Charles A. Beehn." Marshall, Texas: Private papers.
Belmont, Eleanor Robson, *The Fabric of Memory*. New York: Farrar, Straus & Cudahy, 1957.
Binns, Archie (with Olive Kooken), *Mrs. Fiske And the American Theatre*. New York: Crown Publishers, Inc., 1955.
Birnbaum, Martin, *Oscar Wilde, Fragments and Memories*. London: Elkin Mathews, 1920.
Bodeen, DeWitt, "Blanche Sweet," *Films in Review*, November 1965.
Bowen, Catherine Drinker, and Barbara von Meck, *Beloved Friend, The Story of Tchaikowsky and Nadejda von Meck*. New York: Random House, 1937.

Bowers, Claude, *Indianapolis in the "Gay Nineties."* Indiana Historical Society, 1964.

Brady, William A., *Showman.* New York: E. P. Dutton & Co., Inc., 1937.

Brereton, Austin, *Gallery of Players.* Illustrated American Publishing Co., 1894.

Brooks, Van Wyck, *New England: Indian Summer.* New York: E. P. Dutton & Co., 1940.

Brown, T. Allston, *History of the American Stage.* Dick & Fitzgerald, Publishers, 1870.

Carroll, David, *The Matinee Idols.* New York: Arbor House, 1972.

Clapp, Henry A., *Reminiscences of a Dramatic Critic.* Boston: Houghton, Mifflin Co., 1902.

Clapp, John Bouvé, and Edwin Francis Edgett, *Plays of the Present.* New York: Dunlap Society, 1902.

Coleman, Marion Moore, *Fair Rosalind: The American Career of Helena Modjeska.* Cheshire, Ct.: Cherry Hill Books, 1969.

Corbett, James J., *The Roar of the Crowd.* London: Phoenix House Ltd., 1954.

Crane, William H., *Footprints and Echoes.* New York: E. P. Dutton & Co., 1927.

Crawford, Mary Caroline, *Romantic Days in Old Boston.* Boston: Little, Brown & Co., 1910.

Crowninshield, Francis W., *Manners for the Metropolis.* New York: D. Appleton & Co., 1908.

Dale, Alan (Alfred J. Cohen), *Familiar Chats with the Queens of the Stage.* New York: G. W. Dillingham, 1890.

Daly, Joseph Francis, *The Life of Augustin Daly.* New York: The MacMillan Co., 1917.

Davis, Owen, *I'd Like to Do It Again.* New York: Farrar & Rinehart, Inc., 1931.

DeMille, Cecil B., *Autobiography.* Englewood Cliffs, N.J.: Prentice-Hall, Inc., 1959.

Dole, Nathan Haskell, *Joseph Jefferson at Home.* Boston: Estes & Lauriat, 1898.

Dressler, Marie, *The Life Story of an Ugly Duckling.* New York: Robert M. McBride & Co., 1924.

—— (as told to Mildred Harrington), *My Own Story.* Boston: Little, Brown & Co., 1934.

Dudley, Ernest, *The Gilded Lily.* London: Odhams Press, Ltd., 1958.

Eaton, Walter Prichard, *Plays and Players.* Cincinnati: Steward & Kidd Co., 1916.

Eytinge, Rose, *The Memories of Rose Eytinge.* New York: Frederick A. Stokes Co., 1905.

Felheim, Marvin, *The Theater of Augustin Daly.* Cambridge: Harvard University Press, 1956.

Foy, Eddie, and A. F. Harlow, *Clowning Through Life.* New York: E. P. Dutton & Co., 1928.

Frohman, Daniel, *Daniel Frohman Presents.* New York: Kendall & Sharp, 1935.

——, *Encore.* New York: Lee Furman, Inc., 1937.

——, *Memories of a Manager.* New York: Doubleday, Page & Co., 1911.

———, and Isaac F. Marcosson, *Charles Frohman: Manager and Man*. New York: Harper & Bros., 1916.

Gallegly, Joseph, *Footlights on the Border*. Gravenhage: Moulton & Co., 1962.

Genthe, Arnold, *As I Remember*. New York: Reynal & Hitchcock, 1936.

Gilbert, Douglas, *American Vaudeville, Its Life and Times*. New York: McGraw-Hill Book Co., 1940.

Gillmore, Margalo, *Four Flights Up*. Boston: Houghton Mifflin Co., 1964.

Golden, George Fuller, *My Lady Vaudeville and Her White Rats*. New York: White Rats of America, 1909.

Goodwin, Nat C., *Nat Goodwin's Book*. Boston: The Gorham Press, 1914.

Graves, Charles, *The Cochran Story*. London: W. H. Allen.

Gronowicz, Antoni, *Modjeska, Her Life and Loves*. New York: Thomas Yoseloff, Inc., 1956.

Hawtrey, Charles, *The Truth at Last*. London: Thornton Butterworth, Ltd., 1924.

Hayward, Walter Brownell, *Bermuda Past and Present*. New York: Dodd, Mead & Co., 1910.

Hicks, Seymour, *Between Ourselves*. London: Cassell & Co., Ltd., 1930.

Hopper, DeWolf, (with Wesley Winans Stout), *Once a Clown, Always a Clown*. Boston: Little, Brown & Co., 1927.

Horton, Judge William E., *Driftwood of the Stage*. Detroit: Winn & Hammond, 1904.

Huneker, James G., *Steeplejack*, New York: Charles Scribner's Sons, 1922.

In Memoriam, Bronson Howard. New York, 1910.

Izard, Forrest, *Heroines of the Modern Stage*. New York: Sturgis & Walton Co., 1915.

Janis, Elsie, *So Far, So Good!* New York: E. P. Dutton & Co., Inc., 1932.

Jefferson, Joseph, *Autobiography*. New York: The Century Co., 1889.

King, C. Richard, "Maurice Barrymore and the Incident at Marshall." *East Texas Historical Journal*.

Kobbé, Gustav, *Famous Actors & Actresses and Their Homes*. Boston: Little, Brown & Co., 1903.

Langtry, Lillie (Lady de Bathe), *The Days I Knew*. New York: George H. Doran Co., 1925.

Laurie, Joe, Jr., *Vaudeville*. New York: Henry Holt & Co., 1953.

Leeds, Josiah W., *The Theatre: An Essay upon the Non-accordancy of Stageplays with the Christian Profession*. Philadelphia: Published for the Author, 1886.

Leslie, Amy, *Some Players*. Chicago: Herbert S. Stone, 1899.

Linscott, Robert N., *State of Mind, A Boston Reader*. New York: Farrar, Straus & Co., 1948.

Lyght, Charles E., M.D. (ed.), *The Merck Manual* (10th ed.). Rahway, N.J.: Merck Sharp & Dohme Research Labs.

MacKaye, Percy, *Epoch, The Life of Steele MacKaye*. New York: Boni & Liveright, 1927.

Maney, Richard, *Fanfare, The Confessions of a Press Agent*. New York: Harper & Bros., 1957.

"Margaret," *Theatrical Sketches*. New York: Merriam Co., 1894.

Martin, Charlotte M. (ed.), *Stage Reminiscences of Mrs. Gilbert*. New York: Charles Scribner's Sons, 1901.

Matthews, Brander, *The Tocsin of Revolt and Other Essays*. New York: Charles Scribner's Sons, 1922.

Modjeska, Helena, *Memories and Impressions*. New York: Macmillan Co., 1910.

Moody, William Vaughn, *Letters to Harriet*. Boston: Houghton Mifflin Co., 1935.

Morris, Lloyd, *Curtain Time*. New York: Random House, 1953.

——, *Incredible New York*. New York: Random House, 1951.

Morrison, Samuel Eliot, *Maritime History of Massachusetts*. Boston: Houghton Mifflin Co., 1921.

Morse, Frank P., *Backstage with Henry Miller*. New York: E. P. Dutton, 1938.

Moses, Montrose J., and Virginia Gerson, *Clyde Fitch and His Letters*. Boston: Little, Brown, 1924.

——, *Famous Actor Families in America*. New York: Thomas D. Crowell, 1906.

Nathan, George Jean, *Theatre Book of the Year, 1945–46*. New York: Alfred A. Knopf, 1946.

Nesbit, Evelyn (Mrs. Harry K. Thaw), *The Untold Story*. London: John Long, Ltd., 1934.

Parmelee, Deolece, *The Deadly Jewels of Diamond Bessie*. Austin, Texas: D. M. Parmelee, 1968.

Pollock, Channing, *Harvest of My Years*. New York: Bobbs-Merrill, 1943.

Powers, James T., *Twinkle Little Star*. New York: G. P. Putnam's Sons, 1939.

Quinn, Arthur Hobson, *A History of the American Drama*. New York: Appleton-Century-Crofts, Inc., 1927; 2nd ed., 1943.

Rideing, William H., *Many Celebrities and a Few Others*. New York: Doubleday, Page, 1912.

Robbins, Phyllis, *Maude Adams*. New York: G. P. Putnam's Sons, 1956.

Ruggles, Eleanor, *Prince of Players*. New York: W. W. Norton & Co., Inc., 1953.

Ryan, Kate, *Old Boston Museum Days*. Boston: Little, Brown, 1915.

Salvini, Tommaso, *Leaves from the Autobiography of Tommaso Salvini*. New York: Century, 1893.

Sayler, Oliver M., *Our American Theatre*. New York: Brentano's, 1923.

Schriftgiesser, Karl, *Oscar of the Waldorf*. New York: E. P. Dutton, 1943.

Seymour, Clifton, "The Shooting of Maurice Barrymore." *Frontier Times*, April 1927.

Sheean, Vincent, *The Amazing Oscar Hammerstein*. London: Weidenfeld & Nicolson, 1956.

Sichel, Pierre, *The Jersey Lily*. Englewood Cliffs, N.J.: Prentice-Hall, 1958.

Skinner, Cornelia Otis, *Family Circle*. Boston: Houghton Mifflin, 1948.

Skinner, Otis, *Footlights and Spotlights*. Indianapolis: Bobbs-Merrill, 1924.

Smith, Cecil, *Musical Comedy in America*. New York: Robert M. MacGregor, 1950.

Smith, Harry B., *First Nights and First Editions*. Boston: Little, Brown, 1931.

Snow, Edward Rose, *The Romance of Boston Bay*. Boston: Yankee Publishing Co., 1946.

Sothern, E. H. (Fairfax Downey, ed.), *Julia Marlowe's Story*. New York: Rinehart & Co., Inc., 1954.

Stoddart, J. H., *Recollections of a Player*. New York: Century, 1902.

Stone, Henry D., *Personal Recollections of the Drama*. Albany: C. Van Benthuysen, 1873.

Strang, Lewis C., *Famous Actors of the Day in America*. Boston: L. C. Page & Co., Inc., 1900.

Thomas, Augustus, *The Print of My Remembrance*. New York: Charles Scribner's Sons, 1922.

Ticknor, Caroline (ed.), *Dr. Holmes's Boston*. Boston: Houghton Mifflin, 1915.

Timberlake, Craig, *David Belasco, The Bishop of Broadway*. New York: Library Publishers, 1954.

Tomkins, Eugene, *History of the Boston Theatre, 1854–1901*. Boston: Houghton Mifflin, 1908.

Tyler, George C. (with J. C. Furnas), *Whatever Goes Up—* Indianapolis: Bobbs-Merrill, 1934.

Van Every, Edward, *Muldoon: The Solid Man of Sport*. New York: 1928.

Veiller, Bayard, *The Fun I've Had*. New York: Reynal & Hitchcock, 1941.

Wagner, Frederick, and Barbara Brady, *Famous American Actors and Actresses*. New York: Dodd, Mead, 1961.

Walker, Stanley, *The Night Club Era*. New York: Frederick A. Stokes, 1933.

Warde, Frederick, *Fifty Years of Make-Believe*. Los Angeles: Times-Mirror Press, 1923.

Warren, William, *Life and Memoirs*. Boston: James Daly, 1889.

Whiffen, Mrs. Thomas, *Keeping off the Shelf*. New York: E. P. Dutton, 1928.

Whitton, Joseph, *Wags of the Stage*. Philadelphia: George H. Rigby, 1902.

Wilder, Marshall P., *The People I've Smiled With*. New York: Cassell & Co., Ltd., 1889.

Wilson, Francis, *Francis Wilson's Life of Himself*. Boston: Houghton Mifflin, 1924.

——, *Joseph Jefferson*. New York: Charles Scribner's Sons, 1906.

Wilstach, Paul, *Richard Mansfield*. London: Chapman & Hall, 1908.

Winter, William, *Other Days*. New York: Moffat, Yard & Co., 1908.

——, *The Wallet of Time* (2 vols.). New York: Moffat, Yard & Co., 1913.

The many friends who helped in countless ways, some of them by merely sustaining their belief in this project over a period of six years, need no acknowledgment here. Those who made special efforts, however, must endure public gratitude: Martin O'Neill, late of *Time*, and David E. Scherman, of the late *Life*, thought that I might be a writer and generously circulated the notion. Arabella Barron and her parents made possible nearly a year of research and writing in England, enriching the product with their observations and embodiment of British life. Richard Blake Trescott lent his knowledge of the era. Dorothy Dickson enhanced my researching adventures with the lively parade of theatre people, past and present, which graced her London drawing room. Giovanna Breu gave of her time and expertise to trace obscure but vital information in Chicago. My typists, Rose Wiggin and Elizabeth Marston, dealt courageously with the various unwieldy stages of the manuscript. Harry Benson volunteered to take the photograph of the author which appears on the dust jacket. Harvey Loomis scoured the manuscript with an editor's eye. Bartle Bull not only volunteered to handle the legal business of contracts and such but applied his noted attention-to-detail to reading and correcting my original manuscript. My cousin, James John Kotsilibas Davis, lent his support and professionalism from the outset. Agnes Cochran Underwood was responsible for getting the outline of this book, via Ann Friedgood, to Doubleday, where it and the resulting tome were fortuitously embraced by my editor, Lisa Drew, with enthusiasm and, above all, patience.

South Harwich, 1976.

JAMES KOTSILIBAS-DAVIS

Index

and last years, 460–61, 462, 471, 494–95; and father's death, 499–500, 501, 502, 503; *Hangman*, painting by, 473; marriage to Doris Rankin, 491–92, 494; and musical ambition, 470–71, 472, 489; runs away from St. Aloysius Academy, joins father in New York City, 270–72; at Seton Hall, 351, 352–53; and sister, Ethel Barrymore, 475–76, 481–82, 491, 494; and stardom, 486, 494

Barrymore, Mrs. Lionel (Doris Rankin), 491–92, 494, 501

Barrymore, Maurice: acting debut of, 41–42; and animals, love of, 16, 17, 19, 30, 243, 246–47, 254, 270, 299, 306, 341–42, 343–46, 347–51, 372, 375, 377, 392, 393, 426–27, 435ff.; and *Aristocracy* tour, 341–52; arrival in New York City from England, 70ff.; begins playwriting, 120; as beneficiary in father's will, 58–60; and bicycling, 319–20; birth, background, family, (*see under* Blyth, Herbert Arthur Chamberlayne Hunter); birth of daughter Ethel, 114; birth of son John, 165; birth of son Lionel, 119; *Blood Will Tell* as first comedy by, 278, 366–67, 375–76; and bohemian life, 30–31, 34ff., 66, 75ff., 105–6, 265–70, 272, 289, 297, 306, 367–68, 390 (*see also* specific individuals, organizations, places); and boxing and sports, 34–41, 76, 77, 105–6, 177, 232–33, 244, 258, 260, 262–63, 270, 319–20, 488; break and reconciliation with wife, Georgie Drew Barrymore, 295–97, 298ff.; breakdown in health and personality, last years of, 421, 426–27, 435–42, 452–54, 455–69, 470–71, 494–95; and "Buffalo Bill" Cody, 357–58; in *Captain Swift*, 280–83, 284–85, 286, 289, 291, 292, 293, 295, 303, 305–6; changes name from Herbert Blyth to, 57 (*see also* Blyth, Herbert Arthur Chamberlayne Hunter); and Christian Science, 366–67; committed to the Pavilion for the Insane at Bellevue Hos-

pital, 459–69; in Coytesville, New Jersey, 428–30, 432; and critics (theatrical press), 300–1, 325–26, 368–69, 370–71, 379–80, 392–93, 417–18, 421, 424, 436–42, 444–45, 446 (*see also* specific individuals, periodicals, plays); and Daly, 71–72, 74, 106, 109–10, 112 (*see also* Daly, Augustin); and daughter Ethel, 141, 359, 364, 365, 370, 371–73, 395–96, 413 (*see also under* Barrymore, Ethel); death of, 494–95, 499–503; and death of Charley Vandenhoff, 301–2; and death of mother-in-law, Mrs. John Drew, 402, 403–4; and *Debt of Honor*, 153, 156–57, 158–64; debut in New York City, 77ff.; descriptions of, xi, 21, 23–26, 28, 40, 71, 165, 169, 176, 184–85, 192–93, 226, 265, 266–70, 282, 373–74, 467, 484–85, 491–92, 494, 500–1 (*see also* specific individuals, periodicals); disintegration of second marriage, 418, 427, 428, 429; in England with wife Georgie and children, 214–29, 230ff.; first appearance on an American stage, 67; first tour of the American West, 72–74; first trip to the United States, 61, 65ff.; funeral and burial of, 501–3; and Grace Henderson, 252–53, 293–97; growing popularity as a theatrical performer of, 144; and *Homeward Bound*, 160, 164–66, 175; and Lambs' Club 145, 165–66, 265, 268–70, 272, 289, 306 (*see also* Lambs' Club); last will of, 465; last words of, 495; last years at Long Island Home for the Insane, 466, 469, 470–71, 484–85, 491–92, 494–95; and Lillie Langtry, 257–63; in *Man of the World*, 293–94, 297, 301, 303–4, 305, 307, 313; marriage to Georgiana Drew, 105ff.; marriage to second wife, Mamie Floyd, 352, 358–59 (*see also* Floyd, Marie); as a matinee idol, 109, 110, 144, 173, 266, 284; meets Georgiana Drew, 81–82, 104; and memorizing of lines problem, 140–41, 151, 171, 214, 257, 326, 354, 374, 421, 426–27, 435ff.;

India, 6–12, 15–19, 192, 200
Indianapolis, Ind., 416–17
Indianapolis *Journal*, 416–17
In Mizzoura, 330
Irish Emigrant, The, 98
Irish Tutor, The, 92
Irving, Sir Henry, 220, 228, 269, 272, 273, 285, 396, 397–98, 400, 403, 412, 489
Irving, Laurence, 397, 408–9, 412, 414, 480, 481
Irwin, Dick, 25
Irwin, Flora, 303
Irwin, May, 303
Ixion, 57
Izard, Forrest, 424

Jack, or Life in Bohemia, 245, 249–50, 252
Jackson, Andrew, President, 87
Jackson, Dr. C. W., 401
James, Henry, 396, 431, 491
James, Louis, 110
Janis, Elsie, 493
Jarrett, Henry, 238, 273–74
Jay, Colonel William, 106
Jefferson, Joseph (I), 150, 311
Jefferson, Joseph (II), 150
Jefferson, Joseph (III), 87, 95, 118–19, 150–51, 152, 155, 156, 165, 173, 223, 252, 253, 270, 291–92, 311, 312, 319, 329, 363, 382–84, 402–3, 407, 502
Jeffreys-Lewis, replaced by Georgie Drew, 81, 110
Jerome, Jennie (Lady Randolph Churchill), 431, 480, 481
Jerrold, Blanchard, 31
Jersey City, N.J., 341
Jhang, India, 23, 24, 29
Jhansi, India, 15, 18
Jim the Penman, 239–40, 242
Johnson, Dr. Elan, 130–31, 132, 146
Jones, Clarence, 490
Jones, Henry Arthur, 419
Judson, Alice, 93–94, 110, 113–14, 115, 174, 177, 184, 185, 186, 187, 199, 203, 337
Judson, Ally, 178, 184, 185, 186, 299, 337
Judsons, the, 93–94, 101, 110, 113–14, 115, 116, 152, 156, 174, 177–78, 184–87, 199, 203, 299

Kansas City, Mo., 306, 351, 439–40
Kean, Edmund, 89
Keene, Laura, 97
Keith, B. F. (Keith Circuit), 391–92, 393–95, 403, 419, 425, 433, 434
Kelsey, Mrs. Herbert, 304
Kemble, Henry, 220
Kendal, Madge, 220, 227, 246, 267, 292, 319, 413
Kendal, William, 220, 227, 267, 292, 319, 413
Kent, Miller, 344, 345, 346, 348
Kent, Mrs. Miller, 344, 345
Kikurangi Hill estate (Auckland, New Zealand), 118, 120, 193
Kilrain, Jake, 286
Kimball, Moses, 66
King Lear, 125
King's College School (England), 410–11
Kinloch, Adine, 87, 88, 89, 90, 94, 95, 100
Kinloch, Georgiana (later Mrs. Robert L. Stephens), 88, 90, 92, 94, 95–97, 98, 403; death of, 100; marriage of, 96–97, 98
Kinloch, John, 86, 87
Kinloch, Mrs. John (Eliza Trenter Lane), 86–91, 92, 94, 95, 97, 100, 107–8, 125, 141, 156, 173, 192, 285; last days, and death of, 250, 253
Kipling, Rudyard, 443–44
Kiralfy, Imre, 256–57, 263
Kirk's (New York City), 367
Klaw & Erlanger, 405, 406
Knickerbocker Theatre (N.Y.C.), 391, 477, 478
Knowles, Sheridan, 317
Kobbé, Gustav, 165
Kretz, Charlie, 135–36

Lackaye, Wilton, 266, 268–69, 283, 291, 325, 351, 452, 459, 487
Ladies' Battle, The, 102
Lady and the Burglar, The, 444, 445–46
Lady Macbeth. See Macbeth
Lady of Lyons, 55, 193
Lady of the Camellias, The, 171, 372
Lady of the Locket, The, 220
Lady of Venice, A, 357–58, 366
Lady Windermere's Fan, 327–28,

536

537